THE OEDIPUS COLONEUS

OF

SOPHOCLES

T0382377

THE OEDIPUS COLONEUS

OF

SOPHOCLES

WITH A COMMENTARY,
ABRIDGED FROM THE LARGE EDITION

OF

Sir RICHARD C. JEBB

BY

E. S. SHUCKBURGH

CAMBRIDGE:
AT THE UNIVERSITY PRESS
1955

CAMBRIDGE
UNIVERSITY PRESS

University Printing House, Cambridge CB2 8BS, United Kingdom

Cambridge University Press is part of the University of Cambridge.

It furthers the University's mission by disseminating knowledge in the pursuit of education, learning and research at the highest international levels of excellence.

www.cambridge.org
Information on this title: www.cambridge.org/9781107429109

© Cambridge University Press 1903

First published 1903
First edition 1903
Reprinted 1913, 1930, 1955
First paperback edition 2014

A catalogue record for this publication is available from the British Library

ISBN 978-1-107-42910-9 Paperback

PREFACE.

SIR Richard Jebb observed in his preface to the large edition of the Play that "The *Oedipus Coloneus* has its share of textual problems; but, for the modern student, it is more especially a play which demands exegesis." In making my selection from the notes in that edition I have kept this in mind. I have retained discussions on the text when they seemed to be absolutely necessary or to involve important points, whether in Grammar or in the development of the Fable: but I have made it my chief aim to omit nothing which would help the student to realise the scene presented in the play, the coherence and artistic purpose of the plot, or the poet's conception of the dramatic situation and moral standpoint of the characters. For fuller discussion on textual difficulties and controverted interpretation, the advanced student must still go to the larger edition and translation. The work as it now stands is almost wholly Sir Richard Jebb's, though not the whole that he has done for the play. I have in some few instances made obvious corrections, and added a few illustrations, but I have little more credit to claim for the work than that of an arranger and epitomator.

E. S. SHUCKBURGH.

CONTENTS.

	PAGE
INTRODUCTION	vii
MANUSCRIPTS, EDITIONS, AND COMMENTARIES . .	xxxiv
METRICAL ANALYSIS	xxxviii
DRAMATIS PERSONAE ; STRUCTURE	1
TEXT	1
NOTES	65
GREEK INDEX	283
GRAMMATICAL INDEX	295
MAPS :	
I. Map to illustrate Note on vv. 1059 ff. . . .	279
II. Colonus and its neighbourhood, with some of its	
ancient roads	281

INTRODUCTION.

§ 1. At the close of the *Oedipus Tyrannus* the situation is

Situation at the end of the Tyrannus.

briefly this. By the fact of the guilt which has been brought home to him Oedipus is tacitly considered to have forfeited the throne. His two sons being still young boys, their maternal uncle, Creon, succeeds to the direction of affairs. The self-blinded Oedipus, in his first agony of horror and despair, beseeches Creon to send him away from Thebes. Let him no longer pollute it by his presence: let him perish in the wilds of Cithaeron, as his parents would have had it. Creon replies that he cannot assume the responsibility of acceding to the wish of Oedipus: the oracle at Delphi must be consulted. If Apollo says that Oedipus is to be sent away from Thebes, then it shall be done.

Sophocles supposes a long interval—some twenty years,

Events of the interval between the plays.

perhaps—between the two dramas of which Oedipus is the hero. As the exile himself says, "'Tis little to uplift old age, when youth was ruined.' We have to make out the events of this interval, as best we can, from stray hints in the *Coloneus*[1].

---

[1] The Greek title of the play is Οἰδίπους ἐπὶ Κολωνῷ,—the prep. meaning '*at*,' as in such phrases as ἐπ' ἐσχάρῃ (*Od.* 7. 160), ἐπὶ θύραις, etc. It is cited by the authors of the Greek Arguments as ὁ ἐπὶ Κολωνῷ Οἰδίπους. The earlier play was doubtless called simply Οἰδίπους by Sophocles,—Τύραννος having been a later addition (cp. *O. T.* p. 4): but the second play required a distinguishing epithet, and the words ἐπὶ Κολωνῷ must be ascribed to the poet himself. The traditional Latin title, 'Oedipus Coloneus,' is from Cic. *De Sen.* 7, § 21, where it occurs in the accus., *Oedipum Coloneum*.

The promise with which Creon pacified Oedipus at the end of the *Tyrannus* does not appear to have been fulfilled. The oracle was not consulted as to whether Oedipus should remain at Thebes. He remained there; and, as the lapse of time softened his anguish, the blind and discrowned sufferer learned to love the seclusion of the house in which he had once reigned so brilliantly. Creon continued to act as regent. But at last a change took place in the disposition of the Thebans, or at least in Creon's. A feeling grew up that Thebes was harbouring
Expulsion of   a defilement, and it was decided to expel Oedipus.
Oedipus.   There is no mention of an oracle as the cause; indeed, the idea of a divine mandate is incompatible with the tenor of the story, since Oedipus could not then have charged the whole blame on Thebes. One circumstance of his expulsion was bitter to him above the rest. His two sons, who had now reached manhood, said not a word in arrest of his doom.

But his two daughters were nobly loyal. Antigone went forth from Thebes with her blind father,—his sole attendant,— and thenceforth shared the privations of his lot, which could now be only that of a wandering mendicant. Ismene stayed at Thebes, but it was in order to watch the course of events there in her father's interest. We hear of one occasion, at least, on which she risked a secret journey for the purpose of acquainting him with certain oracles which had just been received. The incident marks the uneasy feeling with which the Thebans still regarded the blind exile, and their unwilling-ness that he should share such light on his own destiny as they could obtain from Apollo.

Oedipus had now grown old in his destitute wanderings, when a sacred mission sent from Thebes to Delphi brought back an oracle concerning him which excited a lively interest
The new   in the minds of his former subjects. It was to
oracle.   the effect that the welfare of Thebes depended on Oedipus, not merely while he lived, but also after his death.

The Thebans now conceived the desire of establishing Oedipus somewhere just beyond their border. In this way they thought that they would have him under their control, while at the same time they would avoid the humiliation of confessing themselves wrong, and receiving him back to dwell among them. Their main object was that, on his death, they might secure the guardianship of his grave.

The new oracle obviously made an opportunity for the sons of Oedipus at Thebes, if they were true to their banished father. They could urge that Apollo, by this latest utterance, had condoned any pollution that might still be supposed to attach to the person of Oedipus, and had virtually authorised his recall to his ancient realm. Thebes could not be defiled by the presence of a man whom the god had declared to be the arbiter of its fortunes.

Unhappily, the sons—Polyneices and Eteocles—were no longer in a mood to hear the dictates of filial piety. When they had first reached manhood, they had been oppressed by a sense of the curse on their family, and the taint on their own birth. They had wished to spare Thebes the contamination of their rule; they had been desirous that the regent,— their uncle Creon,—should become king. But presently,— 'moved by some god, and by a sinful mind,'—compelled by the inexorable Fury of their house,—they renounced these intentions of wise self-denial. Not only were they fired with

The strife between the sons. the passion for power, but they fell to striving with each other for the sole power. Eteocles, the younger[1] brother, managed to win over the citizens. The elder brother, Polyneices, was driven out of Thebes. He went to Argos, where he married the daughter of king Adrastus. All the most renowned warriors of the Peloponnesus became his allies, and he made ready to lead a great host against Thebes. But, while the mightiest chieftains were marshalling their followers in his cause, the

[1] See note on v. 375.

voices of prophecy warned him that the issue of his mortal feud depended on the blind and aged beggar whom, years before, he had coldly seen thrust out from house and home. That side would prevail which Oedipus should join.

§ 2.   This is the moment at which our play begins.   The action falls into six principal divisions or chapters, marked off, as usual, by choral lyrics.

Analysis of the play.

The scene, which remains the same throughout the play, is at Colonus, about a mile and a quarter north-west of Athens.   We are in front of a grove sacred to the Furies,—here worshipped under a propitiatory name, as the Eumenides or Kindly Powers.   While the snow still lingers on distant hills (v. 1060), the song of many nightingales is already heard from the thick covert of this grove in the Attic plain; we seem to breathe the air of a bright, calm day at the beginning of April[1].   The blind Oedipus, led by Antigone, enters on the left hand of the spectator.   He is in the squalid garb of a beggar-man,— carrying a wallet, wherein to put alms (v. 1262); the wind plays with his unkempt white hair; the wounds by which, in the prime of manhood, he had destroyed his sight, have left ghastly traces on the worn face; but there is a certain nobleness in his look and bearing which tempers the beholder's sense of pity or repulsion.   The old man is tired with a long day's journey; they have heard from people whom they met

I. Prologue: 1—116.

---

[1] The dates of the nightingale's arrival in Attica, for the years indicated, are thus given by Dr Krüper, the best authority on the birds of Greece ('Greichische Jahrzeiten' for 1875, Heft III., p. 243):—March 29 (1867), April 13 (1873), April 6 (1874).   For this reference I am indebted to Professor Alfred Newton, F.R.S., of Cambridge.   The male birds (who alone sing) arrive some days before the females, as is usually the case with migratory birds, and sing as soon as they come.   Thus it is interesting to notice that the period of the year at which the nightingale's song would first be heard in Attica coincides closely with the celebration of the Great Dionysia, in the last days of March and the first days of April.   If the play was produced at that festival, the allusions to the nightingale (vv. 18, 671) would have been felt as specially appropriate to the season.

on the way that they are near Athens, but they do not know the name of the spot at which they have halted. Antigone seats her father on a rock which is just within the limits of the sacred grove. As she is about to go in search of information, a man belonging to Colonus appears. Oedipus is beginning to accost him, when the stranger cuts his words short by a peremptory command to come off the sacred ground. 'To whom is it sacred?' Oedipus asks. To the Eumenides, is the reply. On hearing that name, Oedipus invokes the grace of those goddesses, and declares that he will never leave the rest which he has found. He begs the stranger to summon Theseus, the king of Athens, 'that by a small service he may find a great gain.' The stranger, who is struck by the noble mien of the blind old man, says that he will go and consult the people of Colonus; and meanwhile he tells Oedipus to stay where he is.

Left alone with Antigone, Oedipus utters a solemn and very beautiful prayer to the Eumenides, which discloses the motive of his refusal to leave the sacred ground. In his early manhood, when he inquired at Delphi concerning his parentage, Apollo predicted the calamities which awaited him; but also promised him rest, so soon as he should reach '*a seat of the Awful Goddesses.*' There he should close his troubled life; and along with the release, he should have his reward,—power to benefit the folk who sheltered him, and to hurt the folk who had cast him out. And when his end was near, there should be a sign from the sky. Apollo and the Eumenides themselves have led him to this grove: he prays the goddesses to receive him, and to give him peace.

Hardly had his prayer been spoken, when Antigone hears footsteps approaching, and retires with her father into the covert of the grove.

The elders of Colonus, who form the Chorus, now enter **Parados:** the orchestra. They have heard that a wanderer **117—253.** has entered the grove, and are in eager search for the perpetrator of so daring an impiety. Oedipus, led by

Antigone, suddenly discovers himself. His appearance is greeted with a cry of horror from the Chorus; but horror gradually yields to pity for his blindness, his age, and his misery. They insist, however, on his coming out of the sacred grove. If he is to speak to them, it must be on lawful ground. Before he consents, he exacts a pledge that he shall not be removed from the ground outside of the grove. They promise this. Antigone then guides him to a seat beyond the sacred precinct. The Chorus now ask him who he is. He implores them to spare the question; but their curiosity has been aroused. They extort an answer. No sooner has the name OEDIPUS passed his lips, than his voice is drowned in a shout of execration. They call upon him to leave Attica instantly. He won their promise by a fraud, and it is void. They refuse to hear him. Antigone makes an imploring appeal.

In answer to her appeal, the Chorus say that they pity both father and daughter, but fear the gods still more; the wanderers must go.

II. First episode: 254—667.

Oedipus now speaks with powerful eloquence, tinged at first with bitter scorn. Is this the traditional compassion of Athens for the oppressed? They have lured him from his sanctuary, and now they are driving him out of their country,—for fear of what? Simply of his name. He is free from moral guilt. He brings a blessing for Athens. What it is, he will reveal when their king arrives. The Chorus agree to await the decision of Theseus. He will come speedily, they are sure, when he hears the name of Oedipus.

At this moment, Antigone descries the approach of her sister Ismene, who has come from Thebes with tidings for her father. Ismene tells him of the fierce strife which has broken out between her brothers,—and how Polyneices has gone to Argos. Then she mentions the new oracle which the Thebans have just received,—that their welfare depends on him, in life and death. Creon will soon come, she adds, in the hope of enticing him back.

Oedipus asks whether *his sons* knew of this oracle. 'Yes,' she reluctantly answers. At that answer the measure of his bitterness is full: he breaks into a prayer that the gods may hear him, and make this new strife fatal to both brothers alike. And then, turning to the Chorus, he assures them that he is destined to be a deliverer of Attica: for his mind is now made up; he has no longer any doubt where his blessing, or his curse, is to descend. The Chorus, in reply, instruct him how a proper atonement may be made to the Eumenides for his trespass on their precinct; and Ismene goes to perform the prescribed rites in a more distant part of the grove.

Here follows a lyric dialogue between the Chorus and (Kommos: Oedipus. They question him on his past deeds, 510—548.) and he pathetically asserts his moral innocence.

Theseus now enters, on the spectator's right hand, as coming from Athens. Addressing Oedipus as 'son of Laïus,' he assures him, with generous courtesy, of protection and sympathy; he has himself known what it is to be an exile. Oedipus explains his desire. He craves to be protected in Attica while he lives, and to be buried there when he is dead. He has certain benefits to bestow in return; but these will not be felt until after his decease. He fears that his sons will seek to remove him to Thebes. If Theseus promises to protect him, it must be at the risk of a struggle. Theseus gives the promise. He publicly adopts Oedipus as a citizen. He then leaves the scene.

Oedipus having now been formally placed under the pro- First tection of Athens, the Chorus appropriately cele- stasimon: brate the land which has become his home. 668—719. Beginning with Colonus, they pass to themes of honour for Attica at large,—the olive, created by Athena and guarded by Zeus,—the horses and horsemanship of the land, gifts of Poseidon,—and his other gift, the empire of the sea. Of all the choral songs in extant Greek drama, this short ode is perhaps the most widely famous; a distinction partly due,

no doubt, to the charm of the subject, and especially to the
manifest glow of a personal sentiment in the verses which
describe Colonus; but, apart from this, the intrinsic poetical
beauty is of the highest and rarest order.

As the choral praises cease, Antigone exclaims that the
moment has come for proving that Athens de-
serves them. Creon enters, with an escort of
guards.

III. Second
episode:
720—1043.

His speech, addressed at first to the Chorus, is short, and
skilfully conceived. They will not suppose that an old man
like himself has been sent to commit an act of violence against
a powerful State. No: he comes on behalf of Thebes, to
plead with his aged kinsman, whose present wandering life
is truly painful for everybody concerned. The honour of the
city and of the family is involved. Oedipus should express
his gratitude to Athens, and then return to a decent privacy
'in the house of his fathers.'

With a burst of scathing indignation, Oedipus replies.
They want him now; but they thrust him out when he was
longing to stay. 'In the house of his fathers!' No, that is
not their design. They intend to plant him somewhere just
beyond their border, for their own purposes. 'That portion
is not for thee,' he tells Creon, 'but this,—my curse upon
your land, ever abiding therein;—and for my sons, this
heritage—room enough in my realm, wherein—to die.'

Failing to move him, Creon drops the semblance of
persuasion. He bluntly announces that he already holds one
hostage;—Ismene, who had gone to perform the rites in the
grove, has been captured by his guards;—and he will soon
have a second. He lays his hand upon Antigone. Another
moment, and his attendants drag her from the scene. He
is himself on the point of seizing Oedipus, when Theseus
enters,—having been startled by the outcry, while engaged
in a sacrifice at the neighbouring altar of Poseidon.

On hearing what has happened, Theseus first sends a

message to Poseidon's altar, directing the Athenians who were present at the sacrifice to start in pursuit of Creon's guards and the captured maidens.—Then, turning to Creon, he upbraids him with his lawless act, and tells him that he shall not leave Attica until the maidens are restored. Creon, with ready effrontery, replies that, in attempting to remove a polluted wretch from Attic soil, he was only doing what the Areiopagus itself would have wished to do; if his manner was somewhat rough, the violence of Oedipus was a provocation. This speech draws from Oedipus an eloquent vindication of his life, which is more than a mere repetition of the defence which he had already made to the Chorus. Here he brings out with vivid force the helplessness of man against fate, and the hypocrisy of his accuser.—Theseus now calls on Creon to lead the way, and show him where the captured maidens are,—adding a hint, characteristically Greek, that no help from Attic accomplices shall avail him. Creon sulkily submits, —with a muttered menace of what he will do when he reaches home. *Exeunt* Theseus and his attendants, with Creon, on the spectator's left.

The Chorus imagine themselves at the scene of the coming

Second stasimon: 1044—1095.

fray, and predict the speedy triumph of the rescuers,—invoking the gods of the land to help. A beautiful trait of this ode is the reference to the 'torch-lit strand' of Eleusis, and to the mysteries which the initiated poet held in devout reverence.

At the close of their chant the Chorus give Oedipus the

IV. Third episode: 1096—1210.

welcome news that they see his daughters approaching, escorted by Theseus and his followers. The first words of Antigone to her blind father express the wish that some wonder-working god could enable him to see their brave deliverer; and then, with much truth to nature, father and daughters are allowed to forget for a while that anyone else is present. When at last Oedipus turns to thank Theseus, his words are eminently noble, and

also touching. His impulse is to salute his benefactor by
kissing his cheek, but it is quickly checked by the thought that
this is not for him ; no, nor can he permit it, if Theseus would.
The line drawn by fate, the line which parts him and his from
human fellowship, is rendered only more sacred by gratitude.

When Antigone is questioned by her father as to the
circumstances of the rescue, she refers him to Theseus; and
Theseus says that it is needless for *him* to vaunt his own deeds,
since Oedipus can hear them at leisure from his daughters.

There is a matter, Theseus adds, on which he should like
to consult Oedipus. A stranger, it seems, has placed himself
as a suppliant at the altar of Poseidon. This happened while
they were all away at the rescue, and no one knows anything
about the man. He is not from Thebes, but he declares that
he is a kinsman of Oedipus, and prays for a few words with
him. It is only guessed whence he comes ; can Oedipus have
any relations at Argos ? Oedipus remembers what Ismene told
him ; he knows who it is ; and he implores Theseus to spare
him the torture of hearing *that* voice. But Antigone's entreaties prevail. Theseus leaves the scene, in order to let the
suppliant know that the interview will be granted.

The choral ode which fills the pause glances forward rather

Third
stasimon
1211—1248.

than backward, though it is suggested by the
presage of some new vexation to Oedipus. It
serves to turn our thoughts towards the approaching end.—Not to be born is best of all ; the next
best thing is to die as soon as possible. And the extreme
of folly is the desire to outlive life's joys. Behold yon aged
and afflicted stranger,—lashed by the waves of trouble from
east and west, from south and north ! But there is one
deliverer, who comes to all at last.

Polyneices now enters,—not attended, like Creon, by

V. Fourth
episode:
1249—1555.

guards, but alone. He is shedding tears ; he
begins by uttering the deepest pity for his father's
plight, and the bitterest self-reproach.—Oedipus,

with averted head makes no reply.—Polyneices appeals to his sisters; will they plead for him? Antigone advises him to state in his own words the object of his visit.—Then Polyneices sets forth his petition. His Argive allies are already gathered before Thebes. He has come as a suppliant to Oedipus, for himself, and for his friends too. Oracles say that victory will be with the side for which Oedipus may declare. Eteocles, in his pride at Thebes, is mocking father and brother alike. 'If thou assist me, I will soon scatter his power, and will stablish thee in thine own house, and stablish myself, when I have cast him out by force.'

Oedipus now breaks silence; but it is in order to let the Chorus know why he does so. His son, he reminds them, has been sent to them by their king.—Then, suddenly turning on Polyneices, he delivers an appalling curse, dooming both his sons to die at Thebes by each other's hands. In concentrated force of tragic passion this passage has few rivals. The great scene is closed by a short dialogue between Polyneices and his elder sister,—one of the delicate links between this play and the poet's earlier *Antigone*. She implores him to abandon his fatal enterprise. But he is not to be dissuaded; he only asks that, if he falls, she and Ismene will give him burial rites; he disengages himself from their embrace, and goes forth, under the shadow of the curse.

A lyric passage now follows, which affords a moment of (Kommos: 1447—1499.) relief to the strained feelings of the spectators, and also serves (like a similar passage before, vv. 510—548) to separate the two principal situations comprised in this chapter of the drama.—The Chorus are commenting on the dread doom which they have just heard pronounced, when they are startled by the sound of thunder. As peal follows peal, and lightnings glare from the darkened sky, the terror-stricken elders of Colonus utter broken prayers to averting gods. But for Oedipus the storm has another meaning; it has filled him with a strange eagerness. He prays Antigone to summon Theseus.

As Theseus had left the scene in order to communicate with the suppliant at Poseidon's altar, no breach of probability is involved in his timely re-appearance. Oedipus announces that, by sure signs, he knows his hour to have come. Unaided by human hand, he will now show the way to the spot where his life must be closed. When he arrives there, to Theseus alone will be revealed the place appointed for his grave. At the approach of death, Theseus shall impart the secret to his heir alone; and, so, from age to age, that sacred knowledge shall descend in the line of the Attic kings. While the secret is religiously guarded, the grave of Oedipus shall protect Attica against invading foemen; Thebes shall be powerless to harm her.—'And now let us set forth, for the divine summons urges me.' As Oedipus utters these words, Theseus and his daughters become aware of a change; the blind eyes are still dark, but the moral conditions of blindness have been annulled; no sense of dependence remains, no trace of hesitation or timidity; like one inspired, the blind man eagerly beckons them on; and so, followed by them, he finally passes from the view of the spectators.

This final exit of Oedipus is magnificently conceived. As the idea of a spiritual illumination is one which pervades the play, so it is fitting that, in the last moment of his presence with us, the inward vision should be manifest in its highest clearness and power.

The elders of Colonus are now alone; they have looked

Fourth stasimon: 1556—1578. their last on Oedipus; and they know that the time of his end has come. The strain of their chant is in harmony with this moment of suspense and stillness. It is a choral litany for the soul which is passing from earth. May the Powers of the unseen world be gracious; may no dread apparition vex the path to the fields below.

A Messenger, one of the attendants of Theseus, relates

VI. Exodos: 1579 —1779. what befell after Oedipus, followed by his daughters and the king, arrived at the spot where he was destined to depart. Theseus was then left alone with him, and to Theseus alone of mortals the manner of his passing is known.

The daughters enter. After the first utterances of grief, one feeling is seen to be foremost in Antigone's mind,—the longing to see her father's grave.

(Kommos: 1670—1750.)

She cannot bear the thought that it should lack a tribute from her hands. Ismene vainly represents that their father's own command makes such a wish unlawful,—impossible. Theseus arrives, and to him Antigone urges her desire. In gentle and solemn words he reminds her of the pledge which he had given to Oedipus. She acquiesces; and now prays that she and Ismene may be sent to Thebes: perhaps they may yet be in time to avert death from their brothers. Theseus consents: and the elders of Colonus say farewell to the Theban maidens in words which speak of submission to the gods: 'Cease lamentation, lift it up no more; for verily these things stand fast.'

§ 3. In the *Oedipus Tyrannus* a man is crushed by the discovery that, without knowing it, he has committed two crimes, parricide and incest. At the moment of discovery he can feel nothing

Relation of the *Coloneus* to the *Tyrannus*.

but the double stain: he cries out that 'he has become most hateful to the gods.' He has, indeed, broken divine laws, and the divine Power has punished him by bringing his deeds to light. This Power does not, in the first instance, regard the intention, but the fact. It does not matter that his unconscious sins were due to the agency of an inherited curse, and that he is morally innocent. He has sinned, and he must suffer.

In the *Oedipus Coloneus* we meet with this man again, after the lapse of several years. In a religious aspect he still rests under the stain, and he knows this. But, in the course of time, he has mentally risen to a point of view from which he can survey his own past more clearly. Consciousness of the stain is now subordinate to another feeling, which in his first despair had not availed to console him. He has gained a firm grasp, not to be lost, on the fact of his moral innocence. He remembers the word of Apollo long ago, which coupled the prediction of his woes with a promise of final rest and reward; and he believes that his moral innocence is recognised by the Power which punished him. Thinking, then, on the two great facts of his life, his defilement and his innocence, he has come to look upon himself as neither pure nor yet guilty, but as a person set apart by the gods to illustrate their will,— as sacred. Hence that apparently strange contrast which belongs to the heart of the *Oedipus Coloneus*. He declines to pollute his benefactor, Theseus, by his touch,—describing himself as one with whom 'all stain of sin hath made its dwelling' (1133). Yet, with equal truth and sincerity, he can assure the Athenians that he has come to them 'as one sacred and pious,'—the suppliant of the Eumenides, the disciple of Apollo (287).

When eternal laws are broken by men, the gods punish the breach, whether wilful or involuntary; but their ultimate judgment depends on the intent. That thought is dominant in the *Oedipus Coloneus*. The contrast between physical blindness and inward vision is an under-note, in harmony with the higher distinction between the form of conduct and its spirit.

§ 4. The Oedipus whom we find at Colonus utters not

The Oedipus of this play. a word of self-reproach, except on one point; he regrets the excess of the former self-reproach which stung him into blinding himself. He has done nothing else that calls for repentance; he has been the passive instrument of destiny. It would be a mistake to aim at bringing the play more into harmony with modern sentiment by suffusing it in a mild and almost Christian radiance, as though Oedipus had been softened, chastened, morally purified by suffering. Suffering has, indeed, taught him endurance (στέργειν), and some degree of caution; he is also exalted in mind by a new sense of power; but he has not been softened. Anger, 'which was ever his bane,' blazes up in him as fiercely as ever. The unrestrained anger of an old man may easily be a very pitiful and deplorable spectacle; it requires the touch of a powerful dramatist to deal successfully with a subject so dangerously near to comedy, and to make a choleric old man tragic; Shakspeare has done it, with pathos of incomparable grasp and range; Sophocles, in a more limited way, has done it too. But probably the chief danger which the *Oedipus Coloneus* runs with modern readers is from the sense of repulsion apt to be excited by this inexorable resentment of Oedipus towards his sons. It is not so when Lear cries—

> 'No, you unnatural hags,
> I will have such revenges on you both,
> That all the world shall—I will do such things,—
> What they are yet, I know not; but they shall be
> The terrors of the earth. You think I'll weep;
> No, I'll not weep.'

Sophocles has left it possible for *us* to abhor the implacable father more than the heartless children. The ancient Greek spectator, however, would have been less likely to experience such a revulsion of sympathy. Nearer to the conditions imagined, he would more quickly feel all that was implied in the attitude of the sons at the moment when Oedipus was expelled from Thebes; his religious sense would demand a nemesis, while his ethical code would not require forgiveness of wrongs; and, lastly, he would feel that the implacability of Oedipus was itself a manifestation of the Fury which pursued the house.

§ 5. On the part of the gods there is nothing that can

The divine amend. properly be called tenderness[1] for Oedipus; we should not convey a true impression if we spoke of him as attaining to final pardon and peace, in the full sense

---

[1] εὔνουν in 1662, and χάρις in 1752, refer mainly to the painless death.

which a Christian would attach to those words. The gods, who
have vexed Oedipus from youth to age, make this amend to
him,—that just before his death he is recognised by men as a
mysteriously sacred person, who has the power to bequeath
a blessing and a malison. They further provide that his
departure out of his wretched life shall be painless, and such
as to distinguish him from other men. But at the very moment
when he passes away, the Fury is busy with his sons. The
total impression made by the play as a work of art depends
essentially on the manner in which the scene of sacred peace
at Colonus is brought into relief against the dark fortunes of
Polyneices and Eteocles.

In the epic version of this story, as also in the versions
adopted by Aeschylus and Euripides, Oedipus cursed his sons
at Thebes, before the strife had broken out between them.
He doomed them to divide their heritage with the sword.
Their subsequent quarrel was the direct consequence of their
father's curse. But, according to Sophocles, the curse had
nothing to do with the quarrel. The strife which broke out
between the sons was inspired by the evil genius of their race,
and by their own sinful thoughts[1]. At that time Oedipus had
uttered no imprecation. His curse was pronounced, *after* the
breach between them, because they had preferred their selfish
ambitions to the opportunity of recalling their father (421)[2].
There is a twofold dramatic advantage in the modification thus
introduced by Sophocles. First, the two sons no longer
appear as helpless victims of fate; they have incurred moral
blame, and are just objects of the paternal anger. Secondly,
when Polyneices—on the eve of combat with his brother—
appeals to Oedipus, the outraged father still holds the weapon
with which to smite him. The curse descends at the supreme
crisis, and with more terrible effect because it has been
delayed.

[1] See vv. 371, 421, 1299.   [2] See note on v. 1375.

§ 6. The secondary persons, like the hero, are best in-
The other characters. terpreted by the play itself; but one or two traits may be briefly noticed. The two scenes in which the removal of Oedipus is attempted are contrasted not merely in outward circumstance—Creon relying on armed force, while Polyneices is a solitary suppliant—but also in regard to the characters of the two visitors. It is idle to look for the Creon of the *Tyrannus* in the Creon of the *Coloneus*: they are different men, and Sophocles has not cared to preserve even a semblance of identity. The Creon of the *Tyrannus* is marked by strong self-respect, and is essentially kind-hearted though undemonstrative; the Creon of this play is a heartless and hypocritical villain. A well-meaning but wrong-headed martinet, such as the Creon of *Antigone*, is a conceivable development of the *Tyrannus* Creon, but at least stands on a much higher level than the Creon of the *Coloneus*. Poly-neices is cold-hearted, selfish, and of somewhat coarse fibre, but he is sincere and straightforward; in the conversation with Antigone he evinces real dignity and fortitude. In the part of Theseus, which might so easily have been commonplace, Sophocles has shown a fine touch; this typical Athenian is more than a walking king; he is a soldier bred in the school of adversity, loyal to gods and men, perfect in courtesy, but stern at need. Comparing the representation of the two sisters in the *Antigone* with that given in this play, we may remark the tact with which the poet has abstained here from tingeing the character of Ismene with anything like selfish timidity. At the end of the play, where the more passionate nature of the heroic Antigone manifests itself, Ismene is the sister whose calm common-sense is not overpowered by grief; but she grieves sincerely and remains, as she has been throughout, entirely loyal.

A word should be added on the conduct of the Chorus in
Attitude of the Chorus. regard to Oedipus. Before they know who he is, they regard him with horror as the man who

has profaned the grove; but their feeling quickly changes to compassion on perceiving that he is blind, aged, and miserable. Then they learn his name, and wish to expel him because they conceive his presence to be a defilement. They next relent, not simply because he says that he brings benefits for Athens,—though they take account of that fact, which is itself a proof that he is at peace with the gods,—but primarily because he is able to assure them that he is 'sacred and pious' (287). They then leave the matter to Theseus. Thus these elders of Colonus represent the conflict of two feelings which the situation might be supposed to arouse in the minds of ordinary Athenians,—fear of the gods, and compassion for human suffering,—the two qualities which Oedipus recognises as distinctly Athenian (260 n.).

§ 7. The topography of the play, in its larger aspects, is Topography. illustrated by the accompanying map[1]. The knoll of whitish earth known as Colonus Hippius, which gave its name to the deme or township of Colonus, was about a mile and a quarter N.W.N. from the Dipylon gate of Athens.

Colonus Hippius. The epithet Hippius belonged to the god Poseidon, as horse-creating and horse-taming (see on 715); it was given to this place because Poseidon Hippius was worshipped there, and served to distinguish this extramural Colonus from the Colonus Agoraeus, or 'Market Hill,' within the walls of Athens[2]. In the absence of a distinguishing epithet, 'Colonus' would usually mean Colonus Hippius; Thucydides calls it simply Colonus, and describes it as 'a sanctuary (ἱερόν) of Poseidon.' The altar of Poseidon in this precinct is not visible to the spectators of our play, but is sup-

---

[1] See p. 281. Reduced, by permission, from part of Plate II. in the 'Atlas von Athen: im Auftrage des Kaiserlich Deutschen Archäologischen Instituts herausgegeben von E. Curtius und J. A. Kaupert' (Berlin, 1878, Dietrich Reimer).

[2] In the district of Melitè, see map II.

posed to be near. When Pausanias visited Colonus (*c.* 180 A.D.), he saw an altar of Poseidon Hippius and Athenc Hippia. A grove and a temple of Poseidon had formerly existed there, but had perished long before the date of his visit. He found, too, that divine honours were paid at Colonus to Peirithous and Theseus, to Oedipus and Adrastus: there were perhaps two shrines or chapels (ἡρῷα), one for each pair of heroes[1]. He does not mention the grove of the Eumenides, which, like that of Poseidon, had doubtless been destroyed at an earlier

Demeter
Euchloüs.

period. About a quarter of a mile N.E.N. of the Colonus Hippius rises a second mound, identified by E. Curtius and others with the 'hill of Demeter Euchloüs' (1600). When Oedipus stood at the spot where he finally disappeared, this hill was 'in full view' (προσόψιος). Traces of an ancient building exist at its southern edge. Similar traces exist at the N.W. edge of the Colonus Hippius. If, as is likely, these ancient buildings were connected with religious purposes, it is possible that the specially sacred region of the ancient Colonus lay between the two mounds.

§ 8. The grove of the Eumenides may have been on the

Probable
site of
the grove.

N. or N.E. side of the Colonus Hippius. But the only condition fixed by the play fails to be precise, viz. that a road, passing by Colonus to Athens, skirted the grove,—the inner or most sacred part of the grove being on the side farthest from the road. The roads

A suggestion.

marked on our map are the ancient roads[2]. It will be observed that one of them passes between Colonus Hippius and the hill of Demeter Euchloüs, going in the direction of Athens. There is no reason why the wandering Oedipus should not be conceived as entering Attica from the N.W.; *i.e.*, as having passed into the Attic plain round the

[1] His use of the singular is ambiguous, owing to its place in the sentence: ἡρῷον δὲ Πειρίθου καὶ Θησέως Οἰδίποδός τε καὶ Ἀδράστου (I. 30. 4).

[2] On these, see the letter-press by Prof. Curtius to the 'Atlas von Athen,' pp. 14 f.

N. end of Aegaleos. And, in that case, the road in question might well represent the route by which Sophocles, familiar with the local details of Colonus in his own day, imagined Oedipus as arriving. Then Oedipus, moving towards Athens, would have the grove of the Eumenides on his right hand[1], if, as we were supposing, this grove was on the N. side of the Colonus Hippius. The part of the grove farthest from him (τοὐκεῖθεν ἄλσους 505) would thus be near the remains of the ancient building at the N.W. edge. When Ismene is sent to that part of the grove, she is told that there is a guardian of the place (ἔποικος 506), who can supply her with anything needful for the rites.

The present aspect of Colonus is thus described by an accomplished scholar, Mr George Wotherspoon (Longman's Magazine, Feb. 1884):—

> Was this the noble dwelling-place he sings,
>   Fair-steeded glistening land, which once t' adorn
>   Gold-reinèd Aphroditè did not scorn,
> And where blithe Bacchus kept his revellings?
> Oh, Time and Change! Of all those goodly things,
>   Of coverts green by nightingales forlorn
>   Lov'd well; of flow'r-bright fields, from morn to morn
> New-water'd by Cephissus' sleepless springs,
> What now survives? This stone-capt mound, the plain
>   Sterile and bare, these meagre groves of shade,
> Pale hedges, the scant stream unfed by rain:
> No more? The genius of the place replied,
>   'Still blooms inspirèd Art tho' Nature fade;
> The memory of Colonus hath not died.'

---

[1] It is scarcely necessary to say that no objection, or topographical inference of any kind, can be drawn from the conventional arrangement of the Greek stage by which Oedipus (as coming from the country) would enter on the spectator's left, and therefore have the scenic grove on his left.

§ 9. When Oedipus knows that his end is near, he leads

The καταρ-
ράκτης ὁδός.

his friends to a place called the καταρράκτης ὁδός, the 'sheer threshold,' 'bound by brazen steps to earth's roots.' There can be no doubt that this 'threshold' denotes a natural fissure or chasm, supposed to be the commencement of a passage leading down to the nether world. Such a chasm exists at the foot of the Areiopagus, where Pausanias saw a tomb of Oedipus in the precinct of the Eumenides. But Sophocles adopts the Colonus-myth unreservedly; nor can I believe that he intended, by any deliberate vagueness, to leave his hearers free to think of the Areiopagus. The chasm called the καταρράκτης ὁδός must be imagined, then, as not very distant from the grove. No such chasm is visible at the present day in the neighbourhood of Colonus. But this fact is insufficient to prove that no appearance of the kind can have existed there in antiquity.

§ 10. Sophocles accurately defines the position of the

The secret
tomb.

'sheer threshold' by naming certain objects near it, familiar, evidently, to the people of the place, though unknown to us[1]. Here it was that Oedipus disappeared. But the place of his 'sacred *tomb*' (1545) was to be a secret, known only to Theseus. The tomb, then, was not at the spot where he disappeared, since that spot was known to all. The poet's conception appears to have been of this kind. At the moment when Oedipus passed away, in the mystic vision which left Theseus dazzled, it was revealed to the king of Athens where the mortal remains of Oedipus would be found. The soul of Oedipus went down to Hades, whether ushered by a conducting god, or miraculously drawn to the embrace of the spirits below (1661); the tenantless body left on earth was wafted by a supernatural agency to the secret tomb appointed for it. When Theseus rejoins the desolate daughters, he already knows where the tomb is, though he is not at liberty to divulge the place (1763).

[1] See on vv. 1593—1595.

§ 11.   The ground on which the grove of the Eumenides

The χαλκοῦς   at Colonus stands is called 'the Brazen Thres-
ὁδός.   hold, the stay of Athens' (57).   How is this
name related to that of the spot at which Oedipus disappeared,
—'the sheer threshold' (1590)?   One view is that the same
spot is meant in both cases.   We have then to suppose that
in verses 1—116 (the 'prologue') the scene is laid at the
καταρράκτης ὁδός, 'the sheer threshold'; and that at v. 117 the
scene changes to another side of the grove, where the rest of
the action takes place.   This supposition is, however, extremely
improbable, and derives no support from any stage arrangements which the opening scene implies.   Rather the 'Brazen
Threshold' of v. 57 was a name derived from the particular
spot which is called the 'sheer threshold,' and applied in
a larger sense to the immediately adjacent region, including
the ground on which the grove stood.   The epithet 'brazen'
properly belonged to the actual chasm or 'threshold,'—the
notion being that a flight of brazen steps connected the upper
world with the Homeric 'brazen threshold' of Hades.   In its
larger application to the neighbouring ground 'brazen' was
a poetical equivalent for 'rocky,' and this ground was called
the 'stay' or 'support' (ἔρεισμα) of Athens, partly in the
physical sense of 'firm basis,' partly also with the notion that
the land had a safeguard in the benevolence of those powers
to whose nether realm the 'threshold' led.

§ 12.   In order to understand the opening part of the play

                (as far as v. 201), it is necessary to form some
Stage ar-   distinct notion of the stage arrangements.   It is
rangements
in the opening of comparatively little moment that we cannot
scene.
                pretend to say exactly how far the aids of scenery
and carpentry were actually employed when the play was first
produced at Athens.   Without knowing this, we can still make
out all that is needful for a clear comprehension of the text.
First, it is evident that the back-scene (the palace-front of so
many plays) must here have been supposed to represent a land-

scape of some sort,—whether the acropolis of Athens was
shown in the distance, or not. Secondly, the sacred grove on
the stage must have been so contrived that Oedipus could
retire into its covert, and then show himself (138) as if in an
opening or glade, along which Antigone gradually leads him
until he is beyond the precinct. If one of the doors in the
back-scene had been used for the exit of Oedipus into the
grove, then it would at least have been necessary to show,
within the door, a tolerably deep vista. It seems more likely
that the doors of the back-scene were not used at all in this
play. I give a diagram to show how the action as far as v. 201
might be managed.

Antigone leads in her blind father on the spectators' left.
She places him on a seat of natural rock (the '1st seat' in the

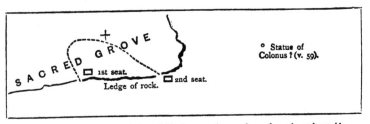

1st seat of Oedipus,—a rock just within the grove (verse 19).—2nd seat (v. 195), outside
the grove, on a low ledge of rock (v. 192). +marks the point at which Oedipus discovers
himself to the Chorus (v. 138), by stepping forward into an open glade of the grove. His
gradual advance in verses 173—191 is from this point to the 2nd seat.

diagram). This rock is just within the bounds of the grove;
which evidently was not surrounded by a fence of any kind,
ingress and egress being free. When the Chorus approach,
Antigone and her father hide in the grove, following the left of
the two dotted lines (113). When Oedipus discloses himself
to the Chorus (138), he is well within the grove. Assured of
safety, he is gradually led forward by Antigone (173—191),
along the right-hand dotted line. At the limit of the grove, in
this part, there is a low ledge of natural rock, forming a sort of

threshold. When he has set foot on this ledge of rock,—being now just outside the grove,—he is told to halt (192). A low seat of natural rock,—the outer edge (ἄκρον) of the rocky threshold,—is now close to him. He has only to take a step sideways (λέχριος) to reach it. Guided by Antigone, he moves to it, and she places him on it (the ' 2nd seat' in the diagram: v. 201).

§ 13. The general voice of ancient tradition attributed the *Oedipus Coloneus* to the latest years of Sophocles,

The Coloneus ascribed to the poet's last years. who is said to have died at the age of ninety, either at the beginning of 405 B.C., or in the latter half of 406 B.C. According to the author of the second Greek argument to the play, it was brought out, after the poet's death, by his grandson and namesake, Sophocles, the son of Ariston, in the archonship of Micon, Ol. 94. 3 (402 B.C.). The ancient belief is expressed by the well-known story for which Cicero is our earliest authority :—

'Sophocles wrote tragedies to extreme old age; and as, owing to this pursuit, he was thought to neglect his property, he was brought by his sons before a court of law, in order that the judges might declare him incapable of managing his affairs,—as Roman law withdraws the control of an estate from the incompetent head of a family. Then, they say, the old man recited to the judges the play on which he was engaged, and which he had last written,—the *Oedipus Coloneus*; and asked whether that poem was suggestive of imbecility. Having recited it, he was acquitted by the verdict of the court.'

Plutarch specifies the part recited,—viz. the first stasimon,

The story of the recitation —not impossible. —which by an oversight he calls the parodos,— quoting vv. 668—673, and adding that Sophocles was escorted from the court with applauding shouts, as from a theatre in which he had triumphed. The story should not be too hastily rejected because, in a modern estimate, it may seem melo-

dramatic or absurd. There was nothing impossible in the
incident supposed. The legal phrase used by the Greek
authorities is correct, describing an action which could be,
and sometimes was, brought by Athenian sons against their
fathers. As to the recitation, a jury of some hundreds of
citizens in an Athenian law-court formed a body to which such
a *coup de théâtre* could be addressed with great effect. The
general spirit of Greek forensic oratory makes it quite intelligible
that a celebrated dramatist should have vindicated his sanity in
the manner supposed. The true ground for doubt is of another
Its probable kind. It appears that an arraignment of the
origin. aged Sophocles, by his son Iophon, before a
court of his clansmen (phratores), had furnished a scene to
a contemporary comedy; and it is highly probable that the
comic poet's invention—founded possibly on gossip about
differences between Sophocles and his sons—was the origin
of the story. This inference is slightly confirmed by the words
which, according to one account, Sophocles used in the law-
court: εἰ μέν εἰμι Σοφοκλῆς, οὐ παραφρονῶ· εἰ δὲ παραφρονῶ, οὐκ
εἰμὶ Σοφοκλῆς. That has the ring of the Old Comedy. The
words are quoted in the anonymous Life of Sophocles as being
recorded by Satyrus, a Peripatetic who lived about 200 B.C.,
and left a collection of biographies. His work appears to have
been of a superficial character, and uncritical. The incident
of the trial, as he found it in a comedy of the time of Sophocles,
would doubtless have found easy acceptance at his hands.
From Satyrus, directly or indirectly, the story was probably
derived by Cicero and later writers.

§ 14. The internal evidence of the play has been inter-
Internal preted in three ways. First, it has been argued
evidence. that it is political in tone and was probably
composed at the beginning of the Peloponnesian War with
the view of kindling Athenian patriotism. Secondly, it has
been suggested that Colonus Hippius may have been in some
special sense the knights' quarter, and that the play being

composed for the Great Dionysia of B.C. 411, just before the
government of the Four Hundred had been established by the
assembly at Colonus, it was adapted to the sympathies of the
oligarchical party, but that the failure of that movement made
its reproduction unsafe until B.C. 402, after the poet's death
But though an Athenian spectator may have found some such
meaning in the play, it is nevertheless from first to last, in great
things and in small, purely a work of ideal art.   Thirdly, the
arguments for its lateness of composition have been rested
(1) on the larger scope given to scenic effects, (2) its
admission of secondary interests other than the single issue,
and its contemplative tendency, which leaves the spectator
at leisure to meditate on such themes as the religious and
moral aspects of the hero's acts, or the probable effect of his
pleas on the Athenian mind, (3) on the fact that it ends with
reconciliation rather than disaster.

   But it is not easy to decide how far these traits are due to
the subject itself, and how far they can safely be regarded as
distinctive of the poet's later manner.   It would be possible to
argue with some plausibility that they are characteristic of
youth ; and on the whole we cannot go beyond the following
conclusion.

   There is no reason to question the external evidence which
refers the *Oedipus Coloneus* to the latest years of

Conclusion.

Sophocles.   But no corroboration of it can be
derived from the internal evidence, except in one general
aspect and one detail,—viz. the choice of an Attic subject,
and the employment of a fourth actor.   The Attic plays of
Euripides belong to the latter part of the Peloponnesian War,
which naturally tended to a concentration of home sympathies.
An Attic theme was the most interesting that a dramatist could
choose ; and he was doing a good work, if, by recalling the
past glories of Athens, he could inspire new courage in her
sons.   If Attica was to furnish a subject, the author of the
Oedipus Tyrannus had no need to look beyond his native

Colonus; and it is conceivable that this general influence of the time should have decided the choice. In three scenes of the play, four actors are on the stage together. This innovation may be allowed as indicating the latest period of Sophocles[1].

[1] See on the Dramatis Personae, pp. l, li.

MANUSCRIPTS, EDITIONS, AND COMMENTARIES.

In the second part of the Introduction to the facsimile of the Florence MS., L, I have concisely stated some reasons for holding that L is not the sole source of our MSS., though it is far the best, and may properly be described as the basis of textual criticism for Sophocles. This play was one of those which were less often copied, and in no one of the seven, perhaps, is the superiority of L more apparent. Among the other MSS. of this play which possess comparative importance, two groups may be broadly distinguished. One group consists of those MSS. which, so far as this play is concerned, are in nearer general agreement with L. Of these the chief is A, cod. 2712 in the National Library at Paris (13th cent.). At the head of the other group is B, cod. 2787 *ib.* (ascribed to the 15th cent.); and within this second group, again, a special character belongs to T (cod. 2711, *ib.*, 15th cent.), as representing the recension of Demetrius Triclinius (14th cent.). These MSS. I have myself collated.

The readings of six other MSS. are recorded by Elmsley in his edition of this play; though, as he truly says, their aid is here of little moment to those who have the testimony of the four named above, L, A, B, and T. Of these six, four may be referred to my first group, and two to the second.

To the first, or L, group belong the following :—(1) F, cod. 2886 in the National Library at Paris (late 15th cent.), derived immediately from L. It usually adopts the corrections of the diorthotes of that MS. (2) R, cod. 34 in the Riccardian Library at Florence. [It has sometimes been ascribed to the 14th cent.; but is pronounced to be of the 16th by Mr P. N. Papageorgius, in his tractate 'Codex Laurentianus von Sophokles und eine neue Kollation im Scholientexte,' Leipzig, Teubner, 1883.] This MS. is nearly akin to A. (3) R², cod. 77 *ib.* (usually said to be of the 15th cent., but, according to Papageorgius, *l. c.*, not older than the 17th). This breaks off at the end of v. 853. (4) L², cod. 31. 10 in the Laurentian Library at Florence (14th cent.), characterised by Elmsley, not without reason, as 'mendosissimus.'

To the second, or B, group belong the following:—(5) Vat., cod. Pal. 287 in the Vatican Library (14th cent.). (6) Farn., cod. II. F. 34 in the National Library at Naples (15th cent.). It is in nearest agreement with T, having the readings of Triclinius. Of these MSS., Elmsley had himself collated R, R², L²: for F, he refers to a collation by Faehsi, and for Vat., to one by Amati. I do not know whether he had himself inspected Farn.

The following emendations of my own are adopted in the text:—121 δή after λεῦσσε.—355 μοι for μου.—541 ἐπωφελήσας for ἐπωφέλησα.—1113 κἀναπνεύσατον for κἀναπαύσατον.—1491 f. εἴτ' ἄκρα | περὶ γύαλ' for εἴτ' ἄκραν | ἐπιγύαλον.—Also these transpositions:—534 σαί τ' εἶσ' ἄρ' for σαί τ' ἄρ' εἰσίν.—1085 ἰὼ θεῶν πάνταρχε, παντ|όπτα Ζεῦ for ἰὼ Ζεῦ πάνταρχε θεῶν, | παντόπτα.—1462 μέγας, ἴδε, μάλ' ὅδ' ἐρείπεται | κτύπος ἄφατος διόβολος for ἴδε μάλα μέγας ἐρείπεται | κτύπος ἄφατος· ὅδε διόβολος.—A few more emendations, not placed in the text, are suggested in the notes. Among these are:—243 τοῦδ' ἀμμόρου for τοῦ μόνου.—385 ὥστ' for ὡς.—868 θεὸς for θεῶν.—896 οἷα καὶ for οἷά περ.—1192 αἰδοῦ νιν for ἀλλ' αὐτόν.—1493 Ποσειδωνίαν for Ποσειδωνίῳ.—1510 καὶ τῷ πέπεισαι for ἐν τῷ δὲ κεῖσαι.—1565 ἂν (or αὖ) τέρματ' ἂν πημάτων ἱκνούμενον for ἂν καὶ μάταν πημάτων ἱκνουμένων.—1604 εἶχ' ἔρωτος for εἶχε δρῶντος.—1702 οὐδ' ἐκεῖ ὢν for οὐδὲ γέρων.—The above list does not include 522 (text) ἤνεγκ' οὖν for ἤνεγκον, since, though the conjecture was made by me independently of Mr R. Whitelaw, the priority belongs to him; nor 153 (text) προσθήσει for προσθήσεις, which, I find, had been proposed by Prof. J. P. Postgate (*Journ. of Phil.* vol. X. p. 90).

The edition of the *Oedipus Coloneus* by Elmsley (Oxford, 1823)

Editions,
Commen-
taries, etc.

is noteworthy as the earliest edition of any Sophoclean play in which L (the Laurentian manuscript) was systematically used. Indeed, for all practical purposes, it was the earliest in which L was used at all. It is probable that Bernard Junta, the editor of the second Juntine edition (Florence, 1547), derived some of his readings from L; but, if so, his use of it was slight and unintelligent. Elmsley, having collated L in 1820, had recognised its paramount value: 'sive antiquitatem spectes, sive bonitatem, primus est.' In order to appreciate the importance of this acknowledgment, it is necessary to recollect what, in outline, the history of the text had been. The *editio princeps* of Sophocles, the Aldine (Venice, 1502), gave a text which, as a whole, is that of the Paris thirteenth-century MS., A. Adrian Turnebus, in his edition (Paris, 1552—3), adopted the Triclinian recension, represented by the Paris fifteenth-century MS., T. This Triclinian text prevailed in the later printed editions of Sophocles down to 1786. In that year Brunck published his first edition, reverting to the Aldine text as his basis, and placing A at the head of his MSS. Thus of the four MSS. mentioned above as principally useful for the *Oedipus Coloneus*,—L, A, B, T,—three correspond with periods of textual history. T represents the period from Turnebus to Brunck, 1553—1786; A, the period from Brunck to Elmsley, 1786—1823; L, the period since 1823.

Another interesting feature of Elmsley's edition is that it embodies what he judged best worth preserving in the work of previous commentators on this play, from Joachim Camerarius (1534) to J. F. Martin (1822). In the sixteenth century, after Camerarius, we have two editors who followed the text of Turnebus,—Henri Estienne (Stephanus, 1568) and William Canter (1579). The readings of Joseph Scaliger, to which John Burton sometimes refers, seem to have been found by the latter in a copy of Estienne's edition. The notes of H. Estienne are given entire,—'magis propter nominis auctoritatem quam quia magnam Sophocli lucem attulit.' So, again, Brunck's notes are given almost entire. The series of eighteenth-century commentators on this play, before Brunck, includes John James Reiske, John Burton, Benjamin Heath, Zachary Mudge, Samuel Musgrave, John Francis Vauvilliers. By 'Lond. A' and 'B' are denoted the anonymous editors of editions published in London in 1722 and 1747. Brunck's edition (Elmsley used the third, of 1788) forms a landmark. The printed texts before Brunck's are often designated collectively by Elmsley as the 'impressi ante Brunckium,'—including Musgrave's edition, since, though it was not published till 1800, Musgrave died in 1780.

Porson, who was twenty-seven when Brunck's first edition appeared (1786), is represented by a few notes on this play published four years after his death in the *Adversaria* (1812), and by a few more which Kidd records. It is right to remember that these jottings, mostly made in youth, supply no measure of the resources which Porson's mature power could have brought to bear ; yet here also some excellent suggestions are due to him (see, *e.g.*, on 709 f. and 1773). In the nineteenth century we have F. H. Bothe, G. H. Schaefer, L. Doederlein, C. Reisig, and J. F. Martin,—thus bringing the catena of Elmsley's predecessors down to the year before that in which his own work appeared. His edition has a permanent historical interest for students of the *Oedipus Coloneus*.

With regard to the work which has been done on the play since Elmsley's time, reference has been made, with varying degrees of frequency, to the complete editions of Sophocles (here named alphabetically) by Bergk, Blaydes, Campbell, Dindorf, Hartung, Hermann, Linwood, Nauck, Schneidewin, Tournier, Wunder. I have also used the new recension of Dindorf's text, in the Teubner series, by S. Mekler (Leipsic, 1885). Separate editions of this play by the following editors have also been consulted:—L. Bellermann (in the Woff-Bellermann ed., Leipsic, 1883): A. Meineke (Berlin, 1863): F. A. Paley (Cambridge, 1881): C. E. Palmer (Cambridge, 1860): N. Wecklein (Munich, 1880). The views of many other scholars are noticed in connection with particular passages. I have found Wecklein's *Ars Sophoclis emendandi* (Würzburg, 1869) especially valuable in giving occasional references to scattered criticisms, in German periodicals or elsewhere, which might otherwise have escaped my notice ; for the sporadic literature of the subject is diffused, often in very minute portions, through a large number of journals and tracts. Mr R. Whitelaw's excellent verse translation of Sophocles (London, Rivingtons, 1883) possesses the further merit, rare in a metrical rendering, of usually showing exactly how he takes the Greek, and thus has in some degree the value of a commentary,—supplemented, in a few cases, by short notes at the end.

METRICAL ANALYSIS.

Ancient Greek metre is the arrangement of syllables according to 'quantity,' *i.e.* according as they are 'short' or 'long.'

Metre.

A 'short' syllable as opposed to a 'long,' is that on which the voice dwells for a shorter time. In Greek verse the short syllable, ⌣, is the unit of measure. Its musical equivalent is the quaver, ♪, ⅛ of 𝅝. The long syllable, –, has twice the value of ⌣, being musically equal to the crotchet, ♩.

Besides ⌣ and –, the only signs used for the lyrics of this play are the following:—

(1) ⌐ for –, when the value of – is increased by *one half*, so that it is equal to ⌣⌣⌣, –⌣, or ⌣–. And ⌐ for –, when the value of – is *doubled*, so that it is equal to –⌣⌣, ⌣⌣–, or ––.

(2) >, to mark an 'irrational syllable,' *i.e.* one bearing a metrical value to which its proper time-value does not entitle it; viz. ⌣ for –, or – for ⌣. Thus ἔργων means that the word serves as a choree, – ⌣, not as a spondee.

(3) ⌣⌣, instead of –⌣⌣, when a dactyl (then called 'cyclic') serves for a choree, – ⌣.

(4) ω, written over two short syllables (as παρά), when they have the value only of one short.

The last syllable of a verse is common (ἀδιάφορος, *anceps*). One practice is to mark it ⌣ or – according to the metre: *e.g.* ἔργων, if the word represents a choree, or ἔργᾱ, if a spondee.

Pauses. At the end of a verse, ∧ marks a pause equal to ⌣, and ∧̄ a pause equal to –

The *anacrusis* of a verse (the part preliminary to its regular metre) is marked off by three dots placed vertically, ⦂

The kinds of metre used are few in number, though they occur in various combinations.

Metres used in this play.

1. *Logaoedic*, or *prose-verse* (λογαοιδικός), was the name given by ancient metrists to a kind of measure which seemed to them something intermediate between verse and prose, owing to its apparent irregularity. Its essential elements are the choree, – ⏑, and the cyclic dactyl, metrically equivalent to a choree, – ⏑ ⏑. Take these words :—

> *Stréngthen our | hánds thou | Lórd of | báttles.*

This is a 'logaoedic' verse of 4 feet (or tetrapody). If '*Oh*' were prefixed to '*strengthen*,' it would represent an 'anacrusis,' or prelude to the regular measure. Such a verse was called '*Glyconic,*' from a lyric poet Glycon, who used it. A dactyl comes first ; then 3 chorees : – ⏑ ⏑ | – ⏑ | – ⏑ | – ⏑. But the dactyl might also stand *second*, as :

> *Líghtly, | mérrily, | spéd the | mórnings :*

or, *third*, as :

> *Lóst one, | foótstep | néver re|túrning.*

According to the place of the dactyl, the verse was called a *First*, *Second*, or *Third* Glyconic.

In this play, the *Second* Glyconic (with anacrusis) is the main theme of the Parodos from 117 as far as 206 (omitting the anapaests); of the First Stasimon (668—719) ; and of the Third Stasimon from 1211 to 1248. It also occurs elsewhere in combination with other forms of logaoedic verse, shorter or longer. Of these other forms, the most important is the verse of 3 feet (or tripody), called 'Pherecratic' from Pherecrates a poet of the Old Comedy. It is merely the Glyconic shortened by one foot, and is called 'First' or 'Second' according as the dactyl comes first or second : so that this is a 'First' Pherecratic,—

> *Hárk to the | crý re|soúnding.*

We have this combined with the Second Glyconic in the opening of the Fourth Stasimon (1556 ff.). Elsewhere in the play we find logaoedic verses twice as long as this, *i.e.* hexapodies. They are combined with the tetrapody, or Glyconic verse, in the epode to the Third Stasimon (1239 ff.), and with the tripody, or Pherecratic, in the kommos at vv. 510 ff.

2. *Dochmiacs* occur in vv. 833—843 = 876—886, and in parts of the kommos, 1447—1499. In the following line, let '*serfs*' and '*wrongs*' be pronounced with as much stress as the second syllable of '*rebel*' and of '*resent*' :—

> *Rebél | Sérfs, rebél | Resént wróngs so díre.*

The first three words form one 'dochmiac' measure; the last four, another; and the whole line is a 'dochmiac dimeter,' written ⏑ ⁝ ‒ ‒ ⏑ |
‒, ⏑ ‖ ‒ ‒ ⏑ | ‒ ∧ ‖. The comma marks the usual caesura, which is preserved in our example. The elements of the dochmiac were thus the bacchius, ‒ ‒ ⏑, equal to 5 shorts, and the (shortened) choree, ‒, equal to 2 shorts. It was a joining of odd and even. No other such combination of *unequal* measures was used by the Greeks. The name δόχμιος, '*slanting*,' '*oblique*,' expressed the resulting effect by a metaphor. It was as if the rhythm diverged sideways from the straight course. The varieties of the dochmiac arose chiefly from resolving one of the long syllables into two shorts; either with, or without, the further substitution of an 'irrational' long for a short in the anacrusis, or in the short syllable of the bacchius.

3. The *Ionic* verse of two feet (dipody) occurs in the Parodos (as v. 214 τέκνον, ὤμοι, τί γεγώνω;). The Ionic measure is ‒ ‒ ⏑ ⏑. Without anacrusis (⏑ ⏑), it is called *ionicus a maiore*: with anacrusis, *ionicus a minore*. Here the Ionic dipody has anacrusis, and should be written ⏑ ⏑ ⁝ ‒ ‒ ⏑ ⏑ |
‒ ‒ ∧ ‖ :

To the híll-tops, to the válleys.

4. Other measures used in the lyrics of this play are *dactylic* (‒ ⏑ ⏑), *choreic* or trochaic (‒ ⏑), *iambic* (⏑ ‒), in various lengths. The only point which calls for notice is the use of the rapid dactylic *tetrapody* to express agitated entreaty (Parodos, 241 ff.). Anapaests of the ordinary type occur in the Parodos and at the close.

In the metrical schemes which are subjoined, the kind of metre used is stated at the beginning of each series of verses, and the scanning of every verse is shown.

I.   Parodos, vv. 117—253.

FIRST STROPHE.—Logaoedic.   The Second Glyconic (seen in v. 3)
is the main theme.

I., II., denote the *First* and *Second Rhythmical Periods*. The sign ‖ marks the end of a *Rythmical Sentence*;] marks that of a *Period*.

I. 1.   ⏑ ⁝ ‒ ⏑ ⏑ | ⌐ | ‒ ⏓ | ‒ ∧ ‖

  2.   ‒ ⏑ ⏑ | ‒ ⏑ ⏑ | ‒ ⏑ | ‒ ⏑ | ⌐ | ‒ ∧ ‖

  3.   ⏑ ⁝ ⌐ | ‒ ⏑ ⏑ | ‒ ⏑ | ‒ ∧]

II. 1. > : ⌞ | ⌞ | – ‿ | – ⌃ ‖
  2. > : ⌞ | ⌞ | – ‿ | – ⌃ ‖
  3. ‿ : ⌞ | – ⌃ ‖
  4. ‿ : ⌞ | ⸌‿ | – ‿ | ⌞ ‖ – > | – ‿‿ |
      – ‿ | ⌞ ‖ – ‿ | – ‿‿ | – ‿ | – ⌃ ‖
  5. – ⸮ | ⸌‿ | – ‿ | ⌞, ‖ ⸌‿ | – ‿ | ⌞ | – ⌃ ‖
  6. ω : – ‿ | – ‿ | – | –, ‿ ‖ ⌞ | ⸌‿ | – ‿ | ⌞ ‖
      – > | ⸌‿ | – ‿ | – ⌃ ‖
  7. > : ⌞ | ⸌‿ | – ‿ | ⌞ ‖ ⸮‿‿ | – ‿ | ⌞ | – ⌃ ‖
  8. ω : – > | ⸌‿ | – ⸌ω | – ⌃ ‖
  9. ω : ⸌‿ | – > | – > | – ⌃ ‖
  10. ω : ⌞ | – ⌃]]

SECOND STROPHE.—Logaoedic.

I.   – > | ⸌‿ | ⌞ ‖ ⸌‿ | ⌞ | ⸌‿ | ⌞ ‖ ⸌‿ | ⌞ | – ⌃ ‖
II. 1. ⸮ : – ω | – ‿ | ⌞ | – ⌃ ‖
  2. ⸮ : – ω | – ‿ | ⌞ | – ⌃ ‖
  3. > : ⸌‿ | – ‿ | – ⌃ ‖
III. ‿‿‿ | ⸌‿ | – ‿ | – ‖ –
      – – – – ⌢
         ‖
      ‿ | ⸌‿ | – ‿ | – ⌃]]

The corresponding words of the strophe are lost. Those of the antistrophe, given above, are regarded by Schmidt as forming a single verse,
which is interrupted by the cry of pain, *ἰὼ μοί μοι*, from Oedipus. The
sign ⌢ shows that *ἰὼ μοί μοι* is a mere parenthesis, not counted in the metre
‖
of the verse.

IV. 1. ‿‿‿ | ⸌‿ | – ‿ | ⌞ ‖ – > | ⸌‿ | – ‿ | – ⌃ ‖
  2. – > | ⸌‿ | ⌞ | – ⌃]]

The words of the strophe are lost.

V. 1. – > | ⸌‿ | – ‿ | – ⌃ ‖
  2. – > | ⸌‿ | – ‿ | – > ‖
  3. ‿ : ‿‿‿ | ‿‿‿ | – ‿ | – ⌃ ‖
  4. ⸌‿ | – ‿ | ⌞ | – ⌃]

After the Second Strophe follows the third system of Anapaests; 188
ἄγε νῦν—191 πολεμῶμεν. After the Second Antistrophe, from 207 (ὦ ξένοι,
ἀπόπτολις) to the end of the Parodos, the correspondence of Strophe and
Antistrophe ceases. The verses are ἀνομοιόστροφα. In some editions the
term ἐπῳδός is applied to them; but, as Schmidt points out (*Gr. Metrik*
p. 451), this is erroneous, as the absence of unity is enough to show. The
ἀνομοιόστροφα fall into six sections, each divided into rhythmical periods.
The rhythms adopted in the successive sections are varied with masterly
skill, according to the emotion which each part interprets.

ANOMOIOSTROPHA.

First Section.—Logaoedic.

1. $>\vdots \cup\cup\cup \mid \smile\cup \mid -\cup \mid \llcorner \parallel \cup\cup\cup \mid -\cup \mid -\cup \mid - \wedge \parallel$
2. $>\vdots \smile\cup \mid -\cup \mid -\cup \mid \llcorner \parallel \smile\cup \mid -\cup \mid -\cup \mid -\cup]\!]$

Second Section.—Ionic.

1. $\cup\cup\vdots --\cup\cup \mid --, \cup\cup \parallel --\cup\cup \mid -- \overline{\wedge} \parallel$
2. $\cup\cup\vdots --\cup\cup \mid \sqcup\cup\cup \parallel --\cup\cup \mid \sqcup \overline{\wedge}]\!]$

Third Section.—Logaoedic.

1. $\smile\cup \mid \smile\cup \mid \llcorner \mid \cup\cup\cup \mid - \wedge \parallel$
2. $\qquad \cup\cup\vdots -\cup\cup \mid -\cup\cup \mid \sqcup \mid - \wedge \parallel$
3. $\smile\cup \mid \smile\cup \mid \llcorner \mid \cup\cup\cup \mid - \wedge \parallel$
4. $\qquad \cup\cup\vdots -\cup\cup \mid -\cup\cup \mid \sqcup \mid - \wedge \parallel$
5. $\smile\cup \mid \smile\cup \mid \llcorner \mid \cup\cup\cup \mid - \wedge \parallel$
6. $\qquad \cup\cup\vdots -\cup\cup \mid -\cup\cup \mid \sqcup \mid - \wedge \parallel$
7. $-\cup\cup \mid -\cup\cup \mid \llcorner \mid \cup\cup\cup \mid - \wedge \parallel$
8. $\qquad \cup\cup\vdots -\cup\cup \mid -\cup\cup \mid \sqcup \mid - \wedge]\!]$

Fourth Section.—Anapaestic.

1. $-\vdots -- \mid -- \mid \cup\cup- \mid - \overline{\wedge} \parallel$
2. $\cup\cup\vdots -\cup\cup \mid -\cup\cup \mid \sqcup \mid - \overline{\wedge} \parallel$
3. $-\vdots -- \mid -- \mid \cup\cup- \mid - \overline{\wedge} \parallel$
4. $\cup\cup\vdots -\cup\cup \mid -\cup\cup \mid \sqcup \mid - \overline{\wedge}]\!]$

Fifth Section.—I. II. Dactylic.   III. Logaoedic.

I. $\quad --\cup \mid -\cup\cup \mid -\cup\cup \mid -\cup\cup \parallel$
$\qquad -\cup\cup \mid -\cup\cup \mid - \overline{\wedge} \parallel$
$\qquad \cup\cup\vdots -\cup\cup \mid -\cup\cup \mid -\cup\cup \mid - \overline{\wedge} \parallel$

II. ⏑⏑⦂–⏑⏑ | –⏑⏑ | –⏑⏑ | –⏑⏑ | –⏑⏑ | – ‾∧ ‖
  ⏑⏑⦂–⏑⏑ | –⏑⏑ ‖ –⏑⏑ | –⏑⏑ | –⏑⏑ | – ‾∧ ‖
III. ⏑⏑⦂~⏑ | ~⏑ | –⏑ | – ‾∧ ‖
  ⏑⦂–⏑ | –⏑ | ⌐ | – ‾∧]

Sixth Section.—I. Dactylic. II. Logaoedic.

I. 1. –⏑⏑ | ⊔ | ⌐⏑ | – ‾∧ ‖
 2. ⌐⏑ | –⏑⏑ | –⏑⏑ | – ‾∧ ‖
 3. –⏑⏑ | –⏑⏑ | –– | – ∧ ‖
 4. –– | –⏑⏑ | ⌐⏑ | –– ‖
 5. –⏑⏑ | –⏑⏑ | –⏑⏑ | –⏑⏑ ‖
 6. –⏑⏑ | ⊔ | ⌐⏑ | – ‾∧ ‖
 7. –⏑⏑ | –– | –⏑⏑ | –⏑⏑ ‖
 8. –⏑⏑ | –⏑⏑ | –⏑⏑ | –⏑⏑ ‖
 9. –⏑⏑ | –⏑⏑ | –⏑⏑ | –⏑⏑ ‖
 10. –⏑⏑ | –⏑⏑ | –⏑⏑ | –⏑⏑ ‖
 11. –– | –⏑⏑ | –⏑⏑ | –⏑⏑
 12. –⏑⏑ | –⏑⏑ | –⏑⏑ | –⏑⏑ ‖
 13. –⏑⏑ | ⊔ | ⌐⏑ | – ‾∧ ‖
 14. –⏑⏑ | –⏑⏑ | –⏑⏑ | –⏑⏑ ‖
 15. –⏑⏑ | –⏑⏑ | –⏑⏑ | –⏑⏑]
II. 1. ~⏑ | ~⏑ | –⏑ | – ∧ ‖
 2. ~⏑ | ⌐ | ⏑⏑⏑ | – ∧ ‖
 3. –⏑ | –⏑ | ⌐ | – ∧]

II. Kommos, vv. 510—548.

FIRST STROPHE.—Logaoedic.

I. 1. –> | ~⏑ | ⌐, ‖ ~⏑ | ⌐, | ~⏑ | ⌐ ‖ ~⏑ | ⌐ | – ∧ ‖
 2. ⊃⦂ ~⏑ | –⏑̆ω | ⌐ | – ∧]
II. 1. ⏑⦂⌐ | – ∧ ‖
 2. >⦂ ⌐ | ⌐ | ~⏑ | –⏑ | ⌐ | – ∧ ‖
 3. >⦂ ~⏑ | –⏑ | ⌐ | – ∧ ‖
 4. >⦂ ~⏑ | –⏑ | ⌐ | – ∧ ‖
 5. >⦂ ~⏑ | –⏑ | ⌐ | – ∧ ‖

6. ∪ ⋮ ⏑⏑ | ⌞ | ⏑⏑ | −∪ ‖
7. > ⋮ ⌞ | ⌞ | ⏑⏑ | −∪ | ⌞ | − ∧ ‖
8. > ⋮ −> | ∪∪∪ | ⌞ | − ∧ ‖
9. ⌞ | − ∧ ‖
10. > ⋮ −> | ⏑⏑ | −∪ | ⌞ | ⌞ | − ∧ ⟧

Second Strophe.—Iambic.

I. 1. > ⋮ −∪ | ∪∪∪ | −∪ | −, > ‖ −∪ | ∪∪∪ | −∪ | − ∧ ‖
2. ∪ ⋮ −∪ | ⌞ | −∪ | −∪ ‖ −∪ | ᪰∪ | −∪ | − ∧ ⟧
II. 1. ∪ ⋮ ∪∪∪ | ∪∪∪ | −∪ | − ∧ ‖
2. ∪ ⋮ −∪ | −∪ | −∪ | ∪∪∪ | −∪ | − ∧ ‖
3. − ω | − ω | − ω | − ω ‖
4. ∪ ⋮ −∪ | −⌣̆ | ∪∪∪ | −∪ | ⌞ | − ∧ ⟧

III. First Stasimon, vv. 668—719.

First Strophe (forming a single period).—Logaoedic, with the Second
Glyconic for main theme.

1. −> | ⏑⏑ | −∪ | ⌞ ‖ −> | ⏑⏑ | −∪ | −∪ | ⌞ | − ∧ ‖
2. ⌣̆ ⋮ ⌞ | ⏑⏑ | −∪ | ⌞ ‖ −⌣̆ | ⏑⏑ | −∪ | − ∧ ‖
3. ⌣̆ ⋮ ⌞ | ⏑⏑ | −∪ | ⌞ ‖ −⌣̆ | ⏑⏑ | ⌞ | − ∧ ‖
4. ⌣̆ ⋮ ⌞ | ⏑⏑ | −∪ | ⌞ ‖ −> | ⏑⏑ | −∪ | − ∧ ‖
5. ⏑⏑ | ⏑⏑ | ⏑⏑ | ⌞ ‖ ∪∪∪ | −∪ | −∪ | −∪ ‖
6. −> | ⏑⏑ | −∪ | ⌞ ‖ −⌣̆ | ⏑⏑ | −∪ | −∪ | ⌞ | −∧ ‖
7. > ⋮ ⏑⏑ | −∪ | ⌞ | − ∧ ⟧

Second Strophe.—Logaoedic,—the Second Glyconic being now varied
by other logaoedic sentences, of 3, 6, or 2 feet. Note the contrast
between the numerous small periods here, and the one great period of
the First Strophe.

I.   −> | ⏑⏑ | ⌞ ‖ ⏑⏑ | ⌞ ‖ ⏑⏑ | ⌞ | − ∧ ⟧
II.   −> | ⏑⏑ | ⌞ ‖ ⏑⏑ | ⌞ | ⏑⏑ | ⌞ ‖ ⏑⏑ | ⌞ | − ∧ ‖
III. 1. > ⋮ −∪ | ⌞ | −∪ | −∪ | ⌞ | − ∧ ‖
2. > ⋮ −∪ | −∪ | −∪ | − ∧ ‖
3. ∪ ⋮ −∪ | ⌞ | −∪ | −∪ | ⌞ | − ∧ ⟧

IV. 1. –> | ⌣⌣⌣ | └ | ⌣⌣⌣ | └ | – ∧ ‖
　　2. > ⫶ –⌣ | └ | ⪦⌣ | –⌣ | └ | – ∧ ⟧
V.　　 └ | └ | ⌣⌣⌣ | └ ‖ ⌣⌣⌣ | └ ‖ ⌣⌣⌣ | ⌣⌣⌣ |–⌣ | – ∧ ‖
VI. 1. –> | ⌣⌣⌣ | –⌣ | – ∧ ‖
　　2. –> | ⌣⌣⌣ | └ | – ∧ ⟧

IV.　Lyrics* in vv. 833—843 = 876—886.—Dochmiac.

I. 1.　⌣ ⫶ └⌣ | – ∧ ‖
　2.　⌣ ⫶ ––⌣ | –, ⌣ ‖ ––⌣ | –, ⌣ ‖ ⌣⌣–⌣ | – ∧ ‖
　3.　> ⫶ ––⌣ | –, ⌣ ‖ ⌣⌣–⌣ | – ∧ ⟧

[Here follow four iambic trimeters, 837—840, = 880—883.]

II. 1.　⌣ ⫶ ––⌣ | –⌣ ‖ ––⌣ | – ∧ ‖
　2.　⌣ ⫶ ⌣⌣–⌣ | –, ⌣ ‖ ⌣⌣–⌣ | – ∧ ‖
　3.　⌣ ⫶ ––⌣ | – ∧ ⟧

V.　Second Stasimon, vv. 1044—1095.

First Strophe.—Dactylic.

I. 1.　– ⫶ –⌣⌣ | └⌣ | – ∧̄ ‖
　2.　– ⫶ –⌣⌣ | └⌣ | – ∧̄ ‖
　3.　– ⫶ –⌣⌣ | └⌣ | – ∧̄ ⟧
II. 1.　– ⫶ └⌣ | –– | └⌣ | –– ‖ –⌣⌣ | –– ‖
　2.　≥ ⫶ └⌣ | └ | –⌣⌣ | –– ‖ └⌣ | – ∧̄ ‖
III. 1.　– ⫶ └⌣ | –– | └⌣ | └ ‖ └⌣ | –– | └⌣ | –– ‖
　2.　└⌣ | –– | └⌣ | –– ‖ └ | └⌣ | –⌣⌣ | – ∧̄ ‖
　3.　–⌣⌣ | └ | └ | └⌣ ‖ –– | –⌣⌣ | └ | – ∧̄ ‖
　4.　└ | └ | └⌣ | –– ‖ └⌣ | └ | –⌣⌣ | –– ⟧

Second Strophe.—Dactylic.

I. 1.　– ⫶ └ | –– | └⌣ | – ∧̄ ‖
　2.　└ | └ | └⌣ | – ∧̄ ‖
　3.　– ⫶ └⌣ | └ | └ | – ∧̄ ⟧

* Schmidt calls this lyric passage simply 'Wechselgesang.' It is not a
κομμόs in the proper sense (cp. n. on 833).

II. 1. > ⋮ ⌊⌣ | —— | ⌊⌣ | —— ‖ ⌊⌣ | —— | ⌊⌣ | – ◌̄ ‖
   2. > ⋮ ⌊⌣ | ⌣⌣ | –⌣⌣ | —— ‖ ⌊⌣ | —— | ⌊⌣ | ——⟧
III. 1. ⌊⌣ | —— | ⌊⌣ | —— ‖ ⌊⌣ | —— ‖
   2. –⌣⌣ | –⌣⌣ | —— ‖ ⌊⌣ | ⌊⌣ | —— ‖
   3. > ⋮ ⌣⌣ | ⌣⌣ | ⌊⌣ | ⌊⌣ ‖ ⌣⌣ | – ◌̄ ⟧

VI. Third Stasimon, vv. 1211—1248.

STROPHE.—Logaoedic, based on the Second Glyconic.

I. 1. –> | ⌣⌣⌣ | –⌣ | ⌊ ‖ –◌ | ⌣⌣⌣ | –⌣ | – ∧ ‖
   2. –> | ⌣⌣⌣ | –⌣ | ⌊ ‖ ⌣⌣⌣ | ⌣⌣⌣ | –⌣ | –⌣ ‖
   3. ◌̆ ⋮ ⌊ | ⌣⌣⌣ | –⌣ | ⌊ ‖ –◌ | ⌣⌣⌣ | –⌣ | – ∧ ‖
   4. ◌̆ ⋮ ⌊ | ⌣⌣⌣ | –⌣ | ⌊ ‖ –⌣ | ⌣̆⌣⌣ | –⌣ | – ∧ ⟧
II. 1. ⌣ ⋮ –⌣ | –⌣ | –⌣ | – ∧ ‖
   2. –⌣ | –⌣ | ⌣⌣⌣ | –⌣ ‖
   3. ⌣⌣⌣ | –⌣ | ⌣⌣⌣ | ⌣⌣◌ | ⌣⌣⌣ | –⌣ ‖
   4. ⌣̄⌣ | ⌣⌣⌣ | ⌣⌣⌣ | –⌣ ‖
   5. ⌣⌣⌣ | –⌣ | ⌊ | – ∧ ⟧

EPODE.—Logaoedic.

I. 1. ⌣ ⋮ ⌊ | ⌊ | –⌣ | –⌣ | –⌣ | – ∧ ‖
   2. –⌣ | –⌣ | –⌣ | –⌣ | ⌊ | – ∧ ⟧
II. 1. ⌣⌣ | ⌊ | ⌣⌣ | –⌣ | ⌊ | – ∧ ‖
   2. –> | ⌣⌣ | ⌊ | – ∧ ‖
   3. –> | ⌣⌣ | ⌊ | – ∧ ‖
   4. ⌊ | ⌣⌣ | ⌣⌣ | –⌣ | ⌊ | – ∧ ⟧*
III. 1. ⌣⌣ | ⌣⌣ | –> | – ∧ ‖
   2. ⌣⌣ | ⌊ | ⌊ | – ∧ ‖
   3. ⌣⌣ | ⌊ | –> | – ∧ ‖
   4. > ⋮ ⌣⌣ | ⌣⌣ | ⌊ | – ∧ ⟧

* Schmidt inserts γ' after κλονέουσιν, when the verse reads

> ⋮ ⌣⌣ | ⌊ | –⌣ | –⌣ | ⌊ | – ∧ ⟧

VII. Kommos, vv. 1447—1456 = 1462—1471 : 1477—1485 = 1491—1499.

FIRST STROPHE.—Iambic in periods I. and II. In III., **v.** 1 is dochmiac, **v.** 2 logaoedic (First Glyconic).

I. 1. ∪ ⦂ ∪ ∪ ∪ | ∪ ∪ ∪ | – ∪ | – ∧ ‖
2. ∪ ⦂ ∪ ∪ ∪ | – ∪ | ∪ ∪ ∪ | – ∪ | – ∧ ‖
3. – ∪ | – ∪ | ⌐ | – ∪ | – ∧ ⟧
II. 1. ∪ ⦂ – ∪ | – ∪ | – ∪ | – ∪, ‖ – ∪ | – ∪ | – ∪ | – ∧ ‖
2. ∪ ⦂ – ∪ | ⌐ | – ∪ | –, ∪ ‖ – ∪ | ⌐ | ∪ ∪ ∪ | – ∧ ⟧
III. 1. ∪ ⦂ ⏤ – ∪ | – ∪ ‖ – – ∪ | – ∧ ‖
2. ∪∪ | – > | ⌐ | – ∧ ⟧

SECOND STROPHE.—Dochmiac in periods I., II., IV.: iambic in III.

I. 1. ∪ ⦂ ∪ ∪ – ⌇ | –, ∪ ‖ – – ∪ | – ∧ ‖
2. ∪ ⦂ ∪ ∪ ∪ ∪ ∪ | ∪ ∪ ∧ ⟧
II. 1. > ⦂ ∪ ∪ – ⌇ | – ⌇ ‖ ∪ ∪ – ∪ | – ∧ ‖
2. > ⦂ ∪ ∪ – ∪ | – ∪ ‖ – – ∪ | – ∧ ⟧
III. ∪ ⦂ – ∪ | – ∪ | – ∪ | – ∪, ‖ – ∪ | – ∪ | – ∪ | – ∧ ⟧
IV. 1. ∪ ⦂ – – ∪ | –, ∪ | – – ∪ | – ∧ ‖
2. > ⦂ ∪ ∪ – > | – ∧ ⟧

VIII. Fourth Stasimon, vv. 1556—1578.

STROPHE.—Logaoedic (the tripody, or Pherecratic verse, in period I.; the tetrapody, or Glyconic, in II.).

I. ∪∪ | – ∪ | ⌐ ‖ ∪∪ | – ⌇ | ⌐ ‖ ∪∪ | – ∪ | – ∪ ⟧
II. 1. ∪∪ | – ∪ | – > | ⌐ ‖ – > | – > | – ⌇ | – ∧ ‖
2. ∪ ∪ ∪* | – ∪ | ∪ ∪ ∪ | ⌐ ‖ ∪∪ | ∪∪ | – ∪ | – ∧ ‖
3. > ⦂ ⌐ | ⌐ | – ∪ | ⌐, ‖ ∪∪ | ∪∪ | – ⌇ | – ∧ ‖
4. > ⦂ – ∪ | ⌐ | – ∪ | ⌐, ‖ – ∪ | – ∪ | – ∪ | – ∧ ‖
5. ∪ ⦂ – ∪ | ⌐ | – ∪ | – ∪ | ⌐ | – ∧ ⟧

---

* Schmidt reads μὴ ἐπίπονα, adding τὸν before ξένον: in the antistr., ὕλακα for φύλακα, adding δὴ before λόγος. This gives ⌇ ⦂ ∪ ∪ ∪ | ∪ ∪ ∪ | ∪ ∪ ∪ | ⌐, ‖ ∪ ∪ | ∪ ∪ | – ∪ | – ∧ ‖

IX. Kommos, vv. 1670—1750.

First Strophe.—Choreic, in verses of 6 or of 4 chorees.

I. 1. > ⋮ └ | └ | – ⏑ | – ⏑ | └ | – ∧ ||
2. – ω | – ω | – ω | – ω ||*
3. ⏑ ⋮ ⏖ ⏑ | – ⏑ | – ⏑ | – ⏑ | └ | – ∧ ||
4. – ω | – ω | – ω | – ω ||
5. – ω | – ω | – ω | – ω | – ω | – ω ||
6. ⏒ ⋮ – ⏑ | – ⏑ | └ | – ∧]]
II. 1. ⏑ ⋮ – ⏑ | └ | – ⏑ | – ⏑ | – ⏑ | – ∧ ||
2. ⏑ ⋮ – ⏑ | – ⏑ | – ⏑ | – ⏑ | – ⏑ | – ∧]]
III. 1. ⏑ ⏑ ⏑ | └ | – ⏑ | – ∧ ||
2. – ⏑ | – ⏑ | – ⏑ | – ⏑ ||
3. – ⏑ | – ⏑ | ⏑ ⏑ ⏑ | – ⏑ ||
4. ⏑ ⏑ ⏑ | └ | ⏑ ⏑ ⏑ | └ | ⏑ ⏑ ⏑ | – ∧]]
IV. 1. ⏑ ⋮ – ⏑ | – ⏑ | – ⏑ | – ∧ ||
2. – ⏑ | – ⏑ | – ⏑ | – ⏑, || ⏕ ⏑ | – ⏑ | – ⏑ | – ∧ ||
3. └ | └ | – ⏑ | –, ⏑ || – ⏑ | – ⏑ | – ⏑ | – ∧ ||
4. ⏑ ⋮ – ⏑ | ⏕ ⏑ | – ⏑ | – ∧]]
V. 1. – ⏑ | – ⏑ | ⏑ ⏑ ⏑ | ⏑ ⏑ ⏑ || – ⏑ | – ⏑ | – ⏑ | – ∧ ||
2. – ⏑ | – ⏑ | └ | – ∧ ||†
[lost in antistrophe]
3. ⏑ ⋮ – ⏑ | – ⏑ | – ⏑ | └ || –⏑ ⏑ | – ⏑ | └ | – ∧ ||
VI. 1. –⏑ ⏑ | – ⏑ | – ⏑ | – ⏒, || ⏑ ⏑ ⏑ | – ⏑ | – ⏑ | – ∧ ||
2. –⏑ ⏑ | – ⏑ | – ⏑ | └, || –⏑ ⏑ | – ⏑ | └ | – ∧]]

* ω means that two short syllables have the value of only one short; so that *οὐ τὸ μέν* (for example) is to be regarded as a choree, – ⏑, not as a cyclic dactyl, –⏑ ⏑. Schmidt has illustrated this by Aesch. *Ag.* 991 *θρῆνον Ἐρινύος αὐτοδίδακτος ἔσωθεν*, which similarly gives – ω | – ω | – ω | – ω | └ | – ∧ ||. In reference to that passage, he remarks:—'The heavy complaint of the Chorus, which breaks forth impetuously, is adequately expressed first by the strong ictus placed each time on –, and then by the quick movement of ω.'

† Schmidt omits *ξυνθανεῖν γεραιῷ*, but retains *πατρί*. Periods V. and VI., as given above, then form only one period.

SECOND STROPHE.—Choreic.

I. 1.   ∪ ⦂ − ∪ | − ∪ | − ∪ ‖ − ∪ | − ∪ | − ∧ ‖
   2.   > ⦂ ∪ ∪ ∪ | ◡◡ ∪ | − ∧ ⟧

II. 1.   > ⦂ ◠◡ ∪ | − ∪ | − ∪ | − ∧ ‖
   2.   ∪ ⦂ − ∪ | − ∪ | − ∪ | − ∧ ‖
   3.   ∪ ⦂ − ∪ | − ∪ | − ∪ | − ∧ ‖

III. 1.   − ∪ | − ⌣̑ | ∪ ∪ ∪ | − ∪ ‖
   2.   ◡◡ ∪ | − ⌣̑ | ∪ ∪ ∪ | − ∪ ‖
   3.   ∪ ∪ ∪ | ∪ ∪ ∪ | ∪ ∪ ∪ | − ∪ ‖
   4.   ∪ ∪ ∪ | ◠◡ ∪ | ∪ ∪ ∪ | ⌣ ∪ ⟧
       − − ⌢
         ‖

IV. 1.   − ∪ | − ∪ | ⌞ | − ∧ ‖
   2.   − ∪ | − ∪ | − ∪ | ∪ ∪ ∪ ‖
   3.   > ⦂ − ∪ | − ∪ | ⌞ | − ∧ ⟧

ΤΑ ΤΟΥ ΔΡΑΜΑΤΟΣ ΠΡΟΣΩΠΑ.

ΟΙΔΙΠΟΥΣ.	ΘΗΣΕΥΣ.
ΑΝΤΙΓΟΝΗ.	ΚΡΕΩΝ.
ΞΕΝΟΣ.	ΠΟΛΥΝΕΙΚΗΣ.
ΧΟΡΟΣ ΑΤΤΙΚΩΝ ΓΕΡΟΝΤΩΝ.	ΑΓΓΕΛΟΣ.
ΙΣΜΗΝΗ.	

The Ἀττικοὶ γέροντες who form the Chorus belong to Colonus. The so-called ξένος is also of Colonus (cp. vv. 78, 297), and derives his traditional title in the Dramatis Personae merely from the fact that Oedipus addresses him as ὦ ξεῖν' (v. 33).

In some parts of this play four persons are on the stage at once; viz. (1) vv. 1096—1210, Oedipus, Antigone, Ismene (mute), Theseus: (2) 1249—1446, Oed., Ant., Ism. (mute), Polyneices: (3) 1486—1555, Oed., Ant., Ism. (mute), Theseus. Two explanations of this fact are possible.

I. A fourth (regular) actor may have been employed. The cast might then have been as follows:—

1. *Protagonist.* Oedipus.
2. *Deuteragonist.* Antigone.
3. *Tritagonist.* Ismene. Creon.
4. *Fourth actor.* Stranger. Theseus. Polyneices. Messenger[1].

---

[1] In order that the same actor should play the Messenger and Theseus, we must suppose that the Messenger leaves the stage in the interval between the entrance of the two sisters (1670) and the entrance of Theseus (1751). The alternative, with or without a fourth actor, is that the Protagonist should take the part of the Messenger as well as that of Oedipus. So in the *Ajax* the Protagonist played both Ajax and Teucer.

Müller (*History of Greek Literature*, vol. 1. p. 403) thinks that
a fourth actor was used. 'The rich and intricate composition
of this noble drama would have been impossible without this
innovation. But even Sophocles himself does not appear to
have dared to introduce it on the stage'—the play having been
produced, after his death, by Sophocles the grandson.

II. The part of Ismene may have been divided between
one of the three regular actors and a 'supernumerary,' who
was a 'mute person' (κωφὸν πρόσωπον). On this view it is
further necessary to divide the part of Theseus. The cast
might then have been as follows:—

1. *Protagonist.* Oedipus. Ismene from 1670.
2. *Deuteragonist.* Stranger. Ismene to 509. Theseus,
except in 887—1043. Creon. Polyneices. Messenger.
3. *Tritagonist.* Antigone. Theseus in 887—1043.
4. *Mute person.* Ismene 1096—1555.

STRUCTURE OF THE PLAY.

1. πρόλογος, verses 1—116.
2. πάροδος, 117—253.

3. ἐπεισόδιον πρῶτον, 254—667, divided into two parts by
a κομμός 510—548.
4. στάσιμον πρῶτον, 668—719.

5. ἐπεισόδιον δεύτερον, 720—1043 (with a kommos-like
passage, 833—843 = 876—886).
6. στάσιμον δεύτερον, 1044—1095.

7. ἐπεισόδιον τρίτον, 1096—1210.
8. στάσιμον τρίτον, 1211—1248.

9. ἐπεισόδιον τέταρτον, 1249—1555, divided into two parts
by a κομμός, 1447—1499.
10. στάσιμον τέταρτον, 1556—1578.

11. ἔξοδος, 1579—1779, including a κομμός 1670—1750.

The Parodos (vv. 117—253) passes at v. 138 into a κομμός: *i.e.* it is not merely the lyric chant with which the Chorus enters the orchestra, but becomes a lyric dialogue, in which Oedipus and Antigone take part with the Chorus. The essence of a κομμός, as defined by Aristotle (*Poet.* 12), was that the *lyric* strains of the Chorus should alternate with the utterances of one or more of the actors. The *actor's* part in the κομμός might be lyric, as here in the Parodos and in the first κομμός (510—548); or it might preserve the ordinary metre of dialogue, as in the second κομμός (1447—1499), where the choral lyrics are interspersed with iambic trimeters spoken by Oedipus and Antigone.

ΟΙΔΙΠΟΥΣ ΕΠΙ ΚΟΛΩΝΩΙ.

TA TOT ΔΡΑΜΑΤΟΣ ΠΡΟΣΩΠΑ.

ΟΙΔΙΠΟΥΣ.
ΑΝΤΙΓΟΝΗ.
ΞΕΝΟΣ.
ΧΟΡΟΣ ΑΤΤΙΚΩΝ ΓΕΡΟΝΤΩΝ.
ΙΣΜΗΝΗ.
ΘΗΣΕΥΣ.
ΚΡΕΩΝ.
ΠΟΛΥΝΕΙΚΗΣ.
ΑΓΓΕΛΟΣ.

ΟΙΔΙΠΟΥΣ ΕΠΙ ΚΟΛΩΝΩΙ.

ΟΙΔΙΠΟΥΣ.

ΤΕΚΝΟΝ τυφλοῦ γέροντος Ἀντιγόνη, τίνας
χώρους ἀφίγμεθ᾽ ἢ τίνων ἀνδρῶν πόλιν;
τίς τὸν πλανήτην Οἰδίπουν καθ᾽ ἡμέραν
τὴν νῦν σπανιστοῖς δέξεται δωρήμασιν;
σμικρὸν μὲν ἐξαιτοῦντα, τοῦ σμικροῦ δ᾽ ἔτι   5
μεῖον φέροντα, καὶ τόδ᾽ ἐξαρκοῦν ἐμοί·
στέργειν γὰρ αἱ πάθαι με χὠ χρόνος ξυνὼν
μακρὸς διδάσκει καὶ τὸ γενναῖον τρίτον.
ἀλλ᾽, ὦ τέκνον, θάκησιν εἴ τινα βλέπεις
ἢ πρὸς βεβήλοις ἢ πρὸς ἄλσεσιν θεῶν,   10
στῆσόν με κἀξίδρυσον, ὡς πυθώμεθα
ὅπου ποτ᾽ ἐσμέν· μανθάνειν γὰρ ἥκομεν
ξένοι πρὸς ἀστῶν, ἃν δ᾽ ἀκούσωμεν τελεῖν.

ΑΝΤΙΓΟΝΗ.

πάτερ ταλαίπωρ᾽ Οἰδίπους, πύργοι μὲν οἳ
πόλιν στέγουσιν, ὡς ἀπ᾽ ὀμμάτων, πρόσω·   15
χῶρος δ᾽ ὅδ᾽ ἱρός, ὡς σάφ᾽ εἰκάσαι, βρύων

---

9 θάκοισιν MSS.: corr. Seidler.   11 πυθοίμεθα MSS.: corr. Brunck.
13 ἃν δ᾽ Elmsley: ἂν L, A: χἂν r.   16 ὡς σάφ᾽ εἰκάσαι A: ὡς
ἀφεικάσαι L (with π written over φ by S): ὡς ἀπεικάσαι vulg.

1—2

δάφνης, ἐλαίας, ἀμπέλου· πυκνόπτεροι δ'
εἴσω κατ' αὐτὸν εὐστομοῦσ' ἀηδόνες·
οὗ κῶλα κάμψον τοῦδ' ἐπ' ἀξέστου πέτρου·
μακρὰν γὰρ ὡς γέροντι προὐστάλης ὁδόν.   20

ΟΙ. κάθιζέ νύν με καὶ φύλασσε τὸν τυφλόν.
ΑΝ. χρόνου μὲν οὕνεκ' οὐ μαθεῖν με δεῖ τόδε.
ΟΙ. ἔχεις διδάξαι δή μ' ὅποι καθέσταμεν;
ΑΝ. τὰς γοῦν Ἀθήνας οἶδα, τὸν δὲ χῶρον οὔ.
ΟΙ. πᾶς γάρ τις ηὔδα τοῦτό γ' ἡμὶν ἐμπόρων.   25
ΑΝ. ἀλλ' ὅστις ὁ τόπος ἦ μάθω μολοῦσά ποι;
ΟΙ. ναί, τέκνον, εἴπερ ἐστί γ' ἐξοικήσιμος.
ΑΝ. ἀλλ' ἐστὶ μὴν οἰκητός· οἴομαι δὲ δεῖν
οὐδέν· πέλας γὰρ ἄνδρα τόνδε νῷν ὁρῶ.
ΟΙ. ἦ δεῦρο προσστείχοντα κἀξορμώμενον;   30
ΑΝ. καὶ δὴ μὲν οὖν παρόντα· χὤ τι σοι λέγειν
εὔκαιρόν ἐστιν, ἔννεφ', ὡς ἀνὴρ ὅδε.
ΟΙ. ὦ ξεῖν', ἀκούων τῆσδε τῆς ὑπέρ τ' ἐμοῦ
αὐτῆς θ' ὁρώσης οὕνεχ' ἡμὶν αἴσιος
σκοπὸς προσήκεις ὧν ἀδηλοῦμεν φράσαι—   35

ΞΕΝΟΣ.

πρίν νυν τὰ πλείον' ἱστορεῖν, ἐκ τῆσδ' ἕδρας
ἔξελθ'· ἔχεις γὰρ χῶρον οὐχ ἁγνὸν πατεῖν.
ΟΙ. τίς δ' ἔσθ' ὁ χῶρος; τοῦ θεῶν νομίζεται;
ΞΕ. ἄθικτος οὐδ' οἰκητός· αἱ γὰρ ἔμφοβοι
θεαί σφ' ἔχουσι, Γῆς τε καὶ Σκότου κόραι.   40
ΟΙ. τίνων τὸ σεμνὸν ὄνομ' ἂν εὐξαίμην κλύων;
ΞΕ. τὰς πάνθ' ὁρώσας Εὐμενίδας ὅ γ' ἐνθάδ' ἂν
εἴποι λεώς νιν· ἄλλα δ' ἀλλαχοῦ καλά.
ΟΙ. ἀλλ' ἵλεῳ μὲν τὸν ἱκέτην δεξαίατο·
ὡς οὐχ ἕδρας γῆς τῆσδ' ἂν ἐξέλθοιμ' ἔτι.   45

30 προσστείχοντα MSS.: corr. Dindorf.   35 ὧν Elmsley: τῶν MSS.
42 ἐνθάδ' ὢν MSS.: corr. Vauvilliers.   45 ὡς Elmsley: ὥστ' MSS.

ΞΕ. τί δ' ἐστὶ τοῦτο; ΟΙ. ξυμφορᾶς ξύνθημ' ἐμῆς.

ΞΕ. ἀλλ' οὐδ' ἐμοί τοι τοὐξανιστάναι πόλεως
δίχ' ἐστὶ θάρσος, πρίν γ' ἂν ἐνδείξω τί δρῶ.

ΟΙ. πρός νυν θεῶν, ὦ ξεῖνε, μή μ' ἀτιμάσῃς,
τοιόνδ' ἀλήτην, ὧν σε προστρέπω φράσαι.   50

ΞΕ. σήμαινε, κοὐκ ἄτιμος ἔκ γ' ἐμοῦ φανεῖ.

ΟΙ. τίς ἔσθ' ὁ χῶρος δῆτ' ἐν ᾧ βεβήκαμεν;

ΞΕ. ὅσ' οἶδα κἀγὼ πάντ' ἐπιστήσει κλύων.
χῶρος μὲν ἱρὸς πᾶς ὅδ' ἔστ'· ἔχει δέ νιν
σεμνὸς Ποσειδῶν· ἐν δ' ὁ πυρφόρος θεὸς   55
Τιτὰν Προμηθεύς· ὃν δ' ἐπιστείβεις τόπον
χθονὸς καλεῖται τῆσδε χαλκόπους ὁδός,
ἔρεισμ' Ἀθηνῶν· οἱ δὲ πλησίοι γύαι
τόνδ' ἱππότην Κολωνὸν εὔχονται σφίσιν
ἀρχηγὸν εἶναι, καὶ φέρουσι τοὔνομα   60
τὸ τοῦδε κοινὸν πάντες ὠνομασμένοι.
τοιαῦτά σοι ταῦτ' ἐστίν, ὦ ξέν', οὐ λόγοις
τιμώμεν', ἀλλὰ τῇ ξυνουσίᾳ πλέον.

ΟΙ. ἦ γάρ τινες ναίουσι τούσδε τοὺς τόπους;

ΞΕ. καὶ κάρτα, τοῦδε τοῦ θεοῦ γ' ἐπώνυμοι.   65

ΟΙ. ἄρχει τις αὐτῶν, ἢ 'πὶ τῷ πλήθει λόγος;

ΞΕ. ἐκ τοῦ κατ' ἄστυ βασιλέως τάδ' ἄρχεται.

ΟΙ. οὗτος δὲ τίς λόγῳ τε καὶ σθένει κρατεῖ;

ΞΕ. Θησεὺς καλεῖται, τοῦ πρὶν Αἰγέως τόκος.

ΟΙ. ἆρ' ἄν τις αὐτῷ πομπὸς ἐξ ὑμῶν μόλοι;   70

ΞΕ. ὡς πρὸς τί λέξων ἢ καταρτύσων μολεῖν;

ΟΙ. ὡς ἂν προσαρκῶν σμικρὰ κερδάνῃ μέγα.

ΞΕ. καὶ τίς πρὸς ἀνδρὸς μὴ βλέποντος ἄρκεσις;

ΟΙ. ὅσ' ἂν λέγωμεν πάνθ' ὁρῶντα λέξομεν.

ΞΕ. οἶσθ', ὦ ξέν', ὡς νῦν μὴ σφαλῇς; ἐπείπερ εἶ   75
γενναῖος, ὡς ἰδόντι, πλὴν τοῦ δαίμονος·
αὐτοῦ μέν', οὗπερ κἀφάνης, ἕως ἐγὼ

τοῖς ἐνθάδ᾽ αὐτοῦ, μὴ κατ᾽ ἄστυ, δημόταις
λέξω τάδ᾽ ἐλθών· οἵδε γὰρ κρινοῦσί σοι
εἰ χρή σε μίμνειν ἢ πορεύεσθαι πάλιν.   80
ΟΙ. ὦ τέκνον, ἦ βέβηκεν ἡμῖν ὁ ξένος;
ΑΝ. βέβηκεν, ὥστε πᾶν ἐν ἡσύχῳ, πάτερ,
ἔξεστι φωνεῖν, ὡς ἐμοῦ μόνης πέλας.
ΟΙ. ὦ πότνιαι δεινῶπες, εὖτε νῦν ἕδρας
πρώτων ἐφ᾽ ὑμῶν τῆσδε γῆς ἔκαμψ᾽ ἐγώ,   85
Φοίβῳ τε κἀμοὶ μὴ γένησθ᾽ ἀγνώμονες,
ὅς μοι, τὰ πόλλ᾽ ἐκεῖν᾽ ὅτ᾽ ἐξέχρη κακά,
ταύτην ἔλεξε παῦλαν ἐν χρόνῳ μακρῷ,
ἐλθόντι χώραν τερμίαν, ὅπου θεῶν
σεμνῶν ἕδραν λάβοιμι καὶ ξενόστασιν,   90
ἐνταῦθα κάμψειν τὸν ταλαίπωρον βίον,
κέρδη μέν, οἰκήσαντα, τοῖς δεδεγμένοις,
ἄτην δὲ τοῖς πέμψασιν, οἵ μ᾽ ἀπήλασαν·
σημεῖα δ᾽ ἥξειν τῶνδέ μοι παρηγγύα,
ἢ σεισμόν, ἢ βροντήν τιν᾽, ἢ Διὸς σέλας.   95
ἔγνωκα μέν νυν ὥς με τήνδε τὴν ὁδὸν
οὐκ ἔσθ᾽ ὅπως οὐ πιστὸν ἐξ ὑμῶν πτερὸν
ἐξήγαγ᾽ εἰς τόδ᾽ ἄλσος. οὐ γὰρ ἄν ποτε
πρώταισιν ὑμῖν ἀντέκυρσ᾽ ὁδοιπορῶν,
νήφων ἀοίνοις, κἀπὶ σεμνὸν ἑζόμην   100
βάθρον τόδ᾽ ἀσκέπαρνον. ἀλλά μοι, θεαί,
βίου κατ᾽ ὀμφὰς τὰς Ἀπόλλωνος δότε
πέρασιν ἤδη καὶ καταστροφήν τινα,
εἰ μὴ δοκῶ τι μειόνως ἔχειν, ἀεὶ
μόχθοις λατρεύων τοῖς ὑπερτάτοις βροτῶν.   105
ἴτ᾽, ὦ γλυκεῖαι παῖδες ἀρχαίου Σκότου,
ἴτ᾽, ὦ μεγίστης Παλλάδος καλούμεναι
πασῶν Ἀθῆναι τιμιωτάτη πόλις,

οἰκτίρατ᾽ ἀνδρὸς Οἰδίπου τόδ᾽ ἄθλιον
εἴδωλον· οὐ γὰρ δὴ τό γ᾽ ἀρχαῖον δέμας. 110
ΑΝ. σίγα. πορεύονται γὰρ οἵδε δή τινες
χρόνῳ παλαιοί, σῆς ἕδρας ἐπίσκοποι.
ΟΙ. σιγήσομαί τε καὶ σύ μ᾽ ἐξ ὁδοῦ πόδα
κρύψον κατ᾽ ἄλσος, τῶνδ᾽ ἕως ἂν ἐκμάθω
τίνας λόγους ἐροῦσιν. ἐν γὰρ τῷ μαθεῖν 115
ἔνεστιν ηὐλάβεια τῶν ποιουμένων.

ΧΟΡΟΣ.

στρ. α΄. ὅρα· τίς ἄρ᾽ ἦν; ποῦ ναίει; 117
2 ποῦ κυρεῖ ἐκτόπιος συθεὶς ὁ πάντων,
3 ὁ πάντων ἀκορέστατος; 120
4 προσδέρκου, λεῦσσε δή,
5 προσπεύθου πανταχῇ·
6 πλανάτας,
7 πλανάτας τις ὁ πρέσβυς, οὐδ᾽ ἔγχωρος· προσέβα
γὰρ οὐκ ἄν ποτ᾽ ἀστιβὲς ἄλσος ἐς 125
8 τᾶνδ᾽ ἀμαιμακετᾶν κορᾶν, ἃς τρέμομεν λέγειν καὶ
9 παραμειβόμεσθ᾽ ἀδέρκτως, ἀφώνως, ἀλόγως τὸ τᾶς
εὐφάμου στόμα φροντίδος 132
10 ἱέντες· τὰ δὲ νῦν τιν᾽ ἥκειν λόγος οὐδὲν ἄζονθ᾽,
11 ὃν ἐγὼ λεύσσων περὶ πᾶν οὔπω 135
12 δύναμαι τέμενος γνῶναι ποῦ μοί
13 ποτε ναίει.

συστ. α΄. ΟΙ. ὅδ᾽ ἐκεῖνος ἐγώ· φωνῇ γὰρ ὁρῶ,
τὸ φατιζόμενον.
ΧΟ. ἰὼ ἰώ, 140
δεινὸς μὲν ὁρᾶν, δεινὸς δὲ κλύειν.

113 ἐξ ὁδοῦ πόδα MSS. : ἐκποδὼν ὁδοῦ conj. H. Keck. 121 λεῦσατ᾽
αὐτὸν προσδέρκου | προσπεύθου πανταχῆι L: προσπεύθου, λεῦσσέ νιν, | προσ-
δέρκου πανταχῇ Hermann: and so Schneidewin, but without transposing
προσδέρκου and προσπεύθου. (δή instead of νιν J.)

8   ΣΟΦΟΚΛΕΟΥΣ

ΟΙ.   μή μ', ἱκετεύω, προσίδητ' ἄνομον.
ΧΟ.   Ζεῦ ἀλεξῆτορ, τίς ποθ' ὁ πρέσβυς;
ΟΙ.   οὐ πάνυ μοίρας εὐδαιμονίσαι
        πρώτης, ὦ τῆσδ' ἔφοροι χώρας.   145
        δηλῶ δ'· οὐ γὰρ ἂν ὧδ' ἀλλοτρίοις
        ὄμμασιν εἶρπον
        κἀπὶ σμικροῖς μέγας ὥρμουν.

ἀντ. ά.   ΧΟ. ἐή· ἀλαῶν ὀμμάτων   149
    2 ἆρα καὶ ἦσθα φυτάλμιος; δυσαίων
    3 μακραίων θ', ὅσ' ἐπεικάσαι.   152
    4 ἀλλ' οὐ μὰν ἔν γ' ἐμοὶ
    5 προσθήσει τάσδ' ἀράς.
    6 περᾷς γάρ,
    7 περᾷς· ἀλλ' ἵνα τῷδ' ἐν ἀφθέγκτῳ μὴ προπέσῃς
        νάπει ποιάεντι, κάθυδρος οὗ   157
    8 κρατὴρ μειλιχίων ποτῶν ῥεύματι συντρέχει· τό,   160
    9 ξένε πάμμορ', εὖ φύλαξαι· μετάσταθ', ἀπόβαθι.
        πολλὰ κέλευθος ἐρατύει·
    10 κλύεις, ὦ πολύμοχθ' ἀλᾶτα; λόγον εἴ τιν' οἴσεις   166
    11 πρὸς ἐμὰν λέσχαν, ἀβάτων ἀποβάς,
    12 ἵνα πᾶσι νόμος, φώνει· πρόσθεν δ'
    13 ἀπερύκου.

σύστ. β'.   ΟΙ. θύγατερ, ποῖ τις φροντίδος ἔλθῃ;   170
ΑΝ.   ὦ πάτερ, ἀστοῖς ἴσα χρὴ μελετᾶν,
        εἴκοντας ἃ δεῖ κἀκούοντας.
ΟΙ.   πρόσθιγέ νύν μου. ΑΝ. ψαύω καὶ δή.
ΟΙ.   ὦ ξεῖνοι, μὴ δῆτ' ἀδικηθῶ
        σοὶ πιστεύσας καὶ μεταναστάς.   175

---

152 ὡς ἐπεικάσαι MSS.: corr. Bothe.   153 προσθήσεις MSS. :
corr. Blaydes and Postgate.   156 προσπέσῃς MSS.: corr. Hermann.
161 τό Heath: τῶν L (τὸν r).   166 εἴ τιν' ἔχεις MSS.: but L has οἴσεις
superscript (prob. by S).   172 κ' οὐκἀκούοντας L: κοὐκ ἀκούοντας or
κοὐκ ἄκοντας r: corr. Musgrave.

στρ. β΄. ΧΟ. οὔ τοι μήποτέ σ᾽ ἐκ τῶνδ᾽ ἑδράνων, ὦ
γέρον, ἄκοντά τις ἄξει.
ΟΙ. 2 ἔτ᾽ οὖν; ΧΟ. ἔτι βαῖνε πόρσω. 178
ΟΙ. 3 ἔτι; ΧΟ. προβίβαζε, κούρα, 180
4 πόρσω· σὺ γὰρ ἀΐεις.
ΑΝ. 5 ⏑⏑⏑ | ⏑⏑ | –⏑ | ‿ ‖ –
ΟΙ. 6 – – – – ‿᷾
ΑΝ. 7 ⏑ | ⏑⏑ | –⏑ | –∧ ⟧
8 ἔπεο μάν, ἔπε᾽ ὧδ᾽ ἀμαυρῷ κώλῳ, πάτερ, ᾇ σ᾽ ἄγω.
ΟΙ. 9 –> | ⏑⏑ | ‿ | –∧ ⟧
ΧΟ. 10 τόλμα ξεῖνος ἐπὶ ξένης,
11 ὦ τλάμων, ὅ τι καὶ πόλις 185
12 τέτροφεν ἄφιλον ἀποστυγεῖν
13 καὶ τὸ φίλον σέβεσθαι.

σύστ. γ΄. ΟΙ. ἄγε νυν σύ με, παῖ,
ἵν᾽ ἂν εὐσεβίας ἐπιβαίνοντες
τὸ μὲν εἴποιμεν, τὸ δ᾽ ἀκούσαιμεν, 190
καὶ μὴ χρείᾳ πολεμῶμεν.

ἀντ. β΄. ΧΟ. αὐτοῦ, μηκέτι τοῦδ᾽ αὐτοπέτρου βήματος
ἔξω πόδα κλίνῃς.
ΟΙ. 2 οὕτως; ΧΟ. ἅλις, ὡς ἀκούεις.
ΟΙ. 3 ἦ ἐσθῶ; ΧΟ. λέχριός γ᾽ ἐπ᾽ ἄκρου 195
4 λᾶος βραχὺς ὀκλάσας.
ΑΝ. 5 πάτερ, ἐμὸν τόδ᾽· ἐν ἡσυχαίᾳ
ΟΙ. 6 ἰώ μοί μοι.
ΑΝ. 7 βάσει βάσιν ἄρμοσαι,
8 γεραὸν ἐς χέρα σῶμα σὸν προκλίνας φιλίαν ἐμάν.
ΟΙ. 9 ὤμοι δύσφρονος ἄτας. 202

178 ἔτ᾽ οὖν ἔτι προβῶ; MSS.: Bothe del. ἔτι προβῶ.—ἐπίβαινε MSS.:
corr. Reiske. 190 εἴποιμεν...ἀκούσαιμεν L: εἴπωμεν...ἀκούσωμεν A.
192 ἀντιπέτρου MSS.: corr. Musgrave. 195 ἦ᾽σθῶ L, with γρ. ἦ στῶ;
197 ἐν ἡσυχίᾳ MSS.: corr. Reisig. 199 ἁρμόσαι MSS.: corr. Elmsley.

ΧΟ. 10 ὦ τλάμων, ὅτε νῦν χαλᾷς,
11 αὔδασον, τίς ἔφυς βροτῶν;
12 τίς ὁ πολύπονος ἄγει; τίν᾽ ἂν 205
13 σοῦ πατρίδ᾽ ἐκπυθοίμαν;

ἀνομοιό- ΟΙ. ὦ ξένοι, ἀπόπτολις· ἀλλὰ μὴ ΧΟ. τί τόδ᾽
στρ. ἀπεννέπεις, γέρον; 209

ΟΙ. μή, μή μ᾽ ἀνέρῃ τίς εἰμι, μηδ᾽ ἐξετάσῃς πέρα
ματεύων.

ΧΟ. τί τόδ᾽; ΟΙ. αἰνὰ φύσις. ΧΟ. αὔδα. ΟΙ. τέκνον,
ὤμοι, τί γεγώνω;

ΧΟ. τίνος εἶ σπέρματος, ὦ ξένε, φώνει, πατρόθεν. 215

ΟΙ. ὤμοι ἐγώ, τί πάθω, τέκνον ἐμόν;

ΑΝ. λέγ᾽, ἐπείπερ ἐπ᾽ ἔσχατα βαίνεις.

ΟΙ. ἀλλ᾽ ἐρῶ· οὐ γὰρ ἔχω κατακρυφάν.

ΧΟ. μακρὰ μέλλετον, ἀλλὰ τάχυνε.

ΟΙ. Λαΐου ἴστε τιν᾽; ὤ. ΧΟ. ἰοὺ ἰού. 220

ΟΙ. τό τε Λαβδακιδᾶν γένος; ΧΟ. ὦ Ζεῦ.

ΟΙ. ἄθλιον Οἰδιπόδαν; ΧΟ. σὺ γὰρ ὅδ᾽ εἶ;

ΟΙ. δέος ἴσχετε μηδὲν ὅσ᾽ αὐδῶ.

ΧΟ. ἰώ, ὦ ὤ· ΟΙ. δύσμορος. ΧΟ. ὦ ὤ.

ΟΙ. θύγατερ, τί ποτ᾽ αὐτίκα κύρσει; 225

ΧΟ. ἔξω πόρσω βαίνετε χώρας.

ΟΙ. ἃ δ᾽ ὑπέσχεο ποῖ καταθήσεις;

ΧΟ. οὐδενὶ μοιριδία τίσις ἔρχεται
ὧν προπάθῃ τὸ τίνειν·
ἀπάτα δ᾽ ἀπάταις ἑτέραις ἑτέρα 230
παραβαλλομένα πόνον, οὐ χάριν, ἀντιδίδωσιν ἔχειν.
σὺ δὲ τῶνδ᾽ ἑδράνων πάλιν ἔκτοπος αὖθις ἄφορμος
ἐμᾶς

210 μὴ μὴ μή μ᾽ MSS.: corr. Hartung. 212 τί τόδε; ΟΙ. δεινὰ
MSS.: corr. Wunder. 217 βαίνεις Triclinius: μένεις L, A, vulg.
219 μέλλετ᾽ L (μέλλετέ γ᾽ Triclinius): corr. Hermann. 220 Λαΐου
ἴστε τιν᾽ ἀπόγονον; MSS.: corr. Reisig.

χθονὸς ἔκθορε, μή τι πέρα χρέος   235
ἐμᾷ πόλει προσάψῃς.

ΑΝ. ὦ ξένοι αἰδόφρονες,
ἀλλ' ἐπεὶ γεραὸν [ἀλαὸν] πατέρα
τόνδ' ἐμὸν οὐκ ἀνέτλατ', ἔργων
ἀκόντων ἀίοντες αὐδάν,   240
ἀλλ' ἐμὲ τὰν μελέαν, ἱκετεύομεν,
ὦ ξένοι, οἰκτίραθ', ἃ
πατρὸς ὑπὲρ τοὐμοῦ μόνου ἄντομαι,
ἄντομαι οὐκ ἀλαοῖς προσορωμένα
ὄμμα σὸν ὄμμασιν, ὥς τις ἀφ' αἵματος   245
ὑμετέρου προφανεῖσα, τὸν ἄθλιον
αἰδοῦς κῦρσαι. ἐν ὕμμι γὰρ ὡς θεῷ
κείμεθα τλάμονες. ἀλλ' ἴτε, νεύσατε
τὰν ἀδόκητον χάριν.
πρός σ' ὅ τι σοι φίλον ἐκ σέθεν ἄντομαι,   250
ἢ τέκνον ἢ λέχος ἢ χρέος ἢ θεός·
οὐ γὰρ ἴδοις ἂν ἀθρῶν βροτῶν
ὅστις ἄν, εἰ θεὸς ἄγοι,
ἐκφυγεῖν δύναιτο.

ΧΟ. ἀλλ' ἴσθι, τέκνον Οἰδίπου, σέ τ' ἐξ ἴσου
οἰκτίρομεν καὶ τόνδε συμφορᾶς χάριν·   255
τὰ δ' ἐκ θεῶν τρέμοντες οὐ σθένοιμεν ἂν
φωνεῖν πέρα τῶν πρὸς σὲ νῦν εἰρημένων.

ΟΙ. τί δῆτα δόξης ἢ τί κληδόνος καλῆς
μάτην ῥεούσης ὠφέλημα γίγνεται,
εἰ τάς γ' Ἀθήνας φασὶ θεοσεβεστάτας   260

238 ἀλαὸν, which was inserted in the text of L by S, is absent from A
and most of the other MSS.   243 τοὐμοῦ μόνου Hermann : τοῦ μόνου
L, A, vulg.: τοὐμοῦ (without μόνου) Triclinius. τοῦδ' ἀμμόρου conj. J.
247 ὕμμι Bergk : ὑμῖν MSS.   251 λέχος Reiske : λόγος MSS.
260 τάς γ' Roman editor of scholia (J. A. Lascaris), A.D. 1518 : τάς τ' L,
A : τὰς T.

εἶναι, μόνας δὲ τὸν κακούμενον ξένον
σῴζειν οἷας τε καὶ μόνας ἀρκεῖν ἔχειν·
κἄμοιγε ποῦ ταῦτ' ἐστίν; οἵτινες βάθρων
ἐκ τῶνδέ μ' ἐξάραντες εἶτ' ἐλαύνετε,
ὄνομα μόνον δείσαντες· οὐ γὰρ δὴ τό γε   265
σῶμ' οὐδὲ τἄργα τἄμ'· ἐπεὶ τά γ' ἔργα μου
πεπονθότ' ἐστὶ μᾶλλον ἢ δεδρακότα,
εἴ σοι τὰ μητρὸς καὶ πατρὸς χρείη λέγειν,
ὧν οὕνεκ' ἐκφοβεῖ με· τοῦτ' ἐγὼ καλῶς
ἔξοιδα. καίτοι πῶς ἐγὼ κακὸς φύσιν,   270
ὅστις παθὼν μὲν ἀντέδρων, ὥστ' εἰ φρονῶν
ἔπρασσον, οὐδ' ἂν ὧδ' ἐγιγνόμην κακός;
νῦν δ' οὐδὲν εἰδὼς ἱκόμην ἵν' ἱκόμην,
ὑφ' ὧν δ' ἔπασχον, εἰδότων ἀπωλλύμην.
ἀνθ' ὧν ἱκνοῦμαι πρὸς θεῶν ὑμᾶς, ξένοι,   275
ὥσπερ με κἀνεστήσαθ', ὧδε σώσατε,
καὶ μὴ θεοὺς τιμῶντες εἶτα τοὺς θεοὺς
μοίραις ποεῖσθε μηδαμῶς· ἡγεῖσθε δὲ
βλέπειν μὲν αὐτοὺς πρὸς τὸν εὐσεβῆ βροτῶν,
βλέπειν δὲ πρὸς τοὺς δυσσεβεῖς, φυγὴν δέ του   280
μήπω γενέσθαι φωτὸς ἀνοσίου βροτῶν.
ξὺν οἷς σὺ μὴ κάλυπτε τὰς εὐδαίμονας
ἔργοις Ἀθήνας ἀνοσίοις ὑπηρετῶν,
ἀλλ' ὥσπερ ἔλαβες τὸν ἱκέτην ἐχέγγυον,
ῥύου με κἀκφύλασσε· μηδέ μου κάρα   285
τὸ δυσπρόσοπτον εἰσορῶν ἀτιμάσῃς.
ἥκω, γὰρ ἱερὸς εὐσεβής τε καὶ φέρων
ὄνησιν ἀστοῖς τοῖσδ'· ὅταν δ' ὁ κύριος
παρῇ τις, ὑμῶν ὅστις ἐστὶν ἡγεμών,
τότ' εἰσακούων πάντ' ἐπιστήσει· τὰ δὲ   290
μεταξὺ τούτου μηδαμῶς γίγνου κακός.
ΧΟ. ταρβεῖν μέν, ὦ γεραιέ, τἀνθυμήματα

278 μοίραις L, A, vulg.: μοίρας r.

πολλή 'στ' ἀνάγκη τἀπὸ σοῦ· λόγοισι γὰρ
οὐκ ὠνόμασται βραχέσι· τοὺς δὲ τῆσδε γῆς
ἄνακτας ἀρκεῖ ταῦτά μοι διειδέναι.   195
ΟΙ. καὶ ποῦ 'σθ' ὁ κραίνων τῆσδε τῆς χώρας, ξένοι;
ΧΟ. πατρῷον ἄστυ γῆς ἔχει· σκοπὸς δέ νιν
ὃς κἀμὲ δεῦρ' ἔπεμψεν οἴχεται στελῶν.
ΟΙ. ἦ καὶ δοκεῖτε τοῦ τυφλοῦ τιν' ἐντροπὴν
ἢ φροντίδ' ἕξειν, αὐτὸν ὥστ' ἐλθεῖν πέλας;   300
ΧΟ. καὶ κάρθ', ὅταν περ τοὔνομ' αἴσθηται τὸ σόν.
ΟΙ. τίς δ' ἔσθ' ὁ κείνῳ τοῦτο τοὔπος ἀγγελῶν;
ΧΟ. μακρὰ κέλευθος· πολλὰ δ' ἐμπόρων ἔπη
φιλεῖ πλανᾶσθαι, τῶν ἐκεῖνος ἀΐων,
θάρσει, παρέσται. πολὺ γάρ, ὦ γέρον, τὸ σὸν 305
ὄνομα διήκει πάντας, ὥστε κεἰ βραδὺς
εὕδει, κλύων σοῦ δεῦρ' ἀφίξεται ταχύς.
ΟΙ. ἀλλ' εὐτυχὴς ἵκοιτο τῇ θ' αὑτοῦ πόλει
ἐμοί τε· τίς γὰρ ἐσθλὸς οὐχ αὑτῷ φίλος;
ΑΝ. ὦ Ζεῦ, τί λέξω; ποῖ φρενῶν ἔλθω, πάτερ;   310
ΟΙ. τί δ' ἔστι, τέκνον Ἀντιγόνη; ΑΝ. γυναῖχ' ὁρῶ
στείχουσαν ἡμῶν ἆσσον, Αἰτναίας ἐπὶ
πώλου βεβῶσαν· κρατὶ δ' ἡλιοστερὴς
κυνῆ πρόσωπα Θεσσαλίς νιν ἀμπέχει.
τί φῶ;   315
ἆρ' ἔστιν; ἆρ' οὐκ ἔστιν; ἢ γνώμη πλανᾷ;
καὶ φημὶ κἀπόφημι κοὐκ ἔχω τί φῶ.
τάλαινα·
οὐκ ἔστιν ἄλλη. φαιδρὰ γοῦν ἀπ' ὀμμάτων
σαίνει με προσστείχουσα· σημαίνει δ' ὅτι   320
μόνης τόδ' ἐστὶ δῆλον Ἰσμήνης κάρα.
ΟΙ. πῶς εἶπας, ὦ παῖ; ΑΝ. παῖδα σήν, ἐμὴν δ' ὁρᾶν
ὅμαιμον· αὐδῇ δ' αὐτίκ' ἔξεστιν μαθεῖν.

300 αὐτὸν ὥστ' Porson: ἀπόνως τ' L, vulg.
321 ἐστὶ δῆλον MSS.: ἔστ' ἀδελφὸν conj. Herwerden, Jacobs.

ΙΣΜΗΝΗ.

ὦ δισσὰ πατρὸς καὶ κασιγνήτης ἐμοὶ
ἥδιστα προσφωνήμαθ', ὡς ὑμᾶς μόλις   325
εὑροῦσα λύπῃ δεύτερον μόλις βλέπω.

ΟΙ. ὦ τέκνον, ἥκεις; ΙΣ. ὦ πάτερ δύσμοιρ' ὁρᾶν.

ΟΙ. τέκνον, πέφηνας; ΙΣ. οὐκ ἄνευ μόχθου γέ μοι.

ΟΙ. πρόσψαυσον, ὦ παῖ. ΙΣ. θιγγάνω δυοῖν ὁμοῦ.

ΟΙ. ὦ σπέρμ' ὅμαιμον. ΙΣ. ὦ δυσάθλιαι τροφαί.   330

ΟΙ. ἦ τῆσδε κἀμοῦ; ΙΣ. δυσμόρου τ' ἐμοῦ τρίτης.

ΟΙ. τέκνον, τί δ' ἦλθες; ΙΣ. σῇ, πάτερ, προμηθίᾳ.

ΟΙ. πότερα πόθοισι; ΙΣ. καὶ λόγων γ' αὐτάγγελος,
ξὺν ᾧπερ εἶχον οἰκετῶν πιστῷ μόνῳ.

ΟΙ. οἱ δ' αὐθόμαιμοι ποῦ νεανίαι πονεῖν;   335

ΙΣ. εἴσ' οὗπέρ εἰσι· δεινὰ τἀν κείνοις τανῦν.

ΟΙ. ὦ πάντ' ἐκείνω τοῖς ἐν Αἰγύπτῳ νόμοις
φύσιν κατεικασθέντε καὶ βίου τροφάς·
ἐκεῖ γὰρ οἱ μὲν ἄρσενες κατὰ στέγας
θακοῦσιν ἱστουργοῦντες, αἱ δὲ σύννομοι   340
τἄξω βίου τροφεῖα πορσύνουσ' ἀεί.
σφῷν δ', ὦ τέκν', οὓς μὲν εἰκὸς ἦν πονεῖν τάδε,
κατ' οἶκον οἰκουροῦσιν ὥστε παρθένοι,
σφὼ δ' ἀντ' ἐκείνων τἀμὰ δυστήνου κακὰ
ὑπερπονεῖτον. ἡ μὲν ἐξ ὅτου νέας   345
τροφῆς ἔληξε καὶ κατίσχυσεν δέμας,
ἀεὶ μεθ' ἡμῶν δύσμορος πλανωμένη
γερονταγωγεῖ, πολλὰ μὲν κατ' ἀγρίαν
ὕλην ἄσιτος νηλίπους τ' ἀλωμένη,
πολλοῖσι δ' ὄμβροις ἡλίου τε καύμασι   350
μοχθοῦσα τλήμων δεύτερ' ἡγεῖται τὰ τῆς

327—330 Order in MSS., 327, 330, 328, 329: corr. Musgrave.
331 δυσμόρου δ' MSS.: corr. Markland.   336 δεινὰ δ' ἐκείνοις L¹,
δεινὰ δ' ἐν κείνοις L²: δεινὰ τἀκείνοις Γ: corr. Schaefer.

οἴκοι διαίτης, εἰ πατὴρ τροφὴν ἔχοι.
σὺ δ', ὦ τέκνον, πρόσθεν μὲν ἐξίκου πατρὶ
μαντεῖ' ἄγουσα πάντα, Καδμείων λάθρᾳ,
ἃ τοῦδ' ἐχρήσθη σώματος, φύλαξ δέ μοι   355
πιστὴ κατέστης, γῆς ὅτ' ἐξηλαυνόμην·
νῦν δ' αὖ τίν' ἥκεις μῦθον, Ἰσμήνη, πατρὶ
φέρουσα; τίς σ' ἐξῆρεν οἴκοθεν στόλος;
ἥκεις γὰρ οὐ κενή γε, τοῦτ' ἐγὼ σαφῶς
ἔξοιδα, μὴ οὐχὶ δεῖμ' ἐμοὶ φέρουσά τι.   360
ΙΣ. ἐγὼ τὰ μὲν παθήμαθ' ἅπαθον, πάτερ,
ζητοῦσα τὴν σὴν ποῦ κατοικοίης τροφήν,
παρεῖσ' ἐάσω· δὶς γὰρ οὐχὶ βούλομαι
πονοῦσά τ' ἀλγεῖν καὶ λέγουσ' αὖθις πάλιν.
ἃ δ' ἀμφὶ τοῖν σοῖν δυσμόροιν παίδοιν κακὰ   365
νῦν ἐστι, ταῦτα σημανοῦσ' ἐλήλυθα.
πρὶν μὲν γὰρ αὐτοῖς ἦν ἔρως Κρέοντί τε
θρόνους ἐᾶσθαι μηδὲ χραίνεσθαι πόλιν,
λόγῳ σκοποῦσι τὴν πάλαι γένους φθοράν,
οἵα κατέσχε τὸν σὸν ἄθλιον δόμον·   370
νῦν δ' ἐκ θεῶν του κἀλιτηρίου φρενὸς
εἰσῆλθε τοῖν τρὶς ἀθλίοιν ἔρις κακή,
ἀρχῆς λαβέσθαι καὶ κράτους τυραννικοῦ.
χὠ μὲν νεάζων καὶ χρόνῳ μείων γεγὼς
τὸν πρόσθε γεννηθέντα Πολυνείκη θρόνων   375
ἀποστερίσκει, κἀξελήλακεν πάτρας.
ὁ δ', ὡς καθ' ἡμᾶς ἔσθ' ὁ πληθύων λόγος,
τὸ κοῖλον Ἄργος βὰς φυγὰς προσλαμβάνει
κῆδός τε καινὸν καὶ ξυνασπιστὰς φίλους,
ὡς αὐτίκ' Ἄργος ἢ τὸ Καδμείων πέδον   380
τιμῇ καθέξον ἢ πρὸς οὐρανὸν βιβῶν.

355 μου MSS.: corr. J.   367 ἔρως T. Tyrwhitt, Musgrave: ἔρις MSS.
371 κἀλιτηρίου Toup: κἀξαλιτηροῦ L, κἀξ ἀλιτηροῦ A: κἀξαλητηροῦ or κἀξ
ἀλητηροῦ r.   381 καθέξον (from καθέξων) A, Brunck: καθέξων L, vulg.

ταῦτ' οὐκ ἀριθμός ἐστιν, ὦ πάτερ, λόγων,
ἀλλ' ἔργα δεινά· τοὺς δὲ σοὺς ὅπου θεοὶ
πόνους κατοικτιοῦσιν οὐκ ἔχω μαθεῖν.

ΟΙ. ἤδη γὰρ ἔσχες ἐλπίδ' ὡς ἐμοῦ θεοὺς 385
ὥραν τιν' ἕξειν, ὥστε σωθῆναί ποτε;

ΙΣ. ἔγωγε τοῖς νῦν γ', ὦ πάτερ, μαντεύμασιν.

ΟΙ. ποίοισι τούτοις; τί δὲ τεθέσπισται, τέκνον;

ΙΣ. σὲ τοῖς ἐκεῖ ζητητὸν ἀνθρώποις ποτὲ
θανόντ' ἔσεσθαι ζῶντά τ' εὐσοίας χάριν. 390

ΟΙ. τίς δ' ἂν τοιοῦδ' ὑπ' ἀνδρὸς εὖ πράξειεν ἄν;

ΙΣ. ἐν σοὶ τὰ κείνων φασὶ γίγνεσθαι κράτη.

ΟΙ. ὅτ' οὐκέτ' εἰμί, τηνικαῦτ' ἄρ' εἴμ' ἀνήρ;

ΙΣ. νῦν γὰρ θεοί σ' ὀρθοῦσι, πρόσθε δ' ὤλλυσαν.

ΟΙ. γέροντα δ' ὀρθοῦν φλαῦρον ὃς νέος πέσῃ. 395

ΙΣ. καὶ μὴν Κρέοντά γ' ἴσθι σοι τούτων χάριν
ἥξοντα βαιοῦ κοὐχὶ μυρίου χρόνου.

ΟΙ. ὅπως τί δράσῃ, θύγατερ; ἑρμήνευέ μοι.

ΙΣ. ὥς σ' ἄγχι γῆς στήσωσι Καδμείας, ὅπως
κρατῶσι μέν σου, γῆς δὲ μὴ 'μβαίνῃς ὅρων. 400

ΟΙ. ἡ δ' ὠφέλησις τίς θύρασι κειμένου;

ΙΣ. κείνοις ὁ τύμβος δυστυχῶν ὁ σὸς βαρύς.

ΟΙ. κἄνευ θεοῦ τις τοῦτό γ' ἂν γνώμῃ μάθοι.

ΙΣ. τούτου χάριν τοίνυν σε προσθέσθαι πέλας
χώρας θέλουσι, μηδ' ἵν' ἂν σαυτοῦ κρατοῖς. 405

ΟΙ. ἡ καὶ κατασκιῶσι Θηβαίᾳ κόνει;

ΙΣ. ἀλλ' οὐκ ἐᾷ τοὔμφυλον αἷμά σ', ὦ πάτερ.

ΟΙ. οὐκ ἄρ' ἐμοῦ γε μὴ κρατήσωσίν ποτε.

ΙΣ. ἔσται ποτ' ἆρα τοῦτο Καδμείοις βάρος.

ΟΙ. ποίας φανείσης, ὦ τέκνον, συναλλαγῆς; 410

ΙΣ. τῆς σῆς ὑπ' ὀργῆς, σοῖς ὅταν στῶσιν τάφοις.

---

383 ὅπου Elmsley (in text), Hartung: ὅποι L, vulg.: ὅπη r.   390 εὐσοίας schol.: εὐνοίας MSS.   391 ὑπ' om. L, add. A and most MSS.
405 κρατῇς MSS.: corr. Brunck.

ΟΙ. ἃ δ' ἐννέπεις, κλύουσα τοῦ λέγεις, τέκνον;

ΙΣ. ἀνδρῶν θεωρῶν Δελφικῆς ἀφ' ἑστίας.

ΟΙ. καὶ ταῦτ' ἐφ' ἡμῖν Φοῖβος εἰρηκὼς κυρεῖ;

ΙΣ. ὥς φασιν οἱ μολόντες εἰς Θήβης πέδον.   415

ΟΙ. παίδων τις οὖν ἤκουσε τῶν ἐμῶν τάδε;

ΙΣ. ἄμφω γ' ὁμοίως, κἀξεπίστασθον καλῶς.

ΟΙ. κᾷθ' οἱ κάκιστοι τῶνδ' ἀκούσαντες πάρος
τοὐμοῦ πόθου προὔθεντο τὴν τυραννίδα;

ΙΣ. ἀλγῶ κλύουσα ταῦτ' ἐγώ, φέρω δ' ὅμως.   420

ΟΙ. ἀλλ' οἱ θεοί σφιν μήτε τὴν πεπρωμένην
ἔριν κατασβέσειαν, ἐν δ' ἐμοὶ τέλος
αὐτοῖν γένοιτο τῆσδε τῆς μάχης πέρι,
ἧς νῦν ἔχονται κἀπαναίρονται δόρυ·
ὡς οὔτ' ἂν ὃς νῦν σκῆπτρα καὶ θρόνους ἔχει   425
μείνειεν, οὔτ' ἂν οὑξεληλυθὼς πάλιν
ἔλθοι ποτ' αὖθις· οἵ γε τὸν φύσαντ' ἐμὲ
οὕτως ἀτίμως πατρίδος ἐξωθούμενον
οὐκ ἔσχον οὐδ' ἤμυναν, ἀλλ' ἀνάστατος
αὐτοῖν ἐπέμφθην κἀξεκηρύχθην φυγάς.   430
εἴποις ἂν ὡς θέλοντι τοῦτ' ἐμοὶ τότε
πόλις τὸ δῶρον εἰκότως κατήνεσεν.
οὐ δῆτ', ἐπεί τοι τὴν μὲν αὐτίχ' ἡμέραν,
ὁπηνίκ' ἔζει θυμός, ἥδιστον δέ μοι
τὸ κατθανεῖν ἦν καὶ τὸ λευσθῆναι πέτροις,   435
οὐδεὶς ἔρωτ' ἐς τόνδ' ἐφαίνετ' ὠφελῶν·
χρόνῳ δ', ὅτ' ἤδη πᾶς ὁ μόχθος ἦν πέπων,
κἀμάνθανον τὸν θυμὸν ἐκδραμόντα μοι
μείζω κολαστὴν τῶν πρὶν ἡμαρτημένων,
τὸ τηνίκ' ἤδη τοῦτο μὲν πόλις βίᾳ   440
ἤλαυνέ μ' ἐκ γῆς χρόνιον, οἱ δ' ἐπωφελεῖν,

421 τὴν πεπρωμένην Γ: τῶν πεπραγμένων L.   424 κἀπαναιροῦνται
MSS.: corr. Hermann.   432 κατήνεσεν Γ: κατήίνυσεν L.   436 ἔρωτος
τοῦδ' MSS.: corr. P. N. Papageorgius.

J. C.   2

18   ΣΟΦΟΚΛΕΟΥΣ

οι τοῦ πατρὸς τῷ πατρί, δυνάμενοι τὸ δρᾶν
οὐκ ἠθέλησαν, ἀλλ' ἔπους σμικροῦ χάριν
φυγάς σφιν ἔξω πτωχὸς ἠλώμην ἀεί.
ἐκ τοῖνδε δ', οὔσαιν παρθένοιν, ὅσον φύσις   445
δίδωσιν αὐτοῖν, καὶ τροφὰς ἔχω βίου
καὶ γῆς ἄδειαν καὶ γένους ἐπάρκεσιν·
τὼ δ' ἀντὶ τοῦ φύσαντος εἰλέσθην θρόνοι·ς
καὶ σκῆπτρα κραίνειν καὶ τυραννεύειν χθονός.
ἀλλ' οὔ τι μὴ λάχωσι τοῦδε συμμάχου,   450
οὐδέ σφιν ἀρχῆς τῆσδε Καδμείας ποτὲ
ὄνησις ἥξει· τοῦτ' ἐγῷδα, τῆσδέ τε
μαντεῖ ἀκούων συννοῶν τε τἀξ ἐμοῦ
παλαίφαθ' ἁμοὶ Φοῖβος ἤνυσέν ποτε.
πρὸς ταῦτα καὶ Κρέοντα πεμπόντων ἐμοῦ   455
μαστῆρα, κεἴ τις ἄλλος ἐν πόλει σθένει.
ἐὰν γὰρ ὑμεῖς, ὦ ξένοι, θέληθ' ὁμοῦ
προστάτισι ταῖς σεμναῖσι δημούχοις θεαῖς
ἀλκὴν ποεῖσθαι, τῇδε μὲν πόλει μέγαν
σωτῆρ' ἀρεῖσθε, τοῖς δ' ἐμοῖς ἐχθροῖς πόνους.   460
ΧΟ. ἐπάξιος μέν, Οἰδίπους, κατοικτίσαι,
αὐτός τε παῖδές θ' αἵδ'· ἐπεὶ δὲ τῆσδε γῆς
σωτῆρα σαυτὸν τῷδ' ἐπεμβάλλεις λόγῳ,
παραινέσαι σοι βούλομαι τὰ σύμφορα.
ΟΙ. ὦ φίλταθ', ὥς νυν πᾶν τελοῦντι προξένει.   465
ΧΟ. θοῦ νῦν καθαρμὸν τῶνδε δαιμόνων, ἐφ' ἃς
τὸ πρῶτον ἵκου καὶ κατέστειψας πέδον.
ΟΙ. τρόποισι ποίοις; ὦ ξένοι, διδάσκετε.
ΧΟ. πρῶτον μὲν ἱρὰς ἐξ ἀειρύτου χοὰς
κρήνης ἐνεγκοῦ, δι' ὁσίων χειρῶν θιγών.   470
ΟΙ. ὅταν δὲ τοῦτο χεῦμ' ἀκήρατον λάβω;

---

451 οὔτε σφιν MSS.: corr. Hermann.   453 τά τ' ἐξ ἐμοῦ MSS.:
corr. Heath.   457 θελητέ μου L, vulg.: θέλητέ μοι r: corr. Dindorf.
458 πρὸ σταῖσι ταῖς L: σὺν ταῖσι ταῖς A, vulg.: corr. Dindorf.

ΧΟ. κρατῆρές εἰσιν, ἀνδρὸς εὐχειρος τέχνη,
ὧν κρᾶτ' ἔρεψον καὶ λαβὰς ἀμφιστόμους.

ΟΙ. θαλλοῖσιν, ἢ κρόκαισιν, ἢ ποίῳ τρόπῳ;

ΧΟ. οἰὸς σὺ νεαρᾶς νεοπόκῳ μαλλῷ λαβών. 475

ΟΙ. εἶεν· τὸ δ' ἔνθεν ποῖ τελευτῆσαί με χρή;

ΧΟ. χοὰς χέασθαι στάντα πρὸς πρώτην ἕω.

ΟΙ. ἢ τοῖσδε κρωσσοῖς οἷς λέγεις χέω τάδε;

ΧΟ. τρισσάς γε πηγάς· τὸν τελευταῖον δ' ὅλον.

ΟΙ. τοῦ τόνδε πλήσας θῶ; δίδασκε καὶ τόδε. 480

ΧΟ. ὕδατος, μελίσσης· μηδὲ προσφέρειν μέθυ.

ΟΙ. ὅταν δὲ τούτων γῆ μελάμφυλλος τύχῃ;

ΧΟ. τρὶς ἐννέ' αὐτῇ κλῶνας ἐξ ἀμφοῖν χεροῖν
τιθεὶς ἐλαίας τάσδ' ἐπεύχεσθαι λιτάς.

ΟΙ. τούτων ἀκοῦσαι βούλομαι· μέγιστα γάρ. 485

ΧΟ. ὥς σφας καλοῦμεν Εὐμενίδας, ἐξ εὐμενῶν
στέρνων δέχεσθαι τὸν ἱκέτην σωτήριον,
αἰτοῦ σύ τ' αὐτὸς κεἴ τις ἄλλος ἀντὶ σοῦ,
ἄπυστα φωνῶν μηδὲ μηκύνων βοήν·
ἔπειτ' ἀφέρπειν ἄστροφος. καὶ ταῦτά σοι 490
δράσαντι θαρσῶν ἂν παρασταίην ἐγώ·
ἄλλως δὲ δειμαίνοιμ' ἄν, ὦ ξέν', ἀμφὶ σοί.

ΟΙ. ὦ παῖδε, κλύετον τῶνδε προσχώρων ξένων;

ΑΝ. ἠκούσαμέν τε χὥ τι δεῖ πρόστασσε δρᾶν.

ΟΙ. ἐμοὶ μὲν οὐχ ὁδωτά· λείπομαι γὰρ ἐν 495
τῷ μὴ δύνασθαι μήδ' ὁρᾶν, δυοῖν κακοῖν·
σφῷν δ' ἀτέρα μολοῦσα πραξάτω τάδε.
ἀρκεῖν γὰρ οἶμαι κἀντὶ μυρίων μίαν
ψυχὴν τάδ' ἐκτίνουσαν, ἢν εὔνους παρῇ.
ἀλλ' ἐν τάχει τι πράσσετον· μόνον δέ με 500
μὴ λείπετ'· οὐ γὰρ ἂν σθένοι τοὐμὸν δέμας
ἔρημον ἕρπειν οὐδ' ὑφηγητοῦ δίχα.

475 σὺ add. Bellermann.   499 ἐκτείνουσαν MSS.: corr. Canter.
502 ὑφηγητοῦ δ' ἄνευ L, vulg. (γ' ἄνευ T): corr. Hermann.

20 ΣΟΦΟΚΛΕΟΥΣ

ΙΣ. ἀλλ' εἰμ' ἐγὼ τελοῦσα· τὸν τόπον δ' ἵνα
χρῆσταί μ' ἐφευρεῖν, τοῦτο βούλομαι μαθεῖν.

ΧΟ. τοὐκεῖθεν ἄλσους, ὦ ξένη, τοῦδ'. ἢν δέ του   505
σπάνιν τιν' ἴσχῃς, ἔστ' ἔποικος, ὃς φράσει.

ΙΣ. χωροῖμ' ἂν ἐς τόδ'· Ἀντιγόνη, σὺ δ' ἐνθάδε
φύλασσε πατέρα τόνδε· τοῖς τεκοῦσι γὰρ
οὐδ' εἰ πονεῖ τις, δεῖ πόνου μνήμην ἔχειν.   509

στρ. α'. ΧΟ. δεινὸν μὲν τὸ πάλαι κείμενον ἤδη κακόν, ὦ
ξεῖν', ἐπεγείρειν·
2 ὅμως δ' ἔραμαι πυθέσθαι

ΟΙ. 3 τί τοῦτο;

ΧΟ. 4 τᾶς δειλαίας ἀπόρου φανείσας
5 ἀλγηδόνος, ᾇ ξυνέστας.

ΟΙ. 6 μὴ πρὸς ξενίας ἀνοίξῃς   515
7 τᾶς σᾶς ἃ πέπονθ' ἀναιδῆ.

ΧΟ. 8 τό τοι πολὺ καὶ μηδαμὰ λῆγον
9 χρῄζω, ξεῖν', ὀρθὸν ἄκουσμ' ἀκοῦσαι.

ΟΙ. 10 ὤμοι.

ΧΟ. 11 στέρξον, ἱκετεύω.

ΟΙ. 12 φεῦ φεῦ.

ΧΟ. 13 πείθου· κἀγὼ γὰρ ὅσον σὺ προσχρήζεις.   520

ἀντ. α'. ΟΙ. ἤνεγκ' οὖν κακότατ', ὦ ξένοι, ἤνεγκ' ἀέκων μέν,
θεὸς ἴστω,
2 τούτων δ' αὐθαίρετον οὐδέν.

ΧΟ. 3 ἀλλ' ἐς τί;

ΟΙ. 4 κακᾷ μ' εὐνᾷ πόλις οὐδὲν ἴδριν   525
5 γάμων ἐνέδησεν ἄτᾳ.

ΧΟ. 6 ἦ ματρόθεν, ὡς ἀκούω,
7 δυσώνυμα λέκτρ' ἐπλήσω;

504 χρῆσται L¹, χρῆ 'σται Lᶜ, r.   516 τᾶς σᾶς· πέπονθ' ἐργ' ἀναιδῆ
MSS. (τὰς σὰς L): corr. Reisig.   522 ἤνεγκον κακότατ' MSS.: corr.
R. Whitelaw.—ἤνεγκον ἄκων MSS.: corr. Martin, Bergk.

ΟΙ. 8 ὤμοι, θάνατος μὲν τάδ᾽ ἀκούειν,
    9 ὢ ξεῖν᾽· αὗται δὲ δύ᾽ ἐξ ἐμοῦ μὲν   530
ΧΟ. 10 πῶς φής;
ΟΙ. 11 παῖδε, δύο δ᾽ ἄτα
ΧΟ. 12 ὢ Ζεῦ.
ΟΙ. 13 ματρὸς κοινᾶς ἀπέβλαστον ὠδῖνος.

στρ. β'. ΧΟ. σαί τ᾽ εἴσ᾽ ἄρ᾽ ἀπόγονοί τε καὶ
ΟΙ. 2 κοιναί γε πατρὸς ἀδελφεαί.   535
ΧΟ. 3 ἰώ. ΟΙ. ἰὼ δῆτα μυρίων γ᾽ ἐπιστροφαὶ κακῶν.
ΧΟ. 4 ἔπαθες ΟΙ. ἔπαθον ἄλαστ᾽ ἔχειν.
ΧΟ. 5 ἔρεξας ΟΙ. οὐκ ἔρεξα. ΧΟ. τί γάρ; ΟΙ. ἐδεξ-
    άμην
    6 δῶρον, ὃ μήποτ᾽ ἐγὼ ταλακάρδιος   540
    7 ἐπωφελήσας πόλεος ἐξελέσθαι.

ἀντ. β'. ΧΟ. δύστανε, τί γάρ; ἔθου φόνον
ΟΙ. 2 τί τοῦτο; τί δ᾽ ἐθέλεις μαθεῖν;
ΧΟ. 3 πατρός; ΟΙ. παπαῖ, δευτέραν ἔπαισας, ἐπὶ νόσῳ
    νόσον.
ΧΟ. 4 ἔκανες ΟΙ. ἔκανον· ἔχει δέ μοι   545
ΧΟ. 5 τί τοῦτο; ΟΙ. πρὸς δίκας τι. ΧΟ. τί γάρ; ΟΙ. ἐγὼ
    φράσω·
    6 καὶ γὰρ ἄν, οὓς ἐφόνευσ᾽, ἔμ᾽ ἀπώλεσαν·
    7 νόμῳ δὲ καθαρός, ἄϊδρις ἐς τόδ᾽ ἦλθον.

ΧΟ. καὶ μὴν ἄναξ ὅδ᾽ ἡμὶν Αἰγέως γόνος
    Θησεὺς κατ᾽ ὀμφὴν σὴν ἐφ᾽ ἁστάλη πάρα.   550

---

530 μὲν add. Elmsley.   532 παῖδες MSS. : corr. Elmsley.
534 σαί τ᾽ ἄρ᾽ εἰσὶν L : σαί τ᾽ ἄρ᾽ εἴσ᾽ A: corr. J.   541 ἐπωφέλησα
MSS. : corr. J.—πόλεως MSS. : corr. Hermann.   547 καὶ γὰρ ἄλλους
ἐφόνευσα καὶ ἀπώλεσα (or κἀπώλεσα) MSS. : corr. Mekler.   550 ἀπε-
στάλη MSS. : corr. Dindorf.

22 ΣΟΦΟΚΛΕΟΥΣ

ΘΗΣΕΥΣ.

πολλῶν ἀκούων ἔν τε τῷ πάρος χρόνῳ
τὰς αἱματηρὰς ὀμμάτων διαφθορὰς
ἔγνωκά σ᾽, ὦ παῖ Λαΐου, τανῦν θ᾽ ὁδοῖς
ἐν ταῖσδ᾽ ἀκούων μᾶλλον ἐξεπίσταμαι.
σκευή τε γάρ σε καὶ τὸ δύστηνον κάρα   555
δηλοῦτον ἡμῖν ὄνθ᾽ ὃς εἶ, καί σ᾽ οἰκτίσας
θέλω ᾽περέσθαι, δύσμορ᾽ Οἰδίπου, τίνα
πόλεως ἐπέστης προστροπὴν ἐμοῦ τ᾽ ἔχων,
αὐτός τε χἠ σὴ δύσμορος παραστάτις.
δίδασκε· δεινὴν γάρ τιν᾽ ἂν πρᾶξιν τύχοις   560
λέξας ὁποίας ἐξαφισταίμην ἐγώ·
ὃς οἶδά γ᾽ αὐτὸς ὡς ἐπαιδεύθην ξένος,
ὥσπερ σύ, χὡς εἰς πλεῖστ᾽ ἀνὴρ ἐπὶ ξένης
ἤθλησα κινδυνεύματ᾽ ἐν τὠμῷ κάρᾳ·
ὥστε ξένον γ᾽ ἂν οὐδέν᾽ ὄνθ᾽, ὥσπερ σὺ νῦν,   565
ὑπεκτραποίμην μὴ οὐ συνεκσῴζειν· ἐπεὶ
ἔξοιδ᾽ ἀνὴρ ὤν, χὤτι τῆς ἐς αὔριον
οὐδὲν πλέον μοι σοῦ μέτεστιν ἡμέρας.

ΟΙ. Θησεῦ, τὸ σὸν γενναῖον ἐν σμικρῷ λόγῳ
παρῆκεν ὥστε βραχέ᾽ ἐμοὶ δεῖσθαι φράσαι.   570
σὺ γάρ μ᾽ ὅς εἰμι, κἀφ᾽ ὅτου πατρὸς γεγὼς
καὶ γῆς ὁποίας ἦλθον, εἰρηκὼς κυρεῖς·
ὥστ᾽ ἐστί μοι τὸ λοιπὸν οὐδὲν ἄλλο πλὴν
εἰπεῖν ἃ χρῄζω, χὡ λόγος διοίχεται.

ΘΗ. τοῦτ᾽ αὐτὸ νῦν δίδασχ᾽, ὅπως ἂν ἐκμάθω.   575

ΟΙ. δώσων ἱκάνω τοὐμὸν ἄθλιον δέμας
σοὶ δῶρον, οὐ σπουδαῖον εἰς ὄψιν· τὰ δὲ
κέρδη παρ᾽ αὐτοῦ κρείσσον᾽ ἢ μορφὴ καλή.

557 ᾽περέσθαι Reisig: τι ἔρεσθαι L (τί r), σ᾽ ἔρεσθαι T.   562 ὡς
οἶδά γ᾽ MSS.: corr. Dindorf.   563 χὡς εἰς Dobree: χῶστις MSS.
574 διοίχεται r: διέρχεται L, A.

ΘΗ. ποῖον δὲ κέρδος ἀξιοῖς ἥκειν φέρων;

ΟΙ. χρόνῳ μάθοις ἄν, οὐχὶ τῷ παρόντι που. 580

ΘΗ. ποίῳ γὰρ ἡ σὴ προσφορὰ δηλώσεται;

ΟΙ. ὅταν θάνω 'γὼ καὶ σύ μου ταφεὺς γένῃ.

ΘΗ. τὰ λοίσθι' αἰτεῖ τοῦ βίου, τὰ δ' ἐν μέσῳ
ἢ λῆστιν ἴσχεις ἢ δι' οὐδενὸς ποεῖ.

ΟΙ. ἐνταῦθα γάρ μοι κεῖνα συγκομίζεται. 585

ΘΗ. ἀλλ' ἐν βραχεῖ δὴ τήνδε μ' ἐξαιτεῖ χάριν.

ΟΙ. ὅρα γε μήν· οὐ σμικρός, οὐχ, ἀγὼν ὅδε.

ΘΗ. πότερα τὰ τῶν σῶν ἐκγόνων κἀμοῦ λέγεις;

ΟΙ. κεῖνοι κομίζειν κεῖσ', ἄναξ, χρῄζουσί με.

ΘΗ. ἀλλ' εἰ θέλοντά γ', οὐδὲ σοὶ φεύγειν καλόν. 590

ΟΙ. ἀλλ' οὐδ', ὅτ' αὐτὸς ἤθελον, παρίεσαν.

ΘΗ. ὦ μῶρε, θυμὸς δ' ἐν κακοῖς οὐ ξύμφορον.

ΟΙ. ὅταν μάθῃς μου, νουθέτει, τανῦν δ' ἔα.

ΘΗ. δίδασκ'· ἄνευ γνώμης γὰρ οὔ με χρὴ λέγειν.

ΟΙ. πέπονθα, Θησεῦ, δεινὰ πρὸς κακοῖς κακά. 591

ΘΗ. ἢ τὴν παλαιὰν ξυμφορὰν γένους ἐρεῖς;

ΟΙ. οὐ δῆτ'· ἐπεὶ πᾶς τοῦτό γ' Ἑλλήνων θροεῖ.

ΘΗ. τί γὰρ τὸ μεῖζον ἢ κατ' ἄνθρωπον νοσεῖς;

ΟΙ. οὕτως ἔχει μοι· γῆς ἐμῆς ἀπηλάθην
πρὸς τῶν ἐμαυτοῦ σπερμάτων· ἔστιν δέ μοι 600
πάλιν κατελθεῖν μήποθ', ὡς πατροκτόνῳ.

ΘΗ. πῶς δῆτά σ' ἂν πεμψαίαθ', ὥστ' οἰκεῖν δίχα;

ΟΙ. τὸ θεῖον αὐτοὺς ἐξαναγκάσει στόμα.

ΘΗ. ποῖον πάθος δείσαντας ἐκ χρηστηρίων;

ΟΙ. ὅτι σφ' ἀνάγκη τῇδε πληγῆναι χθονί. 605

ΘΗ. καὶ πῶς γένοιτ' ἂν τἀμὰ κἀκείνων πικρά;

ΟΙ. ὦ φίλτατ' Αἰγέως παῖ, μόνοις οὐ γίγνεται
θεοῖσι γῆρας οὐδὲ κατθανεῖν ποτε,

---

588 κἀμοῦ Schneidewin: ἢ 'μοῦ MSS.   589 κεῖσ' ἀναγκάζουσί με
L, A, vulg. (κεῖσ' ἀναγκάσουσί με r): corr. Kayser.   590 θέλοντά
γ' r: θέλοντ' ἂν γ' L, A, vulg.

24 ΣΟΦΟΚΛΕΟΥΣ

τὰ δ' ἄλλα συγχεῖ πάνθ' ὁ παγκρατὴς χρόνος.
φθίνει μὲν ἰσχὺς γῆς, φθίνει δὲ σώματος,   610
θνῄσκει δὲ πίστις, βλαστάνει δ' ἀπιστία,
καὶ πνεῦμα ταὐτὸν οὔποτ' οὔτ' ἐν ἀνδράσιν
φίλοις βέβηκεν οὔτε πρὸς πόλιν πόλει.
τοῖς μὲν γὰρ ἤδη τοῖς δ' ἐν ὑστέρῳ χρόνῳ
τὰ τερπνὰ πικρὰ γίγνεται καὖθις φίλα.   615
καὶ ταῖσι Θήβαις εἰ τανῦν εὐημερεῖ
καλῶς τὰ πρὸς σέ, μυρίας ὁ μυρίος
χρόνος τεκνοῦται νύκτας ἡμέρας τ' ἰών,
ἐν αἷς τὰ νῦν ξύμφωνα δεξιώματα
δόρει διασκεδῶσιν ἐκ σμικροῦ λόγου·   620
ἵν' οὑμὸς εὕδων καὶ κεκρυμμένος νέκυς
ψυχρός ποτ' αὐτῶν θερμὸν αἷμα πίεται,
εἰ Ζεὺς ἔτι Ζεὺς χὠ Διὸς Φοῖβος σαφής.
ἀλλ' οὐ γὰρ αὐδᾶν ἡδὺ τἀκίνητ' ἔπη,
ἔα μ' ἐν οἷσιν ἠρξάμην, τὸ σὸν μόνον   625
πιστὸν φυλάσσων· κοὔποτ' Οἰδίπουν ἐρεῖς
ἀχρεῖον οἰκητῆρα δέξασθαι τόπων
τῶν ἐνθάδ', εἴπερ μὴ θεοὶ ψεύσουσί με.
ΧΟ. ἄναξ, πάλαι καὶ ταῦτα καὶ τοιαῦτ' ἔπη
γῇ τῇδ' ὅδ' ἀνὴρ ὡς τελῶν ἐφαίνετο.   630
ΘΗ τίς δῆτ' ἂν ἀνδρὸς εὐμένειαν ἐκβάλοι
τοιοῦδ', ὅτῳ πρῶτον μὲν ἡ δορύξενος
κοινὴ παρ' ἡμῖν αἰέν ἐστιν ἑστία;
ἔπειτα δ' ἱκέτης δαιμόνων ἀφιγμένος
γῇ τῇδε κἀμοὶ δασμὸν οὐ σμικρὸν τίνει.   635
ἀγὼ σεβισθεὶς οὔποτ' ἐκβαλῶ χάριν
τὴν τοῦδε, χώρᾳ δ' ἔμπολιν κατοικιῶ.
εἰ δ' ἐνθάδ' ἡδὺ τῷ ξένῳ μίμνειν, σέ νιν
τάξω φυλάσσειν· εἰ δ' ἐμοῦ στείχειν μέτα

617 τὰ London ed. of 1722 : τε or τὲ MSS.   632 ὅτῳ Suidas
(s. v. δορύξενος) : ὅτου MSS.   637 ἔμπαλιν MSS. : corr. Musgrave.

τόδ᾽ ἡδύ, τούτων, Οἰδίπους, δίδωμί σοι 640
κρίναντι χρῆσθαι· τῇδε γὰρ ξυνοίσομαι.

ΟΙ. ὦ Ζεῦ, διδοίης τοῖσι τοιούτοισιν εὖ.

ΘΗ. τί δῆτα χρῄζεις; ἢ δόμους στείχειν ἐμούς;

ΟΙ. εἴ μοι θέμις γ᾽ ἦν. ἀλλ᾽ ὁ χῶρός ἐσθ᾽ ὅδε,

ΘΗ. ἐν ᾧ τί πράξεις; οὐ γὰρ ἀντιστήσομαι. 645

ΟΙ. ἐν ᾧ κρατήσω τῶν ἔμ᾽ ἐκβεβληκότων.

ΘΗ. μέγ᾽ ἂν λέγοις δώρημα τῆς συνουσίας.

ΟΙ. εἰ σοί γ᾽ ἅπερ φῂς ἐμμενεῖ τελοῦντί μοι.

ΘΗ. θάρσει τὸ τοῦδέ γ᾽ ἀνδρός· οὔ σε μὴ προδῶ.

ΟΙ. οὔτοι σ᾽ ὑφ᾽ ὅρκου γ᾽ ὡς κακὸν πιστώσομαι. 650

ΘΗ. οὔκουν πέρα γ᾽ ἂν οὐδὲν ἢ λόγῳ φέροις.

ΟΙ. πῶς οὖν ποήσεις; ΘΗ. τοῦ μάλιστ᾽ ὄκνος σ᾽ ἔχει;

ΟΙ. ἥξουσιν ἄνδρες ΘΗ. ἀλλὰ τοῖσδ᾽ ἔσται μέλον.

ΟΙ. ὅρα με λείπων ΘΗ. μὴ δίδασχ᾽ ἃ χρή με δρᾶν.

ΟΙ. ὀκνοῦντ᾽ ἀνάγκη. ΘΗ. τοὐμὸν οὐκ ὀκνεῖ κέαρ. 655

ΟΙ. οὐκ οἶσθ᾽ ἀπειλάς ΘΗ. οἶδ᾽ ἐγώ σε μή τινα
ἐνθένδ᾽ ἀπάξοντ᾽ ἄνδρα πρὸς βίαν ἐμοῦ.
πολλαὶ δ᾽ ἀπειλαὶ πολλὰ δὴ μάτην ἔπη
θυμῷ κατηπείλησαν· ἀλλ᾽ ὁ νοῦς ὅταν
αὑτοῦ γένηται, φροῦδα τἀπειλήματα. 660
κείνοις δ᾽ ἴσως κεἰ δείν᾽ ἐπερρώσθη λέγειν
τῆς σῆς ἀγωγῆς, οἶδ᾽ ἐγώ, φανήσεται
μακρὸν τὸ δεῦρο πέλαγος οὐδὲ πλώσιμον.
θαρσεῖν μὲν οὖν ἔγωγε κἄνευ τῆς ἐμῆς
γνώμης ἐπαινῶ, Φοῖβος εἰ προὔπεμψέ σε· 665
ὅμως δὲ κἀμοῦ μὴ παρόντος οἶδ᾽ ὅτι
τοὐμὸν φυλάξει σ᾽ ὄνομα μὴ πάσχειν κακῶς.

στρ. ά. ΧΟ. εὐίππου, ξένε, τᾶσδε χώρας
2 ἵκου τὰ κράτιστα γᾶς ἔπαυλα,
3 τὸν ἀργῆτα Κολωνόν, ἔνθ᾽ 670
4 ἁ λίγεια μινύρεται

5 θαμίζουσα μάλιστ᾽ ἀηδὼν
6 χλωραῖς ὑπὸ βάσσαις,
7 τὸν οἰνωπὸν ἔχουσα κισσὸν
8 καὶ τὰν ἄβατον θεοῦ   675
9 φυλλάδα μυριόκαρπον ἀνήλιον
10 ἀνήνεμόν τε πάντων
11 χειμώνων· ἵν᾽ ὁ βακχιώτας
12 ἀεὶ Διόνυσος ἐμβατεύει
13 θεαῖς ἀμφιπολῶν τιθήναις.   680

ἀντ. α΄.   θάλλει δ᾽ οὐρανίας ὑπ᾽ ἄχνας
2 ὁ καλλίβοτρυς κατ᾽ ἦμαρ ἀεὶ
3 νάρκισσος, μεγάλαιν θεαῖν
4 ἀρχαῖον στεφάνωμ᾽, ὅ τε
5 χρυσαυγὴς κρόκος· οὐδ᾽ ἄϋπνοι   685
6 κρῆναι μινύθουσιν
7 Κηφισοῦ νομάδες ῥεέθρων,
8 ἀλλ᾽ αἰὲν ἐπ᾽ ἤματι
9 ὠκυτόκος πεδίων ἐπινίσσεται
10 ἀκηράτῳ σὺν ὄμβρῳ   690
11 στερνούχου χθονός· οὐδὲ Μουσᾶν
12 χοροί νιν ἀπεστύγησαν, οὐδ᾽ ἁ
13 χρυσάνιος Ἀφροδίτα.

στρ. β΄.   ἔστιν δ᾽ οἷον ἐγὼ γᾶς Ἀσίας οὐκ ἐπακούω,   694
2 οὐδ᾽ ἐν τᾷ μεγάλᾳ Δωρίδι νάσῳ Πέλοπος πώποτε
βλαστὸν
3 φύτευμ᾽ ἀχείρωτον αὐτοποιόν,
4 ἐγχέων φόβημα δαΐων,
5 ὃ τᾷδε θάλλει μέγιστα χώρᾳ,   ʼ700
6 γλαυκᾶς παιδοτρόφου φύλλον ἐλαίας·

674 τὸν οἴνωπ᾽ ἀνέχουσα (made from οἰνωπὰν ἔχουσα) L, vulg.:
οἰνώπαν ἔχουσα r: corr. Erfurdt.   680 θείαις MSS.: corr. Elmsley.
698 ἀχείρωτον A: ἀχείρητον L.—αὐτόποιον MSS.: corr. J.

7 τὸ μέν τις οὐ νεαρὸς οὐδὲ γήρᾳ
8 συνναίων ἁλιώσει χερὶ πέρσας· ὁ γὰρ αἰὲν ὁρῶν
κύκλος
9 λεύσσει νιν Μορίου Διὸς   705
10 χἀ γλαυκῶπις Ἀθάνα.

ἀντ. β'. ἄλλον δ' αἶνον ἔχω ματροπόλει τᾷδε κράτιστον, 707
2 δῶρον τοῦ μεγάλου δαίμονος, εἰπεῖν, χθονὸς αὔχημα
μέγιστον,
3 εὔιππον, εὔπωλον, εὐθάλασσον.   711
4 ὦ παῖ Κρόνου, σὺ γάρ νιν εἰς
5 τόδ' εἷσας αὔχημ', ἄναξ Ποσειδάν,
6 ἵπποισιν τὸν ἀκεστῆρα χαλινὸν
7 πρώταισι ταῖσδε κτίσας ἀγυιαῖς.   715
8 ἁ δ' εὐήρετμος ἔκπαγλ' ἁλία χερσὶ παραπτομένα
πλάτα
9 θρῴσκει, τῶν ἑκατομπόδων
10 Νηρῄδων ἀκόλουθος.

ΑΝ. ὦ πλεῖστ' ἐπαίνοις εὐλογούμενον πέδον,   720
νῦν σὸν τὰ λαμπρὰ ταῦτα δὴ φαίνειν ἔπη.
ΟΙ. τί δ' ἔστιν, ὦ παῖ, καινόν; ΑΝ. ἆσσον ἔρχεται
Κρέων ὅδ' ἡμῖν οὐκ ἄνευ πομπῶν, πάτερ.
ΟΙ. ὦ φίλτατοι γέροντες, ἐξ ὑμῶν ἐμοὶ
φαίνοιτ' ἂν ἤδη τέρμα τῆς σωτηρίας.   725
ΧΟ. θάρσει, παρέσται· καὶ γὰρ εἰ γέρων ἐγώ,
τὸ τῆσδε χώρας οὐ γεγήρακε σθένος.

702 οὔτε νεαρὸς οὔτε MSS. : corr. Porson.   703 συνναίων Blaydes:
σημαίνων MSS.   704 ὁ γὰρ εἰς αἰὲν ὁρῶν L, vulg.: corr. Hermann.
710 χθονὸς add. Porson.   721 σὸν...δὴ Nauck: σοὶ...δὴ L: σοὶ...
δεῖ A, vulg.   726 ἐγὼ L (with κυρῶ superscript by S): κυρῶ A, vulg.

ΚΡΕΩΝ.

ἄνδρες χθονὸς τῆσδ' εὐγενεῖς οἰκήτορες,
ὁρῶ τιν' ὑμᾶς ὀμμάτων εἰληφότας
φόβον νεώρη τῆς ἐμῆς ἐπεισόδου·   730
ὃν μήτ' ὀκνεῖτε μήτ' ἀφῆτ' ἔπος κακόν.
ἥκω γὰρ οὐχ ὡς δρᾶν τι βουληθείς, ἐπεὶ
γέρων μέν εἰμι, πρὸς πόλιν δ' ἐπίσταμαι
σθένουσαν ἥκων, εἴ τιν' Ἑλλάδος, μέγα.
ἀλλ' ἄνδρα τόνδε τηλικόσδ' ἀπεστάλην   735
πείσων ἕπεσθαι πρὸς τὸ Καδμείων πέδον,
οὐκ ἐξ ἑνὸς στείλαντος, ἀλλ' ἀστῶν ὑπὸ
πάντων κελευσθείς, οὕνεχ' ἧκέ μοι γένει
τὰ τοῦδε πενθεῖν πήματ' εἰς πλεῖστον πόλεως.
ἀλλ', ὦ ταλαίπωρ' Οἰδίπους, κλύων ἐμοῦ   740
ἱκοῦ πρὸς οἴκους. πᾶς σε Καδμείων λεὼς
καλεῖ δικαίως, ἐκ δὲ τῶν μάλιστ' ἐγώ,
ὅσῳπερ, εἰ μὴ πλεῖστον ἀνθρώπων ἔφυν
κάκιστος, ἀλγῶ τοῖσι σοῖς κακοῖς, γέρον,
ὁρῶν σε τὸν δύστηνον ὄντα μὲν ξένον,   745
ἀεὶ δ' ἀλήτην κἀπὶ προσπόλου μιᾶς
βιοστερῆ χωροῦντα, τὴν ἐγὼ τάλας
οὐκ ἄν ποτ' ἐς τοσοῦτον αἰκίας πεσεῖν
ἔδοξ', ὅσον πέπτωκεν ἥδε δύσμορος,
ἀεί σε κηδεύουσα καὶ τὸ σὸν κάρα   750
πτωχῷ διαίτῃ, τηλικοῦτος, οὐ γάμων
ἔμπειρος, ἀλλὰ τοὐπιόντος ἁρπάσαι.
ἆρ' ἄθλιον τοὔνειδος, ὦ τάλας ἐγώ,
ὠνείδισ' ἐς σὲ κἀμὲ καὶ τὸ πᾶν γένος;
ἀλλ' οὐ γὰρ ἔστι τἀμφανῆ κρύπτειν· σὺ νυν   755
πρὸς θεῶν πατρῴων, Οἰδίπους, πεισθεὶς ἐμοὶ
κρύψον, θελήσας ἄστυ καὶ δόμους μολεῖν

737 ἀστῶν r: ἀνδρῶν L, vulg.

τοὺς σοὺς πατρῴους, τήνδε τὴν πόλιν φίλως
εἰπών· ἐπαξία γάρ· ἡ δ' οἴκοι πλέον
δίκη σέβοιτ' ἄν, οὖσα σὴ πάλαι τροφός.   760

ΟΙ. ὦ πάντα τολμῶν κἀπὸ παντὸς ἂν φέρων
λόγου δικαίου μηχάνημα ποικίλον,
τί ταῦτα πειρᾷ κἀμὲ δεύτερον θέλεις
ἑλεῖν ἐν οἷς μάλιστ' ἂν ἀλγοίην ἁλούς;
πρόσθεν τε γάρ με τοῖσιν οἰκείοις κακοῖς   765
νοσοῦνθ', ὅτ' ἦν μοι τέρψις ἐκπεσεῖν χθονός,
οὐκ ἤθελες θέλοντι προσθέσθαι χάριν,
ἀλλ' ἡνίκ' ἤδη μεστὸς ἦ θυμούμενος,
καὶ τοὐν δόμοισιν ἦν διαιτᾶσθαι γλυκύ,
τότ' ἐξεώθεις κἀξέβαλλες, οὐδέ σοι   770
τὸ συγγενὲς τοῦτ' οὐδαμῶς τότ' ἦν φίλον·
νῦν τ' αὖθις, ἡνίκ' εἰσορᾷς πόλιν τέ μοι
ξυνοῦσαν εὔνουν τήνδε καὶ γένος τὸ πᾶν,
πειρᾷ μετασπᾶν, σκληρὰ μαλθακῶς λέγων.
καίτοι τίς αὕτη τέρψις, ἄκοντας φιλεῖν;   775
ὥσπερ τις εἰ σοὶ λιπαροῦντι μὲν τυχεῖν
μηδὲν διδοίη μηδ' ἐπαρκέσαι θέλοι,
πλήρη δ' ἔχοντι θυμὸν ὧν χρῄζοις, τότε
δωροῖθ', ὅτ' οὐδὲν ἡ χάρις χάριν φέροι·
ἆρ' ἂν ματαίου τῆσδ' ἂν ἡδονῆς τύχοις;   780
τοιαῦτα μέντοι καὶ σὺ προσφέρεις ἐμοί,
λόγῳ μὲν ἐσθλά, τοῖσι δ' ἔργοισιν κακά.
φράσω δὲ καὶ τοῖσδ', ὥς σε δηλώσω κακόν.
ἥκεις ἔμ' ἄξων, οὐχ ἵν' ἐς δόμους ἄγῃς,
ἀλλ' ὡς πάραυλον οἰκίσῃς, πόλις δέ σοι   785
κακῶν ἄνατος τῆσδ' ἀπαλλαχθῇ χθονός.
οὐκ ἔστι σοι ταῦτ', ἀλλά σοι τάδ' ἔστ', ἐκεῖ
χώρας ἀλάστωρ οὑμὸς ἐνναίων ἀεί·

779 φέροι r: φέρει (with οι above) L, A.
786 τῆσδ' Scaliger: τῶνδ' MSS.

30 ΣΟΦΟΚΛΕΟΥΣ

ἔστιν δὲ παισὶ τοῖς ἐμοῖσι τῆς ἐμῆς
χθονὸς λαχεῖν τοσοῦτον, ἐνθανεῖν μόνον.   790
ἆρ' οὐκ ἄμεινον ἢ σὺ τὰν Θήβαις φρονῶ;
πολλῷ γ', ὅσῳπερ κἀκ σαφεστέρων κλύω,
Φοίβου τε καὐτοῦ Ζηνός, ὃς κείνου πατήρ.
τὸ σὸν δ' ἀφῖκται δεῦρ' ὑπόβλητον στόμα,
πολλὴν ἔχον στόμωσιν· ἐν δὲ τῷ λέγειν   795
κάκ' ἂν λάβοις τὰ πλείον' ἢ σωτήρια.
ἀλλ' οἶδα γάρ σε ταῦτα μὴ πείθων, ἴθι·
ἡμᾶς δ' ἔα ζῆν ἐνθάδ'· οὐ γὰρ ἂν κακῶς
οὐδ' ὧδ' ἔχοντες ζῶμεν, εἰ τερποίμεθα.
ΚΡ. πότερα νομίζεις δυστυχεῖν ἔμ' ἐς τὰ σά,   800
ἢ σ' εἰς τὰ σαυτοῦ μᾶλλον, ἐν τῷ νῦν λόγῳ;
ΟΙ. ἐμοὶ μέν ἐσθ' ἥδιστον εἰ σὺ μήτ' ἐμὲ
πείθειν οἷός τ' εἰ μήτε τούσδε τοὺς πέλας.
ΚΡ. ὦ δύσμορ', οὐδὲ τῷ χρόνῳ φύσας φανεῖ
φρένας ποτ', ἀλλὰ λῦμα τῷ γήρᾳ τρέφει;   805
ΟΙ. γλώσσῃ σὺ δεινός· ἄνδρα δ' οὐδέν' οἶδ' ἐγὼ
δίκαιον, ὅστις ἐξ ἅπαντος εὖ λέγει.
ΚΡ. χωρὶς τό τ' εἰπεῖν πολλὰ καὶ τὰ καίρια.
ΟΙ. ὡς δὴ σὺ βραχέα, ταῦτα δ' ἐν καιρῷ λέγεις.
ΚΡ. οὐ δῆθ' ὅτῳ γε νοῦς ἴσος καὶ σοὶ πάρα.   810
ΟΙ. ἄπελθ', ἐρῶ γὰρ καὶ πρὸ τῶνδε, μηδέ με
φύλασσ' ἐφορμῶν ἔνθα χρὴ ναίειν ἐμέ.
ΚΡ. μαρτύρομαι τούσδ', οὐ σέ· πρὸς δὲ τοὺς φίλους
οἷ' ἀνταμείβει ῥήματ', ἤν σ' ἕλω ποτέ,—
ΟΙ. τίς δ' ἄν με τῶνδε συμμάχων ἕλοι βίᾳ;   815
ΚΡ. ἦ μὴν σὺ κἄνευ τοῦδε λυπηθεὶς ἔσει.
ΟΙ. ποίῳ σὺν ἔργῳ τοῦτ' ἀπειλήσας ἔχεις;
ΚΡ. παίδοιν δυοῖν σοι τὴν μὲν ἀρτίως ἐγὼ
ξυναρπάσας ἔπεμψα, τὴν δ' ἄξω τάχα.

792 κἀκ Doederlein: ἐκ L, vulg.: καὶ A.   808 τὸ καίρια Suidas
(s. v. χωρίς).   816 τοῦδε Musgrave: τῶνδε MSS.

ΟΙ. οἴμοι. ΚΡ. τάχ᾽ ἕξεις μᾶλλον οἰμώζειν τάδε. 820

ΟΙ. τὴν παῖδ᾽ ἔχεις μου; ΚΡ. τήνδε τ᾽ οὐ μακροῦ
χρόνου.

ΟΙ. ἰὼ ξένοι, τί δράσετ᾽; ἢ προδώσετε,
κοὐκ ἐξελᾶτε τὸν ἀσεβῆ τῆσδε χθονός;

ΧΟ. χώρει, ξέν᾽, ἔξω θᾶσσον· οὔτε γὰρ τὰ νῦν
δίκαια πράσσεις οὔθ᾽ ἃ πρόσθεν εἴργασαι. 825

ΚΡ. ὑμῖν ἂν εἴη τήνδε καιρὸς ἐξάγειν
ἄκουσαν, εἰ θέλουσα μὴ πορεύσεται.

ΑΝ. οἴμοι τάλαινα, ποῖ φύγω; ποίαν λάβω
θεῶν ἄρηξιν ἢ βροτῶν; ΧΟ. τί δρᾷς, ξένε;

ΚΡ. οὐχ ἅψομαι τοῦδ᾽ ἀνδρός, ἀλλὰ τῆς ἐμῆς. 830

ΟΙ. ὦ γῆς ἄνακτες. ΧΟ. ὦ ξέν᾽, οὐ δίκαια δρᾷς.

ΚΡ. δίκαια. ΧΟ. πῶς δίκαια; ΚΡ. τοὺς ἐμοὺς ἄγω.

στρ. ΟΙ. ἰὼ πόλις.

ΧΟ. 2 τί δρᾷς, ὦ ξέν᾽; οὐκ ἀφήσεις; τάχ᾽ εἰς βάσανον
εἶ χερῶν. 835

ΚΡ. 3 εἴργου. ΧΟ. σοῦ μὲν οὔ, τάδε γε μωμένου.

ΚΡ. 4 πόλει μαχεῖ γάρ, εἴ τι πημανεῖς ἐμέ.

ΟΙ. 5 οὐκ ἠγόρευον ταῦτ᾽ ἐγώ; ΧΟ. μέθες χεροῖν
6 τὴν παῖδα θᾶσσον. ΚΡ. μὴ 'πίτασσ᾽ ἃ μὴ κρατεῖς.

ΧΟ. 7 χαλᾶν λέγω σοι. ΚΡ. σοὶ δ᾽ ἔγωγ᾽ ὁδοιπορεῖν.

ΧΟ. 8 πρόβαθ᾽ ὧδε, βᾶτε βᾶτ᾽, ἔντοποι. 841
9 πόλις ἐναίρεται, πόλις ἐμά, σθένει.
10 πρόβαθ᾽ ὧδέ μοι.

ΑΝ. ἀφέλκομαι δύστηνος, ὦ ξένοι ξένοι.

ΟΙ. ποῦ, τέκνον, εἶ μοι; ΑΝ. πρὸς βίαν πορεύομαι. 845

ΟΙ. ὄρεξον, ὦ παῖ, χεῖρας. ΑΝ. ἀλλ᾽ οὐδὲν σθένω.

ΚΡ. οὐκ ἄξεθ᾽ ὑμεῖς; ΟΙ. ὦ τάλας ἐγώ, τάλας.

ΚΡ. οὔκουν ποτ᾽ ἐκ τούτοιν γε μὴ σκήπτροιν ἔτι

---

821 τήνδε γ᾽ MSS. : corr. Bothe.   837 πημαίνεις MSS. : corr. Porson.
841 ὧδε, βᾶτε] ὧδ᾽ ἐμβᾶτε MSS. : corr. Triclinius.

32   ΣΟΦΟΚΛΕΟΥΣ

ὁδοιπορήσῃς· ἀλλ' ἐπεὶ νικᾶν θέλεις
πατρίδα τε τὴν σὴν καὶ φίλους, ὑφ' ὧν ἐγὼ   850
ταχθεὶς τάδ' ἔρδω, καὶ τύραννος ὢν ὅμως,
νίκα. χρόνῳ γάρ, οἶδ' ἐγώ, γνώσει τάδε,
ὁθούνεκ' αὐτὸς αὑτὸν οὔτε νῦν καλὰ
δρᾷς οὔτε πρόσθεν εἰργάσω, βίᾳ φίλων
ὀργῇ χάριν δούς, ἥ σ' ἀεὶ λυμαίνεται.   855
ΧΟ. ἐπίσχες αὐτοῦ, ξεῖνε. ΚΡ. μὴ ψαύειν λέγω.
ΧΟ. οὔτοι σ' ἀφήσω, τῶνδέ γ' ἐστερημένος.
ΚΡ. καὶ μεῖζον ἄρα ῥύσιον πόλει τάχα
θήσεις· ἐφάψομαι γὰρ οὐ τούτοιν μόναιν.
ΧΟ. ἀλλ' ἐς τί τρέψει; ΚΡ. τόνδ' ἀπάξομαι λαβών.   860
ΧΟ. δεινὸν λέγοις ἄν. ΚΡ. τοῦτο νῦν πεπράξεται.
ΧΟ. ἢν μή γ' ὁ κραίνων τῆσδε γῆς ἀπειργάθῃ.
ΟΙ. ὦ φθέγμ' ἀναιδές, ἦ σὺ γὰρ ψαύσεις ἐμοῦ;
ΚΡ. αὐδῶ σιωπᾶν. ΟΙ. μὴ γὰρ αἵδε δαίμονες
θεῖέν μ' ἄφωνον τῆσδε τῆς ἀρᾶς ἔτι·   865
ὅς μ', ὦ κάκιστε, ψιλὸν ὄμμ' ἀποσπάσας
πρὸς ὄμμασιν τοῖς πρόσθεν ἐξοίχει βίᾳ.
τοιγάρ σέ τ' αὐτὸν καὶ γένος τὸ σὸν θεῶν
ὁ πάντα λεύσσων Ἥλιος δοίη βίον
τοιοῦτον οἷον κἀμὲ γηρᾶναί ποτε.   870
ΚΡ. ὁρᾶτε ταῦτα, τῆσδε γῆς ἐγχώριοι;
ΟΙ. ὁρῶσι κἀμὲ καὶ σέ, καὶ φρονοῦσ' ὅτι
ἔργοις πεπονθὼς ῥήμασίν σ' ἀμύνομαι.
ΚΡ. οὔτοι καθέξω θυμόν, ἀλλ' ἄξω βίᾳ
κεἰ μοῦνός εἰμι τόνδε καὶ χρόνῳ βραδύς.   875

ἀντ. ΟΙ. ἰὼ τάλας.
ΧΟ. 1 ὅσον λῆμ' ἔχων ἀφίκου, ξέν', εἰ τάδε δοκεῖς τελεῖν.
ΚΡ. 3 δοκῶ. ΧΟ. τάνδ' ἄρ' οὐκέτι νεμῶ πόλιν.

861 λέγοις L, A: λέγεις r. ἄν add. Hermann.
865 τῆς London ed. 1747: γῆς MSS. (from 862).

ΚΡ. 4 τοῖς τοι δικαίοις χὠ βραχὺς νικᾷ μέγαν.   880
ΟΙ. 5 ἀκούεθ' οἷα φθέγγεται; ΧΟ. τά γ' οὐ τελεῖ·
6 Ζεύς μοι ξυνίστω. ΚΡ. Ζεὺς γ' ἂν εἰδείη, σὺ
δ' οὔ.
ΧΟ. 7 ἆρ' οὐχ ὕβρις τάδ'; ΚΡ. ὕβρις, ἀλλ' ἀνεκτέα.
ΧΟ. 8 ἰὼ πᾶς λεώς, ἰὼ γᾶς πρόμοι,
9 μόλετε σὺν τάχει, μόλετ'· ἐπεὶ πέραν   885
10 περῶσ' οἵδε δή.

ΘΗ. τίς ποθ' ἡ βοή; τί τοὔργον; ἐκ τίνος φόβου ποτὲ
βουθυτοῦντά μ' ἀμφὶ βωμὸν ἔσχετ' ἐναλίῳ θεῷ
τοῦδ' ἐπιστάτῃ Κολωνοῦ; λέξαθ', ὡς εἰδῶ τὸ πᾶν,
οὗ χάριν δεῦρ' ᾖξα θᾶσσον ἢ καθ' ἡδονὴν ποδός. 890
ΟΙ. ὦ φίλτατ', ἔγνων γὰρ τὸ προσφώνημά σου,
πέπονθα δεινὰ τοῦδ' ὑπ' ἀνδρὸς ἀρτίως.
ΘΗ. τὰ ποῖα ταῦτα; τίς δ' ὁ πημήνας; λέγε.
ΟΙ. Κρέων ὅδ', ὃν δέδορκας, οἴχεται τέκνων
ἀποσπάσας μου τὴν μόνην ξυνωρίδα.   895
ΘΗ. πῶς εἶπας; ΟΙ. οἷά περ πέπονθ' ἀκήκοας.
ΘΗ. οὔκουν τις ὡς τάχιστα προσπόλων μολὼν
πρὸς τούσδε βωμοὺς πάντ' ἀναγκάσει λεὼν
ἄνιππον ἱππότην τε θυμάτων ἄπο
σπεύδειν ἀπὸ ῥυτῆρος, ἔνθα δίστομοι   900
μάλιστα συμβάλλουσιν ἐμπόρων ὁδοί,
ὡς μὴ παρέλθωσ' αἱ κόραι, γέλως δ' ἐγὼ
ξένῳ γένωμαι τῷδε, χειρωθεὶς βίᾳ.
ἴθ', ὡς ἄνωγα, σὺν τάχει. τοῦτον δ' ἐγώ,
εἰ μὲν δι' ὀργῆς ἧκον ἧς ὅδ' ἄξιος,   905
ἄτρωτον οὐ μεθῆκ' ἂν ἐξ ἐμῆς χερός·

882 Ζεύς μοι ξυνίστω add. J.—Ζεὺς ταῦτ' ἂν εἰδείη, σὺ δ' οὔ MSS.:
corr. Hartung (who supplies ἴστω μέγας Ζεύς before these words).
886 περῶσι δή L, vulg.: περῶσι δῆτα Triclinius: corr. Elmsley.
906 οὐ μεθῆκ' ἂν A: οὐδ' ἀφῆκ' ἂν L (but with οὐ μεθῆκ' ἂν in marg.,
written prob. by the first hand).

νῦν δ' οὕσπερ αὐτὸς τοὺς νόμους εἰσῆλθ' ἔχων,
τούτοισι κοὐκ ἄλλοισιν ἁρμοσθήσεται.
οὐ γάρ ποτ' ἕξει τῆσδε τῆς χώρας, πρὶν ἂν
κείνας ἐναργεῖς δεῦρό μοι στήσῃς ἄγων·   910
ἐπεὶ δέδρακας οὔτ' ἐμοῦ καταξίως
οὔθ' ὧν πέφυκας αὐτὸς οὔτε σῆς χθονός,
ὅστις δίκαι' ἀσκοῦσαν εἰσελθὼν πόλιν
κἄνευ νόμου κραίνουσαν οὐδέν, εἶτ' ἀφεὶς
τὰ τῆσδε τῆς γῆς κύρι' ὧδ' ἐπεισπεσὼν   915
ἄγεις θ' ἃ χρῄζεις καὶ παρίστασαι βίᾳ.
καί μοι πόλιν κένανδρον ἢ δούλην τινὰ
ἔδοξας εἶναι, κἄμ' ἴσον τῷ μηδενί.
καίτοι σε Θῆβαί γ' οὐκ ἐπαίδευσαν κακόν·
οὐ γὰρ φιλοῦσιν ἄνδρας ἐκδίκους τρέφειν,   920
οὐδ' ἄν σ' ἐπαινέσειαν, εἰ πυθοίατο
συλῶντα τἀμὰ καὶ τὰ τῶν θεῶν, βίᾳ
ἄγοντα φωτῶν ἀθλίων ἱκτήρια.
οὔκουν ἔγωγ' ἂν σῆς ἐπεμβαίνων χθονός,
οὐδ' εἰ τὰ πάντων εἶχον ἐνδικώτατα,   925
ἄνευ γε τοῦ κραίνοντος, ὅστις ἦν, χθονὸς
οὔθ' εἷλκον οὔτ' ἂν ἦγον, ἀλλ' ἠπιστάμην
ξένον παρ' ἀστοῖς ὡς διαιτᾶσθαι χρεών.
σὺ δ' ἀξίαν οὐκ οὖσαν αἰσχύνεις πόλιν
τὴν αὐτὸς αὑτοῦ, καί σ' ὁ πληθύων χρόνος   930
γέρονθ' ὁμοῦ τίθησι καὶ τοῦ νοῦ κενόν.
εἶπον μὲν οὖν καὶ πρόσθεν, ἐννέπω δὲ νῦν,
τὰς παῖδας ὡς τάχιστα δεῦρ' ἄγειν τινά,
εἰ μὴ μέτοικος τῆσδε τῆς χώρας θέλεις
εἶναι βίᾳ τε κοὐχ ἑκών· καὶ ταῦτά σοι   935
τῷ νῷ θ' ὁμοίως κἀπὸ τῆς γλώσσης λέγω.
ΧΟ. ὁρᾷς ἵν' ἥκεις, ὦ ξέν'; ὡς ἀφ' ὧν μὲν εἶ
φαίνει δίκαιος, δρῶν δ' ἐφευρίσκει κακά.

907 οὕσπερ Reiske: ὥσπερ MSS.   924. ἐπεμβαίνων r: ἐπιβαίνων L, A.

ΚΡ. ἐγὼ οὔτ' ἄνανδρον τήνδε τὴν πόλιν νέμων,
ὦ τέκνον Αἰγέως, οὔτ' ἄβουλον, ὡς σὺ φής,   940
τοὔργον τόδ' ἐξέπραξα, γιγνώσκων δ' ὅτι
οὐδείς ποτ' αὐτοὺς τῶν ἐμῶν ἂν ἐμπέσοι
ζῆλος ξυναίμων, ὥστ' ἐμοῦ τρέφειν βίᾳ.
ἤδη δ' ὁθούνεκ' ἄνδρα καὶ πατροκτόνον
κἄναγνον οὐ δεξοίατ', οὐδ' ὅτῳ γάμοι   945
ξυνόντες ηὑρέθησαν ἀνόσιοι τέκνων.
τοιοῦτον αὐτοῖς Ἄρεος εὔβουλον πάγον
ἐγὼ ξυνῄδη χθόνιον ὄνθ', ὃς οὐκ ἐᾷ
τοιούσδ' ἀλήτας τῇδ' ὁμοῦ ναίειν πόλει·
ᾧ πίστιν ἴσχων τήνδ' ἐχειρούμην ἄγραν.   950
καὶ ταῦτ' ἂν οὐκ ἔπρασσον, εἰ μή μοι πικρὰς
αὐτῷ τ' ἀρὰς ἠρᾶτο καὶ τῶμῷ γένει·
ἀνθ' ὧν πεπονθὼς ἠξίουν τάδ' ἀντιδρᾶν.
θυμοῦ γὰρ οὐδὲν γῆράς ἐστιν ἄλλο πλὴν
θανεῖν· θανόντων δ' οὐδὲν ἄλγος ἅπτεται.   955
πρὸς ταῦτα πράξεις οἷον ἂν θέλῃς· ἐπεὶ
ἐρημία με, κεἰ δίκαι' ὅμως λέγω,
σμικρὸν τίθησι· πρὸς δὲ τὰς πράξεις ὅμως,
καὶ τηλικόσδ' ὤν, ἀντιδρᾶν πειράσομαι.

ΟΙ. ὦ λῆμ' ἀναιδές, τοῦ καθυβρίζειν δοκεῖς,   960
πότερον ἐμοῦ γέροντος ἢ σαυτοῦ, τόδε;
ὅστις φόνους μοι καὶ γάμους καὶ συμφορὰς
τοῦ σοῦ διῆκας στόματος, ἃς ἐγὼ τάλας
ἤνεγκον ἄκων· θεοῖς γὰρ ἦν οὕτω φίλον,
τάχ' ἄν τι μηνίουσιν εἰς γένος πάλαι.   965
ἐπεὶ καθ' αὑτόν γ' οὐκ ἂν ἐξεύροις ἐμοὶ
ἁμαρτίας ὄνειδος οὐδέν, ἀνθ' ὅτου
τάδ' εἰς ἐμαυτὸν τοὺς ἐμούς θ' ἡμάρτανον.
ἐπεὶ δίδαξον, εἴ τι θέσφατον πατρὶ
χρησμοῖσιν ἱκνεῖθ' ὥστε πρὸς παίδων θανεῖν,   970

945 κἄναγνον A: κἄνανδρον L, vulg.—δεξαίατ' MSS.: corr. Elmsley.

πῶς ἂν δικαίως τοῦτ' ὀνειδίζοις ἐμοί,
ὃς οὔτε βλάστας πω γενεθλίους πατρός,
οὐ μητρὸς εἶχον, ἀλλ' ἀγέννητος τότ' ἦ;
εἰ δ' αὖ φανεὶς δύστηνος, ὡς ἐγὼ 'φάνην,
ἐς χεῖρας ἦλθον πατρὶ καὶ κατέκτανον,   975
μηδὲν ξυνιεὶς ὧν ἔδρων εἰς οὕς τ' ἔδρων,
πῶς ἂν τό γ' ἆκον πρᾶγμ' ἂν εἰκότως ψέγοις;
μητρὸς δέ, τλῆμον, οὐκ ἐπαισχύνει γάμους
οὔσης ὁμαίμου σῆς μ' ἀναγκάζων λέγειν
οἵους ἐρῶ τάχ'· οὐ γὰρ οὖν σιγήσομαι,   980
σοῦ γ' εἰς τόδ' ἐξελθόντος ἀνόσιον στόμα.
ἔτικτε γάρ μ' ἔτικτεν, ὤμοι μοι κακῶν,
οὐκ εἰδότ' οὐκ εἰδυῖα, καὶ τεκοῦσά με
αὑτῆς ὄνειδος παῖδας ἐξέφυσέ μοι.
ἀλλ' ἓν γὰρ οὖν ἔξοιδα, σὲ μὲν ἑκόντ' ἐμὲ   985
κείνην τε ταῦτα δυσστομεῖν· ἐγὼ δέ νιν
ἄκων ἔγημα, φθέγγομαί τ' ἄκων τάδε.
ἀλλ' οὐ γὰρ οὔτ' ἐν τοῖσδ' ἀκούσομαι κακὸς
γάμοισιν οὔθ' οὓς αἰὲν ἐμφορεῖς σύ μοι
φόνους πατρῴους ἐξονειδίζων πικρῶς.   990
ἓν γάρ μ' ἄμειψαι μοῦνον ὧν σ' ἀνιστορῶ.
εἴ τίς σε τὸν δίκαιον αὐτίκ' ἐνθάδε
κτείνοι παραστάς, πότερα πυνθάνοι' ἂν εἰ
πατήρ σ' ὁ καίνων, ἢ τίνοι' ἂν εὐθέως;
δοκῶ μέν, εἴπερ ζῆν φιλεῖς, τὸν αἴτιον   995
τίνοι' ἄν, οὐδὲ τοὔνδικον περιβλέποις.
τοιαῦτα μέντοι καὐτὸς εἰσέβην κακά,
θεῶν ἀγόντων· οἷς ἐγὼ οὐδὲ τὴν πατρὸς
ψυχὴν ἂν οἶμαι ζῶσαν ἀντειπεῖν ἐμοί.
σὺ δ', εἰ γὰρ οὐ δίκαιος, ἀλλ' ἅπαν καλὸν   1000
λέγειν νομίζων, ῥητὸν ἄρρητόν τ' ἔπος,

977 πῶς γ' ἂν MSS.: corr. Elmsley.   989 ἐμφερεῖ̈ς L (with o written
over ε by an early hand): ἐμφέρεις A.

τοιαῦτ' ὀνειδίζεις με τῶνδ' ἐναντίον.
καί σοι τὸ Θησέως ὄνομα θωπεῦσαι καλόν,
καὶ τὰς Ἀθήνας ὡς κατῴκηνται καλῶς·
κᾆθ' ὧδ' ἐπαινῶν πολλὰ τοῦδ' ἐκλανθάνει,   1005
ὁθούνεκ' εἴ τις γῆ θεοὺς ἐπίσταται
τιμαῖς σεβίζειν, ἥδε τῷδ' ὑπερφέρει·
ἀφ' ἧς σὺ κλέψας τὸν ἱκέτην γέροντ' ἐμὲ
αὐτόν τ' ἐχειροῦ τὰς κόρας τ' οἴχει λαβών.
ἀνθ' ὧν ἐγὼ νῦν τάσδε τὰς θεὰς ἐμοὶ   1010
καλῶν ἱκνοῦμαι καὶ κατασκήπτω λιταῖς
ἐλθεῖν ἀρωγοὺς ξυμμάχους θ', ἵν' ἐκμάθῃς
οἵων ὑπ' ἀνδρῶν ἥδε φρουρεῖται πόλις.

ΧΟ. ὁ ξεῖνος, ὦναξ, χρηστός· αἱ δὲ συμφοραὶ
αὐτοῦ πανώλεις, ἄξιαι δ' ἀμυναθεῖν.   1015

ΘΗ. ἅλις λόγων· ὡς οἱ μὲν ἐξειργασμένοι
σπεύδουσιν, ἡμεῖς δ' οἱ παθόντες ἕσταμεν.

ΚΡ. τί δῆτ' ἀμαυρῷ φωτὶ προστάσσεις ποεῖν;

ΘΗ. ὁδοῦ κατάρχειν τῆ ἐκεῖ, πομπὸν δ' ἐμὲ
χωρεῖν, ἵν', εἰ μὲν ἐν τόποισι τοῖσδ' ἔχεις   1020
τὰς παῖδας ἡμῖν, αὐτὸς ἐκδείξῃς ἐμοί·
εἰ δ' ἐγκρατεῖς φεύγουσιν, οὐδὲν δεῖ πονεῖν·
ἄλλοι γὰρ οἱ σπεύδοντες, οὓς οὐ μή ποτε
χώρας φυγόντες τῆσδ' ἐπεύξωνται θεοῖς.
ἀλλ' ἐξυφηγοῦ· γνῶθι δ' ὡς ἔχων ἔχει   1025
καί σ' εἷλε θηρῶνθ' ἡ τύχη· τὰ γὰρ δόλῳ
τῷ μὴ δικαίῳ κτήματ' οὐχὶ σῴζεται.
κοὐκ ἄλλον ἕξεις εἰς τόδ'· ὡς ἔξοιδά σε
οὐ ψιλὸν οὐδ' ἄσκευον ἐς τοσήνδ' ὕβριν
ἥκοντα τόλμης τῆς παρεστώσης τανῦν,   1030

1007 τιμὰς MSS. (the ὰ made in L from ᾶ): corr. Turnebus.—τῷδ'
Kuhnhardt: τοῦδ' L, vulg.: τοῦθ' r.   1016 ἐξηρπασμένην L (-ην made
from -οι): ἐξηρπασμένοι r: corr. F. W. Schmidt.   1019 δέ με MSS.:
corr. Hermann.   1021 ἡμῶν MSS.: corr. Elmsley.

ἀλλ' ἔσθ' ὅτῳ σὺ πιστὸς ὢν ἕδρας τάδε.
ἃ δεῖ μ' ἀθρῆσαι, μηδὲ τήνδε τὴν πόλιν
ἑνὸς ποῆσαι φωτὸς ἀσθενεστέραν.
νοεῖς τι τούτων, ἢ μάτην τὰ νῦν τέ σοι
δοκεῖ λελέχθαι χὦτε ταῦτ' ἐμηχανῶ;   1035
ΚΡ. οὐδὲν σὺ μεμπτὸν ἐνθάδ' ὢν ἐρεῖς ἐμοί·
οἴκοι δὲ χἠμεῖς εἰσόμεσθ' ἃ χρὴ ποεῖν.
ΘΗ. χωρῶν ἀπείλει νῦν· σὺ δ' ἡμίν, Οἰδίπους,
ἔκηλος αὐτοῦ μίμνε, πιστωθεὶς ὅτι,
ἢν μὴ θάνω 'γὼ πρόσθεν, οὐχὶ παύσομαι   1040
πρὶν ἄν σε τῶν σῶν κύριον στήσω τέκνων.
ΟΙ. ὄναιο, Θησεῦ, τοῦ τε γενναίου χάριν
καὶ τῆς πρὸς ἡμᾶς ἐνδίκου προμηθίας.

στρ. α'. ΧΟ. εἴην ὅθι δαΐων
2 ἀνδρῶν τάχ' ἐπιστροφαὶ   1045
3 τὸν χαλκοβόαν Ἄρη
4 μείξουσιν, ἢ πρὸς Πυθίαις
5 ἢ λαμπάσιν ἀκταῖς,
6 οὗ πότνιαι σεμνὰ τιθηνοῦνται τέλη   1050
7 θνατοῖσιν, ὧν καὶ χρυσέα
8 κλῂς ἐπὶ γλώσσᾳ βέβακε
9 προσπόλων Εὐμολπιδᾶν·
10 ἔνθ' οἶμαι τὸν ἐγρεμάχαν
11 Θησέα καὶ τὰς διστόλους   1055
12 ἀδμῆτας ἀδελφὰς
13 αὐτάρκει τάχ' ἐμμείξειν βοᾷ
14 τούσδ' ἀνὰ χώρους·

ἀντ. α'. ἤ που τὸν ἐφέσπερον
2 πέτρας νιφάδος πελῶσ'   1060
3 Οἰάτιδος εἰς νομόν,

1050 σεμναὶ MSS.: corr. Valckenaer.
1061 εἰς νομόν Hartung: ἐκ νομοῦ MSS.

4 πώλοισιν ἢ ῥιμφαρμάτοις
5 φεύγοντες ἀμίλλαις.
6 ἁλώσεται· δεινὸς ὁ προσχώρων Ἄρης,   1065
7 δεινὰ δὲ Θησειδᾶν ἀκμά.
8 πᾶς γὰρ ἀστράπτει χαλινός,
9 πᾶσα δ' ὁρμᾶται καθεῖσ'
10 ἀμπυκτήρια στομίων
11 ἄμβασις, οἳ τὰν ἱππίαν   1070
12 τιμῶσιν Ἀθάναν
13 καὶ τὸν πόντιον γαιάοχον
14 Ῥέας φίλον υἱόν.

στρ. β'.   ἔρδουσ' ἢ μέλλουσιν; ὡς   1074
2 προμνᾶταί τί μοι
3 γνώμα τάχ' ἀντάσειν
4 τὰν δεινὰ τλασᾶν, δεινὰ δ' εὑρουσᾶν πρὸς αὐθαί-
     μων πάθη.
5 τελεῖ τελεῖ Ζεύς τι κατ' ἆμαρ·
6 μάντις εἴμ' ἐσθλῶν ἀγώνων.   1080
7 εἴθ' ἀελλαία ταχύρρωστος πελειὰς
8 αἰθερίας νεφέλας κύρσαιμ' ἄνωθ' ἀγώνων
9 αἰωρήσασα τοὐμὸν ὄμμα.

ἀντ. β'.   ἰὼ θεῶν πάνταρχε, παντ-   1085
2 όπτα Ζεῦ, πόροις
3 γᾶς τᾶσδε δαμούχοις
4 σθένει 'πινικείῳ τὸν εὔαγρον τελειῶσαι λόχον,

1068 καθεῖσ' Schneidewin : κατ' MSS.   1069 ἀμπυκτήρια φάλαρα
πώλων MSS. : corr. Wecklein.   (Bothe and Hermann had deleted φάλαρα.)
1074 ἔρδουσιν MSS. : corr. Elmsley.   1076 ἀντάσειν Buecheler: ἂν
δώσειν MSS.   1077 τὰν δεινὰ τλασᾶν δεινὰ δ' εὑρουσᾶν MSS. : corr. Reisig
(from schol. ιn L).—αἰθαίμων Bothe : αὐθομαίμων MSS.   1083 ἄνωθ'
Hermann : αὐτῶν δ' MSS.   1084 αἰωρήσασα Dindorf (ἐωρήσασα Wun-
der) : θεωρήσασα MSS.   1085 f. ἰὼ Ζεῦ πάνταρχε θεῶν | παντόπτα
πόροις MSS. : corr. J.   1088 ἐπινικείωι σθένει L : ἐπινίκωι σθένει r :
corr. Hermann.

40 ΣΟΦΟΚΛΕΟΥΣ

5 σεμνά τε παῖς Παλλὰς Ἀθάνα. 1090
6 καὶ τὸν ἀγρευτὰν Ἀπόλλω
7 καὶ κασιγνήταν πυκνοστίκτων ὀπαδὸν
8 ὠκυπόδων ἐλάφων στέργω διπλᾶς ἀρωγὰς
9 μολεῖν γᾷ τᾷδε καὶ πολίταις. 1095

ὦ ξεῖν' ἀλῆτα, τῷ σκοπῷ μὲν οὐκ ἐρεῖς
ὡς ψευδόμαντις· τὰς κόρας γὰρ εἰσορῶ
τάσδ' ἆσσον αὖθις ὧδε προσπολουμένας.
ΟΙ. ποῦ ποῦ; τί φής; πῶς εἶπας; ΑΝ. ὦ πάτερ πάτερ,
τίς ἂν θεῶν σοι τόνδ' ἄριστον ἄνδρ' ἰδεῖν 1100
δοίη, τὸν ἡμᾶς δεῦρο προσπέμψαντά σοι;
ΟΙ. ὦ τέκνον, ἦ πάρεστον; ΑΝ. αἵδε γὰρ χέρες
Θησέως ἔσωσαν φιλτάτων τ' ὀπαόνων.
ΟΙ. προσέλθετ', ὦ παῖ, πατρί, καὶ τὸ μηδαμὰ
ἐλπισθὲν ἥξειν σῶμα βαστάσαι δότε. 1105
ΑΝ. αἰτεῖς ἃ τεύξει· σὺν πόθῳ γὰρ ἡ χάρις.
ΟΙ. ποῦ δῆτα, ποῦ 'στόν; ΑΝ. αἵδ' ὁμοῦ πελάζομεν.
ΟΙ. ὦ φίλτατ' ἔρνη. ΑΝ. τῷ τεκόντι πᾶν φίλον.
ΟΙ. ὦ σκῆπτρα φωτός. ΑΝ. δυσμόρου γε δύσμορα.
ΟΙ. ἔχω τὰ φίλτατ', οὐδ' ἔτ' ἂν πανάθλιος 1110
θανὼν ἂν εἴην σφῷν παρεστώσαιν ἐμοί.
ἐρείσατ', ὦ παῖ, πλευρὸν ἀμφιδέξιον
ἐμφύντε τῷ φύσαντι, κἀναπνεύσατον
τοῦ πρόσθ' ἐρήμου τοῦδε δυστήνου πλάνου.
καί μοι τὰ πραχθέντ' εἴπαθ' ὡς βράχιστ', ἐπεὶ
ταῖς τηλικαῖσδε σμικρὸς ἐξαρκεῖ λόγος. 1116
ΑΝ. ὅδ' ἔσθ' ὁ σώσας· τοῦδε χρὴ κλύειν, πάτερ,
οὗ κἄστι τοὔργον· τοὐμὸν ὧδ' ἔσται βραχύ.

1112 ἀμφιδεξιὸν L, ἀμφὶ δεξιὸν r: corr. Mudge. 1113 ἐμφῦσᾶ L
(made by S from ἐμφύσᾶ: a later hand has restored the acute accent, but
without deleting the circumflex): ἐμφῦσα vulg., ἐμφῦτε A: corr. Mudge.—
κἀναπαύσετον L, vulg.: κἀναπαύσατον r: corr. J. 1118 καὶ σοί τε
τοὔργον τοὐμὸν ἔσται βραχύ L: (so the other MSS., except that L² has καὶ
σοί γε: T and Farn., ἔσται δὴ βραχύ :) corr. Wex.

ΟΙ. ὦ ξεῖνε, μὴ θαύμαζε, πρὸς τὸ λιπαρὲς
τέκν' εἰ φανέντ' ἄελπτα μηκύνω λόγον.   1120
ἐπίσταμαι γὰρ τήνδε τὴν ἐς τάσδε μοι
τέρψιν παρ' ἄλλου μηδενὸς πεφασμένην·
σὺ γάρ νιν ἐξέσωσας, οὐκ ἄλλος βροτῶν.
καί σοι θεοὶ πόροιεν ὡς ἐγὼ θέλω,
αὐτῷ τε καὶ γῇ τῇδ'· ἐπεὶ τό γ' εὐσεβὲς   1125
μόνοις παρ' ὑμῖν ηὗρον ἀνθρώπων ἐγὼ
καὶ τοὐπιεικὲς καὶ τὸ μὴ ψευδοστομεῖν.
εἰδὼς δ' ἀμύνω τοῖσδε τοῖς λόγοις τάδε·
ἔχω γὰρ ἅχω διὰ σὲ κοὐκ ἄλλον βροτῶν.
καί μοι χέρ', ὦναξ, δεξιὰν ὄρεξον, ὡς   1130
ψαύσω φιλήσω τ', εἰ θέμις, τὸ σὸν κάρα.
καίτοι τί φωνῶ; πῶς σ' ἂν ἄθλιος γεγὼς
θιγεῖν θελήσαιμ' ἀνδρὸς ᾧ τίς οὐκ ἔνι
κηλὶς κακῶν ξύνοικος; οὐκ ἔγωγέ σε,
οὐδ' οὖν ἐάσω· τοῖς γὰρ ἐμπείροις βροτῶν   1135
μόνοις οἷόν τε συνταλαιπωρεῖν τάδε.
σὺ δ' αὐτόθεν μοι χαῖρε, καὶ τὰ λοιπά μου
μέλου δικαίως, ὥσπερ ἐς τόδ' ἡμέρας.

ΘΗ. οὔτ' εἴ τι μῆκος τῶν λόγων ἔθου πλέον,
τέκνοισι τερφθεὶς τοῖσδε, θαυμάσας ἔχω,   1140
οὔτ' εἰ πρὸ τοὐμοῦ προὔλαβες τὰ τῶνδ' ἔπη·
βάρος γὰρ ἡμᾶς οὐδὲν ἐκ τούτων ἔχει.
οὐ γὰρ λόγοισι τὸν βίον σπουδάζομεν
λαμπρὸν ποεῖσθαι μᾶλλον ἢ τοῖς δρωμένοις.
δείκνυμι δ'· ὧν γὰρ ὤμοσ' οὐκ ἐψευσάμην   1145
οὐδέν σε, πρέσβυ· τάσδε γὰρ πάρειμ' ἄγων
ζώσας, ἀκραιφνεῖς τῶν κατηπειλημένων.
χὤπως μὲν ἀγὼν ᾑρέθη, τί δεῖ μάτην

1130 χέρ' A: χαῖρ' L.   1132 πῶς σ' Hermann: πῶς δ' MSS.
1141 οὔτ' Elmsley: οὐδ' MSS.   1148 χὤπως μὲν ἀγὼν οὗτος ᾑρέθη, τί
δεῖ μάτην MSS.: οὗτος del. Heath.

42   ΣΟΦΟΚΛΕΟΥΣ

κομπεῖν, ἅ γ' εἴσει καὐτὸς ἐκ τούτοιν ξυνών·
λόγος δ' ὃς ἐμπέπτωκεν ἀρτίως ἐμοὶ   1150
στείχοντι δεῦρο, συμβαλοῦ γνώμην, ἐπεὶ
σμικρὸς μὲν εἰπεῖν, ἄξιος δὲ θαυμάσαι·
πρᾶγος δ' ἀτίζειν οὐδὲν ἄνθρωπον χρεών.

ΟΙ. τί δ' ἔστι, τέκνον Αἰγέως; δίδασκέ με,
ὡς μὴ εἰδότ' αὐτὸν μηδὲν ὧν σὺ πυνθάνει.   1155

ΘΗ. φασίν τιν' ἡμῖν ἄνδρα, σοὶ μὲν ἔμπολιν
οὐκ ὄντα, συγγενῆ δέ, προσπεσόντα πως
βωμῷ καθῆσθαι τῷ Ποσειδῶνος, παρ' ᾧ
θύων ἔκυρον ἡνίχ' ὡρμώμην ἐγώ.

ΟΙ. ποδαπόν; τί προσχρῄζοντα τῷ θακήματι;   1160

ΘΗ. οὐκ οἶδα πλὴν ἕν· σοῦ γάρ, ὡς λέγουσί μοι,
βραχύν τιν' αἰτεῖ μῦθον οὐκ ὄγκου πλέων.

ΟΙ. ποῖόν τιν'; οὐ γὰρ ἥδ' ἕδρα σμικροῦ λόγου.

ΘΗ. σοὶ φασὶν αὐτὸν ἐς λόγους ἐλθεῖν μόνον
αἰτεῖν ἀπελθεῖν τ' ἀσφαλῶς τῆς δεῦρ' ὁδοῦ.   1165

ΟΙ. τίς δῆτ' ἂν εἴη τήνδ' ὁ προσθακῶν ἕδραν;

ΘΗ. ὅρα κατ' Ἄργος εἴ τις ὑμὶν ἐγγενὴς
ἔσθ', ὅστις ἄν σου τοῦτο προσχρῄζοι τυχεῖν.

ΟΙ. ὦ φίλτατε, σχὲς οὗπερ εἶ.   ΘΗ. τί δ' ἔστι σοι;

ΟΙ. μή μου δεηθῇς.   ΘΗ. πράγματος ποίου; λέγε.   1170

ΟΙ. ἔξοιδ' ἀκούων τῶνδ' ὅς ἐσθ' ὁ προστάτης.

ΘΗ. καὶ τίς ποτ' ἐστίν, ὅν γ' ἐγὼ ψέξαιμί τι;

ΟΙ. παῖς οὑμός, ὦναξ, στυγνός, οὗ λόγων ἐγὼ
ἄλγιστ' ἂν ἀνδρῶν ἐξανασχοίμην κλύων.

ΘΗ. τί δ'; οὐκ ἀκούειν ἔστι, καὶ μὴ δρᾶν ἃ μὴ   1175
χρῄζεις; τί σοι τοῦδ' ἐστὶ λυπηρὸν κλύειν;

ΟΙ. ἔχθιστον, ὦναξ, φθέγμα τοῦθ' ἥκει πατρί·
καὶ μή μ' ἀνάγκῃ προσβάλῃς τάδ' εἰκαθεῖν.

1164 μόνον Vauvilliers: μολόντ' MSS.   1165 τ' add. Vauvilliers.
1169 ὦ φίλτατ' ἴσχες L (ἐπίσχες A): corr. Heath.   1176 τοῦδ'
Elmsley: τοῦτ' MSS.

ΘΗ. ἀλλ' εἰ τὸ θάκημ' ἐξαναγκάζει, σκόπει·
μή σοι πρόνοι' ᾖ τοῦ θεοῦ φυλακτέα.   1180
ΑΝ. πάτερ, πιθοῦ μοι, κεἰ νέα παραινέσω.
τὸν ἄνδρ' ἔασον τόνδε τῇ θ' αὐτοῦ φρενὶ
χάριν παρασχεῖν τῷ θεῷ θ' ἃ βούλεται,
καὶ νῷν ὕπεικε τὸν κασίγνητον μολεῖν.
οὐ γάρ σε, θάρσει, πρὸς βίαν παρασπάσει   1185
γνώμης, ἃ μή σοι συμφέροντα λέξεται.
λόγων δ' ἀκοῦσαι τίς βλάβη; τά τοι κακῶς
ηὑρημέν' ἔργα τῷ λόγῳ μηνύεται.
ἔφυσας αὐτόν· ὥστε μηδὲ δρῶντά σε
τὰ τῶν κακίστων δυσσεβέστατ', ὦ πάτερ,   1190
θέμις σέ γ' εἶναι κεῖνον ἀντιδρᾶν κακῶς.
ἀλλ' ἔασον· εἰσὶ χἀτέροις γοναὶ κακαὶ
καὶ θυμὸς ὀξύς, ἀλλὰ νουθετούμενοι
φίλων ἐπῳδαῖς ἐξεπᾴδονται φύσιν.
σὺ δ' εἰς ἐκεῖνα, μὴ τὰ νῦν, ἀποσκόπει   1195
πατρῷα καὶ μητρῷα πήμαθ' ἅπαθες·
κἂν κεῖνα λεύσσῃς, οἶδ' ἐγώ, γνώσει κακοῦ
θυμοῦ τελευτὴν ὡς κακὴ προσγίγνεται.
ἔχεις γὰρ οὐχὶ βαιὰ τἀνθυμήματα,
τῶν σῶν ἀδέρκτων ὀμμάτων τητώμενος.   1200
ἀλλ' ἡμὶν εἶκε· λιπαρεῖν γὰρ οὐ καλὸν
δίκαια προσχρῄζουσιν, οὐδ' αὐτὸν μὲν εὖ
πάσχειν, παθόντα δ' οὐκ ἐπίστασθαι τίνειν.
ΟΙ. τέκνον, βαρεῖαν ἡδονὴν νικᾶτέ με
λέγοντες· ἔστω δ' οὖν ὅπως ὑμῖν φίλον.   1205
μόνον, ξέν', εἴπερ κεῖνος ὧδ' ἐλεύσεται,
μηδεὶς κρατείτω τῆς ἐμῆς ψυχῆς ποτε.

1187 κακῶς Hermann: καλῶς MSS.   1190 δυσσεβεστάτων MSS. :
corr. Dawes.   1191 θέμιν conj. Dawes.   1192 ἀλλ' αὐτὸν or
ἀλλ' αὐτὸν MSS.: corr. London ed. of 1722.   1199 οὐχι (sic) βιαια
L, οὐ βιαια r, vulg.: corr. Musgrave.

ΘΗ. ἅπαξ τὰ τοιαῦτ', οὐχὶ δὶς χρῄζω κλύειν,
ὦ πρέσβυ· κομπεῖν δ' οὐχὶ βούλομαι· σὺ δ' ὧν
σῶς ἴσθ', ἐάν περ κἀμέ τις σῴζῃ θεῶν.   1210

στρ.   ΧΟ.   ὅστις τοῦ πλέονος μέρους χρῄζει τοῦ μετρίου
παρεὶς
2 ζώειν, σκαιοσύναν φυλάσσων ἐν ἐμοὶ κατάδηλος
ἔσται.
3 ἐπεὶ πολλὰ μὲν αἱ μακραὶ ἀμέραι κατέθεντο δὴ
4 λύπας ἐγγυτέρω, τὰ τέρποντα δ' οὐκ ἂν ἴδοις ὅπου,
5 ὅταν τις ἐς πλέον πέσῃ
6 τοῦ δέοντος· ὁ δ' ἐπίκουρος ἰσοτέλεστος,   1220
7 Ἄϊδος ὅτε μοῖρ' ἀνυμέναιος
8 ἄλυρος ἄχορος ἀναπέφηνε,
9 θάνατος ἐς τελευτάν.

ἀντ.   μὴ φῦναι τὸν ἅπαντα νικᾷ λόγον· τὸ δ', ἐπεὶ φανῇ,
2 βῆναι κεῖθεν ὅθεν περ ἥκει πολὺ δεύτερον ὡς
τάχιστα.   1228
3 ὡς εὖτ' ἂν τὸ νέον παρῇ κούφας ἀφροσύνας φέρον,
4 τίς πλαγὰ πολύμοχθος ἔξω; τίς οὐ καμάτων ἔνι;
5 φθόνος, στάσεις, ἔρις, μάχαι
6 καὶ φόνοι· τό τε κατάμεμπτον ἐπιλέλογχε   1235
7 πύματον ἀκρατὲς ἀπροσόμιλον
8 γῆρας ἄφιλον, ἵνα πρόπαντα
9 κακὰ κακῶν ξυνοικεῖ.

ἐπ.   ἐν ᾧ τλάμων ὅδ', οὐκ ἐγὼ μόνος,
πάντοθεν βόρειος ὥς τις   1240

1209 σὺ δὲ MSS. (in L δέ σε superscr. by S): corr. Dindorf.   1210 σῶν
MSS.: corr. Scaliger.   1212 παρεὶς] πέρα conj. Schneidewin.   1220 τοῦ
θέλοντος MSS.: corr. Reiske.—ὁ δ' ἐπίκουρος Hermann: οὐδ' ἔπι κοῦρος L :
οὐδ' ἐπὶ κόρος A.   1226 κεῖθεν ὅθεν] κεῖσ' ὁπόθεν conj. Blaydes.
1231 πλαγὰ Herwerden: πλάγχθη MSS.   1233 f.   φόνοι...καὶ φθόνος
MSS.: corr. Faehse.

ἀκτὰ κυματοπλὴξ χειμερία κλονεῖται,
ὡς καὶ τόνδε κατ᾿ ἄκρας
δειναὶ κυματοαγεῖς
ἆται κλονέουσιν ἀεὶ ξυνοῦσαι,
αἱ μὲν ἀπ᾿ ἀελίου δυσμᾶν,   1245
αἱ δ᾿ ἀνατέλλοντος,
αἱ δ᾿ ἀνὰ μέσσαν ἀκτῖν᾿,
αἱ δ᾿ ἐννυχιᾶν ἀπὸ Ῥιπᾶν.

ΑΝ. καὶ μὴν ὅδ᾿ ἡμῖν, ὡς ἔοικεν, ὁ ξένος,
ἀνδρῶν γε μοῦνος, ὦ πάτερ, δι᾿ ὄμματος   1250
ἀστακτὶ λείβων δάκρυον ὧδ᾿ ὁδοιπορεῖ.

ΟΙ. τίς οὗτος; ΑΝ. ὅνπερ καὶ πάλαι κατείχομεν
γνώμῃ, πάρεστι δεῦρο Πολυνείκης ὅδε.

ΠΟΛΥΝΕΙΚΗΣ.

οἴμοι, τί δράσω; πότερα τἀμαυτοῦ κακὰ
πρόσθεν δακρύσω, παῖδες, ἢ τὰ τοῦδ᾿ ὁρῶν   1255
πατρὸς γέροντος; ὃν ξένης ἐπὶ χθονὸς
σὺν σφῷν ἐφηύρηκ᾿ ἐνθάδ᾿ ἐκβεβλημένον
ἐσθῆτι σὺν τοιᾷδε, τῆς ὁ δυσφιλὴς
γέρων γέροντι συγκατῴκηκεν πίνος
πλευρὰν μαραίνων, κρατὶ δ᾿ ὀμματοστερεῖ   1260
κόμη δι᾿ αὔρας ἀκτένιστος ᾄσσεται·
ἀδελφὰ δ᾿, ὡς ἔοικε, τούτοισιν φορεῖ
τὰ τῆς ταλαίνης νηδύος θρεπτήρια.
ἐγὼ πανώλης ὄψ᾿ ἄγαν ἐκμανθάνω·
καὶ μαρτυρῶ κάκιστος ἀνθρώπων τροφαῖς   1265
ταῖς σαῖσιν ἥκειν· τἀμὰ μὴ 'ξ ἄλλων πύθῃ.
ἀλλ᾿ ἔστι γὰρ καὶ Ζηνὶ σύνθακος θρόνων
Αἰδὼς ἐπ᾿ ἔργοις πᾶσι, καὶ πρὸς σοί, πάτερ,

1248 αἱ δὲ νυχίαν L (νυχιᾶν r): corr. Lachmann from schol.
1259 πίνος Scaliger: πόνος MSS.   1266 τἀμὰ Reiske: τἄλλα MSS.

παρασταθήτω· τῶν γὰρ ἡμαρτημένων
ἄκη μὲν ἔστι, προσφορὰ δ᾽ οὐκ ἔστ᾽ ἔτι.   1270
τί σιγᾷς;
φώνησον, ὦ πάτερ, τι· μή μ᾽ ἀποστραφῇς.
οὐδ᾽ ἀνταμείβει μ᾽ οὐδέν, ἀλλ᾽ ἀτιμάσας
πέμψεις ἄναυδος, οὐδ᾽ ἃ μηνίεις φράσας;
ὦ σπέρματ᾽ ἀνδρὸς τοῦδ᾽, ἐμαὶ δ᾽ ὁμαίμονες,   1275
πειράσατ᾽ ἀλλ᾽ ὑμεῖς γε κινῆσαι πατρὸς
τὸ δυσπρόσοιστον κἀπροσήγορον στόμα,
ὡς μή μ᾽ ἄτιμον, τοῦ θεοῦ γε προστάτην,
οὕτως ἀφῇ με, μηδὲν ἀντειπὼν ἔπος.
ΑΝ. λέγ᾽, ὦ ταλαίπωρ᾽, αὐτὸς ὢν χρείᾳ πάρει.   1280
τὰ πολλὰ γάρ τοι ῥήματ᾽ ἢ τέρψαντά τι
ἢ δυσχεράναντ᾽ ἢ κατοικτίσαντά πως
παρέσχε φωνὴν τοῖς ἀφωνήτοις τινά.
ΠΟ. ἀλλ᾽ ἐξερῶ· καλῶς γὰρ ἐξηγεῖ σύ μοι·
πρῶτον μὲν αὐτὸν τὸν θεὸν ποιούμενος   1285
ἀρωγόν, ἔνθεν μ᾽ ὧδ᾽ ἀνέστησεν μολεῖν
ὁ τῆσδε τῆς γῆς κοίρανος, διδοὺς ἐμοὶ
λέξαι τ᾽ ἀκοῦσαί τ᾽ ἀσφαλεῖ σὺν ἐξόδῳ.
καὶ ταῦτ᾽ ἀφ᾽ ὑμῶν, ὦ ξένοι, βουλήσομαι
καὶ τοῖνδ᾽ ἀδελφαῖν καὶ πατρὸς κυρεῖν ἐμοί.   1290
ἃ δ᾽ ἦλθον ἤδη σοι θέλω λέξαι, πάτερ.
γῆς ἐκ πατρῴας ἐξελήλαμαι φυγάς,
τοῖς σοῖς πανάρχοις οὕνεκ᾽ ἐνθακεῖν θρόνοις
γονῇ πεφυκὼς ἠξίουν γεραιτέρᾳ.
ἀνθ᾽ ὧν μ᾽ Ἐτεοκλῆς, ὢν φύσει νεώτερος,   1295
γῆς ἐξέωσεν, οὔτε νικήσας λόγῳ
οὔτ᾽ εἰς ἔλεγχον χειρὸς οὐδ᾽ ἔργου μολών,
πόλιν δὲ πείσας. ὧν ἐγὼ μάλιστα μὲν
τὴν σὴν Ἐρινὺν αἰτίαν εἶναι λέγω·
ἔπειτα κἀπὸ μάντεων ταύτῃ κλύω.   1300

ἐπεὶ γὰρ ἦλθον Ἄργος ἐς τὸ Δωρικόν,
λαβὼν Ἄδραστον πενθερόν, ξυνωμότας
ἔστησ᾽ ἐμαυτῷ γῆς ὅσοιπερ Ἀπίας
πρῶτοι καλοῦνται καὶ τετίμηνται δορί,
ὅπως τὸν ἑπτάλογχον ἐς Θήβας στόλον   1305
ξὺν τοῖσδ᾽ ἀγείρας ἢ θάνοιμι πανδίκως,
ἢ τοὺς τάδ᾽ ἐκπράξαντας ἐκβάλοιμι γῆς.
εἶεν· τί δῆτα νῦν ἀφιγμένος κυρῶ;
σοὶ προστροπαίους, ὦ πάτερ, λιτὰς ἔχων
αὐτός τ᾽ ἐμαυτοῦ ξυμμάχων τε τῶν ἐμῶν,   1310
οἳ νῦν σὺν ἑπτὰ τάξεσιν σὺν ἑπτά τε
λόγχαις τὸ Θήβης πεδίον ἀμφεστᾶσι πᾶν·
οἷος δορυσσοῦς Ἀμφιάρεως, τὰ πρῶτα μὲν
δόρει κρατύνων, πρῶτα δ᾽ οἰωνῶν ὁδοῖς·
ὁ δεύτερος δ᾽ Αἰτωλὸς Οἰνέως τόκος   1315
Τυδεύς· τρίτος δ᾽ Ἐτέοκλος, Ἀργεῖος γεγώς·
τέταρτον Ἱππομέδοντ᾽ ἀπέστειλεν πατὴρ
Ταλαός· ὁ πέμπτος δ᾽ εὔχεται κατασκαφῇ
Καπανεὺς τὸ Θήβης ἄστυ δῃώσειν πυρί·
ἕκτος δὲ Παρθενοπαῖος Ἀρκὰς ὄρνυται,   1320
ἐπώνυμος τῆς πρόσθεν ἀδμήτης χρόνῳ
μητρὸς λοχευθείς, πιστὸς Ἀταλάντης γόνος·
ἐγὼ δὲ σός, κεἰ μὴ σός, ἀλλὰ τοῦ κακοῦ
πότμου φυτευθείς, σός γέ τοι καλούμενος,
ἄγω τὸν Ἄργους ἄφοβον ἐς Θήβας στρατόν.   1325
οἵ σ᾽ ἀντὶ παίδων τῶνδε καὶ ψυχῆς, πάτερ,
ἱκετεύομεν ξύμπαντες ἐξαιτούμενοι
μῆνιν βαρεῖαν εἰκαθεῖν ὁρμωμένῳ
τῷδ᾽ ἀνδρὶ τοὐμοῦ πρὸς κασιγνήτου τίσιν,
ὅς μ᾽ ἐξέωσε κἀπεσύλησεν πάτρας.   1330
εἰ γάρ τι πιστόν ἐστιν ἐκ χρηστηρίων,
οἷς ἂν σὺ προσθῇ, τοῖσδ᾽ ἔφασκ᾽ εἶναι κράτος.

1319 πυρί L, vulg.: τάχα A, R.

πρός νύν σε κρηνῶν καὶ θεῶν ὁμογνίων
αἰτῶ πιθέσθαι καὶ παρεικαθεῖν, ἐπεὶ
πτωχοὶ μὲν ἡμεῖς καὶ ξένοι, ξένος δὲ σύ·   1335
ἄλλους δὲ θωπεύοντες οἰκοῦμεν σύ τε
κἀγώ, τὸν αὐτὸν δαίμον᾽ ἐξειληχότες.
ὁ δ᾽ ἐν δόμοις τύραννος, ὦ τάλας ἐγώ,
κοινῇ καθ᾽ ἡμῶν ἐγγελῶν ἁβρύνεται·
ὅν, εἰ σὺ τῇμῇ ξυμπαραστήσει φρενί,   1340
βραχεῖ σὺν ὄγκῳ καὶ χρόνῳ διασκεδῶ.
ὥστ᾽ ἐν δόμοισι τοῖσι σοῖς στήσω σ᾽ ἄγων,
στήσω δ᾽ ἐμαυτόν, κεῖνον ἐκβαλὼν βίᾳ.
καὶ ταῦτα σοῦ μὲν ξυνθέλοντος ἔστι μοι
κομπεῖν, ἄνευ σοῦ δ᾽ οὐδὲ σωθῆναι σθένω.   1345

ΧΟ.   τὸν ἄνδρα, τοῦ πέμψαντος οὕνεκ᾽, Οἰδίπους,
εἰπὼν ὁποῖα ξύμφορ᾽ ἔκπεμψαι πάλιν.

ΟΙ.   ἀλλ᾽ εἰ μέν, ἄνδρες τῆσδε δημοῦχοι χθονός,
μὴ ᾽τύγχαν᾽ αὐτὸν δεῦρο προσπέμψας ἐμοὶ
Θησεύς, δικαιῶν ὥστ᾽ ἐμοῦ κλύειν λόγους,   1350
οὔ τἄν ποτ᾽ ὀμφῆς τῆς ἐμῆς ἐπῄσθετο·
νῦν δ᾽ ἀξιωθεὶς εἶσι κἀκούσας γ᾽ ἐμοῦ
τοιαῦθ᾽ ἃ τὸν τοῦδ᾽ οὔ ποτ᾽ εὐφρανεῖ βίον·
ὅς γ᾽, ὦ κάκιστε, σκῆπτρα καὶ θρόνους ἔχων,
ἃ νῦν ὁ σὸς ξύναιμος ἐν Θήβαις ἔχει,   1355
τὸν αὐτὸς αὑτοῦ πατέρα τόνδ᾽ ἀπήλασας
κἄθηκας ἄπολιν καὶ στολὰς ταύτας φορεῖν,
ἃς νῦν δακρύεις εἰσορῶν, ὅτ᾽ ἐν πόνῳ
ταὐτῷ βεβηκὼς τυγχάνεις κακῶν ἐμοί.
οὐ κλαυστὰ δ᾽ ἐστίν, ἀλλ᾽ ἐμοὶ μὲν οἰστέα   1360
τάδ᾽, ἕωσπερ ἂν ζῶ, σοῦ φονέως μεμνημένος.
σὺ γάρ με μόχθῳ τῷδ᾽ ἔθηκας ἔντροφον,

1337 ἐξειληχότες r, Brunck: ἐξειληφότες L, vulg.   1340 ξυμπαρα-
στήσεις L, vulg. (-στήσῃ r): corr. Reiske.   1348 δημοῦχοι Lˡ (-ος Lˢ):
δημοῦχος the other MSS.   1361 ἕωσπερ Reiske: ὥσπερ MSS.

σύ μ' ἐξέωσας· ἐκ σέθεν δ' ἀλώμενος
ἄλλους ἐπαιτῶ τὸν καθ' ἡμέραν βίον.
εἰ δ' ἐξέφυσα τάσδε μὴ 'μαυτῷ τροφοὺς   1365
τὰς παῖδας, ἦ τἂν οὐκ ἂν ἦ, τὸ σὸν μέρος·
νῦν δ' αἵδε μ' ἐκσῴζουσιν, αἵδ' ἐμαὶ τροφοί,
αἵδ' ἄνδρες, οὐ γυναῖκες, εἰς τὸ συμπονεῖν·
ὑμεῖς δ' ἀπ' ἄλλου κοὐκ ἐμοῦ πεφύκατον.
τοιγάρ σ' ὁ δαίμων εἰσορᾷ μὲν οὔ τί πω   1370
ὡς αὐτίκ', εἴπερ οἵδε κινοῦνται λόχοι
πρὸς ἄστυ Θήβης. οὐ γὰρ ἔσθ' ὅπως πόλιν
κείνην ἐρείψεις, ἀλλὰ πρόσθεν αἵματι
πεσεῖ μιανθεὶς χὠ σύναιμος ἐξ ἴσου.
τοιάσδ' ἀρὰς σφῷν πρόσθε τ' ἐξανῆκ' ἐγὼ   1375
νῦν τ' ἀνακαλοῦμαι ξυμμάχους ἐλθεῖν ἐμοί,
ἵν' ἀξιῶτον τοὺς φυτεύσαντας σέβειν,
καὶ μὴ 'ξατιμάζητον, εἰ τυφλοῦ πατρὸς
τοιώδ' ἔφυτον. αἵδε γὰρ τάδ' οὐκ ἔδρων.
τοιγὰρ τὸ σὸν θάκημα καὶ τοὺς σοὺς θρόνους   1380
κρατοῦσιν, εἴπερ ἐστὶν ἡ παλαίφατος
Δίκη ξύνεδρος Ζηνὸς ἀρχαίοις νόμοις.
σὺ δ' ἔρρ' ἀπόπτυστός τε κἀπάτωρ ἐμοῦ,
κακῶν κάκιστε, τάσδε συλλαβὼν ἀράς,
ἅς σοι καλοῦμαι, μήτε γῆς ἐμφυλίου   1385
δόρει κρατῆσαι μήτε νοστῆσαί ποτε
τὸ κοῖλον Ἄργος, ἀλλὰ συγγενεῖ χερὶ
θανεῖν κτανεῖν θ' ὑφ' οὗπερ ἐξελήλασαι.
τοιαῦτ' ἀρῶμαι, καὶ καλῶ τὸ Ταρτάρου
στυγνὸν πατρῷον ἔρεβος, ὥς σ' ἀποικίσῃ,   1390
καλῶ δὲ τάσδε δαίμονας, καλῶ δ' Ἄρη
τὸν σφῷν τὸ δεινὸν μῖσος ἐμβεβληκότα.
καὶ ταῦτ' ἀκούσας στεῖχε, κἀξάγγελλ' ἰὼν

1373 ἐρείψεις Turnebus: ἐρεῖ τις (or τίς) MSS.
1386 δορί MSS.: corr. Reisig.   1389 τὸ Hermann: τοῦ MSS.

J. C.   4

50   ΣΟΦΟΚΛΕΟΥΣ

καὶ πᾶσι Καδμείοισι τοῖς σαυτοῦ θ᾽ ἅμα
πιστοῖσι συμμάχοισιν, οὕνεκ᾽ Οἰδίπους   1395
τοιαῦτ᾽ ἔνειμε παισὶ τοῖς αὑτοῦ γέρα.

ΧΟ. Πολύνεικες, οὔτε ταῖς παρελθούσαις ὁδοῖς
ξυνήδομαί σου, νῦν τ᾽ ἴθ᾽ ὡς τάχος πάλιν.

ΠΟ. οἴμοι κελεύθου τῆς τ᾽ ἐμῆς δυσπραξίας,
οἴμοι δ᾽ ἑταίρων· οἷον ἄρ᾽ ὁδοῦ τέλος   1400
Ἄργους ἀφωρμήθημεν, ὦ τάλας ἐγώ·
τοιοῦτον οἷον οὐδὲ φωνῆσαί τινι
ἔξεσθ᾽ ἑταίρων, οὐδ᾽ ἀποστρέψαι πάλιν,
ἀλλ᾽ ὄντ᾽ ἄναυδον τῆδε συγκῦρσαι τύχῃ.
ὦ τοῦδ᾽ ὅμαιμοι παῖδες, ἀλλ᾽ ὑμεῖς, ἐπεὶ   1405
τὰ σκληρὰ πατρὸς κλύετε ταῦτ᾽ ἀρωμένου,
μή τοί με πρὸς θεῶν σφώ γ᾽, ἐὰν αἱ τοῦδ᾽ ἀραὶ
πατρὸς τελῶνται καί τις ὑμὶν ἐς δόμους
νόστος γένηται, μή μ᾽ ἀτιμάσητέ γε,
ἀλλ᾽ ἐν τάφοισι θέσθε κἀν κτερίσμασιν.   1410
καὶ σφῷν ὁ νῦν ἔπαινος, ὃν κομίζετον
τοῦδ᾽ ἀνδρὸς οἷς πονεῖτον, οὐκ ἐλάσσονα
ἔτ᾽ ἄλλον οἴσει τῆς ἐμῆς ὑπουργίας.

ΑΝ. Πολύνεικες, ἱκετεύω σε πεισθῆναί τί μοι.

ΠΟ. ὦ φιλτάτη, τὸ ποῖον, Ἀντιγόνη; λέγε.   1415

ΑΝ. στρέψαι στράτευμ᾽ ἐς Ἄργος ὡς τάχιστά γε,
καὶ μὴ σέ τ᾽ αὐτὸν καὶ πόλιν διεργάσῃ.

ΠΟ. ἀλλ᾽ οὐχ οἷόν τε. πῶς γὰρ αὖθις ἂν πάλιν
στράτευμ᾽ ἄγοιμι ταὐτὸν εἰσάπαξ τρέσας;

ΑΝ. τί δ᾽ αὖθις, ὦ παῖ, δεῖ σε θυμοῦσθαι; τί σοι   1420
πάτραν κατασκάψαντι κέρδος ἔρχεται;

ΠΟ. αἰσχρὸν τὸ φεύγειν, καὶ τὸ πρεσβεύοντ᾽ ἐμὲ

1398 σου Wecklein: σοι MSS.   1402 τινι Tyrwhitt: τινα MSS.
1406 ταῦτ᾽ Sehrwald: τοῦδ᾽ MSS.   1407 σφώ γ᾽, ἐὰν Elmsley: σφῶιν
γ᾽ ἂν L, vulg.   1417 σέ γ᾽ αὐτὸν MSS.: corr. Brunck.   1418 αὖθις
ἂν Vauvilliers: αὖθις αὖ MSS.

οὕτω γελᾶσθαι τοῦ κασιγνήτου πάρα.

ΑΝ. ὁρᾷς τὰ τοῦδ' οὖν ὡς ἐς ὀρθὸν ἐκφέρει
μαντεύμαθ', ὃς σφῷν θάνατον ἐξ ἀμφοῖν θροεῖ;

ΠΟ. χρήζει γάρ· ἡμῖν δ' οὐχὶ συγχωρητέα. 1426

ΑΝ. οἴμοι τάλαινα· τίς δὲ τολμήσει κλύων
τὰ τοῦδ' ἕπεσθαι τἀνδρός, οἳ ἐθέσπισεν;

ΠΟ. οὐδ' ἀγγελοῦμεν φλαῦρ'· ἐπεὶ στρατηλάτου
χρηστοῦ τὰ κρείσσω μηδὲ τἀνδεᾶ λέγειν. 1430

ΑΝ. οὕτως ἄρ', ὦ παῖ, ταῦτά σοι δεδογμένα;

ΠΟ. καὶ μή μ' ἐπίσχῃς γ'· ἀλλ' ἐμοὶ μὲν ἥδ' ὁδὸς
ἔσται μέλουσα, δύσποτμός τε καὶ κακὴ
πρὸς τοῦδε πατρὸς τῶν τε τοῦδ' Ἐρινύων·
σφὼ δ' εὐοδοίη Ζεύς, τάδ' εἰ θανόντι μοι 1435
τελεῖτ', ἐπεὶ οὔ μοι ζῶντί γ' αὖθις ἕξετον.
μέθεσθε δ' ἤδη, χαίρετόν τ'· οὐ γάρ μ' ἔτι
βλέποντ' ἐσόψεσθ' αὖθις. ΑΝ. ὦ τάλαιν' ἐγώ.

ΠΟ. μή τοί μ' ὀδύρου. ΑΝ. καὶ τίς ἄν σ' ὁρμώμενον
εἰς πρ| οὖπτον Ἅιδην οὐ καταστένοι, κάσι; 1440

ΠΟ. εἰ χρή, θανοῦμαι. ΑΝ. μὴ σύ γ', ἀλλ' ἐμοὶ πιθοῦ,

ΠΟ. μὴ πεῖθ' ἃ μὴ δεῖ. ΑΝ. δυστάλαινά τἄρ' ἐγώ,
εἴ σου στερηθῶ. ΠΟ. ταῦτα δ' ἐν τῷ δαίμονι
καὶ τῇδε φῦναι χἀτέρα. σφῷν δ' οὖν ἐγὼ
θεοῖς ἀρῶμαι μή ποτ' ἀντῆσαι κακῶν· 1445
ἀνάξιαι γὰρ πᾶσίν ἐστε δυστυχεῖν.

κομμός. ΧΟ. νέα τάδε νεόθεν ἦλθέ μοι

στρ. α'. 2 κακὰ βαρύποτμα παρ' ἀλαοῦ ξένου,
3 εἴ τι μοῖρα μὴ κιγχάνει. 1450
4 ματᾶν γὰρ οὐδὲν ἀξίωμα δαιμόνων ἔχω φράσαι.

1435 f. σφὼ Hermann: σφῷν MSS.—τάδ' εἰ τελεῖτέ μοι | θανόντ' MSS.:
corr. Lobeck. 1448 βαρύποτμα κακά MSS.: corr. J. H. H. Schmidt.
1450 κιχάνῃ L (made from τυγχάνῃ, prob. by S): κιχάνη or κιχάνει Γ:
corr. Hermann. 1451 ματᾶν Hermann: μάτην MSS.

5 ὁρᾷ ὁρᾷ ταῦτ' ἀεὶ χρόνος, στρέφων μὲν ἕτερα,
6 τὰ δὲ παρ' ἧμαρ αὖθις αὔξων ἄνω.　　1455
7 ἔκτυπεν αἰθήρ, ὦ Ζεῦ.

ΟΙ. ὦ τέκνα τέκνα, πῶς ἄν, εἴ τις ἔντοπος,
τὸν πάντ' ἄριστον δεῦρο Θησέα πόροι;
ΑΝ. πάτερ, τί δ' ἐστὶ τἀξίωμ' ἐφ' ᾧ καλεῖς;
ΟΙ. Διὸς πτερωτὸς ἥδε μ' αὐτίκ' ἄξεται　　1460
βροντὴ πρὸς Ἅιδην. ἀλλὰ πέμψαθ' ὡς τάχος.

ἀντ. α'.　ΧΟ. μέγας, ἴδε, μάλ' ὅδ' ἐρείπεται
2 κτύπος ἄφατος διόβολος· ἐς δ' ἄκραν
3 δεῖμ' ὑπῆλθε κρατὸς φόβαν.　　1465
4 ἔπτηξα θυμόν· οὐρανία γὰρ ἀστραπὴ φλέγει πάλιν.
5 τί μὰν ἀφήσει τέλος; δέδοικα δ'· οὐ γὰρ ἅλιον
6 ἀφορμᾷ ποτ' οὐδ' ἄνευ ξυμφορᾶς.　　1470
7 ὦ μέγας αἰθήρ, ὦ Ζεῦ.

ΟΙ. ὦ παῖδες, ἥκει τῷδ' ἐπ' ἀνδρὶ θέσφατος
βίου τελευτή, κοὐκέτ' ἔστ' ἀποστροφή.
ΑΝ. πῶς οἶσθα; τῷ δὲ τοῦτο συμβαλὼν ἔχεις;
ΟΙ. καλῶς κάτοιδ'· ἀλλ' ὡς τάχιστά μοι μολὼν　　1475
ἄνακτα χώρας τῆσδέ τις πορευσάτω.

στρ. β'.　ΧΟ. ἔα, ἰδοὺ μάλ' αὖθις ἀμφίσταται
2 διαπρύσιος ὄτοβος.
3 ἵλαος, ὦ δαίμων, ἵλαος, εἴ τι γᾷ　　1480
4 ματέρι τυγχάνεις ἀφεγγὲς φέρων.
5 ἐναισίου δὲ σοῦ τύχοιμι, μηδ' ἄλαστον ἄνδρ' ἰδὼν

1454 στρέφων Hartung: ἐπεὶ MSS.　　1455 τὰ δὲ παρ' ἧμαρ Canter
from schol.: τάδε πῆματ' MSS.　　1462 f. ἴδε μάλα μέγας ἐρείπεται | κτύπος
ἄφατος ὅδε | διόβολος MSS.: corr. J.　　1469 δέδοικα δ' Nauck: δέδεια τόδ'
L (δέδια τόδ' r, vulg.): δέδια δ' Triclinius.　　1470 οὐδ' Heath: οὐκ MSS.
1477 ἔα] ἔα ἔα MSS.: corr. Bothe, Seidler.　　1482 σοῦ τύχοιμι Cobet:
συντύχοιμι MSS.

6 ἀκερδῆ χάριν μετάσχοιμί πως·
7 Ζεῦ ἄνα, σοὶ φωνῶ.   1485

ΟΙ. ἆρ' ἐγγὺς ἀνήρ; ἆρ' ἔτ' ἐμψύχου, τέκνα,
     κιχήσεταί μου καὶ κατορθοῦντος φρένα;
ΑΝ. τί δ' ἂν θέλοις τὸ πιστὸν ἐμφῦναι φρενί;
ΟΙ. ἀνθ' ὧν ἔπασχον εὖ, τελεσφόρον χάριν
     δοῦναί σφιν, ἥνπερ τυγχάνων ὑπεσχόμην.   1490

ἀντ. β'. ΧΟ. ἰὼ ἰώ, παῖ, βᾶθι, βᾶθ', εἴτ' ἄκρα
2 περὶ γύαλ' ἐναλίῳ
3 Ποσειδωνίῳ θεῷ τυγχάνεις
4 βούθυτον ἑστίαν ἁγίζων, ἱκοῦ.   1495
5 ὁ γὰρ ξένος σε καὶ πόλισμα καὶ φίλους ἐπαξιοῖ
6 δικαίαν χάριν παρασχεῖν παθών.
7 σπεῦσον, ἄισσ', ὦναξ.

ΘΗ. τίς αὖ παρ' ὑμῶν κοινὸς ἠχεῖται κτύπος,   1500
     σαφὴς μὲν ἀστῶν, ἐμφανὴς δὲ τοῦ ξένου;
     μή τις Διὸς κεραυνός, ἤ τις ὀμβρία
     χάλαζ' ἐπιρράξασα; πάντα γὰρ θεοῦ
     τοιαῦτα χειμάζοντος εἰκάσαι πάρα.
ΟΙ. ἄναξ, ποθοῦντι προὐφάνης, καί σοι θεῶν   1505
     τύχην τις ἐσθλὴν τῆσδ' ἔθηκε τῆς ὁδοῦ.
ΘΗ. τί δ' ἐστίν, ὦ παῖ Λαΐου, νέορτον αὖ;
ΟΙ. ῥοπὴ βίου μοι· καί σ' ἅπερ ξυνήνεσα
     θέλω πόλιν τε τήνδε μὴ ψεύσας θανεῖν.
ΘΗ. ἐν τῷ δὲ κεῖσαι τοῦ μόρου τεκμηρίῳ;   1510
ΟΙ. αὐτοὶ θεοὶ κήρυκες ἀγγέλλουσί μοι,
     ψεύδοντες οὐδὲν σημάτων προκειμένων.

1491 ff. ἰὼ ἰώ Hermann: ἰὼ MSS. —ἄκρα | περὶ γύαλ' J.: ἄκραν | ἐπιγύ-
αλον (or ἐπὶ γύαλον) MSS.   1494 ποσειδωνίῳ Vat.: ποσειδαωνίωι L,
vulg.: ποσειδαονίωι R.   1495 ἁγίζων A (and superscr. by S in L):
ἁγιάζων L.   1499 σπεῦσον add. Triclinius.   1501 ἀστῶν Reiske:
αὐτῶν MSS.   1506 θῆκε τῆσδε MSS.: corr. Heath.

54　ΣΟΦΟΚΛΕΟΥΣ

ΘΗ. πῶς εἶπας, ὦ γεραιέ, δηλοῦσθαι τάδε;
ΟΙ. αἱ πολλὰ βρονταὶ διατελεῖς τὰ πολλά τε
στράψαντα χειρὸς τῆς ἀνικήτου βέλη.　　　　　1515
ΘΙΙ. πείθεις με· πολλὰ γάρ σε θεσπίζονθ᾽ ὁρῶ
κοὐ ψευδόφημα· χὤ τι χρὴ ποεῖν λέγε.
ΟΙ. ἐγὼ διδάξω, τέκνον Αἰγέως, ἅ σοι
γήρως ἄλυπα τῇδε κείσεται πόλει.
χῶρον μὲν αὐτὸς αὐτίκ᾽ ἐξηγήσομαι,　　　　　1520
ἄθικτος ἡγητῆρος, οὔ με χρὴ θανεῖν.
τοῦτον δὲ φράζε μή ποτ᾽ ἀνθρώπων τινί,
μήθ᾽ οὗ κέκευθε μήτ᾽ ἐν οἷς κεῖται τόποις·
ὥς σοι πρὸ πολλῶν ἀσπίδων ἀλκὴν ὅδε
δορός τ᾽ ἐπακτοῦ γειτόνων ἀεὶ τιθῇ.　　　　　1525
ἃ δ᾽ ἐξάγιστα μηδὲ κινεῖται λόγῳ,
αὐτὸς μαθήσει, κεῖσ᾽ ὅταν μόλῃς μόνος·
ὡς οὔτ᾽ ἂν ἀστῶν τῶνδ᾽ ἂν ἐξείποιμί τῳ
οὔτ᾽ ἂν τέκνοισι τοῖς ἐμοῖς, στέργων ὅμως.
ἀλλ᾽ αὐτὸς ἀεὶ σῷζε, χὤταν εἰς τέλος　　　　　1530
τοῦ ζῆν ἀφικνῇ, τῷ προφερτάτῳ μόνῳ
σήμαιν᾽, ὁ δ᾽ ἀεὶ τὠπιόντι δεικνύτω.
χοὕτως ἀδῇον τήνδ᾽ ἐνοικήσεις πόλιν
σπαρτῶν ἀπ᾽ ἀνδρῶν· αἱ δὲ μυρίαι πόλεις,
κἂν εὖ τις οἰκῇ, ῥᾳδίως καθύβρισαν.　　　　　1535
θεοὶ γὰρ εὖ μὲν ὀψὲ δ᾽ εἰσορῶσ᾽, ὅταν
τὰ θεῖ᾽ ἀφείς τις εἰς τὸ μαίνεσθαι τραπῇ·
ὃ μὴ σύ, τέκνον Αἰγέως, βούλου παθεῖν.
τὰ μὲν τοιαῦτ᾽ οὖν εἰδότ᾽ ἐκδιδάσκομεν.
χῶρον δ᾽, ἐπείγει γάρ με τοὐκ θεοῦ παρόν,　　　1540
στείχωμεν ἤδη, μηδ᾽ ἔτ᾽ ἐντρεπώμεθα.
ὦ παῖδες, ὧδ᾽ ἕπεσθ᾽. ἐγὼ γὰρ ἡγεμὼν
σφῷν αὖ πέφασμαι καινός, ὥσπερ σφὼ πατρί.

1515 στρέψαντα MSS. : corr. Pierson.
1541 μηδ᾽ ἔτ᾽ Reisig: μὴ δέ γ᾽ L, vulg.

χωρεῖτε, καὶ μὴ ψαύετ᾽, ἀλλ᾽ ἐᾶτέ με
αὐτὸν τὸν ἱερὸν τύμβον ἐξευρεῖν, ἵνα 1545
μοῖρ᾽ ἀνδρὶ τῷδε τῇδε κρυφθῆναι χθονί.
τῇδ᾽, ὧδε, τῇδε βᾶτε· τῇδε γάρ μ᾽ ἄγει
Ἑρμῆς ὁ πομπὸς ἥ τε νερτέρα θεός.
ὦ φῶς ἀφεγγές, πρόσθε πού ποτ᾽ ἦσθ᾽ ἐμόν,
νῦν δ᾽ ἔσχατόν σου τοὐμὸν ἅπτεται δέμας. 1550
ἤδη γὰρ ἕρπω τὸν τελευταῖον βίον
κρύψων παρ᾽ Ἅιδην· ἀλλά, φίλτατε ξένων,
αὐτός τε χώρα θ᾽ ἥδε πρόσπολοί τε σοὶ
εὐδαίμονες γένοισθε, κἀπ᾽ εὐπραξίᾳ
μέμνησθέ μου θανόντος εὐτυχεῖς ἀεί. 1555

στρ. ΧΟ. εἰ θέμις ἐστί μοι τὰν ἀφανῆ θεὸν
2 καὶ σὲ λιταῖς σεβίζειν,
3 ἐννυχίων ἄναξ,
4 Αἰδωνεῦ, Αἰδωνεῦ, λίσσομαι 1560
5 ἄπονα μηδ᾽ ἐπὶ βαρυαχεῖ
6 ξένον ἐξανύσαι
7 μόρῳ τὰν παγκευθῆ κάτω
8 νεκρῶν πλάκα καὶ Στύγιον δόμον.
9 πολλῶν γὰρ ἂν καὶ μάταν 1565
10 πημάτων ἱκνουμένων
11 πάλιν σφε δαίμων δίκαιος αὔξοι.

ἀντ. ὦ χθόνιαι θεαί, σῶμά τ᾽ ἀνικάτου 1568
2 θηρός, ὃν ἐν πύλαισι
3 ταῖσι πολυξένοις 1570
4 εὐνᾶσθαι κνυζεῖσθαί τ᾽ ἐξ ἄντρων
5 ἀδάματον φύλακα παρ᾽ Ἅιδᾳ

1561 ἄπονα μηδ᾽ Wecklein: μήτ᾽ ἐπιπόνῳ L: μήτ᾽ (or μήποτ᾽) ἐπίπονα r.
1562 ἐξανύσαι Vauvilliers : ἐκτανύσαι MSS. 1564 νεκρῶν Triclinius :
νεκύων MSS. 1565 f. πολλῶν γὰρ αὖ τέρματ᾽ ἂν | πημάτων ἱκνούμενον
conj. J. 1567 σφε Reiske: σε MSS. 1570 ταῖσι Bergk: φασὶ
MSS. 1572 ἀδάμαστον L, vulg. : corr. Brunck.

56 ΣΟΦΟΚΛΕΟΥΣ

6 λόγος αἰὲν ἔχει·
7 τόν, ὦ Γᾶς παῖ καὶ Ταρτάρου,
8 κατεύχομαι ἐν καθαρῷ βῆναι
9 ὁρμωμένῳ νερτέρας
10 τῷ ξένῳ νεκρῶν πλάκας·
11 σέ τοι κικλήσκω τὸν αἰένυπνον.

1575

ΑΓΓΕΛΟΣ.

ἄνδρες πολῖται, ξυντομώτατον μὲν ἂν
τύχοιμι λέξας Οἰδίπουν ὀλωλότα·   1580
ἃ δ᾽ ἦν τὰ πραχθέντ᾽ οὔθ᾽ ὁ μῦθος ἐν βραχεῖ
φράσαι πάρεστιν οὔτε τἄργ᾽ ὅσ᾽ ἦν ἐκεῖ.
ΧΟ. ὄλωλε γὰρ δύστηνος; ΑΓ. ὡς λελοιπότα
κεῖνον τὸν ἀεὶ βίοτον ἐξεπίστασο.
ΧΟ. πῶς; ἆρα θείᾳ κἀπόνῳ τάλας τύχῃ;   1585
ΑΓ. τοῦτ᾽ ἐστὶν ἤδη κἀποθαυμάσαι πρέπον.
ὡς μὲν γὰρ ἐνθένδ᾽ εἶρπε, καὶ σύ που παρὼν
ἔξοισθ᾽, ὑφηγητῆρος οὐδενὸς φίλων,
ἀλλ᾽ αὐτὸς ἡμῖν πᾶσιν ἐξηγούμενος·
ἐπεὶ δ᾽ ἀφῖκτο τὸν καταρράκτην ὁδὸν   1590
χαλκοῖς βάθροισι γῆθεν ἐρριζωμένον,
ἔστη κελεύθων ἐν πολυσχίστων μιᾷ,
κοίλου πέλας κρατῆρος, οὗ τὰ Θησέως
Περίθου τε κεῖται πίστ᾽ ἀεὶ ξυνθήματα·
ἀφ᾽ οὗ μέσος στὰς τοῦ τε Θορικίου πέτρου   1595
κοίλης τ᾽ ἀχέρδου κἀπὸ λαΐνου τάφου
καθέζετ᾽· εἶτ᾽ ἔλυσε δυσπινεῖς στολάς.

1573 ἔχει Triclinius: ἀνέχει L, vulg.   1574 τόν Hermann: ὅν MSS.
1578 αἰὲν ἄϋπνον·L¹, vulg.: αἰέν ὕπνον L³.   1579 ξυντομωτάτως MSS.:
corr. Elmsley.   1584 ἀεὶ L: αἰεὶ A, vulg.   1586 τοῦτ᾽ Γ: ταῦτ᾽
L, vulg.   1588 ὑφηγητῆρος Γ: ὑφ᾽ ἡγητῆρος L.   1595 ἐφ᾽ οὗ
μέσου MSS. (μέσον Vat.): corr. Brunck, Musgrave.   1597 ἔλυσε Γ:
ἔδυσε L, vulg.

κἄπειτ' ἄυσας παῖδας ἠνώγει ῥυτῶν
ὑδάτων ἐνεγκεῖν λουτρὰ καὶ χοάς ποθεν·
τὼ δ' εὐχλόου Δήμητρος εἰς προσόψιον   1600
πάγον μολοῦσαι τάσδ' ἐπιστολὰς πατρὶ
ταχεῖ 'πόρευσαν σὺν χρόνῳ, λουτροῖς τέ νιν
ἐσθῆτί τ' ἐξήσκησαν ᾗ νομίζεται.
ἐπεὶ δὲ παντὸς εἶχε δρῶντος ἡδονήν,
κοὐκ ἦν ἔτ' οὐδὲν ἀργὸν ὧν ἐφίετο,   1605
κτύπησε μὲν Ζεὺς χθόνιος, αἱ δὲ παρθένοι
ῥίγησαν ὡς ἤκουσαν· ἐς δὲ γούνατα
πατρὸς πεσοῦσαι κλαῖον, οὐδ' ἀνίεσαν
στέρνων ἀραγμοὺς οὐδὲ παμμήκεις γόους.
ὁ δ' ὡς ἀκούει φθόγγον ἐξαίφνης πικρόν,   1610
πτύξας ἐπ' αὐταῖς χεῖρας εἶπεν· ὦ τέκνα,
οὐκ ἔστ' ἔθ' ὑμῖν τῇδ' ἐν ἡμέρᾳ πατήρ.
ὄλωλε γὰρ δὴ πάντα τἀμά, κοὐκέτι
τὴν δυσπόνητον ἕξετ' ἀμφ' ἐμοὶ τροφήν·
σκληρὰν μέν, οἶδα, παῖδες· ἀλλ' ἓν γὰρ μόνον   1615
τὰ πάντα λύει ταῦτ' ἔπος μοχθήματα.
τὸ γὰρ φιλεῖν οὐκ ἔστιν ἐξ ὅτου πλέον
ἢ τοῦδε τἀνδρὸς ἔσχεθ', οὗ τητώμεναι
τὸ λοιπὸν ἤδη τὸν βίον διάξετον.
τοιαῦτ' ἐπ' ἀλλήλοισιν ἀμφικείμενοι   1620
λύγδην ἔκλαιον πάντες. ὡς δὲ πρὸς τέλος
γόων ἀφίκοντ' οὐδ' ἔτ' ὠρώρει βοή,
ἦν μὲν σιωπή, φθέγμα δ' ἐξαίφνης τινὸς
θώϋξεν αὐτόν, ὥστε πάντας ὀρθίας
στῆσαι φόβῳ δείσαντας ἐξαίφνης τρίχας.   1625
καλεῖ γὰρ αὐτὸν πολλὰ πολλαχῇ θεός·
ὦ οὗτος οὗτος, Οἰδίπους, τί μέλλομεν
χωρεῖν; πάλαι δὴ τἀπὸ σοῦ βραδύνεται.

1600 προσόψιον L: ἐπόψιον r, vulg.
1619 τὸν βίον] τὸν om. MSS., add. Elmsley. τοῦ βίου Suidas.

ὁ δ᾽ ὡς ἐπῄσθετ᾽ ἐκ θεοῦ καλούμενος,
αὐδᾷ μολεῖν οἱ γῆς ἄνακτα Θησεα.   1630
κἀπεὶ προσῆλθεν, εἶπεν· ὦ φίλον κάρα,
δός μοι χερὸς σῆς πίστιν ὁρκίαν τέκνοις,
ὑμεῖς τε, παῖδες, τῷδε· καὶ καταίνεσον
μήποτε προδώσειν τάσδ᾽ ἑκών, τελεῖν δ᾽ ὅσ᾽ ἂν
μέλλῃς φρονῶν εὖ ξυμφέροντ᾽ αὐταῖς ἀεί.   1635
ὁ δ᾽, ὡς ἀνὴρ γενναῖος, οὐκ οἴκτου μέτα
κατῄνεσεν τάδ᾽ ὅρκιος δράσειν ξένῳ.
ὅπως δὲ ταῦτ᾽ ἔδρασεν, εὐθὺς Οἰδίπους
ψαύσας ἀμαυραῖς χερσὶν ὧν παίδων λέγει·
ὦ παῖδε, τλάσας χρὴ τὸ γενναῖον φρενὶ   1640
χωρεῖν τόπων ἐκ τῶνδε, μηδ᾽ ἃ μὴ θέμις
λεύσσειν δικαιοῦν, μηδὲ φωνούντων κλύειν.
ἀλλ᾽ ἔρπεθ᾽ ὡς τάχιστα· πλὴν ὁ κύριος
Θησεὺς παρέστω μανθάνων τὰ δρώμενα.
τοσαῦτα φωνήσαντος εἰσηκούσαμεν   1645
ξύμπαντες· ἀστακτὶ δὲ σὺν ταῖς παρθένοις
στένοντες ὡμαρτοῦμεν. ὡς δ᾽ ἀπήλθομεν,
χρόνῳ βραχεῖ στραφέντες, ἐξαπείδομεν
τὸν ἄνδρα τὸν μὲν οὐδαμοῦ παρόντ᾽ ἔτι,
ἄνακτα δ᾽ αὐτὸν ὀμμάτων ἐπίσκιον   1650
χεῖρ᾽ ἀντέχοντα κρατός, ὡς δεινοῦ τινος
φόβου φανέντος οὐδ᾽ ἀνασχετοῦ βλέπειν.
ἔπειτα μέντοι βαιὸν οὐδὲ σὺν χρόνῳ
ὁρῶμεν αὐτὸν γῆν τε προσκυνοῦνθ᾽ ἅμα
καὶ τὸν θεῶν Ὄλυμπον ἐν ταὐτῷ λόγῳ.   1655
μόρῳ δ᾽ ὁποίῳ κεῖνος ὤλετ᾽ οὐδ᾽ ἂν εἷς
θνητῶν φράσειε πλὴν τὸ Θησέως κάρα.
οὐ γάρ τις αὐτὸν οὔτε πυρφόρος θεοῦ
κεραυνὸς ἐξέπραξεν οὔτε ποντία

1632 ὁρκίαν P. N. Papageorgius: ἀρχαίαν MSS.
1640 φρενὶ A: φέρειν L.

θύελλα κινηθεῖσα τῷ τότ᾽ ἐν χρόνῳ,   1660
ἀλλ᾽ ἤ τις ἐκ θεῶν πομπός, ἢ τὸ νερτέρων
εὔνουν διαστὰν γῆς ἀλύπητον βάθρον·
ἀνὴρ γὰρ οὐ στενακτὸς οὐδὲ σὺν νόσοις
ἀλγεινὸς ἐξεπέμπετ᾽, ἀλλ᾽ εἴ τις βροτῶν
θαυμαστός. εἰ δὲ μὴ δοκῶ φρονῶν λέγειν,   1665
οὐκ ἂν παρείμην οἶσι μὴ δοκῶ φρονεῖν.

ΧΟ. ποῦ δ᾽ αἵ τε παῖδες χοἰ προπέμψαντες φίλων;

ΑΓ. αἵδ᾽ οὐχ ἑκάς· γόων γὰρ οὐκ ἀσήμονες
φθόγγοι σφε σημαίνουσι δεῦρ᾽ ὁρμωμένας.

στρ. ά. ΑΝ. αἰαῖ, φεῦ· ἔστιν ἔστι νῷν δὴ   1670
2 οὐ τὸ μέν, ἄλλο δὲ μή, πατρὸς ἔμφυτον
3 ἄλαστον αἷμα δυσμόροιν στενάζειν,
4 ᾧτινι τὸν πολὺν
5 ἄλλοτε μὲν πόνον ἔμπεδον εἴχομεν,
6 ἐν πυμάτῳ δ᾽ ἀλόγιστα παροίσομεν   1675
7 ἰδόντε καὶ παθούσα.

ΧΟ. 8 τί δ᾽ ἔστιν; ΑΝ. ἔστιν μὲν εἰκάσαι, φίλοι.

ΧΟ. 9 βέβηκεν; ΑΝ. ὡς μάλιστ᾽ ἂν ἐν πόθῳ λάβοις.

10 τί γάρ, ὅτῳ μήτ᾽ Ἄρης
11 μήτε πόντος ἀντέκυρσεν,   1680
12 ἄσκοποι δὲ πλάκες ἔμαρψαν
13 ἐν ἀφανεῖ τινι μόρῳ φερόμενον.
14 τάλαινα, νῷν δ᾽ ὀλεθρία
15 νὺξ ἐπ᾽ ὄμμασιν βέβακε. πῶς γὰρ ἤ τιν᾽ ἀπίαν
16 γᾶν ἢ πόντιον κλύδων᾽ ἀλώμεναι βίου   1686
17 δύσοιστον ἕξομεν τροφάν;

1662 ἀλύπητον] L. has γρ. ἀλάμπετον written above by the first reviser
(S), and this v. l. is in the text of F (cod. Par. 2886, late 15th cent.), which
usually adopts his corrections.   1669 φθόγγοι σφε r: φθόγγοις δὲ L,
vulg.   1677 ἔστιν μὲν Hermann: οὐκ ἔστι (or -ν) μὲν MSS.   1678 εἰ
πόθῳ L, vulg. (εἰ πόθον r): corr. Canter.   1682 φερόμενον Kuhnhardt
(-αι Hermann): φαινόμεναι L, vulg. (φαινόμενα r).

ΙΣ. 18 οὐ κάτοιδα. κατά με φόνιος Ἀΐδας ἕλοι
19 πατρὶ ξυνθανεῖν γεραιῷ   1690
20 τάλαιναν· ὡς ἔμοιγ' ὁ μέλλων βίος οὐ βιωτός.

ΧΟ. 21 ὦ διδύμα τέκνων ἀρίστα, τὸ φέρον ἐκ θεοῦ
φέρειν,
22 μηδ' ἔτ' ἄγαν φλέγεσθον· οὖτοι κατάμεμπτ'
ἔβητον.   1695

ἀντ. ά. ΑΝ. πόθος τοι καὶ κακῶν ἄρ' ἦν τις.   1697
2 καὶ γὰρ ὁ μηδαμὰ δὴ φίλον ἦν φίλον,
3 ὁπότε γε καὶ τὸν ἐν χεροῖν κατεῖχον.
4 ὦ πάτερ, ὦ φίλος, ὦ τὸν ἀεὶ κατὰ   1700
5 γᾶς σκότον εἱμένος·
6 οὐδέ γ' ἔνερθ' ἀφίλητος ἐμοί ποτε
7 καὶ τᾷδε μὴ κυρήσῃς.
ΧΟ. 8 ἔπραξεν; ΑΝ. ἔπραξεν οἷον ἤθελεν.
ΧΟ. 9 τὸ ποῖον; ΑΝ. ἇς ἔχρῃζε γᾶς ἐπὶ ξένας   1705
10 ἔθανε· κοίταν δ' ἔχει
11 νέρθεν εὐσκίαστον αἰέν,
12 οὐδὲ πένθος ἔλιπ' ἄκλαυτον.
13 ἀνὰ γὰρ ὄμμα σε τόδ', ὦ πάτερ, ἐμὸν
14 στένει δακρῦον, οὐδ' ἔχω   1710
15 πῶς με χρὴ τὸ σὸν τάλαιναν ἀφανίσαι τοσόνδ'
ἄχος.
16 ὤμοι, γᾶς ἐπὶ ξένας θανεῖν ἔχρῃζες, ἀλλ'
17 ἔρημος ἔθανες ὧδέ μοι.

1688—1692 οὐ κάτοιδα...βιωτός. The MSS. give these vv. to Antigone: Turnebus restored them to Ismene. 1694 τὸ φέρον ἐκ θεοῦ φέρειν Wecklein: τὸ φέρον ἐκ θεοῦ καλῶς | φέρειν χρὴ MSS. 1695 μηδ' ἔτ' ἄγαν Bellermann: μηδ' ἄγαν οὔτω MSS. 1697 τοι add. Hartung. 1698 ὁ μηδαμῇι δὴ τὸ φίλον φίλον L (A has ὃ instead of ὁ): corr. Brunck. 1702 οὐδέ γ' ἔνερθ' Wecklein: οὐδὲ γέρων MSS. 1709 ἀνὰ γὰρ Hermann: ἀεὶ γὰρ MSS. 1713 ὤμοι Wecklein: ἰὼ μὴ MSS.

ΙΣ. 18 ὦ τάλαινα, τίς ἄρα με πότμος αὖθις ὧδ'

‿ | ‐ ‿ | ‐ ⋀ ‖   1715

19 ‐ ‿ | ‐ ‿ | ‐ ‿ | ‐ ‿ ‖

20 ἐπαμμένει σέ τ', ὦ φίλα, τὰς πατρὸς ὧδ' ἐρήμας;

ΧΟ. 21 ἀλλ' ἐπεὶ ὀλβίως γ' ἔλυσε τὸ τέλος, ὦ φίλαι, βίου,

22 λήγετε τοῦδ' ἄχους· κακῶν γὰρ δυσάλωτος οὐδείς.

στρ. β'. ΑΝ. πάλιν, φίλα, συθῶμεν.   ΙΣ. ὡς τί ῥέξομεν;

ΑΝ. 2 ἵμερος ἔχει με.   ΙΣ. τίς;   1725

ΑΝ. 3 τὰν χθόνιον ἑστίαν ἰδεῖν

ΙΣ. 4 τίνος;   ΑΝ. πατρός, τάλαιν' ἐγώ.

ΙΣ. 5 θέμις δὲ πῶς τάδ' ἐστί; μῶν

6 οὐχ ὁρᾷς;   ΑΝ. τί τόδ' ἐπέπληξας;   1730

ΙΣ. 7 καὶ τόδ', ὡς   ΑΝ. τί τόδε μάλ' αὖθις;

ΙΣ. 8 ἄταφος ἔπιτνε δίχα τε παντός.

ΑΝ. 9 ἄγε με, καὶ τότ' ἐπενάριξον.

ΙΣ. 10 αἰαῖ· δυστάλαινα, ποῦ δῆτ'

11 αὖθις ὧδ' ἔρημος ἄπορος   1735

12 αἰῶνα τλάμον' ἕξω;

ἀντ. β'. ΧΟ. φίλαι, τρέσητε μηδέν.   ΑΝ. ἀλλὰ ποῖ φύγω;

ΧΟ. 2 καὶ πάρος ἀπέφυγε   ΑΝ. τί;

ΧΟ. 3 τὰ σφῷν τὸ μὴ πίτνειν κακῶς.   1740

ΑΝ. 4 φρονῶ.   ΧΟ. τί δῆθ' ὅπερ νοεῖς;

ΑΝ. 5 ὅπως μολούμεθ' ἐς δόμους

6 οὐκ ἔχω.   ΧΟ. μηδέ γε μάτευε.

ΑΝ. 7 μόγος ἔχει.   ΧΟ. καὶ πάρος ἐπεῖχε.

1715 After αὖθις ὧδ' the MSS. add ἔρημος ἄπορος, prob. borrowed from
1735. To fill the lacuna J. H. H. Schmidt conj. ἀνόλβιος.   1717 ἐπαμμένει Hermann : ἐπιμένει MSS.   1724 ῥέξομεν Α : ῥέξωμεν L, vulg.
1733 ἐνάριξον L, vulg. (ἐξενάριξον r) : corr. Elmsley.   1736 τλάμων
MSS.: corr. Hermann.   1739 f. καὶ πάρος ἀπεφεύγετον | σφῷν τὸ μὴ
πίτνειν κακῶς L, vulg. (μὴ om. L²): corr. Hermann.   1741 ὅπερ νοεῖς
Graser : ὑπερνοεῖς MSS.   1744 ἐπεῖχε Wunder : ἐπεί MSS.

ΑΝ. 8 τοτὲ μὲν ἄπορα, τοτὲ δ' ὕπερθεν.   1745
ΧΟ. 9 μέγ' ἄρα πέλαγος ἐλάχετόν τι.
ΑΝ. 10 φεῦ, φεῦ· ποῖ μόλωμεν, ὦ Ζεῦ;
      11 ἐλπίδων γὰρ ἐς τίν' ἔτι με
      12 δαίμων τανῦν γ' ἐλαύνει;   1750

σύστ. ΘΗ. παύετε θρῆνον, παῖδες· ἐν οἷς γὰρ
        χάρις ἡ χθονία ξύν' ἀπόκειται,
        πενθεῖν οὐ χρή· νέμεσις γάρ.
ΑΝ. ὦ τέκνον Αἰγέως, προσπίτνομέν σοι.
ΘΗ. τίνος, ὦ παῖδες, χρείας ἀνύσαι;   1755
ΑΝ. τύμβον θέλομεν προσιδεῖν αὐταὶ
      πατρὸς ἡμετέρου.
ΘΗ. ἀλλ' οὐ θεμιτόν.
ΑΝ. πῶς εἶπας, ἄναξ, κοίραν' Ἀθηνῶν;
ΘΗ. ὦ παῖδες, ἀπεῖπεν ἐμοὶ κεῖνος   1760
      μήτε πελάζειν ἐς τούσδε τόπους
      μήτ' ἐπιφωνεῖν μηδένα θνητῶν
      θήκην ἱεράν, ἣν κεῖνος ἔχει.
      καὶ ταῦτά μ' ἔφη πράσσοντα καλῶς
      χώραν ἕξειν αἰὲν ἄλυπον.   1765
      ταῦτ' οὖν ἔκλυεν δαίμων ἡμῶν
      χὠ πάντ' ἀΐων Διὸς Ὅρκος.
ΑΝ. ἀλλ' εἰ τάδ' ἔχει κατὰ νοῦν κείνῳ,
      ταῦτ' ἂν ἀπαρκοῖ· Θήβας δ' ἡμᾶς
      τὰς ὠγυγίους πέμψον, ἐάν πως   1770
      διακωλύσωμεν ἰόντα φόνον
      τοῖσιν ὁμαίμοις.

1745 ἄπορα Wunder : πέρα MSS.   1747 Between ἐλάχετόν τι and
φεῦ, φεῦ, the MSS. insert, ΑΝ. ναὶ ναί.   ΧΟ. ξύμφημι καὐτός: del. Dindorf.
1749 ἐς τίν' ἔτι με Hermann: ἐς τί με MSS.   1752 ξυν απόκειται L:
ξυναπόκειται A, vulg. (συναπόκειται r): corr. Reisig.   1754 προσπίτνομεν r: προσπίπτομεν L, vulg.   1758 After θεμιτόν the MSS. add κεῖσε
μολεῖν: del. Bothe.

ΘΗ. δράσω καὶ τάδε, καὶ πάνθ' ὁπόσ' ἂν
μέλλω πράσσειν πρόσφορά θ' ὑμῖν
καὶ τῷ κατὰ γῆς, ὃς νέον ἔρρει,   1775
πρὸς χάριν, οὐ δεῖ μ' ἀποκάμνειν.
ΧΟ. ἀλλ' ἀποπαύετε μηδ' ἐπὶ πλείω
θρῆνον ἐγείρετε·
πάντως γὰρ ἔχει τάδε κῦρος.

1773 ὁπόσ' ἂν Porson: ὅσ' ἂν L, vulg.: ὅσα ἂν A.
1776 οὐ δεῖ Hermann: οὐ γὰρ δεῖ MSS.

NOTES.

Scene:—*At Colonus in Attica, a little more than a mile north-west of the acropolis of Athens. The back-scene shows the sacred grove of the Eumenides, luxuriant with 'laurel, olive, vine' (v. 17). Near the middle of the stage is seen a rock (v. 19), affording a seat which is supposed to be just within the bounds of the grove (v. 37). The hero Colonus is perhaps represented by a statue on the stage (59 τόνδε, cp. 65).*

The blind OEDIPUS (conceived as coming into Attica from the W. or N. W.) enters on the spectator's left, led by ANTIGONE. He is old and way-worn; the haggard face bears the traces of the self-inflicted wounds (δυσπρόσοπτον, v. 286): the garb of both the wanderers betokens indigence and hardship (vv. 747 ff.; δυσπινεῖς στολάς, v. 1597). After replying to his first questions, his daughter leads him to the rocky seat (v. 19).

1—116 Prologue. Oedipus has sat down to rest, when a man of the place warns him that he is on holy ground. It is the grove of the Eumenides. At that word, Oedipus knows that he has found his destined goal; and, when the stranger has gone to summon the men of Colonus, invokes the goddesses.—Steps approach; Oedipus and his daughter hide themselves in the grove.

1 γέροντος. Sophocles marks the length of interval which he supposes between the *O. T.* and the *O. C.* by v. 395, γέροντα δ' ὀρθοῦν φλαῦρον ὃς νέος πέσῃ. In the *O. T.* Oedipus cannot be imagined as much above 40,—his two sons being then about 15 and 14, his two daughters about 13 and 12 respectively. It was 'long' after his fall when Creon drove him into exile (437, 441). It would satisfy the data of both plays to suppose that about 20 years in the life of Oedipus have elapsed between them.

J. C.   5

'Αντιγόνη. An anapaest can hold only the first place in a
tragic trimeter, unless it is contained in a proper name, when
it can hold any place except the sixth. Soph. has the name
'Αντιγόνη only four times in iambics. Here, in 1415, and in
Ant. 11 the anapaest holds the fifth place: in *O. C.* 507, the
4th. But Eur. prefers the anapaest of 'Αντιγόνη in the 4th
place. The anapaest must be wholly in the proper name.

2 χώρους, like *loca*, vaguely, 'region' (so *O. T.* 798): but
sing. χῶρος below (16, 37, 54), of a definite spot. Oed.
already knows that they are near *Athens* (25), but it is time
that the day's journey was ended (20); will this rural region—
or town—supply their needs if they halt?

3 πλανήτην, 'wandering.' Cp. Eur. *Heracl.* 878 ξένοι πλανήτην εἶχετ' ἄθλιον βίον. The word is not in itself opprobrious:
in 123 it is merely opp. to ἔγχωρος: cp. Plat. *Rep.* 371 D
καλοῦμεν...τοὺς...πλανήτας ἐπὶ τὰς πόλεις, ἐμπόρους.

4 σπανιστοῖς, made scanty, given scantily: so Philostratus
(circ. 235 A.D.) p. 611 ἄρωμα...σπανιστόν, 'rare.' This implies
σπανίζω τι as = 'to make a thing scanty' or rare, which occurs
in Greek of the 2nd cent. B.C.: cp. Shaksp. *Lear* 1. 1. 281 *you
have obedience scanted.*

δέξεται: Xen. *Anab.* 5. 5. 24 ξενίοις...δέχεσθαι: Plat. *Legg.*
919 A καταλύσεσιν ἀγαπηταῖς δεχόμενος.

δωρήμασιν, food, and shelter for the night: *Od.* 14. 404 ἐς
κλισίην ἄγαγον καὶ ξείνια δῶκα (whereas δῶρα, or ξεινήϊα δῶρα, in
Hom. usu. = special presents, as of plate or the like, *Od.* 24. 273).

5 ἐξαιτοῦντα, 'asking *earnestly*.' This compound has a like
force in *O. T.* 1255, *Trach.* 10; and so the midd. below, 586,
1327. Cp. ἐξεφίεται, '*straitly* enjoins,' *Ai.* 795. σμικροῦ is
better than μικροῦ, since the rhetorical ἐπαναφορά (cp. 610,
O. T. 25) needs the same form in both places. μικρός having
prevailed in later Attic (as in Xen. and the orators), our MSS.
in the tragic texts often drop the σ. But, metre permitting,
tragedy preferred σμικρός.

6 φέροντα = φερόμενον: *O. T.* 590 πάντ' ἄνευ φόβου φέρω:
cp. 1411. **καὶ τόδ'.** As καὶ οὗτος (like *et is, isque*), or καὶ ταῦτα,
introduces a strengthening circumstance (Her. 6. 11 εἶναι
δούλοισι, καὶ τούτοισι ὡς δρηπέτῃσι), so here καὶ τόδε marks the
last step of a climax. **ἐμοί** after Οἰδίπουν: cp. 1329: as *O. T.*
535 τῆς ἐμῆς after τοῦδε τἀνδρός (like *Tr.* 1073 f.): *Ai.* 865
μυθήσομαι after Αἴας θροεῖ: Plat. *Euthyphro* 5 A οὐδέ τῳ ἂν
διαφέροι Εὐθύφρων τῶν πολλῶν...εἰ μὴ εἰδείην.

Notes 67

7 στέργειν, 'to be patient,' cp. 519, Dem. *Cor.* § 112 εἰ δέ φησιν οὗτος, δειξάτω, κἀγὼ στέρξω καὶ σιωπήσομαι: usu. with accus. Like στέργειν, αἰνεῖν is sometimes absol. in this sense, but ἀγαπᾶν almost always takes a clause with ὅτι, εἰ or ἐάν (*Od.* 21. 289 οὐκ ἀγαπᾷς ὃ ἔκηλος... | δαίνυσαι), or an accus. αἱ πάθαι: Her. 1. 207 τὰ δέ μοι παθήματα ἐόντα ἀχάριτα μαθήματα γέγονε: Aesch. *Ag.* 177 τὸν πάθει μάθος | θέντα κυρίως ἔχειν. ὁ χρόνος, the time (through which I live), attending on me (ξυνών) in long course (μακρός). For ξυνών cp. *O. T.* 863 εἴ μοι ξυνείη... μοῖρα: *Ai.* 622 παλαιᾷ...ἔντροφος ἀμέρᾳ.

8 διδάσκει, verb agreeing with nearest subject: cp. *Ant.* 830, 1133: Plat. *Symp.* 190 C αἱ τιμαὶ γὰρ αὐτοῖς καὶ ἱερὰ τὰ παρὰ τῶν ἀνθρώπων ἠφανίζετο: Cic. *Ad Att.* 9. 10. 2 *nihil libri, nihil litterae, nihil doctrina prodest.* τρίτον, as completing the lucky number: *Ai.* 1174 κόμας ἐμὰς καὶ τῆσδε καὶ σαυτοῦ τρίτου.

9 θάκησιν is in itself a correct form. θάκησις (θακέω) is (1) the act of sitting, (2) the means of sitting, as οἴκησις (οἰκέω) is (1) the act of dwelling, (2) the house. It is not found elsewhere, but cp. *Ph.* 18 ἡλίου διπλῆ | πάρεστιν ἐνθάκησις, a twofold means of sitting in the sun. With the MS. reading θάκοισιν construe:—στῆσόν με ἢ πρὸς θάκοις βεβήλοις, εἴ τινα (θᾶκον) βλέπεις, etc. (We could not render εἴ τινα βλέπεις 'if thou seest any *man*,' since the need for a halt did not depend on that condition.) This is a construction much less clear and simple than that with θάκησιν. βεβήλοις may have induced the change of θάκησιν into θάκοισιν.

10 βεβήλοις, neut. plur. (cp. ἀβάτων ἀποβάς, 167), places which may be trodden, *profana,* opp. to ἱερά, ἄθικτα: cp. Bekker *Anecd.* 325. 13 ἀβέβηλα τὰ ἄβατα χωρία καὶ ἱερὰ καὶ μὴ τοῖς τυχοῦσι βάσιμα, μόνοις δὲ τοῖς θεραπεύουσι τοὺς θεούς. βέβηλα δὲ ἐλέγετο τὰ μὴ ὅσια μηδὲ ἱερά· οὕτω Σοφοκλῆς. (This ignores the classical use of ὅσιος as opp. to ἱερός: in Ar. *Lys.* 743 ὅσιον χωρίον = βέβηλον.)

ἢ πρὸς ἄλσεσιν does not necessarily imply entrance on the ἄλση. But the contrast with πρὸς βεβήλοις is unmeaning unless Oed. thinks of a seat *on* sacred ground, and not merely *near* it. So Antigone, who recognises the grove as sacred (16), seats him within it (19). This grove at Colonus was ἀστιβές (126) because the cult of the Eumenides so prescribed. Sacred groves were often open to visitors, as was the κυκλοτερὲς ἄλσος of the Nymphs, with an altar 'whereon all wayfarers were wont

68   *Oedipus at Colonus*

to make offerings,' ὅθι πάντες ἐπιρρέζεσκον ὁδῖται (*Od.* 17. 208).
Hence Pausanias sometimes mentions that a particular ἄλσος
was *not* open to the public.

11 ἐξίδρυσον, place me in a seat; cp. ἐκ in ἐξορθόω (to
render ὀρθόν). ἐξίδρυσον, without addition, could hardly
mean, 'seat me *apart*,' *i.e.* out of the path. In Eur. fr. 877
(the only other example of ἐξιδρύω) it is the context which
fixes this sense, τηλοῦ γὰρ οἴκων βίοτον ἐξιδρυσάμην, 'I fixed the
seat of my life far apart from men's homes.'

πυθώμεθα. πυθοίμεθα is impossible here. After a primary
tense, the optative in a final clause with ὡς, ὅπως, etc., occurs
only:—(1) in Homeric Greek, where the case is merely
imaginary: *Od.* 17. 250 τόν ποτ' ἐγὼν... | ἄξω τῆλ' Ἰθακῆς, ἵνα
μοι βίοτον πολὺν ἄλφοι: 'him *some day* I will take far from
Ithaca,—so that (if I should do so) he might bring me large
gain,'—implying, εἰ ἄγοιμι, ἄλφοι ἄν. (2) After words expressing
an *aspiration* or *prayer* (and not, like στῆσον here, a simple
order): Aesch. *Eum.* 297 ἔλθοι, κλύει δὲ καὶ πρόσωθεν ὢν
θεός, | ὅπως γένοιτο...λυτήριος: 'may she come—and a god
hears e'en afar—that [so] she might prove my deliverer.'
Aesch. *Suppl.* 670 ff., by which Campb. defends πυθοίμεθα,
would come under (2), if the text were certain, but there τώς
is a *v.l.* for ὡς. (3) More rarely, where the primary tense
implies a secondary: Dem. *In Androt.* § 11 τοῦτον ἔχει τὸν
τρόπον ὁ νόμος...ἵνα μηδὲ πεισθῆναι μηδ' ἐξαπατηθῆναι γένοιτ' ἐπὶ
τῷ δήμῳ: 'the law *stands* thus [=*was made* thus], that the
people *might* not even have the power' etc.: *i.e.* ἔχει implies ἐτέθη.

12 μανθάνειν...ἥκομεν, we have come to learning, = are in
such plight that we must learn: the infin. as after verbs of
duty or fitness (ὀφείλω, προσήκει, etc.). Cp. *O. T.* 1158 εἰς
τόδ' ἥξεις (*sc.* εἰς τὸ ὀλέσθαι).

14 Οἰδίπους, the more frequent voc. (cp. *O. T.* 405 crit. n.):
but Οἰδίπου below, 557, 1346. Athens is a little more than a
mile S.E. of Colonus. The picture which Sophocles meant
πύργοι to suggest probably included both the Acropolis—a
beautiful feature in the view—and the line of city-walls with their
towers. So the city-walls of Thebes are πύργοι, *Ant.* 122.—οἳ at
the end of the verse: cp. *O. T.* 298, *El.* 873, *Tr.* 819.

15 στέγουσιν, the reading of all MSS., is probably right.
It is true that in class. Greek στέγω usually means either
(1) 'cover,' 'conceal,' as *El.* 1118 ἄγγος...σῶμα...στέγον, or
(2) 'keep out,' as Aesch. *Theb.* 216 πύργον στέγειν εὔχεσθε

πολέμιον δόρυ. But the first sense—'cover'—might easily pass into 'protect,' and Xen. *Cyr.* 7. 1. 33 has αἱ ἀσπίδες...στεγάζουσι τὰ σώματα. Wakefield's στέφουσιν ('girdle') is specious; we have στεφάνωμα or στεφάνη πύργων (*Ant.* 122, Eur. *Hec.* 910), Βαβυλῶνα...τείχεσιν ἐστεφάνωσε (Dionys. Periegetes 1006), ὅπλοισιν Μεγάλη πόλις ἐστεφάνωται (Paus. 9. 15). But it does not follow that πύργοι πόλιν στέφουσιν could stand. στέφω never occurs as = 'to be set around,' but either as (1) 'to set around'—ἄνθη περὶ κεφαλὴν στέφεις, or (2) 'to crown'—ἄνθεσι κεφαλὴν στέφεις,—sometimes in the fig. sense of 'honouring,' as with libations or offerings (*Ant.* 431 etc.). ὡς ἀπ' ὀμμάτων, *sc.* εἰκάσαι, to judge from sight (alone), without exact knowledge: schol. ὡς ἔστιν ἐκ προόψεως τεκμήρασθαι: cp. Thuc. 1. 10 εἰκάζεσθαι ἀπὸ τῆς φανερᾶς ὄψεως, to be estimated by the mere external aspect.

16 χῶρος δ' ὅδ' ἱρός. Cp. Plato *Phaedr.* 230 B, where Socrates recognises the sacred character of the spot by the Ilissus : Νυμφῶν τέ τινων καὶ Ἀχελῴου ἱερὸν ἀπὸ τῶν κορῶν τε καὶ ἀγαλμάτων (the votive dolls and images) ἔοικεν εἶναι. There, too, τὸ σύσκιον was a feature.

ὡς σάφ' εἰκάσαι, A's reading, is preferable to ὡς ἀπεικάσαι, which would imply a more diffident guess. The poet of Colonus intends that the sacred character of the grove should at once impress the Theban maiden; and σάφα is confirmed by the emphasis of δάφνης, ἐλαίας, ἀμπέλου. It has been objected that σάφα is inconsistent with εἰκάσαι. But it merely expresses the speaker's own belief that her guess is right; as we can say, 'a certain conjecture.' For the constr. with ὡς, cp. *Tr.* 1220 ὡς γ' ἐπεικάζειν ἐμέ. ὡς is omitted below, 152. βρύων takes a dat. in its literal sense of 'sprouting' (βρύει ἄνθεϊ *Il.* 17. 56), but either a dat. (as Ar. *Nub.* 45) or a gen. in its figurative sense of 'being full.'

17 ἀμπέλου. Cyril (*Jerem. Homil.* 4. 41), speaking of the later pagan practice, says, εἰς ἄλση ὅταν φυτεύωσι ξύλα, φυτεύουσιν οὐ τὰ καρποφόρα, οὐ συκῆν οὐδ' ἄμπελον, ἀλλὰ μόνον τέρψεως χάριν ἄκαρπα ξύλα. But in earlier times, at least, τὰ καρποφόρα were not rare in sacred groves; cp. Xen. *Anab.* 5. 3. 12 (referring to the shrine of the Ephesian Artemis at Scillus) περὶ δ' αὐτὸν τὸν ναὸν ἄλσος ἡμέρων δένδρων ἐφυτεύθη, ὅσα ἐστὶ τρωκτὰ ὡραῖα. Paus. 1. 21. 7 (in an ἄλσος of Apollo at Athens) δένδρων καὶ ἡμέρων καὶ ὅσα τῶν ἀκάρπων ὀσμῆς παρέχεταί τινα ἢ θέας ἡδονήν.

πυκνόπτεροι, 'feathered choir,' poet. for πυκναί, the second
element being equivalent to a separate epithet, πτερούσσαι:
cp. 717 ἑκατομπόδων Νηρῄδων, 1055 δισπόλους, *O. T.* 846 οἰόζωνος
ἀνήρ, a lonely wayfarer (where see n.). The *many* nightingales,
heard to warble from the thick covert, argue the undisturbed
sanctity of the inner grove. Antigone notices an indication
which her blind father can recognise. 8' is elided at the end
of the verse, as *O. T.* 29 (n.), so also τ', as *ib.* 1184 etc., and
once ταῦτα, *ib.* 332: cp. below, 1164.

20 ὡς γέροντι with μακρὰν: cp. Plat. *Soph.* 226 c ταχεῖαν, ὡς
ἐμοί, σκέψιν ἐπιτάττεις ('a rapid process of thought for such as
I am'). Cp. 76. προὐστάλης, 'hast fared forward': a compound
not found elsewhere in Trag., except in Aesch. *Theb.* 415
Δίκη...νιν προστέλλεται, sends him forth as her champion.

22 χρόνου...οὕνεκ'. *O. T.* 857 f.: Her. 3. 122 εἵνεκέν τε
χρημάτων ἄρξεις ἁπάσης τῆς Ἑλλάδος (if it is merely a question
of money): Antiphon or. 5 § 8 κἂν ἀνωμότοις ὑμῖν...ἐπιτρέψαιμι...,
ἕνεκά γε τοῦ πιστεύειν, 'I would leave the verdict to you, though
you were unsworn, if it were only a question of confidence.'

23 ὅποι, since καθέσταμεν implies ἥκομεν: cp. 227, 476:
on the same principle, Ὀλυμπίαζε (not Ὀλυμπίασι) παρεῖναι,
Thuc. 3. 8.

24 γοῦν: 'well (οὖν), I know *Athens* (γε), but not this
place.' Cp. *El.* 233 ἀλλ' οὖν εὐνοίᾳ γ' αὐδῶ, 'well, it is in
kindness that I speak.'

25 ἡμὶν as a trochee is frequent in Soph. (Ellendt counts
26 instances), but does not occur in Eur., nor in Aesch., except
in *Eum.* 347, where Porson's ἁμίν for ἁμῖν seems necessary.
Modern edd., with Dind., usu. write ἡμίν: others, as Nauck
and Ellendt, would always write ἥμιν, for which the old gram-
marians afford some warrant (cp. Chandler, *Accent.* 2nd ed. § 673):
while others, again, would distinguish an emphatic ἡμίν from
a non-emphatic ἥμιν (cp. Hadley and Allen, *Greek Gram.*
§ 264).

26 ἀλλ' ὅστις ὁ τόπος. The tribrach is divided like that in
Eur. *Phoen.* 511 ἐλθόντ|ᾰ σὺν ὅπλ|οις, where σὺν coheres closely
with ὅπλοις, as ὁ with τόπος. But even where no such cohesion
exists, a tribrach may be broken after the second syllable if it
is also broken after the first: *e.g.* δέσποινα, σὺ τάδ' ἔπραξας οἱ
γνώμης ἄτερ is correct: cp. n. on *O. T.* 537. ἢ μάθω, deliberative
subjunct., of which the aor. is more frequent than the pres.:
so *O. T.* 364 εἴπω: see on *O. T.* 651.

Notes

27 ἐξοικήσιμος, capable of being made into a dwelling-place, 'habitable,' here implying 'inhabited.' Adjectives with the suffix σιμο properly denote adaptability. They were primarily formed from substantives in -σι-ς, as χρήσι-μο-ς, fitted for use, from χρῆσις. The noun ἐξοίκησις is found only in the sense of 'emigration,' Plat. *Legg.* 704 C, 850 B. But as from ἱππάζομαι was formed ἱππά-σιμος, though no ἵππασις occurs, so ἐξοικήσιμος here is taken directly from ἐξοικεῖν as = 'to make into a dwelling-place' (Thuc. 2. 17 ἐξῳκήθη).

28 ἀλλ' ἐστὶ μήν, '*nay, but* it *is* inhabited.' Aesch. *Pers.* 233 (in a reply) ἀλλὰ μὴν ἵμειρ', '*nay, but* he was eager' (to take this very city). Especially in rejecting an alternative: Eur. *Helen.* 1047 ἀλλ' οὐδὲ μὴν ναῦς ἔστιν, 'nay, but neither is there a ship.'

30 Impatient for more light, Oed. asks, 'Is he coming forth towards us,—so that it is really needless for thee to move?' **δεῦρο** denotes the goal, **προσ-** the direction, and **ἐξ-** the starting-point. δεῦρο goes with both participles, which form a single expression, = 'coming *towards* us *from* the abodes' implied by οἰκητός (28). Cp. *Ai.* 762 ἀπ' οἴκων... ἐξορμώμενος.

31 καὶ δή, 'already': *Ai.* 49 καὶ δὴ 'πὶ δισσαῖς ἦν στρατηγίσιν πύλαις. μὲν οὖν, 'nay rather' (*imo*); Ar. *Eq.* 13 NI. λέγε σύ. ΔΗ. σὺ μὲν οὖν λέγε.

33 ὦ ξεῖν'. The Ionic voc. occurs even without metrical necessity, Eur. *I. T.* 798 ξεῖν', οὐ δικαίως: Soph. rarely uses ξεῖνος except in voc.: 1014 n. ὑπέρ τ' ἐμοῦ = ὑπὲρ ἐμοῦ τε: as *O. T.* 258 (where see n.), κυρῶ τ' ἐγώ = ἐγώ τε κυρῶ: *Ph.* 1294. Cp. Tennyson's lines 'To the Princess Frederica': *O you that were eyes and light to the King till he past away From the darkness of life. Ant.* 989 (of the blind Teiresias and his guide) δύ' ἐξ ἑνὸς βλέποντε.

34 f. οὕνεχ'...φράσαι: that thou hast come near, αἴσιος σκοπὸς ὤν (= τούτων ἃ) ἀδηλοῦμεν, an opportune inquirer into our doubts, φράσαι, 'so as to explain' (epexegetic infin., cp. 50). σκοπὸς has its ordinary sense of 'scout' (cp. 297). Oedipus supposes that the man has been sent to make inquiry. τούτων (understood in ὤν) is objective gen. after σκοπός.

35 ὤν, by attract.: *O. T.* 788 ὧν...ἱκόμην = (τούτων) ἃ ἱκόμην. ἀδηλοῦμεν, 'we are in doubt about.' Since ἀδηλέω = to be ἄδηλος, (as ἀπειθέω to be ἀπειθής, ἀκοσμέω to be ἄκοσμος,) the form strictly implies that ἄδηλος could mean, 'not *seeing*

clearly': but an act. sense nowhere occurs, for in Eur.
Or. 1318 χρόᾳ δ' ἀδήλῳ τῶν δεδραμένων πέρι means, 'faces
wherein the deeds cannot *be read*' (not, 'which seem to know
nought of them '). Cp. the verbs formed from the active use
of verbal adjectives which were primarily passive, as ἀλαστέω,
to be unforgetting, ἀτλητέω, to be impatient (*O. T.* 515).
Conversely, δηλόω, 'to *make* δῆλος,' sometimes verges on the
sense, ' to *be* δῆλος' (*Ant.* 20, 242).

36 As 78 shows, the man who has just entered is supposed
to belong to Colonus, which, like the rest of Attica, was
subject to the king of Athens (v. 67). τὰ πλείον', 'the' details
foreshadowed by the preamble. Isocr. or. 5 § 63 (in a rapid
sketch of Conon's career) καὶ τί δεῖ τὰ πλείω λέγειν; 'and why
dwell on the details?' So in Soph. *Ph.* 576 μή νύν μ' ἔρῃ τὰ
πλείον', *Tr.* 731 σιγᾶν ἂν ἁρμόζοι σε τὸν πλείω λόγον, the art.
denotes 'the' sequel which the previous discourse promises.
In Eur. *Med.* 609 ὡς οὐ κρινοῦμαι τῶνδέ σοι τὰ πλείονα, the gen.
brings this out: ' Enough—I will not dispute with thee on the
further aspects of this matter.'

37 οὐχ ἁγνὸν πατεῖν, 'which it is not lawful to tread.'
The poets can use ἁγνός either like ἱερός (*e.g.* Eur. *Andr.* 253
ἁγνὸν τέμενος), or, as here, like ὅσιος. For the infin. active,
cp. Plat. *Phaed.* 62 B λόγος οὐ...ῥᾴδιος διιδεῖν, *O. T.* 792
ἄτλητον...ὁρᾶν, and n. on *O. T.* 1204.

38 τοῦ θεῶν νομίζεται; 'to which of the gods is it deemed
to belong?' After verbs of being thought, called, etc., the
gen. expresses 'belonging' (1) to a possessor, as here and *Ant.*
738 οὐ τοῦ κρατοῦντος ἡ πόλις νομίζεται; or (2) to a class, as
Eur. *Andr.* 12 τῶν ἐλευθερωτάτων | οἴκων νομισθεῖσ'. With
(1) here cp. the gen. of the deity after ἱερός (Plat. *Phaed.* 85 B
ἱερὸς τοῦ αὐτοῦ θεοῦ).

39 ἄθικτος οὐδ' οἰκητός, *sc.* ἐστιν, answering τίς ἔσθ' ὁ χῶρος;
cp. 1274 ἄναυδος οὐδ' ἃ μηνίεις φράσας, *Ph.* 2 ἄστειπτος οὐδ'
οἰκουμένη. The second question, τοῦ θεῶν νομίζεται; is
answered by αἱ γὰρ ἔμφοβοι κ.τ.λ.

40 Γῆς τε καὶ Σκότου κόραι: as in Aesch. *Eum.* 416 they
call themselves Νυκτὸς αἰανῆς τέκνα, and invoke μᾶτερ Νύξ (844):
Aesch. does not name the other parent. In Hesiod. *Theog.*
184 the mother is Earth, impregnated by the blood of
Uranus,—the idea being that the Erinyes were called into life
by the crime of a son (Zeus) against a father.

41 τίνων...κλύων; of whom hearing the august name might

I make a prayer? *i.e.* 'who may they be, whose name I am to hear, and to invoke?' The optat. with ἄν gives a reverential tone to the question: ἂν εὐξαίμην refers to such propitiatory words of invocation as were uttered on approaching a shrine. The description has left the Theban stranger in doubt as to the particular deities meant. He might think of other 'Daughters of Darkness,'—as of the Κῆρες (Hes. *Theog.* 217), or of the Μοῖραι,—whom the Eumenides of Aeschylus address as ματροκασιγνῆται, children of the same mother, Νύξ (*Eum.* 961).

42 πάνθ' ὁρώσας, because no crime escapes their ken: *Ai.* 835 f. τὰς ἀεί τε παρθένους | ἀεί θ' ὁρώσας πάντα τὰν βροτοῖς πάθη, | σεμνὰς Ἐρινῦς τανύποδας. Εὐμενίδας, the title of the Erinyes at Sicyon (Paus. 2. 11. 4), was not used by Aeschylus in his play of that name, unless with Herm. we assume that it was in a part of Athena's speech which has dropped out after v. 1028.

43 ἄλλα δ' ἀλλαχοῦ καλά, 'but other names please otherwhere.' Wunder and others quote Plut. *Them.* 27 ὦ ξένε, νόμοι διαφέρουσιν ἀνθρώπων· ἄλλα δ' ἄλλοις καλά. Near Megalopolis, on the road to Messene, there was a shrine of the Μανίαι: δοκεῖν δέ μοι, θεῶν τῶν Εὐμενίδων ἐστὶν ἐπίκλησις, Paus. 8. 34. 1. Aeschines gives the attributes of the Erinyes to the Ποιναί (τοὺς ἠσεβηκότας...ἐλαύνειν καὶ κολάζειν δᾳσὶν ἡμμέναις, or. 1 § 190). As at Athens they were Σεμναί, at Thebes they were Πότνιαι (cp. 84). Another name was Ἀραί (*Eum.* 417).

44 μὲν seems right. It implies a thought answering, rather than opposed, to ἵλεῳ δεξαίατο: *i.e.* 'gracious on their part may be the welcome, (as, on mine, the duty to remain is clear).' Cp. the μέν, without a following δέ, which lightly emphasises rather than contrasts: Xen. *Cyr.* 1. 4. 12 ἐγὼ μὲν οὐκ οἶδα (as others, perhaps, may). τὸν ἱκέτην, without με (which I should at least prefer to 'μὲ or ἐμὲ, if μὲν were changed), is more solemn: cp. 284 ἀλλ' ὥσπερ ἔλαβες τὸν ἱκέτην. δεξαίατο, Ionic: so 921 πυθοίατο, 945 δεξοίατο, *O. T.* 1274 ὀψοίατο, γνωσοίατο, where see n.

45 ὡς is clearly right. The ὥστ' of the MSS. would mean, *and so*' (*i.e.* since they are the Eumenides). It could not mean, 'and in that case,' *i.e.* 'if they prove kind.' ὡς is best taken as simply causal, 'for' (schol. ἐγὼ γὰρ οὐκ ἀναστήσομαι). γῆς: cp. 668 τᾶσδε χώρας | ...ἔπαυλα. ἂν ἐξέλθοιμ' : the optat.

with ἄν calmly expresses a fixed resolve: cp. *O. T.* 343 οὐκ ἄν πέρα φράσαιμι.

46 τί δ᾽ ἐστὶ τοῦτο; 'What means this?' (cp. τί δ᾽ ἔστι; 'what now?' *O. T.* 319 n.). 'What has this sudden resolve to do with the mention of the Eumenides?' ξυμφορᾶς ξύνθημ᾽ ἐμῆς. σύνθημα = something agreed upon (συντίθεμαι), as *e.g.* a military watchword (Her. 9. 98). Apollo had told Oedipus that, when he reached a shrine of the Σεμναί, then he should find rest (90). This was the σύνθημα, the sign preconcerted between them, which Oedipus has now recognised at Colonus (cp. ἔγνωκα, 96). He calls *his own prayer* (44 f.) the σύνθημα of his fate, because it embodies the two points of the σύνθημα,—'Here are the Eumenides,—here I stay.'

47 ἐμοί is indispensable, while οὐδὲ μέντοι would be weak. τοὐξανιστάναι: the art. with the infin. (whether subject or object) is esp. frequent in the dramatists, for the simple reason that it was often metrically convenient: 442: *Ai.* 114 τέρψις ἥδε σοι τὸ δρᾶν: *Ant.* 78 τὸ γὰρ | βίᾳ πολιτῶν δρᾶν ἔφυν ἀμήχανος.

48 δίχ᾽, like ἄνευ or χωρίς, 'without the sanction of': *Ai.* 768 καὶ δίχα | κείνων, 'e'en without the gods' help.' ἐνδείξω τί δρῶ, 'before I have indicated what I am doing': δρῶ is pres. indic.: Plat. *Gorg.* 488 Α ἱκανῶς μοι ἔνδειξαι τί ἐστι τοῦτο. Antiphon or. 6 § 37 ἐνδείξαι τῷ δικαστηρίῳ τὰ ἀδικήματα. The technical ἔνδειξις was an information laid against usurpers of public functions, or, in certain cases, against κακοῦργοι.

49 ξεῖνε: 33. μή μ᾽ ἀτιμάσῃς τούτων (genit. as after verbs of depriving) ἅ σε προστρέπω ('for which I sue to thee,' cp. *Ai.* 831 τοσαῦτά σε...προστρέπω) φράσαι (epexegetic infin.): deny me not the grace of the things for which I supplicate thee, that thou shouldst declare them. Cp. 35.

52 τίς ἔσθ᾽, *i.e.* 'what is it *called*?' In answer to the same query at v. 38 he had only learned that part of it was *sacred.* Cp. 26.

53 κἀγώ. We say:—'What *I* know, *you* also shall know' (ὅσ᾽ οἶδ᾽ ἐγώ, καὶ σὺ ἐπιστήσει). The Greeks could say:— 'What *I also* (=I on my part) know, you (also) shall know.' The second 'also' (καί) is absent here, since σύ is wanting. So Soph. *El.* 1146 οὔτε γάρ ποτε | μητρὸς σύ γ᾽ ἦσθα μᾶλλον ἢ κἀμοῦ φίλος. Cp. below, 870 (κἀμέ): *Ai.* 525: *Ant.* 927.

55 Ποσειδῶν. Paus. I. 30. 4 δείκνυται δὲ καὶ χῶρος καλούμενος Κολωνὸς Ἵππιος...καὶ βωμὸς Ποσειδῶνος Ἱππίου καὶ Ἀθηνᾶς Ἱππίας (1069), ἡρῷον δὲ Πειρίθου καὶ Θησέως (1593), Οἰδίποδός τε καὶ 'Αδράστου. This altar of Poseidon (ἐπιστάτης Κολωνοῦ 889) lies beyond the stage-scene (888). ἐν δ' (adv.), *sc.* ἐστίν : Prometheus did not belong to Colonus itself (as Poseidon did), but to the neighbouring Academy (see on 56): he is named as one of several divine presences in the vicinity. So ἐν δ' adds a new member to a group, *O. T.* 27 (where the same words ἐν δ' ὁ π. θεός refer to the plague), *Ai.* 675.

56 Προμηθεύς is a 'Titan' as son of the Titan Iapetus (Hes. *Theog.* 510). Welcker (*Griech. Götterl.* 2. 254) thinks that 'Titan,' instead of 'Titanid,' is used here only because, like the Titans, Prometheus rebelled against Zeus : but this seems strained. Cp. Cic. *Tusc.* 2. 10. 23 (from the Προμ. Λυόμενος of Aesch., Prometheus speaking) *Titanum suboles, socia nostri sanguinis, Generata caelo.* πυρφόρος (55), because represented with a torch in the right hand : Eur. *Phoen.* 1121 (on the shield of Tydeus) δεξιᾷ δὲ λαμπάδα | Τιτὰν Προμηθεὺς ἔφερεν ὡς πρήσων πόλιν. So πυρφόρος of Artemis (*O. T.* 207), and Capaneus (*Ant.* 135). Cp. Philostratus p. 602 (quoting the Athenian rhetorician Apollonius, circ. 225 A.D.) ἰὼ Προμηθεῦ δᾳδοῦχε καὶ πυρφόρε. His altar was in the Academy, just s. of Colonus, and this was the starting-point of the λαμπαδηφορία (to the Acropolis) at the three torch-festivals. Aesch. wrote both a Πρ. Πυρφόρος (the 1st play of his trilogy) and a satyric Πρ. Πυρκαεύς. τόπον by inverse attraction: Lys. or. 19 § 47 τὴν οὐσίαν ἣν κατέλιπε τῷ υἱεῖ οὐ πλείονος ἀξία ἐστίν κ.τ.λ.: cp. on *O. T.* 449.

57 ὁδός, 'threshold.' Somewhere near the grove of the Eumenides, but not within the stage-scene, was a spot called 'the threshold' of Hades,—a steeply-descending rift or cavern in the rock, at the mouth of which some brazen steps had been made (see on 1590 f.),—in accordance with the epic notion that Hades had a χάλκεος οὐδός (*Il.* 8. 15). From this *spot*, the immediately adjacent *region* (including the grove) was known as '*the brazen threshold*,'—χαλκόπους, borrowed from the literal χαλκᾶ βάθρα (1591), taking the general sense of 'adamantine.' As 'rooted on the nether rock' (γῆθεν ἐρρι-ζωμένον 1591), and also as linked by mystic sanctities with the Powers of the Under-world, this region of the 'brazen threshold' is called ἔρεισμ' 'Αθηνῶν, the *stay* of Athens : a phrase in which the idea of physical basis is joined to that of religious safe-guard. χαλκόπους, with feet of brass (*El.* 491 χ. 'Ερινύς, untiring), *i.e.* furnished with brazen steps.

59 The name—though κολωνός was so familiar a word—is traced in the usual Greek fashion to a hero Colonus, the ἐπώνυμος of the deme; and, to justify the epithet of the place, ἵππιος, he is called ἱππότης, horseman, or knight. In the roads about Colonus (ταῖσδε...ἀγυιαῖς 715) men first learned to use Poseidon's gift of the horse. With τόνδ' cp. 65 τοῦδε τοῦ θεοῦ. A statue of the hero Colonus on the stage would be an effective device for giving greater vividness to the local legend. The speaker could point to it with dramatic fitness, since Antigone is with her blind father.

60 ἀρχηγός, or ἀρχηγέτης, = esp. the founder of a family or clan, or (like κτίστης, οἰκιστής) of a city. ˙Bekker *Anecd.* 1. 449 ἀρχηγέται· ἡγεμόνες οἱ ἐπώνυμοι τῶν φυλῶν, quoting from the Γῆρας of Ar. παρὰ τοὺς ἀρχηγέτας, = by the statues of the ten ἐπώνυμοι ἥρωες of the Attic tribes. Arist. fr. 85 (Berl. ed. p. 1491 *a* 20) ἀρετὴ τοῦ γένους, καὶ εὐγενεῖς οἱ ἀπὸ τούτου τοῦ γένους, οὐκ ἐὰν ὁ πατὴρ εὐγενὴς ᾖ ἀλλ' ἐὰν ὁ ἀρχηγός.

61 And all (the δημόται, supplied κατὰ σύνεσιν from γύαι as = δῆμος) bear his name in common (κοινόν, in their capacity as Κολωνεῖς), being designated thereby. τοὔνομα, acc. of object to φέρουσι, is also cognate accus. to ὠνομασμένοι, which is added to mark the fixity of the deme-name.

62 σοι, ethic dat.: *El.* 761 τοιαῦτά σοι ταῦτ' ἐστίν, ὡς μὲν ἐν λόγῳ | ἀλγεινά, κ.τ.λ. λόγοις, 'story,' legend, generally, but esp. poetry, in which Colonus had not yet figured : the *Iliad* (23. 679) buries Oedipus at Thebes : cp. Paus. 1. 30. 4 (of the Oedipus-myth at Colonus) διάφορα μὲν καὶ ταῦτα τῇ Ὁμήρου ποιήσει.

63 τῇ ξυνουσίᾳ, 'by the dwelling with them': *i.e.* those who live at Colonus feel the charm of its holy places grow upon them. So the Thucydidean Pericles describes the Athenians as τὴν τῆς πόλεως δύναμιν καθ' ἡμέραν ἔργῳ θεωμένους καὶ ἐραστὰς γιγνομένους αὐτῆς (2. 43): cp. the schol. here, τῷ ἔργῳ καὶ τῇ πείρα πλέον τιμώμενα, οὐ τοῖς λόγοις.

64 ἡ γάρ κ.τ.λ. The eager interest of Oed. in this question depends on his knowledge, derived from the oracle, that he brought κέρδη τοῖς δεδεγμένοις (92).

65 καὶ κάρτα: cp. 301: Eur. *Hipp.* 89 ΘΕ. ἆρ' ἄν τί μου δέξαιο...; ΙΙΙ. καὶ κάρτα γ'. θεοῦ, the *hero* Colonus. Though the distinction had lost nothing of its clearness at this date (cp. Antiphon or. 1 § 27 οὔτε θεοὺς οὔθ' ἥρωας οὔτ' ἀνθρώπους δείσασα), θεός is sometimes the generic term for beings who receive divine honours: so Amphion and Zethus, the Theban heroes, are τὼ σιώ (Ar. *Ach.* 905), and Eupolis says ('Αστράτευτοι fr. 3) ἐν εὐσκίοις δρόμοισιν Ἀκαδήμου θεοῦ (the ἐπώνυμος of the 'Ακαδήμεια).

66 Elmsley reads ἄρχει τίς αὐτῶν; '*Who* is their king?' But Oed. rather asks, 'Have they a monarchy or a democracy?' It would be a prosaic objection that the question is hardly suited to the heroic age of πατρικαὶ βασιλεῖαι (Thuc. 1. 13). ἢ 'πὶ τῷ πλ. λόγος; 'or does *power of discussion* rest with the people?' πλήθει, the popular *assembly*, as oft. τὸ ὑμέτερον πλῆθος in the Attic orators. Thuc. 2. 40 (Pericles, on the Athenian democracy) οὐ τοὺς λόγους τοῖς ἔργοις βλάβην ἡγούμενοι. The schol. paraphrases, ἢ ἐν τῷ πλ. ἐστὶν ἡ ἰσχύς; and κράτος is a conject. instead of λόγος. Cp. Eur. *Cycl.* 119 τίνος κλύοντες; (under what king?) ἢ δεδήμευται κράτος;

67 ἐκ, of the head and fount of power: *El.* 264 κἀκ τῶνδ' ἄρχομαι: *Ant.* 63 ἀρχόμεσθ' ἐκ κρεισσόνων.

68 οὗτος...τίς (ὤν)...κρατεῖ; = τίς ἐστιν οὗτος ὃς κρατεῖ; Eur. *Hec.* 501 τίς οὗτος σῶμα τοὐμὸν οὐκ ἐᾷς | κεῖσθαι; λόγῳ τε καὶ σθένει, word (counsel) and might (of deeds): *Od.* 16. 242 (Odysseus) χεῖράς τ' αἰχμητὴν ἔμεναι καὶ ἐπίφρονα βουλήν. So Theseus is described by Thuc. 2. 15 as γενόμενος μετὰ τοῦ ξυνετοῦ καὶ δυνατός.

69 Sophocles conceives the union of the Attic communes (commemorated by the annual festival of the συνοίκια in August) as already accomplished by Theseus. Athens is the capital, all the people of Attica being reckoned as its citizens (ἀπάντων ἤδη ξυντελούντων ἐς αὐτήν, Thuc. 2. 15). Isocr. or. 10 § 18 speaks of Theseus as ὁ λεγόμενος μὲν Αἰγέως, γενόμενος δ' ἐκ Ποσειδῶνος. Aegeus, too, was said to have been king of Athens: see on 297; and was the eponymus of one of the ten Attic tribes (Αἰγηὶς φυλή, Andoc. or. 1 § 62).

70 ἆρ' ἄν τις...μόλοι; 'I wonder if any one would go?' = I wish that some one would go. *Il.* 10. 303 τίς κέν μοι τόδε ἔργον ὑποσχόμενος τελέσειε | δώρῳ ἔπι μεγάλῳ; Cp. infra 1100. αὐτῷ, poet. after the verb of motion: cp. *Il.* 12. 374 ἐπειγομένοισι δ' ἵκοντο: Aesch. *P. V.* 358 ἦλθεν αὐτῷ Ζηνὸς...βέλος: cp. *O. T.* 711. πομπός, one sent to bring a person, *O. T.* 288.

71 ὡς πρὸς τί, 'with what aim?' goes with both participles, μολεῖν with the second only. The Chorus are uncertain whether Oedipus has merely some *message* for Theseus, or wishes to bring him in person to the spot (as πομπός might imply). Our

pointing is better than ὡς πρὸς τί; λ. ἢ κ. μολεῖν. It is
strongly supported by two other places of Soph., in each of
which this formula stands, as here, at the beginning of a
question : *O. T.* 1174 OI. ὡς πρὸς τί χρείας; *Tr.* 1182 ΥΛ.
ὡς πρὸς τί πίστιν τήνδ' ἄγαν ἐπιστρέφεις; The simple πρὸς τί;
(also freq. in Soph.) = merely 'with reference to what?' while
ὡς πρὸς τί = 'with reference to what, in your conception or
intention (ὡς)?'

καταρτύσων μολεῖν, to prepare things (to work upon his mind,
directly or indirectly), so that he shall come : for the inf.
cp. 1286 : Plat. *Rep.* 562 C τὴν πολιτείαν...παρασκευάζει
τυραννίδος δεηθῆναι: and for καταρτύω of mental or moral
influence, Plut. *Mor.* 38 D ἄν...μὴ λόγοις χρηστοῖς ἀφαιρῶν
ἢ παρατρέπων καταρτύῃ τὴν φύσιν.

With L's μόλοι (ὡς being then final), we must render :
'That Theseus might come with what view (πρὸς τί),—to say
or to arrange (what)?' But : (*a*) the double μόλοι, at the end
of two successive verses, is intolerable. (*b*) The antithesis
between λέξων and καταρτύσων is hardly clear.

73 μὴ βλέποντος, conditional : 'if he has not sight.'

74 ὁρῶντα : the blind man's words will be instinct with
mental vision. (Cp. *O. T.* 747.) The insight is ascribed to
the words themselves, not to the speaker, as at 267 πεπονθότα
and δεδρακότα are epithets of the ἔργα, not of the agent.
Cp. Aesch. *Cho.* 854 φρέν'...ὠμματωμένην, *Suppl.* 467 ὠμμάτωσα
...σαφέστερον (λόγον). Milton, *Par. Lost* 3. 51 *So much the
rather thou, Celestial Light, Shine inward, and the mind through
all her powers Irradiate ; there plant eyes.*

75 οἶσθ'...ὡς...μὴ σφαλῇς; 'dost thou know (how to act),—
that thou mayst not come to harm?' A modification of the
phrase οἶσθ' ὡς ποίησον, in which ποίησον is abruptly substituted
for δεῖ σε ποιῆσαι. So, here, οἶσθα eagerly bespeaks attention
to the advice: see on *O. T.* 543.

76 ὡς ἰδόντι, 'to judge by looking.' ὡς has a limiting force
(as above, 20), *Ant.* 1161 ἦν ζηλωτός, ὡς ἐμοί (cp. on *O. T.* 763).
The dat. is that of the person *interested* by the perception,
as in ὡς μὲν συνελόντι εἰπεῖν (Xen. *An.* 3. 1 § 38), πολλὰ καὶ
ἄλλα παραλιπόντι (Thuc. 2. 51), συλλαμβάνοντι κατὰ τὸ ὀρθόν
(for one who rightly comprehends, Her. 7. 143). δαίμονος, *sortis*,
'fortune': so 1337, and oft.: boldly in fr. 587 μὴ σπεῖρε πολλοῖς
τὸν παρόντα δαίμονα, sow not the rumour of thy fate abroad.

78 μὴ κατ' ἄστυ is a comforting parenthesis. μὴ is due to the preceding imperative **μέν'**: but it has, in itself, almost the effect of a reassuring injunction, 'do not suppose that I mean.' We could not make oἱ ἐνθάδ' αὐτοῦ μὴ κατ' ἄστυ δημόται a single phrase, as = such of the folks as are not in the town, but here. **ἐνθάδ' αὐτοῦ**: Solon fr. 36. 11 τοὺς δ' ἐνθάδ' αὐτοῦ (in Attica, as opp. to abroad): so Eupolis fr. inc. 1. 4 τῶν ἐνθάδ' αὑτοῦ, etc. The word δημότης in *Ant.* 690, *Ai.* 1071 = a common man as opp. to a chief. Here, as in Euripides and Pindar (*Nem.* 7. 65), δημόται are the 'citizens' generally; though in this place the term is tinged with the notion of 'demesmen.'

80 εἰ χρή. All our MSS. have ἢ χρή: but, as between ἢ and εἰ in such a case, their authority is small: thus in Aesch. *Cho.* 994, where εἴτ' is certain, L gives the senseless ἦτ'. Epic usage allows ἠὲ (ἤ), answered by ἦε (ἦ), in an indirect question: *Il.* 2. 299 ὄφρα δαῶμεν | ἢ ἐτεὸν Κάλχας μαντεύεται, ἦε καὶ οὐκί. Attic usage prescribed εἰ (or εἴτε) as = '*whether*,' introducing the indirect question: the correlative '*or*' was usu. εἴτε, but sometimes, as here, ἤ. Three instances are indeed alleged from Aesch. (*P. V.* 780, *Cho.* 756, 890), but they are most doubtful.

81 ἡμῖν, ethic dat.: do we find ourselves alone? Cp. 62.

82 ἐν ἡσύχῳ, in quiet case, nearly = ἡσύχως, as 1675 ἐν πυμάτῳ = 'at the last': cp. *El.* 384 νῦν γὰρ ἐν καλῷ φρονεῖν.

83 μόνης πέλας, *sc.* οὔσης, a gen. absol. (we could not understand ὡς ὄντι πέλας ἐμοῦ μόνης): cp. 1588: *O. T.* 966 ὧν ὑφηγητῶν, *sc.* ὄντων.

84 πότνιαι, fitting in his mouth, as being esp. their name at Thebes (43). **δεινῶπες**: as looking sternly on sin (42). The face of the Avengers is still terrible to his inner eye. Sophocles nowhere portrays the lineaments of the Furies, as Aesch. does (*Eum.* 46—54), but he leaves on the mind an impression not less awful. εὖτε νῦν ἔκαμψα ἐπὶ ἕδρας (*gen. sing.*) ὑμῶν πρώτων (possess. gen.) τῆσδε γῆς (partitive gen.). ἐπί can be so placed since ὑμῶν is possessive gen. (= ὑμετέρας): cp. 126, *O. T.* 177 ἀκτὰν πρὸς ἑσπέρου θεοῦ. ἔκαμψα (*sc.* γόνυ) absol., as Eur. *Hec.* 1079 πᾶ βῶ, πᾶ στῶ, πᾶ κάμψω;

86 ἀγνώμονες, without γνώμη, hence, '*inconsiderate*'; and so, '*unfeeling*': *Tr.* 473 φρονοῦσαν θνητὰ κοὐκ ἀγνώμονα, *i.e.* not refusing to make allowance for human frailty. Xen. *Mem.* 2. 8. 5 ἀγνώμονι κριτῇ περιτυχεῖν, to fall in with a judge who makes no allowance. But ἀγνώς = 'undiscerning,' *O. T.* 677.

87 ἐξέχρη, since in Attic χράω contracts in η: Tyrtaeus 3. 3 Ἀπόλλων | χρυσοκόμης ἔχρη πίονος ἐξ ἀδύτου. τὰ πόλλ᾽, cp. *El.* 564 τὰ πολλὰ πνεύματ᾽, those frequent winds. The prophecy was made to Oedipus at Delphi when he went thither in his youth from Corinth, to ask whether he was indeed the son of Polybus, the Corinthian king, and Meropè. The god did not solve his doubt,—ἄλλα δ᾽ ἄθλια καὶ δεινὰ καὶ δύστηνα προΰφηνεν λέγων (*O. T.* 789). Eur. makes Oedipus, while still at Thebes, tell Antigone of a χρησμός which doomed him to die at ἱερὸς Κολωνός (*Phoen.* 1705 ff.). Far more poetical is the conception of Sophocles, that Apollo had appointed the *sign*, but not named the *place*.

88 ταύτην ἔλεξε παῦλαν, 'spoke of this as a rest.' The pronominal object of the verb, instead of being τοῦτο, is assimilated to the gender of the predicate παῦλαν: cp. Lysias or. 12 § 37 ταύτην γὰρ ἐσχάτην δίκην δυνάμεθα παρ᾽ αὐτῶν λαβεῖν, *this* (death) is the extreme penalty which we can exact from them. ἐν χρόνῳ μακρῷ: so *El.* 330: *Ant.* 422, *Ph.* 235, etc.: but 1648 χρόνῳ βραχεῖ (without ἐν). The general Attic rule was to use ἐν in such phrases as ἐν πολλῷ, μακρῷ, ὀλίγῳ, βραχεῖ χρόνῳ, ἐν ὀλίγαις ἡμέραις, ἐν πολλοῖς ἔτεσιν. The ἐν is rarely omitted except in the phrase ὑστέρῳ χρόνῳ which in prose usu. lacks ἐν: it takes it, however, below at 614 and *Tr.* 18.

89 ff. ἐλθόντι...βίον. Apollo said: αὔτη παῦλά σοι ἔσται, ἐλθόντι χώραν τερμίαν, ὅπου ἂν λάβῃς θ. σ. ἕδραν καὶ ξενόστασιν· ἐνταῦθα κάμψεις κ.τ.λ. In the orat. obliqua, if the tense of the principal verb were primary (as λέγει), ὅπου ἂν λάβῃς would become ὅπου ἂν λάβω: since it is secondary (ἔλεξε), we have ὅπου λάβοιμι. The part. ἐλθόντι expresses the first condition to be fulfilled before the παῦλα can be attained. ταύτην is explained by ἐνταῦθα κάμψειν. τερμίαν is proleptic: in whatever land he should find the Semnae, that land was to be for him τερμία, *i.e.* was to contain the goal of his wanderings. The word (elsewhere only in *Ant.* 1331) fits the metaphor of κάμψειν, from rounding the post in the δίαυλος (κάμψαι διαύλου θάτερον κῶλον πάλιν, Aesch. *Ag.* 344), since τέρμα oft. = νύσσα or καμπτήρ, the turning-post (*Il.* 23. 466 εὖ σχεθέειν περὶ τέρμα).

90 σεμνῶν: see on 43. ξενόστασιν, quarters for strangers. Pollux 9. 50 μέρη δὲ καὶ πόλεως καὶ πανδοκεῖον καὶ ξενὼν καὶ ὡς ἐν Ἰνάχῳ Σοφοκλέους (a satyric drama, fr. 253), πανδόκος ξενόστασις. The word occurs only in these two places of Soph.: so ἱππόστασις, βούστασις.

92 f. κέρδη μέν κ. τ. λ.: with advantages, through my having settled there (οἰκήσαντα), for my entertainers, and ruin for the Thebans. The conjecture οἰκίσαντα, 'having founded,' deserves to be carefully weighed. But the blessing to Attica turned on the *personal residence* of Oed. therein at the close of his life: cp. 626 κοῦποτ' Οἰδίπουν ἐρεῖς | ἀχρεῖον οἰκητῆρα δέξασθαι. This favours οἰκήσαντα. κέρδη and ἄτην, accusatives in appos. with the sentence ἐνταῦθα κάμψειν τὸν βίον: the participle οἰκήσαντα (in antithesis with δεδεγμένοις, cp. 13 ξένοι πρὸς ἀστῶν) serves to bring out the point on which the κέρδη and ἄτη depend. For the *plur.* acc. in appos. cp. Eur. *Alc.* 6 καί με θητεύειν πατήρ | ...τῶνδ' ἄποιν' ἠνάγκασεν. It is used here instead of κέρδος (cp. 579) because the 'blessings' were to be felt in many ways and on many occasions (see 1524 ff.).

93 τοῖς πέμψασιν is supplemented by ἀπήλασαν, since πέμπειν can be said of those who 'speed the parting guest': *Od.* 15. 74 χρὴ ξεῖνον παρεόντα φιλεῖν ἐθέλοντα δὲ πέμπειν.

94 παρηγγύα cannot mean 'pledged,' 'promised' (ἠγγυᾶτο), but only 'passed the watchword to me,' *i.e.* '*told* me, as *a sign*.' Xen. *Cyr.* 3. 3. 58 παρηγγύα ὁ Κῦρος σύνθημα, Ζεὺς σύμμαχος καὶ ἡγεμών, 'C. proceeded to pass the watchword, 'Zeus',' etc. παρεγγυάω regularly has this sense (which sometimes passes into that of 'exhorting,' 'encouraging' one another); or else that of 'putting something into another's hand,' 'entrusting' it to him.

95 ἢ σεισμόν, ἢ βροντήν τιν', some such sign as earthquake or thunder (τινά with both): thunder is the sign given at 1606. τιν' suggests that the god spoke merely of 'signs': Oed. interprets.

96 ἔγνωκα μέν is answered (101) by ἀλλά μοι...δότε. νυν, 'then,' seems better than νῦν, (though this could stand,) since the oracle is the basis of his belief. τήνδε τὴν ὁδὸν: acc. of extension in space (with ἐξήγαγε), denoting the ground traversed: cp. 1686: *Ph.* 1223 κέλευθον ἕρπεις.

97 οὐκ ἔσθ' ὅπως οὐ, which in grammatical order immediately follows ὡς, can be thus placed because felt as one adverbial expression = '*assuredly*': so often ἔστιν ὅτε (= 'sometimes'), οὐκ ἔστιν ᾗ ('in no wise'), οὐδεὶς ὅστις οὐ ('everybody'), etc.

πτερὸν: no outward sign had been given. The 'omen'

82   *Oedipus at Colonus*

was in the leading of his will. Cp. *Od.* 16. 282 (Odysseus
to his son, when planning to slay the suitors) ὁππότε κεν
πολύβουλος ἐνὶ φρεσὶ θήσει Ἀθήνη, | νεύσω μέν τοι ἐγὼ
κεφαλῇ: which anticipates such a πτερόν, or divine suggestion,
as is meant here. For πτερόν as = οἰωνός or ὄρνις (= πάνθ'
ὅσαπερ περὶ μαντείας διακρίνει Ar. *Av.* 719) Schneidewin
cp. Callimachus *Lav. Pall.* 124 ποίων (ὀρνίθων) οὐκ ἀγαθαὶ
πτέρυγες, Propert. 4. 10. 11 *felicibus edita pennis* (with happy
auguries).

98 ἐξήγαγ', *i.e.* 'to my goal (ἐξ-),' not, 'aside from the
highway.' Plat. *Phaedo* 66 B κινδυνεύει τοι ὥσπερ ἀτραπός τις
ἐκφέρειν ἡμᾶς (and so Soph. *Ai.* 7). οὐ γὰρ ἄν, 'for *else*,' etc.,
the suppressed protasis being εἰ μὴ ἐξήγαγε: so 125.

100 νήφων ἀοίνοις: the austere wanderer lights first on the
shrine of the austere goddesses (ὡς αἰεὶ τὸν ὅμοιον ἄγει θεὸς ὡς
τὸν ὅμοιον); νήφων implying the thought that he has been in a
manner consecrated to suffering. Water, and honey mixed
with milk (μελίκρατον), formed the χοὰς ἀοίνους, νηφάλια μειλίγ-
ματα (Aesch. *Eum.* 107) of the Furies.

101 ἀσκέπαρνον (cp. 19), not shaped by the adze (σκέ-
παρνος, fr. 724): so Soph. is quoted by Hesychius (1. 90) for
ἀδρέπανον (from δρεπάνη).

102 βίου...πέρασιν...καὶ καταστροφήν τινα, some ending of
life,—some close to my course. βίου πέρασις is τὸ περᾶν
τὸν βίον, a passing through life to its end, a concluding of it
(Eur. *Andr.* 101 τὴν τελευταίαν...περάσας ἡμέραν): καταστροφή
adds the notion of a career which approaches its goal. Thuc.
2. 42 (of those who had fallen in the war) δοκεῖ δέ μοι δηλοῦν
ἀνδρὸς ἀρετὴν πρώτη τε μηνύουσα καὶ τελευταία βεβαιοῦσα ἡ νῦν
τῶνδε καταστροφή (the closing scene of their lives). Polyb. 5. 54
τὴν αὐτὴν ἐποιήσαντο τοῦ βίου καταστροφήν.—ὀμφὰς: see on
550.

104 μειόνως ἔχειν = μείων εἶναι. This euphemistic mode of
expression with the comparative adverb is often found where
censure or disparagement is to be conveyed less bluntly.
Plato *Apol.* 34 C τάχ' ἂν οὖν τις ταῦτα ἐννοήσας αὐθαδέστερον
ἂν πρός με σχοίη, = αὐθαδέστερος ἂν εἴη: *Legg.* 932 A ἐάν τις
ἐν τῇδε τῇ πόλει γονέων ἀμελέστερον ἔχῃ τοῦ δέοντος = ἀμε-
λέστερος ᾖ. Oedipus says to the Furies: 'Grant me rest,
unless haply (τι, adv., as *O. T.* 969, here with bitter irony)
I seem *to be beneath such grace*,—I, who have suffered so much
and so long.' μειόνως ἔχειν means here to be μείων in the sense

Notes

of '*too insignificant,*' '*of too little account,*' in respect of suffering: *i.e.*, one who *has not yet suffered enough.*

105 μόχθοις λατρεύων : Aesch. *Ag.* 217 ἀνάγκας ἔδυ λέπαδνον : Eur. *Suppl.* 877 χρημάτων ζευχθεὶς ὑπο (in bonds to lucre).

106 ἵτ', in urgent petition, as 248, *O. T.* 46 ἴθ'...ἀνόρθωσον : 1413 ἴτ', ἀξιώσατ'. γλυκεῖαι, with blandishment, as *Tr.* 1040 ὦ γλυκὺς Ἀιδας. No other poet of the class. age (I think) ventures on this use of γλυκύς in addressing deities, which, indeed, is somewhat apt to recall the Aristophanic ὦ γλύκων, ὦ γλυκύτατε. Σκότου : on 40.

107 Παλλάδος, possessive gen. with καλούμεναι : 'Athens, thou that art said to belong to Pallas, of all cities most honoured': Eur. *Ion* 8 ἔστιν γὰρ οὐκ ἄσημος Ἑλλήνων πόλις, | τῆς χρυσολόγχου Παλλάδος κεκλημένη : *ib.* 311 Λοξίου κεκλήμεθα, I am called (the servant) of Apollo.

110 εἴδωλον (cp. 393), a mere wraith, with the semblance and speech of the man, ἀτὰρ φρένες οὐκ ἔνι πάμπαν, but the living heart is not therein (as Achilles says of the εἴδωλον of Patroclus, *Il.* 23. 104). So the wraith of Helen is εἴδωλον ἔμπνουν, Eur. *Helen.* 34.

οὐ γὰρ δὴ τό γ'. After τόδ' in 109 a second τόδ' here would be very awkward : and the article, if not necessary, is at least desirable. οὐ γὰρ δή is esp. used in rejecting an alternative to something already stated, and γε is often added with the force of 'at any rate'; below, 265 οὐ γὰρ δὴ τό γε | σῶμ' : *El.* 1020 οὐ γὰρ δὴ κενόν γ' ἀφήσομεν : *Ph.* 246 οὐ γὰρ δὴ σύ γ' ἦσθα ναυβάτης. Without γε *O. T.* 576, *Ant.* 46.

111 The grove being close to the village, the man of the place has done his errand quickly, and the elders of Colonus are already heard approaching (cp. 78).

112 χρόνῳ, dat. of circumstance with παλαιοί, old in respect of their years, *i.e.* 'aged.' The phrase (an unusual one) does not seem to be intensive, as Campbell makes it, 'very old,' but simply pleonastic, as in *Od.* 13. 432 παλαιοῦ...γέροντος, an old man of many years. ἐπίσκοποι here = *speculatores*, explorers, but in *Ant.* 217 overseers, watchers, and *ib.* 1148 or Dionysus, 'master' (of mystic rites).

113 f. καὶ σύ μ' ἐξ ὁδοῦ πόδα κρύψον all MSS. This is usu. explained by partitive apposition (σχῆμα καθ' ὅλον καὶ μέρος), the part πόδα being in appos. with the whole με: 'Hide me, —that is, my foot,—apart from the road.' The construction is common, but the question here is as to the sense. ἄγαγέ

6—2

με πόδα could bear such a sense : but κρύψον με πόδα cannot
do so, unless we grant that κρύπτειν πόδα could mean 'to *guide*
another's steps *to* a hiding-place.' I regard as probable
H. Keck's ἐκποδὼν ὁδοῦ. Cp. Eur. *Phoen.* 978 χθονὸς τῆσδ'
ἐκποδών. No substitute for πόδα is satisfactory: among the
conjectures are κόρα, μέ ποι, πάλιν, πέλας, πέρα, πρόσω, τάχα,
τόδε, τόδ' ἄψ.

114 f. τῶνδ'...ἐκμάθω τίνας λόγους ἐροῦσιν, 'learn *in regard to
these men* what they will say'; not, learn *from* them (by
speaking to them), since his present object is only to overhear
them, unseen. This gen. of connection often goes thus with
verbs of perceiving, etc.: Xen. *Mem.* 3. 6. 17 ἐνθυμοῦ τῶν
εἰδότων ὅτι λέγουσι. Plat. *Gorg.* 517 c ἀγνοοῦντες ἀλλήλων ὅτι
λέγομεν. Distinguish 593 ὅταν μάθῃς μου νουθέτει, when thou
hast learnt *from* me.

115 ἐν γὰρ τῷ μαθεῖν : *i.e.* 'for in learning (how the people
of the place are disposed) consists the caution of (proper for)
all that we are doing': we are poor strangers, who must be
prepared to shape our course according to the mood of the
ἀστοί (13). The spondee can stand in the 5th place, since ἐν,
to which γάρ adheres, itself coheres closely with τῷ μαθεῖν: so
El. 376 εἰ γὰρ τῶνδέ μοι (where, as here, Elms. proposed δὲ
instead of γὰρ): *ib.* 409 τῷ τοῦτ' ἤρεσεν; cp. 664.

116 τῶν ποιουμένων: so *El.* 84 (just before an exit, as here):
ταῦτα γὰρ φέρει | νίκην τ' ἐφ' ἡμῖν καὶ κράτος .τῶν δρωμένων.
The γνώμη here, though perhaps meant to mark the caution
taught by bitter experience (cp. 273), has the tone of Periclean
Athens: cp. Thuc. 2. 40 (it is a mischief) μὴ προδιδαχθῆναι...
λόγῳ πρότερον ἢ ἐπὶ ἃ δεῖ ἔργῳ ἐλθεῖν.

117—253 *Parodos, passing at v.* 138 *into a lyric dialogue*
(κομμός) *between the Chorus and Oedipus* (*see preliminary n.
on the structure of the play*).

The framework is as follows. (1) *1st strophe,* 117 *τίς ἄρ'
ἦν to* 137 *ναίει,* = *1st antistrophe,* 149 *ἐή to* 169 *ἀπερύκου.
Metre. Logaoedic. The 2nd Glyconic is the main theme.*
(2) *2nd strophe,* 176 *οὗτοι to* 187 *σέβεσθαι,* = *2nd antistr.,*
192 *αὐτοῦ to* 206 *ἐκπυθοίμαν: logaoedic. Between the 1st strophe
and the 1st antistrophe is interposed an anapaestic 'system'*
(σύστημα) *of* 11 *verses,* 138 *ὅδ' ἐκεῖνος to* 148 *ὥρμουν* (*Oed.
and Ch.*). *Between the 1st antistr. and the 2nd strophe, a
2nd system of 6 verses,* 170 *θύγατερ to* 175 *μεταναστάς* (*Oed.
and Ant.*). *Between the 2nd strophe and the 2nd antistr., a*

3rd system of 4 *verses,* 188 ἄγε νυν *to* 191 πολεμῶμεν (*Oed.*). *From v.* 207 *to the end* (253), *the verses are without strophic correspondence* (ἀνομοιόστροφα). *A doubt exists as to the genuineness of vv.* 237—253 (ὦ ξένοι—δύναιτο), *and of the* 4 *trimeters which follow* (254—257): *see on* 237.

The Chorus induce Oed. to leave the grove by promising that no one shall remove him from Colonus by force (176), but, on learning who he is (222), revoke the promise, and command him to leave Attica. Antigone appeals to them.

117 ὅρα: cp. Aesch. *Eum.* 255 (the Furies hunting Orestes): ὅρα, ὅρα μάλ' αὖ λεῦσσέ τε πάντα, μὴ | λάθῃ φύγδα βὰς ματροφόνος ἀτίτας: cp. also the scene in which the Chorus of the *Ajax* are seeking the hero (867 πᾶ πᾶ | πᾶ γὰρ οὐκ ἔβαν ἐγώ;). τίς ἄρ' ἦν; imperf. of previous mention (not implying that he *is* not still trespassing): who was he of whom our informant spoke? Plat. *Crito* 47 D ὃ τῷ μὲν δικαίῳ βέλτιον ἐγίγνετο (is, *as we agreed*, made better), τῷ δὲ ἀδίκῳ ἀπώλλυτο. ναίει, of mere *situation* (not habitation), as *Il.* 2. 626 νήσων αἳ ναίουσι πέρην ἁλός: so *Ai.* 597 (of Salamis), and *Tr.* 99 (of a wanderer).

119 ἐκτόπιος instead of ἐκ τόπου: 716 ἁλία...πλάτα | θρώσκει: *O. T.* 1340 ἀπάγετ' ἐκτόπιον: 1411 θαλάσσιον | ἐκρίψατ': *Ant.* 785 φοιτᾷς δ' ὑπερπόντιος: *El.* 419 ἐφέστιον | πῆξαι.

120 ἀκορέστατος, 'most insatiate' (κόρος); hence, reckless of due limit,—shameless: cp. Eur. *Her.* 926 (deprecating ὕβρις), μήποτ' ἐμὸν φρόνημα | ψυχά τ' ἀκόρεστος εἴη. A positive ἀκορής is found in later Greek (Themistius, or. 90 D, 4th cent. A.D.): and as διακορής and κατακορής are classical (Plato, etc.), it may be a mere accident that ἀκορής has no earlier warrant. If referred to ἀκόρεστος, the superl. would be a poet. form like νέατος, μέσατος.

121 This verse is corrupt in the MSS., but two things seem clear: (1) there is no reason to suspect προσδέρκου: (2) the singular λεῦσσε must be restored, and placed *after* προσδέρκου. A long syllable is then wanted to complete the verse προσδέρκου, λεῦσσε. Hermann's νιν has been generally adopted. But λεῦσσέ νιν could only mean '*see* him': not, '*look for* him': λεύσσειν τινά could not stand for ζητεῖν τινα. In 135 ὅν is governed by γνῶναι, not by λεύσσων: and in Aesch. *Eum.* 255 ὅρα, ὅρα μάλ' αὖ, λεῦσσέ τε πάντα (*v. l.* παντᾶ), the sense is, 'scan all the ground.' Cp. *Ai.* 890 ('tis cruel,' the Chorus say, baffled in their quest) ἀμενηνὸν ἄνδρα μὴ λεύσσειν ὅπου.

86   Oedipus at Colonus

122 προσπεύθου (only here) ought to mean 'ask, or learn, *further*' (the reg. sense of προσπυνθάνεσθαι, προσερωτᾶν), but this is weak: here, it seems rather to mean, '*press* the inquiry,' inquire *assiduously*: cp. προσαιτεῖν, προσλιπαρεῖν. προσφθέγγου ('speak to him'), a *v. l.* for προσπεύθου, is plainly unsuitable.

123 πλανάτας, one who has wandered hither from beyond our borders, and so = ξένος: cp. on 3.

125 f. προσέβα γὰρ οὐκ ἄν: cp. 98: for the place of οὐκ, *Ant.* 96.

126 ἄλσος ἐς: see on 84.

127 ἀμαιμακετᾶν, 'with whom none may strive,' used by the poets of any violent force, divine or elemental, with which men cannot cope (as the Chimaera, *Il.* 6. 179; Artemis in her wrath, Pind. *Pyth.* 3. 33; the sea, *ib.* 1. 14; fire, *O. T.* 177), and probably *associated* with ἄμαχος. But the reduplication recalls μαι-μά-ω (cp. πορ-φύρ-ω, ποι-πνύ-ω),—the ἀ being intensive: and if we suppose a secondary development of √ΜΑ as μακ (Fennell on Pind. *P.* 1. 14), the proper sense of ἀμαιμάκετος would be '*very furious.*' The word being of epic coinage, it is conceivable that associations with μάχομαι may have influenced the formation as well as the usage.

130 ff. καὶ παραμειβόμεσθ' κ.τ.λ. In approaching or passing a shrine, it was usual to salute (προσκυνεῖν), and to invoke the deity audibly. But in passing the grove of the Eumenides the people of Colonus avoid looking towards it. No *sound*, no articulate word, escapes them. Their lips only *move* in sign of the prayer which the mind conceives. Cp. on 489. τὸ τᾶς εὐφάμου στόμα φροντίδος ἱέντες = 'moving the lips of (in) reverently-mute thought': ἱέναι (instead of οἴγειν, λύειν, διαίρειν) στόμα has been suggested by the phrases φωνὴν (or γλῶσσαν) ἱέναι: cp. fr. 844. 3 πολλὴν γλῶσσαν ἐκχέας μάτην. εὐφάμου (= *silent*) qualifying the metaphor as when discord is called πῦρ ἀνήφαιστον, Eur. *Or.* 621.

131 ἀφώνως. The ancient custom was to pray aloud, partly from a feeling that one ought not to make any prayer which might not be heard by all *mortals.* Persius 2. 6 *Haud cuivis promptum est murmurque humilesque susurros Tollere de templis et aperto vivere voto.*

133 After ἱέντες we may place either (1) a point,—making τὰ δὲ νῦν begin a new sentence: or (2) merely a comma,—taking ἃς (129) as still the object to ἄξονθ': (1) is best.

134 οὐδὲν (adverb) ἄζονθ', *sc.* αὐτάς: οὐδὲν ἄζονθ' as = 'reverencing *nothing*' would be at least unusual. The act. of ἄζομαι occurs only here; but that fact scarcely seems to warrant a change.

135 ὅν with γνῶναι only: λεύσσων absol.: see on 121.

137 μοι ethic dat. (62, 81): ναίει 117.

138 ἐκεῖνος, of whom ye were speaking: *Ant.* 384: Ar. *Ach.* 41 τοῦτ' ἐκεῖν' ·οὑγὼ 'λεγον: *Nub.* 1167 ὅδ' ἐκεῖνος ἀνήρ: *El.* 665. φωνῇ γὰρ ὁρῶ: (I appear to you), *for* in sound is my sight (*i.e.* I know your presence by your voices). To this announcement of his blindness a certain gentle pathos is added by τὸ φατιζόμ. (acc. in appos.), 'as they say of us the blind': alluding generally, perh., to the fig. use of ὁρᾶν, βλέπειν in ref. to mental sight (as *O. T.* 747, of the blind seer, δέδοικα μὴ βλέπων ὁ μάντις ᾖ), rather than to any special proverb. So Thuc. 7. 87 πανωλεθρίᾳ δή, τὸ λεγόμενον,... οὐδὲν ὅτι οὐκ ἀπώλετο, referring merely to the phrase.

141 ὁρᾶν, κλύειν, epexegetic inf., like χαλεπὸς συζῆν (Plat. *Polit.* 302 B). The cry which bursts from the Chorus merely utters their horror at first *seeing* and *hearing* the wretch who has dared so great an impiety;—they have not yet had time to scan the traces of misery which the blind man's form exhibits (cp. 286).

142 προσίδητ' ἄνομον, regard *as* lawless. The omission of ὡς is remarkable. Doederlein cp. Thuc. 2. 72 δέχεσθε δὲ ἀμφοτέρους φίλους, which is less bold: so, too, is *O. T.* 412 τυφλόν μ' ὠνείδισας. In modern Greek, however, (and the use doubtless goes far back,) θεωρεῖν regularly = 'to consider *as*' (without ὡς).

143 The hiatus allows Ζεῦ to be short. ἀλεξῆτορ: Ar. *Vesp* 161 Ἄπολλον ἀποτρόπαιε, τοῦ μαντεύματος.

144 f. οὐ πάνυ μοίρας πρώτης not wholly of the best fortune, εὐδαιμονίσαι (epexeg. inf., εἰς τὸ εὐδαιμονίσαι schol.) so that men should call him happy. The gen. is a poet. form of the possessive, 'belonging to' the best fortune (as to a category); cp. Pind. *Pyth.* 3. 60 οἵας εἰμὲν αἴσας, of what estate we (mortals) are: Plut. *Num.* 2 κρείττονος ἦν μοίρας.

πρώτης, 'best': *Ant.* 1347 τὸ φρονεῖν | εὐδαιμονίας πρῶτον ὑπάρχει: a sense associated with the idea of first prize (*Il.* 23. 275 τὰ πρῶτα λαβών), τὰ πρωτεῖα: cp. 1313; and so 1228 πολὺ δεύτερον. οὐ πάνυ oft. *means* 'not at all,' but prob as a result of the primary ironical sense, 'not altogether.'

88   *Oedipus at Colonus*

145 ἔφοροι: since the stranger had said κρινοῦσι (79).

146 δηλῶ δ', 'and I make it plain' (like σημεῖον δέ, τεκμήριον δέ), *i.e.*, and this is plain from my being guided by yonder maiden: cp. 1145: *O. T.* 1294 δείξει δὲ καὶ σοί (sc. Οἰδίπους): Ar. *Eccl.* 936 δείξει τάχ' αὐτός: Lys. or. 10 § 20 δηλώσει δέ· οἰχήσεται γὰρ ἀπιών. ἀλλοτρίοις ὄμμ. (instrumental dat.): *Ant.* 989 τοῖς τυφλοῖσι γὰρ | αὕτη κέλευθος ἐκ προηγητοῦ πέλει: Eur. *Phoen.* 834 ἡγοῦ πάροιθε, θύγατερ, ὡς τυφλῷ ποδὶ | ὀφθαλμὸς εἶ σύ.

148 Oedipus is indeed old and worn (110): but **μέγας** contrasts the man of mature age with the girl, his defenceless guide (752). Cp. *Od.* 2. 313 (Telemachus) ἐγὼ δ' ἔτι νήπιος ἦα· | νῦν δ', ὅτε δὴ μέγας εἰμί (*full-grown*).

σμικροῖς: for the allusive (masc.) plur., instead of σμικρᾷ, cp. *O. T.* 366 σὺν τοῖς φιλτάτοις (with Iocasta): for the sense, below, 957 ἐρημία με... | σμικρὸν τίθησι. The antithesis of *persons* suggests that **σμικροῖς** is masc. rather than neut.: so below 880: *Ai.* 158 σμικροί...μεγάλων χωρίς, 160 μετὰ γὰρ μεγάλων βαιὸς ἄριστ' ἂν | καὶ μέγας ὀρθοῖθ' ὑπὸ μικροτέρων. If **σμικροῖς** were neut., it could mean: (*a*) like the masc., weak *persons*: cp. 1 Cor. i. 27 τὰ μωρὰ τοῦ κόσμου ἐξελέξατο ὁ θεός, ἵνα καταισχύνῃ τοὺς σοφούς: (*b*) *fig.*, 'weak *things*,' frail supports. But the neut. plur. σμικρά in such antitheses usu. = 'lowly *fortunes*': Pind. *P.* 3. 107 σμικρὸς ἐν σμικροῖς, μέγας ἐν μεγάλοις | ἔσσομαι: Eur. *El.* 406 εἴπερ εἰσὶν εὐγενεῖς | οὐκ ἔν τε μικροῖς ἔν τε μὴ στέρξουσ' ὁμῶς;

ὥρμουν, 'have been now at anchor': usu. ἐπί τινος: Dem. *De Cor.* § 281 οὐκ ἐπὶ τῆς αὐτῆς (ἀγκύρας) ὁρμεῖ τοῖς πολλοῖς: but also ἐπί τινι: Plut. *Solon* 19 (he added the Βουλή to the Areopagus) οἰόμενος ἐπὶ δυσὶ βουλαῖς ὥσπερ ἀγκύραις ὁρμοῦσαν ἧττον ἐν σάλῳ τὴν πόλιν ἔσεσθαι. For the metaphor cp. Soph. fr. 619 ἀλλ' εἰσὶ μητρὶ παῖδες ἄγκυραι βίου. Eur. fr. 858 ἥδε μοι τροφός, | μήτηρ, ἀδελφή, δμωΐς, ἄγκυρα, στέγη. *Or.* 68 ὡς τά γ' ἄλλ' ἐπ' ἀσθενοῦς | ῥώμης ὀχούμεθ': *Med.* 770 ἐκ τοῦδ' ἀναπτόμεσθα πρυμνήτην κάλων.

149 ἀλαῶν ὀμμάτων. Oedipus has spoken of his own ill fortune as if it consisted primarily in his blindness. The Chorus then ask:—'Ah! and wast thou blind *from thy birth*? Thy life has been long, as well as unhappy, one may judge.' The gen. could depend on ἰή, as oft. on φεῦ, ὦ, οἴμοι, etc., but is better taken with φυτάλμιος, of which the sense (with αὐτῶν *understood*) would else be obscure.

φυτάλμ. = 'generator': *i.e.* didst thou bring them with thee into life? ἔφυσας τυφλὰ ὄμματα; = ἦσθα τυφλὸς ἐκ γενετῆς; *Ai.* 1077 κἂν σῶμα γεννήσῃ μέγα, though one *grow* a great body (= though his frame wax mighty).

152 μακραίων θ', ὅσ' ἐπεικάσαι, 'as far as one may conjecture,' 'to all seeming': for MSS. ὥς, which does not correspond with v. 120: cp. Thuc. 6. 25 ὅσα...ἤδη δοκεῖν αὐτῷ, 'so far as he could now judge.'

153 ('Thou hast *already* suffered;) but verily, within *my* power (ἐν γ' ἐμοί, = if I can help it), thou shalt not add these curses (to thy woes).' μάν strengthens the adversative force of ἀλλά (as in ἀλλὰ μήν, ἀλλ' οὐδὲ μήν): ἐν γ' ἐμοί = ἐν ἐμοί γε. Cp. 247 : *O. T.* 314 (n.): Xen. *Oec.* 7. 14 τίς ἡ ἐμὴ δύναμις; ἀλλ' ἐν σοὶ πάντα ἐστίν. The thought is like that of *Ant.* 556 ἀλλ' οὐκ ἐπ' ἀρρήτοις γε τοῖς ἐμοῖς λόγοις (sc. εἵλου κατθανεῖν). προσθήσει, make thine own, bring on thyself: Aesch. *Pers.* 531 μὴ καί τι πρὸς κακοῖσι προσθῆται κακόν : Eur. *Her.* 146 ἴδια προσθέσθαι κακά : *Andr.* 394 τί δέ με καὶ τεκεῖν ἐχρῆν | ἄχθος τ' ἐπ' ἄχθει τῷδε προσθέσθαι διπλοῦν ; The MSS. have προσθήσεις : but the active word would require either the reflexive pronoun or some dat. such as τοῖς σοῖς κακοῖς : and we cannot legitimately supply either.

154 περᾷς, absol. : 'thou art going too far' (into the grove): Oed., not reassured by their cry (141), has moved some steps back.

156 ff. ἀλλ' ἵνα...μὴ προπέσῃς is answered by μετάσταθ' 162. προπέσῃς ἐν νάπει, advance blindly in the grove, till he stumble (so to say) on its inmost mystery. Cp. Arist. *Eth.* 3. 7. 12 οἱ μὲν θρασεῖς προπετεῖς. Isocr. or. 5 § 90 διὰ τὴν Κύρου προπέτειαν, his precipitancy in rushing at his brother Artaxerxes. ἀφθέγκτῳ : see on 130 ff.

158 ff. οὐ κάθυδρος κρατὴρ συντρέχει ῥεύματι μειλιχίων ποτῶν, where the bowl filled with water is used along with the stream of *sweetened* drink-offering: *i.e.* where libations are poured, first, of *water alone*, and then of *water mingled with honey;* see on vv. 472—479. μειλιχίων π.: schol. γλυκέων ποτῶν, ὅ ἐστι, μέλιτος, οἷς μειλίσσουσι τὰς θεάς (see on 100). συντρέχει, 'is combined with': *Tr.* 295 πολλή 'στ' ἀνάγκη τῇδε (sc. τῇ πράξει) τοῦτο συντρέχειν, this joy of mine must needs attend on this good fortune of my husband. While κρατήρ points to the figurative use of συντρέχει, ῥεύματι *suggests* its literal sense.

161 τό, sc. τὸ προπεσεῖν, for τῶν of most MSS. which cannot be right. To be on one's guard against a thing is always φυλάσσομαί τι, never τινος. In Thuc. 4. 11 φυλασσομένους τῶν νεῶν μὴ ξυντρίψωσιν = acting cautiously *on account of* the ships (where Classen cp. χαλεπῶς φέρειν τινός, 1. 77): in Aesch. *P. V.* 390 τούτου φυλάσσου μήποτ' ἀχθεσθῇ κέαρ, join τούτου κέαρ. τόν (referring to κρατήρ) is less good; and τῷ ('wherefore') would be weak.

164 ἀρατύει, *arcet*, keeps (thee) off (from us), separates: Eur. *Phoen.* 1260 ἐρήτυσον τέκνα | δεινῆς ἀμίλλης. This is said to themselves rather than to Oed.: they are not sure that he has heard their cry, ἀπόβαθι.

166 οἴσεις λόγον πρὸς ἐμὰν λέσχαν = if you have anything to bring forward *to be discussed with us* (cp. *Ant.* 159 σύγκλητον | τήνδε γερόντων προὔθετο λέσχην), not, 'in answer to *our address*,' a sense which λέσχη never has. For οἴσεις cp. *Tr.* 122 ὧν ἐπιμεμφομένα σ' ἀδεῖα (αἰδοῖα Musgrave) μὲν ἀντία δ' οἴσω: for fut. indic. with εἰ of *immediate* purpose, with an imperat. in apodosis, Ar. *Av.* 759 αἶρε πλῆκτρον εἰ μαχεῖ.

167 ἀβάτων: see on 10.

168 ἵνα πᾶσι νόμος, where use suffers all (to speak): for the omission of ἐστί cp. Her. 1. 90 ἐπειρωτᾶν...εἰ ἀχαρίστοισι νόμος εἶναι τοῖς Ἑλληνικοῖσι θεοῖσι.

169 ἀπερύκου, ἀπέχου τοῦ φωνεῖν: schol. πρότερον δὲ μὴ διαλέγου, 'refrain from speech.'

170 ποῖ τις φροντίδος ἔλθῃ; Such phrases present *thought*, *speech*, or the *mind* itself, as a *region* in which the wanderer is bewildered; cp. 310: *El.* 922 οὐκ οἶσθ' ὅποι γῆς οὐδ' ὅποι γνώμης φέρει: 'thou knowest not whither or into what fancies thou art roaming': *ib.* 1174 ποῖ λόγων ... | ἔλθω; *ib.* 390 ποῦ ποτ' εἰ φρενῶν; *Tr.* 705 οὐκ ἔχω...ποῖ γνώμης πέσω.

ἔλθῃ, delib. subjunct., in 3*rd* pers., as Dem. *De Cor.* § 124 πότερόν σέ τις, Αἰσχίνη, τῆς πόλεως ἐχθρὸν ἢ ἐμὸν εἶναι φῇ; L has ἔλθοι, which might be defended as = 'whither can one *possibly* turn?'—a more despairing form of ἔλθῃ.

171 ἀστοῖς ἴσα χρὴ μελετᾶν, we must practise the same customs which they practise. Eur. *Bacch.* 890 οὐ | γὰρ κρεῖσσόν ποτε τῶν νόμων | γιγνώσκειν χρὴ καὶ μελετᾶν: we must never set our theory, or practice, above the laws.

172 Since κἀκούοντας suits both metre and sense, it seems more likely that this was the reading from which, by a scribe's mistake, **κοὐκ ἀκούοντας** arose, than that ἀκούοντας conceals some other participle (such as κατοκνοῦντας or ἀπιθοῦντας).

173 καὶ δή : see on 31.

174 μή...ἀδικηθῶ. The prohibitive subjunct. (esp. aor.) is freq. in the 1st pers. *plur.*, but the 1st pers. *sing.* is very rare : *Tr.* 802 μηδ' αὐτοῦ θάνω : *Il.* 1. 26 μή σε κιχείω : 21. 475 μή σευ ἀκούσω.

175 σοί (the coryphaeus) after ὦ ξεῖνοι (the Chorus) : cp. 208 ὦ ξένοι,...μή μ' ἀνέρῃ : 242 ff. ὦ ξένοι, οἰκτείρατ', followed by ὄμμα σόν. Cp. *O. T.* 1111 πρέσβεις, 1115 σύ.

176 τῶνδ' ἑδράνων, 'these seats,' the resting-place, generally, in front of the grove, rather than the particular rocky seat pointed out at 192 f. : cp. 233 f.

177 ἄξει : for οὐ μή with future in strong denials cp. *El.* 1052 οὔ σοι μή μεθέψομαί ποτε.

179 f. L's ἔτ' οὖν ἔτι προβῶ; metrically answers to οὕτως in 194. The choice seems to lie between ἔτ' οὖν ; and προβῶ ; The latter might easily have been added to explain the former : and ἔτ' οὖν is not too abrupt, since πρόσθιγέ νύν μου (173) has already marked the beginning of his forward movement. ἔτι βαῖνε seems better than ἐπίβαινε in the case of a blind man advancing *step by step*, and asking *at each step* whether he has come far enough. This is well expressed by ἔτ' οὖν ;—ἔτι βαῖνε. —ἔτι; For ἔτι before προβ., cp. *Ant.* 612 τὸ πρίν.

181 ff. After ἄγεις three verses have been lost (the 1st and 3rd for Ant., the 2nd for Oed.), answering to 197 πάτερ—199 ἅρμοσαι : and after ᾇ σ' ἄγω (183) a verse for Oed. answering to 202 ὤμοι...ἄτας.

182 μάν (a stronger μέν, 'verily') may here be simply hortative ('come!') as it oft. is with the imperat.: *Il.* 1. 302 εἰ δ' ἄγε μὴν πείρησαι : 5. 765 ἄγρει μάν : Aesch. *Suppl.* 1018 ἴτε μάν. If the lost words of Oed. uttered a complaint, then μάν may have had an adversative force, 'yet': but this is more oft. γε μήν than μήν alone : cp. 587. ὧδ', in this direction : see on *O. T.* 7.

ἀμαυρῷ κώλῳ = τυφλῷ ποδί (Eur. *Hec.* 1050) : cp. 1639 ἀμαυραῖς χερσίν. In Eur. *Herc. Fur.* 123, however, ποδὸς ἀμαυρὸν ἴχνος = merely 'my *feeble* steps' (for Amphitryon is not *blind*). That might be the meaning here too. But in choosing between the literal sense of ἀμαυρός, 'dim,' and the fig. sense, 'feeble,' we must be guided by the context of each passage ; and the context here favours the former. Cp. 1018.

92   *Oedipus at Colonus*

184 ff. τόλμα 'resolve,' 'incline thine heart.' ξεῖνος ἐπὶ ξένης: *Ph.* 135 τί χρή με, δέσποτ', ἐν ξένᾳ ξένον | στέγειν, ἢ τί λέγειν...;

185 ὦ τλάμων: the nom. can thus stand for the voc. even in direct address, as Eur. *Med.* 1133 μὴ σπέρχου, φίλος: but is sometimes rather a comment, as *ib.* 61 ὦ μῶρος, εἰ χρὴ δεσπότας εἰπεῖν τόδε. Cp. 753, 1471.

186 τέτροφεν ἄφιλον, holds in *settled* dislike:—the perfect tense marking how the sentiment which forbids impiety towards the Eumenides has interwoven itself with the life of the place. τρέφω τι ἄφιλον = to hold a thing (in one's thoughts) as unloveable: cp. ἐν ἐλπίσιν τρέφω τι (*Ant.* 897). For the perfect, denoting a *fixed* view, cp. Her. 3. 38 οὕτω νενομίκασι τὰ περὶ τοὺς νόμους (and so 7. 153, 8. 79). The perf. act. of τρέφω occurs in *Anthol.* Append. 111. 2 (Jacobs vol. 11. p. 795) ἄνδρας ἀγακλειτοὺς τέτροφε Κεκροπίη: in Polybius (12. 25 h in the later form τέτραφα), etc.: but in older Greek only in the Homeric use, as *Od.* 23. 237 περὶ χροῒ τέτροφεν ἅλμη (the brine has hardened on their flesh).

189 ff. ἄν with the optat. verbs, not with ἵνα: '(to a place) where I may speak on the one hand, and hear on the other': so Theocr. 25. 61 ἐγὼ δέ τοι ἡγεμονεύσω | ...ἵνα κεν τέτμοιμεν ἄνακτα (to a place where *we are likely to find* him): Xen. *Anab.* 3. 1. 40 οὐκ οἶδα ὅ τι ἄν τις χρήσαιτο αὐτοῖς (I know not what use one *could make* of them). τὸ μὲν...τὸ δέ are adverbial: cp. Xen. *Anab.* 4. 1. 14 τὰ μέν τι μαχόμενοι, τὰ δὲ καὶ ἀναπαυόμενοι. εἴποιμεν...ἀκούσαιμεν, *i.e.* 'arrive at a mutual understanding,'—a regular phrase: Thuc. 4. 22 ξυνέδρους δὲ σφίσιν ἐκέλευον ἑλέσθαι οἵτινες λέγοντες καὶ ἀκούοντες περὶ ἑκάστου ξυμβήσονται.

εὐσεβίας ἐπιβαίνοντες, *entering on piety*, placing ourselves within its pale: but this figurative sense is here tinged with the notion of 'entering on lawful *ground*' (schol. εὐσεβῶς πατοῦντες). For the fig. sense cp. *Od.* 23. 52 ὄφρα σφῶϊν εὐφροσύνης ἐπιβῆτον | ἀμφοτέρω φίλον ἦτορ, 'that ye may both *enter into* your heart's delight' (Butcher and Lang): *Ph.* 1463 δόξης οὔποτε τῆσδ' ἐπιβάντες, though we had never *entered on* that hope (dared to entertain it).

191 καὶ μὴ χρ. πολ.: *Ant.* 1106 ἀνάγκῃ δ' οὐχὶ δυσμαχητέον. Simonides fr. 5. 21 ἀνάγκᾳ δ' οὐδὲ θεοὶ μάχονται. Eur. fr. 709 χρεία διδάσκει, κἂν βραδύς τις ᾖ, σοφόν.

192 ff. αὐτοῦ. Oed. has now advanced to the verge of the grove. Here a low ledge of natural rock forms a sort of threshold, on which his feet are now set. αὐτοπέτρου βήματος, a 'step,' *i.e.* ledge, *of natural rock*, not shaped by man (as was the ordinary βῆμα or raised place for speakers, etc.), distinct, of course, from the ἄξεστος πέτρος of 19, which was *within* the grove. So αὐτόξυλος (of rough wood, *Ph.* 35), αὐτοπόρφυρος (of natural purple), αὐτόποκος (of simple wool), αὐτόπυρος (of unbolted wheaten flour), αὐτόκομος (with natural hair, Ar. *Ran.* 822), αὐτόροφοι πέτραι (rocks forming a natural roof, Oppian *Halieut.* 1. 22). The ἀντιπέτρου of the MSS. could mean:—(1) 'A ledge *like* rock'; 'a ledge of material firm as rock.' (2) 'A ledge *serving as* a rock.' (3) 'A seat of rock *fronting thee.*' This does not fit the data.

193 πόδα κλίνῃς (aor.) like πόδα τρέπειν (Eur. *Suppl.* 718), since, the seat being now at his side, he *turns away* from it if he moves forward.

195 f. ἦ ἑσθῶ; 'am I to sit down?' deliberative aor. subj. of ἕζομαι. This aor. of the simple verb occurs nowhere else: but ἐκαθέσθην is used in later Greek (as καθεσθέντα Paus. 3. 22. 1). Since ε is the radical vowel, it seems better to suppose a synizesis (ἦ ἑσθῶ;) than an aphaeresis (ἦ 'σθῶ;): the ἦ, though not necessary, is prob. genuine. I have left this questionable ἑσθῶ in the text, on the strength of ἐκαθέσθην: but the *v. l.* ἦ στῶ ('am I to halt?'), preferred by the schol. in L, seems more defensible than it has been thought by recent edd. The answer of the Chorus, no doubt, refers to sitting down. So, however, it could do after ἦ στῶ;

λέχριός γ'...ὀκλάσας, 'yes, moving sideways,'—the rocky seat being near his side—'(sit down), crouching low on the top of the rock.' ὀ-κλάζω (cp. ὀ-δάξ, from √δακ), from κλά-ω, to bend the hams in crouching down; Xen. *An.* 6. 1. 10 τὸ Περσικὸν ὠρχεῖτο,...καὶ ὤκλαζε καὶ ἐξανίστατο, 'he danced the Persian dance, sinking down and rising again by turns' (there was a dance called ὄκλασμα): so ὀκλαδίας = a folding campstool. βραχύς, 'low,' (as μέγας = 'tall,') because the seat is near the ground.

ἄκρου, on the outer edge of the rocky platform (βῆμα 192). λᾶος, gen. of λᾶας, as *Od.* 8. 192 λᾶος ὑπὸ ῥιπῆς. No part of λᾶας occurs in trag., except here and Eur. *Phoen.* 1157 acc. λᾶαν.

197 ff. ἐμὸν τόδ': *i.e.* the office of placing him in his seat

94 — Oedipus at Colonus

(cp. 21 κάθιζέ...με). The words ἐν ἡσυχαίᾳ...ἐμάν are said
as she helps him to sit down. He has to make one step
sideways (195) to the seat. Taking his arm, she says: 'Lean
on me, and join step to quiet step' (ἄρμοσαι aor. imper.
midd.): *i.e.* 'advance one foot to the resting-place, bring the
other up beside it, and then (supported by my arm) sit down.'
Cp. Eur. *Or.* 233 ἢ κἀπὶ γαίας ἁρμόσαι πόδας θέλεις; 'wouldst
thou set thy feet together (plant thy feet) on the ground?'
Pseudo-Simonides 182 ὅπᾳ ποδὸς ἴχνια πρᾶτον | ἁρμόσαμεν,
where we first planted our feet (on the battle-field,—there
we fell).

202 f. δύσφρονος, as the work of a mind clouded by the
gods: *Ant.* 1261 ἰὼ φρενῶν δυσφρόνων ἁμαρτήματα. The gen.
after the exclamation ὤμοι: cp. on 149.

203 τλάμων, see on 185. **χαλᾷς,** 'hast ease' (alluding to his
words betokening pain and exhaustion).

205 f. τίς ὁ πολ.: cp. on 68. **τίν' ἄν.. πατρίδ'.** For the
twofold question, cp. *Ph.* 220 τίνες ποτ' ἐς γῆν τήνδε κατ-
έσχετ';... | ποίας πάτρας ἂν ἢ γένους ὑμᾶς ποτε | τύχοιμ' ἂν
εἰπών; Eur. *Helen.* 86 ἀτὰρ τίς εἶ; πόθεν; τίν' ἐξαυδᾶν σε
χρή;

208 Oed. replies to their *second* question by ἀπόπτολις,
which is almost an exclamation;—'I have *no* πατρίς now':
he deprecates their *first* question (τίς ἄγει;) altogether. Cp.
Aesch. *Ag.* 1410 (the Argive elders to Clytaemnestra) ἀπόπολις
δ' ἔσει, | μῖσος ὄβριμον ἀστοῖς. Soph. has ἀπόπτολις in *O. T.*
1000 (dialogue) and *Tr.* 647 (lyr.). Cp. 1357.

210 μή, μή μ' ἀνέρῃ. As the verses from 207 onwards are
ἀνομοιόστροφα (see on 117), the strophic test is absent, but
μή, μή μ' is metrically preferable to μὴ μὴ μή μ' here. And,
after the preceding ἀλλὰ μή, a *threefold* iteration would rather
weaken than strengthen.

212 Wunder's correction of the MS. δεινὰ to αἰνὰ is required
by the Ionic measure (◡◡ : – ◡◡). **φύσις** = origin, birth: 270:
Tr. 379 (Iolè) λαμπρὰ...φύσιν, | πατρὸς μὲν οὖσα γένεσιν Εὐ-
ρύτου, κ.τ.λ.

214 γεγώνω, delib. perf. subjunct. from γέγωνα: whence,
too, the imper. γέγωνε, *Ph.* 238. Both these could, indeed,
be referred to a pres. γεγώνω, which is implied by other forms,
as ἐγέγωνε (*Il.* 14. 469): cp. Monro *Hom. Gr.* § 27. Poetry
recognised, in fact, three forms,—a perf. γέγωνα, a pres.

γεγώνω, and a pres. γεγωνέω (γεγωνεῖν, *Il.* 12. 337). Cp. ἄνωγα with impf. ἤνωγον.

214 f. τίνος εἶ σπέρματος; possessive gen., denoting the stock, country, etc., to which one *belongs*: cp. on 144: Plat. *Sympos.* 203 A πατρὸς τίνος ἐστὶ καὶ μητρός; *Meno* 94 D οἰκίας μεγάλης ἦν. πατρόθεν with εἶ: the Chorus, whose uneasy curiosity is now thoroughly roused, presses for an explicit answer, and first (as usual) for the *father's* name. Plat. *Legg.* 753 C εἰς πινάκιον γράψαντα τοὔνομα πατρόθεν καὶ φυλῆς καὶ δήμου. *Ai.* 547 ἐμὸς τὰ πατρόθεν.

216 τί πάθω...; 'what is to become of me?' *Tr.* 973 (Hyllus, in his wild grief for his father) τί πάθω; τί δὲ μήσομαι; οἴμοι.

217 ἐπ' ἔσχατα βαίνεις, 'thou art *coming to* the verge,' 'to the last extremity,' since, after the hint αἰνὰ φύσις (212), the full truth cannot long be withheld. Cp. fr. 658 (Orithyia was carried) ἐπ' ἔσχατα χθονός: *Ant.* 853 προβᾶσ' ἐπ' ἔσχατον θράσους: Her. 8. 52 ἐς τὸ ἔσχατον κακοῦ ἀπιγμένοι.

219 Hermann's μέλλετον (for the MS. μέλλετ') is fitting, since Oed. and Ant. have just been speaking together; and is clearly better than μέλλετέ γ' (Triclinius) or μέλλομεν (suggested by Elms.). The sing. τάχυνε rightly follows, since it is from Oed. alone that a reply is sought. μακρά, neut. *plur.* as adv.: *O. T.* 883 ὑπέροπτα (n.): Eur. *Or.* 152 χρόνια... πεσὼν...εὐνάζεται.

220 Λαΐου ἴστε τιν'; The word ἀπόγονον, seemingly a gloss, which follows τιν' in the MSS., is against the metre, which requires − ∪ ∪ − after τιν': it also injures the dramatic force. Each word is wrung from Oed.; the gen. Λαΐου tells all.

221 The family patronymic was taken from Labdacus (the father of Laïus), though the line was traced directly up to Cadmus, father of Polydorus and grandfather of Labdacus (*O. T.* 267; Her. 5. 59).

223 ὅσ' αἰδῶ, 'any words I speak,' is most simply taken as representing an accus., governed by δέος ἴσχετε μηδὲν as = μὴ δειμαίνετε (rather than a genitive depending on δέος): *Tr.* 996 οἵαν μ' ἄρ' ἔθου λώβαν: Dem. *De Fals. Legat.* § 81 ὅ γε δῆμος ὁ τῶν Φωκέων οὕτω κακῶς...διάκειται, ὥστε...τεθνάναι τῷ φόβῳ ...τοὺς Φιλίππου ξένους: Aesch. *Theb.* 289 μέριμναι ζωπυροῦσι τάρβος (= ποιοῦσί με ταρβεῖν) | τὸν ἀμφιτειχῆ λεών: Eur. *Ion* 572 τοῦτο κἄμ' ἔχει πόθος. Cp. below, 583, 1120. In such

instances the acc. might also, however, be taken as one of
'respect.'

224 The MSS. give the one word δύσμορος to Oed., as
uttered by him between the exclamations of the Chorus. It
thus marks his despair at their refusal to hear him. There
is dramatic force in the sentence of expulsion (226) being the
first *articulate* utterance of the Chorus after the disclosure
which has appalled them.

227 ποῖ καταθήσεις; fig. from the payment of a debt in
money. If you will not pay it here and now, 'to what place
will you bring the payment for it?' *i.e.* when, and in what
form, can your promise of a safe refuge (176 f.) be redeemed,
if I am driven from Colonus? ποῖ with a verb pregnantly used,
as in 476. Cp. 383. For καταθήσεις cp. Dem. *In Mid.* § 99
οὐ γάρ ἐστιν ὄφλημα ὅ τι χρὴ καταθέντα ἐπίτιμον γενέσθαι
τουτονί, there is no debt (to the Treasury), by paying which he
can recover the franchise.

228 f. οὐδενὶ μοιριδία τίσις ἔρχεται, to no one comes punishment from fate, ὧν (= τούτων ἅ) προπάθῃ, for things (caus. gen.)
which he has already suffered, τὸ τίνειν (acc.), in respect of his
requiting them, *i.e.* 'if he requites them.' συγγνωστόν ἐστιν
ἐὰν τίνῃ τις ἃ ἂν προπάθῃ. 'Thou didst deceive *us* by getting
our promise before telling thy name; we may requite thy
deceit by deeming our promise void.' τίνειν (with τὸ added,
see on 47) further explains the causal gen. ὧν: 'no one is
punished *for* deeds which have first been done to *him*—that
is, *for repaying* them to the aggressor.' Cp. 1203: Eur. *Or.* 109
τίνοι...τροφάς, *repay* care. ὧν for ὧν ἄν, as 395.

The ὧν of the MSS. is confirmed by other passages where,
instead of an *acc.* governed by the infin., we have a *gen.*
depending on another word, and then the infin. added epexe-
getically: *El.* 542 ἵμερον τέκνων | ...ἔσχε δαίσασθαι: Plat. *Crito*
52 B οὐδ᾽ ἐπιθυμία σε ἄλλης πόλεως οὐδ᾽ ἄλλων νόμων ἔλαβεν
εἰδέναι: *Rep.* 443 B ἀρχόμενοι τῆς πόλεως οἰκίζειν.

230 f. ἀπάτα δ᾽: guile on the one part (ἑτέρα), matching
itself against deeds of guile on the other (ἑτέραις), makes a
recompense of woe, not of grace (as in return for *good* deeds):
ἔχειν, epexeg. '(for the deceiver) to enjoy' (cp. *Il.* 1. 347 δῶκε
δ᾽ ἄγειν). ἀπάτα ἑτέρα, not another *kind* of guile, but another
instance of it, as *Ph.* 138 τέχνα (a king's skill) τέχνας ἑτέρας
προὔχει, excels skill *in another man.* παραβαλλ., as Eur. *I. T.*

1094 ἐγώ σοι παραβάλλομαι θρήνους, *vie with thee* in dirges: *Andr.* 290 παραβαλλόμεναι, abs., 'in rivalry.'

233 f. ἑδράνων with ἔκτοπος (cp. on 118), χθονὸς with ἄφορμος, which adds force to ἔκθορε: cp. *O. T.* 430 οὐκ εἰς ὄλεθρον; οὐχὶ θᾶσσον; οὐ πάλιν | ἄψορρος οἴκων τῶνδ' ἀποστραφεὶς ἄπει; ἄφορμος belongs to ἀφορμᾶν 'rushing from.'

235 f. χρέος...προσάψῃς (like κῦδος, τιμάς, αἰτίαν προσάπτειν), fix a debt or *obligation* on the city, *i.e.* make it liable to expiate a pollution. But χρέος = simply 'matter' in *O. T.* 155, n.

237 αἰδόφρονες: as ye have αἰδώς for the Eumenides, so have αἰδώς for the suppliant. Cp. Dem. or. 37 § 59 ἂν ἑλών τις ἀκουσίου φόνου...μετὰ ταῦτ' αἰδέσηται καὶ ἀφῇ (with ref. to the kinsman of a slain man *pardoning* the involuntary slayer). ἀλλ', 'nay,' opening the appeal: cp. *O. T.* 14. The second ἀλλ' in 241 = 'at least.'

This whole μέλος ἀπὸ σκηνῆς of Antigone (237—253), with the tetrastichon of the Chorus (254—257), was rejected by some of the ancient critics, acc. to the schol. on L: 'for they say it is better that Oed. should *forthwith* address his justification to them.' But, as the schol. rightly adds, it is natural and graceful that an appeal to pity (ἐλεεινολογία),—which the daughter makes,—should precede the father's appeal to reason (τὸ δικαιολογικόν). Though the text is doubtful in some points, the internal evidence cannot be said to afford any good ground for suspicion.

238 γεραὸν...ἐμὸν: the text of this verse is doubtful, and there is no strophic test, but it seems most likely that ἀλαὸν was an interpolation: see crit. n.

240 ἀκόντων, epithet of the agent, instead of that proper to the act (ἀκουσίων): 977: *O. T.* 1229 κακὰ ἑκόντα κοὐκ ἄκοντα. Cp. 74. 267. ἀΐοντες αὐδάν, 'perceiving,' *i.e.* 'being aware of,' 'having heard,' the report of his involuntary deeds. Cp. 792 κλύω Thuc. 6. 20 ὡς ἐγὼ ἀκοῇ αἰσθάνομαι

241 ἀλλ', 'at least,' cp. 1276: fr. 24 κἂν ἄλλο μηδέν, ἀλλὰ τοὐκείνης κάρα.

243 Hermann's τοὐμοῦ μόνου (for the MS. τοῦ μόνου) is metrically right, but μόνου can hardly be sound. It must mean 'for my father alone' (and not for my own sake). ΤΟΥΜΟΝΟΥ may have come from ΤΟΥΔΑΘΛΙΟΥ (Mekler), but τὸν ἄθλιον in 246 is against this (see, however, on 554). Perhaps τοῦδ' ἀμμόρου.

244 οὐκ ἀλαοῖς, as *his* are.

98 *Oedipus at Colonus*

προσορωμένα : for the midd. cp. *El.* 1059 ἐσορώμενοι. The midd. of the simple ὁράω is poet. only (*Ant.* 594): but the midd. of προοράω and περιοράω occurs in Attic prose.

245 ὥς τις κ.τ.λ.: as if I were a young kinswoman of your own, appealing to you, the eldest of my house, for protection. So Creon imagines his niece Antigone appealing to the sacred ties of kinship (*Ant.* 487 Ζηνὸς ἑρκείου: 658 ἐφυμνείτω Δία | ξύναιμον).

247 f. ἐν ὔμμι κείμεθα, 'we are *situated* in your power,' 'we are in your hands': ἐν ὔ., *penes vos*, cp. 392, 422, 1443, *O. T.* 314 (n.), Dem. *De Cor.* § 193 ἐν γὰρ τῷ θεῷ τοῦτο τὸ τέλος ἦν, οὐκ ἐν ἐμοί. The epic forms ὔμμες (nom.), ὔμμι (dat.), ὔμμε (acc.), freq. in Hom., belonged esp. to the Lesbian Aeolic : the acc. occurs in Aesch. *Eum.* 620 βουλῇ πιφαύσκω δ᾽ ὔμμ᾽ ἐπισπέσθαι πατρός: Soph. *Ant.* 846 ξυμμάρτυρας ὔμμ᾽ ἐπικτῶμαι. ἐν ὑμῖν γὰρ (MSS.), but the metre requires a dactyl. κείμεθα, of a critical situation, as *Tr.* 82 ἐν οὖν ῥοπῇ τοιᾷδε κειμένῳ, τέκνον, | οὐκ εἶ ξυνέρξων; (when his fate is thus trembling in the balance). Cp. 1510.

248 f. νεύσατε with acc. of the boon, as *Hom. Hymn.* 5. 445, Eur. *Alc.* 978 Ζεὺς ὅ τι νεύσῃ (more oft. ἐπι- or κατανεύειν). τὰν ἀδόκ. χ., the unlooked-for grace, *i.e.* for which, after your stern words (226), we can scarcely dare to hope,—but which, for that very reason, will be the more gracious.

250 πρός σ᾽: in supplications the poets oft. insert the enclitic σε between πρός and the gen. of that by which one adjures: 1333: *Tr.* 436 μή, πρός σε τοῦ κατ᾽ ἄκρον κ.τ.λ.: *Ph.* 468 πρός νύν σε πατρός, πρός τε μητρός, ὦ τέκνον, | πρός τ᾽ εἴ τί σοι κατ᾽ οἶκόν ἐστι προσφιλές, | ἱκέτης ἱκνοῦμαι. Join ὅ τι σοι φίλον ἐκ σέθεν, 'whatever, *sprung from thyself*, is dear to thee'; the next words repeat this thought, and add to it: 'yea, *by child*—or wife, or possession, or god.' Cp. 530 ἐξ ἐμοῦ.

251 ἢ χρέος ἢ θεός: a designed assonance (παρομοίωσις): cp. Isocr. or. 5 § 134 καὶ τὴν φήμην καὶ τὴν μνήμην: or. 4 § 45 ἀγῶνας...μὴ μόνον τάχους καὶ ῥώμης ἀλλὰ καὶ λόγου καὶ γνώμης. χρέος here = χρῆμα, 'thing,' any cherished possession (cp. *Il.* 23. 618 καί σοι τοῦτο, γέρον, κειμήλιον ἔστω), rather than 'business,' 'office.'

252 ἀθρῶν, though thou look closely. Plat. *Rep.* 577 C τὴν ὁμοιότητα ἀναμιμνησκόμενος τῆς τε πόλεως καὶ τοῦ ἀνδρὸς οὕτω καθ᾽ ἕκαστον ἐν μέρει ἀθρῶν τὰ παθήματα ἑκατέρου λέγε.

253 ἄγοι, *i.e.* draw on to evil: *Ant.* 623 ὅτῳ φρένας | θεὸς ἄγει πρὸς ἄταν. Oedipus was led on to his unwitting deeds by a god. Cp. fr. 615 οὐδ᾽ ἂν εἰς φύγοι | βροτῶν ποθ᾽, ᾧ καὶ Ζεὺς ἐφορμήσῃ κακά: so, too, *El.* 696. For the hiatus after ἄγοι, cp. *O. T.* 1202 f. καλεῖ | ἐμός.

254—667 *First ἐπεισόδιον. Oedipus appeals to the Chorus, who resolve that Theseus shall decide* (295). *Ismene arrives from Thebes* (324), *with news of the war between her two brothers, and presently goes to perform the prescribed rites in the grove of the Eumenides* (509). *After a κομμός* (510—548) *between Oedipus and the Chorus, Theseus enters, and assures Oedipus of protection.*

256 τὰ δ᾽ ἐκ θεῶν, euphemistic: cp. Aesch. *Pers.* 373 οὐ γὰρ τὸ μέλλον ἐκ θεῶν ἠπίστατο. For ἐκ cp. also *Ph.* 1316 τὰς...ἐκ θεῶν | τύχας: Eur. *Phoen.* 1763 τὰς ἐκ θεῶν ἀνάγκας. Similarly *I. A.* 1610 τὰ τῶν θεῶν (=their dispensations).

259 ῥεούσης, when it flows away, perishes, μάτην, 'vainly,' without result: *i.e.* issues in no corresponding deeds. *Tr.* 698 ῥεῖ πᾶν ἄδηλον: *El.* 1000 (our fortune) ἀπορρεῖ κἀπὶ μηδὲν ἔρχεται: *Ai.* 1267 χάρις διαρρεῖ. For μάτην cp. Aesch. *Ch.* 845 λόγοι | ...θνήσκοντες μάτην.

260 εἰ with ind. φασί (*siquidem dicunt*) introduces the actual case which has suggested the general question, τί δῆτα κ.τ.λ.: cp. *El.* 823 ποῦ ποτε κεραυνοὶ Διός, ἢ ποῦ φαέθων | Ἅλιος, εἰ ταῦτ᾽ ἐφορῶντες | κρύπτουσιν ἔκηλοι; γε oft. follows εἰ (and εἴπερ) in such cases, but here is better taken with τάς: it slightly emphasises the name of Athens.

θεοσεβεστάτας. Athens is pre-eminently (1) religious, (2) compassionate towards the oppressed. Pausanias (1. 17. 1) notices that at Athens alone there was an altar of Pity (Ἐλέου) indicating not only kindness to men, but piety to the gods.

261 μόνας, not strictly 'alone,' but 'more than all others': cp. *O. T.* 299 n.

τὸν κακούμενον ξένον. The two standard instances were subsequent, in mythical date, to the time of Oedipus. (1) Theseus, at the prayer of Adrastus king of Argos, compels Creon and his Thebans to permit the burial of the Argive warriors fallen in the war of Eteocles and Polynices. This is the subject of the *Supplices* of Euripides. (2) Demophon, the son of Theseus, protects the children of Hercules against the Argive Eurystheus. This is the subject of the *Heracleidae* of Euripides.

These two examples are cited in Her. 9. 27; in the spurious ἐπιτάφιος ascribed to Lysias (or. 2 §§ 4—16); and in that ascribed to Demosthenes (or. 60 §§ 7, 8). Isocrates quotes them in the *Panegyricus* § 52, in his *Encomium Helenae* § 31, and in his *Panathenaicus* § 168. They figure, too, in the Platonic *Menexenus* 244 E, with the comment that Athens might justly be accused of too great compassion, and too much zeal for 'the weaker cause.' Cp. Her. 8. 142, Andocides or. 3 § 28.

262 σώζειν, to give him a safe refuge: ἀρκεῖν, to come to his rescue (*El.* 322 ἐσθλός, ὥστ᾽ ἀρκεῖν φίλοις), if anyone seeks to take him thence by force. οἵας τε, *sc.* εἶναι, here synonymous with ἔχειν. After οἷός τε this ellipse of εἰμί is frequent.

263 κἄμοιγε ποῦ. The thought of the whole passage is,— τί δόξα μάτην ῥέουσα ὠφελεῖ, εἰ τὰς Ἀθήνας φασὶ (μὲν) θεοσ. εἶναι, ἐμοὶ δὲ ταῦτα μηδαμοῦ ἐστιν; Instead, however, of a clause ἐμοὶ δὲ...κ.τ.λ., thus depending on εἰ, a new sentence is opened by the direct question,—καὶ ἔμοιγε ποῦ ταῦτά ἐστιν;

καί, *prefixed* to interrogative words (as ποῦ, πῶς, ποῖος, τίς), makes the query an indignant comment on a preceding statement: *El.* 236: Dem. *De Fals. Legat.* § 232 καὶ τίς, ὦ ἄνδρες Ἀθηναῖοι, τοῦτ᾽ ἰδὼν τὸ παράδειγμα δίκαιον αὐτὸν παρασχεῖν ἐθελήσει;

οἵτινες, causal, as if παρ᾽ ὑμῖν had preceded: hence = ἐπεὶ ὑμεῖς. Cp. 427, 866; *Ai.* 457 τί χρὴ δρᾶν; ὅστις ἐμφανῶς θεοῖς | ἐχθαίρομαι. Also ὅς: cp. Thuc. 4. 26 ἀθυμίαν τε πλείστην ὁ χρόνος παρεῖχε παρὰ λόγον ἐπιγιγνόμενος, οὓς (= ὅτι αὐτοὺς) ᾤοντο ἡμερῶν ὀλίγων ἐκπολιορκήσειν, *since* they had thought to reduce them in a few days. I. 68 νῦν δὲ τί δεῖ μακρηγορεῖν, ὧν (= ἐπεὶ ἡμῶν) τοὺς μὲν δεδουλωμένους ὁρᾶτε...; Cp. *O. T.* 1228 n.: *Ph.* 1364.

264 As 276 shows, ἐξάραντες refers to his *first* seat, *in* the grove. They had induced him to leave that seat (174 ff.), on a pledge that no one should remove him from the resting-place outside of the grove. Yet now they command him to quit Attica (ἐλαύνετε: 226 ἔξω...βαίνετε χώρας). τάδε βάθρα denote, generally, the seats afforded by the natural rock in or near the grove: here he is thinking specially of the βάθρον ἀσκέπαρνον (101) within its precincts.

265 οὐ γὰρ δὴ τό γε: see on 110. For the art. τό, followed only by γε at the end of the v., with its noun σῶμα in the next v., cp. *Ant.* 67 τὸ γὰρ | ...πράσσειν, *ib.* 78 τὸ δὲ | ...δρᾶν: *Tr.* 92, 742.

Notes

266—270 ἐπεί...ἔξοιδα. I am 'a man more sinned against than sinning' (*Lear* 3. 2. 60),—as would appear, could I unfold to you *my relations with* my parents (τὰ μητρὸς καὶ πατρός), *on account of which* relations (the parricide and the incest—ὧν neuter) ye dread me. Of that I am sure. (For those relations began with their casting out their new-born son to perish. That first wrong led to the rest: hence it was that I knew not the face of my assailant in the pass, or of my bride at Thebes.)

267 πεπονθότ'...δεδρακότα. The agent's activities (τὰ ἔργα μου) here stand for the agent himself; and so, instead of τοῖς ἔργοις πεπονθώς εἰμι (cp. 873), we have τὰ ἔργα μου πεπονθότ' ἐστί. (Cp. 74, 1604.) So a particular activity of a person's mind is sometimes expressed by the active participle (neut.) of a verb to which the person himself would properly be subject: τὸ βουλόμενον, τὸ ὀργιζόμενον τῆς γνώμης (Thuc. 1. 90, 2. 59): τὸ δεδιός, τὸ θαρσοῦν αὐτοῦ (1. 36).

270—274 'Ye shrink from me as from a guilty man. And yet (καίτοι),—evil as were my *acts* (in themselves),—how have I shown an evil *disposition* (φύσιν), or incurred *moral* guilt? Before I struck my father, he had struck me (παθὼν ἀντέδρων: see *O. T.* 809). Even if I had been aware (φρονῶν) who he was, I might plead this in my defence: but, in fact, I did *not* know. Nor did I recognise my mother. *They*, on the other hand, had deliberately tried to kill their babe.'— Note that the clause ὥστ' εἰ φρονῶν...κακός, which could not apply to the incest, limits the reference of ἀντέδρων to the parricide; while ἱκόμην (273) refers to *both* stains.

271 He has two distinct pleas, (1) provocation, and (2) ignorance. These could have been expressed by ἀντέδρων (1) παθὼν μέν, (2) εἰδὼς δ' οὐδέν. But (2) is forestalled by the thought that, if he *had* known, (1) would have excused him. This *hypothesis* is then contrasted with the *fact* (273); and the fact *on his side* is next contrasted with the fact *on the other* (274). Hence παθὼν μέν has no clause really answering to it; for νῦν δ' answers to εἰ φρονῶν, and ὑφ' ὧν δ' to οὐδὲν εἰδώς. The impf. (ἀντέδρων) expresses the *situation* ('I was retaliating'): the aor. (273), an act accomplished at a definite moment.

273 ἱκόμην ἵν' ἱκόμην: cp. 336, 974; *O. T.* 1376 (n.) βλαστοῦσ' ὅπως ἔβλαστε.

274 ὑφ' ὧν δ' ἔπασχον (ὑπὸ τούτων) εἰδότων (predicate) ἀπωλλύμην, impf. of *attempted* act, cp. *O. T.* 1454 οἵ μ' ἀπωλλύτην.

102   *Oedipus at Colonus*

ἔπασχον: when the iron pin was driven through the babe's feet and he was exposed on Cithaeron, *O. T.* 718.

276 ὥσπερ με κἀνεστήσ.: *as ye caused me to leave my seat in the grove, so give me the safety which ye then promised*: see on 264: for καί, on 53. For ἀνιστάναι, of causing ἱκέται to leave sanctuary, cp. Thuc. 1. 126 (Cylon and his adherents) καθίζουσιν ἐπὶ τὸν βωμὸν ἱκέται τὸν ἐν τῇ ἀκροπόλει. ἀναστήσαντες δὲ αὐτοὺς οἱ τῶν Ἀθηναίων ἐπιτετραμμένοι,...ἐφ' ᾧ μηδὲν κακὸν ποιήσουσιν, ἀπαγαγόντες ἀπέκτειναν.

277 θεοὺς...τοὺς θ.: the art. with the repeated word, as 5, *Ph.* 992 θεοὺς προτείνων τοὺς θεοὺς ψευδεῖς τίθης.

278 μοίραις ποεῖσθε could not stand for ἐν μοίραις ποιεῖσθε. The prep. ἐν is indispensable. The gentlest remedy would be μοίρας (*as gen. sing.*), which two MSS. have. As ἐν οὐδενὶ λόγῳ ποιεῖσθαι (Her. 3. 50) and ἐν οὐδεμιᾷ μοίρᾳ ἄγειν (2. 172) are parallel phrases, so οὐδενὸς λόγου ποιεῖσθαι (1. 33) might suggest οὐδεμιᾶς μοίρας ποιεῖσθαι. For the two negatives cp. *El.* 336 καὶ μὴ δοκεῖν μὲν δρᾶν τι πημαίνειν δὲ μή, and *not* to seem active yet do *no* harm. It is hollow, Oed. says, to insist so strictly on the sanctity of a grove (θεοὺς τιμῶντες), and then to refuse the gods their μοῖρα, their due tribute of practical piety. You treat the gods as if they were not, when at their shrines you do ἀνόσια ἔργα (283) by violating your pledge to a suppliant.—ποεῖσθε. Numerous Attic inscriptions of the 5th and 4th cent. B.C. show that in this verb ι was regularly omitted before ει or η (ποεῖ, ποήσει), though never before ου, οι, or ω (ἐποίουν, ποιοίη, ποιῶν: Meisterhans, p. 27). In 584 and 652, as here, L keeps the ι: in the other five places it omits it. In 1517, where the quantity is indifferent, L has ποεῖν.

280 f. The place of του before φωτός (cp. *Ai.* 29 καί μοί τις ὀπτήρ, *Ph.* 519 μὴ νῦν μέν τις εὐχερὴς παρῇς) would be less awkward if φυγὴν and μήπω changed places: but the latter is reserved for the emphatic place at the beginning of the verse.

281 μήπω, not οὔπω, because of the imperat. ἡγεῖσθε (278). After verbs of *thinking*, the negative with the inf. is ordinarily οὐ, though μή is used in asseveration (as with ὄμνυμι), and sometimes in strong expressions of personal conviction: *O. T.* 1455 οἶδα μήτε μ' ἂν νόσον | μήτ' ἄλλο πέρσαι μηδέν, where see n. Thuc. 6. 102 *ad fin.* νομίσαντες μὴ ἄν...ἱκανοὶ γενέσθαι (and id. 4. 18). φωτὸς...βροτῶν, no wight *among mortals*, no one *in the world.* Cp. *Ai.* 1358 τοιοίδε μέντοι φῶτες ἔμπληκτοι βροτῶν:

Od. 17. 587 οὐ γάρ πού τινες ὧδε καταθνητῶν ἀνθρώπων | ἀνέρες ὑβρίζοντες: 23. 187 ἀνδρῶν δ' οὔ κέν τις ζωὸς βροτός.

282 ξὺν οἷς, σὺν τοῖς θεοῖς (schol.), 'with whose help,' since the gods strengthen men to refrain from evil, as well as to do good. μὴ κάλυπτε, as with a veil (κάλυμμα) of dishonour cast over her bright fame: cp. *Il.* 17. 591 τὸν δ' ἄχεος νεφέλη ἐκάλυψε μέλαινα. Thuc. 7. 69 ἀξιῶν...τὰς πατρικὰς ἀρετάς, ὧν ἐπιφανεῖς ἦσαν οἱ πρόγονοι, μὴ ἀφανίζειν. Plut. *Cor.* 31 ἡμαυρωμένος τῇ δόξῃ. τὰς εὐδαίμονας: Her. 8. 111 λέγοντες ὡς κατὰ λόγον ἦσαν ἄρα αἱ Ἀθῆναι μεγάλαι τε καὶ εὐδαίμονες.

284 ἔλαβες, since Oed. put himself into their hands, when he left sanctuary (174 f.). τὸν ἱκέτην, cp. 44, 487. ἐχέγγυον, having received your ἐγγύη, pledge, that I should not be wronged (176). Elsewhere ἐχέγγ. = 'having a good ἐγγύη to *give*,' 'trustworthy.' But Oed. could call himself ἐχέγγυος in *this* sense only as coming with credentials from Apollo; and that is not the point here. Cp. Her. 5. 71 ἀνιστᾶσι (τοὺς ἱκέτας)... οἱ πρυτάνιες,...ὑπεγγύους πλὴν θανάτου, under a pledge that they should stand their trial, but not suffer death.

285 ἐκφύλασσε, 'guard me till I am out of peril': only here, and twice in Eur. as = 'to watch *well*' (*Or.* 1259, *Ion* 741).

286 δυσπρόσοπτον, since the sightless orbs bore traces of his dreadful act (*O. T.* 1268): cp. 577. Continue με with ἀτιμάσῃς

287 f. ἱερός, as now formally the ἱκέτης of the Eumenides (44): εὐσεβής, since he has come thither κατ' ὀμφὰς τὰς Ἀπόλλωνος (102). φέρων | ὄνησιν: the first hint, to the Chorus, of the κέρδη mentioned in the prayer which only his daughter witnessed (92). Cp. 72.

288 f. ὁ κύριος...τις: the master—whoever he be. *O. T.* 107 τοὺς αὐτοέντας...τιμωρεῖν τινας the murderers—whoever they be. The art. implies that the person exists; the indef. pron., that his name is unknown.

290 f. τὰ δὲ μεταξὺ τούτου, in the space between (the present time) and that event (*sc.* τοῦ παρεῖναι αὐτόν): τὰ as in τὰ νῦν, τὸ αὐτίκα, τὸ ἐκ τοῦδε, etc. Dem. *De Cor.* § 26 τὸν μεταξὺ χρόνον...τῶν ὅρκων, the interval between (that time, and) the oaths: Ar. *Av.* 187 ἐν μέσῳ...ἀήρ ἐστι γῆς, between (heaven and) earth: *Ach.* 433 ἄνωθεν τῶν Θυεστείων ῥακῶν, | μεταξὺ τῶν Ἰνοῦς, between (them and) Ino's.

293 τἀπὸ σοῦ, coming from thee, urged on thy part: *Tr.* 844 τὰ δ' ἀπ' ἀλλόθρου | γνώμας μολόντ': *Ant.* 95 τὴν ἐξ ἐμοῦ δυσβουλίαν.

294 ἀνόμασται, 'expressed' (rather than 'mentioned'): cp. Dem. *De Cor.* § 35 οὐ γὰρ τὰ ῥήματα τὰς οἰκειότητας ἔφη βεβαιοῦν, μάλα σεμνῶς ὀνομάζων (expressing himself in very stately language). βραχέσι, not 'short,' but 'light,' 'trivial': Thuc. 1. 78 βουλεύεσθε οὖν βραδέως ὡς οὐ περὶ βραχέων.

295 ἄνακτας, *i.e.* Theseus: Aesch. *Cho.* 53 δεσποτῶν θανάτοισι (Agamemnon's death). Cp. 146, 814, 970. διειδέναι, here, *diiudicare*: usu. = *dignoscere;* Plat. *Phaedr* 262 A τὴν ὁμοιότητα...καὶ ἀνομοιότητα ἀκριβῶς διειδέναι. Cp. *O. T.* 394 διειπεῖν (αἴνιγμα), to solve it.

296 The ξένος΄ had spoken of Theseus as ὁ κατ' ἄστυ βασιλεύς (67), but had not said where he then was.

297 πατρῷον ἄστυ γῆς, not for πατρῴας γῆς ἄστυ, but simply 'his father's city in the land' (the gen. γῆς as 45), *i.e.* the city from which Aegeus (69) had swayed Attica. The poets can use πατρῷος as = πάτριος: but in the mouth of Oed. (*O. T.* 1450) πατρῷον ἄστυ means the city of Laïus

ἔχει = 'is in,' cp. 37.

σκοπὸς refers to the quality in which the man of Colonus had presented himself to Oed. (35), and so helps him at once to know who is meant. The word can mean 'messenger' only in the sense of 'one sent to obtain news'; but we need not change it, as Wecklein does, to πομπός.

298 κἀμέ: see on 53. ἔπεμψεν is better here than ἔπεμπεν, which could only mean, 'was our summoner.' στελῶν, to make him set forth, to fetch him: *O. T.* 860 πέμψον τινὰ στελοῦντα.

299—307 The ξένος must have been sent to Athens by the Chorus before they came to the grove (117), and could not, therefore, know the name of Oedipus (first disclosed at 222). He could only tell Theseus that there was a blind stranger at Colonus, who hinted at his own power to confer benefits (72), and who looked noble (76). Theseus, on entering (551), at once greets Oedipus by name, though he had never seen him before (68). He had divined the identity through a knowledge of the history (553)—*i.e.* he started from Athens on the strength of what the ξένος could tell. And on the way to Colonus (adds Theseus) he has been made *certain* of the fact (554)—*i.e.* he had heard the *name*. The dramatist meant this passage to account for the instant confidence of the recognition by Theseus.

300 Join αὐτὸν with ἐλθεῖν, not with ἕξειν: cp. *O. T.* 6 ἀγὼ δικαιῶν μὴ παρ' ἀγγέλων, τέκνα, | ἄλλων ἀκούειν αὐτὸς ὧδ' ἐλήλυθα.

301 καὶ κάρθ᾿ : cp. 65.

303 ff. κέλευθος: cp. 164. Some wayfarers, passing by
Colonus towards Athens, may have heard the prolonged tumult
of horror which greeted the name of Oedipus (222). As the
distance to the city is more than a mile, there will be many
chances for the news to be caught up from their lips, and
carried to Theseus.

304 πλανᾶσθαι: cp. Cic. *Rep.* I. 17 *speremus nostrum nomen
volitare et vagari latissime*. τῶν refers to ἔπη. ἀΐω and like
verbs can take a gen. either of the *person*, or (as 1187) of the
thing, heard: though the latter is more often in the acc. (as 240).

305 θάρσει, π.: the same words (in another context) 726.
πολύ, with strong rumour: *O.T.* 786 ὑφεῖρπε γὰρ πολύ. Aeschin.
or. 1 § 166 πολὺς μὲν γὰρ ὁ Φίλιππος ἔσται (we shall hear a great
deal of him), ἀναμιχθήσεται δὲ καὶ τὸ τοῦ παιδὸς ὄνομα Ἀλεξάνδρου.

306 f. κεὶ βραδὺς εὕδει, even if he is reposing (from affairs),
and is unwilling to move. εὕδω, in the *fig.* sense (*O. T.* 65),
is more often said of things (as εὕδει πόντος, etc., cp. 621)
than of men: but καθεύδω, at least, was often thus used:
Plut. *Pomp.* 15 ὥρα μέντοι σοι μὴ καθεύδειν ἀλλὰ προσέχειν τοῖς
πράγμασιν. βραδύς here = indisposed to exertion (as βραδύς is
joined with μαλακός in Plat. *Polit.* 307 A, and βραδύτης with
ἡσυχιότης in *Charm.* 160 B).

307 κλύων σοῦ (gen. of connection), hearing *about* thee,
El. 317 τοῦ κασιγνήτου τί φής; *Ph.* 439 ἀναξίου μὲν φωτὸς
ἐξερήσομαι: *Od.* 11. 174 εἰπὲ δέ μοι πατρός τε καὶ υἱέος. Cp. 355.

309 τίς γὰρ ἐσθλός. Oedipus has hinted to the Chorus that
he brings ὄνησιν ἀστοῖς τοῖσδε, but has reserved all explanation
of his meaning until Theseus shall arrive (288). His exclamation
here again touches on his secret; but, instead of interpreting
εὐτυχής, he turns it off, for the present, by a quickly-added
commonplace. 'Does not experience, indeed, teach us that
the benefactor of others is often his own?' The generous
man, though he acts from no calculation of self-interest, actually
serves himself by making zealous friends. Like thoughts are
found in many popular shapes elsewhere: *Il.* 13. 734 (of the
man with νόος ἐσθλός) καί τε πολέας ἐσάωσε, μάλιστά τέ κ᾿ αὐτὸς
ἀνέγνω, ' he saveth many, yea, and he himself best recognises
(the worth of wisdom)': Menander *Sentent.* 141 ἐσθλῷ γὰρ
ἀνδρί [γ᾿] ἐσθλὰ καὶ διδοῖ θεός: *ib.* 391 ξένοις ἐπαρκῶν τῶν ἴσων
τεύξῃ ποτέ.

310 τί λέξω, here prob. fut. ind. rather than aor. subj.

(though 315 τί φῶ;): cp. *O. T.* 1419 οἴμοι, τί δῆτα λέξομεν πρὸς τόνδ᾽ ἔπος; *Ph.* 1233 ὦ Ζεῦ, τί λέξεις; For fut. ind. combined with aor. subj., cp. Eur. *Ion* 758 εἴπωμεν ἢ σιγῶμεν ἢ τί δράσομεν; ποῖ φρενῶν: see on 170.

311 τί δ᾽ ἔστι; (cp. 46) marking surprise, as *O. T.* 319 (n.), 1144 etc.

312 f. Αἰτναίας...πώλου, not seen, of course, by the spectators: Ismene leaves it with her servant (334), and enters on foot (320). Sicily having a reputation both for its horses and its mules, some understand a *mule* here, as that animal (with an easy saddle, ἀστράβη) was much used for such journeys. But though πῶλος, *with a defining word* (as τῶν καμήλων or κύνεοι) could denote the young of animals other than the horse, πῶλος *alone* would always mean a young horse. Αἰτναίας implies some choice breed, as in Theophr. *Char.* xxi the μικροφιλότιμος buys Λακωνικὰς κύνας, Σικελικὰς περιστεράς, etc. In Ar. *Pax* 73 the Αἰτναῖος μέγιστος κάνθαρος is not a mere joke on the Etna breed of *horses*, but alludes to a species of beetle actually found there

313 κρατί: locative dat., 'on her head,' rather than dat. of interest with ἡλιοστ., 'for her head.' The ἡλιοστερής of the MSS. is a very strange word. It ought to mean 'deprived of the sun': cp. βιοστερής 747, ὀμματοστερής 1260. Even with an active sense, 'depriving of the sun,' it is awkward. ἡλιοσκεπής, ἡλιοστεγής, ἡλιοστεγεῖ have been proposed. Θεσσαλὶς κυνῆ, a form of the Thessalian πέτασος, a felt hat (somewhat like our 'wide-awake') with brim, worn esp. by travellers: cp. schol. on Ar. *Av.* 1203 (where Iris enters with a κυνῆ), κυνῆ δέ, ὅτι ἔχει περικεφαλαίαν τὸ πέτασον. In the *Inachus* Soph. made Iris wear an Ἀρκὰς κυνῆ (fr. 251).

314 πρόσωπα (acc. of respect)...νιν: Ar. *Lys.* 542 οὐδὲ γόνατ᾽ ἂν κόπος ἕλοι με.

316 Elms. cp. Eur. *I. T.* 577 ἆρ᾽ εἰσίν; ἆρ᾽ οὐκ εἰσί; τίς φράσειεν ἄν; πλανᾷ, misleads (me): the act. never = 'to wander.' Plat. *Prot.* 356 D αὕτη μὲν (*sc.* ἡ τοῦ φαινομένου δύναμις) ἡμᾶς ἐπλάνα. Hor. *Carm.* 3. 4. 5 *an me ludit amabilis Insania?*

317 τί φῶ, the delib. subj. in a dependent clause (τί might be ὅ τι): cp. *O. T.* 71 n.

319 f. φαιδρά, 'brightly,' neut. acc. plur. as adverb: cp. 1695. σαίνει με, greets me: cp. *Ant.* 1214 παιδός με σαίνει φθόγγος, 'greets mine ear.' [Eur.] *Rhes.* 55 σαίνει μ᾽ ἔννυχος φρυκτωρία, the beacon flashes on my sight.

321 The δῆλον of the MSS. can mean only 'manifest to me' (a very weak sense): for it could not bear the emphatic sense, 'in living presence' (as opp. to 'in my fancy'). Nor, again, can it well be taken as a parenthetic adv., ''tis clear' ('like *Ai.* 906 αὐτὸς πρὸς αὑτοῦ· δῆλον·). The conjecture ἀδελφὸν (cp. *Ant.* 1 ὦ κοινὸν αὐτάδελφον Ἰσμήνης κάρα) may be right.

324 f. Ismene has come from Thebes, where she has hitherto continued to live, in order to bring her father important tidings. The Thebans will shortly make an attempt to fix his home, not within, but near their borders. A war has already broken out between his sons.

There is no contrast in this play, as in the *Antigone*, between the spirit of the sisters. But the contrast between their circumstances indirectly exalts Antigone. She is wandering bare-footed, enduring heat and cold (349 f., 748), while Ismene has at least the ordinary comforts of life. ὦ δισσὰ πατρὸς καὶ κασιγν. κ.τ.λ. = ὦ πάτερ καὶ κασιγνήτη, δισσὰ ἐμοὶ ἥδιστα προσφωνήματα, two names most sweet for me to use.

326 δεύτερον, when I *have* found you. λύπῃ, causal dative.

327 ὁρᾶν, epexeg. inf.: so ἄτλητον...ὁρᾶν, *O. T.* 792. The form δύσμοιρος only here.

330 f. ὦ δυσάθλιαι τροφαί, wretched mode of *life* (338),— referring to the outward signs of suffering and destitution on which Creon dwells, 745 ff.: cp. 1250 ff. By his reply, ἢ τῆσδε κἀμοῦ; Oed. seems to hint that she separates herself from those whom she pities. Ismene with quick sensibility rejoins, δυσμόρου τ' ἐμοῦ τρίτης, the life is to be mine, too, in your company (for τρίτης cp. 8).

ὅμαιμον expresses the sisters' relation to *each other* only. In Soph. ὅμαιμος, ὁμαίμων always refer to brother or sister: 323, 979, 1275, 1405, 1772: *Ant.* 486, 512 f.: *El.* 12, 325, 531: *O. T.* 639.

332 σῇ (caus. dat.) = an objective gen. σοῦ: *O. T.* 969 τὠμῷ πόθῳ (n.).

333 πότερα, instead of πότερον, to avoid an anapaest: *Ai.* 265 n.—πόθοισι; (causal:) was it because thou wast fain to see me after so long a time? (or was there some further *special* cause?) Cp. *Ai.* 531 φόβοισί γ' αὐτὸν ἐξελυσάμην. λόγων αὐτάγγ. object. gen., αὐτὴ λόγους ἀγγέλλουσα. Aesch. *Ag.* 646 πραγμάτων εὐάγγελον.

334 ξὺν ᾧπερ...μόνῳ = ξὺν ⟨τούτῳ⟩ οἰκετῶν ὅνπερ εἶχον πιστὸν μόνον, the attraction of the relative extending to the predicative

108   *Oedipus at Colonus*

adj.: Dem. *De Cor.* § 298 οὔτε φόβος οὔτ' ἄλλο οὐδὲν ἐπῆρεν...
ὧν ἔκρινα δικαίων καὶ συμφερόντων τῇ πόλει οὐδὲν προδοῦναι.

335 πονεῖν, epexeg. infin. with ποῦ (εἰσι): so as to do their part. The infin. was thus used in *affirmative* clauses (esp. after ὅδε), as *Il.* 9. 688 εἰσὶ καὶ οἶδε τάδ' εἰπέμεν, οἵ μοι ἔποντο, here are these also *to tell the tale*, who went with me: Eur. *Hipp.* 294 γυναῖκες αἵδε συγκαθιστάναι νόσον, here are women *to help* in soothing thy trouble. So on the affirmative οἶδε εἰσὶ πονεῖν ('here they are *to serve*') is modelled the interrogative ποῦ εἰσι πονεῖν; 'where are they, that they may serve (as they are bound to do)?' So Eur. *Or.* 1473 ποῦ δῆτ' ἀμύνειν οἱ κατὰ στέγας Φρύγες;

336 οὗπέρ εἰσι: on 273. Schaerer's τἀν is better than the MS. δ' ἐν because the hint is made more impressive by the abruptness. τανῦν is adv.

337 Αἰγύπτῳ. Her. 2. 35 τὰ πολλὰ πάντα ἔμπαλιν τοῖσι ἄλλοισι ἀνθρώποισι ἐστήσαντο ἤθεά τε καὶ νόμους· ἐν τοῖσι αἱ μὲν γυναῖκες ἀγοράζουσι καὶ καπηλεύουσι, οἱ δὲ ἄνδρες κατ' οἴκους ἐόντες ὑφαίνουσι. Soph. certainly seems to have had this passage of his friend's work in view: else it would be strange that v. 341 should correspond so exactly with the special tasks ascribed to the *women* by Her. For other parallels cp. *El.* 62, Her. 4. 95; *Antig.* 905, Her. 3. 119.

338 φύσιν, 270: τροφάς, 330.

340 ἱστουργοῦντες: *Il.* 6. 490 (Hector to Andromache) ἀλλ' εἰς οἶκον ἰοῦσα τὰ σ' αὐτῆς ἔργα κόμιζε, | ἱστόν τ' ἠλακάτην τε, καὶ ἀμφιπόλοισι κέλευε | ἔργον ἐποίχεσθαι· πόλεμος δ' ἄνδρεσσι μελήσει.

341 τἀξω β. τροφεῖα, those means of supporting life which are sought outside of the home,—paraphrasing the ἀγοράζουσι καὶ καπηλεύουσι of Her. 2. 35. Elsewhere τροφεῖα always = 'reward for rearing' (Plat. *Rep.* 520 B, etc.).

342 σφῷν δ', dat. of interest, 'for you two' (Ant. and Ism.), in your case.

343 Not noticing Ismene's hint (336), Oedipus imagines his sons in repose at Thebes. He is soon to learn that one of them, an exile, is levying war against the other (374). οἰκουροῦσιν, not οἰκουρεῖτον, though a dual follows (345): *O. T.* 1511 f. εἰχέτην...εὔχεσθε. ὥστε = ὡς, an epic use freq. in Aesch. and Soph. παρθένοι. [Dem.] *In Neaer.* (or. 59) § 86 ἱκανὸν φόβον ταῖς γυναιξὶ παρασκευάζων τοῦ σωφρονεῖν καὶ μηδὲν ἁμαρτάνειν ἀλλὰ δικαίως οἰκουρεῖν.

344 f. τἀμὰ δυστήνου: *Ph.* 1126 τὰν ἐμὰν μελέου τροφάν: so *nostros vidisti flentis ocellos* Ov. *Her.* 5. 43. τἀμὰ...κακά: cognate acc. to ὑπερπονεῖτον (like πονεῖν πόνους), 'ye *bear* the woes of me hapless *for* me' (δυστήνου, placed between art. and noun, must not be taken with ὑπερπ.).

345 f. νέας τροφῆς ἔληξε, ceased to need the tender care which is given to children. νέα τροφή, here, 'the nurture (*not* 'growth') of the young': so *Ai.* 510 νέας | τροφῆς στερηθείς, bereft of the tendance which childhood needs. κατίσχυσεν, *became* strong (ingressive aor.), δέμας, 'in body' (acc. of respect).

348 γεροντἀγωγεῖ, on the analogy of παιδαγωγεῖν (so, in late Greek, ξεναγωγεῖν for ξεναγεῖν): Ar. *Eq.* 1098 ('I give myself to thee,' says Demus) γεροντἀγωγεῖν κἀναπαιδεύειν πάλιν.

349 νηλίπους, 'barefoot.' Apoll. Rhod. 3. 646 νήλιπος, οἰέανος (shoeless, with only a tunic): Theocr. 4. 56 εἰς ὄρος ὄκχ' ἔρπῃς, μὴ ἀνάλιπος ἔρχεο, Βάττε: where schol. ἤλιψ γὰρ τὸ ὑπόδημα. If the word really comes from an ἤλιψ (of which there is no other trace), then νηλίπους is less correct than νήλιπος, which Blomfield (Aesch. *P. V.* 248) wished to restore here. Eustathius 787. 52 derives νήλιπος from λίπος (fat, unguent), explaining it by αὐχμηρὸς καὶ ἀλιπής ('unkempt').

351 ἡγεῖται. The sentence γεροντἀγωγεῖ, πολλὰ μὲν... ἀλωμένη, πολλοῖσι δ' ὄμβρ. μοχθοῦσα, is so far regular and complete: then we should have expected ἡγουμένη, introducing a comment on the *whole* sentence. Instead, we have ἡγεῖται, which draws μοχθοῦσα to itself, and thus breaks the symmetry of the antithesis. The substitution of a finite verb for a second participial clause is freq. in Greek; but is usu. managed as if here we had πολλὰ μὲν...ἀλωμένη, πολλοῖς δ' ὄμβρ. μοχθεῖ, ἡγουμένη etc. Cp. *El.* 190 οἰκονομῶ θαλάμους πατρός, ὧδε μὲν | ἀεικεῖ σὺν στολᾷ, | κεναῖς δ' ἀμφίσταμαι τραπέζαις (instead of ἀμφισταμένη): *Ph.* 213 ff. οὐ μολπὰν...ἔχων,—...ἀλλὰ...βοᾷ (instead of βοῶν).—τὰ τῆς. There are only three other instances in Soph. of the art. so placed: *Ph.* 263, *Ant.* 409, *El.* 879. Close cohesion in thought and utterance is the excuse for this, as for the elision of δ', τ', ταῦτ' at the end of a verse.

352 εἰ...ἔχοι is an abstract statement of the condition:— '*Supposing* him to have tendance, she is content.' For optat. in protasis, with pres. ind. in apodosis, cp. Antiphanes fr. incert. 51 (Bothe p. 412) εἰ γὰρ ἀφέλοι τις τοῦ βίου τὰς ἡδονάς, | καταλείπετ' οὐδὲν ἕτερον ἢ τεθνηκέναι, '*supposing* one takes away... then nothing is left.' τροφήν, 'tendance': see on 345: cp. 1614.

354 μαντεῖα πάντα implies several oracles, given to the Thebans about Oedipus after he had left Thebes. There is no clue to their purport, and we need not ask: they are invented merely to create a pious office for Ismene. It would not have seemed well that she should have stayed at Thebes all these years without showing any active interest in his fate: on the other hand, the poetic legend required that Antigone should be the sole guide of his wanderings.

355 f. τοῦδε σώματος (without περί), gen. of connection, 'which had been given concerning me'; see on 307. φύλαξ δέ μοι κ.τ.λ., a general description of her part, subjoined to the special instance just given: 'and you constituted yourself a trusty watcher (at Thebes) in my interest, *when I was being driven* from the land,' *i.e.* from the moment when the decision to expel me had been taken, and the act was in contemplation μοι for μου seems necessary: and I suspect that μου first arose from inattention to the exact sense. A gen. after φύλαξ always denotes the object guarded: thus φ. μου ought to mean (not, 'a watcher in my interest,' but) 'a guardian of my person'; this, however, was Antigone's part (21): Ismene had never roamed with him.

358 στόλος, a journey with a purpose, a 'mission': *Ph.* 243 τίνι | στόλῳ προσέσχες; on what mission hast thou touched here?

360 μὴ οὐχὶ...φέρουσα explains the special sense of κενή. 'You have not come empty-handed—*i.e. without bringing* some terror for me.' μὴ οὐ properly stands with a partic. in a negative statement only when μή could stand with it in the corresponding affirmative statement: thus (*a*) affirmative: βραδὺς ἔρχει μὴ φέρων, you (always) come slowly, *if* you are not bringing: (*b*) negative: οὐ βραδὺς ἔρχει, μὴ οὐ φέρων, you never come slowly, *unless* you are bringing. Here μὴ οὐ is irregular, because the affirmative form would be ἥκεις οὐ (not μὴ) φέρουσα, a simple statement of fact; and so the negative should be οὐχ ἥκεις οὐ φέρουσα. But *bringing bad news* is felt here as a *condition* of her coming. Hence μὴ οὐ is used as if the sentence were *formally* conditional: οὐκ ἂν ἦλθες μὴ οὐ φέρουσα.

362 ζητοῦσα τὴν σὴν τροφήν, 'enquiring as to your *way of life*' is supplemented by ποῦ κατοικοίης, *i.e.* '*where* you were living.' Cp. Thuc. 4. 42 ἐπετήρουν τοὺς Ἀθηναίους οἳ κατασχήσουσιν.

365 ἀμφὶ...παίδοιν (dat.), 'about': oft. of encompassing tenderness, as 1614; here, of besetting trouble: unless we take it as merely = 'in the case of': cp. *Tr.* 727 ἀλλ' ἀμφὶ τοῖς σφαλεῖσι μὴ 'ξ ἑκουσίας | ὀργὴ πέπειρα.

367 ff. Eteocles and Polyneices were young boys at the fall of Oedipus, and their uncle Creon (brother of Iocasta) became regent (*O. T.* 1418). As the two brothers grew up, they agreed, at first, in wishing to resign the throne, of which they were joint heirs, to Creon, lest Thebes should be tainted by their own rule; but afterwards they fell to striving with each other for the sole power. ἔρως, desire (436), is a necessary and a certain correction. The MS. ἔρις would have to mean '*emulous* desire,' either (*a*) between the two brothers, if τε... μηδέ = '*both*'...'and not': or (*b*) between the brothers and (τε) Creon. Now, there is no objection to using ἐρίζω, ἔρις of *noble* rivalry. The fatal objection is that the idea of *rivalry* at all is here completely,—almost ludicrously,—out of place. Κρέοντί τε. The τε = 'both,' answering to μηδέ 'and not.' So τε is answered by οὐδέ (instead of οὔτε) Eur. *I. T.* 697, or by δέ Soph. *Ph.* 1312. So, too, οὔτε by δέ, Eur. *Suppl.* 223, etc. Such irregularity is natural when the second thought is opposed to the first. Paley's Κρέοντι δή is, however, highly probable. It would mean, 'to Creon in the next resort.'

368 ἐᾶσθαι, pass., as *Tr.* 329 ἥ δ' οὖν ἐάσθω: Thuc. 1. 142 (ἐασόμενοι): Eur. *I. A.* 331 (ἐάσομαι): *I. T.* 1344 (ἐώμενος): etc. The midd. of ἐάω is not classical. πόλιν: so in *Ant.* 776 ὅπως μίασμα πᾶσ' ὑπεκφύγῃ πόλις, it is implied that the whole State may be polluted by an act of the king.

369 λόγῳ, in the light of reason, with calm reflection (in contrast to the blind passion for power which afterwards seized them), a dat. of manner, cp. 381, *O. T.* 405 ὀργῇ λελέχθαι, *Ant.* 621 σοφίᾳ...ἔπος πέφανται. τὴν πάλαι...φθοράν, beginning with the curse called down on Laïus by Pelops, for robbing him of his son Chrysippus. Cp. *Ant.* 596 (of this Labdacid house) οὐδ' ἀπαλλάσσει γενεὰν γένος, ἀλλ' ἐρείπει | θεῶν τις etc.: one generation doth not free another, but some god brings ruin.

371 καλιτηρίου. The MS. reading, κἀξ ἀλιτηροῦ, is against metre, and gives a form of the adj. which occurs nowhere else. ἀλιτήριος, and the poet. ἀλιτρός, alone are found. Hesychius (1. 236), *s.v.* ἀλιτροσύνη, says that in the Αἰχμαλωτίδες Soph. used the subst. ἀλιτρία (Ar. *Ach.* 907 ὥσπερ πίθακον ἀλιτρίας πολλᾶς πλέων), whence Dindorf κἀξ ἀλιτρίας φρενός, 'from a sin of the mind.' The objection to this is the unexampled lengthening of the second syllable.

372. The dat. after εἰσῆλθε is strictly a dat. of the person interested, but was perh. influenced by the analogy of the dat. in παρέστη μοι, 'it *occurred* to me,' and the like; cp. *Tr.* 298 ἐμοὶ γὰρ οἶκτος...εἰσέβη: Her. 1. 86 (λέγεται) τῷ Κροίσῳ... ἐσελθεῖν...τὸ τοῦ Σόλωνος: but 6. 125 τὸν Κροῖσον γέλως ἐσῆλθε: and so Eur. *Med.* 931 εἰσῆλθέ μ᾽ οἶκτος.

τρὶς ἀθλίοιν for τρισαθλίοιν was first given by Porson, since otherwise there would be no caesura either in the 3rd or in the 4th foot. He compares *Od.* 5. 306 τρὶς μάκαρες Δαναοὶ καὶ τετράκις: Ai. *Plut.* 851 καὶ τρὶς κακοδαίμων καὶ τετράκις, κ.τ.λ. To Hermann's argument, that in any case τρὶς and ἀθλίοιν cohere, the answer is that, for the metre, the degree of coherence makes all the difference.

374 If νεάζων *merely* = νεώτερος ὤν, the pleonasm would be too weak: perh., then, it is tinged with the notion of νεανιευόμενος (as in Eur. *Phoen.* 713: ποῖ; μῶν νεάζων οὐχ ὁρᾷς ἃ χρῆν σ᾽ ὁρᾶν;—said by Creon to Eteocles). Cp. Aesch. *Ag.* 763 φιλεῖ δὲ τίκτειν ὕβρις μὲν παλαιὰ νεάζουσαν ὕβριν.

375 τὸν πρόσθε: Polyneices alludes to his right as the firstborn, 1294, 1422: Eur. (*Phoen.* 71) followed the common account in making Eteocles the elder. The change adopted by Soph. is here a twofold dramatic gain; for (*a*) Polyneices, who is to come on the scene, can be treated as the foremost offender; (*b*) Eteocles has now a special fault, and so the curse on *both* sons is further justified (421).

376 ἀποστερίσκει, historic pres., 'deprives of' (rather than a true pres., 'is excluding from'). The simple στερίσκω was commoner in Attic than this compound.

377 πληθύων, lit., becoming full (of the Nile rising, Her. 2. 19): Aesch. *Ag.* 869 ὡς ἐπλήθυον λόγοι.

378 Ἄργος, the territory, not only the city; called κοῖλον, 'hill-girt,' because the Argive plain is bounded on w., n. and e. by hills, as on s. by the sea. This epithet had already been given to it, acc. to the schol., in the epic called the Ἐπίγονοι, popularly ascribed to Homer (Her. 4. 32, who expresses doubt), and was again used by Soph. in his *Thamyras* (fr. 222).

379 κῆδος, *affinitatem*, with Adrastus, by marrying his daughter Argeia (κῆδος Ἀδράστου λαβών, Eur. *Phoen.* 77); καινόν, in a new quarter (as opp. to his native land). Perhaps Statius, whom Schneid. quotes, was translating this: *iamque ille* novis,

scit fama, superbit | *Conubiis, viresque parat, queis regna capessat*
(*Theb.* 2. 108).

380 f. ὡς κ.τ.λ.: 'as purposing that Argos should either
possess the Theban land in honour, or exalt Thebes to the
skies' (by the glory of having defeated Argos). ὡς...Ἄργος...
καθέξον ἤ...βιβῶν, acc. absol. in the *personal* constr., as *O. T.* 101
ὡς τόδ' αἷμα χειμάζον πόλιν. Eur. *Ion* 964 ΠΑΙΔ. σοὶ δ' ἐς τί
δόξ' εἰσῆλθεν ἐκβαλεῖν τέκνον;—ΚΡΕΟΥΣΑ. ὡς τὸν θεὸν σώσοντα
τόν γ' αὐτοῦ γόνον.

381 τιμῇ, dat. of manner: cp. 369. καθέξον, occupy as
conquerors: Dem. or. 18 § 96 τὰ κύκλῳ τῆς Ἀττικῆς κατεχόντων
ἁρμοσταῖς καὶ φρουραῖς.

ἤ πρὸς οὐρ. βιβῶν, 'or lift it to heaven,' *i.e.* exalt its fame by
being defeated by it: cp. κλέος οὐρανὸν ἵκει (*Od.* 9. 20), κλέος
οὐρανόμηκες (Ar. *Nub.* 459): Eur. *Bacch.* 972 ὥστ' οὐρανῷ
στηρίζον εὑρήσεις κλέος (thou wilt find thy fame towering in the
sky). But the best illustration is Isocr. or. 15 § 134 τὰ μὲν
ἁμαρτανόμενα παρόψονται, τὸ δὲ κατορθωθὲν οὐρανόμηκες
ποιήσουσιν, they will overlook your failures, and exalt your
success to the skies. So Lucr. 1. 78 *religio pedibus subiecta
vicissim Opteritur, nos exaequat victoria caelo.*

382 ἀριθμός...λόγων, 'mere vain words': Eur. *Tro.* 475
κἀνταῦθ' ἀριστεύοντ' ἐγεινάμην τέκνα, | οὐκ ἀριθμὸν ἄλλως, ἀλλ'
ὑπερτάτους Φρυγῶν. Hor. *Epp.* 1. 2. 27 *Nos numerus sumus et
fruges consumere nati.*

383 ὅπου, 'where,' 'at what stage.' If the MS. ὅποι (Vat. ὅπη)
is right, the phrase is harsh beyond example. Note that, in this
context, πόνους=the woes of Oed. generally (mental and physical),
not merely his toils in wandering: this is against the emend.
κατοικιοῦσιν.

385 f. ὡς...θεοὺς...ἕξειν—'that the gods will have some regard
for me'—may be sound. Harsh as it seems to us, usage had
perhaps accustomed the ear to hearing the speaker's own view
introduced by ὡς, even when the corresponding construction did
not follow. ὧδ' ἐμοῦ would be weak. But ὥστ' ἐμοῦ (against which
the presence of ὥστε in 386 is not conclusive, cp. on 544) is worth
weighing: cp. Eur. *Or.* 52 ἐλπίδα δὲ δή τιν' ἔχομεν ὥστε μὴ θανεῖν.

389 f. The purport of this new oracle seems to have
been:—'The welfare of Thebes depends on Oed., alive or
dead.' Ismene paraphrases it:—'It shows that *you will be in
request* with the Thebans *some day* (ποτέ, *i.e.* some day *soon*
397),—not merely after your death, but while you live.'

114   *Oedipus at Colonus*

390 εὐσοίας, used by Soph. also in the *Amphitryon* (fr. 119) ἐπεὶ δὲ βλάστοι, τῶν τριῶν μίαν λαβεῖν | εὔσοιαν ἀρκεῖ, quoted by the scholiast. It does not occur except in Soph.: but Theocr. 24. 8 has εὔσοα τέκνα ('safe and sound').

391 A and other MSS. have τοιοῦδ᾽ ὑπ᾽, which gives a clear constr. It seems arbitrary to assume that in L's reading τίς δ᾽ ἂν τοιοῦδ᾽ ἀνδρὸς εὖ πράξειεν ἂν the syllable lost was rather τι after τίς δ᾽ ἂν, the gen. being one of source. Herm. supports the latter view by *O. T.* 1006 σοῦ πρὸς δόμους ἐλθόντος εὖ πράξαιμί τι, but there the gen. is absolute.

392 ἐν σοί: 247. γίγνεσθαι is never merely εἶναι. ἐν σοὶ γίγνεται τὰ κείνων κράτη = their power *comes to be* in thy hand: *i.e.* the new oracle so appoints. φασὶ with indef. subject, 'people say,' 'report says.' κράτη, political predominance generally, but with esp. ref. to prevalence in war against Athens (1332): the plur. as of royal power (*Ant.* 173 κράτη... καὶ θρόνους).

393 ἀνήρ, emphatic, as oft.: Ar. *Nub.* 823 ὃ σὺ μαθὼν ἀνὴρ ἔσει: Xen. *Cyr.* 4. 2. 25 οὐκέτ᾽ ἀνήρ ἐστιν, ἀλλὰ σκευοφόρος.

394 ὤλλυσαν, imperf. of intention; see on 274. This was their design up to the moment of his fall. From that moment dates the period meant by νῦν.

395 See on 1. ὃς νέος πέσῃ, 'ruined in youth,'—without ἄν, as oft. in poetry, seldom in prose (*O. T.* 1231 n.).

396 καὶ μὴν here = 'Well, however that may be' (even if it *is* φλαῦρον); γε throws back a light stress on Κρέοντα: '*Creon* thinks the matter important.' For a slightly different use of καὶ μήν...γε cp. *O. T.* 345 n.

397 βαιοῦ...χρόνου. The gen. of the 'time *within which*' expresses the period to which the act *belongs*, and might so be viewed as possessive: Plat. *Gorg.* 448 A οὐδείς μέ πω ἠρώτηκε καινὸν οὐδὲν πολλῶν ἐτῶν, *i.e.* non-questioning of me has now been the attribute of many years. κοὐχὶ μ., with warning emphasis: *O. T.* 58 γνωτὰ κοὐκ ἄγνωτα (n.). Cp. 617.

399 στήσωσι, sc. οἱ Θηβαῖοι: Creon himself lays stress on his mission to speak for *all* (737). Schol. κατοικίσωσι. The word has a certain harsh fitness for τὸν πλανήτην (3).

400 ὅρων. ἐμβαίνω usu. takes either dat., or prep. with gen. or accus.: the simple gen. could be explained as partitive, but prob. is rather on the analogy of the gen. with ἐπιβαίνω: cp. *O. T.* 825 ἐμβατεύειν πατρίδος. The gen. with ἐπεμβαίνω (924) is warranted by the first prep.

401—408 The tenor of this fine passage should be observed.

Oedipus took ἐν σοί (392) to mean that the welfare of Thebes depended on his presence there. He is thinking of a restoration to his Theban home (395). He asks, therefore,— 'Of what use can I be to them if I am left at their doors, and not received within their land?' 'They will suffer,' she replies, 'if your *tomb* is neglected.' Oedipus does not see the force of this answer: he still infers (from θανόντα in 390) that, whatever may be his doom in life, he is at least to be *buried* at Thebes. 'Why, of course they will,' he replies (403). '*So*'—pursues the daughter (404)—'they mean to keep you within their grasp.' A new suspicion flashes on him. 'But will they also *bury* me at Thebes?' 'It cannot be.' That is enough. He will never give himself into their hands.—Remark that he was supposing Apollo's former decree (91) to have been cancelled by this later one (389). He now sees that the new oracle does *not* cancel the former, but merely confirms it in one aspect, viz. in the promise of ἄτην τοῖς πέμψασιν (93).

401 θύρασι, *foris*, as Eur. *El.* 2074 οὐδὲν γὰρ αὐτὴν δεῖ θύρασιν εὐπρεπὲς | φαίνειν πρόσωπον (she ought not to show her beauty *abroad*). In θύρασι, θύραζε, θύραθεν, θυραῖος the notion of 'external' is uppermost.

402 κείνοις with βαρύς only. δυστυχῶν = if it does not receive due honours: cp. ἄμοιρος...νέκυς of a corpse denied due rites (*Ant.* 1071). Eur. *Hec.* 319 τύμβον δὲ βουλοίμην ἂν ἀξιούμενον | τὸν ἐμὸν ὁρᾶσθαι. Since in death (390) he was still to sway their destiny, they wished his grave to be where they could make the due offerings (ἐναγίζειν). Such ἐναγισμός would be at least annual (cp. Isae. or. 2 § 46).

403 Cp. *O. T.* 398 γνώμῃ κυρήσας οὐδ' ἀπ' οἰωνῶν μαθών. It needed no oracle to tell one that they would incur divine anger for neglecting the first duties of piety towards their late king.

404 f. σε προσθέσθαι, 'to associate you with them (as a prospective ally) in the neighbourhood of their land, and not (to leave you) in a place where you will be your own master.' Cp. Her. 1. 69 χρήσαντος τοῦ θεοῦ τὸν Ἕλληνα φίλον προσθέσθαι,... ὑμέας...προσκαλέομαι φίλος τε θέλων γενέσθαι καὶ σύμμαχος. With μηδ', etc., a verbal notion such as ἐᾶσαι οἰκεῖν must be supplied from προσθέσθαι: cp. *El.* 71 καὶ μή μ' ἄτιμον τῆσδ' ἀποστείλητε γῆς, | ἀλλ' ἀρχέπλουτον (sc. καταστήσατε). ἂν...

κρατοῖς, nearly = κρατήσεις. See on ἵν' ἄν...εἴποιμεν, 189. With the MS. κρατῆς, ἄν belongs to ἵνα: 'wherever you may be your own master': which is evidently less suitable here.

406 καὶ with **κατασκιῶσι** (not with ἤ, which would imply that he did *not* expect it: 'Having settled me near their land, will they *further* bury me within it?' For κατασκιάζειν cp. *Epigrammata Graeca* 493 (Kaibel, Berl. 1878) θανόντα. .γαῖα κατεσκίασεν.

407 τοὐμφύλον αἷμα, thy blood-guilt for the death of a kinsman: so ἐμφύλιον αἷμα (Pind. *Pyth.* 2. 32), αἷμα συγγενές (Eur. *Suppl.* 148), αἷμα γενέθλιον (*Or.* 89). Oed. was doomed to ἀειφυγία (601). Even to *bury* him in Theban ground would seem impious towards Laïus. So, when Antigone has given the burial-rite to Polyneices, Creon asks, (*Ant.* 514) πῶς δῆτ' ἐκείνῳ δυσσεβῆ τιμᾷς χάριν; 'How, then, canst thou render a grace which is impious towards that other?' (Eteocles).

410 συναλλαγῆς, strictly, a bringing together (by the gods) of persons and circumstances, a 'conjuncture': rarely without the defining gen. (as νόσου ξ., *O. T.* 960).

411 σοῖς...τάφοις, poetical locative dat. (*O. T.* 381 n.), freq. in Homer, as *Il.* 21 389 ἥμενος Οὐλύμπῳ. Some day the Thebans will invade Attica, and will be defeated by the Athenians near the grave of Oedipus. Cp. Aristeides ὑπὲρ τῶν τεττάρων p. 284 (the great men of the Greek past are guardian spirits), καὶ ῥύεσθαί γε τὴν χώραν οὐ χεῖρον ἢ τὸν ἐν Κολωνῷ κείμενον Οἰδίπουν: where the schol. records a vague legend of his epiphany in some fight with Theban invaders. When the Persians (480 B.C.) were repulsed from Delphi, two of the local heroes pursued them (Her. 8. 39). So Theseus was seen at Marathon (Plut. *Thes.* 35); Athene appeared, and the Aeacidae helped, at Salamis (Her. 9. 83 f.).

413 θεωρῶν, 'sacred envoys' sent from Thebes to Delphi, to consult the oracle in solemn form (*O. T.* 114): cp. on 354. ἑστίας, the 'hearth of the Pythian seer' (*O. T.* 965).

414 ἐφ' ἡμῖν, 'in my case.'

415 οἱ μολόντες: schol. οἱ θεωροί.

416 παίδων τις (there being only *two* sons) virtually strengthens the question, as if he asked—'Had my sons any knowledge whatever of this?'

418 f. καὶ εἶτα, 'and after that,' is explained by τῶνδ' ἀκούσαντες. τῶνδ', 'having heard this': see on 304. πάρος... προύθεντο: Eur. *Hipp.* 382 οἱ δ' ἡδονὴν προθέντες ἀντὶ τοῦ καλοῦ |

ἄλλην τιν᾽: Isocr. *Ep.* 9 § 17 ἄλλους ἀνθ᾽ ἡμῶν προκριθῆναι: and so Plat. προτιμᾶν τι ἀντί τινος (*Lys.* 219 D), πρό τινος (*Legg.* 727 D), πλέον τινός (*ib.* 777 D), μᾶλλον ἤ τι (887 B). The complaint of Oed. against his sons is this: Apollo had made him the arbiter, in life and death, of Theban welfare (389). They might have pleaded with the Thebans:—'Apollo has now virtually condoned the ἐμφύλον αἷμα (407). Restore our father to the throne.' But they desired the throne for themselves. Here, as in regard to his expulsion, they neglected an opportunity which natural piety should have seized (441).

419 τοὐμοῦ πόθου, 'the wish for me': the possess. pron. = object. gen. of pers. pron.: see on 332.

420 φέρω δ᾽ ὅμως. The indignant question of Oed. invited a defence. She replies, 'I am pained to hear my brothers charged with such conduct, but I must bear it'—*i.e.* I cannot deny the charge. The contrast between ἀλγῶ and φέρω has thus more point than if φέρω δ᾽ ὅμως = 'but such are my tidings.'

421 ἀλλ᾽. 'Nay, then'—opening the imprecation, as *Ph.* 1040 ἀλλ᾽, ὦ πατρῴα γῆ θεοί τ᾽ ἐγχώριοι, | τείσασθε, τείσασθ᾽.

σφιν, not σφι, was prob. always the form used by Attic tragedy. It is required by metre below, 444, 451, 1490: *Ai.* 570: *El.* 1070: Aesch. *P. V.* 252, 457: *Pers.* 759, 807: fr. 157 (*ap.* Plat. *Rep.* 391 E). Eur. has the dat. in two places where, as here, σφι is *possible*, but in both σφιν has MS. authority, and should probably be read, *Med.* 398 (*v. l.* σφι), *Suppl.* 769. On the other hand there is no place in trag. where metre excludes σφιν.

τὴν πεπρωμένην, 'fated' by the curse in the house of Laïus (369).

422 ἐν δ᾽ after μήτε is harsh, and Elmsley's ἕν τ᾽ may be right. There is, however, a good deal of MS. evidence for τε...δέ in trag.: see on 367. Cp. *Ant.* 1096 τό τ᾽ εἰκαθεῖν γὰρ δεινόν, ἀντιστάντα δὲ κ.τ.λ., n.

ἐν ἐμοί (cp. 247), may the issue for them *come to be* (392) in my hands, *i.e.* may the gods allow me to be the final arbiter, and to doom them *both* by a father's curse.

424 κἀπαναίρονται. The words καὶ ἐπαναίρονται δόρυ do not form a second relative clause,—as if, from the ἧς before ἔχονται, we had to supply the relat. pron. in a different case (ἐφ᾽ ᾗ, or εἰς ἥν) with ἐπαναίρονται. They form an independent sentence,

118   *Oedipus at Colonus*

which is co-ordinated with the relative clause, ἧς ἔχονται, 'which they are setting their hands to.' This is the normal Greek construction. Cp. 467, 731.

ἐπαναιροῦνται δόρυ, the MS. reading, would mean, 'are taking a spear upon them,' the verb being used figuratively (like *in se suscipere*) of obligations or responsibilities (φιλίαν, πόλεμον, τέχνην, λατρείαν etc.); but cp. Eur. *Her.* 313 καὶ μήποτ' ἐς γῆν ἐχθρὸν αἴρεσθαι δόρυ.

425 ὡς, 'for' (if I were to have the decision).

427 οἵ γε, causal : see on οἵτινες 263.

428 ἀτίμως : Soph. has this adv. thrice elsewhere of ignominious or ruthless treatment, *El.* 1181, *Ant.* 1069, fr. 593. 7 : cp. 440, 770.

429 οὐκ ἔσχον, did not stop me (from being expelled). We find such phrases as ἔχω τινὰ ποιοῦντά τι, to check one *in the act* of doing something (*O. C.* 888 βουθυτοῦντά μ'...ἔσχετ'), but not ἔχω τινὰ ἀδικούμενον, to stop one *from being* wronged (like παύω). Here, then, it is better to supply τὸ (or ὥστε) μὴ ἐξωθεῖσθαι than to take ἔσχον with ἐξωθούμενον. Cp. Xen. *An.* 3. 5. 11 πᾶς...ἀσκὸς δύο ἄνδρας ἕξει τὸ (*v.l.* τοῦ) μὴ καταδῦναι· ὥστε δὲ μὴ ὀλισθάνειν, ἡ ὕλη καὶ ἡ γῆ σχήσει.

ἤμυναν, sc. ἐμοί. ἀνάστατος, made to rise up and quit one's abode, 'driven from house and home,' implying ἀειφυγία (601), *Tr.* 39 ἐν Τραχῖνι τῇδ' ἀνάστατοι | ξένῳ παρ' ἀνδρὶ ναίομεν (driven from our home at Argos). Thuc. 1. 8 οἱ...ἐκ τῶν νήσων κακοῦργοι ἀνέστησαν ὑπ' αὐτοῦ (were expelled).

430 αὐτοῖν, not dat. of the agent (very rare except with perf., plpf., or fut. pf. pass.), but dat. of interest ('so far as they were concerned') : cp. *Ph.* 1030 τέθνηχ' ὑμῖν πάλαι : Aesch. *P. V.* 12 σφῷν μὲν ἐντολὴ Διὸς | ἔχει τέλος δή. **ἐξεκηρύχθην,** by a proclamation of Creon (as regent) to the citizens. κήρυγμα is used of the royal *edict, Ant.* 8, 161, etc. Cp. Lys. or. 12 § 95 (of those banished by the Thirty) ἐξεκηρύχθητε...ἐκ τῆς πόλεως.

431 εἴποις ἄν : the figure called ὑποφορά (Lat. *subiectio*, Cornificius 4. 23. 33), the 'suggestion' of an objection, with the reply. Oed. here speaks chiefly to Ism., whose pain for her brothers (420) might suggest the excuse ; though in 445, 457 he addresses the Chorus.

θέλοντι, 'desiring' (not merely 'consenting') : cp. 767 : *O. T.* 1356 θέλοντι κἀμοὶ τοῦτ' ἂν ἦν. The desire of Oed. to be sent away from Thebes is passionately expressed in the

O. T. (1410 ff., 1449 ff.). At the end of that play he repeats the request (1518), and Creon replies that it must be referred to Delphi. τότε with κατήνεσεν, *i.e.* 'when I was banished'; so *Ai.* 650 τότε = 'in those old days.'

432 The ι in L's κατηίνυσεν speaks for κατήνεσεν,—clearly much fitter here than κατήνυσεν. Cp. 1633 καταίνεσον, 1637 κατήνεσεν. The contrast is between exile imposed as a doom or granted as a boon,—not merely between a wish fulfilled or unfulfilled.

433 ἡμέραν: the acc. of duration (cp. *O. T.* 1138) is strictly warrantable, as in Xen. *Cyr.* 6. 3. 11 καὶ ἐχθὲς δὲ καὶ τρίτην ἡμέραν (the day before yesterday) τὸ αὐτὸ τοῦτο ἔπραττον. τὴν αὐτίχ': Thuc. 2. 64 ἔς τε τὸ μέλλον...ἔς τε τὸ αὐτίκα: 3. 112 ἐν τῷ αὐτίκα φόβῳ.

435 λευσθῆναι πέτροις, the typical form of summary vengeance on one who has incurred public execration: *Il.* 3. 56; Aesch. *Ag.* 1616; *Ai.* 254; Her. 9. 5. The redundant πέτροις adds emphasis: so *Ant.* 200 πυρὶ | πρῆσαι κατάκρας. Eur. *Or.* 442 θανεῖν ὑπ' ἀστῶν λευσίμῳ πεπρώματι.

436 ἔρωτ' ἐς τόνδ', the conjecture of Papageorgius is, I think, almost certain. The change supposed is of the slightest kind, such as continually occurs in our MSS.: while ἔρωτος τοῦδ' cannot be defended as either (*a*) gen. of connection, 'helping in regard to this desire,' or (*b*) possessive gen. with ὠφελῶν as = εὐεργέτης, 'helper of this desire.'

437 πέπων, 'assuaged.' The metaphor is not directly from the mellowing of fruit, but from the medical use of the word in ref. to the subsiding of inflammation (as in angry tumours, etc.). Cp. the fig. sense of ὠμός. So πεπαίνεσθαι Hippocr. 1170 B: Arist. *Meteor.* 4. 3 ἡ φυμάτων (tumours) καὶ φλέγματος...πέπανσις: *Anthol. Pal* 12. 80 τί σοι τὸ πεπανθὲν "Ερωτος | τραῦμα διὰ σπλάγχνων αὖθις ἀναφλέγεται; Hence, too, *Tr.* 728 ὀργὴ πέπειρα.

438 ἐκδραμόντα, had rushed out, run to excess: cp. *Ant.* 752 ἢ κἀπαπειλῶν ὧδ' ἐπεξέρχει θρασύς; dost thou e'en *go to the length of* threatening so boldly?

439 The gen. might be taken with μείζω, 'a chastiser *greater than* the sins,' *i.e.* 'severer than they merited' (ἢ κατὰ τὰ ἥμαρτ.); but it is simpler to take it with κολαστήν, 'too great a chastiser of the sins.' As μέγας θυμός is 'violent anger,' so θυμός which is over-violent can be called μείζων κολαστής. The rhythm of the verse will not permit us to disjoin μείζω (as by a comma) from κολαστήν.

440 τὸ τηνίκ' ἤδη, just when that time had come (the art. as in τὸ αὐτίκα, 'at the moment,' Thuc. 2. 41). While τηνικάδε ('at this time of day') was common, the simple τηνίκα occurs nowhere else in class. Attic; it is found, however, in the Alexandrian poets, and in later Greek. τοῦτο μέν is answered by δέ (441) instead of τοῦτο δέ, as by ἔπειτα δέ (*Ant.* 63), τοῦτ' αὖθις (*ib.* 165), εἶτα (*Ph.* 1345), τοῦτ' ἄλλο (*O. T.* 605).

441 χρόνιον, 'after all that time,'—repeating the thought with which he had begun (χρόνῳ 437). Thuc. 1. 141 χρόνιοι... ξυνιόντες, meeting only at long intervals : 3. 29 σχολαῖοι κομισθέντες, having made a leisurely voyage. ἐπωφελεῖν with dat. (like ἐπαρκεῖν) as Eur. *Andr.* 677, elsewhere usu. with acc. (*Ph.* 905, etc.) : cp. the poet. dat. with the simple verb, *Ant.* 560 τοῖς θανοῦσιν ὠφελεῖν.

442 οἱ τοῦ πατρὸς τῷ πατρί blends two forms of antithesis,— (1) οἱ παῖδες τῷ πατρί, and (2) οἱ τοῦ Οἰδίποδος τῷ Οἰδίποδι. The gen. of 'origin,' τοῦ πατρός, really a possessive gen., comes in with peculiar force here, as suggesting that the sons *belong to* the sire. For πάτρὸς...πάτρί cp. 883. τὸ δρᾶν, on 47.

443 ἔπους σμικροῦ χάριν, 'for *lack of* one little word from them,' *i.e.* in his defence. As if one said, 'They incurred all this loss *for the sake of* a petty sum ' (*i.e.* to *save* it). This is a slight deviation from the ordinary use of ἕνεκα, οὕνεκα (22), ἕκατι, χάριν, in such phrases. Cp. fr. 510. 6 κἀμοὶ γὰρ ἂν πατήρ γε δακρύων χάριν | ἀνῆκτ' ἂν εἰς φῶς, would have been brought up, *if tears could bring him*: Aesch. *Pers.* 337 πλήθους... ἕκατι, if numbers could give victory.

444 σφιν, 'as far as they were concerned,' 'for anything they did,' *i.e.* they looked on and did nothing : see on αὐτοῖν 430. ἠλώμην ἀεί = 'I continued to wander.' He can scarcely mean that, *after* his expulsion, they might at any time have recalled him, since he regards the new oracle as having given them an opportunity which did not exist before (418). But he may mean that their silence *at the moment* of his expulsion was the cause of the whole sequel.

445 τοῖνδε, not ταῖνδε, is the form of the fem. dual as found in Attic inscrr. of *c.* 450—320 B.C.: cp. *Ant.* 769 n. But as to the partic., the dual forms in ·α, -αιν, and those in -ε, -οιν, seem to have been used concurrently (cp. 1676 n.).

446 τροφάς: cp. 330, 341.

447 γῆς ἄδειαν, a strange phrase (perh. corrupt), must mean, security *in regard to the land* (where I find myself at any given

time), a secure resting-place. Cp. Thuc. 8. 64 λαβοῦσαι αἱ
πόλεις...ἄδειαν τῶν πρασσομένων, security *in regard to* their
proceedings. His daughters, so far as they can, give him in
exile all that his sons should have given him at Thebes,—
(1) maintenance, (2) safety in his movements, (3) generally, the
support due from kinsfolk.

γένους (subjective gen.) ὑπάρκεσιν = ἦν τὸ γένος παρέχει, 'the
offices of kinship.' Thuc. 7. 34 διὰ τὴν τοῦ ἀνέμου (subject.)
ἄπωσιν τῶν ναυαγίων (object.) = ὅτι ὁ ἄνεμος ἀπωθεῖ τὰ ναυάγια
(Thompson, *Synt.* § 98).

448 f. The constr. is, εἱλέσθην θρόνους, καὶ κραίνειν σκῆπτρα,
etc. κραίνειν = (1) to bring a thing to pass, (2) to exercise
power, to *reign*, sometimes with a *gen.* of the persons ruled
(296, 862, etc.). σκῆπτρα goes with κραίνειν as an almost
adverbial cognate accus., 'to rule with sceptre': as *Ph.* 140
σκῆπτρον ἀνάσσεται (pass.) implies a similar σκῆπτρον ἀνάσσω.

450 f. As most editors since Elmsley have allowed, the MS.
οὔ τι...οὔτε cannot be right. And οὔ τι...οὐδέ is clearly more
forcible than οὔτε...οὔτε. λάχωσι with gen. is less common
than with accus., but is well attested not only in poetry but in
prose, as Plat. *Legg.* 775 E τιμῆς ἐὰν τῆς προσηκούσης...λαγχάνῃ.
τοῦδε, very rare for τοῦδ' ἀνδρός as = ἐμοῦ: so τῆσδε = ἐμοῦ *Tr.* 305,
τῷδε = ἐμοί *ib.* 1012. συμμάχον predicate; cp. 1482 ἐναισίου δὲ
σοῦ τύχοιμι, and 1486.

453 f. The oracle newly brought by Ismene is distinguished
from the oracle given to Oedipus himself at Delphi in former
years (see on 87). He calls the former *her* oracle, because she
brings it. Both oracles alike *concern* him. We must not, then,
change τἀξ to τἀπ' ('concerning me'). τὰ ἐξ ἐμοῦ παλαίφατα =
the earlier predictions which I, on my side, can produce: those
which the resources of my knowledge furnish forth. ἐξ is
appropriate, since they have been so long treasured in his
inmost soul. Cp. on 293.

454 ἤνυσεν, 'fulfilled,' by bringing him to the grove (cp. 87),
in earnest that the requital predicted for the authors of his exile
(93) will also come to pass.

457 f. ὁμοῦ | προστάτισι (predicative), along with them as
your protectors or champions against Theban violence. Oed. is
already under the guard of the Eumenides as their ἱκέτης (284):
if the Coloniates are loyal to the Eumenides, Attica and he will
alike be saved.

For Dindorf's ὁμοῦ | προστάτισι it may be urged :—(1) ταὐτὰ

ταῖς is in all MSS., which would be strange if ταῖσδε ταῖς were genuine; while πρὸς ταῖσι ταῖς is simply explained by προστά(τ)ισι ταῖς. (2) A change of προστάτισι into πρὸς ταῖσι might have produced the change of -θ' ὁμοῦ into -τέ μου. (3) After ἐμοῦ in 455 it is easy to dispense with the pronoun.—Cp. *O. T.* 882 θεὸν οὐ λήξω ποτὲ προστάταν ἴσχων: *Tr.* 209 Ἀπόλλωνα προστάταν: Porphyry *Antr. Nymph.* 12 νύμφαις ὑδάτων προστάτισιν.

458 δημούχοις, holding, reigning among, your people: cp. *O. T.* 160 γαιάοχον... | Ἄρτεμιν: Ar. *Eq.* 581 Παλλὰς πολιοῦχος: Aesch. *Th.* 69 πολισσοῦχοι θεοί. But below, 1087 γᾶς...δαμούχοις = the Athenians, 1348 δημοῦχος χθονός = the king. The word is tinged here with the notion of 'deme': cp. 78.

459 f. ἀλκὴν ποεῖσθαι (for the spelling see 278 n.), a simple periphrasis, = ἀλκαθεῖν: Thuc. I. 124 ποεῖσθαι τιμωρίαν = τιμωρεῖν (to succour), 2. 94 φυλακήν...ἐποιοῦντο = ἐφύλασσον, etc. Distinguish ἀλκὴν τιθέναι τινός (1524), to create a defence against a thing. A *gen.* after ἀλκή as = 'succour' must denote (*a*) the defender, as in Διὸς ἀλκή, or (*b*) the danger;—not the interest defended.

460 ἀρεῖσθε, 'ye will gain.' τοῖς δ' ἐμοῖς: Oedipus is following the train of thought in which benefits to Attica are bound up with retribution for his own wrongs (92); and he thus gives the Chorus another pledge that their interest is one with his.

461 ἐπάξιος, *sc.* εἶ. When the verb is thus omitted, the pron. is usu. added: here, the absence of σύ is excused by Οἰδίπους. This form of the voc. has the best MS. authority in some 12 places of Soph., as against 3 which support Οἰδίπου (more often gen.), viz. below, 557, 1346, and *O. T.* 405 (where see n.). κατοικτίσαι: Thuc. I. 138 ἄξιος θαυμάσαι. The pass. inf. is rarer in this constr., as τίεσθαι δ' ἀξιώτατος Aesch. *Ag.* 531. Cp. 37.

462 αὐτός τε παῖδές θ': cp. 559, 1009, 1125, 1310.

463 ἐπεμβάλλεις, you insert yourself in this plea as a deliverer: *i.e.* to his protest against a breach of their promise (258—291), and his appeal to pity, he adds a promise of benefit to Attica (287, 459). Cp. Her. 2. 4 διὰ τρίτου ἔτεος ἐμβόλιμον ἐπεμβάλλουσι, they *insert* an intercalary month every other year: Plat. *Crat.* 399 A πολλάκις ἐπεμβάλλομεν γράμματα, τὰ δ' ἐξαιροῦμεν, we *insert* letters (in words), or remove them. τῷδε λόγῳ is not instrum. dat., but goes with the verb.

465 f. προξένει, 'grant me thy kindly offices' (of advice and direction), as a man does in his own State to the men of a foreign state which has made him its πρόξενος. ὡς... τελοῦντι, in the assurance that I will perform anything required of me: cp. 13.

466 καθαρμὸν τῶνδε δαιμόνων (poss. gen.), such a lustration as belongs to them, is due to them: not object. gen., since καθαίρειν could not stand for ἱλάσκεσθαι.

467 The libation is due (1) as a greeting to the θεοὶ ἐγχώριοι of Attica, (2) as an atonement for trespass on the grove. The words καὶ κατέστειψας πέδον form an independent sentence, and not a second relative clause (as if ὧν were supplied from ἐφ' ἃς): see on 424. κατέστειψας: Sappho fr. 95 οἴαν τὰν ὑάκινθον ἐν οὔρεσι ποιμένες ἄνδρες | ποσσὶ καταστείβοισι, 'trample on   here the word suggests the rash violation of the χῶρον οὐχ ἁγνὸν πατεῖν (37).

469 ἀειρύτου. The rule is that ρ is doubled when, by inflection or composition, a *simple vowel* precedes it, but remains single when a *diphthong* precedes it: hence νεόρρυτος, but ἀείρυτος. Metre often led the poets to use ρ instead of ρρ, as ἀμφίρυτον (*Ai.* 134), χρυσορύτους (*Ant.* 950), αὐτόριζος (Babrius *fab.* 69); and προρέω, not προρρέω, was the regular form, as euphony plainly required. But there is no classical instance of the opposite anomaly.

470 δι' ὁσίων χειρῶν, *i.e.* after duly washing the hands before entering the sacred precinct. Blood-guilt is not thought of here. Washings, or sprinklings, were required before approaching shrines, and for this purpose περιρραντήρια were set at the entrances of sacred places. Cp. Lucian *Sacrific.* 13 τὸ μὲν πρόγραμμά φησι μὴ παριέναι εἴσω τῶν περιρραντηρίων ὅστις μὴ καθαρός ἐστι τὰς χεῖρας. So *Od.* 4. 750 ἀλλ' ὑδρηναμένη, καθαρὰ χροὶ εἵματ' ἔχουσα,... | εὔχε' Ἀθηναίῃ.

471 τοῦτο, adject., but without art. (cp. 1177), an epic use sometimes allowed by the Attic poets, and not rare in Sophocles. ἀκήρατον: Chrysippus *ap.* Plut. *Stoic. repugn.* 22 commends Hesiod for enjoining on men that they should respect the *purity* of rivers and springs, since thence the gods were served (Hes. *Opp.* 755).

472 κρατῆρές εἰσιν: *i.e.* the priest in charge of the shrine keeps them ready for the use of the worshippers, near the spring in the inner part of the grove (505), from which they were to be filled. The libations to the Eumenides were

124   *Oedipus at Colonus*

wineless (100), but they are associated with the mixing-bowl which was regularly used in libations (of wine) to other deities. Dem. *De Fals. Legat.* § 280 σπονδῶν καὶ κρατήρων κοινωνούς.

εὔχειρος, 'skilful.' Cp. Pind. *Ol.* 9. 111 εὔχειρα, δεξιόγυιον, 'deft-handed, nimble-limbed,' of a wrestler.

τέχνη : fr. 161 ὅπλοις ἀρρῶξιν, Ἡφαίστου τέχνῃ (the *work* of Hephaestus) : a common use of the word in later Greek. Cp. Verg. *Aen.* 5. 359 *clipeum...Didymaonis artes.* Mixing-bowls were made not only of earthenware, but of gold, silver, or bronze : Achilles had an ἀργύρεον κρητῆρα τετυγμένον·...αὐτὰρ κάλλει ἐνίκα πᾶσαν ἐπ' αἶαν | πολλόν· ἐπεὶ Σιδόνες πολυδαίδαλοι εὖ ἤσκησαν (*Il.* 23. 741).

473 κρᾶτ', acc. sing., the 'top,' *i.e.* rim, of each κρατήρ. In *Il.* 19. 93 κράατα is acc. plur., and Pindar is quoted by Eustath. (*Od.* 12. 1715. 63) as having said τρία κρᾶτα (for κράατα). But in *Od.* 8. 92 κρᾶτα is sing., and so always in Attic : Soph. has (τὸ) κρᾶτα several times as acc., and once as nom. An acc. plur. masc. κρᾶτας occurs twice in Eur. (*Phoen.* 1149, *H. F.* 526).

λαβὰς ἀμφιστόμους, handles on each side of the στόμα, or mouth. The festoon of wool, which was to be wreathed round the rim of the bowl, could be secured to these. The crater had various forms, some of them local (Her. 4. 61, 152); but the general type was that of a large bowl, supported by a foot with a broad base, and having a handle at each side (cp. Guhl and Koner, p. 150).

474 θαλλοῖσιν, of olive. κρόκαι are 'woollen cloths' (κρόκη, from κρέκω, to strike the web, in weaving, with the κερκίς, or rod, is the woof, the warp being στήμων).

475 οἰὸς νεαρᾶς, 'of an ewe lamb': with Bellermann, I insert σύ, though Wecklein's τε is also possible. For the iterated νεο- cp. *Ant.* 157 νεοχμὸς νεαραῖσι θεῶν | ἐπὶ συντυχίαις.

λαβών, *sc.* αὐτόν: cp. *Tr.* 1216 (διδούς): Ar. *Av.* 56 σὺ δ' οὖν λίθῳ κόψον λαβών: *Il.* 7. 303 δῶκε ξίφος ἀργυρόηλον—σὺν κολεῷ τε φέρων καὶ ἐϋτμήτῳ τελαμῶνι. The guardian of the grove (506) would supply the μαλλός, 'fleece.'

476 τὸ δ' ἔνθεν, 'and then,' 'and as to the sequel,' rare for τὸ ἐνθένδε, τὸ ἐντεῦθεν, but cp. Aesch. *Ag.* 247 τὰ δ' ἔνθεν οὔτ' εἶδον οὔτ' ἐννέπω. Here prob. adverbial : cp. *Ph.* 895 τί δῆτ' ἂν δρῷμ' ἐγὼ τοὐνθένδε γε; ποῖ τελ., to what conclusion am I to bring the rite? Thus far it has been all preparation. See on 227.

477 χοὰς χέασθαι, 'pour thy drink-offerings.' χοαί were offered to the gods of the under-world (cp. 1599), or to the dead (*Ant.* 431), as σπονδαί to the gods above. Aesch. *Eum.* 107 χοὰς ἀοίνους, of the Eumenides. The midd. verb as *Od.* 10. 518 (χοὴν χεῖσθαι), and Aesch. *Pers.* 219 χρὴ χοὰς | γῇ τε καὶ φθιτοῖς χέασθαι. The verb with cogn. acc. gives solemnity, as in θυσίαν θύειν, σπονδὰς σπένδειν, etc.

πρὸς πρώτην ἔω, not meaning, of course, that the *time* must be dawn. On the contrary it was an ancient custom that sacrifices to the χθόνιοι and to the dead should not be offered till after mid-day.

Statues of gods were oft. set to face the East (Paus. 5. 23. 1, etc.): also, victims about to be sacrificed (Sen. *Oed.* 338). Persons performing expiatory rites (ἐκθύσεις) or purifications (καθαρμοί) faced the East as the region of light and purity; see *El.* 424 f., where Electra ἡλίῳ | δείκνυσι τοὔναρ. Conversely, in pronouncing solemn curses the priests faced the *West*,—waving red banners: [Lys.] *In Andoc.* § 51 στάντες κατηράσαντο πρὸς ἑσπέραν καὶ φοινικίδας ἀνέσεισαν.

478 κρωσσοῖς here = κρατῆρσιν. The word is fitting, since the κρωσσός was more esp. used for *water* (Eur. *Ion* 1173, *Cycl.* 89), though also sometimes for wine (Aesch. fr. 91 κρωσσοὺς | μήτ᾽ οἰνηροὺς μήτ᾽ ὑδατηρούς), also for oil,—or as a cinerary urn. Guhl and Koner (p. 149) think that the krossos resembled the ὑδρία, which, like the κάλπις, was a bulky, short-necked vessel, oft. seen in the vase-paintings as borne by maidens on their heads when fetching water. οἷς by attract. for οὕς. χέω delib. aor. subjunct., 'am I to pour?'

479 πηγάς: here, strictly the gushing of the water from the bowl. From each of the three bowls he is to pour a χοή. The first and second bowls are to be filled with the spring water *only*; and from each of these he is to make a libation without emptying the bowl. The third bowl is to contain water sweetened with honey; and, in making the libation from *this*, he is to empty it. τρισσάς might be distributive, 'three from each bowl' (as the number nine recurs in 483); but in the χοή to the dead in *Od.* 10. 519, at least, there are only three pourings, viz. of (1) hydromel, (2) wine, (3) water. τὸν τελευτ. (κρωσσόν) as if ἔκχεον, not χέον, were understood: cp. Menander fr. 461 τὸν χοᾶ | ἐκκέχυκας, you have emptied the pitcher.

480 θῶ has raised needless doubts. The operator is to fetch water from the spring in the grove (469), fill the bowls

which he will find ready, and *place* them in a convenient
position for the rite. From the distinction just drawn between
the first two bowls and the third, Oed. surmises that the
contents of the latter are not to be of precisely the same
nature as those of the others. He asks, then,—'With what
shall I fill it, before placing it beside the other two,—preparatory to beginning the rite?'

481 μελίσσης = μέλιτος. So πορφύρα (the purple-fish)=purple,
ἐλέφας=ivory, χελώνη=tortoise-shell. προσφέρειν infin. for imper.,
as esp. in precepts or maxims: cp. 490, *O. T.* 1466 αἶν μοι
μέλεσθαι, 1529 μηδέν' ὀλβίζειν.

482 μελάμφυλλος, overshadowed by dense foliage. Pind. *P.* 1.
27 Αἴτνας ἐν μελαμφύλλοις...κορυφαῖς, Ar. *Th.* 997 μ. τ' ὄρη δάσκια.

483 αὐτῇ, *sc.* ἐν τῇ γῇ, locative dat. (411). ἐξ ἀμφοῖν χεροῖν,
perh. laying them with each hand alternately, beginning and
ending with the right, or lucky, hand. The olive-branches
symbolise the fruits of the earth and of the womb, for the
increase of which the Eumenides were esp. invoked, since they
could blight it: Aesch. *Eum.* 907.

484 ἐπεύχεσθαι, 'pray over it,' to complete the rite: the
prayer was to be said while the twigs were being laid; hence
τιθείς, not θείς.

485 τούτων (for the gen. cp. 418), *sc.* τῶν λιτῶν: μέγιστα,
neut. pl. without subject, instead of μέγιστον (cp. 495): *Ai.*
1126 δίκαια γὰρ τόνδ' εὐτυχεῖν κτείναντά με.

486 Εὐμενίδας: see on 42. ἐξ, properly with ref. to the
inner spring of the feeling, but here almost = '*with*': cp. *O. T.*
528 ἐξ ὀμμάτων δ' ὀρθῶν τε κἀξ ὀρθῆς φρενός.

487 τὸν ἱκέτην: cp. 44, 284. σωτήριον = 'with a view to
σωτηρία,'—leaving the hearer to think of that which Oed.
gives, and *also* of that which he receives. σωτήριος is nowhere
definitely pass., as = σῶς, '*saved*'; for in Aesch. *Cho.* 236
σπέρματος σωτηρίου is the seed which is to continue the race.
Hence it is usu. taken here as = 'fraught with good for us,'
with ref. to his promise, σωτὴρ' ἀρεῖσθε (460). That idea is
present, but does not exclude the other.

488 σύ τ', not σύ γ', is right. The constr. is σύ τε αὐτὸς
αἰτοῦ, καὶ (αἰτείσθω) εἴ τις ἄλλος ἀντὶ σοῦ (αἰτεῖται). This is
to be the prayer, *both if* thou thyself prayest, *and if* another
prays for thee. In such statements the conjunctive τε...καί is
equally admissible with the disjunctive εἴτε...εἴτε. Cp. 1444:
Eur. *Hec.* 751 τολμᾶν ἀνάγκη κἂν τύχω κἂν μὴ τύχω.

489 ἄπυστα, 'inaudibly.' The hereditary priests of the Eumenides were called Ἡσυχίδαι. Their eponymous hero, Ἡσυχος, had an ἡρῷον between the Areiopagus and the w. foot of the acropolis, and to him, before a sacrifice, they offered a ram. Priestesses of a like name, serving the Eumenides, are mentioned by Callimachus fr. 123 Ἡσυχίδες.

μηκύνων, 'making loud': a sense found only here (cp. 1609). In μακρὸν ἀϋτεῖν (Hom.), ἠχεῖν (Plat.), etc., the idea of 'loud' comes through that of 'heard afar.'

490 ἀφέρπειν = imperat. (481). ἄστροφος, 'without looking behind': so in Aesch. *Cho.* 98 Electra debates whether, after pouring her mother's offering at Agamemnon's grave, she shall turn away,—καθάρμαθ' ὥς τις ἐκπέμψας, πάλιν | δικοῦσα τεῦχος, ἀστρόφοισιν ὄμμασιν. In Theocr. 24. 92 Teiresias orders the ashes of the serpents which would have strangled the infant Heracles to be cast beyond the borders by one of Alcmena's handmaids: ἂψ δὲ νέεσθαι | ἄστρεπτος. Verg. *Ecl.* 8. 101 *Fer cineres, Amarylli, foras, rivoque fluenti Transque caput iace, neu respexeris.* Ov. *Fasti* 6. 164 *Quique sacris adsunt respicere illa vetat.*

491 παρασταίην, as thy friend and helper: cp. *Ai.* 1383 τούτῳ γὰρ... | μόνος παρέστης χερσίν.

493 προσχώρων, 'dwelling near,' who therefore can judge best (cp. 12).

495 ὁδωτά, plur., as *Ant.* 677 οὕτως ἀμυντέ' ἐστὶ τοῖς κοσμουμένοις, | κοὔτοι γυναικὸς οὐδαμῶς ἡσσητέα: Thuc. 1. 118 ἐπιχειρητέα ἐδόκει εἶναι: cp. 485, 1360. λείπομαι, pass., 'I am at a disadvantage'; usu. with gen. of thing, as *El.* 474 γνώμας λειπομένα σοφᾶς, or person, *Tr.* 266 τῶν ὧν τέκνων λείποιτο. ἐν, 'in the existence of': *O. T.* 1112 ἔν τε γὰρ μακρῷ | γήρᾳ ξυνᾴδει: *Ph.* 185 ἔν τ' ὀδύναις...λιμῷ τ' οἰκτρός.

496 δύνασθαι (*without* σώματι), of bodily strength: cp. the speech of Lysias, or. 24 § 13 οὐ γὰρ δήπου τὸν αὐτὸν ὑμεῖς μὲν ὡς δυνάμενον (as being able-bodied) ἀφαιρήσεσθε τὸ διδόμενον, οἱ δὲ ὡς ἀδύνατον ὄντα κληροῦσθαι κωλύσουσιν: so *ib.* § 12 ὡς εἰμὶ τῶν δυναμένων. μηδ' for μήθ' is a necessary correction here. Cp. 421.

498 f. ἀρκεῖν...παρῇ. The thought is: 'I have trespassed on the grove of the Eumenides, and it might be doubted whether such deities would accept the atonement from any hand but my own. Nay, I believe that they regard the *intention* rather than the outward details. If my deputy

approaches the shrine *in a loyal spirit*, the offering will be accepted—yes, would be accepted, not on behalf of one man alone, but of many.' Clemens Alex. *Strom.* 5. 258 cites verses wrongly ascribed to Menander, θεῷ δὲ θῦε διὰ τέλους δίκαιος ὤν, | μὴ λαμπρὸς ὢν ταῖς χλαμύσιν ὡς τῇ καρδίᾳ. Porphyry *De Abstin.* 2. 19 quotes an inscription from a temple at Epidaurus, ἁγνὸν χρὴ νηοῖο θυώδεος ἐντὸς ἰόντα | ἔμμεναι· ἁγνείη δ' ἐστὶ φρονεῖν ὅσια.

500 ἀλλ' ἐν τάχει τι, 'act then with speed.' For τι cp. *Ant.* 1334 μέλλοντα ταῦτα· τῶν προκειμένων τι χρὴ | πράσσειν

502 δίχα. With γ' ἄνευ the γ' is intolerable, and L's δ' ἄνευ points to a confusion between an original δίχα and a gloss ἄνευ.

503 τελοῦσα, 'to perform,' in its ceremonial sense: cp. *O. T.* 1448 ὀρθῶς τῶν γε σῶν τελεῖς ὕπερ.

τὸν τόπον: βούλομαι δὲ μαθεῖν τοῦτο—ἵνα χρήσει με ἐφευρεῖν τὸν τόπον. The position of the κρήνη (470) had not been indicated.

504 χρῆσται by crasis from χρὴ ἔσται, χρή being a subst., 'need.' This is probable though not certain. I formerly conjectured χρήσει, a fut. of χρή which occurs in Her. 7. 8 and Plat. *Legg.* 809 B.—τοῦτο, resuming the object (τὸν τόπον), with emphasis: *Tr.* 457 n.

505 ἄλσους, gen. after τὸ ἐκεῖθεν, 'on the further side of the grove,' as after τὸ (or τὰ) ἐπ' ἐκεῖνα, τὰ ἐπὶ θάτερα, τὰ πρὸς βορρᾶν, etc.

506 ἔποικος, here, 'guardian,' 'one who dwells close to' the grove,—hardly, *on* the χῶρος οὐκ οἰκητός (39); though the guardians of sacred ἄλση sometimes dwelt within them, as Maron in Apollo's grove (*Od.* 9. 200), and the priest in Athena Kranaa's grove at Elatea (Paus. 10. 34. 7). Elsewhere ἔποικος usu. = 'immigrant.'

507 Ἀντ., σὺ δ': *El.* 150 Νιόβα, σὲ δ' ἔγωγε νέμω θεόν. Cp. 1459.

509 οὐδ' εἰ πονεῖ τις, δεῖ = εἰ καὶ π. τ., οὐ δεῖ.

510—548 A κομμός, which divides the first ἐπεισόδιον into two parts (254—509, 549—667). The metre is logaœdic. (1) *1st strophe,* 510—520 = *1st antistrophe,* 521—532. (2) *2nd strophe,* 533—541 = *2nd antistrophe,* 542—550.

510 κείμενον...ἐπεγείρειν, 'to rouse the old grief so long laid to rest,' Eur. *El.* 41 εὕδοντ' ἂν ἐξήγειρε τὸν | Ἀγαμέμνονος | φόνον. Plato *Phileb.* 15 C μὴ κινεῖν κακὸν εὖ κείμενον ('Let sleeping dogs lie').

513 τί τοῦτο; 'What means this?' Cp. 46 τί δ' ἐστὶ
τοῦτο; He is startled and disquieted. He shrinks from all
cross-questioning on the past, as from a torture (cp. 210).
We lose this dramatic touch if we construe τί τοῦτο (ἔρασαι
πυθέσθαι) as a calm query,—'What is this that thou wouldst
learn?'

514 τᾶς : for the gen. ('concerning'), cp. on. 355. ἀπόρου
φανείσας: because the horror of the discovery consisted in
relationships which could not be changed.

515 ᾇ ξυνέστας, with which you were brought into conflict,—
with which you became involved: Her. 9. 89 λιμῷ συστάντας
καὶ καμάτῳ. Thuc. 4. 55 ξυνεστῶτες...ναυτικῷ ἀγῶνι.

516 τᾶς σᾶς ἃ πέπονθ', 'by thy kindness for a guest, lay not
bare the shame that I have suffered.' The objection to pointing
at σᾶς and understanding ἐστί with ἀναιδῆ (as Herm. proposed)
is that ἀνοίξῃς requires an object. We should then have to
understand ἀλγηδόνα.

517 τὸ πολὺ καὶ μηδαμὰ λῆγον ἄκουσμα χρήζω ἀκοῦσαι ὀρθόν
('aright'): πολὺ, on 305. μηδαμὰ (neut. plur. adv.) with causal
force, 'being such as does not cease.' λῆγον, 'dying away,' of
rumour: *O. T.* 731 ηὐδᾶτο γὰρ ταῦτ', οὐδέ πω λήξαντ' ἔχει. ἄκουσμα,
anything heard,—sometimes in a bad sense, Arist. *Pol.* 7. 17
ἀπελαύνειν ἀπὸ τῶν ἀκουσμάτων καὶ τῶν ὁραμάτων ἀνελευθερίας.

519 στέρξον, be patient of my request, yield to it: cp. 7.

520 κἀγὼ (for καὶ cp. 53) γὰρ (πείθομαί σοι), for I comply
with thee as to all that thou cravest (by allowing him to await
the coming of Theseus, and by instructing him in the rites of
the grove: cp. 465).

522 I read ἤνεγκ' οὖν κακότατ',...ἤνεγκ' ἀέκων. ἤνεγκον was,
indeed, the ordinary form of the aor. in the older Attic, as
inscriptions show, in which ἤνεγκα occurs first about 360 B.C.
(Meisterhans, p. 88); but ἤνεγκα is proved by metre in *El.* 13
and Et.r. *Ion* 38. οὖν is suitable, when he is reluctantly
proceeding to unfold his story in answer to their pressing
demand. ἤνεγκ' emphasises his ruling thought, his great plea—
that he has been a *sufferer*, not a *doer* (267). κακότατ', the
misery of his two involuntary crimes. ἤνεγκον...ἤνεγκ' might
possibly stand, but would be harsh. There is nothing to
offend in ἀέκων μὲν...τούτων δέ, meaning—'The *agent* was not
free—the *acts* were not voluntary.'

In the MS. reading, ἤνεγκον—ἤνεγκον ἄκων μέν, ἄκων is wrong,
since metre requires ∪–(cp. 510).

523 αὐθαίρετον. Heinrich Schmidt keeps this reading, which is not metrically irreconcileable with 512 ὅμως δ' ἔραμαι πυθέσθαι.

525 f. κακᾷ εὐνᾷ, instr. dat., rather than dat. in appos. with ἄτᾳ. γάμων ἄτα, ruin coming from a marriage, like δόκησις λόγων, suspicion resting on mere assertions, *O. T.* 681.

527 f. ἡ ματρόθεν...ἐπλήσω; Didst thou fill thy bed with a mother, δυσώνυμα (prolept.) so as to make it infamous? ματρόθεν is substituted for ματρός by a kind of euphemism: that was the quarter from which the bride was taken. Cp. Aesch. *Theb.* 840 οὐδ' ἀπεῖπεν | πατρόθεν εὐκταία φάτις (the curse of Oed. on his children). The aor. midd. ἐπλησάμην is used by Hom., Her., etc., and (in comp. with ἐν) by Attic writers. The notion of '*filling*' is perh. tinged with that of '*defiling*' (ἀναπιμπλάναι, ἀνάπλεως). The tone of the passage is against rendering 'satisfied,' as if λέκτρα = λέκτρων ἐπιθυμίαν.

529 ἀκούειν: cp. 141.

530 ff. The constr. is αὗται δὲ ἐξ ἐμοῦ δύο μὲν παῖδε, δύο δ' ἄτα...ἀπέβλαστον etc. ἐξ ἐμοῦ, sprung from me: no partic. need be supplied, since the verb ἀπέβλ follows: cp. 250 ὅ τι σοι φίλον ἐκ σέθεν (sc. ἐστί). The cry with which the Chorus interrupts him (πῶς φής;) marks their perception (from his first words αὗται δέ etc.) that the children of *that* marriage were before them. αὗται...παῖδε: cp. Plat. *Laches* p. 187 A αὐτοὶ εὑρεταὶ γεγονότε.

533 Poetical Greek idiom would join κοινᾶς with ὠδῖνος rather than with ματρός. Cp. Aesch. *Eum.* 325 ματρῷον ἄγνισμα κύριον φόνου: *Ant.* 793 νεῖκος ἀνδρῶν ξύναιμον. κοινᾶς = which bore me also.

534 f. σαί τ' εἴσ' ἄρ'. The Chorus have known all along that Oed. had married Iocasta, and also that he was the father of the girls (cp. 170, 322); but they are supposed to learn now for the first time that Iocasta was their mother. In the earlier versions of the Oedipus-myth (as in the *Odyssey*) Iocasta bears no issue to Oed.; his children are borne by a second wife, Euryganeia. The Attic poets seem first to have changed this. The Chorus would say: 'Thine, then, they are by a double tie, at once as children and...as *sisters*?' but Oed. takes out of their mouths the second name which they shrink from uttering, and utters it himself with terrible emphasis. κοιναί, by the same mother: cp. *O. T.* 261 n.: so *Ant.* 1 κοινὸν αὐτάδελφον... κάρα. πατρὸς with ἀδελφεαί only.

536 ἰώ.—ἰὼ δῆτα: cp. *El.* 842 ΗΛ. φεῦ. ΧΟ. φεῦ δῆτ'. γε after μυρίων marks assent. ἐπιστροφαί refers to the revival of the pangs in his soul by this questioning. His troubles are likened to foemen who, when they seem to have been repulsed and to be vanishing in the distance, suddenly wheel about and renew their onset. Cp. 1044 δαΐων | ἀνδρῶν ἐπιστροφαί.

537 ἄλαστ' ἔχειν, unforgettable (dreadful) to endure: ἔχειν epexeg.: see on 231. Trag. borrowed the word from the epic πένθος ἄλαστον (*Il.* 24. 105), ἄλαστον ὀδύρομαι (*Od.* 14. 174): so Aesch. *Pers.* 990 (κακὰ) ἄλαστα στυγνὰ πρόκακα. Cp. 1482.

538 οὐκ ἔριξα: cp. 267, 521. τί γάρ; 'Why, what else?' if not ἔρεξα. Cp. 542.

540 f. δῶρον. The τυραννίς was δωρητόν, οὐκ αἰτητόν (*O. T.* 384),—the reward pressed on him by Thebes for worsting the Sphinx; and with the throne he received the hand of Iocasta.

The MS. ἐπωφέλησα, 'I benefited,' or 'succoured' (cp. 441), cannot be right. The sense required is μήποτε ὤφελον ἐξελέσθαι, 'would that I had never won!' I read the partic. ἐπωφελήσας (which the iambic metre allows), and take ἐξελέσθαι as the absol. infin. expressing a wish :—'and would that I had never received that choice gift from the city, for having served her.' For this absol. infin., with the subject in the nominative, cp. Aesch. *Cho.* 363: ΗΛ. μηδ' ὑπὸ Τρωίας | τείχεσι φθίμενος, πάτερ, | μετ' ἄλλων δουρικμῆτι λαῷ | παρὰ Σκαμάνδρου πόρον τεθάφθαι, | πάρος δ' οἱ κτανόντες νιν οὕτως δαμῆναι. Cp. also *Od.* 24. 376 αἲ γάρ, Ζεῦ τε πάτερ καὶ Ἀθηναίη καὶ Ἄπολλον, | οἷος Νήρικον εἷλον,... | τοῖος ἐών τοι χθιζὸς ἐν ἡμετέροισι δόμοισιν, | τεύχε' ἔχων ὤμοισιν, ἐφεστάμεναι καὶ ἀμύνειν, 'Ah, would to father Zeus,...that, such as I was when I took Nericus,...in such might, and with armour on my shoulders, *I had stood by thee, and had been aiding thee,* yesterday in our house!'

ἐξελέσθαι, ironical as if the bride were a γέρας ἐξαίρετον. The *act.* aor. is used of the army choosing a prize (out of the booty) for a chief, *Il.* 16. 56 κούρην ἥν ἄρα μοι γέρας ἔξελον υἷες Ἀχαιῶν: the *midd.* aor., of the victor choosing his own prize, as *Tr.* 244 ταύτας... | ἐξείλεθ' αὑτῷ κτῆμα. Here πόλεος ἐξελέσθαι is not 'to choose for myself *out* of the city,' but 'to receive as a choice gift *from* the city.'

542 τί γάρ; 'how then?'—marking the transition from the topic of the marriage to that of the parricide. (Cp. *Quid vero?*)

544 δευτέραν, *sc.* πληγήν: Her. 3. 64 καιρίη...τετύφθαι: *Ant.*
1307 τί μ' οὐκ ἀνταίαν | ἔπαισέν τις; Xen. *An.* 5. 8. 12 ἀνέκραγον...
ὡς ὀλίγας παίσειεν. ἐπί...νόσον, 'wound on wound,' accus. in.
apposition: of mental anguish, as *O. T.* 1061 ἅλις νοσοῦσ' ἐγώ.

545 f. ἔχει δέ μοι...πρὸς δίκας τι; but (the deed) has for me
(dat. of interest) something from the quarter of justice; *i.e.* it
has a quality which tends to place it on the side of justice,—
to rank it among justifiable deeds. Cp. *O. T.* 1014 πρὸς δίκης
οὐδὲν τρέμων (n.). The subj. to ἔχει is τὸ ἔργον, easily supplied
from ἵκανον.—This is better than to take ἔχει as impers. with
πρὸς δίκας as = ἐνδίκως, τι being then adv.: 'my case is
in some sort just.'—τί γάρ; *sc.* ἔχει: 'why, what justification
has it?'

547 The MSS. give καὶ γὰρ ἄλλους ἐφόνευσα κ.τ.λ. Many
emendations of ἄλλους have been proposed, but Mekler's καὶ
γὰρ ἄν, οὓς ἐφόνευσ', ἔμ' ἀπώλεσαν best brings out the point on
which Oed. insists, and to which the words νόμῳ καθαρός (548)
refer,—viz. that, in slaying, he was defending his own life.
Cp. 271. After he had returned the blow of Laïus, the
attendants set on him (see on *O. T.* 804—812).

548 νόμῳ...καθαρός, because he had been first struck by
Laïus, and was acting in self-defence. Plat. *Legg.* 869 c
ἀδελφὸς δ' ἐὰν ἀδελφὸν κτείνῃ ἐν στάσεσι μάχης γενομένης ἤ τινι
τρόπῳ τοιούτῳ, ἀμυνόμενος ἄρχοντα χειρῶν πρότερον, καθάπερ
πολέμιον ἀποκτείνας ἔστω καθαρός· καὶ ἐὰν πολίτης πολίτην
ὡσαύτως, ἢ ξένος ξένον. Rhadamanthus himself was cited as the
author of this rule (Apollod. 2. 4. 9). ἐς τόδ' ἦλθον, to this
plight: cp. on 273.

549 καὶ μὴν introducing the new person: cp. 1249: so
Ant. 526, 1180, 1257: *Ai.* 1168, 1223: *El.* 78, 1422.

550 ὀμφήν, his message. Usu. of a divine or oracular voice
(102), but see 1351: Pind. fr. 53 ὀμφαὶ μελέων σὺν αὐλοῖς:
Eur. *Med.* 174 μύθων τ' αὐδαθέντων | ...ὀμφάν (the words of the
Chorus). ἐφ' ἀστάλη = ἐπὶ (ταῦτα) ἐφ' ἃ ἐστάλη (cp. 274), 'to
do that for which he was summoned.'

551 ff. The σκοπός, who did not know the name of Oed.,
could describe the traces of wounds about the sightless eyes,
and brought the mysterious message (72). Theseus then set
out, surmising who it was. Meanwhile the *name* of Oed. had
become known at Colonus (222), and wayfarers who met
Theseus raised his surmise into certain knowledge. Cp. on
299 ff. ἔν τι, answered by τανῦν θ'.

553 ἔγνωκά σ', 'I have recognised thee'—explaining how he is able to greet him by name: not merely, 'I recognise thee.' ἔγνωκα is used (1) with a distinctly perfect sense: Lys. or. 17 § 6 ταῦτα...πρότερον ἐγνώκατε ἡμέτερα εἶναι: Dem. or. 3 § 10 ὅτι...δεῖ βοηθεῖν...πάντες ἐγνώκαμεν. (2) More like a present, yet always with a certain emphasis, '*I have come to know*': Ar. *Eq.* 871 ἔγνωκας οὖν δῆτ' αὐτὸν οἷός ἐστιν; 'have you found out what sort of man he is?' ὁδοῖς ἐν ταῖσδ', 'in the course of my coming here.' The plur. of one journey, as *Ant.* 226 ὁδοῖς κυκλῶν ἐμαυτὸν εἰς ἀναστροφήν, and so *El.* 68: otherwise below, 1397.

554 ἀκούων, after the same word in 551, is awkward. The γάρ in 555 might also suggest that the partic. here referred to the evidence of his own eyes, not to further hearsay by the way. λεύσσων is intrinsically the best substitute that has been proposed· but it has no palaeographic probability. I had thought of ἱκάνων (cp. 576). Doubtless it is possible that ἀκούων was not a corruption of a similar form, but merely an inadvertent repetition from 551. Ancient writers, even the most artistic, were less careful than moderns in avoiding such repetitions of single words. Cp. 631 ἐκβάλοι, 636 ἐκβαλῶ: 638, 640 ἡδύ: 966, 969 ἐπεί: 1000, 1003 καλόν, 1004 καλῶς: *O. T.* 517 φέρον, 519 φέροντι, 520 φέρει: *ib.* 1276, 1278 ὁμοῦ: *Ant.* 73, 76 κείσομαι: *Ai.* 1201, 1204 (τέρψιν). See A. B. Cook in *Classical Review*, vol. xvi. pp. 158 sqq., 256 sqq.

555 σκευή, 'garb,' cp. 1597 εἶτ' ἔλυσε δυσπινεῖς στολάς. The misery of his aspect impresses Creon (747), as it had impressed the Chorus (150). Probably the reference is simply to the tale of long and destitute wanderings which his wretched apparel told (cp. 3 ff.). δύστηνον, as showing how he had blinded himself: cp. 286.

556 ὄνθ' ὃς εἶ, 'that you are the man you are,' *i.e.* Οἰδίπους. Cp. *O. T.* 1036 ὠνομάσθης...ὃς εἶ (Oedipus). *Od.* 24. 159 οὐδέ τις ἡμείων δύνατο γνῶναι τὸν ἐόντα, 'and not one of us could tell that he was the man' (Odysseus).

557 'περέσθαι aor. (used by Thuc., Plat., etc.); the fut. ἐπερήσομαι was also Attic; but the Attic pres. was ἐπερωτάω, ἐπείρομαι being only Ionic.

558 ἐπέστης, hast presented thyself. Plat. *Symp.* 212 D ἐπιστῆναι ἐπὶ τῆς θύρας. Esp. of a sudden and unlooked-for appearance before a place (as in war): Isocr. or. 9 § 58 μικροῦ δεῖν ἔλαθεν αὐτὸν ἐπὶ τὸ βασίλειον ἐπιστάς. πόλεως...ἐμοῦ τ', obj.

gen.: τί προστρέπων πόλιν ἐμέ τε (cp. on 49), 'suit to the city and me.'

560 f. ἄν...τύχοις...ἐξαφισταίμην: 'strange would be the fortune which (= I cannot imagine *what* fortune) you could succeed in mentioning, from which I would hold aloof': another way of saying οὐκ ἂν τύχοις λ. τοιαύτην, ὁποίας ἐξαφισταίμην. When the optat. with ἄν stands in the antecedent clause (as ἄν τύχοις here), the optative *without* ἄν stands in the relative clause : *Il.* 13. 343 μάλα κεν θρασυκάρδιος εἴη, | ὃς τότε γηθήσειεν: he *would be* right bold of heart, *who should* then rejoice. Ar. *Nub.* 1250 οὐκ ἂν ἀποδοίην οὐδ᾽ ἂν ὀβολὸν οὐδενί, | ὅστις καλέσειε κάρδοπον τὴν καρδόπην. Such a relative clause is equivalent to a protasis with εἰ and optat.: as here to εἰ αὐτῆς ἀφισταίμην. Cp. Goodwin, *Moods and Tenses*, § 531. Carefully distinguish the opt. ὃν...ψέξαιμι at 1172, where see n.

πρᾶξιν, 'fortune,' not 'action.' The sing. πρᾶξις in Soph. usu. means 'fortune,' *Ai.* 790, *Tr.* 152, 294 : while the sense of 'action' usu. belongs to the plur. πράξεις, as below, 958, *O. T.* 895, *Ant.* 435. There is only one Sophoclean exception each way : in *Tr.* 879 πρᾶξις = 'mode of doing,' and in *Ant.* 1305 πράξεις = 'fortunes.' Cp. Aesch. *P. V.* 695 πέφρικ᾽ ἐσιδοῦσα πρᾶξιν Ἰοῦς. Her. 3. 65 ἀπέκλαιε τὴν ἑωυτοῦ πρῆξιν.

562 ξένος. Aethra, the mother of Theseus, was daughter of Pittheus, king of Troezen, where Theseus was brought up, in ignorance that his father was Aegeus, king of Athens. On arriving at manhood, he received from his mother the tokens of his birth (σύμβολα, γνωρίσματα)—the sword and sandals left at Troezen by Aegeus—and set out for Attica. There he slew the sons of his uncle Pallas, who were plotting against his father, and was acknowledged by Aegeus as his heir (Plut. *Thes.* 4—13).

563 f. καὶ ὡς ἤθελησα πλεῖστα εἰς ἀνήρ, 'and wrestled with perils to my life as none ever did.' With πλεῖστος the strengthening εἷς or εἷς ἀνήρ is esp. freq.: *Tr.* 460 πλείστας ἀνὴρ εἷς : Eur. *Her.* 8 πλείστων μετέσχον εἷς ἀνήρ: Xen. *Cyr.* 8. 2. 15 θησαυροὺς...πλείστους ἐνὶ ἀνδρί: Thuc. 8. 40 μιᾷ γε πόλει... πλεῖστοι. Cp. *O. T.* 1380 n. With the MS. χώς τις the ὡς before ἐπαιδεύθην must be repeated before ἤθλησα, the constr. being, καὶ (ὡς) ἤθλησα, ὡς ἀνήρ τις πλεῖστα ἤθλησε.

ἐπὶ ξένης : 184.

564 κινδυνεύματ᾽ (acc. of cognate notion), his encounters, on his way overland from Troezen to Attica, with various foes,—the robbers Periphetes, Sinis, Sciron, Procrustes,—the sow of Crommyon,—etc.; his slaying of the Minotaur in Crete; his fighting on the side of the Lapithae against the Centaurs, etc.

ἐν τώμῷ κάρᾳ, at the risk of my own life, **ἐν** denoting the stake: Eur. *Cycl.* 654 ἐν τῷ Καρὶ κινδυνεύσομεν: Plat. *Lach.* 187 B μὴ οὐκ ἐν τῷ Καρὶ ὑμῖν ὁ κίνδυνος κινδυνεύηται, ἀλλ᾽ ἐν τοῖς υἱέσι. Cp. *Od.* 2. 237 παρθέμενοι κεφαλάς, at the risk of their lives. The irreg. dat. **κάρᾳ** from nom. κάρα again *Ant.* 1272, *El.* 445 (*v. l.* κάρα), fr. 141. 2: it occurs first in Theogn. 1018, the Homeric dat. being κάρητι or κρατί.

565 f. ξένον with **ὑπεκτραποίμην,** as well as **συνεκσῴζειν**: cp. Plat. *Phaed.* 108 B τὴν ἀκάθαρτον (ψυχὴν)...ἅπας φεύγει τε καὶ ὑπεκτρέπεται. The notion is that of retiring (ὑπο-) out of the path to avoid meeting a person. Soph. has the act. with gen., *Tr.* 549 τῶν δ᾽ ὑπεκτρέπει πόδα.—**συνεκσῴζειν,** to help in extricating: Antiph. or. 5 § 93 τὸ σῶμα ἀπειρηκὸς ἡ ψυχὴ συνεξέσωσεν.

567 ἀνὴρ = θνητός: *Ant.* 768 φρονείτω μεῖζον ἢ κατ᾽ ἄνδρ᾽ ἰών. Cp. 393.

568 σοῦ = ἢ σοί: *Ant.* 74 πλείων χρόνος | ὃν δεῖ μ᾽ ἀρέσκειν τοῖς ἐκεῖ τῶν ἐνθάδε: Thuc. 1. 85 ἔξεστι δ᾽ ἡμῖν μᾶλλον ἑτέρων.

569 τὸ σὸν γενναῖον: shown in sparing Oed. the painful task of introducing himself and telling his story.

570 παρῆκεν (aor. of παρίημι) closely with **ὥστε...δεῖσθαι**: 'has graciously *permitted* that there should be,' etc. Cp. 591: *El.* 1482 ἀλλά μοι πάρες | κἂν σμικρὸν εἰπεῖν: *Ant.* 1043 (οὐδ᾽ ὡς) θάπτειν παρήσω κεῖνον. For ὥστε cp. Her. 6. 5 οὐ γὰρ ἔπειθε τοὺς Χίους ὥστε ἑωυτῷ δοῦναι νέας: and see on 970. **ὥστε ἐμοὶ δεῖσθαι,** so that there is need for me, **βραχέα φράσαι,** to say but little. **δεῖσθαι** midd., impersonal, = δεῖν. (It could not be *pass.*, with βραχέα for subject.) Bekker *Anecd.* p. 88. 21 δεῖται· ἀντὶ τοῦ δεῖ· ἀπελθεῖν με δεῖται. The only examples (so far as I know), besides our passage, are Plat. *Meno* 79 c δεῖται οὖν σοι πάλιν...τῆς αὐτῆς ἐρωτήσεως. And presently: ἢ οὐ δοκεῖ σοι πάλιν δεῖσθαι τῆς αὐτῆς ἐρωτήσεως; In the former place, while the best MSS. have δεῖται, some have δεῖ. *Rep.* 340 A καὶ τί δεῖται μάρτυρος; *Alc.* II. 149 δοκεῖ μοι πολλῆς φυλακῆς δεῖσθαι. If, however, the text can be trusted, these are clear instances. In Her. 4. 11 δεόμενον (as if = δέον) is plainly corrupt. If we altered **ἐμοὶ** to **ἐμοῦ,** the subject to δεῖσθαι would be τὸ σὸν γενναῖον. But then δεῖσθαι would mean 'requests,' rather than 'requires,' of me.

136 *Oedipus at Colonus*

For the dat. ἐμοί with δεῖσθαι (instead of ἐμέ as subj. to φράσαι) cp. Eur. *Hipp.* 940 θεοῖσι προσβαλεῖν χθονὶ | ἄλλην δεήσει γαῖαν: and see on 721. Wecklein takes ἐμοί with παρῆκεν, *permisit mihi*, but the interposed ὥστε forbids this. The conject. σοι (for ἐμοί), 'to say little *to thee*,' would be very weak.

571 f. Theseus has named Oed. (557) and Laïus (553), but not Thebes. A knowledge of the stranger's country was implied by the rest. Cp. on 205. γῆς could stand with ἦλθον (cp. *O. T.* 152 Πυθῶνος ἔβας, *Ph.* 630 νεὼς ἄγοντα), but is more simply governed by ἀπό.

574 χὠ λόγος διοίχεται, and the statement is at an end. ὁ λόγος is the explanation due from Oedipus after sending for Theseus. Cp. Eur. *Suppl.* 528 (Theseus to the Thebans) εἰ γάρ τι καὶ πεπόνθατ' Ἀργείων ὕπο, | τεθνᾶσιν, ἠμύνασθε πολεμίους καλῶς, | αἰσχρῶς δ' ἐκείνοις, χἠ δίκη διοίχεται: *i.e.*, if you have been wronged, you have had satisfaction, 'and *the cause is closed*.' διέρχεται (L) is certainly corrupt.

575 τοῦτ' αὐτὸ marks eagerness: *O. T.* 545 ΟΙ. ...βαρύν σ' εὕρηκ ἐμοί. ΚΡ. τοῦτ' αὐτὸ νῦν μου πρῶτ' ἄκουσον ὡς ἐρῶ.

577 f. τὰ δὲ | κέρδη: cp. 265, 'but the gains from it are better than beauty.'

580 που, *i.e.* so far as Oed. can conjecture the purpose of Apollo. He could not be sure that the close of his life would *immediately* follow on his arrival at the grove. The promised sign of the end had not yet been given (94).

581 ποίῳ, *sc.* χρόνῳ, asks with surprise for some further definition of the vague χρόνῳ μάθοις ἄν. Theseus naturally assumes that the blessings are to come in the lifetime of Oedipus. And if not now, he asks, then in what contingency? The answer startles him. προσφορά, offering, present. Theophrast. *Char.* xxx it is like the αἰσχροκερδής, γαμοῦντός τινος τῶν φίλων καὶ ἐκδιδομένου θυγατέρα πρὸ χρόνου τινὸς ἀποδημῆσαι, ἵνα μὴ πέμψῃ προσφοράν (a wedding-present). Cp. 1270. δηλώσεται, pass.: see *O. T.* 672 n.

583 f. *i.e.* 'You ask for the last offices which piety can render: you do not ask me for protection during your lifetime.' Through the oracle (389), of which Theseus knows nothing, a *grave* in Attica had become the supreme concern of Oedipus. τὰ δ' ἐν μέσῳ is governed by λῆστιν ἴσχεις as = ἐπιλανθάνει (see on 223), no less than by ποεῖ. To make τὰ δ' ἐν μ. an accus. of respect would suit the first verb, but not the second. δι' οὐδενὸς ποεῖ, 'you disregard,' a solitary instance of this phrase (instead of οὐδενὸς or παρ' οὐδὲν ποεῖσθαι), perh. suggested by the use of the prep. in such phrases as διὰ φυλακῆς ἔχω τι, etc.

585 ἐνταῦθα γάρ, 'yes' for *there*,—in *that* boon (ἐν τῷ θάπτεσθαι),—those other things (τὰ ἐν μέσῳ) are included, lit. brought together for me: *i.e.* if you promise that I shall eventually be buried in Attica, you cannot meanwhile allow me to be forcibly removed to the Theban frontier. He is thinking of protection against Creon's imminent attempt (399). συγκομίζομαι, to collect or store up for oneself, was, like συγκομιδή, esp. said of harvesting (Xen. *Anab.* 6. 6. 37), and that notion perhaps tinges the word here, 'are garnered.'

586 ἐν βραχεῖ in sense = βραχεῖαν: 'this grace which you ask of me lies in a small compass' (*not*, 'you ask me this favour in brief speech'). The adverbial ἐν βραχεῖ does not go with the verb, but is equiv. to a predicative adj. agreeing with χάριν. Such phrases imply the omission of the partic. ὤν: so 29 πέλας γὰρ ἄνδρα τόνδ' ὁρῶ: *Ph.* 26 τοὔργον οὐ μακρὰν λέγεις (the task which you set is not distant): *El.* 899 ὡς δ' ἐν γαλήνῃ πάντ' ἐδερκόμην τόπον. For βραχεῖ cp. 293, Plat. *Legg.* 641 B βραχύ τι...ὄφελος.

587 γε μήν, however: Aesch. *Ag.* 1378 ἦλθε, σὺν χρόνῳ γε μήν. ἀγὼν ὅδε, 'this issue.' *El.* 1491 λόγων γὰρ οὐ | νῦν ἐστιν ἀγών, ἀλλὰ σῆς ψυχῆς πέρι. The word ἀγών is so far ambiguous that it does not necessarily mean a physical *contest*, but can mean an *issue* or *crisis* (Lat. *discrimen, momentum*). Plat. *Rep.* 608 B μέγας...ὁ ἀγὼν...τὸ χρηστὸν ἢ κακὸν γενέσθαι.

588 πότερα. Oed. has said, 'If you pledge yourself to keep me in Attica, a serious issue will be raised.' Theseus :—'Do you mean between your sons and me?' You mean that they will contest my right to retain you? For the MS. ἐκγόνων Hartung reads ἐγγονῶν. But though Theseus does not yet know of the *quarrel* between the father and the sons (599), he knows the sons to exist : they would represent the claim of the ἐγγενεῖς. κἀμοῦ: the MS. ἢ 'μοῦ is certainly wrong. Theseus does not ask—'Will the issue be serious for your kinsmen, or for me?' but, 'In what quarter will the issue arise?' Cp. 606 τἀμὰ κἀκείνων.

589 f. Kayser's ἄναξ, χρῄζουσι (for ἀναγκάζουσι) is exactly what the sense requires, and is fairly near to the MS. reading, while the latter is (I think) certainly corrupt. The verse must not be considered alone, but in close connection with 590,

and with the whole context. We want either: (1) instead of κομίζειν, a word = '*to return*'; but κατελθεῖν is very unlikely, and no other substitute is obvious: or (2) instead of ἀναγκάζουσι, a word = 'they *wish, seek.*' That the fault lies in ἀναγκάζουσι is very strongly suggested by 590, where L has ἀλλ' εἰ θέλοντ' ἄν γ', evidently corrupted, by dittographia of γ', from ἀλλ' εἰ θέλοντά γ', which L² has. This gives a clear and fitting sense, if in 589 we read ἄναξ, χρῄζουσί με. All the trouble, for the mss. and for the edd., has arisen from ἀναγκάζουσι. So far as the tense of ἀναγκάζουσι is concerned, a change to the *fut.* is no gain: it is the pres. of tendency or intention. But the whole mention of *compulsion* or *violence* is premature in 589. Oed. leads very gently up to the disclosure of his sons' unnatural conduct (599).

590 οὐδὲ σοί: while *they*, on their part, call you home, for *you*, on yours, exile is not desirable,—if, indeed, their offer is agreeable to you (*i.e.* if you have no repugnance to Thebes). οὐδὲ is here the negative counterpart of δέ in apodosis: *i.e.* as we can say, εἰ θέλοντά σε ἐκεῖνοι κατάγουσι, σοὶ δὲ κατελθεῖν καλόν, so also οὐδὲ σοὶ φεύγειν καλόν. The same resoluble quality of οὐδέ is seen in its use for ἀλλ' οὐ (*Il.* 24. 25). Cp. on 591. φεύγειν, 'to be an exile' rather than 'to shun them.'

591 ἀλλ' οὐδ' presupposes his refusal, and justifies it: 'Nay, *neither* did they consider my wishes.' παρίεσαν, 'concede,' *sc.* ἐμοὶ κατελθεῖν, cp. 570: not ἐμὲ εἰς τὴν πόλιν, 'admit' (in which sense usu. of allowing armies to enter territory, or the like: Eur. *Suppl.* 468 Ἄδραστον ἐς γῆν τήνδε μὴ παριέναι).

592 θυμὸς δ'. δέ sometimes corrects or objects: *O. T.* 379 (n.) Κρέων δέ σοι πῆμ' οὐδέν ('*Nay*'). ξύμφορον: the neut. as often in maxims, when the masc. or fem. subj. is viewed in its most general aspect: Eur. *Or.* 232 δυσάρεστον οἱ νοσοῦντες: cp. *O. T.* 542 n.

593 ὅταν μάθῃς μου, 'when you have heard (the matter) from me.' Distinguish the gen. with ἐκμάθω in 114, where see n. Cp. *El.* 889 ἄκουσον ὡς μαθοῦσά μου | τὸ λοιπὸν ἢ φρονοῦσαν ἢ μώραν λέγῃς. *O. T.* 545 μανθάνειν δ' ἐγὼ κακὸς | σοῦ.

596 ξυμφοράν euphemistic (*O. T.* 99 n.): cp. 369 τὴν πάλαι γένους φθοράν. Here, as there, γένους = 'race,' not 'birth.' Theseus supposes Oed. to mean that the hereditary curse has fallen on him with especial weight. ἐρεῖς, '*will you* mention,'

Notes   139

i.e. 'do you allude to': cp. *Ph.* 439 ff. ΦΙ. ἀναξίου μὲν φωτὸς ἐξερήσομαι...ΝΕ. ποίου γε τούτου πλὴν Ὀδυσσέως ἐρεῖς; ΦΙ οὐ τοῦτον εἶπον.

598 μεῖζον ἢ κατ' ἄνθρ., 'a grief passing the grief of man': Xen. *Mem.* 4. 4. 24 βελτίονος ἢ κατ' ἄνθρωπον νομοθέτου : Thuc. 7. 75 μεῖζω ἢ κατὰ δάκρυα ἐπεποιθεσαν. If the woe to which he alludes is something greater than the calamity of his house, then it must be superhuman. **νοσεῖς**: see on 544.

601 Instead of οὐκ ἔστι μοι κατελθεῖν ποτε, we have ἔστι μοι κατελθεῖν μήποτε, since ἔστι μοι = 'my doom is,' ζημία κεῖταί μοι.—Cp. on 407.

602 πεμψαίαθ' (cp. on 44), 'summon to themselves': Eur. *Hec.* 977 τί χρῆμ' ἐπέμψω τὸν ἐμὸν ἐκ δόμων πόδα; ὥστ' οἰκεῖν δίχα, *if it is understood* that you cannot live with them in Thebes. **ὥστε** introduces the condition: Thuc. 1. 98 ἑτοῖμοι δὲ εἶναι καὶ ὥστε ἀμφοτέρους μένειν κατὰ χώραν, the Corcyreans said that they were also ready (to make an armistice) *under the condition* that each party should remain where they were.

603 ἐξαναγκάσει. There is no reason for changing fut. to pres. here. The oracle had been given (388), but its effect was to come. Cp. 1179.

605 ὅτι, as if ποῖον χρησμὸν ἀκούσαντας had preceded. Not with δείσαντας: verbs of fearing are sometimes followed by ὡς or ὅπως with indic. (instead of μή with subj.), as in *El.* 1309; but by ὅτι only as = 'because.' τῇδε...χθονί, 'in Attica,' locative dat., not instrum. Oed. interprets Ismene's less explicit statement (411).

606 τἀμὰ κἀκείνων = τὰ ἐμὰ καὶ (τὰ) ἐκείνων: cp. 588: *Tr* 1068: Eur. *El.* 301 τύχας βαρείας τὰς ἐμὰς κἀμοῦ πατρός. Poetry tolerated such omission of the second art. even when the subjects were sharply opposed: *El.* 991: Aesch. *Ag.* 324 καὶ τῶν ἁλόντων καὶ κρατησάντων. Theseus cannot foresee any cause which should trouble the ancient amity between Athens and Thebes (619, 632).

608 γῆρας...κατθανεῖν: for the inf. *without art.* co-ordinated with a noun cp. *Il.* 10. 173 ἐπὶ ξυροῦ ἵσταται ἀκμῆς | ἢ μάλα λυγρὸς ὄλεθρος Ἀχαιοῖς ἠὲ βιῶναι.

609 συγχεῖ, confounds, ruins, effaces: *Tr.* 1229: Her. 7. 136 συγχέαι τὰ πάντων ἀνθρώπων νόμιμα: esp. fitting here, since applicable to breach of treaties, *Il.* 4. 269 σύν γ' ὅρκι' ἔχευαν | Τρῶες. παγκρατὴς, epithet of sleep in *Ai.* 675, and of fire in *Ph.* 986. Cp. Shaksp. *Sonnets* 63, 64 'With Time's injurious hand crush'd and o'erworn': ... 'by Time's fell hand defaced.'

610 φθίνει μὲν...φθίνει δὲ, epanaphora, as 5, *O. T.* 25 φθίνουσα μὲν... | φθίνουσα δ᾽, 259 ἔχων μὲν...ἔχων δέ. γῆs has been needlessly suspected: here, as in the great speech of Ajax (*Ai.* 669—677), human destiny is viewed in relation to the whole order of nature. Cp. Tennyson, *Tithonus* 1 'The woods decay, the woods decay and fall, The vapours weep their burthen to the ground, Man comes and tills the field and lies beneath, And after many a summer dies the swan.'

611 βλαστάνει, comes into existence,—like the other natural growths which wax and wane: fig. of customs and institutions in *Ant.* 296 νόμισμ᾽ ἔβλαστε, *El.* 1095 ἔβλαστε νόμιμα.

612 πνεῦμα is not here the wind of fortune, but the spirit which man breathes towards man, and city towards city; the spirit of friendship or enmity. Cp. Aesch. *Theb.* 705 (where, though fortune is meant, the δαίμων is a person), δαίμων | λήματος ἐν τροπαίᾳ χρονίᾳ μεταλ-|λακτὸς ἴσως ἂν ἔλθοι | θαλερωτέρῳ | πνεύματι. So πνεῖν μένος, κότον, ἔρωτα etc.

613 βέβηκεν, *is set* (cp. 1052). Though (*e.g.*) πνεῦμα φίλιον βέβηκεν ἐν ἀνδράσιν could not mean, 'a friendly spirit *is steady* among men,' yet πνεῦμα ταὐτὸν βέβηκεν can mean, 'the *same* spirit *is set*,' *i.e.* blows steadily. Cp. Ar. *Ran.* 1003 ἡνίκ᾽ ἂν τὸ πνεῦμα λεῖον | καὶ καθεστηκὸς λάβῃς. πόλει ethic dat., on the part of.

614 f. τοῖς μὲν γὰρ ἤδη, for some men *at once* (*i.e.*, after but a brief friendship), for others, later. ἤδη = αὐτίκα here. No relationship between men or states is permanent, *for* the feelings with which they regard each other are liable to change,—from liking to dislike, yes, and back again to liking. καῦθις φίλα, by completing the circle, completes the picture of inconstancy. The maxim ascribed to Bias of Priene (c. 550 B.C.), φιλεῖν ὡς μισήσοντας καὶ μισεῖν ὡς φιλήσοντας (Arist. *Rh.* 2. 13, Cic. *De Amic.* 16. 59 *ita amare oportere ut si aliquando esset osurus*), is paraphrased in *Ai.* 679 ff., with the comment, τοῖς πολλοῖσι γὰρ | βροτῶν ἄπιστός ἐσθ᾽ ἑταιρείας λιμήν: cp. *ib.* 1359 ἢ κάρτα πολλοὶ νῦν φίλοι καῦθις πικροί.

616 Θήβαις dat. of interest, if she has her relations with you in a peaceful state. εὐημερεῖ. εὐημερία = either (1) 'fine weather,' εὐδία, or (2) 'prosperity.' The verb is always figurative.

617 καλῶς, 'satisfactorily,' 'as we could wish.' τὰ πρὸς σέ, 'her relations with you.' ὁ μυρίος: cp. *Ai.* 646 ὁ μακρὸς κἀναρίθμητος χρόνος.

618 τεκνοῦται, 'gives birth to.' The midd. was more commonly used of the mother, the act. of the father (though converse instances occur); the midd. is used figuratively, as here, in Aesch. *Ag.* 754 (ὄλβος), Eur. *I. T.* 1262 (χθών). Ἰών, as it proceeds. Cp. *El.* 1365 πολλαὶ κυκλοῦνται νύκτες ἡμέραι τ' ἴσαι | αἱ ταῦτά σοι δείξουσιν.

619 ἐν αἷς, 'in the course of which': *i.e.* at some moment in them. So *Ant.* 1064 κάτισθι μὴ πολλοὺς ἔτι | τρόχους ἀμιλλητῆρας ἡλίου τελῶν | ἐν οἷσι...ἀμοιβὸν ἀντιδοὺς ἔσει. δεξιώματα, 'pledges' given by placing one's right hand in another's: the word occurs only here, and in Athen. 159 B (poet. anonym.) ὦ χρυσέ, δεξίωμα κάλλιστον βροτοῖς, gift most welcome to men. δεξιοῦσθαι is only 'to greet' or 'welcome': but δεξιὰς διδόναι καὶ λαμβάνειν, etc., suggested the phrase here. Cp. *Il.* 2. 341 σπονδαί τ' ἄκρητοι καὶ δεξιαί, ἧς ἐπέπιθμεν. In Eur. *Suppl.* 930 Theseus says of Polyneices, ξένος γὰρ ἦν μοι, as if alluding to hereditary ξενία between the royal houses. Cp. 632.

620 δόρει διασκεδῶσιν, they will 'throw their pledges to the winds' by an armed invasion of Attica. Cp. *Ant.* 287 νόμους διασκεδῶν, to make havoc of laws. δόρει (instead of the more freq. δορί) is required by metre also in 1314, 1386, Ar. *Pax* 357 σὺν δόρει σὺν ἀσπίδι, *Vesp.* 1081 (where MSS. ξὺν δορὶ ξὺν ἀσπίδι),—all iambic or trochaic.

621 ἵν' could mean, 'at a place where,' at the grave (see on 411), but is better taken as = 'in which case,' 'when,' since the moment of rupture (διασκεδῶσιν) would not be the battle at Colonus, but the preceding declaration of war. εὔδων (cp. on 307), in contrast with the fierce combatants on the ground above him.

622 ψυχρὸς...θερμόν, here of the physical contrast between death and life; but in *Ant.* 88 θερμὴν ἐπὶ ψυχροῖσι καρδίαν ἔχεις, 'thy heart is hot on chilling deeds' (κρυεροῖς). For the idea of the buried dead draining the life-blood of their foes cp. *El.* 1420 παλίρρυτον γὰρ αἷμ' ὑπεξαιροῦσι τῶν | κτανόντων οἱ πάλαι θανόντες.

623 σαφής, true (as a prophet): 792: *O. T.* 1011 ταρβῶ γε μή μοι Φοῖβος ἐξέλθῃ σαφής. So φίλος σαφής, a proved friend (Eur. *Or.* 1155), γραμματεὺς σαφης, an accurate scribe (Aesch. fr. 348).

624 τἀκίνητα, = ἃ μὴ δεῖ λόγῳ κινεῖσθαι (see 1526), secrets which should be allowed to *rest* beyond the veil: so *Ant.* 1060 ὄρσεις με τἀκίνητα διὰ φρενῶν φράσαι, the secrets locked in my soul. (Cp. Gray: 'No farther seeks his merits to disclose, *Or draw his frailties from their dread abode.*')

625 f. ἔα με (ἐν τούτοις) ἃ (λέγων) ἠρξάμην, leave me (permit me to cease) at the point where I began (the prayer for an Attic home). Cp. *Il.* 9. 97 ἐν σοὶ μὲν λήξω, σέο δ' ἄρξομαι. τὸ σόν...πιστὸν φυλάσσων, taking care that thy part is loyally done: cp. *O. T.* 320 τὸ σόν τε σὺ | κἀγὼ διοίσω τοὐμόν (thy part): *Ai.* 1313 ὅρα μὴ τοὐμὸν ἀλλὰ καὶ τὸ σόν (thine interest): *ib.* 99 ὡς τὸ σὸν ξυνῆκ' ἐγώ (thy saying). Both idiom and rhythm are against joining τὸ σὸν πιστόν as 'thy good faith.'

628 εἴπερ μὴ ψεύσουσι, you will find me helpful,—that is to say, if the gods do not disappoint me. εἴπερ marks the point which must be taken for granted, in order that ἐρεῖς (626) should hold good: cp. Eur. *H. F.* 1345 δεῖται γὰρ ὁ θεός, εἴπερ ἔστ' ὄντως θεός (*assuming* him to be so), | οὐδενός.

629 πάλαι: 287, 459. The Chorus, tempering caution with good-nature, testify that the promise of Oedipus is, at least, not merely a device inspired by the arrival of the King.

630 ἐφαίνετο τελῶν (without ὡς) = 'was manifestly intending to perform': ἐφαίνετο ὡς τελῶν = 'appeared *as* one intending to perform,' ὡς marking the aspect in which he presented himself to their minds. *Ai.* 326 καὶ δῆλός ἐστιν ὥς τι δρασείων κακόν.

631 δῆτ', 'then,' a comment on the speech of Oed. rather than on the words of the Chorus. ἐκβάλοι: properly, 'cast out of doors,' as a worthless thing: hence, 'reject,' 'repudiate': Eur. fr. 362. 45 προγόνων παλαιὰ θέσμι' ὅστις ἐκβαλεῖ: Plat. *Crito* 46 B τοὺς δὲ λόγους, οὓς ἐν τῷ ἔμπροσθεν ἔλεγον, οὐ δύναμαι νῦν ἐκβαλεῖν. Others take it literally, 'cast out of the land,' so that ἀνδρὸς εὐμένειαν τοιοῦδε = ἄνδρα εὐμενῆ τοιόνδε. But the notion of rashly scorning what is really precious gives more point both here and in 636.

632 f. ὅτῳ, not ὅτου, is right. Construe: ὅτῳ ἡ δορύξενος ἑστία αἰὲν κοινή ἐστι παρ' ἡμῖν, lit., 'to whom the hearth of an ally is always common among us': κοινή, 'common,' = 'giving *reciprocal* hospitality,' which Theseus could claim at Thebes, as Oedipus at Athens. αἰέν, 'at all times,' *i.e.* 'even if he had not this special claim.' This seems better than to take κοινή

as (1) 'common to him with other Thebans,' (2) 'provided by
our State,' (3) 'common to him with *us*,' or (4) 'accessible,' as
Andoc. or. 2 § 147 οἰκία κοινοτάτη τῷ δεομένῳ.

ἡ δορύξενος ἑστία, 'the hearth of an ally.' δορύξενος as adj.
Aesch. *Cho.* 914. As subst. 'spear-friend,' it is one with whom
one has the tie of ξενία in respect of war : *i.e.* who will make
common cause with one in war. It is applied by Aesch.,
Soph., and Eur. only to princes or chiefs, with an armed force
at their command. Cp. Aesch. *Cho.* 562 ξένος τε καὶ δορύξενος
δόμων, said by Orestes when he presents himself παντελῆ σαγὴν
ἔχων : *i.e.* he comes not merely as the personal ξένος of the
royal house, but as a chief in armed alliance with it.

The ξενία to which Theseus refers is not a personal friend-
ship, but a hereditary alliance between the royal houses, as in
Eur. *Suppl.* 930 Polyneices (whom he had not seen before) is
his ξένος. Cp. on 619.

634 f. ἀφιγμένος, not, 'because,' but, 'while,' he has come.
Besides his public claim (632), Oed. has two personal claims,
(1) as the suppliant of the Eumenides, (2) as a visitor who can
make a valuable return to Athens for protecting him. δασμός,
usu. 'tribute' (*O. T.* 36, and so in Xen.); here fig., 'recompense.'

636 The aor. σεβισθεὶς only here : σεβίζειν 1007, σεβίσασα
Ant. 943, σεβίζομαι (midd.) Aesch. *Suppl.* 922. In later Gk.
the pass. aor. of σεβάζομαι was deponent, as *Anth. P.* 7. 122
αἴ, αἲ Πυθαγόρης τί τόσον κυάμους ἐσεβάσθη; It appears rash to
deny that ἐσεβίσθην could be so used. The deponent use of
ἐσέφθην is attested only by Plat. *Phaedr.* 254 B (σεφθεῖσα), and
Hesych. 1. 1456 ἐσέφθην· ἐσεβάσθην, ἡσύχασα, ᾐσχύνθην.
Σοφοκλῆς Δαιδάλῳ (fr. 168 Nauck). ἐκβαλῶ: cp. 631.

637 ἔμπολιν is Musgrave's certain correction of the MS.
ἔμπαλιν : cp. 1156 σοὶ μὲν ἔμπολιν | οὐκ ὄντα, συγγενῆ δέ, not
thy fellow-citizen, indeed, but thy kinsman. The word does
not occur elsewhere. 'I will establish him in the land,' says
Theseus, 'as a member of our State': he who now is ἄπολις
(cp. 208) shall in Attica have the full protection of our laws.
Campbell objects that with ἔμπολιν 'the opposition of the
clauses would not be sufficiently marked by δέ': but for δέ =
ἀλλά cp. Antiph. or. 5 §§ 4, 5 αἰτήσομαι ὑμᾶς οὐχ ἅπερ οἱ
πολλοί..., τάδε δὲ δέομαι ὑμῶν : Thuc. 4. 86 οὐκ ἐπὶ κακᾷ, ἐπ'
ἐλευθερώσει δὲ τῶν Ἑλλήνων παρελήλυθα.

638 σέ, the Coryphaeus.

639 ff. εἰ δὲ τόδε,—στείχειν μετ᾽ ἐμοῦ,—ἡδύ ἐστι—δίδωμί σοι, τούτων κρίναντι (ὁπότερον βούλει), χρῆσθαι (αὐτῷ). For τόδ᾽ in appos. with στείχειν cp. Xen. *Cyr.* 8. 4. 4 σαφηνίζεσθαι δέ, ὡς ἕκαστον ἐτίμα, τοῦτο ἐδόκει αὐτῷ ἀγαθὸν εἶναι: Aeschin. or. 2 § 106 τὸ μὴ πολυπραγμονεῖν ἡμᾶς τοὺς πρέσβεις μηδέν, τοῦτ᾽ ἀγαθὸν ὑπολαμβάνων εἶναι. Here τόδε similarly follows the word with which it is in appos., though it should properly precede it, as Eur. *Phoen.* 550 μέγ᾽ ἥγησαι τόδε, | περιβλέπεσθαι τίμιον; τούτων partitive gen. with κρίναντι, 'having chosen (one) of these things'; cp. *O. T.* 640 δυοῖν δικαιοῖ δρᾶν ἀποκρίνας κακοῖν, | ἢ γῆς ἀπῶσαι...ἢ κτεῖναι. δίδωμι...χρῆσθαι: cp. Xen *Anab.* 3. 4 §§ 41 f. εἰ βούλει, μένε..., εἰ δὲ χρῄζεις, πορεύου... Ἀλλὰ δίδωμί σοι, ἔφη ὁ Χειρίσοφος, ὁπότερον βούλει ἑλέσθαι

641 τῇδε, 'in that sense,' *i.e.* in whichever course you may prefer, ᾗ ἂν σὺ βούλῃ: cp. 1444: *Ant.* 1111 δόξα τῇδ᾽ ἐπεστράφη: *El.* 1301 ὅπως καὶ σοὶ φίλον | καὶ τοὐμὸν ἔσται τῇδ᾽. ξυνοίσομαι, agree: Antiph. or. 5 § 42 τοῖς μὲν πρώτοις (λόγοις) συνεφέρετο,...τούτοις δὲ διεφέρετο.

642 διδοίης...εὖ: 1435: *O. T.* 1081 (τύχης) τῆς εὖ διδούσης.

643 δόμους στείχειν, 'to go into my house': 1769 Θήβας... | ...πέμψον: *O. T.* 1178 ἄλλην χθόνα | δοκῶν ἀποίσειν.

644 εἰ...ἦν, *sc.* ἔχρηζον ἂν δόμους στείχειν.

645 ἐν ᾧ τί πρόξεις; Cp. *O. T.* 558 OI. πόσον τιν᾽ ἤδη δῆθ᾽ ὁ Λάιος χρόνον | KP. δέδρακε ποῖον ἔργον; οὐ γὰρ ἐννοῶ. | OI. ἄφαντος ἔρρει...etc.: *Ph.* 210 XO. ἀλλ᾽ ἔχε, τέκνον, NE. λέγ᾽ ὅ τι XO. φροντίδας νέας: *El.* 854 ff. An interruption of this kind serves to bespeak the attention of the audience for a point which the dramatist desires to emphasize.

646 κρατήσω: near the shrine he was to close his life (91), and at his grave the Thebans were to be defeated (411, 621).

647 μέγ᾽ ἂν λέγοις δώρημα, = μέγα ἂν εἴη δώρημα ὃ λέγεις, it would be a great benefit of which you speak (sc. εἰ κρατοῖς). Cp. *Ant.* 218. τῆς συνουσίας, 'from your abiding with the people here (at Colonus)': *i.e.* 'You have suggested a strong reason for your staying *here*, rather than for going with me to *Athens*.' Cp. τῇ ξυνουσίᾳ in 63. τῆς σ., gen. of source (ultimately possessive): *O. T.* 170 φροντίδος ἔγχος, a weapon furnished by thought.

648 εἰ σοί γ᾽ | ἅπερ φὴς ἐμμενεῖ, 'yes, if on *your* part (ethic dat.) the promise (of protection and burial) shall be observed, τελοῦντι by your performing it μοι for me' (dat. of interest).

ἐμμένει *alone* might have meant merely, 'if you abstain from withdrawing your promise': τελοῦντι supplements it, marking that good faith must be shown by deeds. We can say either ἐμμένεις οἷς λέγεις or ἐμμένει σοι ἃ λέγεις: cp. Thuc. 2. 2 τέσσαρα μὲν γὰρ καὶ δέκα ἔτη ἐνέμειναν αἱ τριακοντούτεις σπονδαί: Plat. *Phaedr.* 258 B ἐὰν...ἐμμένῃ, if (his proposal) stand good.

649 τὸ τοῦδέ γ' ἀνδρ. might be acc. of respect ('as to'), but is more simply taken with θάρσει: cp. Dem. or. 3 § 7 οὔτε Φίλιππος ἐθάρρει τούτους οὔθ' οὗτοι Φίλιππον: Xen. *Cyr.* 5. 5. 42 εὐώχει αὐτούς, ἵνα σε καὶ θαρρήσωσιν. (Distinguish this acc. with θαρσεῖν, of confidence *in*, from the more freq. acc. of confidence *against*, as θαρσεῖν μάχας.) Cp. τὸ σόν, 625 n.

650 ὡς κακόν, 'as though you were faithless': cp. Shaksp. *Jul. Caes.* 2. 1. 129 ff. 'Swear priests and cowards and men cautelous,— | ...unto bad causes swear | Such creatures as men doubt.' πιστώσομαι. πιστόω is 'to make πιστός': Thuc. 4. 88 πιστώσαντες αὐτὸν τοῖς ὅρκοις, when they had bound him by the oaths (*iureiurando obstrinxerant*): so the pass., *Od.* 15. 435 εἴ μοι ἐθέλοιτέ γε, ναῦται, | ὅρκῳ πιστωθῆναι. The midd. expresses 'in one's own interest,' as here; or reciprocity, as *Il.* 21. 286 χειρὶ δὲ χεῖρα λαβόντες ἐπιστώσαντ' ἐπέεσσιν.

651 ἢ λόγῳ, than by word (without my oath). Dem. or. 27 § 54 καὶ μαρτυρίαν μὲν οὐδεμίαν ἐνεβάλετο τούτων ὁ ταῦτ' εἰπεῖν ἀξιώσας, ψιλῷ δὲ λόγῳ χρησάμενος ὡς πιστευθησόμενος δι' ἐκείνων. Cp. Antiphon or. 5 § 8 quoted on 22. Shaksp. *G. of Verona* 2. 7. 75 'His words are bonds.'

652 τοῦ μάλιστ' ὄκνος σ' ἔχει; not, 'what do you fear *most*?' but, 'What, exactly, do you fear?'—a polite way of asking the question. Plat. *Gorg.* 448 D ΣΩ. ἀλλὰ γὰρ ὃ ὑπέσχετο Χαιρεφῶντι οὐ ποιεῖ. ΓΟΡ. τί μάλιστα, ὦ Σώκρατες;

654 ὅρα με λείπων, like his utterances in 653 and 656, is left unfinished, Theseus striking in: *sc.* μὴ ἐκείνοις προδῷς. Taken as a sentence, the words could mean only 'see that' (*not* 'how') 'you are leaving me.'

655 ὀκνοῦντ' ἀνάγκη: *i.e.*, ὀκνοῦντά με ἀνάγκη διδάσκειν σε,— feeling such fear as I do, I am constrained to be thus urgent with you. (Not, 'I must thus urge you, since you are slack.')

656 οὐκ οἶσθ': Oed. had said nothing of Creon's threatened visit (396). μή, not οὐ, in strong assurance, as with inf. after ὄμνυμι, etr̄.: cp. 281, 797: *Ant.* 1092 ἐπιστάμεσθα... | μήπω ποτ' αὐτὸν ψεῦδος...λακεῖν.

146   *Oedipus at Colonus*

658—660 Many emendations of 658 f. have been proposed, and Wecklein would reject the three verses altogether. To me they seem not only authentic but textually sound. They picture a tumult of passions in the soul, presently quelled by reason. The angry threats and the sobering reason are alike personified. The genuineness of the nominative πολλαὶ δ' ἀπειλαὶ is confirmed by the imagery of the second clause, ἀλλ' ὁ νοῦς ὅταν. For this animated personification of speech or passion, cp. Aesch. *Cho.* 845 ἢ πρὸς γυναικῶν δειματούμενοι λόγοι | πεδάρσιοι θρώσκουσι, θνῄσκοντες μάτην: Eur. *Hipp.* 1416 οὐδὲ γῆς ὑπὸ ζόφῳ | θεᾶς ἄτιμοι Κύπριδος ἐκ προθυμίας | ὀργαὶ κατασκήψουσιν ἐς τὸ σὸν δέμας. The cognate verb κατηπείλησαν (gnomic aorist), instead of the simple ἔλεξαν, gives an emphasis like that which the cogn. accus. would give in πολλοὶ ἀπειλὰς κατηπείλησαν. θυμῷ modal dat., 'in wrath' (not locative, 'in the soul'): cp. Plat. *Legg.* 866 D (ἐὰν θυμῷ ... ᾗ τὸ πεπραγμένον ἐκπραχθέν: *O. T.* 405 ὀργῇ λελέχθαι.

660 αὐτοῦ (possessive) γένηται, become its own master, regain its control over passion: cp. Dem. or. 4 § 7 ἦν ὑμῶν αὐτῶν ἐθελήσητε γενέσθαι: Plat. *Phaedr.* 250 A ἐκπλήττονται καὶ οὐκέθ' αὑτῶν γίγνονται. So Her. I. 119 οὔτε ἐξεπλάγη ἐντός τε ἑωυτοῦ γίνεται, 'was not dismayed, but mastered his feelings.' φροῦδα, there is an end of them: Eur. *Tro.* 1071 (to Zeus) φροῦδαί σοι θυσίαι.

661 f. κείνοις (referring to ἄνδρες in 653) goes both with ἐπερρ. and with φανήσεται. καὶ εἰ ἐπερρώσθη (impersonal) even if courage has come to them δεινὰ λέγειν to say dread things τῆς σῆς ἀγωγῆς about your removal (for the gen. see on 355: for τῆς σῆς as = an objective σου, on 332). The normal phrase would be κεῖνοι ἐπερρώσθησαν, and the use of the impersonal form here is bolder than in the ordinary passive examples (usu. with perf.) such as ἱκανὰ τοῖς...πολεμίοις εὐτύχηται (Thuc. 7. 77).

λέγειν. An inf., which here depends on the notion ἐτόλμησαν, does not elsewhere occur with ἐπιρρώννυσθαι, but stands with the simple pf. ἔρρωμαι as = 'to be bent' on doing' (Lys. or. 13. 31 ἔρρωτο...κακόν τι ἐργάζεσθαι). For the sarcastic ἴσως cp. *Ai.* 962 ἴσως τοι, κεῖ βλέποντα μὴ 'πόθουν, | θανόντ' ἂν οἰμώξειαν. κεῖ here where εἰ καὶ would be natural (as granting the *fact*); whereas in 306 the κεῖ is normal.

663 τὸ δεῦρο, instead of τὸ μεταξύ, since πέλαγος suggests πλοῦς: cp. 1165. If the Thebans attempt an armed invasion, they will find 'a sea of troubles' interposed. Eur. *Hipp.* 822 κακῶν δ', ὦ τάλας, πέλαγος εἰσορῶ | τοσοῦτον ὥστε μήποτ' ἐκνεῦσαι πάλιν, | μήτ' ἐκπερᾶσαι κῦμα τῆσδε συμφορᾶς. Men. ap. Athen. 559 E ἀληθινὸν εἰς πέλαγος αὐτὸν ἐμβαλεῖς γὰρ πραγμάτων. The form πλώσιμον only here: Attic writers elsewhere use πλώϊμος (oft. πλόϊμος in our MSS.), Her. πλωτός: πλεύσιμος is not found.

664 f. θαρσεῖν μὲν οὖν. 'Now (οὖν) you are safe indeed (μὲν), even *without* my protection,—Phoebus being with you; but (δὲ 666) that protection,—superfluous though it be,—will be afforded by my name just as well as by my presence.' For μὲν οὖν with this distributed force cp. *O. T.* 483, *Ant.* 65; for its composite force, *O. T.* 705. κἄνευ τῆς ἐμῆς γνώμης, even apart from my resolve (636) to protect you. Though τῆς ἐμῆς form a cretic, the spondee κἄνευ can stand because the prep. coheres closely with its case. Cp. 115. In 1022 οὐδὲν δεῖ πονεῖν, and 1543 ὥσπερ σφὼ πατρί, the monosyllable excuses the spondee. ἐπαινῶ with inf., 'I advise': *El.* 1322 σιγᾶν ἐπήνεσ'. Φοῖβος: Theseus infers this from 623.

666 ὅμως with μὴ παρόντος: it usu. follows the partic. (as 851, 1529), but sometimes precedes it, as Eur. *Ion* 734 δέσποιν' ὅμως οὖσ'. It would be possible, however, to take ὅμως with οἶδα: 'but nevertheless (though my protection is needless).' Possibly it should be ὁμῶς, 'equally' (*Ai.* 1372 κἀκεῖ κἀνθάδ' ὢν...ὁμῶς).

668—719 *First* στάσιμον. *The first strophe and antistrophe* (668—680 = 681—693) *praise Colonus: the second* (694—706 = 707—719) *praise Attica. But the local theme is skilfully knitted to the national theme. The narcissus and crocus of Colonus introduce the Attic olive* (2nd strophe). *The equestrian fame of Colonus suggests the Attic breed of horses, and this, in turn, suggests Poseidon's other gift to Athens,— the empire of the sea* (2nd antistrophe). *For the metres see Metrical Analysis.*

Cicero (*Cato* 7) is the earliest extant authority for the story of Sophocles reciting this ode before his judges.

668 f. The first word εὔιππον strikes a note which connects Colonus ἵππιος with the fame of Attica. Take γᾶς with κράτιστα. You have come to earth's best abodes (*Colonus*), belonging to this εὔιππος χώρα (*Attica*). The gen. εὔιπ. τ. χώρας is most simply taken as possessive, denoting the country to which the ἔπαυλα belong, though it might also be partitive.

10—2

148   *Oedipus at Colonus*

It precedes ἔπαυλα as the territorial gen. regularly precedes the local name, Her. 3. 136 ἀπίκοντο τῆς Ἰταλίης ἐς Τάραντα.

669 γᾶς is partitive gen. with the superl., as Lys. or. 21 § 6 ἡ ναῦς ἄριστα...ἔπλει παντὸς τοῦ στρατοπέδου. When γῆ stands alone it usu. = 'the earth,' as *O. T.* 480 τὰ μεσόμφαλα γᾶς...μαντεῖα.

ἔπαυλα, prop. a fold for cattle, as in *O. T.* 1138, where σταθμά is its synonym. So ἔπαυλοι in *Od.* 23. 358, and ἔπαυλις in Her. 1. 111. Then, just like σταθμά in poetry, 'home-steads,' 'dwellings': Aesch. *Pers.* 869 πάροικοι | Θρηκίων ἐπαύλων.

670 τὸν: the antistrophic syll. (νάρκ- 683) is long, but it is needless to write τόνδ', since the anacrusis is common.

ἀργῆτα, 'white,' contrasting with χλωραῖς (673). See Tozer, *Geography of Greece* p. 242: 'The site of Colonus is distinguished by two bare knolls of light-coloured earth, the ἀργῆτα Κολωνόν of the poet,—not chalky, as the expositors of that passage often describe it to be.' Schol. τὸν λευκόγεων. From √ARG, denoting 'brightness,' come (*a*) the group of words for 'bright' or white, ἀργός, ἀργής, ἀργινόεις, ἀργεννός, ἄργυφος: (*b*) ἄργυρος: (*c*) ἄργιλος, *argilla*, white clay. Thus the notion of a light-coloured soil was specially associated with this root. And this was certainly one reason why places were called 'white,'—whether the soil was *merely* light-coloured, as at Colonus, or chalky. Pindar puts Cyrene ἐν ἀργινόεντι μαστῷ (*P.* 4. 8), and it is known to have stood on a chalk cliff. Soil is suggested by ἀργείλοφον πὰρ Ζεφυρίων κολώναν (the town Λοκροὶ Ἐπιζεφύριοι on the S.E. coast of Italy, Pind. fr. 200); and soil or light-coloured rocks by Ἀργινοῦσαι, the three islets off the coast of Aeolis (Strabo 617).

671 f. μινύρεται θαμίζουσα inverts the usual constr.; cp. Plat. *Rep.* 328 C ὦ Σώκρατες, οὐδὲ θαμίζεις ἡμῖν καταβαίνων εἰς τὸν Πειραιᾶ. Here, however, θαμίζουσα may be taken separately, 'frequenting' (the place): *Il.* 18. 386 πάρος γε μὲν οὔτι θαμίζεις, 'hitherto thou comest not oft.'

673 χλω. ὑπὸ βάσσαις, 'under' (screened by) green glades,—in the sacred grove (cp. 17) and in the neighbouring Academy. Cp. *Ai.* 198 ἐν εὐανέμοις βάσσαις (Ida's glens).

674 τὸν οἰνωπὸν...κίσσον, 'dwelling amid the wine-dark ivy.' The reading ἀνέχουσα is usually justified by *Ai.* 212 (σε) στέρξας ἀνέχει, 'having conceived a love for thee, he upholds thee'; and Eur. *Hec.* 123 βάκχης ἀνέχων λέκτρ' Ἀγαμέμνων, 'upholding' *i.e.* 'refusing to forsake,' 'remaining constant to.' But how could the bird be said to 'uphold' the ivy in that sense? οἰνωπός is a good Attic form (used four times by Eur.), and οἰνωπὸν ἔχουσα is nearer to the MSS. than Dindorf's οἰνῶπα νέμουσα. The latter word would mean, 'having for her domain.'

675 f. The ivy and the vine (17) being sacred to Dionysus (θεοῦ), the foliage of the place generally is called his. θεοῦ is certainly not the hero Colonus (65). We might desire θεᾶν (the Eumenides), but the φυλλάς meant is not *only* that of the sacred grove; it includes the Academy. μυριόκαρπον refers to the berries of the laurel (παγκάρπου δάφνης *O. T.* 83), the fruit of the olive and of the vine. Cp. on 17.

677 f. ἀνήνεμον...χειμώνων, 'unvexed by wind of any storm,' cp. 786, 1519: *El.* 36 ἄσκενον ἀσπίδων: *ib.* 1002 ἄλυπος ἄτης: *Tr.* 691 ἀλαμπὲς ἡλίου. In these poet. phrases, the gen. might be viewed either as (1) simply a gen. of want, as after καθαρός, etc.: (2) an attrib. gen. depending on the implied noun (here, ανεμοι).

678 βακχιώτας (only here) = βακχευτής, βάκχος, reveller. Cp. *O. T.* 1105 ὁ Βακχεῖος θεός.

679 f. ἐμβατεύει, haunts the ground, Aesch. *Pers.* 449 Πὰν ἐμβατεύει ποντίας ἀκτῆς ἔπι. ἀμφιπολῶν, properly, 'moving around,' so, 'attending on,' 'roaming in company with.' The bold use seems to have been suggested by the noun ἀμφίπολος as = 'follower,' ἀμφιπολεῖν being here to that noun as ὀπαδεῖν to ὀπαδός. τιθήναις, the nymphs of the mythical Nysa, who nurtured the infant god, and were afterwards the companions of his wanderings.

681 ff. θάλλει δ'. After the mention of Dionysus, the narcissus now serves to introduce a mention of Demeter and Persephone (Cora). Under the name of Ἴακχος, Dionysus was associated in the Eleusinian mysteries with the 'two goddesses' (τὼ θεώ): thus *Ant.* 1119 he reigns παγκοίνοις Ἐλευσινίας | Δηοῦς ἐν κόλποις. A relief found at Eleusis in 1859, and referable to the period between Pheidias and Praxiteles, shows Persephone with her right hand on the head of the young Iacchos, who is facing Demeter.

682 καλλίβοτρυς, 'with fair clusters.' As this epithet shows, the νάρκισσος was some thickly-flowering variety: cp. Vergil's 'comantem Narcissum,' *Geo.* 4. 122. Wieseler thinks that a lily is meant here. Bentham (*British Flora*, 4th ed., p. 473) says that the *narcissus poeticus* of the Mediterranean region

'has usually *a solitary flower* of a pure white, except the crown, which is yellow, often edged with orange or crimson.' This does not suit καλλίβοτρυς. But, whatever the true identification may be, the *symbolism* of νάρκισσος in Greek mythology is clear. It is *the flower of imminent death*, being associated, through its narcotic fragrance, with νάρκη,—the pale beauty of the flower helping the thought. It is the *last* flower for which Persephone is stretching forth her hand when Pluto seizes her,—Earth having put forth a wondrous narcissus, with a hundred flowers, on purpose to tempt her: *Hom. Hymn.* 5. 15. Paus. 9. 31. 9 (quoting an ancient hymn by the legendary poet Pamphos) says that Cora was seized οὐκ ἴοις ἀπατηθεῖσαν ἀλλὰ ναρκίσσοις. So Euphorion (220 B.C.) fr. 52 Εὐμενίδες ναρκίσσου ἐπιστεφέες πλοκαμίδας. Narcissus is the fair youth cold to love, whose face seen by himself in the water was the prelude of death.

683 μεγάλαιν θεαῖν: Paus. 8. 31. 1 (at Megalopolis) θεῶν ἱερὸν τῶν μεγάλων· αἱ δέ εἰσιν αἱ μεγάλαι θεαὶ Δημήτηρ καὶ Κόρη. In Attic usu. τὼ θεώ. Indeed θεά is rare in Attic prose except in such phrases as θεοὺς καὶ θεάς. But here, in a lyric passage, and with an epithet added, the poet may have preferred the less familiar θεαῖν.

684 ἀρχαῖον στεφάνωμ'. The narcissus does not figure *specially* as an attribute of the goddesses—as the corn-ears and poppy of Demeter, the pomegranate of Cora, and the myrtle of Iacchos. But, as the flower which Cora was plucking when seized, it was associated with their cult from the first (ἀρχαῖον), and was *one* of the flowers which would be most fitly woven into those floral wreaths which, on the wall-paintings, sometimes replace Demeter's more usual crown of corn-ears. Schneidewin's explanation, '*original* crown,'—before they changed it for others,—is against the myth itself, which makes the narcissus a *new* joy to Cora's eyes (*Hom. Hymn.* 5. 15).

685 χρυσαυγὴς κρόκος. Tozer, *Geogr. of Greece* p. 162 : 'when Sophocles...speaks of the 'crocus with its golden sheen,' we would fain regard this as the same with the splendid flower that displays its golden blossoms close to the snow on Parnassus and the mountains of Arcadia. But, in reality, there can be little doubt that it was the cultivated crocus, from which the saffron was obtained, and which was introduced into Greece from the East, where it was prized as a dye for robes and slippers,—the κροκόβαπτον ποδὸς εὔμαριν of the *Persae* [660]—the sign of royalty and majesty.' Along with roses, violets, 'hyacinth,' 'narcissus,' and 'agallis' (iris?), the 'crocus' is gathered by Cora (*ib.* 6 ff.). At the Thesmophoria (the festivals of Demeter θεσμοφόρος), when wreaths of flowers were not worn, the women appeared in κροκωτοί, saffron-coloured robes (Ar. *Thesm.* 138). The crocus was planted on graves (Juv. *Sat.* 7. 208).

686 κρῆναι, the 'founts.' 'The most distant sources of the river are on the w. side of Mt. Pentelicus and the s. side of Mt. Parnes, and in the intermediate ridge which unites them' (Leake): in particular, a broad stream descends from the steepest part of Parnes. The Cephisus has a course of about 20 miles to the bay of Phalerum.

μινύθουσιν, 'fail.' Soph. has seized a distinctive point. Even at this day, when the plain has much less shade than of old, the *Cephisus* 'never fails,' while in the long droughts of summer the bed of the *Ilissus* is absolutely dry. Cp. *Modern Greece* by H. M. Baird (1856) p. 294: 'The little river Cephisus...scatters fertility and verdure around. Great was the contrast between its banks and the rest of the plain, which in the month of October is dry, parched, and dusty.'—μινύθω is both trans. and intrans. in Homer; intrans. in the Ionic of Hippocr. (who has it of flesh 'wasting'). Aesch. has it twice in lyrics (intrans.); Soph. only here.

687 Κηφισοῦ. Chr. Wordsworth (*Athens and Attica* p. 137) observes that the Athenian poets never praise the *Ilissus* (perhaps because it was too much associated with the prose of daily life), though Plato, in the *Phaedrus*, makes some amends; they keep their praises for the Cephisus (so Eur. *Med.* 835). On the other hand the Ilissus, not the Cephisus, is the representative river of Attica for more distant singers, from Apollonius Rhodius (I. 215) to Milton (*Par. Reg.* 4. 249).

νομάδες, wandering. The word *alludes* to irrigation by ducts or canals (a system still in use), but does so far more poetically than would be the case if we made it active, with ῥεέθρων for object. gen., 'distributing the streams.' There is no example of an adj. of this form having an active sense.

688 ἐπ' ἤματι, a very rare use in Attic, meaning here that *on* (or *for*) each day the river gives what that day requires. Cp. *Il.* 10. 48 (never did I hear ἄνδρ' ἕνα τοσσάδε μέρμερ' ἐπ' ἤματι μητίσασθαι (as one day's work): more oft. ἐπ' ἤματι τῷδε, 'on this day,' *Il.* 13. 234, 19. 110. Herodotus has the gen.

152   *Oedipus at Colonus*

ἐπ' ἡμέρης ἑκάστης in a similar sense (5. 117); this phrase, too, is un-Attic.

689 ὠκυτόκος, 'giving quick increase,' *i.e.* an early reward to the cultivator's labour. ὠκυτόκιον, a medicine used in childbed, Ar. *Th.* 504.

πεδίων ἐπινίσσεται, 'moves over the plains,' a partitive gen. (helped by ἐπι-), cp. ἔρχονται πεδίοιο, *Il.* 2. 801 διέκρησσον πεδίοιο *Il.* 23. 364.

690 ἀκηράτῳ σὺν ὄμβρῳ, 'with stainless tide.' For ὄμβρος = 'water' see *O. T.* 1427.

691 στ. χθονός, possessive gen. with πεδίων.—στερνούχου, having στέρνα: an expressive word for the expanse of the Attic πεδίον, varied by gentle undulations, or by rocky knolls like Colonus itself. Suidas quotes a poet. phrase στέρνα γῆς: cp. the common use of μαστοί for round hills or knolls. Hes. *Theog.* 117 Γαῖ' εὐρύστερνος: Pind. *Nem.* 7. 33 εὐρυκόλπου | ...χθονός. Both στέρνα and νῶτα were applied, says the schol., to τῆς γῆς τὰ πεδιώδη καὶ εὐρέα. The epithet helps, with ὠκυτόκος, to suggest the image of a mighty living frame, quickened by the veins of irrigation.

Μουσᾶν. Paus. 1. 30. 2 (in the Academy, cp. on 55) ἔστι δὲ καὶ Μουσῶν τε βωμὸς καὶ ἕτερος Ἑρμοῦ καὶ ἔνδον Ἀθηνᾶς.

692 f. νιν refers to χθονός in 691: this region generally.

Ἀφροδίτη is not among the divinities of the Academy or Colonus in Paus. 1. 30, though there was an altar of Ἔρως in front of the entrance to the Academy. But she was often associated with Demeter and Cora; and she was also specially connected by an Attic legend with the Cephisus (Eur. *Med.* 835).

χρυσάνιος, 'of the golden rein,' when she drives her chariot drawn by sparrows, doves, or swans. The word occurs only once in *Il.* (6. 205), as epith. of Artemis, and once in *Od.* (8. 285), as epith. of Ares.

694—719 *Thus far the theme has been Colonus and the adjacent region. Now the praises take a larger range. Athena's gift of the olive, Poseidon's gift of the horse, are here celebrated as common to Attica* (τᾷδε χώρᾳ, 700, cp. 668): *though the latter had a special interest for Colonus Hippius, and the former for the Academy, where an olive was shown, said to have sprung up next after the primal olive in the* Πανδροσεῖον *of the Erechtheum* (Paus. 1. 30. 2).

694 γᾶς Ἀσίας, *sc.* ὄν, possessive gen., with ἐπακούω, hear of as belonging to. The poet does not mean, of course, that he has never heard of the olive as *growing* in the Peloponnesus or in Asia Minor. He means that nowhere else has he heard of an olive-tree springing from the earth at a divine command, or flourishing so greatly and so securely under divine protection.

695 f. Δωρίδι, as Schneidewin remarked, is an anachronism (cp. 1301), since legend placed Oedipus before the Trojan war, and the Dorian conquest of the Peloponnesus after it; but Attic tragedy was not fastidious on such points. In Eur. *Hec.* 450 the Peloponnesus is Δωρὶς αἶα. Cp. on 66. νάσῳ: cp. Eust. *ad* Dion. Perieg. 403 ἡ τοῦ Πέλοπος νῆσος ἔστι μὲν κυρίως Χερρόνησος, ὅμως δὲ νῆσος μὲν λέγεται, ὡς παρὰ βραχὺ τοιαύτη οὖσα. In the 10th century we find the Peloponnesus called simply ἡ νῆσος by Constantinus Porphyrogenitus.

Πέλοπος has been regarded by some as a gloss: see on 709 f. But, apart from the fact that 709 f. are shorter by ⏑⏑, it need move no suspicion; for, if not necessary here, it is at least fitting, and is often joined with νῆσος. Tyrtaeus fr. 2 εὐρεῖαν Πέλοπος νᾶσον ἀφικόμεθα. *Cypria* fr. 8 διεδέρκετο νῆσον ἅπασαν | Τανταλίδεω Πέλοπος. Ion *Omphale* fr. 24 ἄμεινον ἢ τὸν Πέλοπος ἐν νήσῳ τρόπον.—Cp. Aesch. *Eum.* 702 (the Areiopagus is a safeguard) οἷον οὔτις ἀνθρώπων ἔχει | οὔτ' ἐν Σκύθαισιν οὔτε Πέλοπος ἐν τόποις.

698 φύτευμ'. φίτευμ', which Blaydes prefers, occurs only once in trag. (Aesch. *Ag.* 1281, of Orestes); it seems more appropriate to a 'scion' (child) than to a plant.

ἀχείρωτον was read here by Pollux (2. 154), and is thus carried back to about 160 A.D.; it is also in A and a majority of our other MSS.; while L's ἀχείρητον is clearly a corruption. The question is whether ἀχείρωτον means (1) '*unvanquished,*' the only sense in which it occurs elsewhere, as Thuc. 6. 10 οἱ Χαλκιδῆς...ἀχείρωτοί εἰσι: or (2) ἀχειρούργητον, as Pollux takes it, '*not cultivated by human hands.*' My reason for preferring '*unvanquished*' is the context. While βλαστόν (697) refers to the miraculous *creation* of the olive by Athena, αὐτοποιόν refers (I think) to its miraculous *self-renewal* after the Persians had burnt it. Her. 8. 55 δευτέρῃ τε ἡμέρῃ ἀπὸ τῆς ἐμπρήσιος Ἀθηναίων οἱ θύειν ὑπὸ βασιλέος κελευόμενοι ὡς ἀνέβησαν ἐς τὸ ἱρόν, ὥρων βλαστὸν ἐκ τοῦ στελέχεος ὅσον τε πηχυαῖον ἀναδεδραμηκότα. This connection of ideas is further indicated by the next phrase, ἐγχέων etc. For αὐτοποιός as 'self-produced' (*i.e.* producing itself from itself), cp. αὐτότοκος, αὐτοφάγος, αὐτοφόνος. All compounds of -ποιος are oxytone: αὐτόποιος

154   *Oedipus at Colonus*

(as our MSS. give it) in this passage 'is the one solitary exception, and therefore probably a false accent' (Chandler).

699 φόβημα. Androtion (circ. 280 B.C.), in his Ἀτθίς, stated that the sacred olives (μορίαι) in Attica had been spared by the Peloponnesian invaders under Archidamus, who sacrificed to Athena. The *Atthis* of Philochorus, a contemporary of Androtion, made the same statement (schol. *ad loc.*).

700 τᾷδε...χώρᾳ, locative dat.: in Attica. μέγιστα, 'most mightily': cp. 219 μακρά, 319 φαιδρά. The light soil of Attica (τὸ λεπτόγεων), and the climate, esp. favoured the olive. For Greece, the olive-zone begins s. of the plains of Thessaly, as for Italy it begins s. of the plains of Lombardy. The olive is found in Phthiotis and Magnesia: in Epeirus, only on the sea-coast.

701 παιδοτρόφου, nourishing the young lives in the land. The epithet is especially fitting here, after the recent allusion to Demeter and Cora, because at the Thesmophoria the prayer to those goddesses associated Earth with them as ἡ κουροτρόφος: see Ar. *Thesm.* 295. Cp. Juv. *Sat.* 3. 84 *quod nostra infantia caelum Hausit Aventini, baca nutrita Sabina* (the olive). Hesych. (*s.v.* στέφανον ἐκφέρειν) says that it was the Attic custom στέφανον ἐλαίας τιθέναι πρὸ τῶν θυρῶν, when a male child was born; as wool, when a female (cp. *foribus suspende coronas: Iam pater es*). But there is no such allusion here. Nor could παιδοτρ. mean 'propagated from the parent olive' on the acropolis, as Schneidewin thought.

702 τὸ μέν τις κ.τ.λ. Two points first claim notice. (1) οὔτε and νεαρός are both in the MSS., but both cannot be right as they exceed the metre. Cp. v. 715. If with Porson the first οὔτε is changed to οὐ, the second οὔτε must certainly be changed to οὐδέ. A single οὔτε cannot follow οὐ, though a repeated οὔτε can (*Tr.* 1058). Elmsley's οὔτε νέος is hardly probable. (2) γήρᾳ σημαίνων seems to me impossible. It surely could not mean either (*a*) 'commanding in old age'— the elderly Archidamus in contrast with the young Xerxes— or (*b*) 'commanding the elderly men.' The difficulty is not in the sense of σημαίνων itself, for which cp. *Il.* 1. 288: it is in the combination with γήρᾳ.

But was the antithesis here between *youth* and *age*, or between some other notions? I incline to believe that the poet indeed meant 'neither young nor old,' but without any personal reference, and merely in this general sense:—'from

generation to generation of men these sacred trees are safe.'
The words ὁ γὰρ αἰὲν ὁρῶν suit this. The conjecture συνναίων
has palaeographic probability (for a cursive text): for the
phrase cp. Eur. fr. 370 μετὰ δ᾽ ἡσυχίας πολιῷ γήραϊ συνοικοίην.

704 κύκλος, the eye of Zeus (so κύκλοι, *Ph.* 1354), not the
'orb' of the sun.

705 Μορίου Διός. *Attic Orators,* vol. I. p. 289: 'Throughout
Attica, besides the olives which were private property (ἴδιαι
ἐλαῖαι, Lys. or. 7 § 10) there were others which, whether on
public or on private lands, were considered as the property of
the state. They were called *moriae* (μορίαι)—the legend being
that they had been propagated (μεμορημέναι) from the original
olive which Athena herself had caused to spring up on the
Acropolis. This theory was convenient for their conservation
as State property, since, by giving them a sacred character,
it placed them directly under the care of the Areiopagus,
which caused them to be visited once a month by Inspectors
(ἐπιμεληταί, Lys. or. 7 § 29), and once a year by special
Commissioners (γνώμονες, *ib.* § 25). To uproot a *moria* was an
offence punishable by banishment and confiscation of goods
(*ib.* § 41).' Μορίου, from the objects protected; so Ζεὺς ἱκέσιος,
κτήσιος, etc.

706 γλαυκῶπις, with grayish-blue eyes: the Homeric epithet
has been suggested by γλαυκᾶς in 701. The altar of Ζεὺς
Μόριος, otherwise called Καταιβάτης, was in the Academy,
where there was also a shrine of Athena close to the μορίαι;
hence the special conjunction of the deities here.

707 ff. This antistrophe is devoted to Poseidon, as the
strophe to Athena. ματρόπολα, 'mother-city' (Athens), since
the men of Colonus, like all other dwellers in Attica, may
deem themselves her children. *Not,* 'capital city,' which
would be prosaic: this sense occurs as early, however, as Xen.,
Anab. 5. 2. 3 ἐν δὲ ἦν χωρίον μητρόπολις αὐτῶν.

709 f. If vv. 696 f. are sound as they stand, the problem
here is to supply ◡ ◡, and Porson's χθονὸς seems best. μεγάλου...μέγιστον, αὔχημα...αὔχημα (713) must not be judged with
modern fastidiousness: see on 554.

711 εὔιππον, εὔπωλον harmonizes with a feeling which
pervades the ode,—that the bounty of the gods to Attica is
continued from day to day and from age to age. The supply
of good ἵπποι is perpetually replenished by good πῶλοι: '*est in
equis patrum Virtus.*' εὔιππον further *suggests* ἱππεῖς, since (as

= 'well-horsed') it is often said of heroes (Pind. *Ol.* 3. 39 εὐ. Τυνδαριδᾶν). For αὔχημα εὔιππον, 'a glory of good horses,' cp. 1062, *P.* 8. 37 νίκαν...θρασύγυιον : *Isth.* 1. 12 καλλίνικον...κῦδος. εὐθάλασσον. The well of salt water shown in the Erechtheum (ὕδωρ θαλάσσιον ἐν φρέατι Paus. 1. 26. 5) was called θάλασσα. It was said to have been created by a blow from Poseidon's trident ; the three holes shown are still visible. Her. 8. 55 Ἐρεχθέος...νηός, ἐν τῷ ἐλαίη τε καὶ θάλασσα ἔνι. Apollod. 3. 14. 1 (Poseidon) ἀνέφηνε θάλασσαν ἣν νῦν Ἐρεχθηῖδα καλοῦσι. εὔιππον, εὐθάλασσον are brought close together as expressing the two great attributes of Poseidon, *Hom. Hymn.* 22. 4 διχθά τοι, Ἐννοσίγαιε, θεοὶ τιμὴν ἐδάσαντο, | ἵππων τε δμητῆρ' ἔμεναι σωτῆρά τε νηῶν.

712 σὺ γάρ, after the voc.: cp. σὺ δέ (507).

713 εἷσας (ἵζω) νιν εἰς τόδ' αὔχημα, didst establish her in this glory, as in a royal throne : cp. Her. 3. 61 τοῦτον...εἷσε ἄγων ἐς τὸν βασιλήιον θρόνον. The phrase is Homeric, *Od.* 1. 130 αὐτὴν δ' ἐς θρόνον εἷσεν ἄγων.

714 ἵπποισιν with τὸν ἀκεστῆρα : cp. *Ai.* 1166 βροτοῖς τὸν ἀείμνηστον | τάφον. ἀκεστῆρα = σωφρονιστήν, 'that cures their rage' and brings them to a calm temper (*Il.* 13. 115 ἀλλ' ἀκεώμεθα θᾶσσον· ἀκεσταί τοι φρένες ἐσθλῶν): cp. Pind. *Ol.* 13. 68 φίλτρον τόδ' ἵππειον, 85 φάρμακον πραΰ, said of the bit (χαλινός) given by Athena to Bellerophon for Pegasus.

715 πρώταισι ταῖσδε...ἀγυιαῖς, first in these roads (about Colonus); locative dat.: κτίσας, 'having instituted,' brought into use among men, as one could say κτίζειν νόμιμα on the analogy of κτίζειν ἑορτήν etc. Greek mythology places Poseidon in two distinct relations to the horse. (*a*) As *creator*. Servius *ad* Verg. *Geo.* 1. 12 *ideo dicitur ecum invenisse quia velox est eius numen et mobile sicut mare.* (*b*) As *tamer*. This was the prominent trait of the Corinthian and Attic legends. At Corinth Poseidon was worshipped as δαμαῖος, and Athena as χαλινῖτις. In Thessaly the horse-*yoking* Poseidon was called ἵμψιος, *i.e.* ζύγιος.

716 ff. 'And the shapely oar, apt to men's hands, hath a wondrous speed on the brine.' Poseidon has taught men to row as well as to ride. He fits the oars to their hands. But, instead of τὰν δὲ πλάταν χερσὶ παράψας, the form is varied to a passive constr. If παραπτομένα is sound, this seems the best account of it,—παρά, 'at the side,' suggesting the notion, 'as an aid.' Cp. Eur. *I. T.* 1405 (χέρας) κώπῃ προσαρμόσαντες.

εὐήρετμος, adj. compounded with a noun cognate in sense to the subst. (πλάτα): cp. βίος μακραίων (*O. T.* 518 n.), λόγος κακόθρους (*Ai.* 138), εὔπαις γόνος (Eur. *I. T.* 1234), εὐπήχεις χεῖρες (*Hipp.* 200). ἔκπαγλα, neut. plur. as adv., cp. 319. ἀλία with θρῴσκει: cp. on 119 ἐκτόπιος.

718 f. τῶν ἑκατομπόδων Νηρῄδων, the Nereids with their hundred feet, the fifty Nereids whose dance and song lead the ship on her way. The choice of the number (though here merely suggesting a *numerous* sisterhood) is not accidental: *fifty* was the number of the Nereids in the earlier Greek poets, as Hesiod *Th.* 264, Pindar *Isthm.* 5. 6, Aesch. fr. 168, Eur. *Ion* 1081. Later it becomes a hundred; Plato *Critias* 116 E; Ovid *Fasti* 6. 499. Νηρεύς (√νυ, νέω, νᾶμα, etc.) and his daughters represent the sea's kindly moods; the Nereids who dance and sing around and before the ship are the waves. In ἑκατομπόδων the second part of the compound suggests 'dancing,' cp. on πυκνόπτεροι (17).

720—1043 *Second ἐπεισόδιον. Creon comes, in the hope of persuading Oed. to return with him. Failing, he causes his attendants to carry off Antigone,—Ismene having already been captured elsewhere. He is about to seize Oed., when Theseus enters, sends pursuers after Creon's men, and compels Creon himself to set out with him to find them.*

721 σὸν...δή, 'it is for thee,'—more poetical and more impressive than σοί...δεῖ: cp. 197, *El.* 1470 οὐκ ἐμὸν τόδ', ἀλλὰ σόν, | τὸ ταῦθ' ὁρᾶν: *Ph.* 15 ἀλλ' ἔργον ἤδη σὸν τὰ λοίφ' ὑπηρετεῖν: Aesch. *Theb.* 232 σὸν δ' αὖ τὸ σιγᾶν. But σοί...δεῖ, though a rare, is an admissible construction. See 570.

φαίνειν τὰ λαμπρὰ ἔπη = φαίνειν τὰς ἀρετὰς δι' ἃς ἐπαινεῖσθε, to *illustrate* the praises by deeds: cp. *Od.* 8. 237 ἀλλ' ἐθέλεις ἀρετὴν σὴν φαινέμεν ἥ τοι ὀπηδεῖ.

722 The ἀντιλαβή (division of the verse between two persons) marks excitement: cp. 652, 1099, 1169.

723 ἡμῖν, ethic dat.: cp. 81.

725 φαίνοιτ' ἄν, a courteous entreaty. Aesch. *Theb.* 261 λέγοις ἂν ὡς τάχιστα. τέρμα τῆς σωτηρίας (defining gen.), the end which consists in safety, cp. τέλος θανάτοιο. When the attack has been made and repulsed, he will feel finally assured.

726 παρέσται, 'it shall be thine,' sc. τὸ τέρμα τῆς σ.—ἐγώ, 'even if *I* am aged, the country's strength hath not grown old.' With γέρων opposed to οὐ γεγήρακε we require ἐγώ opposed to χώρας. It is different when the pers. pron. is omitted because the *main* antithesis is between two verbal notions: as in Aesch. *Eum.* 84 (I will not betray thee) καὶ γὰρ κτανεῖν σ᾽ ἔπεισα, for I *persuaded* (not *I* persuaded) thee to slay.

729 f. ὀμμάτων possessive gen., τῆς ἐμῆς ἐπεισόδου objective gen., both with φόβον: a fear belonging to the eyes (showing itself in them), about my advent. εἰληφότας, 'you have imbibed': *Ai.* 345 τάχ᾽ ἄν τιν᾽ αἰδῶ...λάβοι (conceive): Eur. *Suppl.* 1050 ὀργὴν λάβοις ἄν. νεώρη: cp. on 475.

731 ὅν, relat. to ἐμέ implied in τῆς ἐμῆς (cp. on 263). μήτ᾽ ἀφῆτ᾽ κ.τ.λ. is an independent sentence, co-ordinated with the relat. clause ὅν μήτ᾽ ὀκνεῖτε: see on 424.

732 ὡς with βουληθείς, marking more strongly the agent's own point of view, cp. on 71. δρᾶν τι, euphemistic, to take any forcible measures: so, in a good sense, Thuc. 1. 20 βουλόμενοι ... δράσαντές τι καὶ κινδυνεῦσαι, to do something notable if they must incur the risk.

734 εἴ τιν᾽, instead of εἴτις (σθένει), by assimilation, εἴτις being treated as forming a single adj.: *Ai.* 488 εἴπερ τινός, σθένοντος ἐν πλούτῳ, Φρυγῶν: Thuc. 7. 21 τοῦ τε Γυλίππου καὶ Ἑρμοκράτους καὶ εἴ του ἄλλου πειθόντων.

735 τηλικόσδ᾽, 'old as I am,' confirms the previous assurance that his errand is peaceful, and it harmonises with πείσων. 'I have not come to use *force.* No, I was sent, an aged envoy, to *persuade* him,' etc. If we read τηλικόνδ᾽ Creon's diplomacy is at fault. He should not begin by reminding them that Thebes had suffered Oedipus to wander in misery for so many years.

737 f. οὐκ ἐξ ἑνὸς στείλαντος, not in consequence of one man's sending (στείλαντος predicate): κελευσθείς goes only with ἀστῶν ὑπὸ πάντων. The combination of particles in different cases is esp. freq. when one is a gen. absol. (as if ἐξ were absent here): *Ph.* 170 f. μή του κηδομένου βροτῶν | μηδὲ ξύντροφον ὄμμ᾽ ἔχων: *Tr.* 292: Dem. or. 23 § 156 εἶδεν, εἴτε δή τινος εἰπόντος εἴτ᾽ αὐτὸς συνείς. But it occurs also without gen. abs., as *Ant.* 381.

ἀστῶν marks the public character of his mission from Thebes, while ἀνδρῶν would be intolerably weak. It cannot be justified by Herm.'s argument that Soph. added it in the second clause because he had omitted it in the first, since ἑνὸς needed no addition.

738 ἧκέ μοι γένει, 'it *devolved on me* by kinship.' Cp. Eur. *Alc.* 291 καλῶς μὲν αὐτοῖς κατθανεῖν ἧκον βίου (acc. absol.), when they had reached a time of life mature for dying. The personal constr. occurs in Eur. *Her.* 213 γένους μὲν ἥκεις ὧδε τοῖσδε, thou art related to them *in this degree.* In such examples ἥκει, ἥκω cannot properly be regarded as mere substitutes for προσήκει, προσήκω.

739 εἰς πλεῖστον πόλεως, to the greatest extent of all the citizens, *i.e.* more than any other Theban. εἰς as in εἰς ὑπερβολήν, ἐς τὰ μάλιστα, etc. (cp. ἐπὶ πλέον): the gen. after the superl. adv., as *Ai.* 502 μέγιστον ἴσχυσε στρατοῦ.

740 ἀλλ' opens his direct appeal: cp. 101.

742 δικαίως, 'with right,' since Thebes, which had been his τρόφος so long (760), has a better claim to him than Athens, however hospitable. And Creon has an especial right to urge the claim as being now the guardian of the family honour (755).

ἐκ δὲ τῶν. When the art. stands as demonstr. pron., it is usu. the first word in the clause: but cp. 1699 (τὸν): Aesch. *Eum.* 2 ἐκ δὲ τῆς Θέμιν: Plat. *Euthyd.* 303 c πολλὰ μὲν οὖν καὶ ἄλλα...ἐν δὲ τοῖς καὶ τοῦτο: Eur. *Alc.* 264 οἰκτρὰν φίλοισιν, ἐκ δὲ τῶν μάλιστ' ἐμοί.

743 f. ὅσωπερ, 'even as much as' *sc.* μάλιστα: cp. *Tr.* 312 ἐπεί νιν τῶνδε πλεῖστον ᾤκτισα | βλέπουσ', ὅσωπερ καὶ φρονεῖν οἶδεν μόνη, where πλεῖστον is grammatically needed with ὅσωπερ, though μόνη is added as if ἐπειδή, and not ὅσωπερ, had preceded. Schol. ἐγὼ μάλιστά σε καλῶ, ὅσωπερ πλεῖστον ἀλγῶ τοῖς παθήμασιν.—πλεῖστον...κάκιστος: *Ph.* 631 τῆς πλεῖστον ἐχθίστης: Eur. *Med.* 1323 ὦ μέγιστον ἐχθίστη γύναι: *Alc.* 790 τὴν πλεῖστον ἡδίστην.

745 ff. ξένον would apply to any one living in a country not his own: cp. 562, Xenoph. *Mem.* 2. 1. 13 οὐδ' εἰς πολιτείαν ἐμαυτὸν κατακλείω, ἀλλὰ ξένος πανταχοῦ εἰμι. Oed. is not merely an exile, but a wandering beggar. The rhythm makes it better to take ὄντα with ξένον only, and to connect ἀλήτην with χωροῦντα. ἐπὶ μιᾶς πρ., 'with one handmaid for thy stay,'—the phrase arises from, but does not consciously refer to, the metaphor of an anchor (cp. on 148): Lys. or. 31 § 9 (of a μέτοικος) ἐπὶ προστάτου ᾤκει, he lived under the protection of a citizen as his patron.

747 τήν: Soph. freely uses the art. for the relat. pron., in dialogue no less than in lyrics; but (except in *Tr.* 47) only where metre requires: so in dialogue 1258 (τῆς), *O. T.* 1379 (τῶν), 1427 (τὸ), *Ant.* 1086 (τῶν), *El.* 1144 (τὴν), *Tr.* 47 (τὴν),

160   *Oedipus at Colonus*

381, 728 (τῆς), *Ph.* 14 (τῷ), etc. τάλας has nearly the force of an interjection, 'ah me!': cp. 318.

748 f. οὐκ ἔδοξα πεσεῖν ἄν = ὅτι πέσοι ἄν. ἐς τοσοῦτον αἰκίας, 'to such a depth of misery'; cp. *O. T.* 771 ἐς τοσοῦτον ἐλπίδων | ἐμοῦ βεβῶτος, n. The penult. of αἰκία, as of the epic ἀεικία, is always long; hence the later spelling ἀείκεια, αἴκεια, often found in our MSS. ὅσον, *i.e.* εἰς ὅσον: cp. Dem. or. 19 § 342 ἐπὶ τῆς αὑτῆς ἧσπερ νῦν ἐξουσίας...μενεῖ. Plat. *Rep.* 533 E οὐ περὶ ὀνόματος ἡ ἀμφισβήτησις, οἷς τοσούτων πέρι σκέψις ὅσων ἡμῖν πρόκειται. ἥδε δύσμορος is added as if the preceding statement had been general ('I had not thought that *any* royal maiden,' etc.)

750 τὸ σὸν κάρα, a way of alluding to his blindness without mentioning it: cp. 285.

751 πτωχῷ. The poet. tendency was to treat adjectives with three terminations as if they had only two. Cp. the Homeric πουλὺν ἐφ' ὑγρήν (*Il.* 10. 27): θῆλυς ἐέρση (*Od.* 5. 467), ἡδὺς ἀϋτμή (*Od.* 12. 369), πικρὸν...ὀδμήν (*Od.* 4. 406): below, 1460: *Tr.* 207 κοινὸς...κλαγγά: so *ib.* 478 πατρῷος, and 533 θυραῖος: Eur. *Bacch.* 598 δίου βροντᾶς, 992 ἴτω δίκα φανερός, ἴτω: *Helen.* 623 ὦ ποθεινὸς ἡμέρα.

τηλικοῦτος is fem. only here and *El.* 614. The point of τηλικοῦτος, 'of such an age as she is,' is that her marriageable age is passing by in these perilous wanderings. There is a similar thought in Electra's complaint (*El.* 962). Cp. 1116, 1181.

752 τοὐπιόντος possessive, ἁρπάσαι epexegetic: 'belonging to the first comer,' 'for him to seize.' *O. T.* 393 τό γ' αἴνιγμ' οὐχὶ τοὐπιόντος ἦν | ἀνδρὸς διειπεῖν (n.).

753 ἆρ'; equiv. in *sense* to ἆρ' οὔ; 'are you satisfied that it is so?' *i.e.* 'is it not so?' *O. T.* 822 ἆρ' ἔφυν κακός; | ἆρ' οὐχὶ πᾶς ἄναγνος; ὦ τάλας, nom. instead of voc., cp. 185; so *O. T.* 744 οἴμοι τάλας, n.; below, 847.

754 ff. 'I have uttered a cruel reproach against my kindred and myself. But indeed the reproach is one that cannot be hid, so long as thou and thy daughter are seen wandering thus. Hide it, then, *thou* (no one else can)—by coming home.' Thus in *O. T.* 1424 Creon urges the Theban elders to take Oed. into the house, forbidding them τοιόνδ' ἄγος | ἀκάλυπτον οὕτω δεικνύναι. ἀλλ' οὐ γάρ, is used elliptically, as at 988, *El.* 595, *Tr.* 552. So the schol.: ὥστε συγγνώμης εἰμὶ ἄξιος λέγων· οὐ γὰρ δύναμαι κρύπτειν.

756 πρὸς θεῶν πατρῴων, 'by the gods of thy fathers,' *i.e.* of the Labdacid house, which traced its descent from Agenor, son of Poseidon and father of Cadmus. This peculiarly strong adjuration occurs also *Ant.* 839, *Ph.* 933: cp. *El.* 411 ὦ θεοὶ πατρῷοι, συγγένεσθέ γ᾽ ἀλλὰ νῦν.

757 θελήσας, 'by consenting': cp. *O. T.* 649 πιθοῦ θελήσας φρονήσας τ᾽ (n.). ἄστυ, no less than δόμους, is qualified by τοὺς πατρῴους (cp. 297). Creon's real purpose was to establish Oedipus just beyond the Theban border (399).

759 εἰπών here=προσειπών: so *Il.* 12. 210 δὴ τότε Πουλυδάμας θρασὺν Ἕκτορα εἶπε παραστάς: *Ai.* 764 ὁ μὲν γὰρ αὐτὸν ἐννέπει· τέκνον, etc. Cp. *ib.* 862 τὰ Τρωϊκὰ | πεδία προσαυδῶ· χαίρετ᾽, ὦ τροφῆς ἐμοί: *ib.* 1221 τὰς ἱερὰς ὅπως | προσείποιμεν Ἀθάνας. ἡ δ᾽ οἴκοι (πόλις), 'your own city.' Cp. 351, Aesch. *Suppl.* 390 κατὰ νόμους τοὺς οἴκοθεν (the laws of your country).

761 f. παντὸς with λόγου δικαίου: 'thou who wouldst borrow a crafty device from any plea of right'—as he here uses the λόγος δίκαιος about duty to friends and fatherland for the purpose of enticing Oedipus back. Cp. *Ph.* 407 ἔξοιδα γάρ νιν παντὸς ἂν λόγου κακοῦ | γλώσσῃ θιγόντα: Eur. *I. A.* 97 πάντα προσφέρων λόγον. This is better than to make παντὸς neut., taking λόγου δ. as defining gen. with μηχάνημα: 'thou who from anything wouldst borrow a crafty device consisting in a fair plea': for which, however, we might cp. Eur. *Hec.* 248 πολλῶν λόγων εὑρήμαθ᾽ ὥστε μὴ θανεῖν, *Ant.* 312 ἐξ ἅπαντος...κερδαίνειν, and below, 807. ἂν φέρων = ὃς φέροις ἄν: as in *Ph.* 407 f. (quoted above) ἂν...θιγόντα=ὅτι θίγοι ἄν.

763 f. ταῦτα, 'thus,' is cogn. accus., μου being understood. δεύτερον...ἑλεῖν, to get me *a second time* into thy power. This is explained by vv. 765—771, which set forth how they had abused their *former* control over the blind man. ἐν οἷς = ἐν τούτοις, ἐν οἷς, 'in toils in which it would give me most pain to be caught': cp. *El.* 1476 τίνων ποτ᾽ ἀνδρῶν ἐν μέσοις ἀρκυστάτοις | πέπτωχ᾽ ὁ τλήμων; Eur. *Phoen.* 263 δέδοικα μή με δικτύων ἔσω | λαβόντες οὐκ ἐκφρῶσ᾽. μάλιστ᾽ ἂν ἀλγοίην: because his dearest wish now is that his grave should bless his friends and harm his foes (92). If the Thebans could entice him back, and become masters of his grave, they might baffle that wish; and yet he would not even have burial in Theban soil (406).

765 πρόσθεν τε, answered by νῦν τε in 772. The interval

162   *Oedipus at Colonus*

is somewhat long, but the first τε merely prepares the ear for a statement in two parts. οἰκείοις, due to my own acts: it was horror at his own involuntary crimes that made him eager to quit Thebes: cp. *O. T.* 819 καὶ τάδ᾽ οὖτις ἄλλος ἦν | ἢ 'γὼ 'π' ἐμαυτῷ τάσδ᾽ ἀρὰς ὁ προστιθείς.

766 f. νοσοῦνθ᾽, as if οὐκ ἤθελες ἐκπέμπειν was to follow; but the changed form of phrase requires the dat. θέλοντι. Cp. *O. T.* 350 ἐννέπω σὲ...ἐμμένειν,...ὡς ὄντι (n.).

767 οὐκ ἤθελες θέλοντι κ.τ.λ., the will on my side was not met by will on yours: cp. *Tr.* 198 οὐχ ἑκών, ἑκοῦσι δὲ | ξύνεστιν: *Ant.* 276 πάρειμι δ᾽ ἄκων οὐχ ἑκοῦσιν. προσθέσθαι, 'bestow,' a sense freq. in the active, but somewhat rare in the midd.: cp., however, *Ant.* 40 προσθείμην (πλέον τι, 'contribute'), Aesch. *Eum.* 735 ψῆφον δ᾽ Ὀρέστῃ τήνδ᾽ ἐγὼ προσθήσομαι. The *midd.* usu. = 'to annex' (404), or 'to take on oneself' (*O. T.* 1460 n.). Cp. on προσθήσει, 153.

768 ἦ, the old Attic form, given by L in 973, 1366 (though not elsewhere), and attested by ancient scholia for fr. 406 and *O. T.* 1123, where see n. μεστός, 'satiated,' with partic.: [Dem.] or. 48 § 28 (prob. by a contemporary of Dem.) ἐπειδὴ δὲ μεστὸς ἐγένετο ἀγανακτῶν: Eur. *Hipp.* 664 μισῶν δ᾽ οὔποτ᾽ ἐμπλησθήσομαι | γυναῖκας.

770 ἐξώθεις κἀξέβ., 'you were for thrusting me out': for the impf. cp. 356, 441.

771 τοῦτ᾽, 'this of which you speak,' cp. *Ant.* 96 τὸ δεινὸν τοῦτο.

772 f. πόλιν, the State in the person of its head, Theseus: γένος, the people of Attica, as represented by the elders of Colonus. Cp. *Ai.* 861 κλειναί τ᾽ Ἀθῆναι καὶ τὸ σύντροφον γένος.

774 μετασπᾶν, to snatch to the other side (cp. μετακινεῖν, μεταπείθειν etc.), found only here, but not open to just suspicion, though Blaydes changes it to μ᾽ ἀποσπᾶν. So μεθέλκειν in *Anth. Plan.* 5. 384. σκληρὰ μαλθακῶς λέγων, putting hard purposes into soft words: disguising the ungenerous treatment which was really contemplated (399) under the name of a recall to home and friends (757). For the verbal contrast cp. Arist. *Rhet.* 3. 7. 10 (speaking of the relation to be observed between the *sounds* of words, and the *tones* of the orator's voice) ἐὰν οὖν τὰ μαλακὰ σκληρῶς καὶ τὰ σκληρὰ μαλακῶς λέγηται, ἀπίθανον γίγνεται. Cp. 1406.

775 αὕτη, subject (instead of τοῦτο, see on 88), τίς τέρψις

predicate: **ἄκοντας** object to **φιλεῖν**: What pleasure is this,—
that people should be hospitable to one against one's inclina-
tion? Thuc. 3. 12 τίς οὖν αὕτη ἢ φιλία ἐγίγνετο ἢ ἐλευθερία
πιστή; φιλεῖν, *Il.* 6. 15 πάντας γὰρ φιλέεσκεν ὁδῷ ἔπι οἰκία
ναίων: *Od.* 8. 42 ὄφρα ξεῖνον ἐνὶ μεγάροισι φιλέωμεν. So often
ἀγαπάω. The illustration (776 ff.) shows that **ἄκοντας** refers
to the reluctance of Oed., not to the constraint put by the
oracle on the Thebans.

776 ff. ὥσπερ merely introduces the illustration, like 'For
instance.' Plat. *Gorg.* 451 A ὥσπερ ἄν, εἴ τίς με ἔροιτο...
εἴποιμ' ἄν, 'for instance I should say, if any one were to ask.'
τις before **εἰ** is here a case of 'hyperbaton,' in which Soph.
is sometimes bold: cp. *O. T.* 1251 n. .τυχεῖν: cp. *O. T.* 1435
καὶ τοῦ με χρείας ὧδε λιπαρεῖς τυχεῖν;

778 ὧν χρῄζοις. The verb in the relative clause takes
the optative mood of the verb in the principal clause (ἔχοντι
=ὅτε ἔχοις): cp. Eur. *Hel.* 435 τίς ἂν μόλοι | ὅστις διαγγείλειε,
and n. to *O. T.* 506.

779 ἡ χάρις: when the *benefit* (the thing done) should
bring with it no *sense* of a *favour* conferred: χάρις and χάριν
being used in two different senses: cp. χάριν ἄχαριν...ἐπικρᾶναι
(Aesch. *Ag.* 1545), to grant a boon which gives no pleasure.

780 ἄρ': see on 753. The second ἄν is warranted by the
stress on τῇσδ', and is more likely than τῇσδέ γ': cp. on *O. T.* 339.

781 καὶ σύ, thou on thy part: cp. on 53.

782 λόγῳ...τοῖσι δ' ἔργοισιν: cp. *El.* 60 ὅταν λόγῳ θανὼν |
ἔργοισι σωθῶ: Eur. *Tro.* 1233 ὄνομ' ἔχουσα, τἄργα δ' οὔ.

783 καὶ τοῖσδ'. The Chorus had been present when
Ismene told Oed. of the Theban designs, and when he
uttered an imprecation on his sons (399—460): and Theseus
left the stage at 667. But φράσω refers to the explicit and
public statement of Creon's baseness, now addressed, before
his face, to the Chorus.

785 πάραυλον, having my abode (αὐλή) beside you, *i.e.*
ἄγχι γῆς Καδμείας (399), but outside of it. So *Ai.* 892
τίνος βοὴ πάραυλος ἐξέβη νάπους; 'whose cry burst from the
covert of the wood at our side?': fr. 460 πάραυλος Ἑλλησ-
ποντίς, a neighbour at the Hellespont.

786 κακῶν ἄνατος: see on ἀνήνεμον χειμώνων 677. τῇσδ'
is a certain correction of the ms. τῶνδ', which would be
awkward if masc. (as =the Athenians), and pointless if neut.,
since nothing has yet been said between Creon and Oed.

11—2

about such κακά. The schol., καὶ ἵνα ἡ Θήβη ἀβλαβὴς ἔσται
ἐκ ταύτης τῆς γῆς, confirms τῆσδ'. Join τῆσδε χθονός with
κακῶν, 'evils coming from this land' (gen. of source). ἀπαλλαχθῇ is absol., 'get off,' as *El.* 1002 ἄλυπος ἄτης ἐξαπαλλαχ-
θήσομαι: Ar. *Plut.* 271 ἀπαλλαγῆναι | ἀζήμιος. If it were
joined with τῆσδε χθονός, 'get free of this land,' the words
would naturally mean, 'get safely out of this land.'

787 f. ταῦτα...τάδ', 'that'...'this' (which follows), a good
instance of the normal distinction. Cp. Her. 6. 53 ταῦτα μὲν
Λακεδαιμόνιοι λέγουσι,...τάδε δὲ...ἐγὼ γράφω: Xen. *An.* 2. 1. 20
ταῦτα μὲν δὴ σὺ λέγεις· παρ' ἡμῶν δὲ ἀπάγγελλε τάδε. In
poetry, however, οὗτος often refers to what follows (as *Od.* 2.
306 ταῦτα δέ τοι μάλα πάντα τελευτήσουσιν Ἀχαιοί, | νῆα καὶ
ἐξαίτους ἐρέτας), and ὅδε to what has just preceded: cp. on
1007.

χώρας with ἀλάστωρ, my scourge of the land, the avenging
spirit which, through my curse, will ever haunt the land:
for the gen., cp. *Tr.* 1092 Νεμέας ἔνοικον (the lion), βουκόλων
ἀλάστορα, scourge of herdsmen: Xenarchus (Midd. Comedy,
c. 350 B.C.) Βουταλίων fr. 1. 3 ἀλάστωρ εἰσπέπαικε Πελοπιδῶν,
a very fiend of the Pelopidae has burst in. For ἐνναίων
cp. Aesch. *Suppl.* 415 βαρὺν ξύνοικον...ἀλάστορα.

790 τοσοῦτον ἐνθανεῖν μόνον is bold. The infin. must be
explained as in appos. with τοσοῦτον,—'just thus much right
in the land—the right to die in it.' For the regular construction,
see *O. T.* 1191 τοσοῦτον ὅσον δοκεῖν: Aesch. *Theb.* 730
(in ref. to these same brothers) σίδαρος | χθόνα ναίειν διαπήλας,
ὁπόσαν καὶ φθιμένοισιν κατέχειν, | τῶν μεγάλων πεδίων ἀμοίρους:
Thuc. 1. 2 νεμόμενοι...τὰ αὑτῶν ἕκαστοι ὅσον ἀποζῆν.

ἐνθανεῖν: cp. [Eur.] *Rhes.* 869 ὦ γαῖα πατρίς, πῶς ἂν ἐνθάνοιμί
σοι; a poet. word. Remark that ἐνθανεῖν can mean only
'to *die* in,' not 'to *lie dead* in': but the sense is, 'just enough
ground, with a view to *dying* (instead of *reigning*) on Theban
soil'; *i.e.*, as much as a dead man will need. The phrase is
half-proverbial: Ar. *Eccl.* 592 μηδὲ γεωργεῖν τὸν μὲν πολλήν,
τῷ δ' εἶναι μηδὲ ταφῆναι. Freeman, *Old English History*
p. 313 '...*What will my brother King Harold of England
give to King Harold of Norway?*'...'*Seven foot of the ground
of England, or more perchance, seeing he is taller than other
men.*' Shaksp. *H. IV.* Pt. i. 5. 4. 89 *When that this body did
contain a spirit, A kingdom for it was too small a bound; But
now two paces of the vilest earth Is room enough.*

792 σαφεστέρων, 'as truer are the sources of my knowledge,' see on 623. The καὶ of two MSS. (A, R) is strongly recommended by Greek usage, and is probably to be combined with ἐκ, which, though not necessary with κλύω, has L's support. κλύω, pres., know by hearing, as *Ph.* 261, *Tr.* 68, etc.: cp. 240 n.

794 τὸ σὸν...στόμα, 'thy mouth has come hither suborned': thou hast come as a mere mouthpiece of the Thebans, secretly pledged to aid their designs on me. Cp. *O. T.* 426 (Teiresias says) καὶ Κρέοντα καὶ τοὐμὸν στόμα | προπηλάκιζε, my message from Apollo. ὑπόβλητον: cp. *Ai.* 481 οὐδεὶς ἐρεῖ ποθ' ὡς ὑπόβλητον λόγον, | Αἴας, ἔλεξας, ἀλλὰ τῆς σαυτοῦ φρενός, 'a word not true to thy nature.' So ὑπόπεμπτος of an insidious emissary, Xen. *An.* 3. 3. 4.

795 πολλὴν ἔχον στόμωσιν, with a hard and keen edge,— thoroughly attempered to a shameless and cruel task. στόμωσις was the process of *tempering* iron to receive an edge or point (στόμα); cp. Arist. *Meteor.* 4. 6 τήκεται δὲ καὶ ὁ εἰργασμένος σίδηρος, ὥστε ὑγρὸς γίγνεσθαι καὶ πάλιν πήγνυσθαι. καὶ τὰ στομώματα ποιοῦσιν οὕτως· ὑφίσταται γὰρ καὶ ἀποκαθαίρεται κάτω ἡ σκωρία (dross). ὅταν δὲ πολλάκις πάθῃ καὶ καθαρὸς γένηται, τοῦτο στόμωμα γίγνεται (this makes *tempered iron*). Hence, fig., Ar. *Nub.* 1107 μέμνησο ὅπως | εὖ μοι στομώσεις αὐτόν, ἐπὶ μὲν θάτερα | οἷον δικιδίοις, τὴν δ' ἑτέραν αὐτοῦ γνάθον | στόμωσον οἵαν ἐς τὰ μείζω πράγματα, alluding to a two-edged blade; schol. ὀξυνεῖς...ἀκονήσεις. The double sense of στόμα has suggested the παρήχησις with στόμωσιν: cp. *Ai.* 650 ὃς τὰ δείν' ἐκαρτέρουν τότε, | βαφῇ σίδηρος ὥς, ἐθηλύνθην στόμα: 'I, erst so wondrous firm,—yea, as iron hardened in the dipping,—felt the keen edge of my temper softened.' Cp. *Ai.* 584 γλῶσσα...τεθηγμένη. *Tr.* 1176.

796 κακά and σωτήρια are predicates, 'you will gain more woe than weal': cp. Eur. *Hipp.* 471 ἀλλ' εἰ τὰ πλείω χρηστὰ τῶν κακῶν ἔχεις. Cp. *Ant.* 313. Oed. means: 'By pleading with me to return, you will only illustrate your own heartlessness: you will never win me as a safeguard for Thebes.'

797 If οἶδα is right (as it seems to be), μή can hardly be explained otherwise than by emphasis, *i.e.* by the *strong assurance* which the speaker expresses. But what form should the partic. have? With the MS. πείθων, the sense is: 'However, I am assured that I am not persuading you of this,—go!' In 656 οἶδ' ἐγώ σε μήτινα | ἐνθένδ' ἀπάξοντ' ἄνδρα appears to be

a like case of *strong assurance.* Cp. *O. T.* 1455. In 1121
there is another: ἐπίσταμαι γὰρ τήνδε...τέρψιν παρ' ἄλλου
μηδενὸς πεφασμένην. Here, however, οἶδα μὴ πείθων is so far
stranger, that the emphasis appears less appropriate in stating
the speaker's consciousness *of what he himself is doing.* Other
readings suggested are ἀλλ' οἶσθα γάρ με and αλλ' ἴσθι γάρ με,
and πείσων or πείσοντ' for πείθων.

In later Greek μή with partic., in regard to *fact,* was
common, as Luc. *Dial. Mort.* 16 πῶς οὖν ἀκριβὴς ὁ Αἰακὸς
ὢν οὐ διέγνω σε μὴ ὄντα ἐκεῖνον; 'failed to discern that you
were not he,' where μὴ ὄντα, though it might be paraphrased
by εἰ μὴ ἦσθα, virtually = ὅτι οὐκ ἦσθα. In Mod. Greek the
partic. always takes μή, not δέν. This latter tendency may
conceivably have affected our MSS.: *e.g.* τοιάδ' οὐ πείθων may
have once stood here.

799 εἰ τερποίμεθα, if we should have content therewith:
cp. *Ant.* 1168 πλούτει τε γὰρ κατ' οἶκον, εἰ βούλει, μέγα, | καὶ ζῆ
τύραννον σχῆμ' ἔχων· ἐὰν δ' ἀπῇ | τούτων τὸ χαίρειν, τἆλλ' ἐγὼ
καπνοῦ σκιᾶς | οὐκ ἂν πριαίμην ἀνδρὶ πρὸς τὴν ἡδονήν.

800 f. Which of us do you consider the greater sufferer
by your present attitude? Me, because I am not to bring
you back? Or yourself, when you reject your friends and
country? δυστυχεῖν has been explained as 'to be in error,'
referring to Creon's ignorance of the lot in store for Thebes
(787); but it is simpler to take it of Creon's failure to win
Oedipus. However great that loss may be, Creon means,
the loss to Oed. himself will be greater still. ἐς τὰ σά, 'with
regard to your doings'; cp. 1121 : *O. T.* 980 σὺ δ' εἰς τὰ
μητρὸς μὴ φοβοῦ νυμφεύματα (n.). ἢ σ' εἰς τὰ σαυτοῦ, σὲ being
elided, though emphatic : *O. T.* 64 πόλιν τε κἀμὲ καὶ σ' ὁμοῦ
στένει. ἐν τῷ νῦν λόγῳ, in our present discussion (from 728).

802 f. Creon had said, in effect, ' *Your* happiness is as
much my object as our own.' ' *My* happiness,' Oed. rejoins,
'will be best secured if your application is rejected by the
people of Colonus, as by myself.'

804 φύσας, 'wilt thou shew that even at thy years thou hast
not grown a head of wisdom?' Cp. 150, *El.* 1463 (ὡς) κολαστοῦ
προστυχὼν φύσῃ φρένας : Her. 5. 91 δόξαν...φύσας αὐξάνεται.

805 λῦμα, a 'stain,' or 'reproach.' In the only other
place where Soph. has the word (*Ai.* 655 λύμαθ' ἁγνίσας ἐμά)
it has its primary sense of 'something washed off' (from √ΛΥ,
another form of √ΛΟϜ, whence λούω). τρέφει, pass. (as *O. T.*

374 μιᾶς τρέφει πρὸς νυκτός), thou *livest on* to disgrace thy years by thy folly. Not midd., 'dost nourish a reproach.'

806 Cp. *O. T.* 545 λέγειν σὺ δεινός (Oed. to Creon).

807 ἐξ ἅπαντος, *starting from* anything as the ἀφορμή or ὕλη of discourse; 'on any theme.' So ἐκ marks the conditions from which action sets out (ὡς ἐκ τῶνδ᾿, *Ai.* 537). εὖ λέγει, pleads *speciously*: Eur. *Hec.* 1191 δύνασθαι τἄδικ᾿ εὖ λέγειν.

808 For τὰ καίρια, the reading of the MSS., it may be urged that the phrase is τὰ καίρια (λέγειν, δρᾶν etc.) in Aesch. *Th.* 1, 619, *Suppl.* 446, *Ch.* 582, Eur. *I. A.* 829, Soph. *Ai.* 120. The ellipse of τό is illustrated by 606. τὸ καίρια, the reading of Suidas, is supported by such passages as Aesch. *P. V.* 927 ὅσον τό τ᾿ ἄρχειν καὶ τὸ δουλεύειν δίχα: Eur. *Alc.* 528 χωρὶς τό τ᾿ εἶναι καὶ τὸ μὴ νομίζεται.

809 ὡς δή, *quasi vero*, strictly an elliptical phrase, '(do you mean) forsooth that you speak,' etc. Aesch. *Ag.* 1633 ὡς δὴ σύ μοι τύραννος Ἀργείων ἔσει. Eur. *Andr.* 234 τί σεμνομυθεῖς κεἰς ἀγῶν᾿ ἔρχει λόγων, | ὡς δὴ σὺ σώφρων τἀμὰ δ᾿ οὐχὶ σώφρονα;

810 ὅτῳ = τούτῳ ὅτῳ, 'in the opinion of one who possesses only such sense as yours': for the ethic dat. cp. 1446, *Ant.* 904 καίτοι σ᾿ ἐγὼ ᾿τίμησα τοῖς φρονοῦσιν εὖ. For ἴσος, *only* so much, cp. *O. T.* 810 οὐ μὴν ἴσην γ᾿ ἔτισεν: Her. 2. 3 νομίζων πάντας ἀνθρώπους ἴσον περὶ αὐτῶν ἐπίστασθαι, equally little: for ἴσος καί instead of ὥσπερ, *O. T.* 1187. So also ταὐτὸ καί Herod. 5. 55; 6. 92; 8. 45.

811 πρὸ τῶνδε, 'in the name of these men,' as *O. T.* 10 πρὸ τῶνδε φωνεῖν (n.).

812 ἐφορμῶν with ἔνθα χρή, keeping jealous watch at the place where I am destined to dwell: fig. from a hostile fleet watching a position. με with φύλασσ᾿ only: in class. Gk. ἐφορμεῖν does not take acc.

For με followed by ἐμέ, cp. *El.* 1359 ἀλλά με | λόγοις ἀπώλλυς, ἔργ᾿ ἔχων ἥδιστ᾿ ἐμοί, where ἐμοί is not more emphatic than με. So here, too, it may be doubted whether ἐμέ conveys such an emphasis as would be given by an italicised '*my*,'—implying a reproof of meddlesomeness. The stress is rather on χρή ναίειν: Apollo has brought him to this rest (89).

813 f. This passage, which has been variously altered, appears to me to be sound as it stands in the MSS. Oedipus has undertaken to speak for the men of Attica (ἐρῶ γὰρ καὶ πρὸ τῶνδε). Creon refuses to identify him with them, bitterly reminding the Theban that his real ties are elsewhere. 'I call

them—not thee—to witness my protest': *i.e.* 'I have a just
claim on thee, which thou repellest:—I appeal to a judgment
more impartial than thine own.' The words mark the point
at which he drops persuasion. He now turns to menace.
'But, for the tone of thy reply to kinsmen' (meaning, to
himself, cp. on 148 σμικροῖς), 'if I catch thee'—an aposiopesis.
(Cp. *Il.* 1. 580 εἴπερ γάρ κ' ἐθέλησιν Ὀλύμπιος ἀστεροπητὴς |
ἐξ ἑδέων στυφελίξαι· | ὁ γὰρ πολὺ φέρτερός ἐστιν: Verg. *Aen.* 1.
135 *Quos ego....*)

μαρτύρομαι, *antestor:* cp. Aristoph. *Pax* 1119 TP. ἆ παῖε
παῖε τὸν Βάκιν. IE. μαρτύρομαι. *Av.* 1032 μαρτύρομαι τυπτό-
μενος. *Ach.* 927. *Nub.* 1297.

814 ἀνταμείβει: ἀμείβομαι usu. takes a simple acc. of the
person to whom a reply is made (991); but cp. Her. 8. 60
τότε μὲν ἠπίως πρὸς τὸν Κορίνθιον ἀμείψατο. Even if πρὸς
were not taken with ἀνταμείβει here, it could still mean
'in relation to': cp. *Tr.* 468 κακὸν | πρὸς ἄλλον εἶναι, πρὸς
δ' ἔμ' ἀψευδεῖν ἀεί. οἷα causal = ἐπεὶ τοιαῦτα: cp. on 263.

815 τῶνδε συμμ. with βίᾳ, 'in despite of': cp. 657.

816 ἦ μὴν in a threat, as Aesch. *P. V.* 907 ἦ μὴν ἔτι
Ζεύς, καίπερ αὐθάδη φρονῶν, | ἔσται ταπεινός. κἄνευ τοῦδε, *sc.* τοῦ
ἐλεῖν σε. Cp. *O. T.* 1158 ἀλλ' εἰς τόδ' ἥξεις, *sc.* εἰς τὸ ὀλέσθαι.
The MS. κἄνευ τῶνδε could here mean nothing but 'e'en apart
from these men.' λυπηθεὶς ἔσει = a fut. perf., 'wilt *soon* be
grieved' (though it could also mean, 'wilt suffer a *lasting*
grief'): so *O. T.* 1146 οὐ σιωπήσας ἔσει; *Ant.* 1067 ἀντιδοὺς
ἔσει. In prose the part. with ἔσομαι is the perf., not the aor.

817 ποίῳ σὺν ἔργῳ, 'on the warrant of what deed,'—since
λυπηθεὶς ἔσει implies that something has already been done
to cause the pain which will soon be felt. σὺν has the same
force as in σὺν θεῷ:—'with what deed to *support* the threat.'
Cp. *O. T.* 656 ἐν αἰτίᾳ | σὺν ἀφανεῖ λόγῳ...βαλεῖν, to accuse
one *with the help of* an unproved story. ἀπειλήσας ἔχεις = a
perf.: cp. *O. T.* 577 n.

818 τὴν μὲν, Ismene, who left the scene at 509 to make
the offerings in the grove. Creon may have seized her, as a
hostage, before his entrance at 728; or may have signed to
one of his guards to go and do so, when he found that
Oedipus was stubborn.

820 τάδε might be cognate acc., = τάδε τὰ οἰμώγματα (cp.
Aesch. *Ag.* 1307 ΚΑ. φεῦ, φεῦ. ΧΟ. τί τοῦτ' ἔφευξας;),
but it rather means, 'this capture.'

821 The τήνδε γ' of the MSS. could be retained only if μου were changed to καὶ and given to Creon. οὐ μακρ. χρόνου: see on 397.

823 τὸν ἀσεβῆ, because Oedipus is under the protection of the deities (287), and especially because, as he may well suppose, Ismene had been snatched from the sacred grove (cp. on 818).

824 f. θᾶσσον, oft. in impatient command, as 839, *Ai.* 581 πύκαζε θᾶσσον: *O. T.* 430 οὐκ εἰς ὄλεθρον; οὐχὶ θᾶσσον; Write τὰ νῦν rather than τανῦν, since it is opp. ἃ πρόσθεν: δίκαια, predicate. εἴργασαι (his capture of Ismene) need not be changed to εἰργάσω, since πρόσθεν can mean 'already.'

826 ὑμῖν, addressing his guards (723). ἂν εἴη: here in giving a command with cold sternness. Cp. 725 (in request), *O. T.* 343 (in fixed resolve).

828 f. ποῖ φύγω; cp. on 310. θεῶν...ἢ βροτῶν; *Ai.* 399 οὔτε γὰρ θεῶν γένος οὔθ' ἀμερίων | ἔτ' ἄξιος βλέπειν τιν' εἰς ὄνασιν ἀνθρώπων.

830 οὐχ ἅψομαι. With these words, Creon steps towards Antigone. His actual seizure of her is marked by the words τοὺς ἐμοὺς ἄγω. The fut., therefore, is more dramatic than ἅπτομαι would be. τῆς ἐμῆς, since he considers himself as now the guardian of his nieces,—their father having forfeited all rights at Thebes (cp. *O. T.* 1506 n.).

832 τοὺς ἐμοὺς: cp. 148 σμικροῖς (=Antigone); *Ant.* 48 ἀλλ' οὐδὲν αὐτῷ τῶν ἐμῶν μ' εἴργειν μέτα (*i.e.* from my brother): *O. T.* 1448 ὀρθῶς τῶν γε σῶν τελεῖς ὕπερ (for thy sister).

833—886 *The phrase* τοὺς ἐμοὺς ἄγω *indicates the moment at which Creon lays his hand on Antigone. It is followed by* 11 *verses,* 833—843, *in which the dochmiacs of the Chorus, blended with iambic trimeters, mark excitement. Antistrophic to these are the* 11 *verses,* 876—886, *which in like manner follow the moment at which Creon lays his hand on Oedipus. As a lyric interposition in dialogue, the passage has a kommatic character, though it does not constitute a* κομμός *proper in the same sense as* 510—548, 1447—1499, *or* 1670—1750.

834 ἀφήσεις: 838 μέθες. The former is properly, 'allow to depart,'—the latter, 'release from one's grasp'; but they differ here only as 'let her alone' from the more specific 'unhand her.' Cp. 857 οὔτοι σ' ἀφήσω, I will not allow thee to leave Colonus.

835 εἰς βάσανον εἶ χερῶν, 'you will come to the test of

blows': cp. χειρῶν νόμος, the arbitrament of blows (as opp. to δίκης νόμος), Her. 9. 48 πρὶν...ἢ συμμίξαι ἡμέας ἐς χειρῶν τε νόμον ἀπικέσθαι. **εἰ** as in the common phrase εἰς χεῖρας ἰέναι τινί, or συνιέναι.

836 εἶργον, 'keep back!' said as the Chorus approach him threateningly: cp. *O. T.* 890 τῶν ἀσέπτων ἔρξεται (n.). μωμένου, meditating, designing: a part. used once in dialogue by Soph. (*Tr.* 1136 ἥμαρτε χρηστὰ μωμένη), and twice in lyrics by Aesch. (*Ch.* 45, 441).

837 πόλει: ταῖς Θήβαις.

838 οὐκ ἠγόρευον...; 'did I not say so?' a familiar phrase; Ar. *Ach.* 41 οὐκ ἠγόρευον; τοῦτ' ἐκεῖν' οὑγὼ 'λεγον: *Plut.* 102 οὐκ ἠγόρευον ὅτι παρέξειν πράγματα | ἠμελλέτην μοι; So *O. T.* 973 οὔκουν ἐγώ σοι ταῦτα προὔλεγον πάλαι;—Oed. alludes to 587, 653.

839 μὴ 'πίτασσ' ἃ μὴ κρατεῖς, 'do not give orders in matters where you are not master.' ἃ is not for ὧν, but is cogn. accus. (or acc. of respect), as *O. T.* 1522 πάντα μὴ βούλου κρατεῖν· | καὶ γὰρ ἀκράτησας, οὔ σοι τῷ βίῳ ξυνέσπετο. *Ant.* 664 τοὐπιτάσσειν τοῖς κρατύνουσιν, to dictate to one's masters. Theocr. 15. 90 πασάμενος ἐπίτασσε (wait till you are our master before you give us orders).

840 At Creon's words, when he laid his hand on Antigone (832), one of his guards stepped up, and placed himself at her side. χαλᾶν λέγω σοι, 'let go, I tell you!' like οὐκ ἀφήσεις and μέθες, is said to *Creon*. Creon's σοί, a mocking echo of theirs, is said to *the guard*: 'and *I* tell *thee* to start on the journey.'

841 πρόβαθ'...βᾶτε, as oft. esp. in Eur. *e.g. Or.* 181 διοιχόμεθ', οἰχόμεθ'. ὧδε = δεῦρο: cp. 182. ἔντοποι, the other dwellers at Colonus.

842 πόλις...σθένει: 'our city—yea, our city—is being brought low by sheer strength': ἐναίρεται, because the majesty of the State is destroyed when its asylum is violated. In πόλις ἐμά, the stress is on the first word, not on the second. σθένει with ἐναίρεται, 'is being outraged with the strong hand,' seems to be sufficiently defended by Eur. *Bacch.* 953 οὐ σθένει νικητέον | γυναῖκας, where it differs from βίᾳ only as it differs here,—i.e. as meaning strictly, 'by an exertion of strength,' not, 'by violence': cp. *ib.* 1127 ἀπεσπάραξεν ὦμον, οὐχ ὑπὸ σθένους, not by her own strength (since the god made it easy for her). ὧδε, 'hither.'

845 μοι: ethic dat.; cp. 81.

847 ὦ τάλας: cp. 753.

848 ἐκ τούτοιν...σκήπτροιν, 'by means of these two supports,'—
the art. being omitted, as 471 τοῦτο χεῦμ'. This is simpler
than to construe, 'with the help of these (girls) *as* supports.'
ἐκ refers to the σκῆπτρα as an antecedent condition of his
walking. Essentially the same use, though under slightly
different phases, appears in 807 ἐξ ἄπαντος: *Tr.* 875 (βέβηκεν)
ἐξ ἀκινήτου ποδός: *Ph.* 91 ἐξ ἑνὸς ποδός: *El.* 742 ὠρθοῦθ' ὁ
τλήμων ὀρθὸς ἐξ ὀρθῶν δίφρων. σκήπτροιν, 'crutches' or 'staves':
cp. 1109: Eur. *Hec.* 280 ἥδ' ἀντὶ πολλῶν ἐστί μοι παραψυχή, |
πόλις, τιθήνη, βάκτρον, ἡγεμὼν ὁδοῦ.

849 ὁδοιπορήσῃς. As between -εις and -ῃς in verbal
endings, neither L nor any of our MSS. has authority. The
reason for preferring the aor. subj. here is one of usage.
οὐ μὴ ὁδοιπορήσῃς is a denial: οὐ μὴ ὁδοιπορήσεις, a prohibition.
The latter is grammatically as right as the other, but does not
suit this context. Sometimes (as in Soph. *El.* 1052), but
rarely, οὐ μή with fut. indic. express a denial and not a
prohibition.

νικᾶν, 'to worst,'—by carrying your point against them
(*not* with ref. to future defeats of Thebans by Athenians, 621).

850 ὑφ' ὧν...ταχθείς, 'by whose mandate.'

851 τύραννος, one of the royal house: cp. *Tr.* 316 μὴ τῶν
τυράννων; 'is she of the royal stock?' The Creon of *O. T.*
588 does not wish τύραννος εἶναι (to be *king*) μᾶλλον ἢ τύραννα
δρᾶν: but the captor of the blind man's daughters must seek
a touch of dignity from any source.

852 f. γνώσει τάδε, 'thou wilt understand *these things*'
(= thy present acts in their true bearings),—explained by
ὁθούνεκ', 'namely, that' etc. αὐτὸν = σεαυτόν: so 930, 1356:
but αὐτὸν = ἐμαυτόν 966, *O. T.* 138 (n.).

854 For δρᾷς followed by εἰργάσω, instead of ἔδρασας,
cp. *O. T.* 54 ὡς εἴπερ ἄρξεις...ὥσπερ κρατεῖς (n.). βίᾳ φίλων
(cp. 815) applies to his *former* conduct, since, in searching
out his origin, he acted against the passionate entreaties
of Iocasta (*O. T.* 1060 ff.). Greek idiom uses a parataxis,
οὔτε νῦν...οὔτε πρόσθεν, where ours would subordinate the second
clause to the first, 'now, *as* before': cp. 308.

855 ὀργῇ χάριν δούς, 'having indulged anger': cp. 1182:
El. 331 θυμῷ ματαίῳ μὴ χαρίζεσθαι κενά: Cratinus fr. inc. 146
ἔσθιε καὶ σῇ γαστρὶ δίδου χάριν. We remember his blow at

Laïus (παίω δι' ὀργῆς *O. T.* 807)—his anger with Teiresias (ὡς ὀργῆς ἔχω, *ib.* 345)—his anger with Iocasta (*ib.* 1067)— his frantic self-blinding (*ib.* 1268).

856 The guards, carrying off Antigone, have already left the scene (847); cp. 875 μοῦνος. Creon is now about to follow them, when the Chorus again approach him, and protest that he shall not leave Colonus unless the two maidens are restored.

857 τῶνδε. So the *plur.* αἵδε of the two sisters below, 1107, 1367, 1379 (immediately after the *masc.* dual τοιώδ', referring to the brothers), 1668; τάσδ' 1121, 1146, 1634, *O. T.* 1507, *Ant.* 579. On the other hand the *dual* of ὅδε occurs only thrice in Soph.; above, 445 τοῖνδε: τώδε *El.* 981 f. *bis.* It is surely needless, then, to write τοῖνδε here. In 859 (merely two) Creon uses the dual because he is thinking of the two sisters *together* as the '*two supports*' of Oed. (848, 445). The plur. differs from the dual simply by the *absence* of any stress on the notion of 'a pair.'

858 f. ῥύσιον: Then thou shalt soon deposit even a greater security for my city. πόλει = Thebes, as in Creon's former words, 837 πόλει μαχεῖ. ῥύσιος denotes what one draws to oneself, carries off, (1) as booty, (2) as a security, (3) in reprisal.   Here θήσεις points to (2), since ἐνέχυρον τιθέναι, to deposit a pledge, was a regular phrase: Ar. *Eccl.* 754 πότερον μετοικιζόμενος ἐξενήνοχας | αὔτ', ἢ φέρεις ἐνέχυρα θήσων; 'or are you taking them to be deposited as securities?' Plat. *Legg.* 820 E ἐνέχυρα...τοὺς θέντας (those who have given the pledges)...τοὺς θεμένους (those to whom they have been given). πόλει dat. of interest, as ὑποτιθέναι 'to mortgage' takes a dat. of the mortgagee: Dem. or. 27 § 25 ὁ ὑποθεὶς τῷ πατρὶ τἀνδράποδα.

ἐφάψομαι: Aesch. *Suppl.* 412 καὶ μήτε δῆρις ῥυσίων ἐφάψεται, (and so) 'that the foeman shall not lay hands on you as prizes' (where the king of Argos is speaking to the Danaïdes whom he protects).

861 After δεινὸν λέγοις (L), or λέγεις, a syllable has to be supplied conjecturally. Triclinius added ὡς ('be sure that,' 45) before τοῦτο: but this mars the rhythm: and the *simple* fut. (as in 860) is more forcible. The optat. λέγοις of L, which is not likely to be a mere error for λέγεις, strongly favours Hermann's simple remedy, δεινὸν λέγοις ἄν, ''twere a dread deed that thou threatenest' (if only thou couldst *do* it): cp. on 647 μέγ' ἂν λέγοις δώρημα. Next to this, I should prefer Wecklein's δεινὸς λόγοις εἶ.

πεπράξεται, 'will have been done': *i.e.* will be done forth-with: Dem. or. 19 § 74 ἔφη...ταῦτα πεπράξεσθαι δυοῖν ἢ τριῶν ἡμερῶν. Cp. *O. T.* 1146 n.

862 ἦν μή γ'. Piderit is clearly right (I think) in giving this verse to the Chorus, not to Creon. Creon, who has long since dropped the semblance of courtesy with which he began (759), cannot, of course, mean to express serious deference for the wishes of Theseus; while, as an ironical defiance, the words would be extremely tame. In the mouth of the Chorus, however, the threat has point, since they know their king's public resolve (656); it has also dramatic force, since he is soon to appear (887). The words of Oed. (863) refer to 861. ἀπειργάθῃ, 'hinder': cp. *El.* 1271 εἰργαθεῖν (and so Eur.): Aesch. *Eum.* 566 κατειργαθοῦ (aor. imper. midd.). The forms ἐέργαθεν, ἀποέργαθε (aor., or, as some would call them, impf.) are Homeric.

863 φθέγμ', 'voice,' rather than 'word.' The future ψαύσεις is more natural than the present, and expresses indignation with greater force.

864 f. αὐδῶ σιωπᾶν. Creon forbids the utterance of the curse which he forebodes; and the injunction reminds Oedipus that he is near the Awful Goddesses who impose abstinence from all ill-omened words. 'Nay (γάρ),' he cries, 'may they suffer me to utter one imprecation more (ἔτι).' γάρ implies, 'I will not yet be mute'; cp. also its use in wishes, εἰ γάρ, εἴθε γάρ, etc. ἔτι recalls the former imprecation on his sons (421 ff.).—ἄφωνον...ἀρᾶς, 'without voice to utter this curse': cp. on 677 ἀνήνεμον...χειμώνων.

866 ὅς, with caus. force, 'since thou hast...': see on οἵτινες, 263. ψιλὸν ὄμμ' can mean only 'a defenceless eye,' *i.e.* a defenceless maiden (Antigone) who was to him as eyesight. The phrase has bitter point, since Creon himself, in his smooth speech, had pathetically described Antigone as τοὐπιόντος ἁρπάσαι 'for any one to seize' (752). It is also less bold in Greek than in English, owing to the common figurative use of ὄμμα, as if he had said, 'my defenceless *darling*' (cp. on *O. T.* 987). ψιλὸν should not be taken as acc. *masc.* with με: this would be tame and forced. Cp. below 1029 οὐ ψιλὸν οὐδ' ἄσκευον, not *without allies* or instruments. ἀποσπάσας takes a double acc. (like ἀφαιρεῖν, etc.).

867 ἔοιχει, as 894 οἴχεται...ἀποσπάσας, though he is still present: so 1009 οἴχει λαβών. ἔοιχει merely adds the notion of '*away*' to ἀποσπάσας, 'you have torn and taken away.'— Cp. *El.* 809 ἀποσπάσας γὰρ τῆς ἐμῆς οἴχει φρενός, etc.

868 σέ τ' αὐτὸν seems preferable to σὲ καὐτὸν, since τε...καὶ was usual in such formulas with αὐτός, cp. 462, 559, 952, 1009, 1125: though τε was sometimes omitted when a third clause followed, as Antiph. or. 5 § 11 ἐξώλειαν αὐτῷ καὶ γένει καὶ οἰκίᾳ τῇ σῇ ἐπαρώμενον. I hardly think that θεῶν can be right. It would be partitive, 'of the gods, the all-seeing Sun.' But as there is no stress on '*gods*' as opp. to other beings, I should prefer θεὸς, from which θεῶν may have arisen by the carelessness of a copyist who connected it with γένος.

869 f. Ἥλιος: invoked *O. T.* 660 (n.) οὐ τὸν πάντων θεῶν θεὸν πρόμον Ἅλιον, as the all-seeing god whom no deceit can escape. βίον cogn. acc., instead of γῆρας, 'to pass an old age.' κἀμέ: see on 53. In the *Antigone* Creon's wife Eurydicè and his son Haemon commit suicide,—another son, Megareus, having already devoted his life for Thebes. But in Creon's own person, at least, the curse was fulfilled by his surviving all that he loved best. (Cp. *Ant.* 1317 ff.)

871 ὁρᾶτε: he calls on them to witness the unnatural imprecation: cp. 813 μαρτύρομαι.

873 ἔργοις: cp. on 782. ῥήμασιν is said with a bitter consciousness of impotence at this critical moment.

875 μοῦνος, as 991, 1250: cp. *O. T.* 1418 n.

876 ἰὼ τάλας: see on 833.

879 τάνδε (πόλιν) οὐκέτι νεμῶ πόλιν, 'I will no longer reckon Athens a city.' Cp. *O. T.* 1080 ἐμαυτὸν παῖδα τῆς Τύχης νέμων: *El.* 597 καί σ' ἔγωγε δεσπότιν | ἢ μητέρ' οὐκ ἐλάσσον εἰς ἡμᾶς νέμω. The *fut.* is better than the *pres.* here, since the latter would assume Creon's triumph.

880 τοῖς...δικαίοις, instrumental dat., by means of τὰ δίκαια, *i.e.* by having justice on one's side. 'In a just cause, the feeble man vanquishes the strong.' Cp. fr. 76 τοῖς γὰρ δικαίοις ἀντέχειν οὐ ῥᾴδιον: fr. 78 καὶ γὰρ δικοίη γλῶσσα' ἔχει κράτος μέγα. Here she speaks of the moral force with which Δίκη inspires her champion, while in 957 he admits himself to be physically helpless—κεῖ δίκαι' ὅμως λέγω. βραχὺς, of slight physical strength: cp. 586: and for μέγαν cp. on 148.

881 τά = ἅ: cp. on 747.

882 Ζεύς γ' ἄν...σὺ δ' οὔ. The lacuna certainly *preceded*

these words. The words in the strophe answering to τά γ' οὐ
τελεῖ and to the lacuna are 838 f. XO. μέθες χεροῖν | τὴν
παῖδα θᾶσσον. It is probable, then, that the lost words here
belonged to the Chorus, being such as Ζεύς μοι ξυνίστω.

883 ὕβρις: for the quantity, cp. 442 n. ἀνεκτέα, nom. neut.
plur.: cp. on 495 ὁδωτά.

884 πρόμοι, invoking a higher power than the ἔντοποι of
Colonus (841), prepares the entrance of the king. For the
plur., meaning Theseus, cp. ἄνακτας 295 n., 1667.

885 f. πέραν περῶσ' οἵδε δή, 'yonder men' (with a gesture in
the direction taken by Creon's guards) 'are already passing
towards the other side.' πέρα (which Elmsley wrote here) is
ultra, 'to some point beyond,' a line which is either left to be
understood, or expressed in the gen.: πέραν is *trans*, 'on, or *to*,
the *further side*' of a river, sea, or intervening space. περῶσι
implies only that the fugitives are *on their way to* the border of
Boeotia,—not that they are now actually crossing it. δή nearly
= ἤδη: *O. T.* 968 n.

888 f. βωμόν, Poseidon's altar at Colonus: see on 55.
ἔσχετ' : see on 429.

890 θᾶσσον ἢ καθ' ἡδονὴν ποδός, 'quicker than it is pleasant
to walk': see on 598.

891 ἔγνων: so *O. T.* 1325 γιγνώσκω σαφῶς, | καίπερ
σκοτεινός, τήν γε σὴν αὐδὴν ὅμως.

893 τὰ ποῖα ταῦτα; The art. is prefixed to ποῖος when
it asks for further definition: Plat. *Crat.* 395 D ΣΩ. εἰ ἀληθῆ
(ἐστὶ) τὰ περὶ αὐτὸν λεγόμενα. ΕΡΜ. τὰ ποῖα ταῦτα;

894 f. οἴχεται: cp. on 867.—τὴν μόνην: his sons are as
dead to him (cp. 445).

896 περ in the thesis of the 3rd foot is remarkable, and
very unpleasing. Rhythm and sense would both gain if we
could read οἷα καὶ πέπονθ' ('indeed suffered').

897 f. οὔκουν τις...ἀναγκάσει, 'will not some one, then,
compel?'='then let some one compel': cp. *O. T.* 430 n.
τούσδε βωμούς: the plur. might be merely poetical for the sing.
(888, cp. *Ant.* 1006), but here perh. refers to the association
of Poseidon Ἵππιος with Athena Ἱππία (1069).

899 ff. Join σπεύδειν ἀπὸ θυμάτων, ἄνιππον, ἱππότην τε ἀπὸ
ῥυτῆρος: 'to hasten from the sacrifice, some on foot, others on
horseback, with slack rein.' The worshippers of the Ἵππιος
and Ἱππία are in part ἱππεῖς (cp. 1070), and have their horses
with them. The place of ἀπὸ ῥ. is due to the fact that these

horsemen are the important pursuers, ἄνιππον being added
merely to give the notion of a pursuit *en masse*.

ἀπὸ ῥυτῆρος, 'away from the rein,' *i.e.* 'unchecked by the
rein,' *immissis habenis*: Phrynichus *ap.* Bekker *Anecd.* p. 24
ἀπὸ ῥυτῆρος τρέχειν ἵππον· οἷον ἀπὸ χαλινοῦ ἢ ἄνευ χαλινοῦ.
Cp. *El.* 1127 ἀπ' ἐλπίδων, contrary to my hopes: *Tr.* 389 οὐκ
ἀπὸ γνώμης, not against my judgment: and so οὐκ ἀπὸ τρόπου
(not unreasonably), οὐκ ἀπὸ καιροῦ, etc. Plut. *Dion* 42
οὗτοι διελάσαντες τὴν ὁδὸν ἵπποις ἀπὸ ῥυτῆρος ἧκον εἰς
Λεοντίνους τῆς ἡμέρας ἤδη καταφερομένης, 'having ridden the
whole distance *at full speed*.' For the ō in ἀπὸ before ῥ,
cp. *Ant.* 712 n.

δίστομοι...ὁδοί, 'where two high-roads meet.' See map II.
at the end of this volume. The two roads meant are probably:—(1) A road leading from Colonus, north of the Sacred
Way, to the pass now called Daphnè, a depression in the range
of Mount Aegaleos through which the Sacred Way issued from
the plain of Athens, after which it skirted the shores of the bay
of Eleusis. (2) A road diverging from the former in a N.W.
direction, and going round the N. end of the same range of
Aegaleos, at a point some miles N. of the Daphnè pass, into
the Thriasian plain. By either route the captors could gain the
pass of Dryoscephalae, over Mount Cithaeron, leading from
Attica into Boeotia. The hope of Theseus is that the pursuers
may reach the point of bifurcation before the captors, since
it is conceivable that the latter should wait to be joined by
their master, Creon. See on 1054 ff.

μάλιστα with ἔνθα, lit., 'to *about* the place where': cp. Her.
1. 191 ἀνδρὶ ὡς ἐς μέσον μηρὸν μάλιστά κῃ, 'just about to the
height of a man's thigh.'

904 ἴθ', said to the πρόσπολος (897).

905 δι' ὀργῆς ἧκον, 'were in such wrath,' rather than,
'had come hither in such wrath.' Cp. Eur. *Or.* 757 λέξον·
διὰ φόβου γὰρ ἔρχομαι, 'for I begin to fear.' Her. 1. 169
διὰ μάχης...ἀπίκοντο Ἁρπάγῳ, gave him battle. Cp. on *O. T.*
773.

906 μεθῆκ', suggesting a relaxed grasp, is better than the
more general ἀφῆκ' here: cp. 834.

907 οὕσπερ...τοὺς νόμους, *sc.* the law of force: antecedent
drawn into relative clause: cp. *Ant.* 404 θάπτουσαν ὃν σὺ τὸν
νεκρὸν | ἀπεῖπας, where the schol. quotes Cratinus (fr. 159),
ὅνπερ Φιλοκλέης τὸν λόγον διέφθορεν.

908 τούτοισι, instrum. dat., ἁρμοσθήσεται, he shall be brought to order, regulated: Ar. *Eq.* 1235 ΚΛ. παῖς ὢν ἐφοίτας ἐς τίνος διδασκάλου; | ΑΛ. ἐν ταῖσιν εὐστραις κονδύλοις ἡρμοττόμην, 'was *kept in order*' by blows: Lucian *Toxaris* 17 τὸν ἁρμοστὴν ὃς ἥρμοζε τὴν Ἀσίαν τότε.

909 Theseus now addresses Creon.

910 ἐναργεῖς, before my eyes: *Tr.* 223 τάδ' ἀντίπρωρα δή σοι | βλέπειν πάρεστ' ἐναργῆ.—ἄγων, as *Il.* 2. 558 στῆσε δ' ἄγων: below, 1342. Cp. 475 λαβών.

911 κατάξια δρᾶν would be more usual than καταξίως δρᾶν: but the latter is no more incorrect than is ὀρθῶς or καλῶς δρᾶν.

912 ὧν = τούτων ὧν, possessive gen., here denoting origin: cp. on 214.

913 f. Athens 'practises justice,' *i.e.* respects the rights of other States; and ' determines (κραίνουσαν) nothing without law,' *i.e.* admits no claim which the laws do not sanction. Oedipus had placed himself and his daughters under the protection of Attic law. Creon should have sought legal warrant for their removal. Instead of doing so, he has used violence.

914 εἶτ', 'after that,' 'nevertheless': cp. 418, 1005. ἀφείς, 'having put aside': cp. 1537.

915 τὰ...κύρια, the constituted authorities, like τὰ τέλη, a phrase suggestive of *constitutional* monarchy, in which the citizens have some voice: as Theseus himself says in Eur. *Suppl.* 350 ἀλλὰ τοῦ λόγου | προσδοὺς ἔχοιμ' ἂν δῆμον εὐμενέστερον (proposing to refer a question to the people), and describes himself (*ib.* 353) as ἐλευθερώσας τήνδ' ἰσόψηφον πόλιν.

ἐπεισπεσών, of an abrupt or violent entrance, as Xen. *Cyr.* 7. 5. 27 οἱ δ' ἐπὶ τοὺς φύλακας ταχθέντες ἐπεισπίπτουσιν αὐτοῖς πίνουσι.

916 ἄγεις, of taking captive, as in ἄγειν καὶ φέρειν: παρίστασαι, 'bring to your own side,' 'subjugate'; Thuc. 1. 98 Ναξίοις...ἐπολέμησαν καὶ πολιορκίᾳ παρεστήσαντο.

917 κένανδρον ἢ δούλην τινά, some State destitute of inhabitants, or else only peopled by spiritless slaves. Cp. *O. T.* 56, and Thuc. 7. 77 ἄνδρες γὰρ πόλις, καὶ οὐ τείχη οὐδὲ νῆες ἀνδρῶν κεναί. So in Aesch. *Suppl.* 913 the king of Argos asks the insolent herald, ἀλλ' ἦ γυναικῶν ἐς πόλιν δοκεῖς μολεῖν;

918 τῷ μηδενί, dat. of τὸ μηδέν: cp. *Tr.* 1107 κἂν τὸ μηδὲν ὦ. Her. 8. 106 ὅτι με ἀντ' ἀνδρὸς ἐποίησας τὸ μηδὲν εἶναι (*sc.* εὐνοῦχον). Cp. *O. T.* 638, 1019.

178 *Oedipus at Colonus*

919 Θῆβαι. A courteous exoneration of Thebes accords with the hereditary ξενία which this play supposes: see on 632. and cp. the compliments to Thebes in 929, 937. ἐπαίδευσαν, more than ἔθρεψαν, implying a moral and mental training: cp. Pind. fr. 180 οὔτοι με ξένον | οὐδ᾽ ἀδαήμονα Μοισᾶν ἐπαίδευσαν κλυταὶ | Θῆβαι: so of the Spartan public training, Thuc. 1. 84 ἀμαθέστερον τῶν νόμων τῆς ὑπεροψίας παιδευόμενοι. Athens is τῆς Ἑλλάδος παίδευσις (id. 2. 41).

921 πυθοίατο, cp. 945, and n. on 44.

922 f. συλῶντα κ.τ.λ., 'forcibly carrying off what belongs to me,—yes, and what belongs to the *gods*, when you seek to lead captive unhappy men who are suppliants.' It is best to put a comma after τὰ τῶν θεῶν, which is explained by βίᾳ ἄγοντα, etc. He robs the *gods* when he seeks to seize the sacred suppliant of the Eumenides (44, 287). He robs Theseus (τἀμὰ) when he seizes persons who are under the protection of Attic law (915). If τὰ τῶν θεῶν φωτῶν ἀθλ. ἱκτήρια were joined (as Blaydes prefers), the double gen. would be very awkward.

φωτῶν ἀθλίων ἱκτήρια = literally 'suppliant objects consisting in hapless persons,' = φῶτας ἀθλίους ἱκτηρίους. The gen. defines the 'material,' or nature, of the ἱκτήρια, as in *El.* 758 σῶμα δειλαίας σποδοῦ is a body consisting in (reduced to) ashes. We could not render, 'the emblems of supplication brought by hapless persons.' Nor, again, 'the suppliants belonging to a wretched man' (the two maidens).

924 ἐπεμβαίνων: cp. on 400. Theseus points his reproof, as Oed. did in 776 ff., by asking Creon to imagine their respective situations reversed.

925 εἶχον, since ἐνδικώτατα = μέγιστα δικαιώματα: Thuc. 1. 41 δικαιώματα τάδε πρὸς ὑμᾶς ἔχομεν: and so id. 3. 54 παρεχό-μενοι...ἃ ἔχομεν δίκαια, advancing the just pleas which are ours.

926 ἄνευ γε τοῦ κραίνοντος, *iniussu dominatoris*, cp. *Il.* 15 213 ἄνευ ἐμέθεν καὶ Ἀθηναίης ἀγελείης, *without* my *consent* and hers. χθονὸς, gen. with κρ., as *Ai.* 1050 ὃς κραίνει στρατοῦ. ὅστις ἦν: the verb in the relative clause is assimilated to the form of the conditional sentence: cp. Plat. *Men.* 89 B εἰ φύσει οἱ ἀγαθοὶ ἐγίγνοντο, ἦσάν πού ἂν ἡμῖν οἳ ἐγίγνωσκον τῶν νέων τοὺς ἀγαθοὺς τὰς φύσεις.

927 οὔθ᾽ εἷλκον οὔτ᾽ ἂν ἦγον. The chief protasis is contained in the partic. ἐπεμβαίνων (924), = εἰ ἐπενέβαινον, while εἰ...εἶχον merely subjoins a special case in which the

Notes 179

apodosis would still hold good :—εἰ ἐπενέβαινον, οὐκ ἂν εἷλκον, οὐδὲ (εἷλκον ἂν) εἰ εἶχον. Remark that the form of the apodosis, οὔθ' εἷλκον...ἂν etc., does not logically imply, 'I *am* now dragging,' but merely, 'I am *not* now *forbearing to* drag': there is no opportunity for such abstention, since the fact supposed by ἐπεμβαίνων ('If I were on Theban soil') is non-existent. The conditional form with the imperf. indic. has been preferred to that with the optative (used in the similar illustration at 776), because Theseus is thinking of what Creon is actually doing.

928 ξένον, for whom the first rule should be, ἀστοῖς ἴσα μελετᾶν (171, cp. 13). Cp. Aesch. *Suppl.* 917 (the Argive king to the Egyptian herald who threatens to drag off the Danaïdes by force), ξένος μὲν εἶναι πρῶτον οὐκ ἐπίστασαι.

929 ἀξίαν οὐκ οὖσαν, *immeritam*, 'that does not deserve such treatment'; Dem. or. 21 § 217 εἰμὶ δ' οὐ τούτων ὑμῖν ἄξιος, 'I do not deserve such (harsh) treatment at your hands': cp. ἀξιοῦν τινά τινος, *to condemn* one to a punishment, *O. T.* 1449 (n.).

930 τὴν αὐτὸς αὐτοῦ: cp. 1356, *Ai.* 1132 τούς γ' αὐτὸς αὐτοῦ πολεμίους: Aesch. *P. V.* 921 ἐπ' αὐτὸς αὐτῷ: *ib.* 762 πρὸς αὐτὸς αὐτοῦ κενοφρόνων βουλευμάτων. In this hyperbaton αὐτός merely adds emphasis to the reflexive. If αὐτός is meant to stand out with its full separate force, it precedes the prep., as αὐτὸς πρὸς αὑτοῦ twice in Soph. (*Ant.* 1177, *Ai.* 906).

930 f. ὁ πληθύων χρόνος, the growing number of thy years; cp. on 377 and 7. τοῦ νοῦ, 'good sense,' which is just what old age ought to bring: fr. 240 καίπερ γέρων ὤν· ἀλλὰ τῷ γήρᾳ φιλεῖ | χὠ νοῦς ὁμαρτεῖν καὶ τὸ βουλεύειν ἃ δεῖ: Aesch. fr. 391 γῆρας γὰρ ἥβης ἐστὶν ἐνδικώτερον.

933 τινά, simply 'some one': not here a threatening substitute for σέ (as in *Ai.* 1138, *Ant.* 751). Indifference as to the *agent* strengthens insistence on the *act*.

934 The essence of the notion conveyed by μέτοικος, in ordinary Attic usage, was a voluntary sojourn, terminable at the will of the sojourner. Hence the irony here. With a similar force the Attic poets apply it to one who has found his 'last, long home' in foreign earth. Aesch. *Cho.* 683 εἴτ' οὖν κομίζειν δόξα νικήσει φίλων, | εἴτ' οὖν μέτοικον, εἰς τὸ πᾶν ἀεὶ ξένον, | θάπτειν: 'whether his friends decide to bring his ashes home, or to bury him among strangers, an alien utterly for ever': so a Persian whose corpse was left at Salamis is

12—2

180   *Oedipus at Colonus*

σκληρᾶς μέτοικος γῆς ἐκεῖ (*Pers.* 319): Eur. *Her.* 1033 μέτοικος
ἀεὶ κείσομαι κατὰ χθονός (the Argive Eurystheus buried in
Attica). Cp. *O. T.* 452 n.

935 βίᾳ τε κοὐχ ἐκ. as *O. T.* 1275 πολλάκις τε κοὐχ ἅπαξ.
κοὐχ ἐκών, not καὶ μὴ ἐκών, though dependent on εἰ, since οὐχ
ἐκών = ἄκων: cp. *Ai.* 1131 εἰ τοὺς θανόντας οὐκ-ἐᾷς θάπτειν:
Lys. or. 13 § 62 εἰ μὲν οὖν οὐ-πολλοὶ ἦσαν.

936 The words τῷ νῷ have been suspected by recent
criticism. They seem to me sound, The sense is, 'these
things, which I say to you, are *purposed by my mind* as really
as they are uttered by my tongue.' With τῷ νῷ a verb
meaning 'I intend' (*e.g.* διανοοῦμαι) should strictly have been
used; but the verb appropriate to ἀπὸ τῆς γλώσσης is made to
serve for both. ἀπὸ γλώσσης usu. = 'by word of mouth'
(as opp. to 'by letter'), as in Thuc. 7. 10.—For the antithesis
cp. Plat. *Symp.* 199 A ἡ γλῶττα οὖν ὑπέσχετο, ἡ δὲ φρὴν οὔ
(alluding to Eur. *Hipp.* 612).

937 f. ὁρᾷς ἵν' ἥκεις; 'do you see your position?' an
indignant reproach, as *O. T.* 687. ἀφ' ὧν = ἀπὸ τούτων, ἀφ' ὧν
(cp. on 274): '*To judge by* the folk *from whom* thou art sprung
(the Thebans, cp. 919), thou seemest just'—*i.e.* a member of
a just race. For ἀπό of judging *by* a thing, cp. on 15. The
Greek sense of the prep. with the relative here is really the
same as with the supplied antecedent. It is our idiom which
makes them seem different.

939 f. ἐγὼ οὔτ': so 998: *O. T.* 332 ἐγὼ οὔτ' ἐμαυτόν:
Ant. 458 ἐγὼ οὐκ ἔμελλον: *Ph.* 585 ἐγώ εἰμ' Ἀτρείδαις.—
νέμων (for λέγω) 'counting' is clearly right: cp. on 879.
While ἄνανδρον answers to κένανδρον ἢ δούλην in 917, ἄβουλον
(940), which implies the lack of a guiding mind, answers to
κἄμ' ἴσον τῷ μηδενί in 918.—Creon's speech is as clever as it is
impudent. He has only anticipated what the Athenians
themselves would have wished. Indeed, he has acted in
reliance on the Areiopagus (950). If his *method* has been
rough, he was provoked by the violence of Oedipus.

942 αὐτούς, the people implied in τὴν πόλιν (939). Cp.
Eur. *Bacch.* 961 κόμιζε διὰ μέσης με Θηβαίας χθονός, | μόνος γὰρ
αὐτῶν εἰμ' ἀνὴρ τολμῶν τάδε. So in *Her.* 5. 63 αὐτοὺς after
Θεσσαλίης, and 8. 121 αὐτῶν after Κάρυστον. ἐμπέσοι has here
the constr. of ἕλοι: cp. Eur. *I. A.* 808 δεινὸς ἐμπέπτωκ' ἔρως |
τῆσδε στρατείας Ἑλλάδ', οὐκ ἄνευ θεῶν. This is decisive
against here reading αὐτοῖς, the commoner constr.

943 ζῆλος, 'desire for.' ξυναίμων, 'kinsfolk' *i.e.* Oedipus, Antigone, and Ismene.

945 κἄναγνον. Cp. *O. T.* 821 λέχη δὲ τοῦ θανόντος ἐν χεροῖν ἐμαῖν | χραίνω, δι' ὧνπερ ὤλετ'· ἆρ' ἔφυν κακός; | ἆρ' οὐχὶ πᾶς ἄναγνος; So here, too, ἄναγνον refers to the taint of murder, aggravated by union with the wife of the slain. '*Both* a parricide, *and*, in a complex sense, impure,—yea, guilty of incest.'—δεξοίατ': cp. on 44. The fut. optat. after a secondary tense, as *O. T.* 538 f., 792, 796, 1271 ff.

946 ηὑρέθησαν. Attic inscriptions nearly as old as the poet's time confirm ηὑ- against εὑ-: cp. *O. T.* 546 n. τέκνων has been suspected. The literal meaning of ἀνόσιοι γάμοι τέκνων can be nothing but 'unholy nuptials *with children*' (such as Iocasta's with Oed.). But here the sense should be, 'unholy nuptials *with parents*': cp. 978 μητρὸς...γάμους. But ξυνόντες suggests the *consort*. Hence ἀνόσιοι γάμοι τέκνων is said, with poetical boldness and also with a certain designed obscurity, in this sense:—'*a woman who has made an unholy marriage with her son.*'

947 τοιοῦτον, introducing a reason for a preceding statement, as *Ai.* 164 (τοιούτων), 218 (τοιαῦτ'), 251 (τοίας), 562 (τοῖον).—εὔβουλον suggests the title of the Court, ἡ ἐξ Ἀρείου πάγου βουλή. If the Council of the Areiopagus (Creon assumes) became aware that a polluted person, such as Oedipus, was in Attica, it would take steps for his expulsion. Such a proceeding would doubtless have come within the limits of the general moral censorship actually possessed by the Areiopagus, at least in the earlier days of the Athenian democracy. Indeed that court is found exercising authority of a like kind (though only by special warrant) even after the reforms of Pericles and Ephialtes. Cp. Deinarchus or. 1 § 58, where the Ecclesia commissions the Areiopagus to inquire into the conduct of a merely suspected person, and the Areiopagus, having done so, reports to the Ecclesia. See also Plut. *Sol.* 22, Isocr. or. 7 §§ 36—55, and my *Attic Orators* vol. II. p. 211.

948 χθόνιον = ἐγχώριον, 'in their land,' a use found in *Ai.* 202 χθονίων ἀπ' Ἐρεχθειδᾶν (= αὐτοχθόνων), and fr. adesp. (Nauck²) χθονίους Ἰναχίδας.

954 f. θυμοῦ, the anger which moved Creon to make the seizure: cp. 874 οὔτοι καθέξω θυμόν. Theseus had said that Creon's violence disgraced his years (931). Creon replies,

'There is no old age for anger, except death'; *i.e.* 'anger, under gross insult, ceases to be felt only when a man is dead, and can feel nothing.' Cp. Aesch. *Theb.* 682 οὐκ ἔστι γῆρας τοῦδε τοῦ μιάσματος. Here, too, γῆρας is figurative,—'decay,' 'abatement,' of anger; while θανεῖν has its literal sense, the subject being τινά understood.—θανόντων: *El.* 1170 τοὺς γὰρ θανόντας οὐχ ὁρῶ λυπουμένους: *Tr.* 1173 τοῖς γὰρ θανοῦσι μόχθος οὐ προσγίγνεται.

957 ff. κεἰ here = εἰ καὶ 'although': cp. 661.—σμικρὸν: cp. 148 (σμικροῖς), 880 (βραχύς), where see n.—πρὸς...τὰς πράξεις, 'against your deeds,' *i.e.* any measures that you may take to deprive me of my captives. Cp. Arist. *Pol.* 6. 5. 3 πρὸς ταῦτα ἀντιπράττειν. He hints that, though he cannot resist now, he will take steps, when he returns to Thebes, for obtaining redress by force of arms: cp. 1036. Note the repeated ἀντιδρᾶν (953, 959) and ὅμως (957 f.): cp. 554 n.

960 τοῦ [= τίνος]. Which is more disgraced by your words,—the involuntary sufferer, or the author of deliberate insults to an unhappy kinsman?

962 f. μοι, dat. of interest, 'for my reproach,' διῆκας, *sent through* thy mouth,—poured forth: cp. *El.* 596 ἢ πᾶσαν ἵης γλῶσσαν: fr. 844. 3 πολλὴν γλῶσσαν ἐκχέας μάτην. In *Tr.* 323 διήσει γλῶσσαν is Wakefield's correction of διοίσει.

964 ἄκων: cp. on 521.—θεοῖς: the synizesis as in *O. T.* 1519, and about 26 other places of dialogue in Soph.: he admits it also in lyrics, as *O. T.* 215.

965 ἄν cannot go with μηνίουσιν, since the partic. does not represent an apodosis, as ἂν φέρων does in 761 (n.). On the other hand, ἄν does not here give any conditional force to ἦν, which is a simple statement of fact. Rather τάχ'- ἄν is here felt as one word, = 'perhaps.' 'It was dear to the gods,— perhaps because they were wroth.' Cp. *O. T.* 523 ἀλλ' ἦλθε μὲν δὴ τοῦτο τοὔνειδος τάχ' ἂν | ὀργῇ βιασθέν, 'this reproach came under stress, perchance, of anger.' The origin of this usage was an ellipse: θεοῖς ἦν φίλον, τάχα (δ') ἂν (φίλον εἴη) μηνίουσιν, 'and perhaps (it would be dear) because they were wroth': where the supplied εἴη expresses a conjecture about a past fact, as in Her. 1. 2 εἴησαν δ' ἂν οὗτοι Κρῆτες.

966 ff. ἐπεὶ καθ' αὑτόν γ'. 'My fate must have been a divine judgment upon me for the sins of ancestors. For you could not discover against me (ἐμοί, dat. of interest, cp. 962),— taken *by myself* (καθ' αὑτόν, apart from those ancestors),—any charge of sin, *in retribution for which* (ἀνθ' ὅτου) I proceeded to sin (impf. ἡμάρτανον) against myself and my kindred.' If any *voluntary* crime on his part had preceded his *involuntary* crimes, the latter might have been ascribed to an ἄτη sent on him by angry gods. But he had committed *no* such voluntary crime. For αὑτόν = ἐμαυτόν see on 852 f.

Others take ἀνθ' ὅτου as = 'in that,' '*because,*' and understand:—' For you cannot charge any guilt on me *personally* (καθ' αὑτόν), in that I sinned against myself and my kindred.' But (1) καθ' αὑτόν contrasts the man with the γένος, not with his acts. (2) ἀνθ' ὅτου regularly (if not always) = 'in return for which,' 'wherefore': *e.g. El.* 585 δίδαξον ἀνθ' ὅτου τανῦν | αἴσχιστα πάντων ἔργα δρῶσα τυγχάνεις: Eur. *Alc.* 246 οὐδὲν θεοὺς δράσαντας ἀνθ' ὅτου θανεῖ.

969 f. ἐπεὶ δίδαξον: 'for *else*—if this is *not* so—tell me': the controversial ἐπεί, on which see *O. T.* 390 n. Note the early repetition (after 966): see on 554: cp. ἀλλ' 985, 988.

εἴ τι θέσφατον: 'if, by oracles (χρησμ., instrum. dat.) some divine doom was coming on my sire, that he should die,' etc.: ἱκνεῖτο, *impf.*, because the doom was impending from the moment at which the Delphic oracle spoke. The simple inf. θανεῖν could have depended on θέσφατον, but ὥστε is added, as below 1350; Plat. *Prot.* 338 C ἀδύνατον ἡμῖν ἄστε Πρωταγόρου τοῦδε σοφώτερόν τινα ἐλέσθαι: Eur. *Hipp.* 1327 Κύπρις γὰρ ἤθελ' ὥστε γίγνεσθαι τάδε.—παίδων, allusive plur. for sing., cp. 295 ἄνακτας (n.).

972 f. οὔτε...οὐ: cp. *Ant.* 249 οὔτε του γενῆδος ἦν | πλῆγμ', οὐ δικέλλης ἐκβολή: Eur. *Or.* 41 ὧν οὔτε σῖτα διὰ δέρης ἐδέξατο, | οὐ λούτρ' ἔδωκε χρωτί: Her. 8. 98 οὔτε νιφετός, οὐκ ὄμβρος, οὐ καῦμα, οὐ νύξ. But of the converse, οὐ...οὔτε, there is no certain example.—βλάστας, plur., *O. T.* 717: πατρὸς and μητρός, gen. of origin with βλ. γεν. εἶχον as = ἔβλαστον: he was not yet begotten or conceived.

974 φανεὶς δύστηνος, having been born to misery (as being fated to slay his sire): so 1225 ἐπεὶ φανῇ, when one has come into the world. This is better here than, 'having proved unfortunate.' ἐγὼ 'φάνην: for the prodelision of the temporal augment in the 6th place, cp. *Ant.* 457: *Ai.* 557 ἐξ οἵου 'τράφης.

975 ἐς χεῖρας: cp. on 835.

976 μηδὲν is adjective with ὧν (= τούτων ἅ), and adverb with (τούτους) εἰς οὕς.

977 The MSS. have πῶς γ' ἄν, but γ' should probably be omitted, for the first γ' would weaken the second, while πῶς needs no strengthening. There is, however, no objection to a doubled γε where each of two words in the same sentence is to be emphasised (Her. 1. 187).—ἄκον = ἀκούσιον: see on 240.

980 οὖν here = 'indeed'; in 985 'at all events.'

981 εἰς τόδ' ἐξελθ. ἀνόσιον στόμα, having gone to such lengths of impious speech, *i.e.* having outraged the most sacred ties of kinship by these public taunts. Cp. 438 ἐκδραμόντα (n.). ἀνόσιον στόμα agrees with τόδ', depending on εἰς. Since στόμα was familiar to poetry in the sense of λόγος (cp. *O. T.* 426), this version is clearly preferable to taking εἰς τόδ' separately and ἀνόσ. στ. as accus. of respect.

982—984 He has just said, 'why force me to speak of Iocasta's marriage, when it was *such as I will tell?*' (980). In these three vv. he tells of what sort it was,—viz., incestuous, but unconsciously so;—a double reason why Creon should have spared the taunt.

ἔτικτεν = 'she was my mother'—she, who was becoming my bride—though neither of us knew it at the time of the marriage. Cp. Eur. *Ion* 1560 ἥδε τίκτει σ', 'she is thy mother'; and *O. T.* 437, 870. αὐτῆς ὄνειδος, because, although she was morally guiltless in the marriage, yet such a union was, in fact, shameful: cp. *O. T.* 1494, 1500. Rhetoric of a similar cast, and prompted by the same thought, occurs in *O. T.* 1403 ff., 1496 ff.

986 δυσστομεῖν (only here) with acc., as *El.* 596 τὴν μητέρα | κακοστομοῦμεν.

987 ἄκων. A single τε linking whole sentences is not rare in Soph. (*e.g.* 1437, *O. T.* 995); but ἄκων τ' (Vat.) may be right here.

988 ἀλλ' οὐ γάρ. Distinguish two uses of this formula. (1) With an ellipse, as here,—'but (your charges are untrue), *for.*' In this, γάρ may be represented by '*in fact*,' or '*indeed*.' Cp. on 755. (2) When there is no ellipse, as *O. T.* 1409 ἀλλ' οὐ γὰρ αὐδᾶν ἔσθ' ἃ μηδὲ δρᾶν καλόν,...καλύψατ'. Then γάρ = '*since.*' The MS. ἀκούσομαι κακὸς = 'will be *pronounced* evil' (in the report of fairminded men): cp. *Ph.* 1074 ἀκούσομαι μὲν ὡς ἔφυν οἴκτου πλέως | πρὸς τοῦδ': 'I shall be reproached, as full of pity, by yon man': some read ἁλώσομαι 'I shall be found guilty.'

989 f. ἐμφορεῖς (*ingeris*), 'heapest on me,' 'urgest against me,' is supported, as against ἐμφέρεις, by the common use of the word in later Greek, as Plut. *Pomp.* 3 πολλὰς ἐνεφόρει πληγὰς τοῖς στρώμασιν : Alciphro 1. 9 ἐπὶ τῷ σφετέρῳ κέρδει εἰς τοὺς ἀπράγμονας ἐμφοροῦσιν ὕβρεις, 'for their own gain they heap insults on quiet people.'—φόνους : the rhetorical pl., as 962.

991 ἄμειψαι : cp. on 814 ἀνταμείβει.

992 f. εἴ τις...κτείνοι, should *attempt* to slay ; cp. *Od.* 16. 432 παῖδά τ' ἀποκτείνεις, 'and *art seeking to* slay his son': Antiph. or. 5 § 7 ὅταν δ' ἄνευ κινδύνων τι διαπράσσωνται, are *seeking to* effect. (For the parallel use of the imperf., see 274.) The optat. in putting the imaginary case, as 776 : cp. on 927. αὐτίκα (not, 'for instance,' but) with ἐνθάδε, at this moment and on this spot, cp. *nunc iam ilico* (Ter. *Ad.* 2. 1. 2).—τὸν δίκ. : for the ironical article cp. *Ant.* 31 τὸν ἀγαθὸν Κρέοντα.

995 δοκῶ μέν, 'I should think so,' with the emphasis on the verb, not on the 1st pers. : *El.* 61 δοκῶ μέν, οὐδὲν ῥῆμα σὺν κέρδει κακόν : fr. 83 δοκῶ μέν, οὐδείς.

996 τοὔνδικον περιβλέποις, 'look around for thy warrant.' This compound occurs nowhere else in Soph., nor does he use περίβλεπτος. But Eur. uses them five times (*Andr.* 89, *H. F.* 508, *Ion* 624, *I. A.* 429, *Phoen.* 551), and Ar. has the verb once (*Eccl.* 403). In all six places, as here, the ι is made long. On the other hand, the ι of περιδρομή and its cognates is usually, if not always, short.

997 ff. εἰσέβην suits the imagery of ἀγόντων (see on 253): cp. Aesch. *Suppl.* 470 ἄτης δ' ἄβυσσον πέλαγος οὐ μάλ' εὔπορον | τόδ' ἐσβέβηκα.

After ἀντειπεῖν and like words the *person* gainsaid is denoted by the dat. ; the *argument*, by περί τινος or πρός τι. Here we begin with a neut. dat. οἷς (instead of πρὸς ἃ or περὶ ὧν), which implies a personification of the λόγος. Then, at the end of the sentence, ἐμοί is pleonastically added, by a sort of after-thought. This double dative, though irregular, does not seem to warrant the change of ἐμοί into ἔχειν. ἐμοί gives greater vividness to the thought of the dead brought face to face with the living.—ἂν with ἀντειπεῖν.—ἐγὼ οὐδὲ : cp. 939.

πατρὸς ψυχὴν...ζῶσαν = 'my father's life, if it could live again,'= simply πατέρα ζῶντα : not, 'his departed spirit, if it could visit this world.' ψυχή in the trag. never means 'a departed spirit' (*Il.* 23. 104 ψυχὴ καὶ εἴδωλον), but always the *anima* of the living: cp. Aesch. *Ag.* 1456 (of Helen) μία τὰς πολλὰς... | ψυχὰς ὀλέσασ' ὑπὸ Τροίᾳ. For the periphrasis here cp. *El.* 1126 ὦ φιλτάτου μνημεῖον ἀνθρώπων ἐμοὶ | ψυχῆς Ὀρέστου λοιπόν: *Ant.* 559 ἡ δ' ἐμὴ ψυχὴ πάλαι | τέθνηκεν.

1000 f. ἄπαν, 'anything,' cp. on 761: καλὸν with λέγειν, *dictu honestum*, 'fitting to be said,' cp. on 37.—ῥητὸν ἄρρ.: Dem. or. 18 § 122 βοᾶς ῥητὰ καὶ ἄρρητα ὀνομάζων: or. 21 § 79 πάντας ἡμᾶς ῥητὰ καὶ ἄρρητα κακὰ ἐξεῖπον. Remark that in neither place does Dem. place a καὶ *before* ῥητά, or a τε after it. The form which he gives was doubtless the familiar one. Cp. Verg. *Aen.* 1. 543 *deos memores fandi atque nefandi*: Hor. *Epp.* 1. 7. 72 *dicenda tacenda locutus*.

1003 τὸ Θ. ὄνομα θωπ., 'to pay court to the great name of Th. (to the renowned Th.).' Creon had been courteous to Theseus, as Theseus towards Thebes, and nothing more: there is no θωπεία in 940. But Oed. is incensed by the contrast between the rough words spoken of himself (944 ff.) by Creon and the fair words to Theseus. θωπεῦσαι: cp. 1336. —καλόν, not as in 1000, but = '*seasonable*': cp. *O. T.* 78 εἰς καλὸν...εἶπας (n.): *El.* 384 νῦν γὰρ ἐν καλῷ φρονεῖν.

1004 ὡς κατῴκηνται καλῶς, lit. 'that it has been administered well,' the perf. here denoting that a good administration is thoroughly *established* in it (cp. on τέτροφεν, 186). The political senses of κατοικέω and κατοικίζω should be carefully distinguished. (1) ἡ πόλις καλῶς κατοικεῖται = the city *is dwelt-in* on good principles, 'is well administered': see Plat. *Legg.* 683 A. (2) ἡ πόλις καλῶς κατῴκισται = the city *has been established* on good principles, 'has a good constitution': see *Legg.* 752 B. Oed: refers to Creon's implied praise of Athenian loyalty (941 ff.), and esp. to his mention of the Areiopagus (947 ff.).

1005 κᾆθ': cp. on 914.—πολλὰ with ὧδ'.

1006 εἴ τις γῆ θεοὺς: see on 260.

1007 τῷδ', referring to what has just *preceded* (cp. on 787), as *Ant.* 464, 666, *Ai.* 1080. The dat., marking *the point in which* the excellence is shown, is the usu. constr.: so Thuc. has προέχειν δυνάμει (1. 9), ναυτικῷ (1. 25), πλήθει...καὶ ἐμπειρίᾳ (1. 121), γνώμῃ (2. 62), etc.: Xen. *An.* 3. 2. 19 ἑνὶ δὲ μόνῳ προέχουσιν ἡμᾶς: *Lac.* 15. 3 πλούτῳ ὑπερφέρειν: Her. 8. 138 ῥόδα ὀδμῇ ὑπερφέροντα: 8. 144 χώρη κάλλεϊ καὶ ἀρετῇ μέγα ὑπερφέρουσα. Surely, then, usage is strongly for τῷδ' as against τοῦθ'.

1008 κλέψας, in purpose (so far as Oed. himself is concerned), though not in fact: *Ai.* 1126 δίκαια γὰρ τόνδ᾽ εὐτυχεῖν, κτείναντά με; Eur. *Ion* 1500 ἔκτεινά σ᾽ ἄκουσ᾽ (Creusa to her living son), 'doomed thee to perish.' Tr. 'Whence thou hadst planned to steal me, the suppliant, the old man, and didst seek to seize me, and hast actually carried off my daughters.'

1009 ἐχαροῦ, impf. of endeavour: see 274: cp. 950. οὔχει: see on 867.

1011 κατασκήπτω λιταῖς, '*enjoin on* you with prayers,' is an unexampled use of this compound. On the other hand ἐπισκήπτω was often used in entreaty, as Aeschin. or. 3 § 157 κλαίοντας, ἱκετεύοντας,...ἐπισκήπτοντας μηδενὶ τρόπῳ τὸν...ἀλιτή-ριον στεφανοῦν.

1014 f. ξεῖνος: cp. 33. Elsewhere, with the exception of fr. 726. 4, Sophocles uses in dialogue only the vocative of the Ionic form.—αἱ δὲ σ.: while *he* is innocent, his *fortunes* have been appalling, ἄξιαι δ᾽ ἀμ., *but* (all the more) deserve sympathy.

1015 ἄξιαι...ἀμυναθεῖν, worthy that one should succour them. The forms in -θον have not always an aoristic force, *e.g.* in *El.* 1014 εἰκαθεῖν has no such force (cp. on *O. T.* 651): but here, at least, as 461 ἐπάξιος...κατοικτίσαι shows, an aorist inf. is not less fitting than a present. For the *act.* inf., see on 461.

1016 f. 'The doers of the deed are in flight, whilst we, the sufferers, stand still.' The contrast with παθόντες, and the impossibility (as I think) of justifying ἐξηρπασμένοι, confirm F. W. Schmidt's ἐξειργασμένοι. Since E also represented H in the older Ionic alphabet, the origin of the vulgate is at once explained if it is supposed that in ΕΞΕΡΓΑΣΜΕΝΟΙ the Γ became Π,—one of the slightest and easiest of all errors in uncial writing.

There is no other instance of ἐξηρπασμένοι in the middle, which would therefore mean 'The captured ones are speeding.' But σπεύδουσιν is most strange as = 'are being carried off': it should imply eagerness. The masc. plur. also is strangely used when *two girls* are definitely meant. It is different when a woman, speaking of *herself* in the *plur.*, uses the masc. (*El.* 399),—when the masc. sing. is used by the leader of a female Chorus (Eur. *Hipp.* 1105),—or when the masc. sing. is used in an abstract statement, though with allusion to a woman (*El.* 145).

188   *Oedipus at Colonus*

1017 ἕσταμεν : the same form in *O. T.* 1442, *Tr.* 1145.

1018 ἀμ. φωτί, 'a helpless man,' *i.e.* Creon himself. The tone is half sulky, half whining. He has given up the game. ἀμαυρῷ here 'feeble' (cp. 880 βραχύς, 958 σμικρόν), but in 182 'dim' (where see n.). Cp. 391 τοιοῦδ᾽ ὑπ᾽ ἀνδρός, said by Oed. of himself ; and so 1109 φωτός.

1019 f. τῆς ἐκεῖ = τῆς ἐκεῖσε, 'the road thither,' in 'their track': Her. 9. 108 ἐκεῖ...ἀπίκετο : Thuc. 3. 71 τοὺς ἐκεῖ καταπεφευγότας.

πομπὸν δ᾽ κ.τ.λ. The construction is :—(προστάσσω σὲ μὲν) κατάρχειν ὁδοῦ τῆς ἐκεῖ, ἐμὲ δὲ πομπὸν χωρεῖν : 'my pleasure is,— that you should show the way thither (*i.e.* to where the maidens are), and that I should go as your escort.' The governing verb which is supplied, προστάσσω, contains the general notion δοκεῖ μοι, 'it seems good to me,' 'it is my pleasure.' For ἐμέ with inf. where ἐγώ is subj., cp. *Od.* 8. 221 τῶν δ᾽ ἄλλων ἐμέ φημι πολὺ προφερέστερον εἶναι. Schaefer well cites *Il.* 3. 88 ἄλλους μὲν κέλεται... | τεύχεα κάλ᾽ ἀποθέσθαι..., | αὐτὸν δ᾽ ἐν μέσσῳ καὶ ἀρηΐφιλον Μενέλαον | ...μάχεσθαι, where αὐτόν, referring to the subject of κέλεται, is parallel with ἐμέ here : 'Paris urges that *the others* should lay their arms aside, but that *he* and Menelaus should fight.' The accusative occurs where there is emphatic contrast, Xen. *Cyr.* 1. 4. 4. The word πομπόν (used in 723 of Creon's own followers) has here a touch of grim irony: cp. *Il.* 13. 416 ἐπεί ῥά οἱ ὤπασα πομπόν, 'given him a companion,'—*i.e.* sent his slayer to the shades along with him.

Other explanations are (1) to read μοι :—'that you should go as my guide.' The following clause ἵν᾽...ἐκδείξῃς ἐμοί makes this somewhat weak. (2) Governing με by πομπόν: 'that you should guide me on the way.' This was the view of Erfurdt and Reisig: it was also held by Shilleto. But this construction, always rare, is extremely harsh here, where πομπόν would naturally be taken as agreeing with με.

1021 ἡμῖν, 'for us,' *i.e.* so that we may find them : ethic dat. (cp. 81). τὰς παῖδας ἡμῶν could mean only '*our* maidens,'—which is hardly to be justified as the language of a paternal government.

1022 ἐγκρατεῖς, sc. τῶν παίδων: φεύγουσιν, sc. οἱ ἐξειργασμένοι (1016), Creon's guards. Theseus is not sure whether these guards have merely carried the sisters to some spot in Attica,

at which they are to await Creon himself, or are already in
full flight with them to Boeotia.

1023 f. ἄλλοι: the horsemen who at 900 were told σπεύδειν
ἀπὸ ῥυτῆρος.

οὓς χώρας τῆσδε φυγόντες οὐ μή ποτε ἐπεύξωνται θεοῖς, 'from
whom having escaped out of this land, never shall they make
grateful (ἐπ-) vows to the gods.' φεύγω can take a gen. of
separation, denoting the thing, or the region, *from which* one
escapes: *Od.* 1. 18 οὐδ' ἔνθα πεφυγμένος ἦεν ἀέθλων. This gen.
is here combined with an acc., as in Eur. *Suppl.* 148 Τυδεὺς
μὲν αἷμα συγγενὲς φεύγων χθονός, flying from the land, from
(the penalties of) a brother's murder: cp. *Or.* 1506 ποῦ 'στιν
οὗτος ὃς πέφευγε τοὐμὸν ἐκ δόμων ξίφος. ἐπεύξωνται implies a
vow of thank-offerings for safety: cp. Aesch. *Theb.* 276 (θεοῖς)
ἐπεύχομαι | θήσειν τρόπαια. The partic. φυγόντες expresses the
cause to which ἐπί in the compound refers: cp. *Ant.* 483
δεδρακυῖαν γελᾶν.

1025 ἀλλ', 'nay'; cp. 237. In ἐξυφηγοῦ (only here), ἐκ
refers to the moment of starting, while ὑπό = 'onward,' as in
ὑπάγω.

ἔχων ἔχει [pass.], cp. our phrase, 'the biter bitten.' Aesch.
Ag. 340 οὔ τἂν ἑλόντες αὖθις ἀνθαλοῖεν ἄν. Hor. *Ep.* 2. 1. 156
capta ferum victorem cepit. Isaiah xiv. 2 *and they shall take
them captives, whose captives they were.*

1026 f. θηρῶνθ' recalls the metaphor used by Creon himself,
τήνδ' ἐχειρούμην ἄγραν (950). ἡ τύχη = Destiny: see on *O. T.*
977 τί δ' ἂν φοβοῖτ' ἄνθρωπος, ᾧ τὰ τῆς τύχης | κρατεῖ. The
'irony of fate' is better denoted by τύχη than by the proposed
substitute Δίκη.

τὰ...δόλῳ κτήματα = τὰ δόλῳ κατακτηθέντα, 'gains got by
wrongful arts': the instrum. dat. with the noun as with the
cognate partic.: *Tr.* 668 τῶν σῶν Ἡρακλεῖ δωρημάτων: Plat.
Soph. 261 E τῶν τῇ φωνῇ περὶ τὴν οὐσίαν δηλωμάτων. τῷ μὴ
δικαίῳ: cp. 73.

1028 ff. κοὐκ ἄλλον ἕξεις εἰς τόδ', and you will not have
another (to aid you) with a view to this (*i.e.* to the removal of
the captives). For this use of ἔχειν cp. Andoc. or. 1 § 63
ἕξεις ἡμᾶς ἐπιτηδείους: for εἰς τόδ' cp. 507. ὡς ἔξοιδα, '(I speak
of 'another,') *for* I know,' etc.: ὡς causal; cp. 45.

οὐ ψιλόν: see on 866. ἄσκευον: *El.* 36 ἄσκευον αὐτὸν
ἀσπίδων τε καὶ στρατοῦ. The allusion is to some Attic
accomplices, whose secret aid had emboldened Creon to

make the attempt (1031). The Greek was quick to explain disaster by treason; thus it instantly occurs to Oedipus that some Theban must have been concerned in the murder of Laïus (*O. T.* 124). After Aegospotami, 'the general belief... held that the Athenian fleet had been sold to perdition by some of its own commanders' (Grote VIII. 300). Theseus had no definite ground for his suspicion, but its utterance serves to place him (for a Greek audience) on the proper level of wary sagacity.

1029 f. ἐς τοσήνδ' ὕβριν...τόλμης. The τόλμα is the audacious spirit manifested in the ὕβρις, or outrageous action. The gen. τόλμης seems best taken as partitive, ἐς τοσήνδ' ὕβριν ἥκοντα being equiv. to ἐς τοσοῦτον ἥκοντα (cp. Isocr. 8 § 31 εἰς τοῦτο γάρ τινες ἀνοίας ἐληλύθασιν): 'you have come to such a point of violence *in* the daring which now possesses you.' If the gen. is taken as possessive, ὕβρις τόλμης nearly = ὕβρις τολμηρά: but the addition of τῆς παρεστώσης τανῦν makes this awkward.

1031 ἀλλ' ἔσθ' ὅτῳ, 'there is some one in whom.' Cp. Ar. *Nub.* 1347 ὡς οὗτος, εἰ μή τῳ 'πεποίθειν, οὐκ ἂν ἦν | οὕτως ἀκόλαστος· | ἀλλ' ἔσθ' ὅτῳ θρασύνεται. πιστὸς, active, 'trusting': Aesch. *P. V.* 916 θαρσῶν καθήσθω τοῖς πεδαρσίοις κτύποις | πιστός. So μεμπτός, 'blaming' (*Tr.* 446); ὕποπτος, 'suspecting' (Eur. *Hec.* 1135); ἀφόβητος, 'not fearing' (*O. T.* 885); ἄψαυστος, 'not having touched' (*ib.* 969); ἀμφίπληκτος, 'beating around' (*Ph.* 688).

1034 f. τι τούτων, ironical for ταῦτα : *O. T.* 1140 λέγω τι τούτων, ἢ οὐ λέγω πεπραγμένον;

τὰ νῦν—'Or do the things *said just now* seem to you no less vain than (*the things said*) at the time when you were plotting these deeds?' alluding to the remonstrances and menaces of the Chorus, 829 ff. τὰ νῦν τε χὤτε is then like τἀμὰ κἀκείνων (606), one article doing double duty. τανῦν would mean 'Or do these things seem to you to have been said in vain, *both now, and when* you were plotting these deeds?' But it is natural that Theseus should refer to his own *words* rather than to thoughts which the Chorus had suggested before him.

1036 ἐνθάδ' ὤν has been generally suspected, because the qualification, 'while here,' seems to suit Creon better than Theseus. But, though ἐνθάδ' ὄντ' ἐρεῖς ἐμέ lies near, the vulgate is right. '*While here*,' said of Theseus, means, 'since this is your own realm, in which you have force at command.'

μεμπτὸν ἐμοί, predicate; 'you will say nothing to my dissatisfaction': *i.e.* 'you can say what you please,—I shall not dispute it.' It is vain to argue with a master of legions.

1038 χωρῶν ἀπείλει νῦν, 'threaten (if you will) now—only set out.' The enclitic νυν ('well then') would be weak here: νῦν takes point from 1037. For the partic. expressing *the leading idea of the sentence*, cp. *Tr.* 592 ἀλλ' εἰδέναι χρὴ δρῶσαν: Thuc. I. 20 Ἵππαρχον οἴονται τύραννον ὄντα ἀποθανεῖν, 'was *reigning* when he was killed': 4. 11 τὰς σφετέρας ναῦς, βιαζομένους τὴν ἀπόβασιν, καταγνύναι ἐκέλευε: "he cried, 'Wreck your ships, if you must—but force your way ashore.'"

1039 πιστωθείς, 'assured,' 'with my pledge,' as *Od.* 21. 218 ὄφρα μ' ἐῢ γνῶτον πιστωθῆτόν γ' ἐνὶ θυμῷ, that ye twain may be *assured* in your minds: but elsewhere ἐπιστώθην is said of him who *gives* the pledge, cp. on 650.

1042 ὄναιο, a blessing, usu. with simple gen., as Eur. *I. A.* 1359 ὄναιο τῶν φρενῶν, 'bless thee for thy kindness,' or a defining partic., as *Or.* 1677 γήμας ὄναιο: but there is no reason to suspect χάριν, for which Blaydes suggests τρόπου. Cp. 569 τὸ σὸν γενναῖον.

[Exeunt Theseus and attendants, with Creon.]

1044—1095 *Second στάσιμον.—1st strophe* (1044—1058) = *1st antistr.* (1059—1073). *2nd strophe* (1074—1084)= *2nd antistr.* (1085—1095). *The metre is Dactylic.—The Chorus utter their longing to be at the scene of the fight between the Theban captors and the Attic rescuers. They predict the speedy victory of the latter, and invoke the gods to help.*

1044 εἴην ὅθι: cp. *Ai.* 1218 (Chorus) γενοίμαν ἵν' ὑλᾶεν ἔπεστι πόντου | πρόβλημ', etc.: Eur. *Hipp.* 732 (Chorus) ἁλιβάτοις ὑπὸ κευθμῶσι γενοίμαν, | ἵνα etc.

1045 ἐπιστροφαί, the wheeling-about of Creon's guards, carrying off their captives, when overtaken by the Attic pursuers. For the military use of the word see on 536. ἀνδρῶν ἐπιστροφαί=ἄνδρες ἐπιστρεφθέντες: cp. *El.* 417 εἰσιδεῖν πατρὸς...δευτέραν ὁμιλίαν: Eur. *Alc.* 606 ἀνδρῶν Φεραίων εὐμενὴς παρουσία.

1046 ff. χαλκοβόαν cannot be resolved into two separate epithets,—'brass-clad,' and 'clamorous': rather it seems to mean, 'with noise of brass,'—the clatter of shields and swords in battle. Cp. *O. T.* 190, where the Death-god (the plague) is an Ares who is ἄχαλκος ἀσπίδων, yet περιβόατος.—μείξουσιν: cp. *Il.* 15. 510 ἢ αὐτοσχεδίῃ μῖξαι χεῖράς τε μένος τε. The

Attic spelling in the age of Sophocles was μείζω (not μίζω), ἔμειξα, verb adj. μεικτός: and so in the proper names Μειξίας, Μείξιππος, etc.: see Meisterhans pp. 25, 87.

ἢ πρὸς Πυθίαις ἢ λαμπάσιν ἀκταῖς. The Chorus here imagine the Athenians as pursuing the Thebans through the pass of Daphnè, over Mount Aegaleos, towards Eleusis. Two points are mentioned as possible scenes for a fight.

(1) Πύθιαι ἀκταί, *the Pythian shores*; the shore of the bay of Eleusis just beyond the pass of Daphnè on the N.W., near the salt-springs called 'Ρειτοί (Thuc. 2. 19). The distance from Colonus is about six miles. Πύθιαι alludes to the Πύθιον, an Ionic temple of Apollo (some fragments from which are among the Elgin marbles in the British Museum), situated on the site of the present monastery of Daphnè, in the narrowest and highest part of the pass. (Cp. Leake, *Demes* pp. 144 f.: Paus. 1. 37. 6.)

(2) λαμπάδες ἀκταί, '*the torch-lit shores*' (cp. Harpocr. 184, quoted on 56, ἑορτὰς λαμπάδας): the coast of the same bay of Eleusis at a point about 5 miles W.N.W. of the former point,— viz. at Eleusis itself. The yearly celebration of the great Eleusinia began on or about the 16th of Boedromion (September). On the 20th of that month an image of Iacchus was borne in a torch-light procession along the ἱερὰ ὁδός from Athens to Eleusis. This procession is indicated by the χορὸς μυστῶν in Ar. *Ran.* 316 ff.: see *ib.* 340. The search of Demeter for Persephone was also represented at Eleusis in a παννυχίς of torch-bearing mystae. Cp. Aesch. fr. 376 (speaking of Eleusis) λαμπραῖσιν ἀστραπαῖσι λαμπάδων σθένει. Ar. *Th.* 1151.

1050 πότνιαι, Demeter and Persephone (Cora). Cp. 683. τιθηνοῦνται, 'cherish' as the spiritual nurturers of their faithful votaries. τέλη: Plat. *Rep.* 560 E τελουμένου ψυχὴν μεγάλοισι τέλεσι: Eur. *Hipp.* 25 σεμνῶν ἐς ὄψιν καὶ τέλη μυστηρίων: Aesch. fr. 377 μυστικοῦ τέλους: in prose usu. τελεταί.

1051 θνατοῖσιν, 'for mortals,' esp. fitting here, since the highest value of the Eleusinia consisted in opening a prospect of bliss after death. Soph. fr. 753 ὡς τρὶς ὄλβιοι | κεῖνοι βροτῶν, οἳ ταῦτα δερχθέντες τέλη | μόλωσ' ἐς Ἅιδου· τοῖσδε γὰρ μόνοις ἐκεῖ | ζῆν ἔστι, τοῖς δ' ἄλλοισι πάντ' ἐκεῖ κακά. Pindar fr. 114 ὄλβιος ὅστις ἰδὼν κεῖν' εἶσ' ὑπὸ χθόν'· οἶδε μὲν βίου τελευτάν, οἶδεν δὲ διόσδοτον ἀρχάν. Isocr. or. 4 § 28 ἧς (τελετῆς) οἱ μετασχόντες περί τε τῆς τοῦ βίου τελευτῆς καὶ τοῦ σύμπαντος αἰῶνος ἡδίους τὰς ἐλπίδας ἔχουσιν.

ὧν καὶ χρυσία κ.τ.λ.: ὧν refers to θνατοῖσιν: καὶ ('also') has the effect of limiting the reference to those persons on whom the pledge of secrecy has been imposed;—'*those mortals on whose lips has been set the divine seal of the ministrant Eumolpidae*': *i.e.* those who have been duly initiated by the Eumolpid Hierophant at Eleusis, and have been bound by him to secrecy. κλῇς Εὐμολπιδᾶν (possessive gen.), the silence which they impose. Perhaps we should read βέβακ' ἐκ. The Eumolpidae figure here as interpreters between the Two Goddesses and mortals, not as guardians of a secret which they may not communicate.

1052 κλῄς, 'that which closes,' cannot well be rendered '*key*' here, any more than in Aesch. fr. 309 ἀλλ' ἔστι κἀμοὶ κλῇς ἐπὶ γλώσσῃ φύλαξ. The apparent boldness of a Greek metaphor is sometimes thus mitigated by the poet's consciousness of the literal sense; as when Pindar calls an inspiring thought an ἀκόνη,—literally, 'sharpener,' conventionally 'whetstone'); or when he calls the master, who tempers a chorus into harmony, a κρατήρ (*Ol.* 6. 82, 91). Cp. Eur. *Med.* 660 καθαρὰν ἀνοίξ|αντα κλῆδα φρενῶν, 'having unlocked his heart in sincerity.' κληδοῦχος was said either of a tutelar deity or of a priestess, and on the vases the symbolic key, adorned with woollen threads, is sometimes borne by the priestess: but there is no evidence for the Eleusinian Hierophant actually *putting a key* to the lips of the initiated. χρυσία, divine, precious,—because of the truths revealed: *O. T.* 157 χρυσέας τέκνον Ἐλπίδος.

1053 προσπόλων Εὐμολπιδᾶν. The Eleusinia had four chief ministrants. 1. The ἱεροφάντης. This office was hereditary in the Eumolpid gens. 2. The δᾳδοῦχος: hereditary in the gens of Callias and Hipponicus, which traced itself from Triptolemus. 3. The ἱεροκῆρυξ: hereditary in the gens of the Κηρυκίδαι (or Κήρυκες). 4. The altar-priest, ἱερεὺς ὁ ἐπὶ βωμῷ, or ἐπιβώμιος, who offered the sacrifice. It is not known whether this office was hereditary. As some relationship seems to have existed between the Eumolpidae and the two other gentes, προσπόλων here possibly includes (2) and (3), but is more naturally taken of the ἱεροφάντης only. A hydria found at Cumae exhibits an Eleusinian group of deities and priests, among whom the ἱεροφάντης is distinguished by a long white stole partly embroidered with gold, a myrtle wreath, and the thyrsus.

J. C.   13

194   *Oedipus at Colonus*

1054 ἐγρεμάχαν, 'rousing the fight,' is a fit epithet for the champion who overtakes the captors, and forces them to a contest. Elsewhere we find only the fem. ἐγρεμάχη, as epithet of Pallas, *Hom. Hymn.* 5. 424. Cp. Bacchyl. 12. 100 [= 13. 67 of Kenyon's ed.] ἀερσιμάχους.

1055 Θησέα has the final a long in 1458, but short here: cp. Eur. *Hec.* 882 ξὺν ταῖσδε τὸν ἐμὸν φονέα τιμωρήσομαι, = 870 ed. Porson, who adds Philemon *ap.* Athen. 7. 307 E κεστρέ᾽ ὀπτόν. ἐμμείξειν is here intrans., like ἐπι-, προσ-, συμμιγνύναι: and the sense is, 'Theseus and the two maidens will soon *meet* amid a battle-cry of confident prowess.' Thus with ἐμμείξειν we are to understand ἀλλήλοις. The verb is fitting, because the maidens, though their sympathies are with Theseus, are *in the midst of the hostile force.* αὐτάρκει βοᾷ is dat. of circumstance, 'amid a war cry of men strong to save.' δισσόλους = 'two journeying' sisters,—as borne off by their captors: see on 17 πυκνόπτεροι. Not, 'separately carried off,' with ref. to two bands of Thebans (cp. 818).—αὐτάρκει, 'self-sufficing,' and so 'self-reliant,' giving confident promise of victorious rescue. τούσδ᾽ ἀνὰ χ.: *i.e.* in Attica, before the border can be passed.

1059 ff. Hartung's εἰς νομόν for the MS. ἐκ νομοῦ is certain. The rare acc. with πελάζω could be supported by Eur. *Andr.* 1167 δῶμα πελάζει: but the ellipse of χῶρον with τὸν ἐφέσπερον is surely impossible. νομοῦ, being always masc., could not agree with Οἰάτιδος, and the latter, without art., could not stand for Οἰάτιδος γῆς. πελῶσ᾽, if sound, must be *fut.* of πελάζω, as πελᾶν clearly is in *El.* 497. The evidence for a pres. πελάω is scanty, and the fut. seems defensible here, as = 'they will (presently) approach': though Hartung's περῶσ᾽ may be right. Construe, then:—ἤ που πελῶσ᾽ εἰς ἐφέσπερον πέτρ. νιφ. Οἰάτιδος νομόν: 'or perchance they will presently approach the pastures to the west of the snowy rock of Oea.'

The place meant is not certain. The scholiast takes the νιφὰς πέτρα to be a rock or crag of Mount Aegaleos;—the same which was called λεία πέτρα, 'the smooth rock,' by Istros, a writer on Attica, c. 240 B.C., whom he quotes. The schol. then explains Οἰάτιδος by the fact that Aegaleos ἐπ᾽ ἐσχάτων ἐστὶ τοῦ δήμου τούτου, 'skirts that deme,'—namely, of Οἴη. The meaning will then be:—'Or perhaps the captors did not take the road through the pass of Daphnè, which goes by the sea-coast to Eleusis. Perhaps they went round the N. end of

Aegaleos, and will soon be emerging on the Thriasian plain, to the west of Aegaleos, near the deme of Oea.' See the map I, in which *A* and *B* mark the two possible points at which the δίστομοι ὁδοί may be placed.

1062 f. ῥιμφαρμάτοις...ἀμίλλαις = ἀμίλλαις ῥίμφα φερομένων ἁρμάτων (see on 710 αὔχημα...εὔιππον), emulous careers of swift chariots, as *El.* 861 χαλαργοῖς ἐν ἀμίλλαις, races of swift steeds: cp. *Ant.* 1065 τροχοὺς ἀμιλλητῆρας ἡλίου, *rapid* courses of the sun. Pind. *Olymp.* 3. 37 περὶ ῥιμφάρματος διφρηλασίας.

1065 ἁλώσεται, *sc.* ὁ Κρέων, 'he will be worsted' (not, 'captured,' since he was already in the hands of Theseus): cp. Thuc. 1. 121 μιᾷ...νικῇ...ἁλίσκονται, they are sure to be *overthrown* by one victory of ours. For the ellipse of the subject, where the mind could readily supply it, cp. Xen. *Cyr.* 2. 4. 24 πορεύσομαί διὰ τοῦ πεδίου εὐθὺς πρὸς τὰ βασίλεια. καὶ ἢν μὲν ἀνθιστῆται, 'and if the enemy (the king) resist....' This is better than (1) 'the fugitive will be captured,' supplying ὁ φεύγων from φεύγοντες: (2) 'a capture will be made,'—taking the verb as impers.: or (3) 'the battle will be won,' ἁλώσεται ὁ ἀγών, as Elms. takes it, comparing 1148 ἀγὼν ἡρέθη.

1065 f. προσχώρων, the neighbours of the grove, the Coloniates (cp. 493); not, 'our neighbours the Thebans,' for the Chorus are predicting an easy victory over the Thebans, not a tough fight with them. Colonus and its neighbourhood had furnished a contingent to the party of rescue (897). Θησειδᾶν, schol. Ἀθηναίων: cp. Κεκροπίδαι, Ἐρεχθεῖδαι, Aeneadae, etc.: here, followers of Theseus from *Athens*, as distinct from the Coloniates. ἀκμά, vigour, might: Pind. *Isthm.* 3. 68 ἀλλ' ὀνοτὸς μὲν ἰδέσθαι, | συμπεσεῖν δ' ἀκμᾷ βαρύς, 'dread to grapple with in his strength.'

1068 f. We require ∪ – instead of the MS. κατ'. Bothe gets this by supposing non-elision of κατὰ before ἀμπυκτήρια. This, though rare, is possible: cp. *Ai.* 425 χθονὸς μολόντ' ἀπὸ | Ἑλλανίδος: *Tr.* 510 Βακχίας ἄπο | ἦλθε. But I cannot believe κατὰ | ἀμπυκτήρια to be Greek, as meaning either (1) 'according to the full speed given by the headgear,' *i.e.* by shaking the reins,—Paley: or (2) 'in the direction of the bridles,'—*i.e.* 'every horseman gives his steed its head,' Campbell. Instead of κατ', Hermann gives χαλῶσ': Schneidewin proposed καθεῖσ', 'slacking,' 'with slack rein.' This, if it had become κατεῖσ', might easily have shrunk to the MS. κατ', through the rest of the word being taken for εἰς.

ἀμπυκτήρια φάλαρα πώλων is the MS. reading. Hesychius
s.v. has: ἀμπυκτήρια· τὰ φάλαρα. Σοφοκλῆς Οἰδίποδι ἐν
Κολωνῷ. This proves what the metre already hinted,—that
φάλαρα is a gloss. ἀμπυκτήριον here = 'bridle,' as ἀμπυκτήρ in
Aesch. *Theb.* 461 ἵππους δ' ἐν ἀμπυκτήρσιν ἐμβριμωμένας: where
the schol. (minor) expressly says that ἄμπυξ (properly the
head band) was similarly used: κυρίως οἱ περὶ τὴν κεφαλὴν
ἱμάντες τοῦ χαλινοῦ ἄμπυξ καλοῦνται: and so Quintus Smyr-
naeus uses ἄμπυξ, 4. 511. It is but a slight poetical extension
of meaning to use ἀμπυκτήρια as including the *bridle-reins*.
The MS. πώλων is against the metre, and may have been tacked on
to the gloss φάλαρα. Wecklein's conjecture, ἀμπυκτήρια στομίων
('the *reins* of the *bits*') gives an exact correspondence with 1054
ἔνθ' οἶμαι τὸν ἐγρεμάχαν. Nothing better has been suggested.

1070 ἄμβασις, 'knighthood,' for ἀναβάται, as φυγαί for
φυγάδες (Herod. 3. 138), δουλεία for δοῦλοι (Thucyd. 5. 23)
and the like. For the apocopè, cp. *Ant.* 1275 ἀντρέπων, n.
οἵ, as if ἀναβάται had gone before: cp. *Ai.* 235 ὧν after ποίμνην:
Her. 8. 128 περιέδραμε ὅμιλος,...οἵ etc. Cp. 942 n. (αὐτούς
after πόλιν). τὰν ἱππίαν: see on 55.

1072 f. γαιάοχον, in the Homeric use, is most simply
explained as 'earth-embracer,' with ref. to the Homeric idea of
Ὠκεανός flowing round the earth: though some take it here
as = '*guarding our land*,' like γ. Ἄρτεμιν in *O. T.* 160: and this
certainly has more special point here. But would the constant
Homeric epithet of Poseidon be applied to *him* in a sense
different from the Homeric? All Greek hearers would think
of the γαιήοχος Ἐννοσίγαιος. Ῥέας, here a monosyllable, as in
Il. 15. 187. Rhea, in the Greek theogony, is daughter of
Uranos and Gaia, wife of Cronus, and 'mother of the gods.'
The cult was that of the 'Phrygian Mother' Cybele in a
special phase, and came very early to Greece from Lydia:
in Attica it was intimately connected with the Eleusinian cult
of Demeter.

1074 ἔρδουσ': 'are they (the pursuers) in action, or on the
point of being so? *for* (ὡς) I have a foreboding, etc.' μέλλουσιν,
sc. ἔρξειν: cp. *Tr.* 74 Εὐβοῖδα χώραν φασίν, Εὐρύτου πόλιν, |
ἐπιστρατεύειν αὐτὸν ἢ μέλλειν ἔτι: *Ph.* 567 ὡς ταῦτ' ἐπίστω
δρώμεν', οὐ μέλλοντ' ἔτι.

1075 f. γνώμα μοι, 'my mind,' προμνᾶταί τι (adv.), 'somehow
pleads for the belief,' 'presages.' προμνᾶσθαι means (1) *to woo*
for another, κόρην τινί: (2) fig., to seek to obtain anything for

another, *e.g.* δῶρά τινι. The bold use here comes through the notion of *pleading*, or *speaking persuasively*, as the προμνήστρια to the maiden on behalf of the lover.

1076 ἀντάσειν (Buecheler),—a conjecture which had occurred independently to myself,—seems the most probable correction of ἄν δώσειν. The Chorus express a presentiment that they will soon again be brought face to face with the maidens who were dragged away before their eyes; and this prepares for the approaching entrance of Antigone and Ismene, **1097** τὰς κόρας γὰρ εἰσορῶ. ἀντάω usu. takes a dat. of *meeting a person*, but sometimes a gen., as *Il.* 16. 423 ἀντήσω γὰρ ἐγὼ τοῦδ' ἀνέρος (in battle). With the gen., ἀντάω also = κυρεῖν, τυγχάνειν: *Od.* 3. 97 ἤντησας ὀπωπῆς: Her. 2. 119 ξεινίων ἤντησε μεγάλων. Cp. Soph. *Ant.* 982 ἄντασ' Ἐρεχθειδᾶν, she *attained unto* them (traced her lineage back to them). Here the idea of *obtaining back* is blended with that of being brought *face to face*. It is not, then, a valid objection that the Chorus do not *move to meet* the maidens.

1079 κατ' ἆμαρ here = κατ' ἦμαρ...τὸ νῦν (*Ai.* 753), as μοῖρα καθαμερία (*El.* 1414) = 'the doom of *to-day.*'

1081 ἀελλαία: *O. T.* 466 ἀελλάδων | ἵππων. ταχύρρωστος goes closely with it in sense, 'with a swift, strong impetus, as of the storm,' cp. *Il.* 23. 367 ἐρρώοντο μετὰ πνοιῆς ἀνέμοιο.

1083 ff. 'That I might reach an airy cloud, with gaze lifted above the fray.' Hermann's ἄνωθ' for the αὐτῶν δ' of the MSS., with αἰωρήσασα for θεωρήσασα, gives the most probable correction of the passage. ἄνωθε, for ἄνωθεν, though it does not occur elsewhere in trag., is once used by Ar. *Eccl.* 698 (ἄνωθ' ἐξ ὑπερῴου), and we can hardly doubt that a tragic poet would have admitted it,—at least in lyrics,—when metre required. Wecklein makes the gen. depend on αἰωρήσασα, as = 'having lifted *above*': but the gen. would mean '*from,*' as *Ant.* 417 χθονὸς | ...ἀείρας: and the rise here is not *from* the fight below. He has since conjectured αὐτῶν ἄνωθεν: which is near to the letters of L: but αὐτῶν (referring to ἀγώνων in 1080) seems a little weak; and in any case I should prefer ἄνωθεν αὐτῶν. I had thought of τῶνδ' ἀγώνων | ὕπερθ' ἄρασα, but prefer Herm.'s remedy.—αἰωρεῖν, not ἐωρεῖν, is the classical Attic form: cp. on *O. T.* 1264.

1085 f. In the MS. order of the words, ἰὼ Ζεῦ, πάνταρχε θεῶν (monosyll.) = 1074 ἔρδουσ' ἢ μέλλουσιν; ὥς, and παντόπτα, πόροις = 1075 προμναται τί μοι. This requires the final α of the voc. παντόπτα to be long, which is impossible, though some edd. tacitly assume it. Meineke's remedy, παντόπτ᾽ ὦ, is not probable: and παντόπτας (nom. for voc.) could not stand here. The simple transposition which I have made in the text removes the difficulty.

1087 δαμούχοις (cp. on 458), the people of Attica.

1088 σθένει: cp. *Tr.* 497 μέγα τι σθένος ἁ Κύπρις ἐκφέρεται νίκας ἀεί. ἐπινικείῳ for ἐπινικίῳ, 'triumphant.' τὸν εὔαγρον τελεῶσαι λόχον (grant to the Athenians) to accomplish the successful surprise,—the way-laying of Creon's guards, by which the Athenians will secure their quarry (ἄγρα), viz. the maidens. τὸν εὔαγρον, proleptic: cp. *Tr.* 477 τῆσδ᾽ οὕνεχ᾽ ἡ πολύφθορος | καθῃρέθη πατρῷος Οἰχαλία δόρει. λόχον, 'ambuscade,' seems here to have the more general sense, 'scheme of capture' (cp. *Od.* 4. 395 φράζευ σὺ λόχον θείοιο γέροντος, a *way to take* him): though there is nothing in the scanty references to the pursuit which necessarily excludes the idea of a literal ambush. Taking λόχον as = 'company,' we could render, 'grant this to our folk,—that thou shouldst *crown* the successful band *with victory*' (τελειῶσαι): cp. *El.* 1508 ὦ σπέρμ᾽ Ἀτρέως... | τῇ νῦν ὁρμῇ τελεωθέν, 'crowned with peace by this day's effort': but the construction thus supposed is less simple, while the frequent poetical association of λόχος with capture points to the other sense.

1090 σεμνά τε παῖς, *sc.* πόροι (from πόροις, 1086).

1091 τὸν ἀγρευτὰν, the hunter. Cp. Aesch. fr. 195 (Heracles, in the Προμηθεὺς Λυόμενος, when aiming his shaft at the eagle) Ἀγρεὺς δ᾽ Ἀπόλλων ὀρθὸν ἰθύνοι βέλος. Paus. (1. 41. 3) saw at Megara a temple dedicated to Ἀγροτέραν Ἄρτεμιν καὶ Ἀπόλλωνα Ἀγραῖον. Xenophon, in his treatise on hunting, bids the hunter pray τῷ Ἀπόλλωνι καὶ τῇ Ἀρτέμιδι τῇ Ἀγροτέρᾳ μεταδοῦναι τῆς θήρας (*Cyneg.* 6. 13).—Note the change from vocative (Ζεῦ), and 3rd pers. (παῖς, *sc.* πόροι) with optat., to the constr. of acc. and infin. with στέργω. Cp. *O. T.* 204 Λύκει᾽ ἄναξ...209 τὸν χρυσομίτραν τε κικλήσκω: Aesch. *P. V.* 88 ὦ δῖος αἰθήρ etc....καὶ τὸν πανόπτην κύκλον ἡλίου καλῶ.

1092 f. ὀπαδὸν...ἐλάφων, as following them in the chase. Artemis Ἀγροτέρα had a temple at Athens in the suburb Ἄγραι, on an eminence by the Ilissus; and to her, as 'smiter of deer,' the festival of the Ἐλαφηβόλια was held in the month thence named (Mar.—Apr.). *Hom. Hymn.* 27. 2 ἐλαφηβόλον, ἰοχέαιραν,... | ἢ κατ᾽ ὄρη σκιόεντα καὶ ἄκριας ἠνεμοέσσας | ἄγρῃ τερπομένη παγχρύσεα τόξα τιταίνει. She is also ἐλλοφόνος,

Corp. Inscr. 5943 (ἐλλίς, a fawn), θηροκτόνος, θηροφόνος, etc.
—πυκνοστίκτων: cp. Eur. *Hipp.* 215 εἶμι πρὸς ὕλαν | καὶ παρὰ
πεύκας, ἵνα θηροφόνοι | στείβουσι κύνες, | βαλιαῖς ἐλάφοις
ἐγχριμπτομένα: *Bacch.* 111 στικτῶν ἔνδυτα νεβρίδων.

1094 στέργω, 'I desire.' Its primary sense is, 'to love,'
whence poetry could easily draw the neighbouring sense,
'to desire.' So in *O. T.* 11 στέρξαντες = 'having formed a
desire.' Hermann and others take στέργω here as = 'I entreat,'
—getting the idea of 'praying' through that of 'revering'
(as implied in the στοργή of children for parents, etc.).
Hermann so takes the word in the Orphic *Argonautica* 772
μειλιχίοις στέρξοι τε παραιφάμενος ἐπέεσσιν ('entreat him'),
where Ruhnken conjectured θέλξοι.

διπλᾶς ἀρωγὰς, two aids (abstract for concrete), Apollo and
Artemis. Cp. *O. T.* 164 τρισσοὶ ἀλεξίμοροι προφάνητέ μοι
(Zeus, Apollo, Artemis).

1096—1210 *Third ἐπεισόδιον. The maidens are restored
to their father by Theseus; who also brings word that an
unknown suppliant has placed himself at the altar of Poseidon,
praying to speak with Oedipus.*

1096 τῷ σκοπῷ μὲν, 'to thy watcher at least' (cp. 802
ἐμοὶ μέν). The Chorus, left alone with the blind man, has
acted as his watchman. μέν implies, 'if my mere *presage* (1075)
did not persuade, my eye, at least, may be trusted.'

1098 προσπολουμένας, 'coming under escort.' The verb
προσπολεῖν elsewhere occurs only in the act. as = to be a
πρόσπολος (with dat., Eur.). So δορυφορεῖν = to be a body-
guard, ῥαβδουχεῖν to be a lictor. And if the passives
δορυφορεῖσθαι (Plat., etc.) and ῥαβδουχεῖσθαι (Plut. *Num.* 10)
can mean to be escorted by δορυφόροι or ῥαβδοῦχοι, it is
not plain why the pass. προσπολεῖσθαι should not mean to be
escorted by πρόσπολοι. The attendants are the ὀπάονες (1103)
of Theseus.

1099 *Enter Antigone and Ismene with Theseus and his
attendants.*

1100 f. τίς ἄν...δοίη, 'who would give?' = 'oh that some one
would give!' Aesch. *Ag.* 1448 τίς ἄν... | μόλοι φέρουσ' ἐν
ἡμῖν | μοῖρ' ἀτέλευτον ὕπνον. So more often πῶς ἄν. δοίη, by a
sudden gift of sight to the blind eyes.

1104 f. μηδαμά, οὐδαμά are used by the poets when the
final must be short; μηδαμῇ, οὐδαμῇ, when it must be long.
Where, as here, either form is possible, L is not a safe guide in

choosing between them. The μη-adverb occurs 5 times in Soph.: here L has μηδαμᾶ: in *Ph.* 789 (a like case) μηδαμῆι. Above, 517, where μηδαμά is necessary, L has μηδαμᾶ: in 1698 (a like case), μηδαμῆι. The οὐ-adv. occurs 4 times in Soph., and L has always οὐδαμᾶι, which is necessary only in *Ant.* 874, while οὐδαμά is necessary *ib.* 830: either could stand *ib.* 763, *Tr.* 323. Thus L's perispomenon form has displaced a *necessary* -ά in 3 places, while only one place of all 9 requires the long form.

τὸ **μηδαμὰ** ἐλπισθὲν ἥξειν, the generic μή, *one* which was never expected, etc.,—and which, therefore, is the more welcome. Cp. *O. T.* 397 ὁ μηδὲν εἰδώς, n.—**βαστάσαι,** 'to embrace': Eur. *Alc.* 917 φιλίας ἀλόχου χέρα βαστάζων.

1106 ἃ τεύξει need not be explained as an attraction for ἃν τεύξει, since the neut. plur. acc. of pronouns and adjectives can stand after τυγχάνειν and κυρεῖν, rather as a cognate or adverbial acc. than as directly governed by the verb: cp. Aesch. *Cho.* 711 τυγχάνειν τὰ πρόσφορα, and see on *O. T.* 1298.—**σὺν πόθῳ...ἡ χάρις,** the grace shown (by granting thy wish) is combined with a desire (on our own part).

1108 ἔρνη, like θάλος (which, however, was used only in nom. and acc. sing.).—**τῷ τεκόντι** as Aesch. *Cho.* 690: so the allusive *plur.*, *O. T.* 1176. πᾶν, *sc.* τεχθέν.

1109 σκῆπτρα: see on 848. φωτός: cp. 1018.

1111 θανὼν can mean only, 'having died,'—'after my death': but the reading, which has been suspected, seems sound. The sense is:—'were I to die now, I could not after my death be said to have been altogether unhappy, when my last hours had been thus cheered.'

1112 ἐρείσατε...πλευρὸν ἀμφιδέξιον, 'press each her side (to mine) on right and left'—Antigone on his one hand, Ismene on the other. Cp. *O. T.* 1243 ἀμφιδεξίοις ἀκμαῖς, with the fingers of both hands.

1113 f. ἐμφύντε, clinging close, like the Homeric ἐν δ' ἄρα οἱ φῦ χειρί (*Il.* 6. 253), ἔφυν ἐν χερσὶν ἕκαστος *Od.* 10. 397, *clasped* my hands, each and all. For the paronomasia with **φύσαντι** cp. *O. T.* 878 (χρησίμῳ χρῆται) n.: for the masc. ending, see on 1676 ἰδόντε.

κἀναπνεύσατον, 'repose from': for the gen. cp. *Ai.* 274 ἔληξε κἀνέπνευσε τῆς νόσου: *Il.* 11. 382 ἀνέπνευσαν κακότητος: 15. 235 ἀναπνεύσωσι πόνοιο. At such a moment it is surely natural that the father should have a word of sympathy for the late terror and distress of his helpless daughters, instead of dwelling solely on the pain to *himself* of being left without their support. κἀναπαύσατον (note that L has κἀναπαύσετον) is taken to mean, 'and give me relief from this hapless wandering, desolate before,'—*i.e.* since Antigone was carried off (844). πλάνου, then, must mean, 'wanderer's doom,' for we cannot explain it merely of restless movements on the scene since his daughter's departure. But this seems forced. Wecklein explains it *figuratively*, of the insecurity felt by a blind man who has no guide. But how could πλάνου *alone* denote this mental state? Schneidewin (rightly, I think) referred πλάνου to the carrying away of the maidens by Creon's guards, rendering, '*repose from* your late forlorn and hapless wandering.' But ἀναπαύσατον could not thus stand for the midd.: when the act. seems to do so, there is an acc. to be mentally supplied, as Thuc. 4. 11 ἀναπαύοντες ἐν τῷ μέρει, (not 'resting,' but) 'relieving (their comrades) in turn': Xen. *H.* 5. 1. 21 ἡσυχίαν εἶχε καὶ ἀνέπαυε (*sc.* τὰς ναῦς).

1116 ταῖς τηλικαῖσδε: *i.e.* it is not fitting for young maidens to make long speeches in such a presence. The epithet need not be pressed as implying extreme youthfulness (cp. 751).

1117 ὅδ'...τοῦδε: cp. *El.* 981 τούτω φιλεῖν χρή, τώδε χρὴ πάντας σέβειν· | τώδ' ἐν θ' ἑορταῖς etc.: *Ant.* 384 ἥδ' ἔστ' ἐκείνη..., | τήνδ' εἵλομεν etc.

1118 I have little doubt that Wex is right, or nearly so, in his οὐ κἄστι τοὔργον. The λόγος should be his to whom belongs the ἔργον. The words τοὐμὸν ὧδ' ἔσται βραχὺ then mean, 'my part will thus be brief' (as you desire it to be, 1115)—consisting simply in referring Oed. to Theseus. This supposes an accidental loss of οὐ, after which κἄστι grew into καὶ σοί τε of the MS.

Hermann's change of the MS. τοὐμὸν into τοῦτ' ἐμοί τ' has been accepted by many edd. But the sense is most unsatisfactory. If τοὔργον means the deed of rescue, as is most natural, the meaning will be : 'this deed will be a short story both for thee and for me': *i.e.* '*I* shall not have to relate it, and *you* will be so much interested in listening to Theseus that you will not find it tedious.' But is this tolerable,— to say nothing of the somewhat ungracious suggestion that the account of their deliverer's exploit would otherwise be fatiguing? The alternative version would be worse still:

'this *task* (viz. that of reciting, or of hearing) will be short both for thee and me.'

1119 Take πρὸς τὸ λιπαρὲς with μηκύνω λόγον: 'do not wonder if with eager insistence I prolong my words to my children, now that they have appeared unexpectedly': πρὸς τὸ λ. = λιπαρῶς, as πρὸς βίαν = βιαίως, πρὸς ἡδονήν = ἡδέως: *Ai.* 38 πρὸς καιρόν = καιρίως: *El.* 464 πρὸς εὐσέβειαν (λέγει) = εὐσεβῶς. It is possible to join πρὸς τὸ λ. with θαύμαζε, as Schneidewin and others do, comparing *Tr.* 1211 φοβεῖ πρὸς τοῦτο: but such a constr. for θαυμάζειν is without example. τέκνα, acc. governed by μηκύνω λόγον as = διὰ μακρῶν προσηγορῶ: see on 223: cp. 583, 1150. ἄελπτα, adv.: cp. 319.

1121 τὴν ἐς τάσδε, having reference to them, *i.e.* caused by their return. Cp. εἰς in τό γ εἰς ἑαυτόν (*O. T.* 706 n.), Eur. *Or.* 542 ηὐτύχησεν ἐς τέκνα.

1122 μηδενὸς, instead of οὐδενός, gives the emphasis of strong assurance: cp. on 797.

1124 ὡς instead of ἅ or οἷα: cp. the phrase διδόναι εὖ (642). Schneidewin cp. *Hom. Hymn.* 5. 136 δοῖεν...τέκνα τεκέσθαι | ὡς ἐθέλουσι τοκῆες: *Ant.* 706 ὡς φὴς σύ, κοὐδὲν ἄλλο, τοῦτ' ὀρθῶς ἔχειν.

1125 αὐτῷ τε κ.τ.λ.: see 462 n., and cp. 308.

1125 f. τό γ' εὐσεβές: see on 260. μόνοις: on 261.

1127 τοὐπιεικὲς: an equitable and humane disposition. Arist. *Eth. N.* 5. 10 τὸ ἐπιεικὲς δίκαιον μέν ἐστιν, οὐ τὸ κατὰ νόμον δέ, ἀλλ' ἐπανόρθωμα νομίμου δικαίου. Her. 3. 53 τῶν δικαίων τὰ ἐπιεικέστερα προτιθεῖσι, 'prefer the more equitable course to the letter of their right.' Soph. fr. 699 ὃς οὔτε τοὐπιεικὲς οὔτε τὴν χάριν | οἶδεν, μόνην δ' ἔστερξε τὴν ἁπλῶς δίκην (speaking of Hades).

1128 εἰδὼς δ' ἀμύνω κ.τ.λ., 'and I have experienced these qualities which I *requite* (acknowledge) with these words': cp. *Ph.* 602 (the gods) ἔργ' ἀμύνουσιν κακά, requite evil deeds. The stress is on εἰδώς, which is interpreted by the next v., ἔχω γάρ etc. Others render: 'And as one who has had experience I thus support these sayings (about Athens),' τάδε being an adverbial cogn. acc., as *O. T.* 264 τάδ' ὡσπερεὶ τοὐμοῦ πατρὸς | ὑπερμαχοῦμαι. But τοῖσδε τοῖς λόγοις would then refer to what others say of Athens, whereas it plainly refers to what he himself has just said.

1131 f. ψαύσω, *sc.* αὐτῆς. εἰ θέμις, 'if it is lawful,'—a reverential or courteous formula usu. employed when the speaker believes that the act *is* lawful, as fr. 856. 14 **εἰ μοι θέμις, θέμις δὲ τἀληθῆ λέγειν, | Διὸς τυραννεῖ πλευμόνων,**—if it is lawful to say so,—and it *is* lawful to say the truth,—she (Aphrodite) sways the heart of Zeus: so *Tr.* 809 f., etc. Here, however, the impulse of Oed. is abruptly checked by the thought that he is defiled:—**καίτοι τί φωνῶ;** 'but what am I saying?'

1132 ff. πῶς σ', 'how could I wish you to touch a man.' Hermann's change of δ' to σ' is necessary, since otherwise the sense would be, 'and how could I wish to touch *a man*,— I who,' etc.; when **ἀνδρός** would be unendurably weak. But the words **ἄθλιος γεγὼς** are clearly sound, ἄθλιος being a euphemism like συμφορά said of a defilement or crime (*O. T.* 99).

τίς οὐκ = πᾶσα: cp. *O. T.* 1526 οὗ τίς οὐ ζήλῳ πολιτῶν ταῖς τύχαις ἐπέβλεπεν. **κηλὶς κακῶν,** 'stain of sin,' *O. T.* 833 κηλῖδ' ἐμαυτῷ συμφορᾶς ἀφιγμένην. **ξύνοικος,** 'abides in,' Plat. *Phileb.* 63 D ἆρ' ἔτι προσδεῖσθ' ὑμῖν τὰς μεγίστας ἡδονὰς ξυνοίκους εἶναι.... —**οὐκ ἔγωγέ σε,** sc. θέλω θιγεῖν: οὐδ' οὖν, nor *indeed* will I allow it (εἰ καὶ σὺ θέλεις).

Oedipus is indeed ἱερός (287), as the suppliant of the Eumenides, and εὐσεβής (*ib.*), as obeying the word of Apollo; but at this moment he feels that, in the eye of religious law, he is still formally what Creon has just called him—πατροκτόνος and ἄναγνος (944).

1135 βροτῶν is changed by Nauck to κακῶν, and by Dindorf to ἐμῶν ('my affairs'), on the ground that ἐμπείροις needs definition. But if the preceding words leave any need for such definition, it is supplied in the next v. by **συνταλαιπωρεῖν τάδε.** Only those who, like his daughters, are already involved in the family sorrows can show him the offices of affection without fear of a new stain from the contact.

1137 αὐτόθεν, *i.e.* 'from where thou now art,'—without drawing near to receive an embrace. Cp. *Il.* 19. 76 τοῖσι δὲ καὶ μετέειπεν ἄναξ ἀνδρῶν Ἀγαμέμνων | αὐτόθεν ἐξ ἕδρης, οὐδ' ἐν μέσσοισιν ἀναστάς,—from where he sat, without rising.

1138 ἐς τόδ' ἡμέρας: cp. *El.* 14 τοσόνδ' ἐς ἥβης: *ib.* 961 ἐς τοσόνδε τοῦ χρόνου (to this time of thy life).

1139 f. οὔτ' εἴ τι κ.τ.λ.: lit. 'if you have used somewhat great (πλέον) length of speech': ἔθου = ἐποιήσω. Cp. Thuc. 5. 89 οὔτε μετ' ὀνομάτων καλῶν...μῆκος λόγων ἄπιστον παρέξομεν. **τι,** adv., courteously softens the phrase.—**θαυμάσας ἔχω = τεθαύμακα**:

204 *Oedipus at Colonus*

cp. 817: Plat. *Phaedr.* 257 C τὸν λόγον δέ σου πάλαι θαυμάσας ἔχω.

1141 πρὸ τοὐμοῦ προὔλαβες κ.τ.λ., received their words first, in preference to speech with me. We need not supply ἔπους with τοὐμοῦ, which = 'my part,' 'what I had to say'; cp. *Tr.* 1068 εἰ τοὐμὸν ἀλγεῖς μᾶλλον. The verb προλαμβάνειν nowhere = προαιρεῖσθαί τί τινος, to *prefer* one thing to another. It is πρὸ τοὐμοῦ which here suggests preference, while προὔλαβες merely expresses priority in time.

1142 γὰρ = 'indeed,' conveying an assurance.

1145 δείκνυμι δ': cp. on 146 δηλῶ δ'.

1145 f. The usu. constr. is ψεύδειν τινά τινος, while ψεύδειν τινά τι is comparatively rare: and so here οὐδέν seems to be adv., while ὧν (= τούτων ἅ) is gen. after ἐψευσάμην. So I should take Plat. *Legg.* 921 A τὴν τιμὴν τῶν ἔργων ὀφειλέτω ὧν ἂν τὸν ἐκδόντα ψεύσηται, 'of which he has disappointed the contractor,'—though an attraction of acc. into gen. is equally possible. ὤμοσα: 1040.

1147 For the gen. with ἀκραιφνεῖς cp. 1519: Eur. *Hipp.* 949 κακῶν ἀκήρατος.

1148 ᾑρέθη: cp. Her. 9. 35 οὕτω δὴ πέντε σφι...ἀγῶνας τοὺς μεγίστους...συγκαταιρέει, helps them to *conquer in* five of the most important contests.

1150 f. λόγος, by inverse attraction, instead of an acc. λόγον governed by συμβαλοῦ γνώμην as = συνδιάσκεψαι (cp. on 223). When the antecedent is thus drawn into the case of the relat., the case is more often the acc.: see on 56 τόπον. λόγος here = a subject for consideration (cp. our 'argument' in the old sense of 'theme'). ἐμπέπτωκεν, has presented itself to me: so Plat. *Prot.* 314 C περί τινος λόγου διελεγόμεθα ὃς ἡμῖν κατὰ τὴν ὁδὸν ἐνέπεσεν.

συμβαλοῦ γνώμην, 'contribute your opinion,' *i.e.* help me to decide what should be done. Her. 8. 61 (Adeimantus in the council) πόλιν...τὸν Θεμιστοκλέα παρεχόμενον οὕτω ἐκέλευε γνώμας συμβάλλεσθαι, 'he said that T. should have a city to represent before he contributed his views.' *ib.* 5. 92 § 1.

1152 εἰπεῖν...θαυμάσαι: for the inf. act., cp. on 37, 461. So *O. T.* 777 (τύχη) θαυμάσαι μὲν ἀξία, | σπουδῆς γε μέντοι τῆς ἐμῆς οὐκ ἀξία.

1153 ἄνθρωπον, emphatic (as *O. T.* 977, cp. *ib.* 1528 θνητὸν ὄντ'). A mortal cannot read the future, and therefore can never be sure that an incident, seemingly trivial, will not prove momentous.

1154 f. τί δ' ἔστι; cp. 311.—διδασκέ με, ὡς μὴ εἰδότ', 'instruct me, since I do not know.' The μή is due to the imperative: cp. *Ph.* 253 ὡς μηδὲν εἰδότ' ἴσθι μ' ὧν ἀνιστορεῖς: *ib.* 415 ὡς μηκέτ' ὄντα κεῖνον ἐν φάει νόει. ὡς οὐ, instead of ὡς μή, sometimes stands, however, with the partic. (esp. in gen. or acc. absol.), although the verb is imperative: Eur. *Med.* 1311 ὡς οὐκέτ' ὄντων σῶν τέκνων, φρόντιζε δή: Lys. or. 27 § 16 μὴ... ἀζημίους ἀφίετε,...ὥσπερ τοῦ ὀνείδους ἀλλ' οὐ τῆς ζημίας αὐτοῖς μέλον. And when the verb is *not* imperative, ὡς οὐ in such cases is normal, as Thuc. 4. 5 ἐν ὀλιγωρίᾳ ἐποιοῦντο, ὡς...οὐχ ὑπομενοῦντας: 6. 24 ἔρως ἐνέπεσε τοῖς πᾶσιν...ἐκπλεῦσαι,...ὡς... οὐδὲν ἂν σφαλεῖσαν μεγάλην δύναμιν. This is against referring μὴ εἰδότ' here to a cause independent of the imperative, viz. to the mental conception implied by ὡς.

1156 ff. ἡμῖν, ethic dat. (81).—ἔμπολιν: cp. 637. As Theseus was returning from the rescue, word had been brought him that a stranger had seated himself as a suppliant on the steps of the altar of Poseidon at Colonus (see on 55). This man said merely that he was a kinsman of Oedipus; and that he wished to speak a few words to him (1162). The fact that he was not from Thebes, but from Argos (1167), seems to have been inferred from something in his dress, for Theseus says that he does not *know* whence the man had come (cp. 1161). Polyneices took this precaution of becoming a ἱκέτης because he did not know what power might now be at the command of the paternal anger which he foresaw (cp. 1165).

προσπεσόντα πως: lit. 'having somehow rushed to' the altar: *i.e.* he had come in the absence of those Coloniates who had hurried from the sacrifice to the rescue (899), and no one had witnessed his arrival. (Cp. 156 προπέσῃς, 915 ἐπεισπεσών.) πως could not mean, 'for an unknown reason.'

1158 f. βωμῷ with προσπεσόντα, rather than locative dat. with καθῆσθαι: with the latter cp. 1160 θάκημα, 1163 ἕδρα (*O. T.* 15 προσήμεθα, *ib.* 20 θακεῖ, and *ib.* 2 n.).—ἔκυρον. In Eur. *Hipp.* 746 κύρων was restored by Heath from MS. κυρῶν (*v. l.* ναίων): elsewhere Attic poets have only κυρέω. *Il.* 23. 821 has κῦρον: *Hom. Hymn.* 5. 189 κῦρε: and the form was used by the Alexandrian poets.—ἠνίχ' ὡρμώμην, 'when I *first* set out,' lit. 'when I proceeded to set out': *i.e.* when he left the sacrifice, summoned by the cry of the Chorus, 887.

206 Oedipus at Colonus

1160 τῷ θακήματι, instrum. dat.: προσ- as in προσαιτεῖν (cp. on 122).

1161 f. σοῦ seems to be an objective gen. with μῦθον, 'a colloquy with thee' (cp. ἐμὰν λέσχαν, 167). We find αἰτῶ τινα, παρά τινος, πρός τινος, etc., but never the simple gen. αἰτῶ τινος (like δέομαί τινος).—οὐκ ὄγκον πλέων, on a subject of no great pretensions,—i.e. not so important as to demand any great exertion from the old man. Cp. Eur. Phoen. 717 ἔχει τιν' ὄγκον τἄργος Ἑλλήνων πάρα. This seems better than to take ὄγκου here as = 'effort,' a sense which it bears (in a different context) below, 1341 βραχεῖ σὺν ὄγκῳ (non magna mole).

1164 f. ἐς λόγους ἐλθεῖν μόνον, 'they say that he asks no more than to come to speech with you.' Vauvilliers seems clearly right in restoring μόνον from the MS. μολόντ'. The latter would go with ἐλθεῖν: 'they say that he asks that, having approached, he may confer with you': but this is weak; and it would be even worse to take μολόντ' as = 'after his arrival' (at Colonus). μόνον fits the tone of the context. The suitor prefers his request in as modest a strain as possible.

1167 f. κατ' Ἄργος. This brings the first flash of light to Oed.,—he remembers Ismene's words (378). Cp. on 1156. τοῦτο is best taken as acc. after τυχεῖν: cp. 1106 n., and O. T. 1155 τί προσχρῄζων μαθεῖν; But it might, of course, be acc. after προσχρῄζοι, τυχεῖν being epexegetic inf.

1169 σχὲς οὗπερ εἶ, 'stop where thou art,' i.e. 'say no more'— do not go on to urge that I should receive this visitor. Cp. Eur. I. A. 1467 σχές, μή με προλίπῃς. This correction (Heath's) of the MS. ἴσχες is much better than Doederlein's ἴσχε σ'. While the intrans. ἔχε is common as 'hold!' we never find ἔχε σε in that sense.—τί δ' ἐστι σοι; 'what is the matter with thee?' Cp. 311.

1170 πράγματος ποίου; 'what?' The construction δέομαί σού τινος, though less freq. than δέομαί σού τι, occurs in good prose, as Xen. Cyr. 8. 3. 19 δεόμενοι Κύρου ἄλλος ἄλλης πράξεως.

1171 ἀκούων τῶνδ', hearing these words (1167): cp. 418: for τῶνδ' referring to what precedes, 787.—ὅς = ὅστις: O. T. 1068 μήποτε γνοίης ὃς εἶ: Ai. 1259 μαθὼν ὃς εἶ. Her. 9. 71 γενομένης λέσχης ὃς γένοιτο αὐτῶν ἄριστος.

προστάτης, one who presents himself before a god as a suppliant: so 1278: schol. ὁ ἱκέτης, ὁ προσεστηκὼς τῷ βωμῷ. Elsewhere the word always = 'protector' or 'patron.' But cp.

El. 1377 ἤ σε (*sc.* τὸν Ἀπόλλωνα) πολλὰ δὴ | ἀφ' ὧν ἔχοιμι
λιπαρεῖ προΰστην χερί, 'have oft *come before thee* with offerings
of my best in suppliant hand.'

1172 ὅν γ' ἐγὼ ψέξαιμι, who is he, to whom I could possibly
have any objection? Cp. Aesch. *P. V.* 292 οὐκ ἔστιν ὅτῳ | μείζονα
μοῖραν νείμαιμ' ἢ σοί. Distinguish 561 ὁποίας ἐξαφισταίμην,
which is not strictly similar (see n. there).

1173 f. στυγνός has greater force through its position:
'my son, king—a son whom I hate': cp. 1615 σκληράν.
λόγων: for the gen. cp. 418. ἄλγιστα ἀνδρῶν, = ἄλγιον ἢ παντὸς
ἄλλου ἀνδρὸς (λόγων), 'whose words would give me pain as
those of no one else.' The usage is similar to that by which
a Greek could say, πυραμίδα ἀπελίπετο ἐλάσσω τοῦ πατρός
(Her. 2. 134), instead of τῆς τ. π., or ἢν ὁ πατήρ. Cp. *O. T.*
467 n. More often the words would mean, ἄλγιον ἢ πᾶς ἄλλος
ἀνήρ (so οἶμαι κάλλιστ' ἀνθρώπων λέγειν, Plat. *Ion* 530 c).

1175 ἅ μὴ: '*such* things *as* thou dost not wish' (*quae non
cupias*): cp. 1186, 73 n.

1176 The emphasis is on κλύειν, not on τοῦδ': 'why is it
painful to thee to give this man a *hearing?*' Theseus has no
need to ask, 'why is it painful to thee to hear *this man?*'—for
he knows already how Oed. has been treated by his sons (599).
The sense is thus the same as if we kept the MS. τοῦτ': 'why
is this thing painful to thee,—namely, to hear?' But, when
the question has already been put in an abstract form (οὐκ
ἀκούειν ἔστι etc.), it would be tame to reiterate it in the same
form. By τοῦδε it is adapted to the particular case. Cp. 1117
τοῦδε χρὴ κλύειν.

1177 φθέγμα τοῦθ' (art. omitted, as 629), 'that voice'—his
son's. The blind man could not express loathing more
vividly: cp. 863. ἧκει, 'has come to be': *O. T.* 1519 θεοῖς γ'
ἔχθιστος ἥκω.

1178 μή μ' ἀνάγκῃ προσβάλῃς, 'do not force me to the
necessity' of yielding,—the ἀνάγκη being, as it were, a rock on
which his course is driven: cp. Aesch. *Eum.* 564 τὸν πρὶν
ὄλβον | ἕρματι προσβαλὼν...ὤλετ'. We cannot properly call
this 'an inverted expression' for μή μοι ἀνάγκην προσβάλῃς,
which would suggest a wholly different image.—εἰκαθεῖν: cp.
862, 1015.

1179 f. τὸ θάκημ' (1160), his suppliant ἕδρα at the altar of
Poseidon, in whose name he implored the boon. ἐξαναγκάζει:
cp. 603. If we point at σκόπει, as is best, then μή...ῇ is

elliptical: '(beware, I say) lest.' Cp. Plat. *Gorg.* 462 E
ΠΩΛ. τίνος λέγεις ταύτης; ('what calling do you mean?')
ΣΩ. μὴ ἀγροικότερον ᾖ τὸ ἀληθὲς εἰπεῖν, 'I fear it may be
scarcely courteous to say the truth.'

πρόνοια...τοῦ θεοῦ, respect for the god: Andoc. or. 1 § 56
εἶπον...ἃ ἤκουσα..., προνοίᾳ μὲν τῶν συγγενῶν καὶ τῶν φίλων,
προνοίᾳ δὲ τῆς πόλεως ἁπάσης. Cp. on *O. T.* 978. φυλακτέα,
must be *observed*, like φυλάσσειν νόμον, ὅρκια, etc. For slightly
different, though kindred, uses of the verb, cp. 626, 1213.

1181 πιθοῦ μοι, 'comply with me,' grant this wish, as *El.*
1207, *Tr.* 470 (n.): while πείθου is rather, 'be persuaded,' as
El. 1015, and above, 520.—κεἰ where εἰ καί would be normal:
cp. 661. νέα: see on 751: cp. 1116.

1182 f. τὸν ἄνδρα τόνδε, Theseus (cp. 1100). 'Allow him
at once to gratify his own mind (that Polyneices should be
heard, 1175), and to gratify Poseidon as he wishes to do,'
i.e. by granting the prayer made in Poseidon's name. χάριν
παρασχεῖν belongs to both clauses; ἃ is acc. of respect. The
subj. to βούλεται is Theseus.—These two vv. mark two leading
traits in the character of Theseus—his sense of justice (φρενί),
and his piety (θεῷ).

1184 ὕπεικε here = συγχώρει, '*concede to* us that...'; so
παρείκειν in prose.

1185 f. παρασπάσει, sc. ὁ κασίγνητος. Cp. *Ant.* 791 σὺ καὶ
δικαίων ἀδίκους | φρένας παρασπᾷς ἐπὶ λώβᾳ, 'thou wrenchest
the minds e'en of the just unto injustice, for their bane.'—
ἃ μή = (ταῦτα) ἃ μή (1175), 'in respect of such words as shall
not be spoken for thy good,'—a tribute, marked by feminine
tact, to her father's judgment. λέξεται is always pass. in trag.:
cp. 581 δηλώσεται.

1187 κακῶς is Hermann's easy and certain correction of
the MS. καλῶς. 'Evilly devised deeds are disclosed by speech':
i.e. even supposing that Polyneices *is* harbouring ill designs,
the best way to discover them is to converse with him.
Cp. *Ant.* 493 φιλεῖ δ' ὁ θυμὸς πρόσθεν ᾑρῆσθαι κλοπεύς, | τῶν
μηδὲν ὀρθῶς ἐν σκότῳ τεχνωμένων,—where the bad conscience is
supposed to bewray itself even before (πρόσθεν) investigation.
With καλῶς, the words are merely 'a rhetorical generality,'
as Campbell (who retains it) says: *i.e.* speech is a good thing,
'for it is by speech that all man's best discoveries are revealed.'
But surely we need something more relevant to the matter in
hand.

1189 ff. Meineke rejects the three verses, 1189—1191, because (1) ἔφυσας αὐτόν is too abrupt: (2) it is too much to tell Oed. that he must bear anything from his son: (3) the phrase τὰ τῶν κακίστων etc. is indefensible. As to (1), few readers can fail to perceive that the 'abruptness' is both forcible and pathetic at the moment when she turns from colder and more external arguments to the plea of natural affection. As to (2), it is enough to observe that Antigone means, 'The relationship between parent and child is indelibly sacred. No wickedness on your son's part can alter the fact that he is your son.' As to (3), see next n.

1190 δυσσεβέστατ', ὦ (Dawes) seems right: it amends the MS. τὰ τῶν κακίστων δυσσεβεστάτων by simply striking off the final ν. 'The most *impious* among the *worst* of deeds' is a vehement phrase suited to the passion of the appeal. Among evil deeds, τὰ κακά, those which outrage gods or kinsfolk form a class, τὰ δυσσεβῆ. If κακίστων were changed to κάκιστα, the latter must be an adv., and τῶν δυσσεβεστάτων must be masc.: 'the deeds of men who in the worst way are most impious.' κἀσεβεστάτων ('the deeds of the worst and most impious men') is less probable.

1191 θέμις σέ γ' εἶναι. The MSS. here agree in the nominative. Is θέμις, then, indeclinable in this phrase? That is now the received view. It rests, however, solely on the fact that our MSS. have θέμις, and not θέμιν, here, and in four other places. Porson believed that, with Dawes, we ought to read θέμιν. That is my own opinion; but, as the question must be considered doubtful, I have preferred to leave θέμις in the text.

1192 ἀλλ' ἔασον, 'Nay, allow (him to come),' is perhaps the best remedy for the MS. αὐτόν, since we can suppose αὐτόν to have been an explanatory gloss which supplanted the verb. It is a robust faith which can accept ἀλλ' αὐτόν as an aposiopesis. For the synizesis cp. *O. T.* 1451 ἀλλ' ἔα με, n. ἀλλ' ἔα αὐτόν as = – – ◡ is surely impossible for tragedy. Musgrave's ἀλλ' εἶξον is intrinsically preferable to either, but leaves the corruption unexplained. I had thought of αἰδοῦ νιν ('have compassion on him'). If αὐτόν had supplanted νιν, ΑΙΔ might have become ΑΛΛ.

1194 ἐξεπᾴδονται φύσιν, 'are charmed out of their nature': lit. 'are subdued by the charm, in their nature' (acc. of respect). Plat. *Phaed.* 77 E ἀλλ' ἴσως ἔνι τις καὶ ἐν ἡμῖν παῖς, ὅστις τὰ τοιαῦτα φοβεῖται· τοῦτον οὖν πειρώμεθα πείθειν μὴ δεδιέναι τὸν θάνατον ὥσπερ τὰ μορμολύκεια. Ἀλλὰ χρή, ἔφη ὁ Σωκράτης, ἐπᾴδειν αὐτῷ ἑκάστης ἡμέρας, ἕως ἂν ἐξεπᾴσητε ('charm him out of us'). Plut. *De Iside et Os.* 384 A τὰ κρούματα τῆς λύρας, οἷς ἐχρῶντο πρὸ τῶν ὕπνων οἱ Πυθαγόρειοι, τὸ ἐμπαθὲς καὶ ἄλογον τῆς ψυχῆς ἐξεπᾴδοντες οὕτω καὶ θεραπεύοντες, 'subduing by the charm (of music) the passionate and unreasoning part of the soul.' See also Plat. *Phaedr.* 267 D: Aesch. *P. V.* 172. The frequency of the metaphor is due to the regular use of ἐπῳδαί in the medical practice of the age: thus Pindar describes Cheiron as using (1) incantations, (2) draughts, (3) amulets, (4) surgery (*Pyth.* 3. 51), and Plato's list of remedies is the same, with καύσεις added (*Rep.* 426 B). In *Od.* 19. 457 an ἐπῳδή stops hemorrhage, and in [Dem.] or. 25 § 80 is applied to epilepsy. See also Sophocles *Tr.* 1001; *Ai.* 582; Lucian *Philops.* 9. Cp. Shaksp. *Cymbeline* 1. 6. 115 '´tis your graces | That from my mutest conscience to my tongue | Charms this report out.'

1195 f. ἐκεῖνα, away yonder, in the past. πατρῷα καὶ μ., connected with them: so *Ant.* 856 πατρῷον δ᾽ ἐκτίνεις τιν᾽ ἆθλον. He is to turn from his present causes for anger (τὰ νῦν) to the issues of his former anger—when he slew his sire. μητρῷα, because the slaying prepared the marriage.

1198 τελευτήν, result: Her. 7. 157 τῷ δὲ εὖ βουλευθέντι πρήγματι τελευτὴ ὡς τὸ ἐπίπαν χρηστὴ ἐθέλει ἐπιγίνεσθαι. For the constr. cp. *Ant.* 1242 δείξας ἐν ἀνθρώποισι τὴν ἀβουλίαν | ὅσῳ μέγιστον ἀνδρὶ πρόσκειται κακόν.

1199 f. τἀνθυμήματα (cp. 292), 'the food for meditation' (on the evils of anger) which his *blindness* might furnish—itself due to an act of anger, the climax of acts traceable to the anger in which he slew Laïus. Cp. 855.

1200 ἀδέρκτων: 'being deprived of thy sightless eyes,' = 'being deprived of thine eyes, so that they shall see no more,' the adj. being proleptic: cp. 1088 τὸν εὔαγρον n. τητώμενος: the pres. τητᾶσθαι denotes a state ('to be without'), not an act ('to lose'); cp. Hes. *Op.* 408 μὴ σὺ μὲν αἰτῇς ἄλλον, ὁ δ᾽ ἀρνῆται, σὺ δὲ τητᾷ, 'and thou *remain in* want.'

1202 f. Notice the dat. προσχρῄζουσιν (with καλόν), followed by the acc. αὐτόν with πάσχειν, and παθόντα with ἐπίστασθαι. A literal version shows the reason:—'It is not fitting *for* the askers of just things to sue long, nor *that* a man should himself be well-treated, and then not know how to

Notes

211

requite it.' *Importunity* is here viewed as touching the dignity of the suppliants; *ingratitude*, in its moral aspect.—οὐδ', *sc.* καλόν ἐστι. Cp. Isocr. or. 4 § 175 ἄξιον ἐπισχεῖν, ἀλλ' οὐκ ἐπειχθῆναι.—οὐκ ἐπίστασθαι: with the inf. after οὐ καλόν ἐστι the normal negative would be μή, or μὴ οὔ: but οὐ is treated as forming one word with the inf.: cp. *Il.* 24. 296 εἰ δέ τοι οὐ-δώσει. τίνειν = ἀμείβεσθαι: see on 229.

The structure of οὐδ' αὐτὸν...τίνειν illustrates the Greek tendency to co-ordinate clauses. We sometimes meet with the same construction in English: *e.g.* 'For one thing I am sorry, and that is *that the English Government might have prevented the conflict with one single word, and* yet has not thought it necessary to interfere.'

1204 f. The stress is on βαρεῖαν: 'Grievous (for me) is the gratification (to yourselves) in regard to which ye prevail over me by your words; however (δ' οὖν) it shall be as ye wish.' ἡδονὴν is a bold acc. of respect with νικᾶτε, suggested by the constr. with a cognate acc., νίκην νικᾶτε, since the pleasure is secured by the victory. Cp. on 849 νικᾶν. We cannot well take ἡδ. with λέγοντες, 'ye prevail over me in' (or 'by') '*speaking of* a pleasure' etc.—δ' οὖν: cp. *Ai.* 115 σὺ δ' οὖν... | χρῶ χειρί, 'well, then, (if thou must).'

1206 ἐλεύσεται: this form occurs *Tr.* 595, Aesch. *P. V.* 854, *Suppl.* 522: not in Eur., Comedy, or Attic prose, unless it be genuine in Lys. or. 22. 11. The Att. fut. is εἶμι.

1207 κρατείτω τῆς ἐ. ψυχῆς, 'become master of my life,' acquire the power to dispose of me,—alluding to the Thebans' plan for establishing him on their border (cp. 408). τῆς ἐμ. ψ. is merely a pathetic periphrasis for ἐμοῦ: see on 998.

1208 κλύειν is not perfectly courteous, as Wecklein says, who reads λέγειν,—perhaps rightly. But for κλύειν it may be pleaded that, just after so signal a proof of good-faith and valour, Theseus might be excused if he showed a little impatience at the reiterated fears of Oedipus. Cp. their conversation at 648—656. Besides, τὰ τοιαῦτ', a phrase which implies some annoyance, must refer to the fears just uttered, rather than to pledges which should allay them.

1209 f. If δ' is omitted (with Wecklein) after κομπεῖν, we must either make κομπεῖν οὐχὶ βούλομαι a parenthesis (as he does), or else point thus: κλύειν· | ὦ πρέσβυ, etc. The abruptness would add a certain spirit to the words. But the δ' after κομπεῖν may well be genuine, if we conceive him as

14—2

212 *Oedipus at Colonus*

checking the impulse to remind Oed. of the prowess already shown:—'however, I do not wish to boast.' σὺ δὲ | σῶς ἴσθι could not mean, 'know that you are safe': ὤν is indispensable.

1211—1248 *Third stasimon.* (1) *Strophe* 1211—1224 = *antistr.* 1225—1238. (2) *Epode* 1239—1248. *The metre is logaoedic.—The old men of Colonus comment on the folly of desiring that life should be prolonged into years at which man's strength is 'but labour and sorrow.' The helpless and afflicted stranger before them suggests the theme, which serves to attune our sympathy, as the solemn moment of his final release draws nearer.*

1211 ff. ὅστις τοῦ πλέονος μ. χρῄζει, whoever desires the ampler portion, ζώειν (epexeg. inf.), that he should live (through it), παρείς, having neglected, *i.e.* not being content, τοῦ μετρίου (χρῄζειν), to desire a moderate portion: *i.e.* 'whoever desires the larger part (of the extreme period allotted to human life), and is not satisfied with moderate length of days.' χρῄζ. with gen., as *Ai.* 473 τοῦ μακροῦ χρῄζειν βίου, which also illustrates the art. with πλέονος: cp. *O. T.* 518 οὗτοι βίου μοι τοῦ μακραίωνος πόθος. For χρῄζ. τοῦ πλ. μ., ζώειν, instead of χρῄζ. ζώειν τὸ πλέον μέρος, cp. 1755: Plat. *Crito* 52 B οὐδ' ἐπιθυμία σε ἄλλης πόλεως οὐδ' ἄλλων νόμων ἔλαβεν εἰδέναι.

παρείς, if sound, must be construed in one of two ways: (1) as above, which is best: or (2) in Hermann's way, παρεὶς τοῦ μετρίου (χρῄζων) ζώειν, 'negligens vivere modicam partem expetens,' scorning to live with desire of a modest span only. Others make it govern μετρίου, 'neglecting the moderate portion.' But the active παριέναι never governs a gen. (in the nautical παριέναι τοῦ ποδός, 'to slack away the sheet,' the gen. is partitive). Though the phrase τὸ μέτριον παρείς ('in neglect of due limit') occurs in Plato *Legg.* 691 C, it seems very doubtful whether παρείς is sound here. The conjecture πέρα (Schneidewin) is possible. Verrall ingeniously proposes παρέκ, which, however, does not occur in Tragedy. Possibly τοῦ μετρίου προθείς, 'in preference to the moderate portion.'

σκαιοσ., 'perversity,' 'folly': cp. *Ant.* 1028 αὐθαδία τοι σκαιότητ' ὀφλισκάνει. φυλάσσων, 'cleaving to': Eur. *Ion* 735 ἄξι' ἀξίων γεννητόρων | ἤθη φυλάσσεις. Cp. 626, 1180. ἐν ἐμοί, *me iudice*, ἐν denoting the tribunal, as *O. T.* 677 (n.) ἐν...τοῖσδ' ἴσος, 'just in their sight': Plat. *Legg.* 916 B διαδικαζέσθω δὲ ἔν τισι τῶν ἰατρῶν.

1214 ff. αἱ μακραὶ | ἁμ., the long days (of any given long life), πολλὰ μὲν δὴ κατέθεντο, 'are wont' (gnomic aor.) 'to lay up full many things,' λύπας (gen. sing.), ἐγγυτέρω 'somewhat near to grief': *i.e.* advancing years are apt to accumulate around men a store of cares, regrets, sorrows,—in brief, a store of things which are nearer to pain than to joy; while in the mean time the joys of earlier days have vanished.

λύπας ἐγγυτέρω is a sort of euphemism: cp. *Ant.* 933 οἴμοι, θανάτου τοῦτ᾽ ἐγγυτάτω | τοῦπος ἀφῖκται, 'this word hath come very nigh unto death'—*i.e.* threatens imminent death.

The middle κατατίθεσθαι is continually used in Attic of '*storing up*,'—either literally, as καρπούς, θησαυρούς, σῖτον,—or figuratively, as χάριν, κλέος, φιλίαν, ἔχθραν. Therefore I would not render κατέθεντο simply, '*set down*,' as if the meaning were that many things, once 'near to joy,' are moved by the years, and set down nearer to grief; though this view is tenable.

οὐκ ἂν ἴδοις ὅπου (*sc.* ἐστί, as *Ai.* 890 ἄνδρα μὴ λεύσσειν ὅπου), 'you will not see where they are,' *i.e.* they will be invisible to you: cp. Aesch. *Eum.* 301 τὸ χαίρειν μὴ μαθόνθ᾽ ὅπου φρενῶν, 'knowing not where to find joy in thy soul.'

1220 f. τοῦ δέοντος (Reiske) is indicated by the schol. in L, τοῦ μετρίου, τοῦ ἱκανοῦ, and is, I think, true. The phrase, ὅταν πέσῃ τις ἐς πλέον τοῦ δέοντος, means, '*when one has lapsed into excess of due limit*' in respect of prolonged life, *i.e.* when one has outlived those years which alone are enjoyable, and at which the line of the μέτριον μέρος (1212) is drawn. πέσῃ (cp. πίπτειν εἰς κακά, etc.) suggests a joyless decline of life, with decay of the faculties.

The vulgate τοῦ θέλοντος would be gen. of τὸ θέλον (see on 267): 'when a man has lapsed into excess of wish,' *i.e.* of wish *for prolonged life*; not, of *self-indulgence*; for the whole gist of the passage is that joy is left behind by simply living on: the satiety of jaded appetite (which can befall the young) is not in point here. Assuredly τοῦ θέλοντος in this context is not Greek.

ὁ δ᾽ ἐπίκουρος ἰσοτέλεστος, 'and the succourer (*i.e.* the deliverer from life's troubles) comes at the last to all alike,'—when the doom of Hades has appeared,—'namely, Death at the end.' The man who is to attain *long* life has the same *end* before him as the man of shorter span,—viz. death; the only difference is that the long-lived man has to go through years of suffering which the other escapes, until death comes to him as a welcome ἐπίκουρος. Cp. *Ai.* 475.

ἰσοτέλεστος might be defended as act., '*making an end for all alike*' (see examples on 1031), but is better taken as pass., lit. '*accomplished for* all alike,' *i.e.* forming the τέλος for them. The phrase τέλος θανάτοιο was in the poet's mind, and has blended itself with the image of a personal deliverer.—Whitelaw takes ἰσοτέλεστος (as pass.) with μοῖρα, a doom paid alike by all. This may be right; but the accumulation of epithets on μοῖρα becomes somewhat heavy, while ἐπίκουρος is left in a long suspense.

1222 f. ἀνυμέναιος: to death belongs the θρῆνος, not the joyous song of the marriage procession, or the music of the lyre, with dancing: cp. Eur. *I. T.* 144 θρήνοις ἔγκειμαι, | τᾶς οὐκ εὐμούσου μολπᾶς | ἀλύροις ἐλέγοις. So Aesch. (*Suppl.* 681) calls war ἄχορον ἀκίθαριν δακρυογόνον Ἄρη: cp. Eur. *Tro.* 121 ἄτας κελαδεῖν ἀχορεύτους: Aesch. *Eum.* 331 ὕμνος ἐξ Ἐρινύων | ...ἀφόρμικτος.

ἀναπέφηνε, hath *suddenly* appeared: *Il.* 11. 173 (oxen) ἅς τε λέων ἐφόβησε μολὼν ἐν νυκτὸς ἀμολγῷ | πάσας· τῇ δέ τ' ἰῇ ἀναφαίνεται αἰπὺς ὄλεθρος: 'he turns all to flight, and to one of them sheer death appeareth *instantly*.' Cp. ἀνακύπτω.

1225 μὴ φῦναι τὸν ἅπ. νικᾷ λόγον, lit. 'Not to be born *exceeds every possible estimate*,'—of the gain, as compared with the loss, of being born. ὁ ἅπας λόγος is strictly, *the whole* range of possible appreciation : for the art. with ἅπας cp. Thuc. 6. 16 περὶ τῶν ἁπάντων ἀγωνίζεσθαι, for *the sum* of their fortunes : *ib.* 6 τὴν ἅπασαν δύναμιν τῆς Σικελίας, *the total* power. Rate the gain of being born as high as you please; the gain of *not* being born is higher.

The form hints that Soph. was thinking of the verses of Theognis (425 ff.) which the schol. quotes, without naming that poet, as familiar (τὸ λεγόμενον):—πάντων μὲν μὴ φῦναι ἐπιχθονίοισιν ἄριστον, | μηδ' ἐσιδεῖν αὐγὰς ὀξέος ἠελίου, | φύντα δ' ὅπως ὤκιστα πύλας Ἀΐδαο περῆσαι | καὶ κεῖσθαι πολλὴν γῆν ἐπιεσσάμενον. Diog. Laert. 10. 1. 126 quotes Epicurus as censuring these lines, and remarking that a man who really thought so ought to quit life,—ἐν ἑτοίμῳ γὰρ αὐτῷ τοῦτ' ἔστιν. Cic. *Tusc.* 1. 48. 115 *Non nasci homini longe optimum esse, proximum autem quam primum mori*: where he translates the lines of Eur. (fr. 452) ἐχρῆν γὰρ ἡμᾶς σύλλογον ποιουμένους | τὸν φύντα θρηνεῖν εἰς ὅσ' ἔρχεται κακά· | τὸν δ' αὖ θανόντα καὶ πόνων πεπαυμένον | χαίροντας εὐφημοῦντας ἐκπέμπειν δόμων. Alexis (Midd. Com., 350 B.C.) Μανδραγοριζομένη 1. 14 οὐκοῦν

τὸ πολλοῖς τῶν σοφῶν εἰρημένον, | τὸ μὴ γενέσθαι μὲν κράτιστόι
ἐστ' ἀεί, | ἐπὰν γένηται δ', ὡς τάχιστ' ἔχειν τέλος.
ἐπεὶ φανῇ, when he has been born, cp. 974: for subj., 395.

1226 The MS. **βῆναι κεῖθεν ὅθεν περ ἥκει** is usu. defended as
an instance of 'attraction'; but it is harsher than any example
that can be produced. **βῆναι** and **ἥκει** being sharply opposed,
each verb requires its proper adverb. I should prefer to read
κεῖσ' ὁπόθεν, as Blaydes proposed. Cp. Tennyson, 'The Coming
of Arthur' (of man's destiny), 'From the great deep to the
great deep he goes.'

πολὺ δεύτερον: easily the second-best thing: Thuc. **2.** 97
ἡ βασιλεία (ἡ τῶν Ὀδρυσῶν)...τῶν...ἐν τῇ Εὐρώπῃ...μεγίστη
ἐγένετο χρημάτων προσόδῳ,...ἰσχύϊ δὲ μάχης καὶ στρατοῦ πλήθει
πολὺ δευτέρα μετὰ τὴν τῶν Σκυθῶν (where 'easily second' suits
the context better than 'decidedly inferior'). **πολὺ** with
compar., as *Il.* 6. 158 πολὺ φέρτερος, Thuc. 1. 35 πολὺ...ἐν
πλείονι αἰτίᾳ, etc. (but πολλῷ...πρῶτον *Ant.* 1347).

1229 f. ὡς εὖτ' ἄν...καμάτων ἔνι; The first point to decide
in this vexed passage is :—Does Sophocles here speak of **τὸ νέον**
as a brief space of *joy* before the troubles of life begin? Or is
τὸ νέον itself the period of fierce passions and troubles? The
former, I think. Cp. *Ai.* 552 ff. (Ajax speaking to his young
son) καίτοι σε καὶ νῦν τοῦτό γε ζηλοῦν ἔχω, | ὁθούνεκ' οὐδὲν τῶνδ'
ἐπαισθάνει κακῶν. | ἐν τῷ φρονεῖν γὰρ μηδὲν ἥδιστος βίος, | ἕως τὸ
χαίρειν καὶ τὸ λυπεῖσθαι μάθῃς. | ...τέως δὲ κούφοις πνεύμασιν
βόσκου, νέαν | ψυχὴν ἀτάλλων. Cp. *Tr.* 144.

παρῇ, then, must be taken from παρίημι, 'when he hath let
youth go by,' not from πάρειμι. For **παρῇ** ('remit,' 'give
up'), cp. Eur. *Tro.* 645 παρεῖσα πόθον: Plat. *Rep.* 460 E
ἐπειδὰν τὴν ὀξυτάτην δρόμου ἀκμὴν παρῇ.

1231 τίς πλαγὰ (Herwerden) is the best correction yet
proposed for the MS. **τις πλάγχθη**. Cp. Aesch. *Pers.* 251 ὡς ἐν
μιᾷ πληγῇ κατέφθαρται πολὺς | ὄλβος: *Eum.* 933 πληγαὶ βιότου.
Hartung reads παρεὶς for παρῇ and τις πλαγχθῇ depending on
εὖτ' ἄν: 'When, having let youth go by, a man wanders out
into life's many troubles.'

1233 φθόνος, the root of so much evil, is more naturally
placed before **στάσεις**, while **φόνοι** is more fitting as a climax
than at the beginning of the list.

1235 ff. κατάμεμπτον, 'disparaged,' because often spoken
of as dreary (cp. ὀλοῷ ἐπὶ γήραος οὐδῷ, γήραϊ λυγρῷ, etc.).
Shaksp. *As You Like It* 2. 3. 41 'When service should in

216 *Oedipus at Colonus*

my old limbs lie lame, And unregarded age, in corners thrown.'

ἐπιλέλογχε, 'next (ἐπι-) falls to his lot.' Cp. Pind. *O.* 1. 53 ἀκέρδεια λέλογχεν θαμινὰ κακαγόρος (Dor. acc. pl.), 'sore loss hath oft come on evil-speakers,' a *gnomic* perf., as here. Here, too, we might understand τὸν ἄνθρωπον: but the verb seems rather to be intrans., as oft.: Eur. *Hel.* 213 αἰὼν δυσαίων τις ἔλαχεν, ἔλαχεν: *Od.* 9. 159 ἐς δὲ ἑκάστην | ἐννέα λάγχανον αἶγες, 'fell to the portion of each ship': Plat. *Legg.* 745 D καθιερῶσαι τὸ λαχὸν μέρος ἑκάστῳ τῷ θεῷ.

ἀκρατές, 'weak': Eustath. 790. 92 ἀκρατὲς ἐκεῖνός φησιν, οὐ τὸ ἀκόλαστον, ἀλλὰ τὸ ποιοῦν πάρεσιν, ὡς μὴ ἔχοντα τὸν γέροντα κρατεῖν ἑαυτοῦ. Cp. *Ph.* 486 καίπερ ὢν ἀκράτωρ ὁ τλήμων, χωλός. Perhaps an Ionic use of ἀκρατής, for Hippocr. has it in this sense (*Aph.* 1247): in Attic *prose* it always means 'without control' over passion or desire (*impotens*). For ἄφιλον placed after γῆρας, cp. *Ph.* 392 n.

1238 κακὰ κακῶν, 'ills of ills,'='worst of ills': *O. T.* 465 ἄρρητ' ἀρρήτων (n.).—ξυνοικεῖ: cp. 1134.

1240 f. βόρειος ἀκτὰ, a shore exposed to the north wind, and so lashed by the waves (κυματοπλὴξ) which that wind raises χειμερία, in the stormy season. Cp. *Ant.* 592 στόνῳ βρέμουσιν ἀντιπλῆγες ἀκταί (in a like comparison). So *Tr.* 112 πολλὰ γὰρ ὥστ' ἀκάμαντος ἢ νότου ἢ βορέα τις | κύματ'...ἴδοι (of the troubles of Heracles).

1241 f. κατ' ἄκρας, 'utterly,' in the sense of 'violently': perh. with a reminiscence of *Od.* 5. 313 (quoted by Campbell) ὡς ἄρα μιν εἰπόντ' ἔλασεν μέγα κῦμα κατ' ἄκρης, 'the great wave smote down on him' (Odysseus on his raft): in *Ant.* 201 πρῆσαι κατ' ἄκρας (of destroying a city). κυματοᾱγεῖς, breaking like billows.

1245 ff. Compare this poet. indication of the four points of the compass with the prose phraseology in Xen. *Anab.* 3. 5. 15, πρὸς ἕω, πρὸς ἑσπέραν, πρὸς μεσημβρίαν, πρὸς ἄρκτον.— ἀνὰ μέσσαν ἀκτῖν' = 'in the region of the noon-tide ray,' *i.e. these* waves of trouble are supposed to be driven by a south wind (cp. *Tr.* 112, n. on 1240).

1248 'Ριπᾶν. Arist. *Meteor.* 1. 13 (Berl. ed. 350 b 6) ὑπ' αὐτὴν δὲ τὴν ἄρκτον ὑπὲρ τῆς ἐσχάτης Σκυθίας αἱ καλούμεναι 'Ρῖπαι, περὶ ὧν τοῦ μεγέθους λίαν εἰσὶν οἱ λεγόμενοι λόγοι μυθώδεις. It is fortunate that this passage is extant, showing, as I think it does beyond all reasonable doubt, that Soph. here named the Rhipaean mountains, 'beyond utmost Scythia,' as representing the *North*. Aristotle's words prove that the name 'Ρῖπαι for these mountains was thoroughly familiar. Cp. Alcman of Sparta (660 B.C.) fr. 51 (Bergk), 'Ρίπας, ὄρος ἔνθεον (ἀνθέον Lobeck) ὕλᾳ, | Νυκτὸς μελαίνας στέρνον. Hellanicus (circ. 450 B.C.) fr. 96 (Müller) τοὺς δὲ Ὑπερβορέους ὑπὲρ τὰ 'Ρίπαια ὄρη οἰκεῖν ἱστορεῖ. Damastes of Sigeum (his younger contemporary) fr. 1 ἄνω δ' Ἀριμασπῶν τὰ 'Ρίπαια ὄρη, ἐξ ὧν τὸν βορέαν πνεῖν, χιόνα δ' αὐτὰ μήποτε ἐλλείπειν· ὑπὲρ δὲ τὰ ὄρη ταῦτα Ὑπερβορέους καθήκειν εἰς τὴν ἑτέραν θάλασσαν. For the age of Sophocles, these mountains belonged wholly to the region of myth, and so were all the more suitable for his purpose here. The Roman poets, too, used the 'Rhipaei montes' to denote the uttermost North (Verg. *Geo.* 1. 240, etc.). The name 'Ρῖπαι was only ῥιπαί,—the 'blasts' of Boreas coming thence. ἐννυχιᾶν, wrapped in gloom and storm: cp. 1558.

Others, not taking ῥιπᾶν as a name, render: (1) 'From the nocturnal blasts,'—but this would not sufficiently indicate the *north*. (2) 'From the vibrating star-rays of night,' like *El.* 105 παμφεγγεῖς ἄστρων | ῥιπάς. But there would be no point in saying that troubles come on Oedipus from the *West*, the *East*, the *South*, and—*the stars*. There is, indeed, a secondary contrast between the *brightness* of the South and the *gloom* of the North ; but the primary contrast is between the *regions*.

1249—1555 *Fourth* ἐπεισόδιον, *divided by a* κομμός (1447 —1499). *Polyneices is dismissed with his father's curse. Hardly has he departed, when thunder is heard* (1456). *Theseus is summoned, and receives the last injunctions of Oedipus, who knows that his hour has come. Then Oedipus, followed by his daughters and by Theseus, leads the way to the place where he is destined to pass out of life* (1555).

1249 καὶ μήν, introducing the new comer (549): ἡμῖν ethic dat. (81).

1250 ἀνδρῶν γε μοῦνος (cp. 875), 'with no escort at least,' in contrast to Creon, 722 ἆσσον ἔρχεται | Κρέων ὅδ' ἡμῖν οὐκ ἄνευ πομπῶν, πάτερ. Oedipus dreaded that his son, like Creon, would make an attempt to carry him off by violence : cp. 1206 εἴπερ κεῖνος ὧδ' ἐλεύσεται, | μηδεὶς κρατείτω etc. : and Antigone hastens to assure him at once that Polyneices comes otherwise than as Creon came. He is *alone*, and in tears. For the gen. cp. *Ai.* 511 σοῦ...μόνος.

218   *Oedipus at Colonus*

1251 ἀστακτὶ has ῑ in 1646. The general rule is that such adverbs, when from nouns in η or α, end in ει (as αὐτοβοεί): when from nouns in ος, in ι, which is more often short, but sometimes long. For ῐ cp. ἐγερτί (*Ant.* 413), νεωστί (*El.* 1049), σκυθιστί (fr. 429), ἀωρί (Ar. *Eccl.* 741), ἀνδριστί (*ib.* 149), δωριστί (*Eq.* 989), the Homeric ἀμογητί, μεγαλωστί, etc. For ῑ, ἀνοιμωκτί (*Ai.* 1227), ἀνιδρωτί (*Il.* 15. 228), ἀσπουδί (8. 512), ἀνωιστί (*Od.* 4. 92), etc.—ἀστακτὶ, 'in streams,' not στάγδην (*stillatim*): Plat. *Phaed.* 117 c ἐμοῦ γε...ἀστακτὶ ἐχώρει τὰ δάκρυα. So Eur. *I. T.* 1242 ἀστάκτων...ὑδάτων, and Apoll. Rh. 3. 804 ἀσταγές.—ὧδε = δεῦρο: cp. 1286, *O. T.* 7.

1252 κατείχομεν γνώμῃ, apprehended: Plat. *Men.* 72 D οὐ μέντοι ὡς βούλομαί γέ πω κατέχω τὸ ἐρωτώμενον.

1254 f. δράσω, probably aor. subj. (cp. 478), though it might be fut.: cp. *Tr.* 973 τί πάθω; τί δὲ μήσομαι; οἴμοι. So Eur. *Phoen.* 1310 οἴμοι, τί δράσω; πότερ' ἐμαυτὸν ἢ πόλιν | στένω δακρύσας, etc. The *Phoenissae* being the earlier play, it is possible that Soph. had it in mind, but it is quite as likely that the coincidence is accidental: it is at any rate trivial.

1257 ἐνθάδ' ἐκβεβλημένον, in exile here: Plat. *Gorg.* 468 D εἴ τις ἀποκτείνει τινὰ ἢ ἐκβάλλει ἐκ πόλεως ἢ ἀφαιρεῖται χρήματα (cp. ἐκπίπτειν, of being exiled). We might understand, 'shipwrecked here,' ἐκβάλλω being regularly used of casting ashore; but I prefer the simpler version.

1258 f. σὺν: cp. *El.* 191 ἀεικεῖ σὺν στολᾷ—τῆς: see on 747.—γέρων...πίνος, 'foul squalor': *Od.* 22. 184 σάκος εὐρὺ γέρον, πεπαλαγμένον ἄζῃ (stained with rust): Theocr. 7. 17 ἀμφὶ δέ οἱ στήθεσσι γέρων ἐσφίγγετο πέπλος (cp. *anus charta*, Catull. 68. 46). So Ar. *Lys.* 1207 ἄρτος...νεανίας. συγκατῴκηκεν, has made an *abiding* home, emphatic perf., cp. 186 τέτροφεν (n.), 1004.

1260 πλευρὰν μαραίνων, 'a very blight upon his flesh,' can mean only that the squalor of the raiment is unwholesome for the body to which it clings. Cp. Aesch. *P. V.* 596 νόσον...|...ἅ μαραίνει με.

1260 f. κρατὶ ὀμματοστερεῖ, locative dat.: cp. on 313.—ἀκτένιστος: Her. 7. 208 (the Lacedaemonians before Thermopylae) τοὺς μὲν δὴ ὥρα γυμναζομένους τῶν ἀνδρῶν, τοὺς δὲ τὰς κόμας κτενιζομένους. The κτείς was usu. of boxwood, ivory, or metal.—ᾄσσεται, 'flutters': *Il.* 6. 510 ἀμφὶ δὲ χαῖται | ὤμοις ἀΐσσονται.

1262 ἀδελφά...τούτοισιν, 'matching with these things': but

Notes 219

Ant. 192 ἀδελφὰ τῶνδε. The dat. occurs elsewhere (as Plat. *Tim.* 67 E), but the gen. is much commoner.

φορεῖ is taken by some as 'obtains by begging'; but a *conjecture* to that effect would be hardly in place. Obviously it means simply '*carries*,' and alludes to a wallet (πήρα) carried by Oed., for the reception of the σπανιστὰ δωρήματα (4). This was a part of the conventional outfit for the wandering beggar; so, when Athena turned Odysseus into that guise, she gave him σκῆπτρον καὶ ἀεικέα πήρην, | πυκνὰ ῥωγαλέην· ἐν δὲ στρόφος ἦεν ἀορτήρ: 'a staff, and a mean, much-tattered wallet; and therewith was a cord to hang it' (*Od.* 13. 437).

1265 f. 'And I testify that I have come to be, have proved myself, most vile in regard to thy maintenance': ἥκειν as 1177 ἔχθιστον...ἥκει (n.).—τροφ. ταῖς σαῖσιν, dat. of respect. —μὴ 'ξ ἄλλων, *i.e.* from myself: *El.* 1225 ΗΛ. ὦ φθέγμ', ἀφίκου; ΟΡ. μηκέτ' ἄλλοθεν πύθῃ.

1267 f. ἀλλά...γάρ, 'but *since*': see on 988. Ζηνὶ σύνθακος θρόνων, a sharer with Zeus on his throne: cp. on 1382. Where we should say, 'an *attribute*' of godhead, the Greeks often use the image of assessor. Αἰδώς, here compassion; see on 237. Αἰδώς, as well as Ἔλεος, had an altar at Athens (see Paus. 1. 17. 1, cited on 260). Shaksp. *Merch.* 4. 1. 193 (mercy): 'It is enthroned in the hearts of kings, It is an attribute to God Himself; And earthly power doth then show likest God's, When mercy seasons justice.'

ἐπ' ἔργοις πᾶσι, in all deeds: cp. *Il.* 4. 178 αἴθ' οὕτως ἐπὶ πᾶσι χόλον τελέσει' Ἀγαμέμνων, 'in all cases' (as in this).

καὶ πρὸς σοί, '*nigh to* thee also.' In this sense πρός is usu. said of places (see 10), very seldom of persons (except in such phrases as ἃ πρὸς τοῖς θεσμοθέταις ἔλεγε, *before* their tribunal, Dem. or. 20 § 98). In *Ant.* 1188 κλίνομαι | ...πρὸς δμωαῖσι='sink into their arms': in *Ai.* 95 ἔβαψας ἔγχος εὖ πρὸς Ἀργείων στρατῷ=*on* them; and so *ib.* 97 πρὸς Ἀτρείδαισιν.

1269 f. τῶν γὰρ ἡμαρτημένων: 'there are remedies for the faults committed (*i.e.* if Oed. will return to Thebes with Polyneices), while there is no possibility of adding to them.' In this appeal for pardon, the 'faults' most naturally mean those committed by the speaker; but the vague phrase which he has chosen permits the thought that there have been errors on both sides. προσφορά implies at once a confession and an assurance; the son has behaved as ill as possible; he could not, even if he would, add to his offence.

1271 τί σιγᾷς; An anxious pause, while Oed. remains silent: cp. 315, 318.

1272 f. μή μ' ἀποστραφῇς, 'turn not away from me': Xen. *Cyr.* 5. 5. 36 ἢ καὶ φιλήσω σε; Εἰ σὺ βούλει, ἔφη. Καὶ οὐκ ἀποστρέψει με ὥσπερ ἄρτι; But the *place* from which one turns is put in the gen., as *O. T.* 431 οἴκων τῶνδ' ἀποστραφείς.— ἀτιμάσας, of rejecting a suppliant, cp. 49, 286.

1275 ὦ σπέρματ': for the plur. cp. 600. The *v.l.* σπέρμα τἀνδρὸς might be defended by *Tr.* 1147 κάλει τὸ πᾶν μοι σπέρμα σῶν ὁμαιμόνων (cp. *ib.* 304); but the sing., when it refers to more than one person, is usu. rather 'race,' like σπέρμα Πελοπιδῶν Aesch. *Cho.* 503. Cp. 330.

ἐμαὶ δ'. When different relationships of the same person are expressed, the second is introduced by δέ, without a preceding μέν: Aesch. *Pers.* 151 μήτηρ βασιλέως, | βασίλεια δ' ἐμή: Eur. *Med.* 970 πατρὸς νέαν γυναῖκα, δεσπότιν δ' ἐμήν: Her. 7. 10 πατρὶ τῷ σῷ, ἀδελφῷ δὲ ἐμῷ: 8. 54 Ἀθηναίων τοὺς φυγάδας, ἑωυτῷ δὲ ἑπομένους.

1276 ἀλλ' ὑμεῖς γε, '*Ye* at least' (since I have failed): cp. *El.* 411 συγγένεσθέ γ' ἀλλὰ νῦν (*now*, at least): *ib.* 415 λέγ' ἀλλὰ τοῦτο (*this*, at least): *ib.* 1013 νοῦν σχὲς ἀλλὰ τῷ χρόνῳ ποτέ: *Tr.* 320 εἴπ', ὦ τάλαιν', ἀλλ' ἡμίν: Dem. or. 3 § 33 ἐὰν οὖν ἀλλὰ νῦν γ' ἔτι...ἐθελήσητε.

1277 δυσπρόσοιστον = χαλεπὸν προσφέρεσθαι (midd.), hard for one to hold intercourse with. Cp. Plat. *Lys.* 223 B ἐδόκουν ἡμῖν...ἄποροι εἶναι προσφέρεσθαι, they 'seemed to us hard to deal with.' The epithet refers to his *sullen silence*, and is defined by ἀπροσήγορον, 'our sire's implacable, inexorable silence.'

1278 f. ὡς μή μ' ἄτιμον...οὕτως ἀφῇ με. The objection to ἀφῇ γε is that a second γε (though possible, see on 387) is here weak after θεοῦ γε. As to its place after ἀφῇ, that is paralleled by 1409. On the other hand a repeated με, in the utterance of impassioned entreaty, may be defended by 1507 ff. μή τοί με...μή μ' ἀτιμάσητέ γε: cp. *Tr.* 218 ἰδού μ' ἀναταράσσει | εὐοῖ μ' ὁ κισσός: Eur. *Phoen.* 497 ἐμοὶ μέν, εἰ καὶ μὴ καθ' Ἑλλήνων χθόνα | τεθράμμεθ', ἀλλ' οὖν ξυνετά μοι δοκεῖς λέγειν.

Elmsley's conjecture οὕτως ἀφιῇ, which Hartung adopts, is unmetrical. ἵημι has ῐ *always* in pres. subj. and opt.: *Il.* 13. 234 μεθίῃσι μάχεσθαι: *Hom. Hymn.* 4. 152 προίῃ βέλεα στονόεντα: Theogn. 94 γλῶσσαν ἱῇσι κακήν: *Od.* 2. 185 ὧδ' ἀνιείης. In the pres. indic., imper., inf., and part., ῑ is normal, but Homeric verse usually has ῐ in *thesis* (as when ἵενται ends

Notes

a line); and the part. ἱείς (ῑ in Ar. *Eq.* 522) occurs with ῐ in Trag. (Aesch. *Th.* 493, etc.). Cp. *El.* 131 n.

τοῦ θεοῦ γε, Poseidon (1158): **γε** emphasises the whole phrase, to which ὄντα would usu. be added (cp. 83): cp. *O.T.* 929 ὀλβία... | γένοιτ᾽, ἐκείνου γ᾽ οὖσα παντελὴς δάμαρ.—προστάτην: cp. on 1171.—**οὕτως,** so contemptuously: cp. *O. T.* 256, *Ant.* 315.

1280 χρείᾳ, a causal (rather than modal) dat., cp. 333 πόθοισι: *Ph.* 162 φορβῆς χρείᾳ | στίβον ὀγμεύει.

1281 f. **τὰ πολλὰ ῥήματα,** 'the many words' (of any given long speech), with gnomic aor., as 1214 αἱ μακραὶ | ἁμέραι κατέθεντο. Distinguish 87 τὰ πόλλ᾽ ἐκεῖνα κακά, '*those* many,' in a definite allusion. (τὰ πολλὰ must not be taken separately as adv., 'oft.')—ἢ τέρψαντά τι etc.: 'by giving some pleasure,— or by some utterance of indignation, or of pity.' Not, 'by *exciting* some indignation or some pity.' Neither δυσχεραίνειν nor κατοικτίζειν is ever causative in classical Greek. In Eur. *I. A.* 686 κατῳκτίσθην is not, 'I was moved to pity,' but 'I bewailed myself,' the pass. aor. in midd. sense, as often. The emotion of the speaker will awaken a response in the hearer.

1283 ἀφωνήτοις, 'to the dumb,' in act. sense: so ἀναύδατος (*Tr.* 968), ἄφθεγκτος (Aesch. *Eum.* 245); cp. ἀφόβητος, 'fearless,' *O. T.* 885: and n. above on 1031.

1284 ἐξηγεῖ, 'admonish' (but otherwise in 1520). Cp. *Ai.* 320 ἐξηγεῖτ᾽, 'he ever taught' (Tecmessa recalling the utterances of Ajax).

1285 f. ποιούμενος ἀρωγόν, 'making my helper,' *i.e.* appealing to his name: cp. *O. T.* 240 (τὸν ἄνδρα) κοινὸν ποεῖσθαι, 'make him partner': Theognis 113 μήποτε τὸν κακὸν ἄνδρα φίλον ποιεῖσθαι ἑταῖρον.—ὧδε with μολεῖν (epex. inf.), 'that I should come hither': cp. 1251. ἀνέστησεν: cp. 276.

1288 λέξαι τ᾽ ἀκοῦσαί τ᾽: see on 190.—ἐξόδῳ: see 1165.

1289 βουλήσομαι, 'I shall wish' (*i.e.* until the hoped-for fulfilment of the wish has been attained). So *O. T.* 1077 (where see n.), *Ai.* 681, etc.

1291 θέλω δὲ λέξαι (ταῦτα) ἃ ἦλθον, those things *for which* I came; cognate acc. of errand, as *O. T.* 1005 τοῦτ᾽ ἀφικόμην: Plat. *Prot.* 310 E αὐτὰ ταῦτα καὶ νῦν ἥκω. See n. on *O. T.* 788.

1293 f. πανάρχοις is fitting, since each brother claimed the sole power (373).—γονῇ γεραιτέρᾳ: the phrase, 'brought into

222   *Oedipus at Colonus*

being by the *elder birth*,' is a poetical fusion of γονῇ προτέρᾳ πεφυκώς with γεραίτερος πεφυκώς.

In Attic prose the comparative of γεραιός always implies the contrast between youth and a more advanced period of life (Thuc. 6. 18 ἅμα νέοι γεραιτέροις βουλεύοντες). The use in the text, to denote merely *priority of birth* (Attic πρεσβύτερος), is Ionic, as Her. 6. 52 ἀμφότερα τὰ παιδία ἡγήσασθαι βασιλέας, τιμᾶν δὲ μᾶλλον τὸν γεραίτερον : and poetical, as Theocr. 15. 139 ὁ γεραίτατος εἴκατι παίδων.

1295 ἀνθ᾽ ὧν, 'wherefore': cp. *O. T.* 264 n.—In Ἐτεοκλῆς the o might be either long or short (cp. on 1): elsewhere Soph. has the name only in *Ant* 23. 194 (Ἐτεοκλέα beginning both verses).

1296 f. λόγῳ, in an argument upon the claim, before a competent tribunal.—εἰς ἔλεγχον : cp. 835 τάχ᾽ εἰς βάσανον εἶ χερῶν. χειρὸς οὐδ᾽ ἔργου is a species of hendiadys,—the practical test of single combat: cp. *Ai.* 814 τάχος γὰρ ἔργου καὶ ποδῶν ἅμ᾽ ἕψεται.

1298 ff. μάλιστα μὲν with λέγω, not with τὴν σὴν Ἐρ. : 'and of these things I hold (as the most probable account) that the curse on thy race is the cause ;—then from seers also I hear in this sense.' Cp. *El.* 932 οἶμαι μάλιστ᾽ ἔγωγε τοῦ τεθνηκότος | μνημεῖ᾽ Ὀρέστου ταῦτα προσθεῖναί τινα, 'I think it *most likely* that...': *Ph.* 617 οἴοιτο μὲν μάλισθ᾽ ἑκούσιον λαβών, 'he thought it most likely that he (could bring him) without compulsion.' The μέν after μάλιστα opposes *this* view, the most likely, to *other* views (not stated) which are possible, though less probable : ἔπειτα is not opposed to μέν, but introduces the fact which confirms his conjecture.

τὴν σὴν Ἐρινὺν, the Fury who pursues thee and thy race, the family curse, 369 τὴν πάλαι γένους φθοράν (cp. 965), as Oed. himself called his sons' strife πεπρωμένην (421). Not, '*thy* curse on thy sons': Polyneices knows nothing of the imprecation uttered at 421 ff. It is a distinctive point in the Sophoclean treatment of the story that the curse of Oed. on his sons comes *after* the outbreak of war between them, not *before* it, as with Aesch. and Euripides.

μάντεων, at Argos, probably alluding to Amphiaraus (1313). This Argive utterance as to the *cause* of the brothers' strife may be conceived as a part of the oracles noticed at 1331, which also concerned the *issue*.

1301 f. The γάρ seems meant to introduce a further

account of what the μάντεις at Argos had said; but no such explanation is given. γάρ cannot be explained, at this point in the story, as the mere preface to narrative (*O. T.* 277); that should have stood in 1292. Yet I would not write δ' ἄρ'. The hearers are left to understand that he found the seers among his new allies.—τὸ Δωρικόν, simply as being in the Δωρίδι νάσῳ Πέλοπος (see on 695); cp. on 378 (προσλαμβάνει).

1303 f. γῆς 'Απίας, a name for the Peloponnesus (Aesch. *Ag.* 256), from the mythical king 'Απις, who crossed over from Naupactus, 'before Pelops had come to Olympia,' as Paus. says, and purged the land of monsters. The Sicyon myth made him son of Telchin (Paus. 2. 5. 7); Aesch. calls him ἰατρόμαντις παῖς 'Απόλλωνος (*Suppl.* 263). Distinguish 1685 ἀπίαν γᾶν, 'a far land' (ἀπό).

1304 τετίμηνται: for the pf., expressing *fixed* repute, cp. on 186, 1004: Thuc. 2. 45 φθόνος γὰρ τοῖς ζῶσι πρὸς τὸ ἀντίπαλον, τὸ δὲ μὴ ἐμποδὼν ἀνανταγωνίστῳ εὐνοίᾳ τετίμηται, is in permanent honour.—δορί: see on 620. This was the ordinary form, *i.e.* the form used in prose, as by Thuc. In the iambic verse of tragedy it is only once necessary (Eur. *Hec.* 5 κίνδυνος ἔσχε δορὶ πεσεῖν 'Ελληνικῷ). In lyrics it was freely used by Aesch. and Eur. But neither the iambics nor the lyrics of Soph. anywhere require it, while they thrice require δόρει. On general grounds it is more probable that Soph. should have admitted both forms.

1305 τὸν ἑπτάλογχον...στόλον, 'the expedition with seven bodies of spearmen'; *i.e.* the compound adj. is equivalent to two separate epithets, 'sevenfold,' and 'armed with spears': cp. on 17 πυκνόπτεροι. The art. τόν, because the expedition is no longer a project, but a fact (1312).

1306 f. πανδίκως, as asserting just claims in fair fight. The device on the shield of the Aeschylean Polyneices is Δίκη leading a man in golden armour (*Theb.* 647).—τοὺς τάδ' ἐκπρ., Eteocles: for pl., cp. on 148.

1308 εἶεν, 'well!' marks a pause after a statement, before the speaker proceeds to comment or argument: so *El.* 534: Eur. *Med.* 386 εἶεν· | καὶ δὴ τεθνᾶσι· τίς με δέξεται πόλις;

1310 αὐτός τ': cp. 462. The genitives are simply subjective, 'prayers of mine and of theirs,' *i.e.* made by us (cp. 1326), rather than gen. of connection, 'about myself,' etc.

1311 f. τάξεσιν...λόγχαις. The 'allies' are the chieftains. They have marched 'with their seven hosts and their seven spears,' because each, carrying his spear, rides at the head of his own body of spearmen. Polyneices, who is one of the seven, thinks of himself for the moment as present with his comrades in arms.

1313 f. δορυσσοῦς = δορυσσόος, a word used also by Hes. and Aesch. (not Hom.), and usu. rendered 'spear-*brandishing*.' But this seems to confuse σεύω with σείω. On the analogy of the Homeric λαοσσόος, 'urging on the host' (epith. of Ares etc.), and the Pindaric ἱπποσόας, 'steed-urging,' δορυσσόος should mean rather 'spear-*hurling*,' since the epic δόρυ is rather a missile than a cavalry-lance.

Ἀμφιάρεως (–∪∪–, cp. on 1), son of Oecles, 'at once the Achilles and the Calchas of the war' (Schneidewin), is the most pathetic figure of the legend. He foresees the issue; but his wife Eriphylè, the sister of Adrastus, persuades him to go (having been bribed by Polyneices with Harmonia's necklace); and when all the chiefs save Adrastus have fallen, the Theban soil opens, and swallows up Amphiaraus and his chariot: *El.* 837: Pind. *Nem.* 9. 24: 10. 8. Cp. *Ol.* 6. 15. Aesch. makes him the type of ill-fated virtue (*Theb.* 597). In contrast with the ὕβρις of the other chiefs, his σωφροσύνη is marked by the absence of any device on his shield (*ib.* 591, Eur. *Phoen.* 1112). τὰ πρῶτα μὲν...πρῶτα δέ: the art. is to be repeated with the second clause. For the epanaphora cp. 5: *Il.* 1. 258 οἳ περὶ μὲν βουλὴν Δαναῶν, περὶ δ᾽ ἐστὲ μάχεσθαι.

οἰωνῶν ὁδοῖς, in respect to the paths of birds of omen, *i.e.* in applying the rules of augury to their flights. Cp. *Il.* 12. 237 τύνη δ᾽ οἰωνοῖσι τανυπτερύγεσσι κελεύεις | πείθεσθαι· τῶν οὔ τι μετατρέπω οὐδ᾽ ἀλεγίζω, | εἴτ᾽ ἐπὶ δεξί᾽ ἴωσι, etc.

1315 ff. The thirteen lines (1313—1325) which contain the list of chiefs illustrate the poet's tact. There is no pomp of description, no superfluous detail; but the three most interesting points are lightly touched,—the character of Amphiaraus, the character of Capaneus, and the parentage of Parthenopaeus. The dramatic purpose is to dignify the strife, and to heighten the terror of the father's curse, which falls not only on the guilty son, but on his allies (cp 1400).

The list agrees in names, though not in order, with Aesch. *Th.* 377—652, where each name is associated with one of the seven gates of Thebes, as probably in the epic Thebaid. Eur. *Phoen.* 1104—1188 also has this list, except that Eteoclus is omitted, and Adrastus (the one survivor) substituted. In his *Supplices* Eteoclus and Adrastus are both included, while either Hippomedon or Amphiaraus seems to be omitted.

1318 f. κατασκαφῇ...δηώσειν πυρί = 'to destroy it with fire, in such a manner as to raze it to the ground': πυρί is instrum. dat., and coheres closely with the verb; κατασκαφῇ is dat. of manner, but with proleptic force, like *O. T.* 51 ἀλλ' ἀσφαλείᾳ τήνδ' ἀνόρθωσον πόλιν, = ὥστε ἀσφαλῆ εἶναι. Καπανεύς is the giant in whom the ὕβρις of the assailants takes its most daring and impious form, the Goliath or Mezentius of the story: cp. *Ant.* 133, Aesch. *Th.* 422 ff. In *Phoen.* 1128 Eur. follows this conception; but in *Suppl.* 861 ff. he presents Capaneus in a totally new light, as no less modest than trusty.

1320 ff. Παρθενοπαῖος, son of Atalanta by Meilanion, her vanquisher in the foot-race. Another version made Ares the father. ἐπώνυμος τῆς πρόσθεν ἀδμήτης, 'so named after her who before was a virgin,' χρόνῳ μητρὸς λοχευθείς, 'having been born of her when at last she became a mother.'—χρόνῳ (437), after her long virginity. The gen. μητρός as *O. T.* 1082 τῆς γὰρ πέφυκα μητρός.

1323 f. ἐγὼ δὲ σός : 'And I, thy son,—*or* (the corrective καί), if not really thy son,...thine at least in name.' πότμου : for gen., cp. last n. He does not mean, 'thou art not to blame for my tainted birth,' but,—'disowned by thee, I have no sire but evil Destiny.' For γέ τοι 'at least' cp. *O. T.* 1171 κείνου γέ τοι δὴ παῖς ἐκλῄζεθ'.

1326 f. ἀντὶ παίδων...ἱκετεύομεν here=πρὸς παίδων, '*by* them,' *i.e.* 'as you love them,' a very rare use of ἀντί, but one which comes easily from its ordinary sense, 'in return for,' 'as an equivalent for.' It would be as much as their lives are worth to refuse the prayer.

1328 f. μῆνιν...εἰκαθεῖν, *concede* thy wrath to me, *i.e.* remit it. This is better than to make μῆνιν acc. of respect.—For the form of εἰκ., cp. 862.—τοὐμοῦ after τῷδ' ἀνδρί, as *O. T.* 533 τὰς ἐμάς followed by τοῦδε τἀνδρός: cp. on 6.

1330 Since πάτρας must clearly go with both verbs, it would seem that, aided by ἐξέωσε, the poet has used ἀπεσύλησεν with the constr. of ἀπεστέρησεν. Elsewhere we find only ἀποσυλᾶν τί τινος, to strip a thing from a man (cp. 922), or ἀποσυλᾶν τινά τι to strip a man of a thing. We cannot here take πάτρας as gen. of the person robbed, ('snatched me from my country,') since ἐξέωσε implies that the expeller is within the

226   *Oedipus at Colonus*

country. Nor could we well read πάτραν ('took my country from me').

1331 f. χρηστηρίων. The oracle brought to Oed. by Ismene (389) had been received at Thebes (apparently) before the expulsion of Polyneices, since Oed. complains that the two brothers did not avail themselves of it in order to recall him (418). But the reference here is rather to a special oracle concerning the war between the brothers, which Polyneices has heard from the μάντεις at Argos (cp. 1300).

προσθῇ: join thyself: cp. [Dem.] or. 11 §6 (speaking of the Persian king's power in the Peloponnesian war) ὁποτέροις πρόσθοιτο (the 'Attic' alternative for προσθεῖτο, cp. Buttmann *Gr.* § 107, *Obs.* 3), τούτους ἐποίει κρατεῖν τῶν ἑτέρων. So in the genuine Dem. or. 6 § 12 εἰ δ' ἐκείνοις προσθεῖτο, and in Thuc. (3. 11; 6. 80; 8. 48, 87) etc.—Cp. n. on 404.—ἔφασκ': *sc.* τὰ χρηστήρια.

1333 κρηνῶν: so *Ant.* 844 Antigone cries, ἰώ, Διρκαῖαι κρῆναι Θήβας τ' | εὐαρμάτου ἄλσος. So Ajax at Troy, when dying, invokes κρῆναί τε ποταμοί θ' οἶδε along with the Sun-god. Orestes, returning to Argos, brings an offering to the Inachus (Aesch. *Cho.* 6). Wecklein quotes an inscription from Rangabé *Antiqu. Hellen.* nr. 2447 καὶ [ὀμνύω] ἥρωας καὶ ἡρωάσσας καὶ κράνας καὶ ποταμοὺς καὶ θεοὺς πάντας καὶ πάσας. ὁμόγνιοι θεοί = gods which belong to (protect) the same γένος, here, the gods of the Labdacid γένος (369): cp. 756.

1334 f. πιθέσθαι: cp. 1181.

1336 θωπεύοντες, the word used by Creon in taunting Oed. (1003), is unpleasant, but Polyneices means it to be so; his aim is to move Oedipus to loathing of his present lot. To the Athenian ἐλεύθερος the very essence of a free man's dignity was αὐτάρκεια: hence it is a trait of the μεγαλόψυχος (Ar. *Eth. N.* 4. 8), πρὸς ἄλλον μὴ δύνασθαι ζῆν ἀλλ' ἢ πρὸς φίλον· δουλικὸν γάρ: where the saving clause would apply to Oedipus.

1337 δαίμον': cp. 76.—ἐξειληχότες, 'having had allotted to us,' is clearly right; cp. Eur. fr. 115, Ar. *Th.* 1070 τί ποτ' Ἀνδρομέδα περίαλλα κακῶν | μέρος ἐξέλαχον; Soph. has the verb *El.* 760 πατρῴας τύμβον ἐκλάχῃ χθονός. ἐξειληφότες was defended by Herm. as 'having received from Eteocles,'—the dispenser of our fortunes :—which seems far-fetched.

1338 f. τάλας, nom. for voc., as 753: cp. on 185.—ἁβρύνεται, not merely, 'lives softly,' but 'waxes proud.' In

Attic the midd. and pass. ἀβρύνομαι seems always to have this further sense, *e.g.* Plat. *Apol.* 20 c ἐκαλλυνόμην τε καὶ ἠβρυνόμην ἄν, εἰ ἠπιστάμην ταῦτα. The *act.*, however, approaches the simpler sense in Aesch. *Ag.* 918 μὴ γυναικὸς ἐν τρόποις ἐμὲ | ἄβρυνε, 'make me luxurious.'

1340 φρενί, 'wish,' 'purpose': cp. 1182 : *Ant.* 993 οὔκουν πάρος γε σῆς ἀπεστάτουν φρενός. The decisive objection to the conjecture χερί is that the assistance meant by ξυμπαρασῄσει is moral, and φρενί marks this.

1341 ff. ὄγκῳ, 'trouble,' see on 1162. σὺν: cp. 1602 ταχεῖ...σὺν χρόνῳ.—διασκεδῶ, 'I will scatter his power to the winds': cp. 620.—στήσω...στήσω δ': for the omission of μέν, cp. *Ant.* 806 ff. n.—ἄγων: cp. on 910.

1345 οὐδὲ σωθῆναι, *not even* to *return alive* from the expedition (much less conquer): a freq. Attic sense of σώζομαι, as Xen. *An.* 3. 1. 6 ὁ Ξενοφῶν ἐπήρετο τὸν Ἀπόλλω τίνι ἂν θεῶν θύων...ἄριστα ἔλθοι τὴν ὁδὸν ἣν ἐπινοεῖ, καὶ καλῶς πράξας σωθείη.

1346 f. τοῦ πέμψαντος, Theseus, who, on leaving the scene at 1210, brought, or sent, word to the suppliant. Cp. 298.—εἰπών...ἐκπέμψαι, *say*, ere thou dismiss : see on 1038.

1348 δημοῦχοι (cp. 1087 γᾶς τᾶσδε δαμούχοις), the reading of the first hand in L, is clearly preferable to δημοῦχος. For (1) it is precisely in the formal ἄνδρες τῆσδε δημοῦχοι χθονός that we catch the note of suppressed passion; (2) Θησεύς, so emphatic as the first word in 1350, would be *weakened* by δημοῦχος in 1348: and (3) with δημοῦχος we should here need the article. The elders of Colonus are addressed as 'guardians of this land' because, in the temporary absence of Theseus, they represent him. So 145 ὦ τῆσδ' ἔφοροι χώρας.

1350 δικαιῶν ὥστ' : see on 970.

1351 ὀμφῆς. We should press the word too much if we rendered, 'my *prophetic* voice'; though it always has a certain solemnity, owing to its traditional poetic use in reference to a god or an oracle: see on 550.

1352 f. ἀξιωθεὶς...κἀκούσας γ', 'having been deemed worthy thereof (*sc.* ἐπαισθέσθαι ὀμφῆς τῆς ἐμῆς), yea, and having heard,' etc. This is simpler than to supply τοιούτων with ἀξ. from τοιαῦτα.

τοιαῦθ' followed by ἃ instead of οἷα, as *O. T.* 441, *Ant.* 691,

Thuc. 1. 41 and oft.; so Lat. *talis qui*, old Eng. *such...which* (Shaksp. *Wint.* 1. 1. 26, etc.).

1354 ὅς γ', ὦ κάκιστε: cp. 866 ὅς μ', ὦ κάκιστε (to Creon) · for the causal ὅς, see on 263. Oedipus first explains *to the Chorus* why he deigns a reply at all, and then suddenly turns on his son. Profound resentment could not be more dramatically expressed.—σκῆπτρα καὶ θρόνους: cp. 425, 448.

1355 ἅ, *which things*: the neut. plur. of ὅς being used substantivally, with ref. to the masc. θρόνους no less than to σκῆπτρα: cp. Isocr. or. 9 § 22 κάλλος καὶ ῥώμην καὶ σωφροσύνην, ἅπερ τῶν ἀγαθῶν πρεπωδέστατα τοῖς τηλικούτοις ἐστίν.

1356 f. τὸν αὐτὸς αὑτοῦ: see on 930.—ἔθηκας ἄπολιν καὶ... φορεῖν, didst *make* me homeless, and *cause* me to wear: so in Pind. *Pyth.* 1. 40 ἐθελήσαις ταῦτα νόῳ τιθέμεν εὐανδρόν τε χώραν, 'mayst thou *take* these things into thy providence, and *make* the land happy in her sons.' The constr. of τίθημι with acc. and inf. is not rare in poetry: cp. Eur. *Hec.* 357, *Her.* 990, *Med.* 717, etc.—ἄπολιν: cp. 208.—ταύτας without τάς: cp. 629.

1358 f. πόνῳ...κακῶν = πολυπόνοις κακοῖς, the gen. being added to define πόνῳ more closely. Cp. such phrases as δυσοίστων πόνων | ἆθλ' (*Ph.* 508), πόνων | λατρεύματ' (*Tr.* 356), ἆεθλ' ἀγώνων (*ib.* 506).—βεβηκώς, as *El.* 1056 ὅταν γὰρ ἐν κακοῖς | ἤδη βεβήκῃς: *ib.* 1094 μοίρᾳ μὲν οὐκ ἐν ἐσθλᾷ | βεβῶσαν.—ἐμοί depending on ταὐτῷ.

1360 κλαυστά...οἰστέα: for the plur., see on 495. There is no sound basis for the view that κλαυστός = *deflendus*, κλαυτός = *defletus*. Whether with or without the σ, the verbal adj. meant simply 'bewept,' and took on a potential sense only as *invictus* could mean 'unconquerable.'—ἐμοὶ μὲν, 'by me, on my part,' has no clause formally answering to it: but the antithesis is implied in the doom of Polyneices (1370 ff.).

1361 I have little doubt that τάδ', ἕωσπερ, not τάδ', ὥσπερ, is the true reading here. The synizesis of ἕως was familiar through Homer: *Od.* 2. 148 τὼ δ' ἕως μέν ῥ' ἐπέτοντο μετὰ πνοιῇς ἀνέμοιο: *Il.* 17. 727 ἕως μὲν γάρ τε θέουσι διαρραῖσαι μεμαῶτες. ἕωσπερ here could not be trisyllabic, since the anapaest in the first place must be contained in one word, the only exception being the prep. and its case, as ἐπὶ τῷδε δ' ἠγόρευε Διομήδης ἄναξ, Eur. *Or.* 898. With ὥσπερ the sense is, '*however* I may live,'—*i.e.* whether my remaining life be less, or even more, wretched than now. Clearly, however, the sense wanted is not this, but, '*as long as* I live.'—φονέως, 'as a murderer' (predicative), a strong word, as *O. T.* 534 (Oed. to Creon) φονεὺς ὢν τοῦδε τἀνδρὸς ἐμφανῶς.—μεμνημένος, nom., by attraction to ἕωσπερ ἂν ζῶ, instead of a dat. agreeing with ἐμοί: cp. *Il.* 7. 186 τὸν ἵκανε. | ὅς μιν ἐπιγράψας κυνέῃ βάλε, φαίδιμος Αἴας.

1362 f. μόχθῳ...ἔντροφον, 'acquainted with anguish': cp. *Ai.* 622 παλαιᾷ μὲν σύντροφος ἁμέρᾳ, | λευκῷ δὲ γήρᾳ.—ἐκ σέθεν, since the brothers had passively sanctioned his expulsion (441): ἐκ of the prime cause, as *O. T.* 1454.

1364 ἐπαιτῶ, act., used by Soph. only here and *O. T.* 1416 (of a humble request): midd. once, *El.* 1124. The author of the *Rhesus*, also, has used it of mendicancy, 715 βίον δ' ἐπαιτῶν εἶρπ' ἀγύρτης τις λάτρις.

1365 f. εἰ δ' ἐξέφυσα...μή: for the hyperbaton of μή cp. *O. T.* 329 τἄμ', ὡς ἂν εἴπω μὴ τὰ σ', ἐκφήνω κακά, *Ph.* 66 εἰ δ' ἐργάσει | μὴ ταῦτα.—τὸ σὸν μέρος, acc. of respect, 'as far as you were concerned'; so *Ant.* 1062: cp. *O. T.* 1509 πάντων ἐρήμους, πλὴν ὅσον τὸ σὸν μέρος.

1368 f. εἰς τὸ συμπονεῖν: cp. 335, and for εἰς, 1028.— ἀπ' ἄλλου: cp. *Ai.* 547 (he will not flinch) εἴπερ δικαίως ἔστ' ἐμὸς τὰ πατρόθεν.

1370 f. τοιγάρ σ' ὁ δαίμων. The thought is: 'Therefore the avenging deity has his eyes upon thee; not yet, however, with a gaze so fierce as that which he will turn on thee anon, if (as thou tellest me) these hosts are marching against Thebes.' A certain measure of retribution has already come on the wicked son, who is 'a beggar and an exile' (1335); and the measure will soon be filled by a fratricide's death. For εἰσορᾷ cp. 1536: so βλέπειν πρός τινα, 279. The μὲν after εἰσορᾷ properly implies such a statement as this:—εἰσορᾷ μὲν νῦν, αὐτίκα δὲ καὶ μᾶλλον εἰσόψεται. Instead of the second clause, a more reticent and more impressive form of speech is abruptly substituted,—οὔ τί πω ὡς αὐτίκ', 'not yet as they will look anon.'

εἴπερ refers to the statement made by Polyneices, which it does not call in question, but merely notes as the condition. κινοῦνται refers to the march from Argos.

1372 γάρ, I say 'moving against the city,' for that you should *take* it is impossible.

1373 f. κείνην ἐρείψεις, 'overthrow,' is a certain correction (by Turnebus, Paris, ann. 1553) of κείνην ἐρεῖ τις, and has been accepted by nearly all subsequent editors. Cp. the threat Θήβης ἄστυ δῃώσειν πυρί, 1319: and κατασκάψαντι, 1421. It was necessary to take Thebes by storm before Polyneices could establish his power. The only natural sense for the MS. reading is, 'for it is impossible that any one shall call Thebes a city.'—αἵματι...μιανθείς, not merely 'covered with (thine own) blood,' but 'stained with a brother's blood,' as *Ant.* 171 (of these brothers) παίσαντές τε καὶ | πληγέντες αὐτόχειρι σὺν μιάσματι.

1375 τοιάσδ'. His former imprecation, uttered on hearing Ismene's tidings, implied the same doom which is more plainly denounced here (421—427: 451 f.). Manifestly it is to this that πρόσθε refers. See on 1298 and Introduction.

ἐξανῆκ', *sent up, from* my inmost soul: the notion being that the ἀραί, when they have once passed the father's lips, are thenceforth personal agencies of vengeance: hence 1376 ξυμμάχους. So ἐξανιέναι is said of the earth 'sending up,'— calling into activity,—plagues or dread beings (Eur. *Phoen.* 670, etc.). Distinguish ἀφῆκα (*Ant.* 1085), ἐφῆκας (Eur. *Hipp.* 1324), of *launching* curses, etc., like missiles.

1376 ἀνακαλοῦμαι, simply, 'I invoke,' not, 'I invoke *again*.' In this compound the prep. has two different meanings, (1) '*aloud*,' as in ἀναβοᾶν, ἀνακηρύσσειν, and (2) '*up*' or '*back*,' as in ἀνιέναι. Cp. Her. 9. 90 θεούς...ἀνακαλέων, 'calling aloud on the gods.' So in Eur. *Suppl.* 626 κεκλημένους μὲν ἀνακαλούμεθ' αὖ θεούς = 'again (αὖ) we call *aloud*,' etc.

1377 f. ἵν' ἀξιῶτον. The thought is, 'I call the Curses (to *destroy* you twain), that ye may deign to revere parents,' etc.: a Greek way of saying, 'that ye may rue your neglect to revere them.' The irony consists in the lesson being learned only when it is too late to practise it. Cp. *Ant.* 310 (ye shall *die*), ἵν' εἰδότες τὸ κέρδος ἔνθεν οἰστέον | τὸ λοιπὸν ἁρπάζητε (cp. the form of threat, 'I'll teach thee to do such things').

τοὺς φυτεύσαντας σέβειν. Attic law disfranchised a son convicted of neglecting to support a parent in sickness or old age (γηροβοσκεῖν), or of other grave failure in filial duty. In a case of κάκωσις γονέων the accuser could speak at any length (ἄνευ ὕδατος), and was not liable to the ἐπωβελία, or fine in ⅙th of the damages laid, if he failed to gain a fifth of the votes. Diog. L. 1. 2. 55 δοκεῖ δὲ (Solon) κάλλιστα νομοθετῆσαι· ἐάν τις

μὴ τρέφῃ τοὺς γονέας, ἄτιμος ἔστω. Aeschin. or. 1 § 28 ἐάν τις
λέγῃ ἐν τῷ δήμῳ, τὸν πατέρα τύπτων ἢ τὴν μητέρα, ἢ μὴ τρέφων,
ἢ μὴ παρέχων οἴκησιν, τοῦτον οὐκ ἐᾷ λέγειν (ὁ νόμος).

1378 f. καὶ μὴ ᾽ξατιμάζητον, *sc.* τοὺς φυτεύσαντας: 'and that
ye may not utterly scorn your parents, because the father
(εἰ = ὅτι) is *blind* from whom ye, such evil sons, have sprung—
for your sisters did not thus.' τυφλοῦ has the chief emphasis:
the father's blindness emboldened the impiety of the base sons,
while it only stimulated the devotion of the daughters. For
the gen. cp. 1322.—Others understand: 'do not *think it a light
matter that* ye have been such sons of a blind sire' (εἰ as after
θαυμάζω, ἐλεῶ, etc.): but this sense for ἐξατιμάζητον seems much
less natural.

ἔφυτον is the MS. reading, as 1696 ἔβητον, 1746 ἐλάχετον:
and there are about 10 other places in Attic writers where the
MSS. give -τον for the 2nd pers. dual of secondary tenses.
Against this group is to be set a smaller group (of some
9 passages) in which -την is established, εἰχέτην ἤδη, *O. T.* 1511,
being the only one proved by metre. But, in the absence of
better proof that -τον had been wholly discarded, a consensus
of MSS. seems entitled to the benefit of the doubt. I cannot
find any evidence on this point from the best source,—inscriptions.

1380 τοιγάρ τὸ σὸν θ.: 'wherefore they (*sc.* αἱ Ἀραί) have
the control over thy *supplication* (to Poseidon) and *thy throne*'
(said bitterly—'the throne of which thou dreamest'). τὸ σόν
(etc.) is like the ironical use of inverted commas: cp. *El.* 1110,
Ph. 1251, *Ant.* 573. Polyneices has two pleas: (1) As ἱκέτης
of Poseidon, he had adjured his father to remember Αἰδώς,
who is enthroned with Zeus, and to bless his enterprise, 1267.
(2) As eldest-born, he claimed the throne by right, 1293.
Oedipus answers that Δίκη, no less than Αἰδώς, sits with Zeus.
The son has broken the eternal laws (ἀρχαῖοι νόμοι) of natural
duty. Therefore this highest Δίκη annuls both his pleas. His
father's curse has the final control.

θάκημα as 1160, 1179: to make it a mere hendiadys with
θρόνους would grievously enfeeble these words.—κρατοῦσιν, with
acc., not of the person *conquered* (as more often), but of the
domain over which the rule extends: cp. Aesch. *Suppl.* 254
καὶ πᾶσαν αἶαν... | ...κρατῶ.

1381 f. ἡ παλαίφατος, declared from of old (by inspired
poets and seers), a freq. epithet of oracles, etc., and significant

here, where the higher law is opposed to the conventional
right of the elder-born.—ξύνεδρος with Ζηνός: Pind. *Ol.* 8. 21
ἔνθα Σώτειρα, Διὸς ξενίου | πάρεδρος, ἀσκεῖται Θέμις:· cp. on
1267.

ἀρχαίοις νόμοις, causal dat., 'by,' 'under sanction of,' the
ἄγραπτα κἀσφαλῆ θεῶν | νόμιμα... | οὐ γάρ τι νῦν τε κἀχθὲς ἀλλ'
ἀεί ποτε | ζῇ ταῦτα, *Ant.* 454. See on *O. T.* 865.

1383 κἀπάτωρ ἐμοῦ, and without a father in me: for the
gen. cp. on 677 ἀνήνεμον...χειμώνων. Plat. *Legg.* 928 E τὸν
ἀπάτορα (the disowned child). From ἐμοῦ supply ἐμοί with
ἀπόπτυστος (cp. Aesch. *Eum.* 191).

1384 f. συλλαβών, taking them with thee,—a colloquial
phrase, bitter here: cp. *Ph.* 577 ἔκπλει σεαυτὸν συλλαβών:
sometimes playful, as in Ar. *Av.* 1469 ἀπίωμεν...συλλαβόντες
τὰ πτερά: see on *O. T.* 971.—**καλοῦμαι.** The midd. (rare in
Attic except as a law-term, to cite one before a court, Ar. *Nub.*
1221) is fitting here, since the Ἀραί are *his* creatures, and do
his work.—**ἐμφυλίου,** stronger than πατρῴας, and suggestive of
the unnatural strife: cp. *Ant.* 1263 κτανόντας τε καὶ | θανόντας
βλέποντες ἐμφυλίους.

1386 f. δόρει: see on 620.—**νοστῆσαι** with acc., as Eur.
I. T. 534 οὔπω νενόστηκ' οἶκον. Cp. 1769.—**τὸ κοῖλον Ἄργος:**
on 378.

1390 πατρῷον. What is meant by the 'horrible *paternal*
gloom of Tartarus'? Clearly πατρῷον must have *some* reference
to the personal relationships of the speaker, but that reference
might be variously defined.   (1) The primeval Darkness,
father of all (as Apollo is πατρῷος διὰ τὴν τοῦ Ἴωνος γένεσιν,
Plat. *Euthyd.* 302 C). Ar. *Av.* 693 Χάος ἦν καὶ Νὺξ Ἔρεβός τε
μέλαν πρῶτον καὶ Τάρταρος εὐρύς: cp. Hes. *Th.* 116. The
point will then be *twofold*; the Furies are παῖδες ἀρχαίου
Σκότου (see on 40); and Darkness, father of all, is invoked by
the father who is cursing his son,—as Ζεὺς πατρῷος is the god
to whom an outraged father appeals (Ar. *Nub.* 1468).   (2) The
nether gloom *which hides Laïus.* The thought will then be
that the family ἀρά which slew Laïus is to slay Polyneices.
But it is not the fit moment for Oed. to recall his own parricidal
act.   (3) The nether gloom *which is to be thy sole patrimony,*
πατρῷον being proleptic. This seems too subtle for the direct
vehemence of the curse.   (4) A darkness *like that in which
thy blind father dwells*: cp. *O. T.* 1314 ἰὼ σκότου | νέφος ἐμὸν
ἀπότροπον.

I prefer (1), but suspect that the poet used πατρῷον with some deliberate vagueness, leaving hearers to choose between its possible associations, or to blend them. No emendation seems probable.

ἀποικίσῃ, 'to take you to another home,' cp. *Tr.* 954 γένοιτ' ἔπουρος ἑστιῶτις αὔρα, | ἥτις μ' ἀποικίσειεν ἐκ τόπων.

1391 τάσδε δαίμονας: the Eumenides, one of whose general attributes it was to punish sins against kinsfolk, are invoked separately from the personal Ἀραί of the sufferer (1375): so *El.* 111 Πότνι' Ἀρά, | σεμναί τε θεῶν παῖδες Ἐρινύες. The *Curse* calls the *Furies* into action. Cp. on 1434.—Ἄρη, Ares the Destroyer, whether by strife, as here, or by pestilence (*O. T.* 190).

1393 f. ἐξάγγελλε, 'publish,'—with bitter irony, since the son dares not tell it even to a bosom-friend: see 1402.—The word was used esp. of traitors who carried news out of a city or camp to the enemy (cp. n. on *O. T.* 1223).—καὶ πᾶσι, *e'en* to all. (καί...τε could not stand for τε...καί as 'both...and': cp. *O. T.* 347 n.)

1396 γέρα, a fit word, since used esp. of royal prerogatives: Thuc. I. 13 ἐπὶ ῥητοῖς γέρασι πατρικαὶ βασιλεῖαι.

1397 f. οὔτε...τε, as *O. T.* 653, *Ph.* 1321, *Ant.* 763, *El.* 350, 1078. The converse, τε...οὔτε, is not found (n. on 367).— ὁδοῖς, his journeys from Thebes to Argos, and from Argos to Attica. *Ant.* 1212 δυστυχεστάτην | κέλευθον ἕρπω τῶν παρελ- θουσῶν ὁδῶν.

Wecklein reads ξυνήδομαί σου (for σοι): rightly, I think. With σοι, ταῖς παρελθούσαις ὁδοῖς is usu. taken as causal, '*on account of* thy past journeys': but such a dat., in addition to the dat. of the *person*, is most awkward. ξυνήδομαι was constantly used with a dat. of the *thing* in which one takes joy, or of which one approves: Eur. *Med.* 136 οὐδὲ συνήδομαι ...ἄλγεσι δώματος: *Hipp.* 1286 τί...τοῖσδε συνήδει; (these *deeds*): *Rhes.* 958 οὐ μὴν θανόντι γ' οὐδαμῶς συνήδομαι (his death).

1399 οἴμοι with gen., as *Ai.* 367, *Ant.* 82, *El.* 1143. τῆς ἐμῆς with κελεύθου also: cp. *O. T.* 417 μητρός τε καὶ τοῦ σοῦ πατρός.

1400 f. οἶον...ὁδοῦ τέλος, a compressed phrase for οἶον τέλος μέλλουσαν ἕξειν ὁδόν, 'on a journey destined to have what an end.' Such a compression becomes intelligible when it is remembered that the *purpose* or *end* of a journey could be expressed in Greek by a bold use of the ' internal ' accus., as in ἀγγελίην ἐλθόντα (*Il.* 11. 140), etc.—τάλας: cp. 753, 847.

1402 ff. οἷον, acc., is object to φωνῆσαι only, but exerts a causal force over ἀποστρέψαι also (as ὥστε would have done): the first οὐδ' = 'not even,' the second links the two infinitives:— '*such that* 'tis not lawful even to utter it to any of my comrades, or to turn them back.' The utterance *would* turn them back: but the curse is too dreadful to be revealed.—ἀλλ' ὄντ': *sc.* δεῖ, evolved from the negative οὐδ' ἔξεστι: cp. *O. T.* 817 ὃν μὴ ξένων ἔξεστι μηδ' ἀστῶν τινι | δόμοις δέχεσθαι... | ὠθεῖν δ' ἀπ' οἴκων.

1405 f. τοῦδ' is often taken here as = ἐμοῦ (450), when it would go with ὅμαιμοι: but it rather means Oed., like τοῦδ' in 1407. A change of reference, within three vv., would be awkward. Cp. 331.—ἀλλ' begins the appeal (237): it might be 'at least' (1276), but the other view is better, esp. as σφώ γ' follows.

1406 τὰ σκληρά: cp. 774.—ταῦτ', for the ms. τοῦδ', seems a true correction, since (1) the threefold τοῦδ' in three lines exceeds the limit of probable repetition; and (2) it appears a decided gain to have ταῦτα with τὰ σκληρά.

1407 ff. μή τοί με...μή μ': see on 1278 f.

1410 θέσθε ἐν τάφοισι = 'lay me in the tomb': θέσθε ἐν κτερίσμασι = 'give me a share of funeral honours': cp. Her. 3. 3 τὴν δὲ...ἐν τιμῇ τίθεται. There is thus a slight zeugma of the verb (cp. 1357). κτερίσματα (only plur.) for the Homeric κτέρεα, gifts to the dead, or funeral rites: *Od.* 1. 291 σῆμά τέ οἱ χεῦαι καὶ ἐπὶ κτέρεα κτερεΐξαι. In *El.* 434, 931 κτερίσματα are the libations, flowers, etc., brought to Agamemnon's grave. Cp. *Ant.* 203 τάφῳ | κτερίζειν.

The poet's allusion to his own *Antigone* is lightly and happily made. Polyneices here naturally prays for regular funeral rites. That was not to be: yet the κτερίσματα for which he asks are represented by the χοαὶ τρίσπονδοι which his sister pours, after the symbolic rite of scattering dust on the unburied corpse (*Ant.* 431).

1411 ff. κομίζετον, 'win,' = κομίζεσθον, with gen. of the person from whom, as *O. T.* 580 πάντ' ἐμοῦ κομίζεται. Cp. 6 φέροντα = φερόμενον. The same use of the act. κομίζω occurs in Homer (as *Il.* 11. 738 κόμισσα δὲ μώνυχας ἵππους), Pind. *Nem.* 2. 19 νίκας ἐκόμιξαν, etc.—οἷς = τούτοις ἅ, by reason of (causal dat.) the services which you render.—οἴσει, 'will bring,'

i.e. will have added to it. Cp. *Ai.* 866 πόνος πόνῳ πόνον φέρει.
As ὁ νῦν ἔπαινος is the praise for εὐσέβεια, the thought is:—
'The natural piety, which brings you *this* praise for serving
your father, will bring you further praise for serving your
brother.'—τῆς ἐμῆς ὑπουργίας, causal gen. with ἔπαινον (understood): ἐμῆς = shown to me: cp. 419.

1414—1446 The dialogue between sister and brother
illustrates her affection for him, and thus strengthens the link
(1405 ff.) between this play and the *Antigone*. It has, however,
a further dramatic purpose. The version of the paternal
curse adopted by Sophocles tended to suggest this question
to the spectator:—Why should Polyneices persevere in the
war, when his defeat and death had been definitely foretold
to him? For he plainly believes the prediction (cp. 1407,
1435), though he affects to think that there is a chance of
escape (1444). The answer is furnished by the traits of his
character which this dialogue brings out.

1415 τὸ ποῖον : the art. marks the lively interest felt
by the speaker : see 893. The *v. l.* ὦ φιλτάτη μοι, ποῖον, is
inferior.

1416 ὡς τάχιστά γε. Instead of γε, we should rather expect δή : but γε, emphasising τάχιστα, will not seem weak
if we regard the clause as supplementary : 'turn back thy
host—yes, and with all speed too.'

1417 πόλιν, Thebes, rather than his *adopted* city, Argos.
Oedipus had declared, indeed, that his son should not destroy
Thebes (1372): but in any case, Thebes would suffer the
scourge of war.

1418 f. The MS. πῶς γὰρ αὖθις αὖ πάλιν | στράτευμ' ἄγοιμι
ταὐτόν is defensible if we take πῶς ἄγοιμι as dubitative, 'How
could I *possibly* lead?' But there is at least a strong probability
that the poet used ἄν here, instead of employing the much
rarer construction. I prefer αὖθις ἄν...ἄγοιμι to αὖθις αὖ...
ἄγοιμ' ἄν, because ἄν is thus more forcibly placed, and serves
also to bring out αὖθις. We have αὖθις αὖ πάλιν in *Ph.* 952,
but usually αὖθις πάλιν (364: *Ph.* 127, 342, 1232: *Tr.* 342:
Ai. 305: fr. 444. 3).

ταὐτόν has been needlessly suspected and altered. 'The
same host' means an army to which the same realms should
again send contingents,—not necessarily, of course, an army
composed throughout of the same men.

1420 f. αὖθις, an echo of his word: cp. *O. T.* 570, 622, 1004.—πάτραν, native *city*: cp. *O. T.* 1524 ὦ πάτρας Θήβης ἔνοικοι: hence κατασκάψαντι. So *Ant.* 199 ff. γῆν πατρῴαν... | πρῆσαι.

1422 f. πρεσβεύοντ' = πρεσβύτερον ὄντα, 'though the elder,' as often in good prose: Thuc. 6. 55 γέγραπται μετὰ τὸν πατέρα ...διὰ τὸ πρεσβεύειν ἀπ' αὐτοῦ (because he was his eldest son). —οὕτω goes best with γελᾶσθαι: cp. 1339.

1424 The MS. ἐκφέρει is usu. taken as intrans., 'come to fulfilment.' The only relevant support for this is *Tr.* 824 ὁπότε τελεόμηνος ἐκφέροι | δωδέκατος ἄροτος, 'come to an end.' But ἐκφέρει may be also 2nd pers. pres. midd., 'fulfil for thyself.' Cp. the use of the active in *Il.* 21. 450 μισθοῖο τέλος...Ὧραι | ἐξέφερον, accomplished the term of our hire: Pind. *Nem.* 4. 60 Χείρων | ...τὸ μόρσιμον ἔκφερεν. Soph. has ἐκφέρεται as = 'she achieves for herself' in *Tr.* 497. Here, '*thou* art fulfilling,' has clearly more point than, 'they are being fulfilled.' —ἐς ὀρθόν, *recte*, so that the event is parallel with the prediction: *Ant.* 1178 ὦ μάντι, τοὔπος ὡς ἄρ' ὀρθὸν ἤνυσας: cp. *O. T.* 506 n.

1425 ἐξ ἀμφοῖν instead of ἐξ ἀλλήλοιν. Death is to proceed *from you both*: the phrase leaves it to be understood that the death which proceeds from *each* is for the *other*.

1426 χρῄζει γάρ: 'aye, for he wishes it': implying that the wish may have prompted the prophecy.

1428 ἕπεσθαι, 'to follow *you*': for the irregular order of words, cp. *O. T.* 1251 χὤπως μὲν ἐκ τῶνδ' οὐκέτ' οἶδ' ἀπόλλυται (n.): *Ant.* 682 n.

1429 f. οὐδ', not even (to begin with); cp. Her. 3. 39 τῷ γὰρ φίλῳ ἔφη χαριεῖσθαι μᾶλλον ἀποδιδοὺς τὰ ἔλαβε ἢ ἀρχὴν μηδὲ λαβών, 'than if he had not taken them *at all*.'—φλαῦρ', a euphemism for κακά: cp. Arist. *Rhet.* 2. 13. 1 (old men are persuaded) τὰ πλείω φαῦλα εἶναι τῶν πραγμάτων, 'unsatisfactory.'—So τἀνδεᾶ for τὰ χείρω: the defects or weak points in one's case, the things which threaten failure: cp. Her. 7. 48 εἰ ...ταύτῃ φαίνεται ἐνδεέστερα εἶναι τὰ ἡμέτερα πρήγματα, if our side seems somewhat weak here.

1433 f. ἔσται μέλουσα: cp. 653.—κακή, *dira*, ill-omened (like κακὸς ὄρνις), with πρὸς τοῦδε κ.τ.λ.—τοῦδ' Ἐριν.: cp. 1299: so *Od.* 11. 280 μητρὸς Ἐρινύες: Her. 4. 149 Ἐρινύων τῶν Λαΐου τε καὶ Οἰδιπόδεω. '*His* Erinyes' are those whom his

'Αραί summon: *Il.* 9. 454 πολλὰ κατηρᾶτο στυγερὰς δ' ἐπε-
κέκλετ' 'Ερινῦς: though the Curse and the Fury are sometimes identified, as Aesch. *Th.* 70 'Αρά τ', 'Ερινὺς πατρὸς ἡ
μεγασθενής.

1435 f. εὐοδοίη, 'may he make your path bright,' in contrast with his own ὁδός. The conjecture εὖ διδοίη (Burges),
accepted by some of the best edd., effaces a natural and
pathetic touch. The MS. σφῷν, if right, might be compared
with the dat. after words of showing favour (εὐμενής etc.):
perhaps also with the dat. after ἡγεῖσθαι and ὁδοποιεῖν. But
in 1407, where σφώ is certain, the MSS. have σφῷν: and the
acc. with εὐοδοῦν is slightly recommended by the analogy
of ὁδοῦν, ὁδηγεῖν.

τάδ' εἰ θανόντι μοι | τελεῖτ'. The MSS. have τελεῖτε... | θανόντ'.
With Lobeck, I hold the simple transposition to be the true
remedy. The ι of the dative could be elided in Homeric
Greek; but among the alleged instances in Attic drama there
is not one which bears examination.—ἐπεὶ οὐ = ◡ –, a frequent
synizesis, which Soph. has again *Ph.* 446, 948, 1037.—ἕξετον,
sc. τελεῖν τι. The sense is:—'if ye will perform these things
(*i.e.* the last rites, 1410) for me in my death,—as ye will
no more be able (*to do aught*) for me in life.' Since τελεῖν
was specially appropriate to ritual (see 503), there is a certain
awkwardness in the transition to its general sense (630 etc.) as
merely = ὑπουργεῖν. But it is less than that of zeugmas such as
Greek idiom permitted (cp. 1357), and does not seem to
warrant the view that the verse is spurious. It has been said
that the thought is repeated in οὐ γάρ μ' ἔτι | βλέποντ' ἐσόψεσθ'
αὖθις: but the latter is a different statement, and a climax—
'Ye will be able to *serve* me no more while I live—nay, ye
will no more *see* me alive.'

1437 μέθεσθε, *sc.* ἐμοῦ: cp. 838. *He disengages himself
from the embrace of his sisters.*

1439 The change of persons within the verse (ἀντιλαβή)
marks excitement: cp. 652, 820, 1169.

1439 f. καὶ τίς: cp. 606.—προὖπτον, since his father has
prophesied the end (1385 ff.): cp. on 1414.

1441 f. μὴ σύ γ', a *caressing* remonstrance: so Eur. *Hec.*
405 (Polyxena to her aged mother) βούλει πεσεῖν πρὸς οὖδας;...
μὴ σύ γ'· οὐ γὰρ ἄξιον: *Phoen.* 531 (Iocasta to her son
Eteocles) τί τῆς κακίστης δαιμόνων ἐφίεσαι | φιλοτιμίας, παῖ;·
μὴ σύ γ'· ἄδικος ἡ θεός.—ἃ μὴ δεῖ: cp. 73.

238   *Oedipus at Colonus*

1443 f. εἰ...στερηθῶ, an epic use sometimes admitted by the Attic poets: see on *O. T.* 198.—ταῦτα δ', '*Nay*, these things rest with Fortune, that they should be either thus or otherwise' (that I should die, or survive). ταῦτα, nomin.: φῦναι, epexeget. infin.: this δέ in reply modifies or corrects the last speaker's statement. ἐν τῷ δ., dependent on: see on 247.— φῦναι with adv. is equivalent to the intrans. ἔχειν, as elsewhere in poetry it is sometimes little more than εἶναι. *El.* 860 πᾶσι θνατοῖς ἔφυ μόρος. Cp. Aesch. *P. V.* 511 οὐ ταῦτα ταύτῃ μοῖρά πω τελεσφόρος | κρᾶναι πέπρωται. For καί...καί, instead of ἤ...ἤ, cp. 488.

The MS. σφῷν is better than σφώ, to which some edd., following Elmsley, have needlessly changed it. '*For you two* my prayer is—that ye ne'er meet with ills.' The contrast between his own case and theirs is thus more impressively marked. For the dat. of the person in whose interest the prayer is made, cp. *O. T.* 269, *Ph.* 1019, *Ai.* 392. For ἀρῶμαι in a *good* sense cp. *Tr.* 48, *Ai.* 509, *Il.* 9. 240, Her. 1. 132 (ἑωυτῷ...ἀρᾶσθαι ἀγαθά).

1446 πᾶσιν, ethic dat., 'in the sight of all': cp. 810 n.

1447—1499 *Kommos. 1st strophe* 1447—1456 = *1st antistr.* 1462—1471: *2nd str.* 1477—1485 = *2nd antistr.* 1491—1499. *Each strophe is separated from the next by five trimeters, spoken by Oed. and Ant. At the close of the 2nd antistrophe Theseus enters, and he also has five trimeters.*

The dramatic purpose is to divide the two great scenes of the fourth ἐπεισόδιον (1249—1555). *Sophocles here shows himself a master of stage-effect in the highest sense. This momentary pause in the action gives a wonderful impressiveness to the sudden signal from heaven* (1456).

1447 ff. νέα τάδε...κιγχάνει. Two views are admissible: I prefer that which'is here placed first. (1) ἦλθέ μοι = 'have come in my hearing,' not, 'have come *on* me,' μοι being ethic dative (81). The Chorus alludes to the doom pronounced on Polyneices and his brother. 'Here are new ills whose coming from the blind stranger I have witnessed,—unless perchance, Fate is finding fulfilment.' The Chorus correct their first phrase by surmising that haply this fate, not Oedipus, is the real agent of the doom on the brothers.

(2) Others suppose that a low rumbling of thunder was heard immediately after the exit of Polyneices, and that ἔκτυπεν αἰθήρ in 1456 merely marks the first *loud* sound. νέα

τάδε...κακά are then the evils which the Chorus forebode from the *incipient* thunder: ἦλθέ μοι='have come *upon* me.' εἰ τι μοῖρα μὴ κιγχάνει is then taken either as before, or thus;—'if haply *his end* is not coming upon him.' But (*a*) It is much more natural to suppose that the *beginning* of the thunder is denoted by ἔκτυπεν. The whole effect of the passage depends on the moralising of the Chorus (1451 ff.) being interrupted by the sudden crash at 1456. (*b*) After the exit of Polyneices, we naturally expect from the Chorus some comment on the father's curse and the son's doom. (*c*) If νέα κακά meant 'new ills' brought *on the Chorus* by Oed., the language would rather imply that they had suffered something else from him before,— which is not the case.

νεόθεν strengthens νέα, and might mean, 'from a new occasion' (the visit of Polyneices); but it seems more probable that the poet used it merely in the sense of 'newly' (lit., 'from a recent moment'); schol. νεωστί. For the form cp. *Il.* 7. 97 λώβη τάδε γ' ἔσσεται αἰνόθεν αἰνῶς, 'with horrors of horrors': *ib.* 39 οἰόθεν οἶος, 'singly and alone.'—εἰ τι μοῖρα μὴ κιγχάνει: for τι = 'perchance,' cp. *O. T.* 124 (n.): the formula εἴ τι μή is used in noticing an alternative which occurs to one as an afterthought, *ib.* 969.—κιγχάνει, '*is overtaking*' (its victims), the acc. being understood, as *Il.* 17. 671 πᾶσιν γὰρ ἐπίστατο μείλιχος εἶναι | ζωὸς ἐών· νῦν αὖ θάνατος καὶ μοῖρα κιχάνει.

1451 f. ματᾶν. The MS. μάτην seems plainly corrupt. The sense is: 'for I cannot say that any decree of deities *is in vain*': *i.e.* μάτην must stand for μάταιον εἶναι. Isocr. or. 4 § 5 has ὥστ' ἤδη μάτην εἶναι τὸ μεμνῆσθαι περὶ τούτων (=μάταιον): but that does not justify the use of the adv. *alone* here. Nor can it go with φράσαι. For ματᾶν cp. Aesch. *Eum.* 142 ἰδώμεθ' εἴ τι τοῦδε φροιμίου ματᾷ, 'is in vain.'—ἀξίωμα, prop. 'what one thinks right'; here, 'decree,' 'ordinance'; in 1459 'request.' Cp. Dem. or. 18 § 210 τὰ τῶν προγόνων ἀξιώματα, their political maxims.—φράσαι: these words are a comment on the last. Perchance it is Fate that is being fulfilled; *for* a heaven-appointed fate *never fails* of fulfilment.

1453 f. ταῦτ' = ἀξιώματα δαιμόνων. With στρέφων (for the corrupt ἐπεί), the sense is :—' Watchful, ever watchful of these divine decrees is Time,—*overthrowing* some fortunes, and the next day, again, exalting others on high.' Cp. Eur. fr. 424 μί' ἡμέρα | τὰ μὲν καθεῖλεν ὑψόθεν, τὰ δ' ἦρ' ἄνω.—ὁρᾷ, as *Ph.* 843 τάδε μὲν θεὸς ὄψεται, 'will look to' this. Time is the vigilant minister of Fate. The mighty are humbled (as the Labdacıdae have been); the lowly, again, are exalted. The last words contain an unconscious hint that the sufferings of Oedipus are well-nigh finished, and that honour is coming to him. At that instant, the thunder is heard.

The MS. words ἐπὶ μὲν ἕτερα...ἄνω are thus paraphrased by the schol.: πολλὰ μὲν αὔξων παρ' ἦμαρ, πολλὰ δὲ εἰς τὸ ἔμπαλιν τρέπων. This makes it certain that, instead of ἐπεί (which is here untranslatable), the schol. had some *participle*, as the form of the sentence plainly requires. For στρέφων cp. Eur fr. 540 φεῦ, τὰ τῶν εὐδαιμονούντων ὡς τάχα στρέφει θεός. Soph. *Tr.* 116 τὸν Καδμογενῆ | στρέφει, τὸ δ' αὔξει βιότου | πολύπονον, the troubles of his life now bring reverse, now glory, to Heracles. This was a poetical use of στρέφω, which the schol.'s words εἰς τὸ ἔμπαλιν τρέπων were meant to explain. τρέπω itself was not used alone as=ἀνατρέπω, though often in phrases with that sense.

1456 ἔκτυπεν, the epic aor., only here in Attic: elsewhere ἐκτύπησα.

1457 f. πῶς ἄν: cp. on 1100.—εἴ τις ἔντοπος, 'on the spot,'—other, that is, than the Chorus: some one who could be sent on the errand. Cp. 70, 297.—δεῦρο...πόροι, 'cause him to come hither.' πορεῖν, to give, is never found as = πορεύειν, to make to come (1476): and here the phrase is strictly a compressed one, 'enable me to speak to him, (by bringing him) hither.' But the associations of πόρος and πορεύειν have doubtless influenced it. Cp. *El.* 1267 εἴ σε θεὸς ἐπόρισεν | ἁμέτερα πρὸς μέλαθρα.—Cp. Pind. *Pyth.* 3. 45 καί ῥά νιν Μάγνητι φέρων πόρε Κενταύρῳ διδάξαι ('gave,' with the like notion as here of bringing to).—πάντ', adv.: *Ai.* 911 ὁ πάντα κωφός: *O. T.* 475 n.

1459 τί δ', after the voc.: cp. 507.—τάξίωμ': see on 1451.

1460 f. πτερωτὸς: Verg. *Aen.* 5. 319 *et ventis et fulminis ocior alis.*—ἄξεται: the fut. midd. here merely = ἄξει, for 'cause me to be led' would be strained. In *Od.* 21. 322 οὗ τί σε τόνδ' ἄξεσθαι ὀΐομεθ' ('wed thee'), the midd. has its proper special force: cp. *ib.* 214. In Eur. *Hipp.* 625 it is doubtful. In Aesch. *Ag.* 1632 etc. it is passive.

1462 f. While the MS. words ἴδε μάλα μέγας ἐρείπεται correspond with the first verse of the strophe (1447), the second verse here exceeds its strophic counterpart by ⏑⏑. Hermann supplied νέα in the strophe after βαρύποτμα:

Heinrich Schmidt omits ὅδε here.   But if we write μέγας, ἴδε, μάλ᾽ ὅδ᾽ ἐρείπεται | κτύπος ἄφατος διόβολος, we get an exact correspondence, without either adding to the strophe or taking from the antistrophe.   ἐρείπεται, *ruit* (cp. *Ai.* 309 n.); the very sky seems to come down with the crash: so Valerius Flaccus 8. 334 *ruina poli* of thunder.—κτύπος...διόβολος, the noise of a bolt hurled by Zeus: cp. on 710 αὔχημα...εὔιππον.— ἄκραν, the tips, not the roots, *i.e.* my hair stands on end with fright: cp. 1624.

1466 ἔπτηξα, aor. referring to a moment just past, where we should ordinarily use the pres.: *Ai.* 693 ἔφριξ᾽ ἔρωτι.   Cp. *O. T.* 337 n.—θυμόν, acc. of part affected.

οὐρανία, 'in the sky.'   Heinrich Schmidt defends οὐρανία as – ‿ –: others deny that such a synizesis is possible.   But in Aesch. *Th.* 288 καρδίας answers metrically to ἐχθροῖς (305); in his *Suppl.* 71 καρδίαν=the last two syllables of στυγοῦντες (80); and *ib.* 799 καρδίας=the first two of γαιάοχε (816).

1468 τί...ἀφήσει τέλος; 'what end (event) will (the lightning) bring forth?'   For ἀφιέναι as = 'to emit,' 'produce from one's self,' cp. Arist. *Hist. An.* 6. 14 ἀφιᾶσι τὸ κύημα,...τῆς θηλείας ἀφιείσης τὸ ᾠόν.   This use, which was common, suggests how the word might be figuratively said of the storm *giving birth* to some disastrous issue.   μῶν, 'verily,' here nearly = an exclamation, such as 'ah!'   Cp. on 182.

1469 L has δέδεια τόδ᾽, which might easily have grown out of δέδοικα δ᾽ (Nauck).   The latter is recommended by metre, giving an exact correspondence if in 1454 we read στρέφων: cp. on 1453 f.

1470 f. ἀφορμᾷ, *sc.* ἡ ἀστραπή, 'rushes forth' (from the sky),—better here than the *v. l.* ἐφορμᾷ.—ξυμφορᾶς, not definitely 'misfortune,' but rather, more generally, 'grave issue.'   The thought is merely that something momentous always follows such a storm.   Cp. *O. T.* 44 τὰς ξυμφορὰς...τῶν βουλευμάτων, the issues or effects of counsels.

1471 ὦ μέγας αἰθήρ is a cry rather than an address like ὦ Ζεῦ: yet in Aesch. *P. V.* 88, in a direct address, we have ὦ δῖος αἰθήρ, followed by the voc. παμμῆτόρ τε γῆ.

1472 ἥκει τῷδ᾽ ἐπ᾽ ἀνδρί.   We may render the prep. 'upon' me, but properly it is rather 'against' me;—the doom, from which there is no ἀποστροφή, advances to take him.   Cp. *O. T.* 509 ἐπ᾽ αὐτῷ πτερόεσσ᾽ ἦλθε κόρα.

1474 συμβαλὼν ἔχεις (cp. 817, 1140), 'hast inferred,' a

242 *Oedipus at Colonus*

frequent sense of the act. in Attic: Her. in this sense prefers the midd. As ὦ παῖδες (1472) evidently means the daughters, this v. is rightly given to Antigone; but her question reminds us that she, and she only, had heard Oed. speak of the signs which should announce his end (95).

1475 μοι, ethic dat., 'I pray you': cp. *O. T.* 1512 τοῦτ εὔχεσθέ μοι, 'I would have this to be your prayer.'

1477 f. ἔα is the cry of one startled by a sight or sound (Aesch. *P. V.* 298 ἔα· τί χρῆμα λεύσσω;): only here in Soph.— μάλ' αὖθις, 'again, and loudly': *El.* 1410 ἰδοὺ μάλ' αὖ θροεῖ τις.—ἀμφίσταται, because the peals of thunder, now at their loudest, seem to be around them on every side. Cp. *Od.* 6. 122 ὥστε με κουράων ἀμφήλυθε θῆλυς ἀϋτή: so περὶ...ἤλυθ ἰωὴ | φόρμιγγος (17. 261), ἄσημα περιβαίνει βοῆς (*Ant.* 1209): but the phrase here is more vigorous, suggesting the image of a threatening foe.— διαπρύσιος, as with κέλαδος, Eur. *Hel.* 1308; ὀλολυγαί, *Hom. Hymn.* 4. 19: in Homer only as adv., ἤϋσεν δὲ διαπρύσιον (*Il.* 8. 227): properly, 'going through' the ear, 'piercing,' like τορός, διατόρος.

1480 f. For ὦ δαίμων cp. on 185.—ἵλαος (*sc.* ἴσθι), as usually in Homer, etc., though ἵλαος also occurs (as *Il.* 1. 583, *Hymn.* 5. 204, Hes. *Op.* 340, Aesch. *Eum.* 1040).

1481 f. γᾷ ματέρι, Attica: cp. 707 ματροπόλει τᾷδε. Plat. *Rep.* 414 E δεῖ ὡς περὶ μητρὸς καὶ τροφοῦ τῆς χώρας ἐν ᾗ εἰσὶ βουλεύεσθαι.—ἀφεγγὲς, 'gloomy,' as the thunder-cloud.

1482 σοῦ τύχοιμι is a certain correction, 'gracious may I find thee.'

ἄλαστον ἄνδρ', 'a man accursed,' Oedipus. With Homer, this adj. is always the epithet of πένθος or ἄχος, except in *Il.* 22. 261 (Achilles), Ἕκτορ, μή μοι, ἄλαστε, συνημοσύνας ἀγόρευε, '*Wretch*, prate not to me of covenants,'—the epithet of the *act* (537, 1672) is transferred to the *agent*,—the doer of ἄλαστα being called ἄλαστος in the general sense of 'wretch,' 'accursed one.'—ἰδὼν, since, in the old Greek belief, even casual association with a polluted man was perilous: Antiph. or. 5 § 82 πολλοὶ ἤδη ἄνθρωποι μὴ καθαροὶ χεῖρας ἢ ἄλλο τι μίασμα ἔχοντες συνεισβάντες εἰς τὸ πλοῖον συναπώλεσαν μετὰ τῆς αὐτῶν ψυχῆς τοὺς ὁσίως διακειμένους τὰ πρὸς τοὺς θεούς. Cp. Aesch. *Th.* 597 ff., Eur. *El.* 1354, Xen. *Cyr.* 8. 1. 25, Hor. *Carm.* 3. 2. 26.

1484 ἀκερδῆ χάριν μετάσχ., have for my portion an unprofitable recompense (in return for the sympathy shown

Notes

243

to Oed.); cp. Aesch. *P. V.* 544 ἄχαρις χάρις ('a thankless favour'), Soph. *Ai.* 665 ἄδωρα δῶρα. Pind. *Ol.* 1. 54 ἀκέρδεια = disaster (with a similar euphemism).—In the verb, μετά here = 'along with Oedipus,' 'as my share in his curse': χάριν is acc., not gen., because it denotes the share, not the thing shared. μετέχω takes (1) gen. of thing shared, (2) acc. of share, (3) dat. of partner: but when (3) is present, (2) is usu. absent, unless equality is affirmed or denied, as Xen. *Cyr.* 7. 2. 28 εὐφρο-συνῶν πασῶν ἐμοὶ τὸ ἴσον μετεῖχε. *Hiero* 2. 7 τούτου (τοῦ κακοῦ) πλεῖστον μέρος οἱ τύραννοι μετέχουσιν. The peculiarity here is only in the use of the acc. *alone*, without a gen. (as τῆς ἀρᾶς).

1487 κιχήσεται with gen., on the analogy of τυγχάνειν. Elsewhere κιχάνω always governs acc. We might take ἐμψύχου...μου (*sc.* ὄντος, cp. 83) καὶ κατορθοῦντος as gen. absol., but this is less probable.—κατορθοῦντος intrans., φρένα acc. of respect: cp. ἐξ ὀρθῆς φρενός, *O. T.* 528. The *intrans.* κατορθόω usu. = 'to succeed' (Thuc. 6. 12 ἢ κατορθώσαντας,...ἢ πταίσαντας), but also 'to be right or correct,' as Plat. *Legg.* 654 C ὃς ἂν τῇ μὲν φωνῇ καὶ τῷ σώματι μὴ πάνυ δυνατὸς ᾖ κατορθοῦν (in song and dance).

1488 ἐμφῦναι φρενί, 'and what is the pledge which thou wouldst have fixed in thy mind?' Many recent critics have held that φρενί has come in from 1487, but the explanation of the Scholiast (ἐμβαλεῖν τῇ φρενὶ ἐκείνου) proves the antiquity of it, and so far as the mere *repetition* is an argument, we must be cautious in applying it: cp. 70 f., and n. on 554. The sense must be either:—'And what is *the pledge* which thou wouldst have fixed (1) in *his* mind?'—*i.e.* 'What is it that thou wouldst tell him in confidence, under his pledge of secrecy?'— or else (2) 'in *thy* mind?'—*i.e.* 'what promise wouldst thou obtain from him before death?' Here (2) is recommended by the fact that the φρήν is then the same in both vv. Nor is the reply of Oed. (1489) inconsistent with it; since the fulfilment of his promise (580) to Theseus involves a pledge from Theseus to keep the secret (1530). It is, of course, possible that Soph. wrote ἐμφῆναι ξένῳ, or the like: but the vulgate is at least defensible.

1489 f. For the pause in sense after εὖ, cp. 52, 288, 610, *El.* 1036, Aesch. *Eum.* 87.—τελεσφόρον χάριν, a requital (1484) fraught with fulfilment (of my promise).

σφιν is most naturally taken here, with the schol., as = αὐτῷ,

16—2

244   *Oedipus at Colonus*

seeing that vv. 1486 f. refer to Theseus alone; though it is
tenable as = αὐτοῖς, *i.e.* Theseus and his people. The evidence
for σφιν as dat. sing. is slender; but in *Hom. Hymn.* 19. 19
σὺν δέ σφιν ought to mean σὺν Πανί, and in *Hymn.* 30. 9 we
have βρίθει μέν σφιν ἄρουρα φερέσβιος, ἠδὲ κατ' ἀγροὺς | κτήνεσιν
εὐθηνεῖ, οἶκος δ' ἐμπίπλαται ἐσθλῶν, where σφιν should refer
to ὁ δ' ὄλβιος shortly before, and the subject to εὐθηνεῖ
seems clearly to be *the man*, not ἄρουρα. Aesch. *Pers.* 759 is
exactly parallel with this: *i.e.* σφιν would most naturally
refer to Xerxes alone, but *might* refer to Xerxes and his
advisers. In Pind. *Pyth.* 9. 116, again, σφιν might mean
Antaeus and his family. Lycophron 1142 seems to have
meant σφι for αὐτῷ, as the schol. thought. On the whole,
it appears unsafe to deny that poetry sometimes admitted
the use.

τυγχάνων = ὅτε ἐτύγχανον (ὧν ᾔτησα), cp. 579 ff. The absol.
use is made easier by ἀνθ' ὧν ἔπασχον εὖ.

1491—1495 εἴτ' ἄκρα...ικοῦ. A corrupt passage. Reading
ἄκρα | περὶ γύαλ' for ἄκραν | ἐπὶ γύαλον, I take the sense to be:
'*or if* (εἴτ'), in the furthest recesses of the glade, for the honour
of the Poseidonian sea-god, thou art hallowing his altar with
sacrifice, (yet) come.' The precinct of Poseidon at Colonus
was large enough for an ecclesia to be held within it (Thuc. 8.
67). It included the ἄλσος and ναός mentioned by Paus. 1. 30
§ 4. For γύαλον, 'a hollow,' used in the plur. of hollow *ground*,
valleys, or dells, cp. Aesch. *Supp.* 550 Λύδιά τ' ἂγ γύαλα | καὶ
δι' ὀρῶν Κιλίκων. It would apply to the depressions between
the gentle eminences of this στερνούχου χθονός (691),—as *e.g.*
between the two neighbouring knolls at Colonus (cp. 1600).
ἄκρα' περὶ γύαλα means that the altar of Poseidon is in the part
of the large τέμενος furthest from the Chorus. When Theseus
left the scene (1210), his purpose was to send the suppliant
Polyneices from this same altar to Oedipus (cp. 1349). The
Chorus surmise that Theseus may have stayed at the altar to
complete his interrupted sacrifice (888).

In 1491 εἴτ' is intelligible if we suppose the thought to
be,—Come (if thou art near, and at leisure),—*or if* thou art
sacrificing, nevertheless quit the altar, and come.—βούθυτον
proleptic with ἁγίζων: to sacrifice on the altar *is* to 'hallow' it.
—ἑστίαν = βωμόν (888, 1158): Aesch. *Th.* 275 μήλοισιν αἱμάσ-
σοντας ἑστίας θεῶν.—Ποσειδωνίῳ θεῷ = Ποσειδῶνι, not really like
ὁ Βακχεῖος θεός (*O. T.* 1105), 'the god of Βάκχοι' (cp. 678), but

Notes

somewhat similar to the Homeric βίη Ἡρακληείη, etc. Perhaps Ποσειδωνίαν (with ἑστίαν): cp. Pind. N. 6. 46 Ποσειδάνιον ἂν τέμενος.

1496 ἐπαξιοῖ: lit. 'he *deems* thee, thy city, and thy friends *worthy* (of a recompense),—*that he should make a due return*, after receiving benefits.' The inf. is added epexegetically, outside of the construction with the principal verb (cp. 752 ἁρπάσαι, 1212 ζώειν). This is, however, unusually bold, since we should have expected δικαίας χάριτος.

πόλισμα in Attic prose usu. implies a town of the *smaller* kind, as Thuc. 4. 109 (of Thracian tribes) κατὰ δὲ μικρὰ πολίσματα οἰκοῦσι. But Eur. *Med.* 771 has ἄστυ καὶ πόλισμα Παλλάδος, 'the *town* and *stronghold* of Pallas' (Athens), *Bacch.* 919 πόλισμ' ἑπτάστομον (Thebes): so it is used of the grand Cloud-city (Ar. *Av.* 553, 1565): and Her. applies it to Ecbatana (1. 98).—**παθών** does not require us to *supply* anything: it is strictly, 'for treatment received,'—χάριν sufficing to mark that this treatment was good. Cp. 1203.

1500 f. *Enter Theseus.* **αὖ:** cp. 887.—ἠχεῖται is probably pass., as we find ἠχῶ γόους, ὕμνον, etc.—σαφής would ordinarily have been repeated in the second clause (cp. 5); but the equivalent ἐμφανής takes its place: cp. *O. T.* 54 ἄρξεις...κρατεῖς: *Ant.* 669 καλῶς...εὖ: also *El.* 986 f.: *Ai.* 647, 1323. The two adjectives could not be *contrasted.*—ἀστῶν is a certain correction of αὐτῶν, which, as = 'you *yourselves*,' would be very awkward after ὑμῶν and κοινός.

1502 ff. μή τις: 'Can it be some thunderbolt of Zeus, or the rushing onset of some hail-storm (that has scared you)?' —ἐξέπληξεν ὑμᾶς, or the like. Theseus must, of course, be supposed to have heard the thunder which was pealing a few moments before; the doubt implied by μή is merely as to whether the thunder is the cause of the summons.—ὀμβρία χάλαζα, hail falling in a *shower*: cp. *O. T.* 1279 ὄμβρος χαλάζης (n.).—ἐπιρράξασα, from ἐπιρράσσω, which is either (1) trans., 'to dash one thing against another,' as *O.T.* 1244 πύλας...ἐπιρράξασ', 'having dashed the doors together' at her back: or (2) intrans., as here, 'to dash or burst on one': so with Diod. 15. 84 τοῖς Μαντινεῦσιν...ἐπέρραξεν, 'he dashed upon' them.

1504 τοιαῦτα: 'for one might forebode anything when the god sends such a storm as this' (on διοσημίαι see n. to 95):—a courteous way of hinting that their alarm was not unnatural.

1505 f. ποθοῦντι προὐφάνης: cp. *O. T.* 1356 θέλοντι κἀμοὶ
τοῦτ᾽ ἂν ἦν, n.: *Il.* 12. 374 ἐπειγομένοισι δ᾽ ἵκοντο.—καί σοι θεῶν:
'and some god (cp. 1100) hath ordained for thee the good
fortune of this coming': τύχην...ὁδοῦ, a fortune belonging to
(connected with) it.—The MS. θῆκε was a mere blunder caused
by transposition. Cp. above, 974.

1508 f. ῥοπὴ βίου μοι, the turn of the scale (*momentum*)
for my life,—the moment which is to bring it down to death.
Cp. *O. T.* 961 σμικρὰ παλαιὰ σώματ᾽ εὐνάζει ῥοπή.

καὶ θέλω θανεῖν μὴ ψεύσας σε πόλιν τε τήνδε (τούτων) ἅπερ
ξυνῄνεσα, 'and I wish to die without having defrauded thee
and this city of the things on which I agreed.' For the constr.
of ψεύσας cp. on 1145, and for the chief stress on the partic.,
1038: for ξυνῄνεσα, Xen. *Cyr.* 4. 2. 47 ταῦτα συνῄνουν, they
agreed to these terms.

1510 ἐν τῷ δὲ κεῖσαι: usu. explained, 'And on what sign
of thine end *dost thou rely*?' But κεῖμαι ἔν τινι (see on 247)=
'to be situated in a person's power': an analogous use of
κεῖμαι here would give us, 'on what sign *doth thy fate depend*?'
In *Tr.* 82, however, we have ἐν οὖν ῥοπῇ τοιᾷδε κειμένῳ: and,
if the text be sound, κεῖσαι has (I think) a like sense here:
lit., 'at what sign of thy fate art thou in suspense?' The
phrase is thus *virtually* equivalent to ἐν τίνι ῥοπῇ κεῖσαι;—the
τεκμήριον itself standing for the crisis which it marks. The
phrase seems to me possible (for our poet), but slightly
suspicious. We might conjecture καὶ τῷ πέπεισαι: cp. Eur. *Hel.*
1190 ἐννύχοις πεπεισμένη | στένεις ὀνείροις.

1511 f. αὐτοὶ with κήρυκες: the gods herald their own
interposition in his fate. No μάντις, but Heaven itself, gives
the warning.

ψεύδοντες οὐδὲν σημάτων προκ., 'disappointing me in no way
(οὐδὲν adv., cp. 1145) of the signs appointed beforehand' (94):
as Her. 2. 38 (of the Apis) εἰ καθαρὴ (ἡ γλῶσσα) τῶν προκειμένων
σημηίων, the marks *appointed* by sacred law.

1514 The usual order would be αἱ πολλὰ διατελεῖς βρονταί,
'the long-continued thunderings.' But an adj. or partic. is
sometimes thus placed *after* the subst., when the art. and an
adv. (or adverbial phrase) stands *before* it: cp. *O. T.* 1245
τὸν ἤδη Λάιον πάλαι νεκρόν = τὸν ἤδη πάλαι νεκρὸν Λ., the
already long-dead L.: where see n.—πολλὰ = 'very,' with the
adj.: cp. *Ant.* 1046 χοὶ πολλὰ δεινοί: *Ph.* 254 ὦ πόλλ᾽ ἐγὼ
μοχθηρός: *El.* 1326 ὦ πλεῖστα μῶροι: *Il.* 11. 557 πόλλ᾽ ἀέκων.

1515 στράψαντα. στράπτω is not extant in classical Attic, but occurs in Apollonius Rhodius (2nd cent. B.C.) and Oppian (2nd cent. A.D.), also in an Orphic hymn of uncertain date, and in the Anthology. The learned Alexandrian poets had often earlier warrant for this or that word which, as it happens, we cannot trace above them. (Cp. on ἀκορέστατος, 120.) With ἀστράπτω and στράπτω, cp. ἀστεροπή and στεροπή, ἀσπαίρω and σπαίρω, ἀσταφίς and σταφίς, ἄσταχυς and στάχυς, and many other instances in which the longer form and the shorter both belong to the classical age.—χειρὸς τῆς ἀν., gen. of point *whence* with στρ. (*O. T.* 152 Πυθῶνος...ἔβας) rather than possess. gen. with βέλη, 'hurled from the unconquered hand.'

1516 f. θεσπίζονθ': as Oed. had predicted trouble from Thebes at a time when Theseus thought it impossible (606 ff.); Creon had fulfilled the prediction, and had even hinted at future war (1037).

1518 f. σοι ethic dat., τῆδε πόλει dat. of interest; 'which thou shalt have stored up for Athens.' The ethic dat. is often combined with another, as [Eur.] *Rhes.* 644 ἐχθρῶν τις ἡμῖν χρίμπτεται στρατεύματι, we have some foeman approaching our camp. The *v. l.* σῇ τε came of not seeing this.—γήρως ἄλυπα, 'not to be marred by age': see on 677 ἀνήνεμον...χειμώνων.

1520 f. χῶρον...ἐξηγήσομαι, show the way to the place: the literal notion being blended with that of expounding (as the ἐξηγηταί expounded the sacred law). Cp. Her. 3. 4 ἐξηγέεται...τὴν ἔλασιν, expounds the route for the march.—ἄθικτος, pass., as always in Attic: *Tr.* 685 ἀκτῖνός τ' ἀεὶ | θερμῆς ἄθικτον. The act. sense, 'not touching,' occurs later.

1522 f. τοῦτον refers to χῶρον, the place where he was to 'die,' *i.e.* disappear. This place is accurately described at 1590. It was the *grave* (1545) that was to remain secret. But here, by a slip, the poet identifies them. We should not change τοῦτον to τύμβον.—Note how Soph. uses the vagueness of the local legend as to the *grave*. Secrecy was imposed by the dying breath of Oed. himself.

μήθ' οὗ κέκευθε: neither where (precisely) it is concealed, nor (even) whereabouts it is situated.

1524 f. ὥς σοι...τιθῇ. Like τοῦτον in 1522, ὅδε refers to χῶρον (1520), 'this spot'. it is not for ἀνὴρ ὅδε (450). For πρὸ cp. Thuc. 1. 33 ἦν ὑμεῖς ἂν πρὸ πολλῶν χρημάτων καὶ χάριτος

248 Oedipus at Colonus

ἐτιμήσασθε δύναμιν ὑμῖν προσγενέσθαι, αὕτη πάρεστιν αὐτεπάγγελτος.—δορός τ' ἐπακτοῦ. As the hoplite was armed with a δόρυ no less than with a shield, there is no contrast here between infantry and cavalry, but only between citizens and foreign allies. Cp. Isocr. or. 10 § 37 οὐδ' ἐπακτῷ δυνάμει (foreign mercenaries) τὴν ἀρχὴν διαφυλάττων, ἀλλὰ τῇ τῶν πολιτῶν εὐνοίᾳ δορυφορούμενος.

Others join ἀλκήν...γειτόνων, 'a defence against neighbours' (the Thebans, 1534), but, though the objective gen. is quite correct (see on *O. T.* 218), the order of the words makes it hardly possible to disjoin γειτόνων from δορός τ' ἐπακτοῦ.

1526 f. ἃ δ' ἐξάγιστα, 'but as to things which are *banned*' (which cannot be uttered without impiety). Cp. Aeschin. or. 3 § 113 οἱ Λοκροὶ οἱ Ἀμφισσεῖς...τὸν λιμένα τὸν ἐξάγιστον καὶ ἐπάρατον πάλιν ἐτείχισαν: 'the harbour which was *banned* and accursed,'—the Amphictyons having pronounced an ἀρά, which said of the transgressor, ἐναγὴς ἔστω (*ib.* § 110). ἁγίζω = to make ἅγιος (1495): ἐξαγίζω= to devote to avenging gods (cp. ἐξοσιόω, to dedicate), rather than (as some explain it) 'to *de*-consecrate.'

μηδὲ κινεῖται λόγῳ, 'and such things as (μηδέ of the class, cp. 73) are not to be touched upon in speech' (see on 624 τἀκίνητ' ἔπη). The pres. κινεῖται expresses what fate has decreed (*Ph.* 113 αἱρεῖ).—μαθήσει, by sight as well as by hearing: see 1641, 1650.

1530 f. αὐτὸς...σῷζε, 'guard them for thyself alone,'—not merely, 'remember' them, a sense peculiar to the midd. σῴζομαι (Plat. *Theaet.* 153 B, etc., n. on *O. T.* 318).

τῷ προφερτάτῳ μόνῳ: 'but to one, | *Thy chiefest*' (Whitelaw), which well gives the vagueness of the phrase. While the hereditary monarchy lasted, the προφέρτατος would, in fact, be the king's eldest son: afterwards it would be the man whose place in the State made him the proper guardian of the secret. The poet chose a phrase which would cover priestly tradition. I would not, then, change μόνῳ, with Nauck, to γόνῳ. In fr. 401 ἢ γὰρ φίλη 'γὼ τῶνδε τοῦ προφερτέρου, the sense 'elder' is possible, but not certain. The nearest parallel to our passage is Hes. *Th.* 361 προφερεστάτη ἐστιν ἁπασέων, *foremost* among the daughters of Oceanus is Styx; and at 777 she is called πρεσβυτάτη. So, here, the word *suggests* seniority, but without excluding pre-eminence of other kinds.

1533 ff. ἀδῆον contr. for ἀδήϊον, 'unravaged,' from δῆϊος (δῆος Theogn. 552, always Dor. δάϊος in trag.), 'ravaging': σπαρτῶν ἀπ᾽ ἀνδρῶν, 'on the part of,' 'from the quarter of' the Thebans. For ἀπό, cp. Plat. *Phaed.* 83 B οὐδὲν τοσοῦτον κακὸν ἔπαθεν ἀπ᾽ αὐτῶν. Schaefer's ὑπό is admissible (Plat. *Rep.* 366 A ἀζήμιοι...ὑπὸ θεῶν): but ἀπό is fitter here as including all peril from that *region*. When Cadmus was founding Thebes, he required water from a well guarded by a dragon, the off-spring of Ares. He killed the dragon, and sowed its teeth in the ground. Armed men sprang up, who slew each other, all save five. These five, of whom Echion was chief, became the ancestors of the Cadmeans.

αἱ δὲ μυρίαι πόλεις, justifying his hint of possible danger from Thebes. 'Most cities are apt (gnomic aor.) to enter on aggression with a light heart (ῥᾳδίως), even though their neigh-bour is well-behaved.' Cp. what he said of the Thebans in 619 f., where ἐκ σμικροῦ λόγου answers to ῥᾳδίως here.

Greek writers often use μυρίοι to express the notion of *many probabilities against one*. Cp. Her. 8. 119 ἐν μυρίῃσι γνώμῃσι μίαν οὐκ ἔχω ἀντίξοον, 'among ten thousand opinions I have not one against me': *i.e.* not one man in 10,000 would dispute it. Xen. *An.* 2. 1. 19 ἐγώ, εἰ μὲν τῶν μυρίων ἐλπίδων μία τις ὑμῖν ἐστι σωθῆναι πολεμοῦντας βασιλεῖ, συμβουλεύω μὴ παραδιδόναι τὰ ὅπλα: 'if among the ten thousand forebodings (which the situation might suggest) there is one chance of your escape,' etc. So, of 'facing fearful odds, Eur. fr. 588 εἷς τοι δίκαιος μυρίων οὐκ ἐνδίκων | κρατεῖ. It is something more than a mere synonym for αἱ πολλαί. It suggests:— 'Be Athens never so just, there are countless chances to one that Thebes will some day attack it.'—κἄν εὖ τις οἰκῇ, 'even though one (*i.e.* a neighbour) lives aright': cp. Plat. *Rep.* 423 A ἕως ἂν ἡ πόλις σοι οἰκῇ σωφρόνως. (It might also be transitive, 'governs,' *sc.* τὴν πόλιν.) A compliment to Theseus and to Athens is implied: cp. 1125.

1536 γὰρ refers to ῥᾳδίως. '(Outrage is lightly committed), *for* the gods are late, though they are sure, in visiting sin,' and so the hope of *present* impunity emboldens the wicked. See 1370. Cp. *Orac. Sibyll.* 8. 14 ὀψὲ θεῶν ἀλέουσι μύλοι, ἀλέουσι δὲ λεπτά. Longfellow, 'Retribution': *Though the mills of God grind slowly, yet they grind exceeding small.* Hor. *Carm.* 3. 2. 32 *pede Poena claudo.*

εὖ μὲν ὀψὲ δ᾽. When two clauses are co-ordinated by μέν

and δέ, if we wish to subordinate one to the other we must take care that the subordinated clause is that which has μέν. Thus here :—'late, *though* surely.' ' 'Surely, *though* late,' would be ὀψὲ μὲν εὖ δέ. So *O. T.* 419 (n.) βλέποντα νῦν μὲν ὄρθ', ἔπειτα δὲ σκότον=sightless then, though seeing now. It is the necessity of giving the chief emphasis to ὀψέ, not to εὖ, that decides the true relation of this verse to the preceding.

1537 τὰ θεῖ' ἀφείς, having set religion at nought : cp. *O. T.* 910 ἔρρει δὲ τὰ θεῖα.—μαίνεσθαι, the madness of passions which are no longer controlled by religion,—as the frenzy of ambition (371), and of hatred (1392).

1538 f. ὃ μὴ σὺ...βούλου παθεῖν, referring to τὰ θεῖ' ἀφείς etc. To divulge the ἐξάγιστα (1526) would be ἀφεῖναι τὰ θεῖα. The next verse turns off this light reminder by adding that Theseus does not require it. ' Well (οὖν), thou knowest such things, without my precepts.' Thuc. 2. 36 μακρηγορεῖν ἐν εἰδόσιν οὐ βουλόμενος: *Il.* 10. 250 εἰδόσι γάρ τοι ταῦτα μετ' Ἀργείοις ἀγορεύεις. Cp. on 1038.

1540 f. χῶρον : cp. 644.—τοὐκ θεοῦ παρόν : 'that which has come from the god,' (cp. 1694 τὸ φέρον ἐκ θεοῦ,)—the summons as conveyed both by the storm and by an inward prompting.

μηδ' ἔτ' ἐντρεπώμεθα, 'nor longer *hesitate*,' ὀκνῶμεν, μέλλωμεν. ἐντρέπεσθαι (1) 'to turn about': (2) 'to give heed to,' with gen., as *O. T.* 724 : (3) then, absol., *'to feel a scruple or misgiving*,' to hesitate, as here. Intelligible as the third use is, this is perh. the only clear example of it in classical Attic : but cp. Polyb. 31. 12. The hesitation which Oed. deprecates is that which the *others* might feel in acknowledging that the hour of his end had come.

1542—1555 A more splendid dramatic effect than Sophocles has created here could hardly be conceived. Hitherto, throughout the play, Oedipus has been strongly characterised by that timidity in movement, and that sense of physical dependence, which are normal accompaniments of blindness. (Cp. 21, 173 ff., 495 ff., 1206, etc.) Now, suddenly inspired by the Unseen Power which calls him, he becomes the guide of his guides. Now it is they who shrink. Eager and unfaltering, the blind man beckons them on. And so he finally passes from the eyes of the spectators.

1542 f. ὧδ' : see 182.—καινός, of a novel *kind*, 'in strange wise': cp. Plat. *Euthyd.* 271 B καινοί τινες...σοφισταί ..καὶ τίς ἡ σοφία;

Notes 251

1547 τῆδ', ὧδε, τῆδε, lit. 'this way,—hither,—this way';— marking that he is already sure of his path.

1548 ὁ πομπὸς: *Ai.* 831 καλῶ δ' ἅμα | πομπαῖον Ἑρμῆν χθόνιον εὖ με κοιμίσαι: hence ψυχοπομπός (Diod. 1. 96): Hor. *Carm.* I. 10. 17 *Tu pias laetis animas reponis Sedibus.* He was also the guide of the living on errands of danger or guile (*El.* 1395, *Ph.* 133 Ἑ. ὁ πέμπων δόλιος).—ἥ τε νερτέρα θεός: Persephone: *Ant.* 893 ὧν ἀριθμὸν ἐν νεκροῖς | πλεῖστον δέδεκται Περσέφασσ' ὀλωλότων.

1549 f. φῶς ἀφεγγές, light which, for the blind, is no light: cp. 'darkness of life' in Tennyson's lines quoted on 33: σκότον βλέπειν, ἐν σκότῳ ὁρᾶν (*O. T.* 419, 1273). The dying bid farewell to the sunlight, as *Ai.* 856 σὲ δ', ὦ φαεννῆς ἡμέρας τὸ νῦν σέλας | ...προσεννέπω | πανύστατον δή. So here the blind man, for whom light has long been changed to darkness, bids farewell to his *memory* of it.—πρόσθε, before he blinded himself (cp. *O. T.* 1183). The full thought is,—'Once I *saw* thee, but for long I have only *felt* thee, and now I *feel* thee for the last time.' Whitelaw cp. *Par. Lost* 3. 21, *Thee I revisit safe,* | *And* feel *thy sovran vital* lamp; *but thou* | *Revisit'st not these eyes.* And *Lear* 4. 1. 23 *Might I but live to see thee* in my touch, | *I'd say I had eyes again.*

1551 f. τὸν τελευταῖον βίον is most simply taken (1) as = 'the last part of my life,' its close. He is going '*to hide the close of his life with Hades*' (παρ' Ἅιδην since motion is implied), not merely because he is about to quit life, but because he is destined to quit it by a strange passing not beheld of men.—(2) We might also take τελευταῖον as proleptic adj. *with art.* (see on 1089 τὸν εὔαγρον): 'to hide my life, so that it shall be ended.' I prefer (1).

1553 αὐτός τε: cp. on 448. Theseus and his realm are identified, as 308 f., 1125, 1496.—πρόσπολοι, like ὀπάονες (1103). Here his Attic lieges generally seem meant, rather than his followers from *Athens* as opposed to the Coloniates (1066). So 1496 σε καὶ πόλισμα καὶ φίλους.

1554 f. κἄπ' εὐπραξίᾳ: 'and *in* your prosperous *state*,' ἐπί expressing the attendant condition (as it denotes the terms of a treaty): cp. *El.* 108 ἐπὶ κωκυτῷ... | ...ἠχώ...προφωνεῖν: *Ant.* 759 ἐπὶ ψόγοισι δεννάζειν: Aesch. *Eum.* 1047 ὀλολύξατε νῦν ἐπὶ μολπαῖς: Thuc. 7. 81 § 5 ἐπ' εὐπραγίᾳ ἤδη σαφεῖ ('when success was now assured').—μέμνησθε, imper., not μεμνῆσθε, optat.: for this depends on them, but their weal (εὐδ. γένοισθε) on the gods.—**εὐτυχεῖς ἀεί**: (remember me), for your lasting welfare. If they duly revere his memory, their good-fortune will abide.

1556—1578 *Fourth stasimon.* *Strophe* 1556—1567 = *antistr.* 1568—1578.—*The metre is logaoedic.*—'*May Persephone and Pluto suffer Oedipus to pass painlessly to the place of the dead. May the Erinyes and Cerberus spare to vex his path. Hear us, O Death.*'

1556 εἰ θέμις ἐστί: a propitiatory address, since Pluto and the other χθόνιοι θεοί are stern to human prayers. So Hades is δίχα παιάνων (Eur. *I. T.* 185), ἀμείλιχος ἠδ᾽ ἀδάμαστος (*Il.* 9. 158). Hor. *Carm.* 2. 14. 5 *Non si tricenis, quotquot eunt dies, Amice, places illacrimabilem Plutona tauris.*—**τὰν ἀφανῆ θεόν**, 'the Unseen goddess,' Persephone (1548), an unusual title, perhaps suggested by the literal sense of Ἅιδης: cp. Pind. fr. 207 Ταρτάρου πυθμὴν πιέζει σ᾽ ἀφανοῦς: Aesch. *Th.* 859 τὰν ἀνάλιον | πάνδοκον εἰς ἀφανῆ τε χέρσον.

1558 f. ἐννυχίων ἄναξ (*Tr.* 501 τον ἔννυχον Ἅιδαν), suggested by *Il.* 20. 61 ἄναξ ἐνέρων Ἀϊδωνεύς. This poetically lengthened form of Ἅιδης (trisyllabic only here) occurs also *Il.* 5. 190, Hes. *Theog.* 913, and oft. in later poets. A stream of the Troad on Mt Ida was called Ἀϊδωνεύς from its disappearing into the ground, Paus. 10. 12. 3 f.

λίσσομαι = ἐξ ἄντρων in the antistrophe (1571): but, since the first syll. of ἄντρων is 'irrational,' *i.e.* a long syllable doing duty for a short, the normal choree λισσο is defensible. The schol. had in his text δίδου μοι,—not instead of λίσσομαι, but (as his words show) in addition to it. As the construction of λίσσομαι was clear enough, δίδου μοι would rather seem to have been a gloss on some imperat. with μοι. Possibly νεῦσόν μοι (cp. *Ph.* 484 νεῦσον,...πείσθητι: Pind. *P.* 1. 71 νεῦσον, Κρονίων) which may have been current as a *v. l.* for λίσσομαι.

1561 ff. L gives μήτ᾽ ἐπιπόνω (*sic*) μήτ᾽ ἐπιβαρυαχεῖ. In the antistrophic verse (1572) the words φύλακα παρ᾽ Ἅιδᾳ tally metrically with ἐπὶ βαρυᾶχεῖ, Doric for βαρυηχεῖ. The question is:—How are the words μήτ᾽ ἐπιπόνω μήτ᾽ to be so corrected, that they shall metrically answer to ἀδάματόν? The absence of the ι subscript agrees with the hypothesis of an original μητ᾽ ἐπιπόνως. If, with Wecklein, we regard this as having been a gloss on a genuine ἄπονα (adv. neut. pl., 319), and read ἄπονα μηδ᾽ ἐπὶ βαρυαχεῖ, an exact correspondence is obtained, without further change in the strophe, and without any change in the antistrophe. The sense is also clear.

ἐπὶ βαρναχεῖ...μόρῳ, 'by a doom exciting sore lament': for the prep. (= 'with') see on 1554. This prayer to Pluto needed the preface εἰ θέμις (1556), since he στεναγμοῖς καὶ γόοις πλουτίζεται (*O. T.* 30).

ἐξανύσαι, reach: *Ai.* 607 ἀνύσειν...Ἀιδαν: *Ant.* 804 τὸν παγκοίτην...θάλαμον | ...ἀνύτουσαν. Eur. *Or.* 1684 λαμπρῶν ἄστρων πόλον ἐξανύσας.—παγκευθῆ, 'all-enshrouding,' as Hades is πάνδοκος (n. 1556), πολυδέγμων (*Hom. Hymn.* 5. 31), παγκοίτας (*Ant.* 810), πολύκοινος (*Ai.* 1193).—πλάκα (1577, 1681), a plain: cp. the *lugentes campi* of Vergil's Inferno (*Aen.* 6. 441).

1565 f. The traditional text, πολλῶν γὰρ ἂν καὶ μάταν πημάτων ἰκνουμένων, is usu. understood: 'for, whereas sorrows were *coming upon him* in great number *and without cause* (καὶ μάταν), a just god may now lift him up once more.'

In this there are two difficulties. (1) ἰκνουμένων is thus the partic. of the *imperf.*,=ἐπεὶ ἰκνεῖτο. But manifestly the partic. ought here to have a *pres.* sense, '*are* coming on him.' When the pres. partic. (or inf.) serves for the imperf., there is usually something in the context which prevents too great ambiguity, as is the case in 1587 (παρών), and *O. T.* 835 τοῦ παρόντος, where see n.

(2) μάταν is strange in the sense '*without cause*' as = '*undeservedly*.' Another proposed version, 'without any good result so far,' seems inadmissible. Nor can the sense be 'wildly' (*temere*). Hence there is ground for suspecting καὶ μάταν. I would suggest ἰκνούμενον, and, for ἂν καὶ μάταν, αὖ (or ἂν) τέρματ' ἂν: '*now that he is coming to the goal of many sorrows.*' So the pl. *El.* 686 δρόμου...τὰ τέρματα. A doubled ἂν would not be unsuitable here, as expressing earnest hope; but αὖ, which MSS. often confuse with ἂν, would well mark the turning-point: and for its combination with πάλιν cp. 1418.

1567. The MS. σε is possible; but Reiske's σφε has very strong probability. Changes to, and from, apostrophe are certainly not rare in choral odes; but this would (to my mind) be a somewhat harsh example.—αὔξοι, 'uplift,' 'raise to honour: cp. *O. T.* 1092 (n.), *Tr.* 116 (n. on 1453 f.).

1568. χθόνιαι θεαί: schol. Ἐρινύες. Hardly Demeter and Persephone (683), who would not be thus associated with the fell Cerberus.—σῶμά τ', 'dread form of the unconquered hound': the periphrasis suggests a more vivid image of the dread monster: cp. *Tr.* 508 φάσμα ταύρου: Verg. *Aen.* 6. 289 *et forma tricorporis umbrae* (Geryon). Eur. *Phoen.* 1508 Σφιγγὸς ἀοιδοῦ σῶμα: *Her. Fur.* 24 τρισώματον κύνα. Cp. *Tr.* 1097 τόν θ᾽ ὑπὸ χθονὸς | ᾽Αιδου τρίκρανον σκύλακ᾽, ἀπρόσμαχον τέρας. Homer mentions 'the dog of Hades' only in reference to Eurystheus sending Heracles ἐξ ᾽Ερέβευς ἄξοντα κύνα στυγεροῦ ᾽Αΐδαο (*Il.* 8. 368, *Od.* 11. 625). The name Cerberus occurs first in Hes. *Th.* 311, where he is the offspring of Typhaon and Echidna, and has fifty heads: Horace makes him *centiceps*, *Carm.* 2. 13. 34.

1569 ff. It seems clear that the φασὶ after πύλαισι in the MSS. is an interpolated gloss on λόγος ἔχει. If φασὶ were genuine, it must go with εὐνᾶσθαι only, κνυζεῖσθαι depending on λόγος ἔχει: a construction awkward beyond example. πολυξένοις for πολυξέστοις appears certain: cp. Aesch. *Suppl.* 157 τὸν πολυξενώτατον | Ζῆνα τῶν κεκμηκότων | ἱξόμεσθα σὺν κλάδοις | ἀρτάναις θανοῦσαι. See above on παγκευθῆ (n. 1561 ff.), and cp. *Ant.* 893 in n. on 1548.

1571 While κνυζᾶσθαι is the form recommended by the analogy of like words for the sounds of animals (βληχάομαι, μυκάομαι, ὑλάομαι, etc.), κνυζεῖσθαι has L's support, and also seems better just after εὐνᾶσθαι. If right here, it is, however, much the rarer form of the two.—ἐξ ἄντρων: Verg. *Aen.* 6. 417 *Cerberus haec ingens latratu regna trifauci Personat, adverso recubans immanis in antro.*

1572 f. φύλακα. Hes. *Th.* 767 ἔνθα θεοῦ χθονίου πρόσθεν δόμοι ἠχήεντες... | ἑστᾶσιν· δεινὸς δὲ κύων προπάροιθε φυλάσσει. He fawns on those who enter: ἐξελθεῖν δ᾽ οὐκ αὖτις ἐᾷ πάλιν, ἀλλὰ δοκεύων | ἐσθίει ὅν κε λάβῃσι πυλέων ἔκτοσθεν ἰόντα.— λόγος...ἔχει, transitive, like Pind. *P.* 1. 96 ἐχθρὰ Φάλαριν κατέχει...φάτις, rather than intransitive like ὁ λόγος κατέχει ('the report *prevails* that...') Thuc. 1. 10 § 2. Cp. Paus. 9. 3 § 9 μαντεύεσθαι δὲ τὰς νύμφας τὸ ἀρχαῖον αὐτόθι ἔχει λόγος.

1574 τόν (as relat.) is more probable than ὅν after the vowel: cp. *O. T.* 199 ἔρχεται· | τόν, ὦ τᾶν πυρφόρων.—Γᾶς παῖ. This cannot mean Pluto, who was the son of Cronus and Rhea; nor Cerberus (usu. called son of Typhaon and Echidna), unless with Nauck we change τόν to δός. Thanatos is not elsewhere thus described, (in Hes. *Th.* 211 he is the son of Νύξ, no father being named,)—but is probably meant here. The invocation in 1578 is certainly addressed to him.

1575 f. The MSS. have ἐν καθαρῷ βῆναι. 'And I pray that he (Cerberus)...may *leave a clear path* for the stranger,' as he passes to Hades. βῆναι ἐν καθαρῷ τῷ ξένῳ must mean strictly, 'to go *on to clear ground* for the stranger,' *i.e.* to pass to ground which *he* will not traverse, leaving *his* path clear. ἐν καθαρῷ is thus virtually equivalent to ἐκποδών. Madvig's ἐκ καθαροῦ is proleptic:—'go out of the path, *so as to leave it clear.*' I suspect the text to be unsound. Two views are possible. (1) τόν in 1574 may be corrupt. If (*e.g.*) Hartung's τόδ' were read, the sense would be:—'This is my prayer for the stranger..., that he may *move in a clear path.*' Such a view best suits the natural sense of ἐν καθαρῷ βῆναι. (2) τόν may be sound, while ἐν καθαρῷ may have supplanted something like ἐκ καθόδου. Or βῆναι may have come (*e.g.*) from φθῆναι: 'I pray for the stranger that he speed safely past Cerberus to clear ground.'—πλάκας: see on 1564.

1578 τὸν αἰένυπνον, Death, the giver of eternal sleep, the ἀτέρμονα νήγρετον ὕπνον (Moschus 3. 105): in contrast with his brother who λύει πεδήσας (*Ai.* 676).

1579—1779 *Exodos. The passing of Oedipus is told. His daughters make lament. Antigone prays of Theseus that he send them to Thebes, if haply they may avert the coming strife of their brothers; and he promises to do so.*

1579 f. ξυντομώτατον (neut. as adv.) is the best correction of the MS. ξυντομωτάτως. A few such forms in -ως have MS. authority among good writers, though they are mostly comparatives, as βεβαιοτέρως, ἐρρωμενεστέρως (Isocr.), καλλιόνως, σαφεστέρως, etc. In Eur. *Suppl.* 967 γηράσκω δυστηνότατος | οὔτ' is corrected by Reiske to δυστηνοτάτως, which metre commends: but this is an almost isolated example. There is thus a strong presumption in favour of the form in -ον where, as here, it can easily be restored.—λέξας...ὀλωλότα, 'I should give my news most briefly if I said that Oedipus is gone': cp. *O. T.* 463 εἶπε...τελέσαντα, n.

1581 f. ἃ δ' ἦν τὰ πραχθέντ'. ἅ = ἅτινα: see on 1171. 'But as to what the occurrences were, *neither* is the tale possible for me to tell in brief compass, *nor* (were) the events (brief) which happened there': *sc.* οὔτε (βραχέα ἦν) τἄργ'. That is, resolving the parataxis with οὔτε—οὔτε:—'But as to what occurred, the tale cannot be briefly told, *as neither* were the occurrences themselves brief.' φράσαι (epexeg. inf.) further defines πάρεστιν.

1584 The MS. words τὸν ἀεί (or ἀἰεί) certainly conceal a fault, which is perhaps very old. We cannot supply χρόνον ('for ever'). Nor do I see how τὸν ἀεὶ βίοτον could mean,

256   *Oedipus at Colonus*

'the life of all his days' ('What life, life-long, was his,'
Whitelaw). The schol. gives nothing better than a fatuous
interpretation of τὸν ἀεὶ βίοτον as τὸ μακρὸν γῆρας. The first
question is whether the fault is confined to ἀεί. (1) If so, τόν
being sound, ἀεί may conceal another adv., or an adj.: or may
have arisen from some ancient mutilation of ἄνδρα. The very
simplicity of κεῖνον τὸν ἄνδρα has a solemnity which is not
unfitting here. (2) If τόν is corrupt, then there are these
possibilities. (a) τὸν ἀεί may conceal one word, such (e.g.) as
πάνοιζυν, 'all-wretched,' Aesch. *Cho.* 49. (b) τόν may have
been inserted to supply a lost syllable. This view suits (e.g.)
ἐκεῖνον ἄρτι, or Hermann's κεῖνόν γ' ἐσαιεί (to which, however,
the γ' is fatal).

1585 f. ἀπόνῳ, as they themselves had just prayed for him
Cp. the prayer of Ajax to Hermes Chthonios that he may die
ἀσφάδαστος (*Ai.* 833).—τοῦτ'...ἤδη means, 'here we come to
the point which is indeed (καί) worthy of wonder': cp. Plat.
Sympos. 204 B δῆλον δὴ, ..τοῦτό γε ἤδη καὶ παιδί, ὅτι, etc.

1588 ὑφηγητῆρος is supported against ὑφ' ἡγητῆρος (a) by
such examples as 83, ὡς ἐμοῦ μόνης πέλας, (b) by the fact that
the compound with ὑπό is suitable where, as here, the sense
is that no one so much as hinted or indicated the way.
Cp. Plat. *Crito* 54 E πράττωμεν ταύτῃ, ἐπειδὴ ταύτῃ ὁ θεὸς
ὑφηγεῖται. So *O. T.* 966 ὧν ὑφηγητῶν ('on whose showing'):
ib. 1260 ὡς ὑφηγητοῦ τινος.

1590 καταρράκτην (from ῥάσσω to strike hard, or dash,
cp. 1503), lit. 'dashing or rushing down'; Strabo 10. 640
τηρήσας καταρράκτην ὄμβρον: here, of a cleft *descending abruptly*
into the ground, 'the sheer threshold.'

1591 χαλκοῖς βάθροισι. *Il.* 8. 13 ἐς Τάρταρον ἠερόεντα, | τῆλε
μάλ' ἧχι βάθιστον ὑπὸ χθονός ἐστι βέρεθρον, | ἔνθα σιδήρειαί τε
πύλαι καὶ χάλκεος οὐδός. Hes. *Theog.* 811 (of Tartarus) ἔνθα
δὲ μαρμάρεαί τε πύλαι καὶ χάλκεος οὐδός, | ἀστεμφής, ῥίζῃσι
διηνεκέεσσιν ἀρηρώς, | αὐτοφυής: 'a brazen threshold, im-
moveable, *fixed in the earth by roots without a break,* of
natural growth,' *i.e.* not wrought by human hands. The rift
or cavern at Colonus, from which the adjoining region took
the name of the χαλκοῦς ὁδός (see on 57), was locally supposed
to be connected with the 'brazen threshold' below by brazen
steps reaching down into the under-world. The stress laid on
the χαλκοῖς βάθροισι here, and the name 'Brazen Threshold'
itself, rather suggest that the myth was visibly symbolised by

some artificial steps made at the top of the steep rift.—γῆθεν, 'in the earth,' 'deep down.'

1592 πολυσχίστων. Several paths converged at the καταρ-ράκτης ὁδός. We are reminded, perhaps designedly, of that σχιστὴ ὁδός in Phocis at which the misfortunes of his early manhood began (*O. T.* 733).

1593 κοίλου...κρατῆρος. (1) Schneidewin takes this to mean *a large brazen vessel* set in a rift of the ground, over which Theseus and Peirithous slew the victims when they made their pact (ὅρκια ἔταμον). He cites Eur. *Suppl.* 1201, where Theseus is directed thus to make a covenant with Adrastus; the throats of nine sheep are to be cut over a bronze τρίπους, and the terms of the pact (ὅρκοι) are then to be graven in its basin (τρίποδος ἐν κοίλῳ κύτει). (2) The schol., whose view is more likely, understands a *basin or hollow in the rock*; and took this κρατήρ or μυχός in the rock to be the actual cavity in which the καταρράκτης ὁδός began. In each case the κρατήρ was close to the ὁδός. Thus Plat. *Phaedo* 111 D says of the subterranean cavities, συντετρῆσθαί τε πολλαχῇ...καὶ διεξόδους ἔχειν, ᾗ πολὺ μὲν ὕδωρ ῥεῖν ἐξ ἀλλήλων εἰς ἀλλήλους ὥσπερ εἰς κρατῆρας.

Θησέως. Theseus went down to Hades with Peirithous, king of the Thessalian Lapithae, to help him in carrying off Persephone. Both heroes were made prisoners by Pluto. Theseus was afterwards delivered by Heracles, when sent by Eurystheus to capture Cerberus. According to another version, Heracles delivered Peirithous also.

1594 Περίθου. Elsewhere in extant classical literature the form is Πειρίθοος or (Attic) Πειρίθους. But a form Περίθους is sufficiently attested by the name of the Attic deme of which this hero was eponymus. Vases and inscriptions also give it. There is no need, then, to write Πειρίθου Θησέως τε, as Blaydes does.

κεῖται...ξυνθήματα: schol. οἷον ὑπομνήματα τῆς πίστεως ἧς ἔθεντο πρὸς ἀλλήλους: *i.e.* he understood by κεῖται some visible memorial. This seems clearly right. The local belief probably pointed to characters or marks on the rock. See the schol. on Ar. *Eq.* 785 ἔστι δὲ καὶ ἀγέλαστος πέτρα καλουμένη παρὰ τοῖς Ἀθηναίοις, ὅπου καθίσαι φασὶ Θησέα μέλλοντα καταβαίνειν εἰς Ἅδου. Wherever this ἀγέλαστος πέτρα was, there must have been a cavern suggestive of the descent to Hades. The phrase, παρὰ τοῖς Ἀθηναίοις, would cover Colonus.

1595 μέσος usu. takes a simple gen. of the extremes, and is not elsewhere found with ἀπό, but the latter is natural (Plat. *Parm.* 145 B τό γε μέσον ἴσον τῶν ἐσχάτων ἀπέχει). The κρατήρ is then one of the four points from which the point denoted by μέσος is measured. The second ἀπό may be taken with ἀχέρδου also: cp. *O. T.* 734, 761. With L's ἐφ' οὗ: '*At* which' (the κρατήρ) he halted, midway between' the other objects, cp. *Il.* 22. 153 ἔνθα δ' ἐπ' αὐτάων πλυνοὶ εὐρέες ἐγγὺς ἔασιν, *at* the springs. With ἐφ', L's μέσον is possible; 'at which, midway as it is.' With Brunck's ἀφ' οὗ, it becomes necessary to read μέσος.

τοῦ τε Θορικίου πέτρου. It was from Thoricus (Apollod. 2. 4. 7) that 'radiant Eos caught up Cephalus to the gods' (Eur. *Hipp.* 455). Hence the name of that place may have been associated in the Athenian mind with the idea of removal to another world. Θορικός was a town and deme of Attica, belonging to the tribe Ἀκαμαντίς, on the S.E. coast, about 6 miles N. of Sunium, and 42 S.E. of Colonus. If Θορικίου is unsound, the familiarity of Θορίκιοι as a deme-name may have suggested it. Schneidewin's τρικορύφου rests on the schol. to 57: καί τις τῶν χρησμοποιῶν φησί· Βοιωτοὶ δ' ἵπποιο ποτιστείχουσι Κολωνόν, | ἔνθα λίθος τρικάρανος ἔχει καὶ χάλκεος οὐδός. But, if Θορικίου came from τρικορύφου, the genuine word must have been well-nigh obliterated.

1596 κοίλης τ' ἀχέρδου: schol. τῆς τὸν πυθμένα ἐχούσης ὑπόκενον, σαπέντα. The wild pear gave its name to the Attic deme Ἀχερδοῦς (Ἀχερδούσιοι); as in its other form, ἀχράς, to Ἀχραδίνη, the E. quarter of Syracuse. If, as the schol. states (n. 1593), the local myth placed the rape of Persephone here, this old tree may have been pointed out as the spot whence she was snatched. An ἐρινεός (wild fig-tree) by the Cephisus was connected with a like legend (Paus. 1. 38. 5). A wild olive-tree (κότινος) at Troezen was associated with the disaster of Hippolytus (2. 32. 10), as the στρεπτὴ ἐλαία at Epidaurus (see on 694) with Heracles.—κἀπὸ λαῖνου τάφου, 'and from the marble tomb.' The λάϊνος τάφος is opposed to a τύμβος of earth or a λάρναξ of wood (Thuc. 2. 34): it would commonly denote an oblong monument with a flat slab (τράπεζα) on top, the sides being sometimes sculptured.

The power and beauty of this passage are in no way lessened for us because we know nothing of the basin or the stone, the tree or the tomb. Rather it might be said that the

very fact of our ignorance illustrates the spirit in which these
details are introduced. They show us how the blind man,
who had never been at Colonus before, placed himself at
precisely the due point in the midst of its complex sanctities.
The god made him as one who had the most intimate and
minute knowledge of the ground.

1597 ἔλυσε, as *Tr.* 924 λύει τὸν αὐτῆς πέπλον: while the
midd. in *Il.* 17. 318 λύοντο δὲ τεύχεα refers to Greeks stripping
Trojans.—δυσπινεῖς: cp. 1258. He prepares to put on the garb
of the dead.

1598 ῥυτῶν (ῥέω), flowing, ἐξ ἀειρύτου κρήνης (469).

1600 f. They go to a hillock a little way off, on which
was a shrine of Demeter Euchloös. See map II.—εὐχλόου,
as protecting the young green corn and other young vegetation
(χλόη), Paus. 1. 22. 3 ἔστι δὲ (at Athens) καὶ Γῆς κουροτρόφου
καὶ Δήμητρος ἱερὸν Χλόης. She was associated with Γῆ κουροτρόφος and with Apollo in the Χλόεια held on 6th Thargelion
(latter part of May).

προσόψιον, not found elsewhere, is read by L and Suidas.
'The hill of Demeter, in full view': rather than, 'the hill
looking on Demeter.' The act. sense is possible (*Ph.* 1040
θεοί τ' ἐπόψιοι), but the other seems better here: cp. *Ant.* 1110
ὁρμᾶσθ'...εἰς ἐπόψιον τόπον.

1602 f. 'πόρευσαν and πόρευσαν are alike admissible in this
ῥῆσις (cp. 1606 ff.), but the former seems preferable on the
general principle of not multiplying omissions of augment
without necessity. (Cp. *Tr.* 560 μισθοῦ 'πόρευε.) '*Brought*
this behest,' *i.e.* the water for which he had asked. Eur.
Phoen. 984 MEN. χρημάτων δὲ τίς πόρος; | ΚΡ. ἐγὼ πορεύσω
χρυσόν. Cp. on 1458 πόροι.—ταχεῖ σὺν χρ.: cp. 885: *Tr.* 395
σὺν χρόνῳ βραδεῖ μολών.—λουτροῖς, as the dead were washed:
Lucian *De Luctu* 11 μετὰ ταῦτα δὲ λούσαντες αὐτούς...προτίθενται.
So *Ai.* 1405 λουτρῶν ὁσίων (for the dead Ajax).

1603 ᾗ νομίζεται, as the dead were usually dressed for
burial, *i.e.* in white.

1604 παντὸς...δρῶντος. (1) Usu. explained:—'when he
had content of all *service*,' *i.e.* when his daughters had done
for him all that he wished. Then πᾶν δρῶν will be 'every
activity' of attendants: cp. the Homeric δρηστῆρες, δρήστειραι,
of servants, *Od.* 10. 349 etc. (2) A better view is: 'when
of doing all he had content' (as Whitelaw), when πᾶν δρῶν
is his *own* activity. Cp. τὸ βουλόμενον τῆς γνώμης and similar

phrases (see on 267): also Thuc. I. 142 ἐν τῷ μὴ μελετῶντι, 'in the absence of practice.' But the absence of the art. makes πᾶν δρῶν a bolder expression than any of these; nor can the adverbial ἐν ἀμείβοντι, 'alternately,' (Pind. *N.* 11. 42,) be properly compared. I suspect, then, that the text is corrupt. The obvious ἔρωτος ('desire') should not be too lightly rejected: cp. 436.

1605 ἀργὸν, neglected: see on *O. T.* 287.

1606 κτύπησε: for the omission of the augment, see on *O. T.* 1249. Ζεὺς χθ.: *Il.* 9. 457 Ζεύς τε καταχθόνιος καὶ ἐπαινὴ Περσεφόνεια. At Corinth Pausanias saw three images of Zeus, one being Χθόνιος, another Ὕψιστος, the third nameless (2. 2. 8). The Zeus Chthonios was a benevolent Pluto, associated with Demeter in the prayers of the husbandman (Hes. *Op.* 465).

1608 f. οὐδ' ἀνίεσαν, 'did not remit' (cp. ἀνιέναι φυλακήν, ἄσκησιν, ἔχθραν, etc.); *not*, 'did not send up' (as in *O. T.* 1277, a different context). κλαυθμός was commonly associated with κομμός (*planctus*) and γόος. If Soph. had meant otherwise, he would have added another verse with ἀλλά.—παμμήκεις, very loud: see on 489.

1610 ἐξαίφνης, because they burst into their wail when the sudden peal of thunder was heard.

1613 πάντα τἀμά, all that concerns my earthly life.

1614 ff. τὴν δυσπόν.: cp. 509: Aesch. *Pers.* 515 ὦ δυσπόνητε δαῖμον.—ἀμφ' ἐμοί: cp. *El.* 1143 quoted on 345; τροφήν, *ib.* and 352.—ἀλλά...γάρ, 'but (I need not speak of hardship), *for*':='but indeed': cp. on 988.—ἐν...ἔπος, 'one word,' viz. φιλεῖν. Cp. *Ant.* 53 μήτηρ καὶ γυνή, διπλοῦν ἔπος. (This is better than 'one *saying*,' *i.e.* reflection.)—λύει, cancels.

1618 f. τητώμεναι: cp. on 1200.—The simplest view of the MS. τὸ λοιπὸν ἤδη βίοτον διάξετον is Elmsley's, that βίοτον was written by a mistake for τὸν βίον. But τοῦ βίου (Suidas) is equally possible: cp. *O. T.* 1487 νοούμενος τὰ λοιπὰ τοῦ πικροῦ βίου. The constr. τὸν λοιπὸν...τοῦ βίου would be a rare one: Dem. or. 15 § 16 πρὸς τὸν λοιπὸν τοῦ χρόνου, Xen. *Cyr.* 4. 5. 1 τοῦ σίτου...τὸν ἥμισυν: so ἡ πολλὴ τῆς γῆς, etc.

1620 f. ἐπ' ἀλλήλ. ἀμφικ.: *i.e.* each of the daughters had twined their arms about her father, while he had also embraced them. Cp. *Od.* 8. 523 ὡς δὲ γυνὴ κλαίῃσι φίλον πόσιν ἀμφιπεσοῦσα.—λύγδην from λύζω, *singultare*. *Anthol. Pal.* 15. 28. 3 λιγέως ὀλοφύρετο μήτηρ, | λύγδην, ἱσταμένη.

1623 σιωπή, a moment of absolute stillness, after the wails

Notes

261

had subsided. Job iv. 15 'Then a spirit passed before my face; the hair of my flesh stood up. It stood still, but I could not discern the appearance thereof; a form was before mine eyes: there was silence, and I heard a voice.'—τινὸς: Eur. *Andr.* 1147 πρὶν δή τις ἀδύτων ἐκ μέσων ἐφθέγξατο | δεινόν τι καὶ φρικῶδες.

1624 f. θώϋξεν αὐτόν. Porson on Eur. *Phoen.* 5 wished to read θεῶν ἐθώϋξ' (omitting αὐτόν). But the change is unnecessary, if occasional omission of the augment is conceded to such ῥήσεις as this: cp. 1606. θωΰσσω denotes a loud, urgent cry (cp. Eur. *Hipp.* 219 κυσὶ θωΰξαι): here with acc. of the person called.—πάντας, subject to στῆσαι. For this phrase, instead of πᾶσι στῆναι τρίχας, see on 150 φυτάλμιος. Cp. 1464.—φόβῳ is causal dat. with στῆσαι, rather than modal dat. with δείσαντας.—ἐξαίφνης, though it has come in 1623 (and 1610): see on 554.

1626 πολλὰ πολλαχῇ, 'with repeated and manifold calling.' There seems to be no genuine instance of πολλαχῇ meaning simply πολλάκις. It is always 'by many routes' (as Xen. *An.* 7. 3. 12), 'in many ways' (Her. 6. 21), or 'on many grounds' (*id.* 1. 42). The phrase here, then, cannot mean '*loudly*' (πολλά) and *often*': nor can it be merely, 'again and again.' But πολλαχῇ need not refer to different *forms of words*. It is enough to understand it of varying tones in which the name was sounded, or of the voice seeming to come from different points at successive moments.

1627 ὦ οὗτος. So the goddess Athena, calling Ajax to come forth from his tent; *Ai.* 71 οὗτος, σὲ τὸν τὰς etc.: 89 ὦ οὗτος, Αἴας, δεύτερόν σε προσκαλῶ, where Αἴας is voc. (*ib.* 482), as Οἰδίπους here (cp. 461). οὗτος ('Ho there!'), thus used, implies that the person addressed is not duly heeding the speaker; here it helps to express impatience. So, when Medea turns her face away from Jason's smooth words, he cries to her, αὕτη, τί χλωροῖς δακρύοις τέγγεις κόρας; etc. (*Med.* 922). There is nothing of *roughness* in the phrase, except in the particular combination οὗτος σύ (*O. T.* 532, 1121: Eur. *Hec.* 1280).

1628 χωρεῖν: cp. the emphatic place of δεῖξαι, *O. T.* 278. Nauck's μέλλομεν; | χώρει· by the change to the singular number, breaks the companionship of Oedipus with the Unseen.—τἀπὸ σοῦ adv., βραδύνεται pass. impers.: delay is made on thy part. Cp. Eur. *Tro.* 74 ἕτοιμ' ἃ βούλει τἀπ' ἐμοῦ: Ar. *Plut.* 100 ἄφετον με νῦν· ἴστον γὰρ ἤδη τἀπ᾽ ἐμοῦ (for in both places it is ἀπό rather than ἐπί). Cp. 293.

1630 οἱ, ethic dat., 'for him,' as a grace to him: cp. 81. The enclitic almost adheres to μολεῖν, while γῆς is naturally drawn to ἄνακτα: thus the two monosyllables in the 3rd foot do not hurt the rhythm.—Theseus, with attendants, had followed Oed. to the ὁδός (see 1589), but had remained apart while the daughters ministered to their father (1598—1603). He is now summoned to approach them.

1632 ὁρκίαν, the conjecture of P. N. Papageorgius, is the best emendation of the certainly corrupt ἀρχαίαν. It gives exactly what we need, viz. such an epithet for πίστιν as marks the special solemnity of the pledge. Cp. Plat. *Legg.* 843 A φιλίαν τε καὶ ἔχθραν ἔνορκον. The occurrence of ὅρκιος in 1637 cannot be made an objection (cp. 544 n.); on the contrary, it rather confirms ὁρκίαν here. Theseus did just what Oedipus asked.

ἀρχαίαν has been explained as follows:—(1) 'Thy right hand, *that time-honoured pledge.*' (2) Thy pledge, '*which some day will be old,*' *i.e.* which you are sure to observe permanently. (3) 'A pledge of such good faith as you have always observed.' (4) A modification of the last view refers ἀρχαίαν to v. 631, as = 'the pledge given at the beginning (of our intercourse).'

(1) Two other conjectures claim notice. ἀρθμίαν (Wecklein) = 'in a friendly compact.' Cp. *Od.* 16. 427 οἱ δ᾽ ἡμῖν ἄρθμιοι ἦσαν, 'they were in amity with us.' But this epithet does not strengthen πίστιν. (2) ἀρκίαν (L. Schmidt) = 'sure.' The only support for this is the epic phrase μισθὸς ἄρκιος (*Il.* 10. 304, *Od.* 18. 358, Hes. *Op.* 368).

1634 ἑκών, 'if thou canst help it': cp. Plat. *Prot.* 345 D ὃς ἂν ἑκὼν μηδὲν κακὸν ποιῇ: in prose more often with εἶναι added, as *Symp.* 214 E ἑκὼν γὰρ εἶναι οὐδὲν ψεύσομαι: almost always in sentences which contain or imply a negative; but Her. 7. 164 has ἑκών τε εἶναι καὶ δεινοῦ ἐπιόντος οὐδενὸς... καταθεὶς τὴν ἀρχήν.

1635 μέλλῃς, *sc.* τελεῖν: φρονῶν εὖ, 'wishing them well.' Cp. *O. T.* 1066 καὶ μὴν φρονοῦσά γ᾽ εὖ τὰ λῷστά σοι λέγω. 'To do all that, *as their well-wisher,* thou seemest likely (to do) with advantage to them.' As a well-wisher will do *his best,* εὖ φρονῶν thus practically means, 'to the best of thy judgment'; but that is not the first sense of the words.

1636 οὐκ οἴκτου μέτα, 'without making lamentation,'—

controlling his feelings in presence of the afflicted girls. Vauvilliers: 'οἶκτος hic est quod nos Galli dicimus *foiblesse.*' Cp. Plat. *Phaedo* 117 C καὶ ἡμῶν οἱ πολλοὶ τέως μὲν ἐπιεικῶς οἷοί τε ἦσαν κατέχειν τὸ μὴ δακρύειν, ὡς δὲ εἴδομεν πίνοντά τε καὶ πεπωκότα, (that Socrates had drunk the hemlock,) οὐκέτι, ἀλλ' ἐμοῦ γε βίᾳ καὶ αὐτοῦ (*in spite of myself*) ἀστακτὶ ἐχώρει τὰ δάκρυα. If the men of the old Greek world were more easily moved to tears than modern men, at least they knew very well when a man is bound to repress his emotion, if he can. Why, then, obliterate a noble touch by changing οἶκτου— as Wecklein does with Wex and Bothe—to the wretchedly feeble ὄκνου?

1637 ὅρκιος, 'on his oath': *Ant.* 305 ὅρκιος δέ σοι λέγω.

1639 ἀμαυραῖς, 'dark,' not guided by eyes: cp. 182 ἀμαυρῷ | κώλῳ. Not 'feeble' (1018), for no increase of physical weakness is among the signs that his end is near: rather is he lifted above his former helplessness (1587).

1640 τλάσας...τὸ γενναῖον φρενί, 'ye must make a brave effort of the mind, and depart': τὸ γενναῖον, acc. governed by τλάσας. It might also be adv., like κάμνοντι τὸ καρτερόν Theocr. 1. 41, but an absolute use of τλάσας seems slightly less probable here.—φρενί, in or with it. L's φέρειν is conceivably genuine, but in that case τὸ γενναῖον can hardly be so.

1641 f. ἃ μὴ: '*such things as* 'tis not lawful,' etc.: cp. 73.— φωνούντων, masc.

1643 ὁ κύριος, the master, he who has control of all; since to him alone the ἐξάγιστα (1526) are to be confided. The word has a further fitness here, since the maidens had been committed to the care of Theseus (cp. n. on *O. T.* 1506).

1645 f. εἰσηκούσαμεν, simply 'heard' (rather than 'obeyed'), as *Ant.* 9, *Ai.* 318, *Tr.* 351, 424.—ξύμπαντες, the attendants of Theseus, who had remained apart when their master was summoned to approach Oedipus (1630).—ἀστακτὶ: see on 1251.

1648 f. ἐξαπείδομεν, 'we could see from a distance.' This compound occurs only here, but is not intrinsically more questionable than the Homeric ἐξαποβαίνω, ἐξαποδύνω, etc. While ἐξορᾶν = 'to see *at a distance*' (used in pass. by Eur. *Her.* 675 etc.), ἀφορᾶν *alone* usu. = merely 'to regard': hence the double compound is really less pleonastic than those just mentioned. So ἐκπροτιμᾶν occurs only in *Ant.* 913.—τὸν ἄνδρα τὸν μὲν: 'we saw Oedipus,—*him*, I say,—no longer present anywhere, but *Theseus*, etc.' The τὸν μὲν comes in, by an afterthought, to prepare the distinction: cp. *Od*. I. 115 εἴ ποθεν ἐλθὼν | μνηστήρων τῶν μὲν σκέδασιν κατὰ δώματα θείη, | τιμὴν δ᾽ αὐτὸς ἔχοι: 'make a scattering of the wooers,— *those men there*,—in the house, but *himself* have honour,' etc.

1650 αὐτὸν, 'alone': Ar. *Ach*. 504 αὐτοὶ γάρ ἐσμεν οὑπὶ Ληναίῳ τ᾽ ἀγών (citizens without foreigners): cp. *O. T*. 221 n.— ὄμμ. (object. gen.) ἐπίσκιον, predicative, ὥστε ἐπισκιάζειν τὰ ὄμματα, 'holding his hand before his face to screen his eyes.'

1651 ἀντέχοντα, holding over against, from the primary sense of ἀντί: so with dat. (ὄμμασι) *Ph*. 830.—Perhaps nothing else in Greek literature leaves on the mind an impression so nearly akin to that of the awful vision in Job (iv. 15, 16).

1654 f. γῆν τε...καὶ..."Ὄλυμπον. Theseus bows down and kisses the earth, then suddenly rises, and with upturned face stretches forth his hands towards the sky. The vision which he had just seen moved him to adore both the χθόνιοι and the ὕπατοι. This touch is finely conceived so as to leave the mystery unbroken. Cp. *Ph*. 1408 στεῖχε προσκύσας χθόνα: *Ant*. 758 τόνδ᾽ Ὄλυμπον (the heaven above us).—ἐν ταὐτῷ λόγῳ, 'in the same address (or prayer),' *i.e.* one immediately after the other: not, 'on the same account.'

1659 f. ἐξέπραξεν, like διειργάσατο, διεχρήσατο, *confecit*, 'took his life'; cp. Eur. *Hec*. 515 πῶς καί νιν ἐξεπράξατ'; 'how indeed did ye take her life?'—ποντία θύελλα κινηθεῖσα, 'a whirlwind from the sea, suddenly aroused,'—so as to sweep inland on Colonus, and snatch him out of men's sight. For the locative force of ποντία as = ποντόθεν, cp. on 118 ἐκτόπιος. Cp. *Il*. 6. 345 (Helen's wish) ὥς μ᾽ ὄφελ᾽ ἤματι τῷ ὅτε με πρῶτον τέκε μήτηρ | οἴχεσθαι προφέρουσα κακὴ ἀνέμοιο θύελλα | εἰς ὄρος ἢ εἰς κῦμα πολυφλοίσβοιο θαλάσσης.

1661 f. πομπός: cp. 1548.—ἢ τὸ νερτέρων...γῆς...βάθρον, the nether world on which the upper world rests. γῆς βάθρον, earth's firm floor, rocky base: cp. Milton, 'Hymn on the Nativity,' *And cast the dark foundations deep*. So *Ai*. 860 ἑστίας βάθρον is the ground on which the home stands.

ἀλύπητον, the MS. reading, is incomparably better than the variant ἀλάμπετον (not attested in the classical age though occurring in the Anthology), which I believe to have been merely one of those conjectures in which the old transcribers and commentators sometimes indulged. By ἀλύπητον the poet meant, '*without pain*' (to Oed.); though it does not follow that he used the word with definite consciousness of an active sense. Cp. *Ph.* 687 ἀμφιπλήκτων ῥοθίων, the billows that beat around him: *O. T.* 969 ἄψαυστος, 'not touching,' etc. (*ib.* 885 ἀφόβητος, 'not fearing,' is not properly similar, since ἐφοβήθην was deponent). Plat. *Legg.* 958 E τὰ τῶν τετελευτηκότων σώματα μάλιστα ἀλυπήτως τοῖς ζῶσι...κρύπτειν, to bury the dead *with least annoyance* to the living. The passive sense, 'not pained,'— *i.e.*, where all earthly pain is over,—seems less suitable.

1663 f. οὐ στενακτός, 'not with wailing.' Some assume a definitely active sense, '*not wailing*'; see last n., and add μεμπτός 'blaming' (*Tr.* 446). Others make it definitely passive, '*not bewailed.*' The thought is that his end was 'not accompanied by στεναγμοί,' and the poet probably meant to suggest both ideas. Cp. on σωτήριον 487.—σὺν νόσοις: cp. *O. T.* 17 σὺν γήρᾳ βαρεῖς.—ἀλγεινός, associated with ἄλγος, here as *feeling*, not as *causing*, it: thus only here. Analogous is Pind. *Ol.* 1. 26 καθαροῦ λέβητος, the cauldron of cleansing, where Fennell cp. Theocr. 24. 95 καθαρῷ δὲ πυρώσατε δῶμα θεείῳ.

1665 f. εἰ δὲ μὴ δοκῶ, 'But if I seem not to speak with understanding' (*i.e.* if my narrative is thought incredible and foolish), 'I would not crave belief from those to whom I seem not sane.'—οὐκ ἂν παρείμην. παρίεμαι = 'to win over to one's own side,' and so either (1) with *gen.* of pers., Plat. *Rep.* 341 B οὐδέν (adv.) σου παρίεμαι, I ask no favour, no mercy, *from* you: or (2) with *acc.* of pers., *Legg.* 742 B παρέμενος...τοὺς ἄρχοντας ἀποδημείτω, 'when he has persuaded the rulers,'—obtained their permission: so again *ib.* 951 A. Here it seems better to understand τούτων than τούτους. He scorns to deprecate their unbelief. To the ancient Greek, who enjoyed discussion, there was something peculiarly impressive in declining it.

1667 f. χοἱ προπέμψ.: meaning Theseus (295 n.), though the plur. might also be explained of Theseus *with* his attendants (1646).—ἀσήμονες = ἄσημοι, only here.

1670—1750 *Kommos.* *1st str.* 1670—1696 = *1st antistr.* 1697—1723. *2nd str.* 1724—1736 = *2nd antistr.* 1737—1750. *The metre is choreic.*

1670 ff. αἰαῖ, φεῦ. To delete φεῦ here seems a less probable remedy than to supply τοι in 1697, where the neighbourhood of καί may have caused its loss.

ἔστιν ἔστι νῷν δή. The passage is simple if it is only remembered that οὐ τὸ μέν, ἄλλο δὲ μή is an adverbial phrase.

equivalent to παντελῶς. 'It is indeed for us twain *in no incomplete sense* to bewail the accurst blood of our father which was born in us, hapless that we are.' While he lived, they suffered with him. Now, his fate has snatched him from them in strange and terrible sort, leaving them destitute. οὐ τὸ μέν, ἄλλο δὲ μή (μή, instead of οὐ, because it goes with the inf. στενάζειν), 'not in *one* respect merely, with the exception of some other'; not merely *partially*. This phrase is frequent where the notion of *completeness* or *universality* is to be brought out with greater emphasis than would be given by the mere use of πᾶς or like words. Aesch. *Pers.* 802 συμβαίνει γὰρ οὐ τὰ μὲν τὰ δ᾽ οὔ, *i.e.* 'for our disasters are complete.' Her. 1. 139 οὐ τὰ μέν, τὰ δ᾽ οὔ, ἀλλὰ πάντα ὁμοίως. The idiom strikingly illustrates three tendencies of Greek; (1) love of antithesis, (2) love of parataxis, (3) the tendency to treat whole clauses as virtually adverbs (cp. οὐκ ἔσθ᾽ ὅπως οὐ, οἶδ᾽ ὅτι, etc.).

1671 f. ἔμφυτον, 'planted in us at our birth': whereby they are sharers in the hereditary ἀρά on the Labdacid race.— ἄλαστον: cp. on 1482.—αἷμα, as kinsfolk are of the same 'blood': cp. Eur. *Phoen.* 246 κοινὸν αἷμα, κοινὰ τέκεα: *O. T.* 1406 αἷμ᾽ ἐμφύλιον, an incestuous kinship.

1673 ᾦτινι, dat. of interest, 'for whom': cp. 508 τοῖς τεκοῦσι γάρ | οὐδ᾽ εἰ πονεῖ τις.—τὸν πολὺν: for the art. cp. on 87.

1675 f. ἐν πυμάτῳ, 'at the last,' *i.e.* 'at his death,' as opp. to ἄλλοτε μέν, *i.e.* 'during his life.'—ἀλόγιστα, things which baffle λογισμός, things which transcend human reason. As ἰδόντε shows, the reference is to the mysterious manner of their father's death, while παθοῦσα maiks their loss by that death.

παροίσομεν can only be explained, with Hermann, as = 'we shall bring forward,' 'allege.' 'And *we shall have to tell* of things baffling reason, as seen and suffered by us at the end.' This will seem less strained, I think, if we observe that Antigone need not be supposed to know of the *Messenger's* narrative. She may believe that she is bringing the Chorus the first intelligence of the event; and, if so, ἀλόγιστα παροίσομεν would be no unsuitable preface. This view agrees with the next words of the Chorus, who ask τί δ᾽ ἔστιν; as if uncertain what she means; and βέβηκεν; as if they did not *know* that Oedipus was gone. A wish to check the flow of her sorrow, to which utterance will be a relief.—Though the phrase is certainly strange, yet the defence indicated may at least avail in arrest of judgment. If παροίσομεν were to be altered, I should be disposed to suggest ἐπεράσαμεν ('we have gone through,' cp. περᾶν κίνδυνον etc.). The more obvious ἄπορ' οἴσομεν and ἀπορήσομεν are barred by the context.

1676 ἰδόντε καὶ παθούσα. The difficulty is to explain how, if παθόντε originally stood here, it was changed in the MSS. to παθούσα, when ἰδόντε (which metre requires) was more likely to cause an opposite change. I therefore leave παθούσα in the text. And it is important to notice that a similar combination of forms (both attested by metre) occurs in an Attic inscription of about the second cent. B.C., edited by Kaibel, *Epigr.* 1110: λευκοῖσιν φάρεσσι καλυψαμένα χρόα καλὸν | ἀθανάτων μετὰ φῦλον ἴτον προλιπόντ' ἀνθρώπους | Αἰδὼς Εὐνομίη τε.—Cp. Eur. *Andr.* 1214 ὦ κακὰ παθὼν ἰδών τε.

1677 The Chorus ask, 'And what is it?' She replies, ἔστιν μὲν εἰκάσαι, 'we may *conjecture*' (τὸ δὲ σαφὲς οὐδεὶς οἶδε). Cp. Eur. fr. 18 δοξάσαι ἔστι, κόραι· τὸ δ' ἐτήτυμον οὐκ ἔχω εἰπεῖν. So 1656 μόρῳ δ' ὁποίῳ κεῖνος ὤλετ' οὐδ' ἂν εἷς | θνητῶν φράσειε. Better thus than, '*you* can guess.'—The MS. οὐκ ἔστιν μὲν = 'we cannot conjecture.' οὐκ requires us to omit μέν or else to alter v. 1704, where see n.

1678 ὡς μάλιστ' ἂν ἐν πόθῳ λάβοις, as thou mightest most desire (that he should pass away). λαμβάνειν τι ἐν πόθῳ, to take a thing into one's desires, to conceive a wish for it; cp. *Ant.* 897 ἐν ἐλπίσιν τρέφω: ἐν ὀργῇ ἔχειν τινά (Thuc. 2. 21). For λαμβάνειν of mental conception, cp. 729.—The MS. εἰ (for ἐν) seems a mere mistake. The construction ὡς μάλιστα ἂν πόθῳ λάβοις, εἰ (λάβοις) is intolerable here.

1679 f. τί γάρ, ὅτῳ: 'How else, when he,' etc. For the causal use of the relat. see on 263.—μήτ' Ἄρης μήτε πόντος. His death was *sudden*, yet not *violent*. Death in battle and death by drowning are taken as types of the death which is both sudden and violent. Schol.: ᾧτινι μήτε πόλεμος μήτε νόσος ἐπῆλθεν. This certainly looks as if he read something else than πόντος. Cp. *Ant.* 819 οὔτε φθινάσιν πληγεῖσα νόσοις | οὔτε ξιφέων ἐπίχειρα λαχοῦσ'. Hence the conjecture νοῦσος, a form which the Attic poets nowhere use. I think that the schol.'s νόσος was a paraphrase of πόνος, a corruption of πόντος which actually appears in the Vatican MS. here.

1681 f. ἄσκοποι...πλάκες, the 'viewless fields' of the nether world (cp. on 1564).—φερόμενον, pass., is clearly right, 'borne away,' helping ἔμαρψαν to express sudden and swift disappearance. Plat. *Phaed.* 98 B ἀπὸ δὴ θαυμαστῆς ἐλπίδος...ᾠχόμην φερόμενος, 'from what a summit of hope was I hurled *headlong.*' The midd. φερόμεναι, as 'carrying off to themselves,' would be somewhat strange, and also much less forcible.

1683 f. ὀλεθρία νύξ, 'night as of death': cp. *O. T.* 1222 κατεκοίμησα τοὐμὸν ὄμμα, I have closed my eyes (as in death),— said, as here, in despairing grief.

1685 ff. ἀπίαν γᾶν, some distant land, the Homeric 'ἀπίη γαίη (*Il.* 1. 270 etc.). If the regular quantity, 'ἀπίαν, is to be kept here, we must read τόσον, with Arndt, for τοσόνδ', in 1712. But τοσόνδ' is there confirmed by metre.   In this word ᾱ is not found elsewhere.   But, by a converse license, Ἀπία (see on 1303) had sometimes ᾰ in later epos; and if, in poetical usage, the quantity of Ἀπία could thus be affected by association with ἀπίη, it is conceivable that the influence should have been reciprocal.—ἀλώμεναι with acc. of space traversed, as *Ai.* 30 πηδῶντα πεδία.—δύσοιστον, not -ον, since βίου—τροφάν form one notion; cp. *Ant.* 793 νεῖκος—ἀνδρῶν ξύναιμον.

1689 ff. κατά...ἕλοι = καθέλοι: so 1709 ἀνά...στένει (cp. *O. T.* 199 n.).—φόνιος here = 'deadly,' in a general sense, as *O. T.* 24 (n.) φοινίου σάλου (of the plague).

In this and some following passages the correspondence of strophe and antistrophe has been disturbed by interpolations and omissions in the MSS.   A κομμός of this kind was peculiarly liable to corruption by the actors, and that has doubtless been one of the causes at work. (Cp. on 1737.)   At some points it is now impossible to restore the text with certainty; but the whole extent of the mischief is small.

1690 The words πατρὶ ξυνθανεῖν γεραιῷ are not suspicious in themselves; but they are in metrical excess of 1715 f.   Now, if ξυνθανεῖν γεραιῷ is omitted, πατρί must go also, or be altered. For ἕλοι πατρί could not mean 'take *for*' (*i.e.* to join) 'my father.'   I prefer to leave πατρὶ ξυνθανεῖν γεραιῷ, and to suppose a lacuna after 1715.   The sense is: 'may deadly Hades lay me low (καθέλοι), so that I may share the death of mine aged sire.' Cp. *Ai.* 516 καὶ μητέρ' ἄλλη μοῖρα τὸν φύσαντά τε | καθεῖλεν Ἅιδου θανασίμους οἰκήτορας.

1693 f. The MSS. give τὸ φέρον ἐκ θεοῦ καλῶς φέρειν χρή. There has certainly been an interpolation, equivalent to ∪ ∪ –. Wecklein, with whom I agree, rejects καλῶς and χρή, keeping φέρειν.   Then τὸ φέρον ἐκ θεοῦ φέρειν = '*bear* the fate from heaven,' the inf. standing for imperat., a use fitting in such a precept

(*O. T.* 1529). The origin of the interpolated words is thus clear: χρή explained the use of the inf., while καλῶς was meant to fix the sense of φέρειν, lest τὸ φέρον should obscure it.

τὸ φέρον ἐκ θεοῦ, = the fortune from the god. τὸ φέρον in this sense admits of two explanations. (1) '*That which brings*' good or evil. This view seems confirmed by the analogy of *fors, fortuna* (*ferre*): Ter. *Ph.* 1. 2. 88 *quod fors feret, feremus:* Cic. *Att.* 7. 14 *ut fors tulerit*, etc. (2) '*That which carries*' or '*leads*' us forward, in a course which we cannot control (cp. ἡ ὁδὸς φέρει ἐκεῖσε, and like phrases).—The conjecture τὸ παρὸν (cp. 1540) would be plausible only if there were reasons for thinking that τὸ φέρον in this sense was a phrase of post-classical date.

1694 The MS. μηδ' ἄγαν οὕτω answers to λήγετε τοῦδ' in 1722. The question is, Are we (1) to compress the former, or (2) to expand the latter? Dindorf and others prefer (1), and so eject οὕτω, reading μηδ' ἔτ' (or μηδὲν) ἄγαν, = λήγετε τοῦδ'. This view agrees with the metre, and is adopted by Heinrich Schmidt. If, on the other hand, οὕτω is kept here, then Hermann's λήγετ' <ἤδη> τοῦδ' is the simplest supplement in 1722.

1695 οὔτοι κατάμεμπτ' ἔβητον, 'ye have fared not blameably': ye cannot justly complain of the destiny which has removed your father, in old age, by a painless death (cp. 1678). κατάμεμπτα, neut. pl. as adv.: cp. on 319. βαίνειν does not occur elsewhere in a strictly similar use, for we cannot compare the *perf.* εὖ βεβηκώς (*El.* 979) as = '*placed* well,' 'prosperous.' But there is at least some analogy in such figurative uses of it as Eur. *Her.* 625 ἁ δ' ἀρετὰ βαίνει διὰ μόχθων, the path of virtue lies through troubles; *H. F.* 630 ὧδ' ἔβητ' ἐπὶ ξυροῦ; 'had ye come into such peril?' *Phoen.* 20 σὸς οἶκος βήσεται δι' αἵματος, 'will pass through deeds of blood':—where a certain course of *fortune* is expressed.

1697 τοι: see on 1670.—ἆρ' ἦν. The impf. of *new perception:* 'there was such a thing, then' (all the time), though I did not know it before: *Ph.* 978 ὅδ' ἦν ἄρα | ὁ ξυλλαβών με: Eur. fr. 807 μέγιστον ἄρ' ἦν ἡ φύσις: Plat. *Gorg.* 508 C ἃ Πῶλον αἰσχύνη ᾤου συγχωρεῖν, ἀληθῆ ἄρα ἦν, 'were true all the time.'

1698 f. The MS. τὸ φίλον φίλον can only mean: 'that which is in no way τὸ φίλον (was) φίλον.' But the article is unendurable here, making her say, in effect, that her former

Oedipus at Colonus

duty was not *the ideal* of what is pleasant. It came in to patch the metre, when ἦν had dropped out. For μηδαμά instead of οὐδαμά cp. 73: for the neut. pl. form, 1104.—τόν = αὐτόν: cp. 742.

1700 f. ὦ φίλος: for the nom. cp. on 185.—Join τὸν ἀεὶ κατὰ γᾶς σκότον, the eternal darkness beneath the earth: there is no warrant for τὸν ἀεί with ellipse of χρόνον as = 'for ever' (cp. 1584).—εἱμένος, 'thou that hast put on': Pind. *N.* 11. 15 θνατὰ μεμνάσθω περιστέλλων μέλη, | καὶ τελευτὰν ἀπάντων γᾶν ἐπιεσσόμενος: Xen. *Cyr.* 6. 4. 6 ἐπομνύω...βούλεσθαι ἄν...γῆν ἐπιέσσασθαι μᾶλλον ἢ ζῆν.

1702 οὐδέ γ' ἔνερθ', 'not even in Hades,' is Wecklein's correction of the corrupt οὐδὲ γέρων which yields no intelligible sense. In Linwood's οὐδὲ γὰρ ὣς (which Hartung and Blaydes adopt), γάρ will refer to her addressing him as ὦ φίλος (1700).

1704 The first ἔπραξεν is itself an argument for the second. A simple repetition is more fitting than ἐξέπραξεν. Cp. on 1677. Cp. *Ai.* 966 ἐμοὶ πικρὸς τέθνηκεν ἢ κείνοις γλυκύς, | αὐτῷ δὲ τερπνός· ὧν γὰρ ἠράσθη τυχεῖν | ἐκτήσαθ' αὐτῷ, θάνατον ὅνπερ ἤθελεν.

1707 f. εὐσκίαστον: cp. on 406, Pind. *P.* 11. 21 Ἀχέροντος ἀκτὰν παρ' εὔσκιον.—πένθος...ἄκλαυτον: lit. 'he did not leave behind him a mourning unhonoured by tears,'—*i.e.* he is duly mourned by weeping friends, as the spirits of the dead desired. Solon fr. 21 μηδέ μοι ἄκλαυτος θάνατος μόλοι, ἀλλὰ φίλοισιν | ποιήσαιμι θανὼν ἄλγεα καὶ στοναχάς.

1709. In τόδ' ἐμὸν ὄμμα δακρῦον ἀναστένει (tmesis, 1689) σε, 'I bewail you with streaming eyes,'—it is truer to regard ἐμὸν ὄμμα as a periphrasis for ἐγώ than ἀναστένει as a mere synonym for 'mourns.' Cp. *Ai.* 139 πεφόβημαι | πτηνῆς ὡς ὄμμα πελείας, *ib.* 977 ὦ φίλτατ' Αἴας, ὦ ξύναιμον ὄμμ' ἐμοί.

1711 f. τὸ σὸν ἄχος, grief for thee: cp. 419 n.—ἀφανίσαι, do away with, overcome (not, 'conceal').—τόσον, Arndt's correction of τοσόνδ', would give us the normal 'ἀπίαν in 1685 (n.).

1713 f. ὤμοι is Wecklein's correction of ἰὼ μή. That μή was an error for μοι had already been surmised by some old corrector. Render:—'Ah me, it was thy *wish* to die in a strange land (and so far thy death is well): but thus (by this manner of death) thou hast died *forlorn in regard to me*' (μοι ethic dat.). She means, 'I have had no opportunity of rendering thee the due rites, and now I do not know the place

of thy grave, so as to make the ἐναγίσματα at it.' Hence her
passionate desire to find his grave (1724 ff.), which Theseus
with difficulty allays by reminding her of his solemn promise
(1760). The preparatory offices rendered at 1602 f. could
not be viewed as taking the place of a daughter's tribute to
the dead. Like 1410, this trait serves to recall the special
manifestation of her piety in the earlier play.—Not merely:—
'It was your wish; but it was sad for me to see you die
forlorn,'—*i.e.* in exile. Though ἐπὶ ξένης, he was *not* in this
sense ἔρημος,—he who, in his own words, had 'Athens and all
her people' for his friends (772).—Cp. 1705 ᾶς ἔχρῃζε...ἔθανε.

1715 f. Cp. 1735 αὖθις ὧδ' ἔρημος ἄπορος. Almost all
critics are now agreed that the words ἔρημος ἄπορος were
borrowed thence, to supply a gap here. But opinions differ
as to whether we should here retain αὖθις, or ὧδ', or both.
I retain both.

1720 f. ἔλυσε τὸ τέλος...βίου, lit. 'closed the end of life,'
a pleonasm which blends ἔλυσε βίου and ἀφίκετο τὸ τέλος βίου:
so Eur. *El.* 956 τέλος κάμψῃ βίου instead of the simple κάμψῃς
βίου (*Helen.* 1666). The phrase λύειν βίον occurs Eur. *I. T.*
692, καταλύειν βίοτον *Suppl.* 1004.

1722 λήγετε: cp. on 1694.—κακῶν δυσάλωτος, hard for
calamity to capture. Every mortal is an easy prey to misfortune. The gen. as 1519: *Ai.* 910 ἄφρακτος φίλων, *Ant.* 847
φίλων ἄκλαυτος, *ib.* 1034 μαντικῆς | ἄπρακτος. In prose a
prep. would usu. be added, as Xen. *Ages.* 8. 8. 8 τείχη ἀνάλωτα
...ὑπὸ πολεμίων.—Cp. Shaksp. *Hen. VI.* Pt. iii. 1. 4. 115
'their woes, *whom fortune captivates.*'

1724 f. πάλιν...συθῶμεν, hasten back (601) to the neighbourhood of the καταρράκτης ὁδός (1590).—ὡς τί ῥέξομεν; ὡς
with the fut. indic., depending on συθῶμεν, is the object-clause
after a verb implying effort: Xen. *Cyr.* 3. 2. 13 ὡς δὲ καλῶς
ἕξει τὰ ὑμέτερα, ἐμοὶ μελήσει. With the fut. indic., however,
ὅπως is much commoner than ὡς.

1725 The MS. text of this verse does not answer metrically to 1739. Bergk and Gleditsch alter both verses. Hermann, whose remedy is simplest, leaves this v. intact, and in
1739 reads ΧΟ. καὶ πάρος ἀπέφυγε ΑΝ. τί; See n. there.

1727 τὰν χθόνιον ἑστίαν, the home, resting-place, in the
ground (1763 θήκην ἱεράν). Oedipus had himself spoken in
her hearing of the ἱερὸς τύμβος (1545) where he was to rest.

1729 f. θέμις...τάδ': cp. 883: *O. T.* 1329.—μῶν οὐχ ὁρᾷς;

dost thou not see for thyself that it cannot be?—since Oedipus solemnly forbade it (1529, 1640). μῶν οὐ is a strong '*nonne?*' (Aesch. *Suppl.* 417, Eur. *Med.* 733, Plat. *Polit.* 291 D, etc.).— ἐπέπληξας, *sc. μοι*: 'what is this reproof of thine to me?'

1731 f. καὶ τόδ' still depends on οὐχ ὁρᾶς;—μάλ' αὖθις; cp. 1477.—ἔπιτνε, impf., must be either (1) 'was appointed to perish,' or (2) 'was perishing' when we last saw him. (2) seems best.—δίχα τε παντός, 'apart from all': *i.e.* without any eye-witness (save Theseus).—Better thus than 'in a manner different from all other men.'—Ismene opposes her sister's desire as (1) unlawful, and (2) impossible.

1733 ἄγε με. 'Lead me (to the spot where we last saw our father), and then slay me *also*.' In ἐπενάριξον the prep. = 'in addition' (*i.e.* to my father). *Not,* 'slay me *at his grave*' (Eur. *Hec.* 505 κἄμ' ἐπισφάξαι τάφῳ). She could not intend this after Ismene's words ἄταφος ἔπιτνε, to which she had been attentive. Cp. Ismene's wish 1689.

1734 ff. The MS. ποῖ δῆτ'...ἔξω has been defended in two ways, neither of which is satisfactory: (1) by an ellipse of μολοῦσα: (2) as = 'until *when?*' As in 383 (n.) we should read ὅπου for ὅποι, and in 335 (n.) ποῦ for ποῖ, so here I feel sure that ποῦ is right. It suits the sense better than *v. l.* πῇ, besides being closer to the MSS. The *v. l.* ἄξω, (which would justify ποῖ,) is plainly a mere corruption of ἔξω.—αὖθις, lit. 'now again,' *i.e.* after this new turn in our unhappy fortunes.

1737—1750 In these verses the utterances usually assigned to Antigone all turn on her anxiety as to a refuge, and her desire to return to Thebes. Such feelings, at this moment, are more in harmony with the character of Ismene (cp. 1735). Antigone is at present absorbed in the yearning to visit her father's tomb, or at least the spot where she last saw him alive (1724). When Theseus appears, it is this wish which she instantly presses on him. Only when it has been put aside does she think of a return to Thebes (1769).

Ought we, then, to read ΙΣ. for ΑΝ. throughout vv. 1737—1750? The Laur. MS. leaves the question open. I am disposed to think that Sophocles wrote the words for Ismene, but that the fourth-actor difficulty had led to a fluctuation of stage-practice, which helps to account for the ambiguity of the MS. tradition.

1738 φύγω: cp. on 170.

1739 f. The MS. ἀπεφεύγετον is most simply corrected to

ἀπεφύγετον. But then we must either (1) add τί δή, and expand
v. 1726, as Bergk and Gleditsch do (cr. n. *ad l.*): or (2),
leaving v. 1726 intact, suppose that vv. 1739, 1740 are spoken
by the Chorus without any interpellation by Antigone. This,
however, is improbable, and also injurious to the point of
v. 1740. I therefore incline to Hermann's ἀπέφυγε ΑΝ. τί;
'Long ago *there was an escape*'—ΑΝ. 'For what?' [lit. '*what
escaped?*']—CH. '*For your fortunes*, from falling out ill.'
The merits of this reading are:—(1) it leaves v. 1725, which
seems quite sound, unaltered: (2) by making τὰ σφῷν nom.
to ἀπέφυγε, it smooths v. 1740.

1741 φρονῶ, I am conscious of that,—'I know it well,'—
in quick and grateful response to their allusion. Theseus
and the men of Attica had indeed rescued her and her sister
in their extremity.—τί δῆθ' ὅπερ νοεῖς; 'What then is thy
thought?' The MS. ὑπερνοεῖς is corrupt. It occurs only here,
and could not mean (1) 'why art thou too anxious?' nor
(2) 'what *further* hast thou in thy thoughts?'

1742 ὅπως μολούμεθ': 'how we are to return to Thebes,
I know not':—for Oedipus had predicted that both her
brothers would soon fall in the war (1373), and Creon, the
next heir to the throne, was no friend. This continues the
thought ποῖ φύγω; (1737). The interposed words of the
Chorus do not touch her difficulty.

1743 μηδέ γε μάτευε: 'No, (thou canst not return to Thebes,)
nor seek to do so,'—but stay in Attica under the protection of
Theseus.

1744 μόγος ἔχει, *sc. ἡμᾶς.*—ἐπεῖχε, 'bore hardly on you,'
sc. ὑμῖν or ἐφ' ὑμᾶς: for μόγος ἐπεῖχεν ὑμᾶς would mean, 're-
strained you.' The MS. ἐπεί doubtless arose from a contraction
of ἐπεῖχε.

1745 τοτὲ μέν...ὕπερθεν. Whitelaw: 'Oh then past cure,
but worst is now grown worse.' The neut. plur. is most
simply taken as adverb (319), referring to μόγος ἐπεῖχε: though
we might also construe, ἄπορα (ἦν τὰ ἡμέτερα). τοτὲ μέν...τοτὲ
δέ, 'at one time' (*i.e.* while Oed. lived)...'at another time'
(*i.e.* now that he is dead). ὕπερθεν, hyperbolic, since ἄπορα
already='hopeless': cp. fr. 188 ὦ πᾶν σὺ τολμήσασα καὶ πέρα,
γύναι.

1746 πέλαγος, without κακῶν or the like, is excused by the
familiarity of the metaphor in Greek: cp. on 663.

1747 φεῦ, φεῦ. Dindorf substitutes αἰαῖ, because he supposes the latter to_have generated the ναὶ ναί which, with the words ξύμφημι καὐτός, he ejects. But so common a form as αἰαῖ was not very likely to be thus corrupted. It is simpler to suppose that the ejected phrase was a mere interpolation, perhaps due to actors.

1748 f. ἐλπίδων γὰρ ἐς τίν': lit., '(we may well ask whither we are to go,) *for* towards what remaining (ἔτι) hope of (all possible) hopes is fate now urging us?' What hope now remains for us, in the course on which we are driven? For ἔτι, which here is virtually equiv. to an adj. λοιπήν, cp. 865 τῆσδε τῆς ἀρᾶς ἔτι—ἐλπίδων in its good sense, rather than neutral or sinister ('bodings'): cp. *El.* 958 ποῖ γὰρ μενεῖς ῥάθυμος, ἐς τίν' ἐλπίδων | βλέψασ' ἔτ' ὀρθήν;

1751 ff. θρῆνον, not θρήνων, is clearly right. The 2nd per. *sing.* imper., παῦε, is the only part of παύω which is used intransitively by the classical Attic writers,—being, in fact, an exclamation (like our '*stop!*'), though sometimes joined with a gen. (παῦε τοῦ λόγου, Ar. *Ran.* 580).

ξύν' ἀπόκειται for the MS. ξυναπόκειται is (I think) right. The literal sense is:—ἐν οἷς γὰρ 'for in a case where' (*neut. pl.*), χάρις ἡ χθονία 'the kindness shown by the χθόνιοι,' ξύν' ἀπόκειται 'is stored up as a common benefit' (ξυνά, neut. pl. as adv.),—common, namely, to Oedipus and the Athenians. That is:—'By the death of Oedipus, the Powers below have given *him* the everlasting rest which he desired, and *us* the abiding safeguard which he promised' (*i.e.* his grave). To mourn here would be to provoke the deities who have ordered all things well for him and for us.—ἀπόκειται, is laid up in store: cp. [Dem.] or. 23 § 42 τὸ τῆς συγγνώμης ὠφέλιμον...ὅτῳ ποτὲ τῶν πάντων ἀπόκειται ἄδηλον ὄν, it being uncertain for whom the benefit of compassion *is laid up*,—*i.e.* who may need to draw upon it.—For ξυνά (adv.) cp. *Ant.* 546 μή μοι θάνῃς σὺ κοινά, *along with* me: *Ai.* 577 τὰ δ' ἄλλα τεύχη κοίν' ἐμοὶ τεθάψεται.

1753 νέμεσις γάρ, *sc.* πενθεῖν ἐστί: it is provocative of divine anger to mourn, as if insensible of the divine beneficence. *Il.* 14. 80 οὐ γάρ τις νέμεσις φυγέειν κακόν, ''tis no matter for indignation that one should flee from ill': *Od.* 1. 350 τούτῳ δ' οὐ νέμεσις...ἀείδειν: where, however, the νέμεσις is human, not, as here, divine. Cp. *El.* 1467 εἰ δ' ἔπεστι νέμεσις, οὐ λέγω (in revoking words which might offend *the gods*).

1755 f. τίνος...χρείας. '*for* what request,'—depending on the idea of δεόμεθα, χρήζομεν, implied in προσπίτνομεν: ἀνύσαι (*sc.* αὐτήν), epexegetic inf., 'so that ye should obtain it': cp. 1211 (n.).—For the use of χρείας, cp. *O. T.* 1435 καὶ τοῦ με χρείας ὧδε λιπαρεῖς τυχεῖν;—αὐταὶ, with our own eyes (instead of merely hearing that it exists).

1758 The MS. words κεῖσε μολεῖν, which I omit, were almost certainly a gloss upon ἀλλ' οὐ θεμιτόν. If we keep them, then we must add something more, so as to make an anapaestic dimeter.

1760 f. ἀπεῖπεν, forbade, takes μή after it, as is usual (cp. *O. T.* 236 ἀπαυδῶ...μή); Aeschin. or. 1 § 138 ταῦτα τοῖς δούλοις ἀπεῖπον μὴ ποιεῖν.

1762 μήτ' ἐπιφωνεῖν...θήκην must be carefully distinguished from ἐπιφωνεῖν θήκῃ. The former must mean strictly (not, 'to utter *over* the grave,' but) '*to approach* the grave *with utterance*,'—the notion being that of invading the secret silence around it. Invocations and prayers to the dead were often made aloud at a grave: Eur. *Helen.* 961 λέξω τάδ' ἀμφὶ μνῆμα σοῦ πατρὸς πόθῳ · | ὦ γέρον, ὃς οἰκεῖς τόνδε λάϊνον τάφον, etc.— The alternative is to take ἐπιφωνεῖν as='mention to another': but this is unfitting, since Theseus *alone* knows the place.

θήκην ἱεράν: cp. 1545. Thuc. I. 8 τῶν θηκῶν ἀναιρεθεισῶν ὅσαι ἦσαν τῶν τεθνεώτων ἐν τῇ νήσῳ.

1764 f. καλῶς with πράσσοντα (not with ἕξειν), 'performing in a seemly manner,' 'duly' (Lat. *rite*): cp. 617: *O. T.* 879 τὸ καλῶς δ' ἔχον | πόλει πάλαισμα. The fact that πράσσοντα καλῶς usually meant 'faring well' is no objection. The ancient Greek instinct for words was remarkably free from bondage to phrases. Cp. *Ant.* 989 n.—ἄλυπον: an echo of the expression used by Oed. (1519).

1766 f. ταῦτ' οὖν: '*These things*, then, (οὖν, according to the injunctions of Oedipus,) I was heard to promise by the god,' etc. ταῦτ' is short for 'the promise to do these things,' as if ὑπισχνουμένων stood with ἡμῶν. For ἔκλυεν with both gen. and acc. cp. *O. T.* 235.—δαίμων: the Divine Power that called Oedipus away (1626).

1767 πάντ' ἀΐων: cp. 42. The α of ἀΐω *short*, as in 240 and *Ph.* 1410: whereas it is *long* in 181, 304, *Ai.* 1263.— Διὸς Ὅρκος, as the servant of Zeus. Hes. *Op.* 803 ἐν πέμπτῃ γάρ φασιν Ἐρινύας ἀμφιπολεύειν | Ὅρκον γεινόμενον, τὸν Ἔρις τέκε πῆμ' ἐπιόρκοις. This personified Horkos is a deity who witnesses an oath, and punishes perjury (Hes. *Theog.* 231).

He is the son of Eris, because strife gives birth to treaties; he
is attended at his birth by the Erinyes, because they avenge
broken faith. And he is the servant of Zeus, because Ζεὺς
Ὅρκιος is the *supreme* guardian of good-faith—represented in
the βουλευτήριον at Olympia by a Zeus with lightnings in both
hands.

1768 f. κατὰ νοῦν. Ar. *Eq.* 549 κατὰ νοῦν πράξας : so oft.
κατὰ γνώμην.—τάδ'...ταῦτ': cp. on 787.

1770 τὰς ὠγυγίους, a specially fit epithet, since the mythical
Ὠγύγης was represented (in one legend at least) as son of
Boeotus, and first ruler of Thebes (Paus. 9. 5. 1). Another
legend connected him with Attica (Paus. 1. 38. 7). The trait
common to the two legends is a great inundation which
happened in his reign. The adj. is applied by Aesch. to
Thebes (*Th.* 321 πόλιν ὠγυγίαν, *Pers.* 37 τάς τ' ὠγυγίους Θήβας),
and also to Athens (*Pers.* 974). The Attic poets used it in
the general sense of 'very ancient,' as *Ph.* 142 κράτος ὠγύγιον,
'royalty inherited from of old.'

1771 f. ἰόντα, a pres., not fut., partic. (*O. T.* 773 n.),
'coming on them': *El.* 374 κακὸν...εἰς αὐτὴν ἰόν: Plat. *Legg.*
873 E παρὰ θεοῦ...βέλος ἰόν. So *Ant.* 185 τὴν ἄτην ὁρῶν |
στείχουσαν ἀστοῖς.—ὁμαίμοις: see on 330.

Antigone suggests that she and Ismene may yet be in time
to plead with their two brothers, and so to avert the doom
of mutual destruction pronounced on them by their father
(1373). Thus the close of this drama is linked by the poet
with the beginning of his earlier *Antigone*, which opens at
a moment just after the deaths of the brothers. The sisters
are then living at Thebes, where Creon has succeeded to the
throne. An additional pathos is lent to Antigone's part there
by the suggestion here of a previous intercession. In Aesch.
Theb. it is the Chorus (of Theban maidens) that endeavours to
dissuade Eteocles from going to meet his brother (677 ff.): in
Eur. *Phoen.* it is their mother Iocasta who seeks to reconcile
them (452 ff.).

1773—1776 After οὐ in 1776 the MS. γάρ must be struck
out, as Hermann saw, so that the anapaests spoken by Theseus
may end with a paroemiac. When anapaests spoken by the
Chorus close a tragedy, these always form a system separate
from the anapaests (if any) which precede them. This was
plainly necessary, in order to avoid an unduly abrupt ending.
But if we point thus:—πρὸς χάριν· οὐ δεῖ μ' ἀποκάμνειν the

asyndeton has a crude effect. Hence, placing only a comma after πρὸς χάριν, we should render:—'Not only will I do these things, but *in all things* which I am likely to do for your advantage (etc.) I must not *wax weary*.' The sentence begins as if the constr. was to be δράσω καὶ τάδε καὶ πάντα. But the new verb added at the end requires πάντα to be acc. with ἀποκάμνειν. (Cp. on 351.)

1773 ὁπόσ' ἂν seems slightly preferable to ὅσα γ' ἂν as a correction of the MS. ὅσ' ἂν (or ὅσα ἂν), because the qualification which γ' would imply is sufficiently provided for by πρόσφορα etc.: cp. 1634 τελεῖν δ' ὅσ' ἂν | μέλλῃς φρονῶν εὖ ξυμφέροντ' αὐταῖς ἀεί.

1774 ff. πράσσειν, *pres.* inf. with μέλλω, as in eight other places of Sophocles. He has the *fut.* inf. with it ten times, including *O. T.* 967, weshe the MS. κτανεῖν, if sound, would be the only instance of the *aor.* inf. with μέλλω in Soph.; but there the fut. κτενεῖν is clearly right. Where μέλλω means 'to delay,' the pres. inf. is naturally preferred: cp. 1627: *O. T.* 678 τί μέλλεις κομίζειν δόμων τόνδ' ἔσω;

πρόσφορά θ' ὑμῖν, καὶ πρὸς χάριν τῷ κατὰ γῆς: at once for your advantage, and to the gratification of the dead. πρόσφορα, 'suitable' for a given purpose, and so 'useful,' 'profitable': so often in Attic prose, as Thuc. 1. 125; 2. 46, 65; 7. 62. πρὸς χάριν: cp. *O.T.* 1152 n.

ἔρρει is justified by the *sudden and swift* removal of Oedipus, as *O. T.* 560 ἄφαντος ἔρρει, he hath been *swept* from men's sight. In *El.* 57 τοὐμὸν ὡς ἔρρει δέμας | φλογιστὸν ἤδη, it is little more than οἴχεται. More commonly ἔρρειν implies either an evil end, or at least some feeling of contempt on the speaker's part, as Eur. *Suppl.* 1112 οὓς χρῆν, ἐπειδὰν μηδὲν ὠφελῶσι γῆν, | θανόντας ἔρρειν κἀκποδὼν εἶναι νέοις.

1776 ἀποκάμνειν, 'to cease from labouring,' can take an acc. of the labour avoided: hence πάνθ' in 1773 need not be merely acc. of respect. Xen. *H.* 7. 5. 19 πόνον...μηδένα ἀποκάμνειν, 'to flinch from no toil.' Also with inf., Plat. *Crito* 45 B μὴ ἀποκάμῃς σαυτὸν σῶσαι, 'do no abandon the effort to save yourself.' For the form of the sentence cp. Plat. *Rep.* 445 B ἐπειδὴ ἐνταῦθα ἐληλύθαμεν, ὅσον οἶόν τε σαφέστατα κατιδεῖν ὅτι ταῦτα οὕτως ἔχει, οὐ χρὴ ἀποκάμνειν. For this force of ἀπό cp. ἀπαλγέω, ἀπανθέω, ἀποζέω, ἀποκηδεύω, ἀπολοφύρομαι.

1777 ff. ἀλλ' introduces the final words of comfort which the elders of Colonus address to the Theban maidens; cp. 101.

—ἀποπαύετε, no less than the following verb, governs θρῆνον: cp. on 1751.—Though the neut. pl. πλείω *alone* is sometimes adverbial, there seems to be no instance of ἐπὶ πλείω as=ἐπὶ πλέον: indeed, such a phrase is hardly conceivable. ἐπὶ must therefore belong to ἐγείρετε: for the tmesis cp. on 1689.

1779 ἔχει...κῦρος, lit., 'have validity,' = κεκύρωται, *sancta sunt.* Cp. *El.* 919 πολλῶν...κῦρος...καλῶν ('sanction of'), Aesch. *Suppl.* 391 οὐκ ἔχουσι κῦρος...ἀμφὶ σοῦ, 'authority over thee.'— Two meanings are possible: (1) '*These promises of Theseus* are certain to hold good': or, more generally, (2) '*These events* have assuredly been ordained past recall' (by the gods). Most commentators prefer (1). But (2) seems more fitting at the conclusion. The last soothing words of the Chorus convey a precept of resignation to the divine will.

I

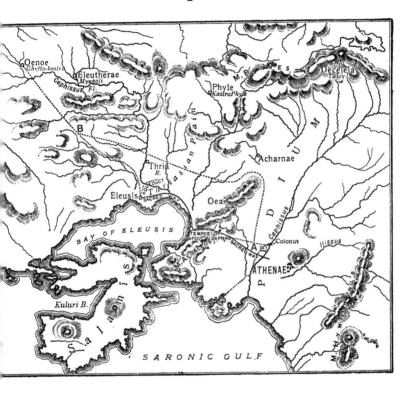

Map to illustrate Note on vv. 1059 *ff.*

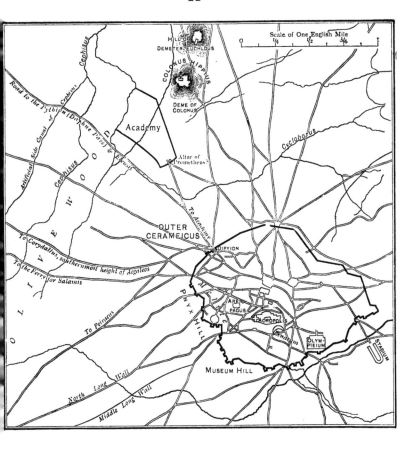

COLONUS AND ITS NEIGHBOURHOOD,
with some of the ancient roads.

INDICES.

I. GREEK.

The number denotes the verse, in the English note on which the word or matter is illustrated. When the reference is to a *page*, p. is prefixed to the number.)(means, 'as distinguished from.'

α before γν, quantity of, 547
α, final, in Θησέα, 1055
ἀβρύνεσθαι, 1338 f.
ἄγειν, to take captive, 916
ἀγέλαστος πέτρα, 1594
ἀγνώμων, 10
ἀγρευτής, epith. of Apollo, 1091
ἄγων, quasi-pleonastic, 910
ἀγών, senses of, 587
ἄδεια γῆς, 447
ἀδελφός, with gen. or dat., 1262
ἀδηλέω, 35
ἀδῇος, 1533 ff.
ἀείρυτος, not ἀείρρυτος, 469
ἀελλαῖος, 1081
ἄξω, the active, only in 134
ἄθικτος, pass., 1520
ἀθρεῖν, 252
αἰδόφρων, 237
᾿Αϊδωνεύς, 1558 f.
Αἰδώς, 1267 f.
ἀΐειν, 240 : ᾱ or ᾰ in, 1767
αἰένυπνος, ὁ, 1578
αἰκία, penult. of, long, 748 f.
αἱρεῖν ἀγῶνα, 1148
ἀΐσσεσθαι, 1260 f.
αἰωρεῖν, 1083 ff.
ἀκεστήρ, 714
ἀκίνητος, 624

ἀκμή, 1065 f.
ἀκορέστατος, 120
ἀκούειν, with genit. of thing heard,
    418 f., 485, 1171, 1173 ; ἀκούειν
    κακός, 988
ἄκουσμα, 517
ἀκρατής, sense of, 1235 f.
ἀκτένιστος, 1260 f.
ἄκων = ἀκούσιος, 240, 977
ἀλάμπετος, 1661 f.
ἄλαστος, 537, 1483
ἀλάστωρ, 787 f.
ἀλγεινός = feeling pain, 1663 f.
ἀλιτεῖν, derivatives of, 371
ἀλκὴν ποιεῖσθαι, 459 f.
ἀλλά, in appeal, 'nay,' 237, 421,
    1405 f.: ἀλλά, 'at least,' 241,
    1276 ; ἀλλὰ μήν, in reply, 28 ;
    ἀλλ᾿ οὐ γάρ, two uses of, 988 ;
    ἀλλ᾿ οὐ μήν, 153
ἄλλα ἀλλαχοῦ καλά, 43
ἄλλων, μὴ πύθῃ ἐξ, 1265 f.
ἀλύπητος, 1661 f.
ἀμαιμάκετος, 127
ἀμαυρός, senses of, 182, 1018, 1639
ἄμβασις = ἀναβάται, 1070
ἀμείβεσθαι, constr. of, 814
ἄμιλλαι ῥιμφάρματοι, 1062 f.
ἀμπυκτήρια, 1069 f.

ἀμυναθεῖν, 1015
ἀμύνειν, to requite, 1128
ἀμφί, with dat., 365, 1614
Ἀμφιάρεως, 1313
ἀμφιδέξιον πλευρόν, 1112
ἀμφικείμενος, 1620 f.
ἀμφιπολεῖν, 679 f.
ἀμφίστασθαι, of sound, 1477 f.
ἀμφίστομοι λαβαί, 473
ἀμφοῖν for ἀλλήλοιν, 1425
ἄν, doubled, 780; ἄν, with past
  tenses of indic., p. 284
ἀναδιδόναι)(ἀποδιδόναι, 1076
ἀνακαλεῖσθαι, 1376
ἀναπαύειν, 1113 f.
ἀναπνεῖν, 1113 f.
ἀνάστατος, 429
ἀναφαίνεσθαι, 1222 f.
ἄνευ τινός, without his command,
  926
ἀνέχειν, senses of, 674
ἀνήρ, emphatic, 393; ἀνήρ = θνητός,
  567
ἀνθ' ὅτου, 'wherefore,' 966 ff.
ἄνθρωπος, emphatic, 1153
ἀνθ' ὧν, 'wherefore,' 1295
ἀνιέναι, to remit, 1608 f.
ἀνιστάναι ἱκέτην, 276
ἀντᾶν, constr. of, 1076
ἀντειπεῖν, constr. of, 997 ff.
ἀντέχειν with genit., 1651
ἀντί, in compound adjectives, 192 ff.;
  ἀντί τινος, (to adjure) 'by,' 1326 f.
ἀντιλαβή (division of verse), 652,
  722, 820, 1099, 1169, 1439
ἀνυμέναιος, 1222 f.
ἄξιος, of demerit, 929
ἀξίωμα, a decree, 1451 f.
ἄξομαι, midd. or pass., 1460 f.
ἄοινος, epith. of Furies, 100
ἄπαν, 'anything,' 1000 f.
ἀπάτωρ, 1383
ἀπειπεῖν μή, 1760 f.
ἀπειργαθεῖν, 862
Ἀπία γῆ (ἄ), 1303 f.
ἀπίη γαίη (usu. ἄ), 1685 ff.
ἀπὸ γλώσσης, opp. to τῷ νῷ, 936;
  ἀπὸ ῥυτῆρος, 899 ff.; ἀπὸ σοῦ, τό,
  293, 1628; ἀπό τινος, from his
  quarter (πάσχειν τι), 1533 ff.;
  ἀπό τινος εἰκάζειν etc., 15, 937 f.

ἀποικίζειν, 1390
ἀποκάμνειν, constr. of, 1776
ἀπόκεισθαι, 1751 ff.
ἀπόπτολις, 208
ἀποστερίσκω, 376
ἀποστρέφεσθαί τινα, 1272 f.
ἀποσυλᾶν, 1330
ἀπόφημι)(φημί, 317
ἀπροσήγορος, 1277
ἄπυστος, 'inaudible,' 489
ἆρα equiv. in sense to ἆρ' οὐ, 753
Ἀραί, and Furies, distinguished,
  1391 : identified, 43, 1433 f.
ἀρᾶσθαι, in good sense, 1443 f.
ἀργής, ἀργινόεις, of places, 670
ἀργός, 1605
ἀριθμὸς λόγων, 382
ἁρμόζειν πόδας, etc., 197 ff.
ἁρμόζεσθαι, to be brought to order,
  908
ἀρχαῖος, senses of, 1632
ἀρχηγός, 60
ἀσκέπαρνος, 101
ἄσκευος, 1028 ff.
ἀστακτί, 1251
ἄστροφος, 490
ἀτιμάζω, 49 : with genit., 1272 f.
ἀτίμως, 428
αὐθαίρετος, 523
αὖθις πάλιν 1418 f.
αὐτάρκης βοή, 1055
αὐτίκα with ἐνθάδε, 992 f.; αὐτίκα,
  ὁ, 433
αὐτόθεν, 1137
αὐτοῖν for ἀλλήλοιν, 1425
αὐτόπετρος, 192 ff.
αὐτοποιός, 698
αὐτός, 'alone,' 1650; αὐτός, between art. and αὐτοῦ, 930; αὐτὸς
  κῆρυξ, 1511 f.; αὐτός τε καί, etc.,
  868
ἀφανὴς θεός, ἡ, 1556
ἀφιέναι, to emit, 1468; ἀφιέναι)(
  μεθιέναι, 834
ἄφορμος, 233 f.
ἀφώνητος, 'mute,' 1183
ἀχείρωτος, 698
ἄχερδος, 1595 f.
ἄχορος, 1222 f.

βάθρον γῆς, 1661 f.

I. Greek 285

βαίνειν, fig. uses of, 1695
βακχιώτης, 678
βαρυάχης, Dor. for -ηχής, 1561 f.
βάσανος χερῶν, 835
βαστάζειν, 1104 f.
βεβηκέναι, sense of, 613 ; βεβηκώς, 1358 f.
βέβηλος, 10
βῆσσα, 673
βλάστας ἔχειν, 972 f.
βουλήσομαι, 1289
βοῦς ἐπὶ γλώσσῃ, 1052
βραχύς, 'trivial,' 294; 'weak,' 880
βρύω, 16

γαιάοχος, 1071 f.
γάρ = 'indeed,' 1142
γε, emphasising a whole phrase, 1278 f.; γε, twice in one sentence, 387, 1278 f. ; γε with ὡς τάχιστα, 1416; γε μήν, 587 ; γέ τοι, 1323 f.
γεγώνω, 214
γένος, the (Attic) people, 772 f.
γέρα, 1396
γεραίτερος, 1293 f.
γέρων as adj., 1258 f.
γῆθεν, 1591
γλαυκῶπις, 706
γλυκύς, said to a deity, 106
γοῦν and οὖν...γε, 24
γύαλον, 1491

δᾳδοῦχος, at Eleusis, 1053
δασμός, 634
δέ after voc., 507, 1459
δέ, corrects or objects, 592, 1443 f.; δέ, elided at end of verse, 17; δέ, irregularly answering to τε, 367 ff. ; δέ, without μέν, marking a second relationship (πατὴρ ὁ σός, ἀδελφὸς δ ἐμός), 1275; δὲ οὖν, 1204 f.
δεῖ understood from οὐκ ἔξεστι, 1402 ff.
δείκνυμι δέ, 1145
δεινῶπες, as epith. of Furies, 84
δείνωσις, rhetorical, 1336
δεῖσθαι, midd., = δεῖν (impers.), 570; δεῖσθαι, with double gen., 1170
δεξίωμα, 619
δεῦρο, τό, πέλαγος, 663
δεύτερον, adverb, 326

δεύτερος, second-best, 1226
δή, of succession, 367 ff.
δηλῶ δέ, like τικμήριον δέ, 146
δημότης, in tragedy, 78
δημοῦχος, 458
δῆτα, in echo, 536; δῆτα, 'then,' in comment, 631
διὰ ὀργῆς ἥκειν, 905; διὰ οὐδενὸς ποιεῖσθαι, 583 f.
διαπρύσιος, 1477 f.
διασκεδαννύναι, fig., 620, 1341 f.
διδόναι, εὖ, 642
διειδέναι, 225
διιέναι στόματός τι, 962 f.
δίκαια, τά, the just cause, 880
Δίκη, 1380
διοσημία, 95
δίστολος, 1055
δίχα τινός, without his sanction, 48
δοκῶ μέν, 995
δόρει and δορί, 620, 1304
δορύξενος, 632
δορυσσοῦς, 1313 f.
δρᾶν τι, euphemistic, 732
δρῶντος, παντός, 1904
δύνασθαι absol., of the body, 496
δυσπρόσοιστος, 1277
δυσστομεῖν, spelling of, 986
δύσφρων, 202 f.

ἔα, 1477 f.
ἔασον, as -◡ (conjectured), 1192
ἑαυτόν = ἐμαυτόν, 966: = σεαυτόν, 852 f.
ἐγγυτέρω λύπης, 1214 ff.
ἔγνωκα, uses of, 553
ἐγρεμάχας, 1054
ἐγὼ οὔτ' (synizesis), 939
ἔδρανα, 176
ἐή, 149
εἰ with fut. indic., 166; εἰ with pres. indic., 260 ; εἰ with indic. after θαυμάζω, etc., 1378 f.; εἰ with subjunct., 1443 f.; εἰ...ἤ, 'whether'...'or,' 80 ; εἰ θέμις, 1131 f., 1556
εἰδότα διδάσκειν, etc., 1538 f.
εἴδωλον, 110
εἶεν, 1308
εἴην ὅθι, etc., 1044
εἰκαθεῖν μῆνιν, 1328 f.
εἱμένος σκότον, 1700 f.

286   Indices

εἰπεῖν = προσειπεῖν, 759
εἴπερ, with fut. ind., 628; with pres.,
1370 f.
εἰς = 'in reference to,' 1121: 'with
a view to,' 1028, 1368 f.; εἰς
πλεῖστον, with genit., 739; εἰς
πλέον, with gen., 1220 f.; εἰς
τόδ' ἡμέρας, 1138
εἰς ἀνήρ, with πλεῖστος, 563 f.
εἰσακούειν, 1645 f.
εἰσορᾶν, of visiting sin, 1370, 1536
εἶτά, nevertheless, 914
εἴτις, assimilated to the case of a
partic., 734
ἐκ, of the antecedent condition,
807, 848; ἐκ, of the parent, 250,
530 ff.; ἐκ, of the ultimate agent,
67, 737 f.
ἑκατόμποδες, of the Nereids, 718 f.
ἐκβάλλειν, 631, 1257
ἐκεῖ = ἐκεῖσε, 1019 f.
ἐκεῖνα, said of the past, 1195 f.;
ἐκεῖνος = of whom ye spoke, 138
ἐκκηρύσσειν, 430
ἐκλαγχάνω, 1337
ἐκπράσσειν, to destroy, 1659 f.
ἐκφέρειν and ἐκφέρεσθαι, 1424
ἐκφυλάσσειν, 285
ἑκών in negative sentences, 1634;
ἑκὼν δέκοντί γε θυμῷ, 522
ἔλεγχος χειρός, 1296 f.
ἐλεύσομαι, 1206
ἐλπίδων, τίς, 1748 f.
ἐμβαίνω, with genit., 400
ἐμβατεύειν, 679 f.
ἐμέ, with inf., where ἐγώ is subject,
1019 f.
ἐμμένειν, of promises, 'to hold good,'
648
ἐμμιγνύναι, intrans., 1055
ἐμοί, οἱ, of one relative (masc. or
fem.), 832
ἐμπίπτειν, to occur to one, 1150 f.:
with accus., 942
ἔμπολις, 637
ἐμφορεῖν, 989 f.
ἐμφύλιος γῆ, 1384 f.
ἔμφυλον αἷμα, 407
ἐμφῦναι, 1113 f., 1488
ἐν (adv.) δέ, 55; ἐν, of circumstance,
495; ἐν, the last word of a verse,
495; ἐν, with plur. of days, etc.,

'within,' 619; ἐν, with πολλῷ
χρόνῳ, etc., 88; ἐν βραχεῖ, 586;
ἐν ἐμοί, penes me, 153, 422,
1443 f.; me iudice, 1211 f.; ἐν
ἡσύχῳ (neut.), 82; ἐν πυμάτῳ,
1675 f.; ἐν τὠμῷ κάρᾳ, at the
risk of, 564
ἐναγίζειν, 402
ἐναίρεσθαι, fig., 842
ἐναργής, 910
ἐνδεής, 1429 f.
ἐνδεικνύναι, 48
ἐνδιδόναι, 1076
ἐνέχυρα τιθέναι, τίθεσθαι, 858 f.
ἐνθάδ' αὐτοῦ, οἱ, 78
ἐνθνήσκω, 790
ἐνθυμήματα, 'food for thought,'
1199 f.
ἐννυχίων ἄναξ, 1558 f.
ἐντρέπεσθαι, senses of, 1540 f.
ἔντροφος, with dat., 1362 f.
ἐξ ἐμοῦ, τά, what can I produce,
453 f.; ἐξ εὐμενῶν στέρνων, 486
ἐξάγειν, lead to a goal, 98
ἐξάγιστος, 1526 f.
ἐξαιρεῖν)(ἐξαιρεῖσθαι, of prizes, 580 f.
ἐξαιτεῖν, 5
ἐξανιέναι, 1375
ἐξανύειν, to reach, 1561 f.
ἐξαφοράω, 1648 f.
ἐξεπᾴδειν, 1194
ἐξέρχεσθαι, to go to excess, 981
ἐξηγεῖσθαι, 1520: fig., 1284
ἐξηρπασμένοι, prob. corrupt, 1016 f.
ἐξιδρύω, 11
ἐξοικήσιμος, 27
ἐξορμᾶσθαι, 30
ἐξυφηγεῖσθαι 1025
ἐπαινεῖν, with infin., 'to advise,'
664 f.
ἐπαιτεῖν, 1364
ἐπακτὸν δόρυ, 1524 f.
ἐπαναίρεσθαι)(ἐπαναιρεῖσθαι, 424
ἐπαναφορά, figure of, 5, 610
ἔπαυλα, 669
ἐπεγείρειν, fig., 510
ἐπεί = 'for else,' 969 f.; ἐπεὶ οὔ,
1435 f.
ἐπεισπίπτειν, 915
ἐπεμβάλλειν, 463
ἐπεναρίζειν, 1733
ἐπερέσθαι, aor., 557

ἐπεύχεσθαι, 484: senses of, 1023 f.
ἐπέχειν τινί)(τινά, 1744
ἐπί after its case, 84; ἐπί with
genit. as = 'at,' 1595 f.; ἐπί with
dat. as = 'against,' 1472; ἐπί
βωμῷ, ὁ, 1053; ἐπί (ἔργοις), 'in,'
1267 f., 1554 f., 1561 f.; ἐπί
ἤματι, 688; ἐπί μιᾶς προσπόλου,
745 ff.; ἐπί ξένης, 184, 563 f.;
ἐπί τινι, 'in his case,' 414
ἐπιβαίνειν with genit., 186 ff.
ἐπιεικές, τό, 1126
ἐπιλαγχάνω, 1235 f.
ἐπινίκειος = ἐπινίκιος, 1088
ἐπιρράσσειν, 1502 ff.
ἐπιρρώννυσθαι, 661 f.
ἐπίσκοποι = explorers, 112
ἐπιστῆναι, 558
ἐπιστροφή, 536
ἐπιτάσσειν, 839
ἐπιφωνεῖν θήκην)(θήκῃ, 1762
ἐπλησάμην, 527 f.
ἔποικος, 506
ἔπος, ἔν, 1614 ff.
ἐπῳδαί, 1194
ἐπωφελεῖν, 441, 540 f.
ἔργοις, opp. to λόγῳ, 782: to ῥήμασιν, 873
ἐρητύειν, 164
Ἐρινύες, with gen. of person, 1433 f.
ἔρρειν, without bad sense, 1774 ff.
ἐσθῶ, a doubtful form, 195 f.
ἔσομαι, with pres. part., 653, 1433 f.:
with aor. part., 816
ἔσταμεν, 1017
ἑστία = βωμός, 1491 ff.: = τάφος,
1727
ἔσχατα, βαίνειν ἐπ', 217
Ἐτεοκλῆς, 1295
ἕτερος, use of, 230 f.
ἔτι nearly = adj. λοιπός, 1748 f.
εὖ λέγειν, in a bad sense, 807
εὕδειν, fig. use of, 306 f., 621
εὐημερεῖν, 616
εὔιππος, force of, 711
εὐοδόω, constr. of, 1435 f.
εὔπωλος, 711
εὐσκίαστος, of the grave, 1707 f.
εὔσοια, 390
εὔχειρ, 472
Εὔχλοος, 1600 f.
ἐφάπτεσθαι, 858 f.

ἐφορμεῖν, 812
ἐχέγγυος, 284
ἔχειν, epexegetic, 230 f., 537; ἔχειν,
to check, hinder, 429; ἔχειν with
aor. partic., 817, 1139 f., 1474;
ἔχειν κῦρος, 1779; ἔχειν τινὰ εἰς
τι, 1028 ff.; ἔχειν τόπον, to be in
it, 297; ἔχων ἔχει, 1025
ἔχρη from χράω, 87
ἔως, as a monosyllable, 1361
-έως, -έων, from nouns in -εύς,
metrical treatment of, 946

ῇ, 1st pers. sing. imperf. of εἰμί, 768
ἤ γάρ, in eager question, 64
ἤ...ἤ, 'whether,'...'or,' doubtful in
Attic, 80, p. 275
ἤ κατά after compar. adj., 598, 890
ἤ μήν, in a threat, 816
ἤδη used like αὐτίκα, 614 f.; ἤδη,
with τοῦτο, 1585 f.
ἤκει μοι, it devolves on me, 738;
ἤκειν, to have become, 1177,
1265 f.; ἤκω, with infin., 12
Ἥλιος invoked, 869 f.
ἡλιοστερής, 313
ἡμίν, as trochee, 25
ἡχεῖσθαι, 1500 f.

θάκημα, 1179 f.
θάκησις, 9
θάλασσα, in Erechtheum, 711
θαμίζειν, constr. of, 671 f.
θαρσεῖν, with accus., 649
θᾶσσον, in commands, 824 f.
θεαῖν, or -οῖν, 683
θεῖα, τά, 1537
θελήσας, 757
θέμις (nom.) before εἶναι, 1191
θεοὶ πατρῷοι, 756; θεός = ἥρως, 65
θήκη, a tomb, 1762
Θησέα, quantity of α in, 1055
Θησεῖδαι, 1065 f.
θύρασι)(ἐπί θύραις, 401
-θω, verbal forms in, 862, 1015, 1178,
1328 f.
θωπεύειν, 1003, 1336
θωΰσσειν, 1624 f.

ῑ before βλ, 996; ῐ or ῑ in ἀστακτί,
etc., 1251; in ἴημι, 1278 f.; ι of
dative, not elided in trag., 1435 f.

-ια, synizesis of, 1466
ἰέναι στόμα, 130; ἰέναι τινί, to be coming on him, 1771 f.
ἱεροκῆρυξ at Eleusis, 1053
ἱεροφάντης at Eleusis, 1053
ἴζειν εἴς τι, 713
ἴθι, ἴτε, in urgent prayer, 106
ἱκόμην ἵν' ἱκόμην, 273
ἵλαος and ἵλᾱος, 1480 f.
ἵνα, 'in which case,' 621
ἴσος, *only* so much, 810
ἰσοτέλεστος, 1220 f.
ἰών, pres. part., 1771 f.

καθ' αὑτόν, 'taken by oneself,' 966 f.
καθαρμός, with gen. of god, 466
καθαρῷ, βῆναι ἐν, 1575
καί after ἴσος, 810; καί before interrogatives, 263; καί, corrective, 1323 f.; καί='e'en,' followed by τε, 1393 f.; καὶ δή, 31; καὶ ἐγώ='I on my part,' 53, 520, 781, 869 f.; καὶ εἰ)(εἰ καί, 661 f., 957; καὶ κάρτα, 65; καὶ μήν, 396: introduces a new person, 549, 1249
καινός, 1542 f.
κακὰ κακῶν, 1238; κακός, 'ill-omened,' 1433
κάκωσις γονέων, 1377 f.
καλόν, 'seasonable,' 1003
καλοῦμαι, midd., 1384 f.
καλύπτειν, fig. sense of, 282
καλῶς with a compound of εὖ, 617
κάμπτειν, absol., 84; βίον, 89 ff.
καρπός, of berries or fruit, 675 f.
κατ' ἄκρας, 1241 f.; κατ' ἦμαρ= σήμερον, 1079; κατὰ νοῦν, 1768 f.
καταινέω, 432
κατάμεμπτον γῆρας, 1234
καταπειλεῖν, 658 ff.
καταρράκτης, 1590
καταρτύω, 71
κατασκαφῇ, 1218 f.
κατασκήπτειν λιταῖς, 1011
κατασκιάζειν, of burial, 406
καταστείβειν, 467
καταστροφή, 102
κατατιθέναι, of payment, 227
κατατίθεσθαι, 1214 ff.
κατέχειν γνώμῃ, 1252

κατισχύω, 345
κατοικεῖν)(κατοικίζειν, 1004
κατοικίζειν, 1281 f.
κατορθόω, intrans., 1487
κεῖθεν ὅθεν for κεῖσε ὅθεν, 1226
κείμενον μὴ κινεῖν (prov.), 510; κεῖσθαι ἔν τινι, 247 f., 1510
κῆδος, 379
κηλὶς κακῶν, 1132 ff.
κιγχάνειν, 1447 ff.: with gen., 1487
κλαυστός and κλαυτός, 1360
κλῄς, sense of, 1052
κλίνειν πόδα, 193
κνυζεῖσθαι and -ᾶσθαι, 1571
κοῖλος, of land, 378
κοινός, born of the same mother, 534 f.: other senses of, 632
κομίζειν=κομίζεσθαι, 1411 ff.
κραίνειν σκῆπτρα, 448 f.
κρᾶτα, 473
κρατεῖν with accus., 1380
κράτη, senses of, 392
κρατήρ for libation, 427 f.: the κοῖλος, 1593
κρίνειν, to select, 639 ff.
κρόκη, 474
κρωσσός, 478
κτερίσματα, 1410
κτίζειν, of usages, 715
κτυπεῖν, aorist of, 1456
κύκλος, 'eye,' 704
κύρειν, 1158 f.
κύρια, τά, 915; κύριος, ὁ, 288, 1643
κῦρος, 1779

λαβών, quasi-pleonastic, 475
-λαγχάνειν, with gen., 450 f.: intrans., 1235 f.
λαμβάνειν, to conceive (a feeling), 729 f.: ἐν πόθῳ τι, 1679
λαμπάδες, at Eleusis, 1046 ff.
λᾶος *versus* λάου, 195 ff.
λατρεύειν μόχθοις, 105
λέγειν καὶ ἀκούειν, 189 ff., 1288
λείπεσθαι, to be at a disadvantage, 495
λέξομαι, pass., 1185 f.
λέσχη, sense of, 166
λεύσσειν τινά, never=ζητεῖν, 121
λόγος, one's bare word (opp. to ὅρκος), 651; λόγος=power of discussion, 66; λόγος, the guide

of ἔργα, 116; λόγος ἔχει τινά, 1572 f.; λόγος, ὁ ἅπας, sense of, 1225; λόγῳ σκοπεῖν, 369: νικᾶν, 1296 f.
λόχος, sense of, 1088
λύγδην, 1620 f.
λύειν στολάς, 1597: τέλος βίου, 1720 f.
λῦμα, 805

μάλ' αὖθις, 1477, 1731 f.
μάλιστα with οἶμαι, 1298 ff.; with τίς, 652: with ἔνθα, 899 ff.
μανθάνειν, double sense of genit. with, 114, 593
μαραίνειν, 1260
μαρτύρεσθαι, *antestari*, 813 f.
ματᾶν, 1451 f.
μάτην, senses ascribed to, 1565 f.
ματρόθεν, by euphemism for ματρός, 527 f.
με followed by ἐμέ, 812; με repeated, 1278 f., 1407 ff.
μέγας, a full-grown man, 148
μειόνως ἔχειν = μείων εἶναι, 104
μελάμφυλλοι, 482
μελετᾶν, of observing usages, 171
μέλισσα = μέλι, 481
μέλλειν, with pres. inf., 1774 ff.: with verb understood, 1074
μέν...δέ, in co-ordinate clauses, 1536; μέν without δέ, 44, 1298 ff., 1360, 1370 f., 1677; μὲν οὖν = *imo*, 31: with distributed force, 664 f.
μέσος with genit. and ἀπό, 1595 f.
μεστός, with partic., 768
μετασπᾶν, 774
μετέχειν, constr. of, 1484
μέτοικος, poet. use of, 934
μή marking condition or cause, 73, 517, 1026 f., 1175, 1186, 1441 f., 1526 f., 1641 f., 1698 f.; μή, double, p. 277; μή due to a preceding imperative, 78, 281, 1104 f., 1154 f.; μή, interrogative, 1502 ff.; μή placed after its verb, 1365 f.; μή (or τὸ μή) with inf. after φεύγειν, etc., 1739 f.; μή with inf. after verbs expressing strong assurance, 281, 656, 797, 1122; μή with inf. instead of οὐ

with principal verb, 601; μή with partic. in later Greek, 797; μή with subjunct., (beware) lest, 1179 f.; μὴ οὐ with partic., 360; μὴ σύ γε)(μή μοι σύ, 1441 f.
μηδαμά and μηδαμῇ, 1104 f.
μηδέ, required instead of μήτε, 496
μηδέν, τό, 918
μῆκος λόγων, 1139 f.
μηκύνειν βοήν, 489, 1608 f.
μήν, hortative, with imperat., 182: with τί, 1468
μήτηρ γῆ, 1481 f.
μητρόπολις, 707 ff.
μιγνύναι Ἄρη, 1046 ff.
μινύθω, 686
μοι as ethic dat. (ἦλθέ μοι, ' I have seen come '), 1447 ff., 1475
μοῖρα, phrases with, 278, p. 277
μόνος = ' pre-eminently,' 261; with genit., 1250
Μόριος, Ζεύς, 705
μυρίος, ὁ, 617: in plur., 1533 ff.
μώμενος, 836
μῶν οὐ; 1729 f.

ναίειν, of mere situation (not dwelling), 117
νεάζειν, 374
νεαλής, Attic sense of, 475
νέμειν, to deem, 879
νέμεσις γάρ (ἐστι), 1753
νεόθεν, 1447 ff.
νεύειν with accus., 248 f.
νεώρης, 475
νηλίπους, 349
νῆσος, of the Peloponnesus, 695 f.
νικᾶν with double accus., 1204 f.
νιφὰς πέτρα, 1059 ff.
νομάς, epith. of streams, 687
νομίζεσθαι with genit., 38
νόμοι ἀρχαῖοι, 1381 f.; νόμος with ἐστί understood, 168
νοστεῖν with acc., 1386 f.
νυν and νῦν, 96, 465 f.
νὺξ ὀλεθρία (of death), 1683 f.

ξεῖν', where metre would admit ξέν', 33
ξεῖνος in dialogue, 1014 f.
ξένη sc. γῆ, 184, 563
ξενόστασις, 90

290 *Indices*

ξυνά as adv., 1751 f.

ὄγκος, senses of, 1161 f.
ὅδ' ἐκεῖνος, 138; ὅδε and οὗτος, 787;
ὅδε, for ἀνὴρ ὅδε as = ἐγώ, 450;
ὅδε, rhetorically repeated, 1117
ὁδοί = ὁδός, 553; ὁδοὶ οἰωνῶν, 1313 f.
ὁδός, χαλκοῦς, 57
Οἰδίπους, vocative, 461
οἰκεῖν, said of a State, 1533 ff.
οἴκοι, ὁ, 759
οἷος with infin., 1402 ff.
οἶσθ' ὡς μὴ σφαλῇς, 75
οἴχομαι, with aor. part., 867
ὀκλάζω, 195 f.
Ὄλυμπος, the sky, 1654 f.
ὅμαιμος, of brother and sister, 330
ὀμβρία χάλαζα, 1502 ff.
ὄμβρος = water, 690
ὄμμα in periphrasis, 1709
ὀμματοστερής, 1260 f.
ὁμόγνιοι θεοί, 1333
ὀμφή, divine, 102: human, 550
ὅμως, preceding the partic., 666
ὄναιο, 1042
ὄνομα in periphrasis, 1003
ὀνομάζειν, to phrase, 294
ὅποι, where motion is implied, 23,
383
ὅπου, with ἐστί understood, 1214 ff.
ὅρα, with partic., 654; ὁρᾶν, of
mental sight, 74, 138; ὁρᾶν, to
watch over, 1453 f.; ὁρᾷς ἵν'
ἥκεις; 937 f.
ὁρκία πίστις, 1632
Ὅρκιος, Ζεύς, 1767
Ὅρκος personified, 1767
ὁρμεῖν ἐπί τινος or ἐπί τινι, 148
ὅς for ὅστις (indirect question), 1171,
1581 f.
ὅσα = ὅσον, or ὡς, with inf., 152
ὅσῳπερ, constr. of, 743 f.
ὅτι, after verbs of fearing, 605
οὐ, irregular for μή, after εἰ, 935:
with inf., 1202 f.; οὐ, with infin.
after verbs of thinking, 281; οὐ
γὰρ ἄν, with suppressed protasis,
98, 125; οὐ γὰρ δή (...γε) in rejecting an alternative, 110, 265;
οὐ μή with fut. indic., 177, 849;
οὐ πάνυ, 144 f.; οὐ τὰ μὲν τὰ δ'
οὔ, etc., 1670 ff.

οὐδαμά and οὐδαμῇ, 1104 f.
οὐδέ negatively, = δέ of apodosis,
590; οὐδέ = not even (to begin
with), 1429 f.
οὐκ ἔσθ' ὅπως οὐ = 'assuredly,' 97;
οὐκ ἠγόρευον, 838
οὖν, 980, 1135, 1538 f.
οὕνεκα χρόνου, so far as concerns it, 22
οὐρανία as - ⏑ -, 1466
οὐρανόν, βιβάζειν πρός, 381
οὔτε, corrected to οὐδέ, 702 : vice
versa, 1141; οὔτε...οὐ, 972 f.;
οὔτε...τε, 1397 f.
οὗτος, adj., without art., 471, 629,
848, 1177, 1356 f.; οὗτος, in voc.,
1627

παγκευθής, 1561 f.
παιδεύειν, said of the State, 919
παιδοτρόφος, of the olive, 701
παλαίφατος Δίκη, 1381 f.
πανδίκως, 1306 f.
πάντα, adv., with adj., 1457 f.
παρά with acc. after κρύπτειν, 1551 f.;
παρ' ἦμαρ, on the morrow, 1453 f.
παραβάλλομαι, 230 f.
παράπτειν, 716 ff.
παρασπᾶν, 1185 f.
πάραυλος, 785
παραφέρειν, 1675 f.
παρεγγυάω, 94
παρήχησις, rhetorical, 795
παριέναι, constr. of, 1211 f. : 'to
give up,' 1229 f.; παριέναι, per-
mittere, 570, 591; παρίεσθαι, to
win over, 1665 f.
παρίστασθαι, to subjugate, 916
πατρόθεν, 214 f.
πατρῷα πήματα, sense of, 1195 f.;
πατρῷος, senses of, 1390
παῦε, 1751 f.
πείθου)(πιθοῦ, 1181
πελῶ, fut. of πελάζω, 1059 ff.
πέμπειν, of expelling, 93
πέπον, in familiar address, 516
πέπων, medical use of, 437
περ in thesis of 3rd foot, 896
πέρα)(πέραν, 885 f., p. 283
περιβλέπειν, ῑ in, 996
Περίθους = Πειρίθους, 1594
πήρα, the beggar's, 1262
πιστός, active sense of, 1031

πιστόω, 650, 1039
πλανάω, to mislead, 316
πλανήτης, 3, 123
πλάξ, of the nether world, 1561 f.
πλείονα, τά, the details, 36
πλεῖστον, with superlat., 743 f.
πληγή, a calamity, 1231
πληγήν understood (with δευτέραν), 544
πλῆθος, τό, the civic body, 66
πληθύω, 377, 930 f.
πλώσιμος, 663
πνεῦμα, sense of, 612
πόδα, supposed redundant use of, 113
ποῖ, where motion is implied, 227, 476, 1734 ff.; ποῖ φροντίδος, etc., 170
ποιεῖσθαι ἀρωγόν, 1285 f.
ποῖος, ὁ, 893, 1415
ποιούμενα, τά, the matter in hand, 116
πόλισμα, 1496
πολλά, adv., with adj., 1514
πολλαχῇ, 1626
πολύ, adv., with comparative, 1226
πολύξενος, 1569 f.
πολύς, of rumour, 305, 517
πομπός, of Hermes, 1548; πομπός, with ironical sense, 1019 f.
πόνος κακῶν, 1358 f.
πορεῖν and πορεύειν, 1457 f.
Ποσειδώνιος θεός, 1491 ff.
πότνιαι, Demeter and Cora, 1050; πότνιαι, Theban name of Furies, 43, 84
πρᾶξις)(πράξεις, in Soph., 560 f.
πράσσειν καλῶς, sense of, 1764 f.
πρεσβεύειν, 1422 f.
πρό, 'in preference to,' 1524 f.
προκεῖσθαι, to be pre-ordained, 1511 f.
προλαμβάνειν, 1141
προμνᾶσθαι, usage of, 1075 f.
πρόνοια with object. gen. 1179 f.
προξενεῖν, 465 f.
προπετής, 156
προπίπτειν, 156
πρός, force of, in some compound verbs, 122, 1160; πρὸς δίκης, ἔχειν τι, 545 f.; πρός σοι, 'near thee,' 1267 f.; πρὸς τὸ λιπαρές, 1119

προσβάλλειν ἀνάγκη τινά, 1178
προσορᾶν, peculiar use of, 142 : midd., 244
προσόψιος, 1600 f.
προσπεύθεσθαι, sense of, 122
προσπίπτειν, 1158 f.
προσπολεῖσθαι, pass., 1098
προστάτης, senses of, 1171 ; πρόστα-τις, a guardian goddess, 457 f.
προστιθέναι and προστίθεσθαι, 153, 767 ; προστίθεσθαι (φίλον, etc.), 404 f.: (τινί), 1331 f.
προσφέρεσθαι (midd.), 1277
προσφορά, 581, 1269 f.
πρόσφορος, senses of, 1774 ff.
προσφώνημα, etc., poetical use of, 324 f.
προσχρῄζειν, 1160, 1202 f.
πρόσχωρος, 1065 f.
προτίθεσθαι, with prep. added, 418 f.
προφέρτατος, 1530 f.
πρῶτος = best, 144 f.
πτερόν, an omen, 97
Πύθιαι ἀκταί, 1046 ff.; Πύθιον, the, in Daphnè pass, 1046 ff.
πυμάτῳ, ἐν, 1675 f.
πύργοι, of a city, 14
πυρφόρος = torch-bearing, 56

ρ, when doubled, 469
Ρέα, 1071 f.
ρεῖν, to come to nought, 259
ρητὸν ἄρρητόν τε, 1000 f.
'Ρῖπαι, αἱ, name of hills, 1248
ροπή, 1508 f.
ρύσιον, 858 f.
ρυτὸν ὕδωρ, 1598

σαίνειν, 319 f.
σάφα with εἰκάζω, 16
σαφής, true (of a prophet), 623, 792
σέ elided, though emphatic, 800 f.; σε (enclitic) between πρός and genit., 250
σεβισθείς, 636
σεμναί, epith. of Furies, 43, 90
σημαίνειν, military sense of, 702
σθένει)(βίᾳ, 842
σκαιοσύνη, 1211 ff.
σκῆπτρον, fig., 848
σκληρὰ μαλθακῶς λέγειν, 774

σκοπός, 34, 297, 1096
σμικρός, of persons, 'weak,' 148
σόν (ἐστι), ''tis thy part,' 721; σόν,
τό, thy part, 625 f.; σός, ὁ, ' of
which you speak,' 1380
σπανιστός, 4
σπαρτοὶ ἄνδρες, 1533 ff.
σπέρμα)(σπέρματα, 1275
σσ or σ in compounds with δυσ-,
986
στέγειν, uses of, 15
στέλλειν, to fetch, 298
στενακτός, 1663 f.
στέργειν, absol., 7 : in prayer, 1094
στερνοῦχος, 691
στέφειν, uses of, 15
στόλος, 358
στόμα in periphrasis, 1277; στόμα
ἰέναι, 130; στόμα, of an envoy,
794
στόμωσις, 795
στράπτω and ἀστράπτω, 1515
στρέφειν, to overthrow, 1453 f.
σὺ γάρ, after voc., 712
συγκομίζομαι, 585
συγχεῖν, 609
συλλαβών, force of, 1384 f.
συμβάλλειν, conicere, 1474; συμβάλλεσθαι γνώμην, 1150 f.
συμφέρεσθαι, to agree, 639 ff.
συμφορά, euphemistic, 596; σύμφορά,
sense of, 1470 f.
σύν, with the help of, 817:= ' combined with,' 1106: σ. ἐσθῆτι,
1258 f.: σ. βραχεῖ χρόνῳ, 1341 f.:
σ. νόσοις, 1663 f.
συναινεῖν, 1508 f.
συναλλαγή, 410
σύνεδρος, with gen., 1381 f.
συνεῖναι, of age, fortune, etc., 7
συνεκσώζειν, 565 f.
συνήδεσθαι, constr. of, 1397 f.
σύνθακος with both gen. and dat.,
1267 f.
σύνθημα, 46
συνίστασθαι ἀγῶνι, etc., 515
συνναίειν γήρᾳ, 702
συνοικεῖν, fig., 1238
σύνοικος, fig., 1132 ff.
συνουσία, of dwelling in a place, 63,
647
συντρέχειν, senses of, 158 ff.

σφιν and σφι, 421; as dat. sing.,
1489 f.
σχές, 1169
σῴζειν)(σῴζεσθαι, 1530 f.: σῴζεσθαι, of a safe return, 1345
σῶμα in periphrasis, 1568
σωτήριος, 487

τὰ ἐκ θεῶν, 236, 1540 f.; τὰ μεταξύ,
adverbial, 290 f.; τὰ νῦν and
τανῦν, 1034 f.; τὰ πλείονα, the
details, 39; τὰ πολλά, 'those
many,' 87
ταύτην (instead of τοῦτο) ἔλεξε παῦλαν, 88
τάχ' ἄν, elliptical use of, 965
ταχύρρωστος, 1081
τε misplaced, 33; τε (single) linking
sentences, 987; τε...δέ, 422;
τε...καί instead of εἴτε...εἴτε, 488;
τε...οὔτε (or μήτε) not found,
367 ff.; τε...τε, long interval
between, 765
τεκών, ὁ, the father, 1108
τελεῖν, of ritual, 504
τελειοῦν, senses of, 1088
τελευταῖος βίος, ὁ, 1551 f.
τελευτή, result, 1198
τέλη, of rites, 1050
τέλος ὁδοῦ ἀφορμᾶσθαι, 1400 f.
τέρμιος, 89
τετίμημαι, 1304
τέτροφα, Homeric, and later, 186
τέχνη = a work of art, 472
τῇδε, 'in that sense,' 639 ff.; τῇδ
repeated, 1547
τηλικοῦτος fem., 751
τηνίκα, 440
τητᾶσθαι, 1200
τι, adverb, 1139 f., 1447 ff.; τι
with πράσσειν, 500; τί γάρ; 538,
542, 545 f., 1680 f.; τί δ' ἐστὶ
τοῦτο; 'what means it?' 46; τί
δ' ἔστι; 311, 1154 f.; τί τοῦτο;
513; τι τούτων, iron. for ταῦτα,
1034 f.
τιθέναι in a double sense, 1356 f.;
τίθεσθαι in a double sense, 1410;
τίθεσθαι = ποιεῖσθαι, 1139 f.
τιθηνεῖσθαι, fig., 1050
τίνειν, opposed to πάσχειν, 228 f.
τις, after a noun with art., 288; τις

as=either of two, 416; τις, enclitic, before its noun, 280 f.; τις, of a supernatural being, 1623; τις, vague (βροντήν τιν', 'haply'), 95; τίς ἄγει=τίς εἶ, ὃς ἄγει, 205 f.; τίς οὐ=πᾶς, 1132

τὸ ἔνθεν=τὸ ἐνθένδε, 476; τὸ μή with inf. after φεύγειν, etc., 1739 f.; τὸ σὸν μέρος, 1365 f.; τὸ φατιζόμενον, 'as the saying is,' 138

τόδε in appos. with a preceding word, 639 ff.

τοιοῦτος, introducing the reason for a statement, 947; followed by ὅς, 1352 f.

-τον and -την in 2nd pers. dual, 1378 f.

τοσοῦτον and inf. (without ὅσον), 790

τοὐμόν, 'my part,' 1118

τοῦτ' αὐτό, 575; τοῦτο, ironical force of, 771; τοῦτο μέν answered by δέ only, 440

τρέφειν, of mental habit, 186

τρικόρυφος πέτρος, 1595 f.

τρὶς ἄθλιος versus τρισάθλιος, 372

τρίτος, 8, 330 f.

τροφεῖα, 341

τροφή, or -αί, way of life, 330, 362; τροφὴ νέα, nurture of youth, 345

τυγχάνειν with accus. of pron. or adj., 1106

τύραννος, one of the royal house, 851

τύχη, ἡ, Destiny, 1026 f.

τῶν as 1st syll. of 3rd foot, 257

ὔμμι, 247

ὔπεικε=συγχώρει, 1184

ὑπεκτρέπεσθαι with acc., 565 f.

ὑπόβλητος, 794

ὑποφορά, figure of, 431

φαίνειν, to illustrate, 721; φαίνεσθαι, of birth, 974: with ὡς and partic., 630

φέρειν=φέρεσθαι, 6; φέρειν, *proferre*, in debate, 166; φέρειν, to bring (an addition), 1411 ff.; φερόμενος=swiftly or suddenly, 1681 f.; φέρον, τό, of fortune, 1693 f.

φεύγειν with both gen. and acc., 1023 f.

φήμη, 1516 f.

φιλεῖν, of hospitality, 775

φλαῦρος, euphem. for κακός, 1429 f.

φονεύς, fig., 1361

φόνιος, in a general sense, 1689 ff.

φρήν, 'purpose,' 1340

φύειν φρένας, etc., 804

φύλαξ, gen. or dat. after, 355 f.

φυλάσσειν, to cleave to, 1211 ff.

φυλάσσομαι, constr. of, 161

φυτάλμιος ἀλαῶν ὀμμάτων, 149

φύτευμα)(φίτευμα, 698

φώς, said by speaker of himself, 1018, 1109

φῶς ἀφεγγές, 1549 f.

χαλκοβόας, 1046 ff.

χαλκόπους ὁδός, 57

χάριν διδόναι ὀργῇ, 855; χάριν τινός, 'for lack of it,' 443; χάρις, in two senses, 779

χειρὸς οὐδ' ἔργου, 1296 f.; χειρῶν νόμος, 835

χείρωμα, 698

χεῖσθαι, midd., 477

χθόνιος=ἐγχώριος, 948 : Ζεύς, 1606

Χλόη, Δημήτηρ, 1600 f.

χοαί)(σπονδαί, 477

χρεία = necessity, 191 : request, 1755 f.; χρεία τινός, 1280

χρέος προσάπτειν, 235

χρῄζειν with gen., 1211 ff.

χρήσει, 504

χρῆσται, etc., 504, p. 280

χρόνος, ὁ, of life-time, 7, 930 f.

χρυσέος, fig., 1052

χρυσήνιος, 692

χῶροι)(χῶρος, 2

ψεύδειν, constr. of, 1145 f., 1508 f., 1511 f.

ψιλός, 866, 1028 ff.

ψυχή in periphrasis, 997 ff., 1207

ψυχρός, of death, 622

ὠγύγιος, 1770

ὧδε='hither,' 182, 1251

ὠκυτόκος, 689

ὤν omitted, 83, 586, 694, 1278 f., 1588

-ωs, adverbs in, of compar. or superl., 1579

ὡs, an unusual omission of, 142; ὡs, causal (=' for'), 45, 1028 ff.; ὡs, limiting, 20, 76; ὡs with διδόναι (instead of ἅ), 1124; ὡs with fut. ind. in object clause, 1724; ὡs with infin. instead of indic., 385 f.; ὡs with partic., marking speaker's point of view,

71, 732; ὡs ἀπ' ὀμμάτων, 15; ὡs δή, 809; ὡs οὐ with partic., 1154 f.

ὥσπερ prefacing an illustration, 776 ff.

ὥστε redundant with inf., after verbs of persuading, etc., 570, 969 f., 1350; ὥστε with inf. of condition, 602; ὥστε = ως, 343

ὠφελεῖν with gen., wrong, 436

ὤφελον to be understood, 540 f.

GRAMMATICAL INDEX.

abstract (ἀρωγή) for concrete, 1094
accent of compounds in -ποιος, 698
accus. absol. in personal constr.,
380 f. ; after phrase equiv. to
transitive verb, 223, 583, 1119,
1150 f.; after θαρσεῖν, two senses
of, 649; cognate, of errand (ἃ
ἦλθον), 1291, 1400 f. ; cognate
(ὑπερπονεῖν κακά), 344 f., 564 :
with νικᾶν, 1204 f.: sometimes
gives solemnity, 477; governed by
verbal adj., 1019 f. ; in appos.
with sentence, 92 f., 138; of motion
to, 643, 1386 f.; of pron. or adj.
with τυγχάνειν, 1106; of respect,
314; of space traversed, 96, 1685
ff.; temporal, 433; with dat., before inf., 1202 f.
active infin. after adjective, 37; infin.
after ἄξιος, etc., 461
adj. agreeing with pers., instead of
subst. with prep. (ἐκτόπιος = ἐκ
τόπου), 119, 441, 716 ff., 1659 f.;
alone, instead of adj. with ὤν, 83;
as epithet of a compound phrase
(κοινὰ ὠδὶς μητρός, instead of
κοινᾶς), 533 ; compound, = two
distinct epithets, 17, 1055, 1305 ;
compound, equiv. to adj. and subst.
in gen. (αὔχημα εὔιππον), 711,
1462 f.; compounded with noun
of like sense with the subst.
(εὐήρετμος πλάτη), 716 ff.; in apposition, 1614 ff.; in periphrasis,
for proper name (Ποσειδώνιος θεός),
1491 ff.; in -σιμο, 27; masc. or
fem., with partit. gen. (ἡ πολλὴ
τῆς γῆς), 1616 f.; neut. plur., with
defining gen. (φωτῶν ἀθλίων ἱκτήρια), 922 f.; neut., with art., as
adv. (τὸ καρτερόν), 1640; of three
terms., treated by poets as of two,
751; placed after art., adv., subst.

(αἱπολλὰ βρονταὶ διατελεῖς), though
not the predicate, 1514; qualifying
a metaphor, 130; verbal, with act.
sense, 1031, 1283; with second of
two nouns, but belonging to the
first also, 1399
adv., compar., with ἔχειν, euphemistic, 104
agent, epithet of, given to his act,
74, 267
anapaest, in proper names, 1, 1313 f.
anapaests, final, of a play, 1773 ff.
antecedent, attracted into case of
relative (nom.), 1150 f.: (accus.),
56, 907
anteced. in acc. understood before
relat. with prep. (κτανεῖν ὑφ' οὗπερ
ἔφυγες), 1388
aor., ingressive, 345; of moment
just past, 1466
aposiopesis, 813 f.
apposition of whole and part (μέθες
με χεῖρα), 113
art. as demonstr. pron., 742, 1698 f.;
as relat. pron., 747, 1574; before
ποῖος, 893; ironical (ὁ δίκαιος),
992 f.; omitted before second of
two subjects, 606, 808, 1034 f.;
omitted with adjectival οὗτος, 471,
629, 848, 1177, 1356 f.; generic
(τὰ πολλὰ ῥήματα), 1281 f.; with
a repeated word, 277; with infin.,
instead of simple infin., 47, 228 f.,
442; with noun, after dependent
dat., 714; with ἅπας, 1225; with
or without γε, at end of verse, 265,
351; with μέν added to noun and
art. (τὸν ἄνδρα τὸν μέν...), 1648 f.;
with πολύς, 87, 1673
assimilation of εἴτις ὅστις to the case
of a partic., 734
assonance (παρομοίωσις), 251
attraction, inverse (nom.), 1150 f. ;

(acc.) 56, 907; of adverbs (ἄλλοσε, for ἄλλοθι, before ὅποι), 1226; of relative extended to predicate, 334; of relative (into gen.), 35, 228 f.

augment, omission of, 1602, 1606: prodelision of, 974, 1602

caesura, 372

cases, different, required by two adjectives, 1383

compound form before simple (προβᾶτε...βᾶτε), 841

compressed phrase, a, 1400 f., 1766 f.

construction, changed as sentence proceeds, 263, 351, 766 f., 1773 ff.

co-ordination of clauses (parataxis), 854, 1202 f., 1536, 1581 f.

cretic preceded by γάρ, 115

'dappled,' Greek words for, 1092 f.

dative, after δεῖ, 570, 721; after εἰσέρχομαι, 372; after ὁ αὐτός, 1358 f.; causal, 333, 738, 1280, 1381 f., 1411 ff., 1624 f.; ethic, 62, 81, 723, 845, 1021, 1156 f., 1249, 1447 ff., 1630, 1713 f.; ethic, combined with another, 1518 f.; ethic, in ποθοῦντι προὐφάνης, 1505 f.; ethic, of judgment (πᾶσιν, 'in the eyes of all'), 810, 1446; instrum., 880, 908, 1160: combined with object. dat., 525 f.: with modal, 1318 f.; locative, 313, 411, 483, 605, 700, 1260 f.; modal, 381, 658 ff.; object., after ἰέναι, 'to come upon,' 1771 f.; of circumstance (χρόνῳ παλαιός), 112; of interest, 342, 430 f., 444, 616, 1673; of interest, followed by art. and noun, 714; of percipient (ὡς ἰδόντι), 76; of person for whom a prayer is made, 1443 f.; of respect, with verbs of excelling, 1007, 1265 f., 1313 f.; or acc., before inf., 1202 f.; to be supplied with the first of two adjectives, from a gen. after the second, 1383; with noun (τὰ δόλῳ κτήματα), 1026 f., 1594

disjunctive statement in conjunctive form, 488

division of verse between two speakers, 722

dual and plur., concurrent use of, 857; and plur. verbs combined, 343; partic. in -ντε (fem.), 1113 f., p. 293; pron., supposed distributive use of, 342; 2nd pers., forms of, 1378 f.

echo of the last speaker's phrase, 1420 f., 1704

elision of datival ι in trag., 1435 f., p. 289; of δ' (etc.) at end of verse, 17

epanaphora, 5, 610

epithet placed *after* a subst. which has art. and adv. *before* it, 1514

future indic. with deliber. aor. subj., 310, 1254 f.; indic. with εἰ, 166; indic. with ὡς, 1724; interrog. with οὐ, in commands, 897; midd. as pass., 581, 1185 f.; of intention (ἐρεῖς=μέλλεις ἐρεῖν), 596; of wish, etc. (βουλήσομαι), 1289; perf., 816, 861

genitive absol. of noun, without partic., 83, 1588; after adj. implying 'free from,' 1147, 1518 f.; after compar., instead of dat. with ἤ (πλέον σοῦ=πλέον ἢ σοί), 568; after compound adj. with a privative (ἀνήνεμος χειμώνων), 677 f.; after pers. pron. (τἀμὰ δυστήνου), 344; after verb of receiving, etc., 1411 ff.; after γίγνομαι, 660; after εἰς πλέον, 1220 f.; after τὸ ἐκεῖθεν, 505; after ὤμοι, etc., 202, 982 f., 1399; causal, 228 f., 1411 f.; defining (τέλος θανάτου), 725, 835, 922 f.; double, after δεῖσθαι, 1170; object., after adj. of active sense, 1650: of passive sense, 1722; object., after προσπίτνειν as=δεῖσθαι, 1755 f.; object., with adj. (λόγων αὐτάγγελος), 333; object., with μῦθος, 1161 f.; of class or category (οὐκ ἐσμὲν πρώτης μοίρας), 144; of connection, after verbs of perceiving (ἐνθυμοῦ τῶν εἰδότων ὅτι λέγουσι), 114 f.; of connection, after verbs of saying or hearing, etc. (τινός, *about* one), 307, 355 f.,

514; of connection, after a subst. (τύχη ὁδοῦ), 1506; of parentage, etc., 214 f., 1320 ff.; of place whence, 1515; of the land to which a place belongs, 45, 297; of *thing*, after αἴω, etc., 304, 418 f.; of time within which, 397, 821; of source, 647, 786, 972 f.; of subject and object combined, 447, 729 f.; partitive, after εἶς τοῦτο ἥκειν, etc., 1029 f.; partitive, in κακὰ κακῶν, 1238; partitive, with superlat., 669, 739, 1173 f.; possessive, after ἐπακούω, 694; possessive, with inf. (τοὐπιόντος ἁρπάσαι), 752; with ἀτιμάζω, 49; with καλούμενος, 107

gnomic aorist, 1214 ff.

hendiadys, 1297
hiatus, Ζεῦ short before, 143
hyperbaton (τις before εἰ), 776 ff.: (αὐτός between τήν and αὑτοῦ), 930: (μή), 1365 f.
hyperbole, 1745

imperf., inceptive (ὡρμώμην), 1158 f.; in conditional sentence, 927; of a new perception, 1697; of intention, 274, 394, 770; of previous mention, 117; of τίκτω, 'was the parent,' 982 f.; of what was doomed to happen, 969 f.
impers. pass. (βραδύνεται), 1628
infin. active after ἀγνός, ἄξιος, etc., 37, 461, 1015, 1152; after ἥκω, 12; after τιθέναι, 1356 f.; epexegetic, 34 f., 49, 230 f., 1581 f.; defining an adj., 141, 327, 537; epexegetic, added to a verb governing a different case (χρῄζει τούτων, εἰδέναι), 1211 f., 1496, 1755 f.; epexegetic, after τοῦ ἐστί; 335; for imperat., 481, 490; in appos. with τοσοῦτον, 790; in wishes, ὤφελον being understood, 540 f.; *without art.*, co-ordinate with another noun, 608
intention described as fact, 1008
interruption in stichomuthia, dramatic use of, 645

Ionicisms in dialogue, 33, 44, 602, 875, 945, 1293 f.
ironical form of threat, 1377 f.

masc. plur., alluding to a woman, 832
midd. of ὁράω and compounds, 244
monosyllable in 5th foot (spondee) before cretic, 115

neut. adj. (plur.) with defining gen. (φωτῶν ἀθλίων ἱκτήρια), 922 f.; predicate of masc. or fem. subject (θυμὸς οὐ ξύμφορον), 592; plur. without subst., 10, 167; sing. of superl. adj. as adv., 1579
nominative for voc., 185, 203, 753, 1338 f., 1480, 1700 f.; (in exclamation) with voc., 1471

optative, dubitative, without ἄν, 170, 1172, p. 275; in final clause after primary tense, 11; in protasis, with pres. ind. in apodosis, 352; in relative clause, 560 f., 778; with ἄν, after ἵνα ('where'), 189 ff., 404 f.; in courteous entreaty, 725; of fixed resolve, 45, 826; in question expressing wish, 70, 1100, 1457 f.
oratio obliqua, 89 ff.
order of words, irregular, 1428

paroemiac, 1757, 1773 ff.
paronomasia, 1113 f.
participle active neut. in τὸ θαρσοῦν αὑτοῦ, etc., 267, 1604; expressing the leading idea of the sentence, 1038, 1128, 1346 f., 1508 f., 1538 f.; in different cases combined, 737 f.; of εἰμί omitted, 83, 586, 694, 1278 f.; with ἄν, 761 f.
pause, in sense after a word which ends the 3rd foot, 1489 f.; marked by words *extra metrum*, 1271
perfect, emphatic, 186, 1004, 1139 f., 1258 f., 1304; forms, alternatively pass. or midd., 1016 f.; pass. of κατοικέω, sense of, 1004
person, transition from 1st to 3rd, 6, 1328 f.; pers. constr. in expressing

'it is plain': δηλῶ δέ, 146 : δείκνυμι δέ, 1145

pleonasm (παλαιὸς γέρων), 112, 435

plural, allusive, for sing., 148, 295, 832, 884, 969 f., 1306 f.; and dual, concurrently used, 857; marking moments of the same feeling (πόθοισι), 333; neut. of adj. as adverb, 219, 319, 716 ff., 1119, 1695, 1745, 1751 ff.; neut. of adj. as subst., 10, 167; neut. of adj. without subject (ἀδύνατά ἐστι), 485, 495, 883, 1360; poet. for sing. (as σκῆπτρα for σκῆπτρον), 425, 553, 897 f., 972 f., 989 f.

position, adding force to a word, 1173 f., 1628

positive and negative joined, 397, 935

positive verb evolved from negative (δεῖ from οὐκ ἔξεστι), 1402 ff.

prep. added to προτίθεσθαι, etc., 418 f.; following its case, 84; supplied to relat. pron. from antecedent, 748 f., 937 f.

pres. partic. as partic. of imperf., 1565 f.; of attempt (κτείνει, seeks to kill), 992 f.

prodelision, 974, 1602

proleptic use of adjective, 89, 527 f. : with art., 1088, 1200, 1491 ff.

pronoun assimilated to predicate (ταύτην ἔλεξε παῦλαν, instead of τοῦτο), 88 ; pers., when omitted, 726, 995; (plur.), referring to persons implied in a collective noun (αὐτούς after πόλιν), 942, 1070; possessive, = objective gen. (σὸς πόθος), 332; reflexive, 3rd pers. for 1st or 2nd, 852 f.; relat., before two verbs, in a case which suits only the first, 424, 467, 731; relat., neut. plur., where one of the antecedents is masc. or fem., 1355; relat., of pers., evolved from

possessive pron., 731; relat., with causal force (ὅς=ἐπεὶ σύ, etc.), 263 : (antecedent understood), 427, 1354

relative clause, verb of, assimilated to form of conditional sentence, 926; pron. with optative, 560 f., 778

repetitions of words, 554, 969, 1406

rhetorical epanaphora, 5, 610, 1500 f. : hypophora, 431 : parechesis, 795 : paronomasia, 1113 f.

singular, change from plur. to, in addressing Chorus, 175 ; verb, with nearest of several subjects, 8

speech personified, 658 ff.

subject to verb understood, 1065

subjunct. after ἐπεί (lyr.), 1225 : after εἰ, 1443 f.; after ὅs without ἄν, 228 f.; deliberative, 26, 170 (3rd pers.), 195, 216, 1254; prohibitive, with μή, rare in 1st pers. sing., 174

superlat. with πλεῖστον added, 743 f.

synizesis, 939, 946, 964, 1192, 1361, 1435 f., 1466

synonym used, instead of repeating the same word, 1500 f.

tmesis, 1689 ff., 1777 ff.

tribrach, in 2nd place, 26

verb, agrees in number with nearest subject, 8 ; compound and simple forms together, 841; substituted for a participial clause, 351

verse divided between two speakers, 311, 652, 722, 820, 1099, 1169, 1439; ending with art., 351 ; ending with ἐν, 495

zeugma of τιθέναι, 1356 f. : of τιθέσθαι, 1410

For EU product safety concerns, contact us at Calle de José Abascal, 56–1°, 28003 Madrid, Spain or eugpsr@cambridge.org.